Lecture Notes in Computer Science 3754

Commenced Publication in 1973
Founding and Former Series Editors:
Gerhard Goos, Juris Hartmanis, and Jan van Leeuwen

Jordi Dalmau Royo   Go Hasegawa (Eds.)

Management of Multimedia Networks and Services

8th International Conference on Management
of Multimedia Networks and Services, MMNS 2005
Barcelona, Spain, October 24-26, 2005
Proceedings

 Springer

Volume Editors

Jordi Dalmau Royo
Abertis Telecom
Gran Via de les Corts Catalanes, 130-136, 08038 Barcelona, Spain
E-mail: jordi.dalmau@retevision.es

Go Hasegawa
Osaka University, Cybermedia Center
1-32, Machikaneyama-cho, Toyonaka, Osaka, 560-0043, Japan
E-mail: hasegawa@cmc.osaka-u.ac.jp

Library of Congress Control Number: 2005934300

CR Subject Classification (1998): C.2, H.5.1, H.3, H.5, K.3, H.4

ISSN   0302-9743
ISBN-10   3-540-29641-7 Springer Berlin Heidelberg New York
ISBN-13   978-3-540-29641-6 Springer Berlin Heidelberg New York

Springer is a part of Springer Science+Business Media

springeronline.com

© 2005 IFIP International Federation for Information Processing, Hofstrasse 3, 2361 Laxenburg, Austria
Printed in Germany

Typesetting: Camera-ready by author, data conversion by Scientific Publishing Services, Chennai, India
Printed on acid-free paper   SPIN: 11572831   06/3142   5 4 3 2 1 0

Preface

We are delighted to present the proceedings of the *8th IFIP/IEEE International Conference on Management of Multimedia Networks and Services (MMNS 2005)*.

The MMNS 2005 conference was held in Barcelona, Spain on October 24–26, 2005. As in previous years, the conference brought together an international audience of researchers and scientists from industry and academia who are researching and developing state-of-the-art management systems, while creating a public venue for results dissemination and intellectual collaboration.

This year marked a challenging chapter in the advancement of management systems for the wider management research community, with the growing complexities of the "so-called" multimedia over Internet, the proliferation of alternative wireless networks (WLL, WiFi and WiMAX) and 3G mobile services, intelligent and high-speed networks, scalable multimedia services, and the convergence of computing and communications for data, voice and video delivery. Contributions from the research community met this challenge with 65 paper submissions; 33 high-quality papers were subsequently selected to form the MMNS 2005 technical program. The diverse topics in this year's program included wireless networking technologies, wireless network applications, quality of services, multimedia, Web applications, overlay network management, and bandwidth management.

The conference chairs would first like to thank all those authors who contributed to an outstanding MMNS 2005 technical program, second the Program Committee and Organizing Committee chairs for their support throughout the development of the program and conference, third the worldwide experts who assisted in a rigorous review process, and fourth the sponsors, Universitat Politecnica de Catalunya, IFIP and IEEE, without whose support we would not have had such a professional conference. Last and certainly not least, we express sincere thanks to the company sponsors who were instrumental in helping to ensure a top-quality MMNS 2005.

We truly feel that this year's proceedings mark another significant point in the development of MMNS as a primary venue for the advancement of network and service management, and also novel architectures and designs in technology and network services, to enable multimedia proliferation.

October 2005

Jordi Dalmau and Go Hasegawa

Organization

Table of Contents

Wireless Networking Technologies

Wireless Network Applications

Overlay Network Management (1)

Multimedia (1)

Multimedia (2)

Web Applications

Overlay Network Management (2)

Quality of Services

Bandwidth Management

A New Performance Parameter for IEEE 802.11 DCF*

Yun Li, Ke-Ping Long, Wei-Liang Zhao, Qian-Bin Chen,
and Yu-Jun Kuang

Special Research Centre for Optical Internet & Wireless Information Networks,
ChongQing University of Posts & Telecommunications,
ChongQing 400065, China
{liyun, longkp, zhaowl}@cqupt.edu.cn

Abstract. In this paper, we define a new performance parameter, named *PPT*, for 802.11 DCF, which binds successful transmission probability and saturation throughput together. An expression of optimal minimum contention windows (CW_{min}) is obtained analytically for maximizing PPT. For simplicity, we give a name DCF-PPT to the 802.11 DCF that sets its CW_{min} according this expression. The simulation results indicate that, compared to 802.11 DCF, DCF-PPT can significantly increase the PPT and successful transmission probability (about 0.95) in condition that the saturation throughput is not decreased.

1 Introduction

Much research has been conducted on the performance of IEEE802.11 DCF[1]. In [2] and [3], the author gave a Markov chain model for the backoff procedure of 802.11 DCF and studied its saturation throughout. Haitao Wu *et al.* [4] considered the maximum retransmit count and improved the model given in [3]. In [5], the authors evaluated the performance of 802.11 DCF in terms of the spatial reuse. Wang C. et al. [6] proposed a new efficient collision resolution mechanism to reduce the collision probability. In [7], an enhancement for DCF is proposed to augment the saturation throughput by adaptively adjusting the contention window.

Although saturation throughput is an important performance parameter for 802.11 DCF because enhancing saturation throughput can utilizes the channel more efficiently, increasing the successful transmission probability is also important for 802.11 DCF. In this paper, we define a novel performance parameter, named Product of successful transmission Probability and saturation Throughput (PPT), for 802.11 DCF. The analysis is given to maximize PPT.

The rest of this paper is organized as follows: In section 2, we define PPT, and analyze how to maximize PPT. In section 3, the performance of DCF-PPT is simulated with different stations on terms of saturation throughput, successful transmission probability and PPT. We conclude this paper in section 4.

* Supported by the Research Project of Chongqing Municipal Education Commission of China (050310, KJ050503), the Research Grants by the Science & Tech. Commission of Chongqing(8817), the Research grants by the Ministry of Personnel of China.

J. Dalmau and G. Hasegawa (Eds.): MMNS 2005, LNCS 3754, pp. 1 – 10, 2005.
© IFIP International Federation for Information Processing 2005

2 PPT: Defining and Maximizing

Before defining PPT, we give the same definition of saturation throughput as in [3] as follows:

Definition 1: The saturation throughput of 802.11 DCF, S, is the limit throughput reached by the system as the offered load increase, which represent the maximum throughput in system's stable condition.

Definition 2: The system's stable condition is the condition on which the transmission queue of each station is nonempty.
   We define the successful transmission probability as follows:

Definition 3: The successful transmission probability P is the probability that a given transmission occurring on a slot is successful.
   Based on Definition 1 and Definition 3, we define PPT as follows:

Definition 4: The PPT is the product of successful transmission probability and saturation throughput, that is

$$PPT = S \times P \tag{1}$$

The definition of PPT binds saturation throughput and successful transmission probability together. Maximizing PPT can increases the saturation throughput while keeping high successful transmission probability, which is illustrated in the following.
   In [3], the author gave a two-dimensional Markov chain $\{b(t),s(t)\}$ to analyze the performance of 802.11 DCF, and obtained the saturation throughput S as follows:

$$S = \frac{P_s \cdot P_{tr} \cdot E[P]}{(1 - P_{tr}) \cdot \sigma + P_{tr} \cdot P_s \cdot T_s + P_{tr}(1 - P_s) \cdot T_c} \tag{2}$$

where, $E[P]$ is the average packet payload size, T_s is the average time the channel is sensed busy because of a successful transmission, T_c is the average time the channel is sensed busy during a collision, σ is the duration of an empty slot time, P_{tr} is the probability that there is at least one transmission in the considered slot time, P_s is the probability that a transmission occurring on the channel is successful, and

$$P_{tr} = 1 - (1 - \tau)^n \tag{3}$$

$$P_s = \frac{n\tau \cdot (1 - \tau)^{n-1}}{1 - (1 - \tau)^n} \tag{4}$$

where, τ is the probability that a station transmits in a randomly chosen slot, which can be expressed as follows[3]:

$$\tau = \frac{2 \cdot (1 - 2p)}{(1 - 2p) \cdot (w + 1) + p \cdot w \cdot \left(1 - (2p)^m\right)} \tag{5}$$

where, w is the contention windows, m is the maximum backoff stage, p is the probability that a transmitted packet encounters a collision, which is expressed as

$$p = 1 - (1 - \tau)^{n-1} \qquad (6)$$

Note that in definition 3, P is the probability that a given transmission occurring on a slot is successful, and a given transmission occurring on a slot is successful if and only if the $n\text{-}1$ remaining stations don't transmit in the same slot, so it is easy to obtain that

$$P = (1 - \tau)^{n-1} \qquad (7)$$

Plugging expression (2) and (7) into (1), we obtain

$$PPT = \frac{P_s \cdot P_{tr} \cdot E[P]}{(1 - P_{tr}) \cdot \sigma + P_{tr} \cdot P_s \cdot T_s + P_{tr}(1 - P_s) \cdot T_c} \cdot (1 - \tau)^{n-1} \qquad (8)$$

Given the expression of (3) and (4), (8) can be rewritten as:

$$PPT = \frac{n\tau \cdot (1 - \tau)^{n-1} \cdot E[P]}{(1 - \tau)^n \cdot \sigma + n\tau \cdot (1 - \tau)^{n-1} \cdot T_s + \left[1 - (1 - \tau + n\tau) \cdot (1 - \tau)^{n-1}\right] \cdot T_c} \cdot (1 - \tau)^{n-1} \qquad (9)$$

Expressions (2) and (7) denote that S and P are the function of τ, but the curves of S vs. τ and P vs. τ, which are shown in Fig. 1, are very different. Maximizing S does not means maximizing P simultaneously. However, maximizing PPT can obtain high S and P simultaneously because PPT is their product.

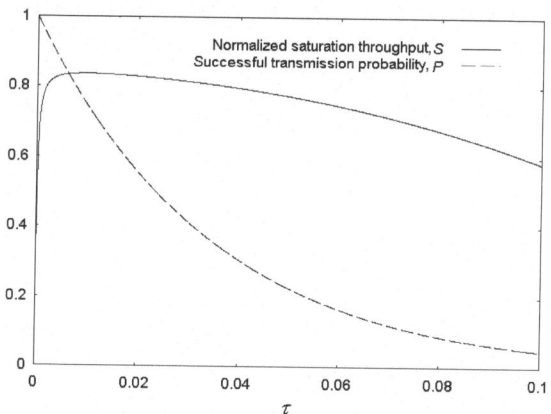

Fig. 1. S vs. τ, P vs. τ, $0 \le \tau \le 0.1$, $n=30$

Fig.2 indicates that PPT has a maximum value. We will deduce the optimal τ in the following.

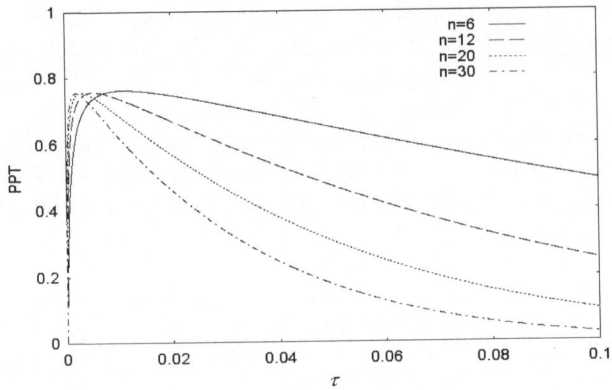

Fig. 2. PPT vs. τ, $0 \le \tau \le 0.1$

Taking the derivative of (1) with respect to τ, and imposing it equal to 0, we obtain the following equation:

$$\frac{d(PPT)}{d\tau} = \frac{d(S \cdot P)}{d\tau} = \frac{dS}{d\tau} \cdot P + \frac{dP}{d\tau} \cdot S = 0 \tag{10}$$

Note that

$$S = \frac{n\tau \cdot (1-\tau)^{n-1} \cdot E[P]}{(1-\tau)^n \cdot \sigma + n\tau \cdot (1-\tau)^{n-1} \cdot T_s + \left[1 - (1-\tau+n\tau) \cdot (1-\tau)^{n-1}\right] \cdot T_c} \tag{11}$$

Taking the derivative of S with respect to τ, and making some simplification, we obtain

$$\frac{dS}{d\tau} = \frac{\left[n \cdot (1-\tau)^{n-1} - n\tau(n-1) \cdot (1-\tau)^{n-2}\right] \cdot f(\tau) - n\tau \cdot n \cdot (1-\tau)^{n-1} \cdot f'(\tau)}{f^2(\tau)} \cdot E[P] \tag{12}$$

where,

$$f(\tau) = (1-\tau)^n \cdot \sigma + n\tau \cdot (1-\tau)^{n-1} \cdot T_s + \left[1 - (1-\tau+n\tau) \cdot (1-\tau)^{n-1}\right] \cdot T_c \tag{13}$$

$$f'(\tau) = -n(1-\tau)^{n-1}\sigma + (n - n^2\tau) \cdot (1-\tau)^{n-2} T_s + n\tau \cdot (n-1) \cdot (1-\tau)^{n-2} T_c \tag{14}$$

Taking the derivative of P with respect to τ, we obtain

$$\frac{dP}{d\tau} = -(n-1) \cdot (1-\tau)^{n-2} \tag{15}$$

Plugging expression (12) and (15) into (10), and making some simplification, we obtain

$$(1 + \tau - 2n\tau) \cdot f(\tau) - \tau \cdot (1-\tau) \cdot f'(\tau) = 0 \tag{16}$$

Moreover, plugging expression (13) and (14) into (16), and making some simplification, we obtain

$$\left(1+\tau-n\tau-n\tau^2\right)\sigma+\left(n\tau^2-n^2\cdot\tau^2\right)T_s$$
$$+\left[\frac{1+\tau-2n\tau}{(1-\tau)^{n-1}}-\left(1 \quad n\tau-\tau^2-n^2\tau^2+2n\tau^2\right)\right]T_c=0 \tag{17}$$

(17) is an equation in one variable of degree n. Noting that $\tau \ll 1$, we can obtain $(1-\tau)^{n-1}\approx 1$. Moreover, ignoring the τ^2 items, (17) was simplified to a linear equation as follows:

$$(n-1)\cdot T_c \cdot \tau+(n-1)\cdot \sigma \cdot \tau-\sigma = 0 \tag{18}$$

The approximate optimal τ, denoted as τ_{opt}, can be obtain from (18) as follows:

$$\tau_{opt} = \frac{1}{(n-1)\cdot T_c^* +n-1} \tag{19}$$

where, $T_c^* =\dfrac{T_c}{\sigma}$, which is the duration of a collision measured in slot time unit σ.

Expression (5) and (6) show that for given n, τ depends on the system parameters m and w. In [1], the default value of m is 5. In [3], the author have point out that the saturation throughput don't change obviously after the value of m is beyond 5. So, we let m keep on its default value 5, and only consider how to adjust w to maximize PPT.

Plugging (19) into (6), we can obtain

$$p =1-\left(1-\frac{1}{(n-1)\cdot T_c^* +n-1}\right)^{n-1} \tag{20}$$

From (5), we can obtain

$$w = \frac{(1-2p)\cdot (2-\tau)}{\tau - p\cdot \tau - p\cdot \tau\cdot (2p)^m} \tag{21}$$

Plugging (19) and (20) into (21), the expression of optimal w, denoted as w_{opt}, can be written as

$$w_{opt} = \frac{\left(-1+2\cdot\left(1-\dfrac{1}{(n-1)\cdot T_c^* +n-1}\right)^{n-1}\right)\cdot\left(2-\dfrac{1}{(n-1)\cdot T_c^* +n-1}\right)}{\dfrac{1}{(n-1)(T_c^* +1)}\left(\left(1-\dfrac{1}{(n-1)(T_c^* +1)}\right)^{n-1}-2^m\left(1-\left(1-\dfrac{1}{(n-1)(T_c^* +1)}\right)^{n-1}\right)^{m+1}\right)} \tag{22}$$

Expression (22) shows that we can adjust the values w (and consequently τ) to maximize the PPT.

In order to simplify the computation of w_{opt}, we approximate the expression (22) in the following.

Let

$$x = \left(1 - \frac{1}{(n-1)\cdot T_c^* + n - 1}\right)^n = \left(1 - \frac{1}{n\cdot\left(\frac{n-1}{n}T_c^* + \frac{n-1}{n}\right)}\right)^n = \left(1 - \frac{1}{nk}\right)^n$$

where, $k = \frac{n-1}{n}T_c^* + \frac{n-1}{n}$.

Note that $nk \gg 1$, x can be approximate as $x = e^{-\frac{1}{x}}$. As $p = x/\left(1 - \left(\frac{1}{nk}\right)\right)$, p can

be approximated as

$$p = 1 - \frac{1}{e^{1/k}\cdot\left(1 - \frac{1}{nk}\right)} \tag{23}$$

Plugging (19) and (23) into (21), we can obtain the approximated expression of w_{opt} as follows:

$$w_{opt} = \frac{\left(-1 + \frac{2}{e^{1/k}\cdot\left(1 - \frac{1}{nk}\right)}\right)\cdot\left(2 - \frac{1}{(n-1)\cdot T_c^* + n - 1}\right)}{\frac{1}{(n-1)\left(T_c^* + 1\right)}\left(\frac{1}{e^{1/k}\cdot\left(1 - \frac{1}{nk}\right)} - 2^m\left(1 - \frac{1}{e^{1/k}\cdot\left(1 - \frac{1}{nk}\right)}\right)\right)^{m+1}} \tag{24}$$

where,

$$k = \frac{n-1}{n}T_c^* + \frac{n-1}{n} \tag{25}$$

Moreover, if $n \gg 1$, then $\frac{n-1}{n} \approx 1$, $k = T_c^* + 1$, w_{opt} can be further approximated as

$$w_{opt} = \frac{\left(-1 + \frac{2}{e^{1/k}\cdot\left(1 - \frac{1}{nk}\right)}\right)\cdot\left(2 - \frac{1}{(n-1)\cdot T_c^* + n - 1}\right)}{\frac{1}{(n-1)\left(T_c^* + 1\right)}\cdot\left(\frac{1}{e^{1/k}\cdot\left(1 - \frac{1}{nk}\right)} - 2^m\cdot\left(1 - \frac{1}{e^{1/k}\cdot\left(1 - \frac{1}{nk}\right)}\right)\right)^{m+1}} \tag{26}$$

where, $k = T_c^* + 1$.

The computation of expression (24) and (26) is less complex than expression (22) after approximating the expression p. If the network size is small $(n \leq 10)$, we make use of (24) to calculate w_{opt}, and if the network size is huge $(n > 10)$, we make use of (26) to calculate w_{opt}. For simplicity, in section 3, we only make use of expression (24) to calculate w_{opt}.

3 Simulation

In this section, we firstly simulate the PPT, which is maximized by adjusting w_{opt} according to expression (24), and compare the simulated result to the numerically calculated maximum PTT. Then, we compare DCF-PPT to 802.11 DCF in terms of PPT, successful transmission probability and saturation throughput. The simulation platform is NS-2 [8]. The physical layer is DSSS. The stations transmit packets by means of RTS/CTS mechanism, and the simulation parameters are shown in table 1.

Table 1. Simulation Parameters

Channel Bit Rate	2Mbit/s
Slot Time	20μs
SIFS	10μs
DIFS	50μs
PHYHeader	192bits
MACHeader	144bits
RTS Length	160bits
CTS Length	112bits
CW_{min}	32
CW_{max}	1024
CBR Packet Size	1024Bytes

To calculate w_{opt} from expression (24), we must obtain the T_c. T_c is the average time the channel is sensed busy during a collision. In [3], when 802.11 DCF transmit packet by means of RTS/CTS mechanism, the author gave the expression of T_c as $T_c = RTS + DIFS + \sigma$. In this paper, we revised expression of T_c as

$$T_c = RTS + EIFS + \sigma \tag{27}$$

where, $EIFS = SIFS + ACK + DIFS$.

Making use of the expression (24), (25) and (27), we calculated the w_{opt} as in Table 2, according to different number of stations.

Table 2. Calculated w_{opt} for different number of stations

Number of stations	w_{opt}
6	147
12	386
20	696
30	1083

3.1 Comparing Simulated PPT to Numerical PPT

The maximum numerical PPT curve and the simulated PPT curve are drawn in Fig. 3, in different number of stations. In the simulation, we select the minimum contention windows (CW_{min}) according to table 2.

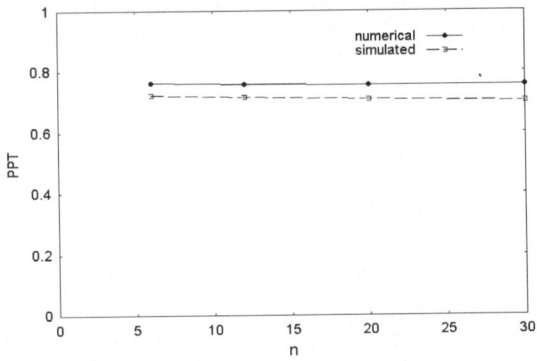

Fig. 3. Maximum PPT vs. n

Fig.3 shows that the simulated PPT is smaller than numerical PPT because we make some approximation to obtain the expression of w_{opt} in section 2, as make the calculated w_{opt} departure from the ideal value a bit . But the difference between the simulated PPT and the numerical PPT is less than 8%.

3.2 Comparing DCF-PPT to 802.11 DCF

According to different number of stations, the saturation throughput, successful transmission probability and PPT of DCF-PPT and 802.11 DCF are drawn in Fig. 4, Fig. 5 and Fig. 6, respectively.

Fig. 4 shows that the saturation throughput of DCF-PPT for all selected number of stations, except 12, is higher than 802.11 DCF. This is due to that we adaptively adjust CW_{min} according to the number of stations.

Fig. 5 shows that the successful transmission probability of DCF-PPT (about 0.95) is much higher than 802.11 DCF, and it does not decrease obviously with the number of stations increasing, as is also attributed to that we adjust CW_{min} adaptively according to the number of stations.

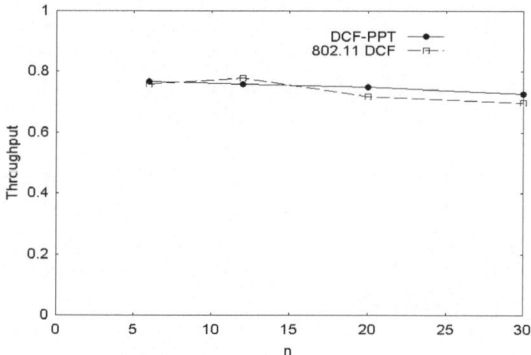

Fig. 4. The normalized throughput of DCF-PPT and 802.11 DCF

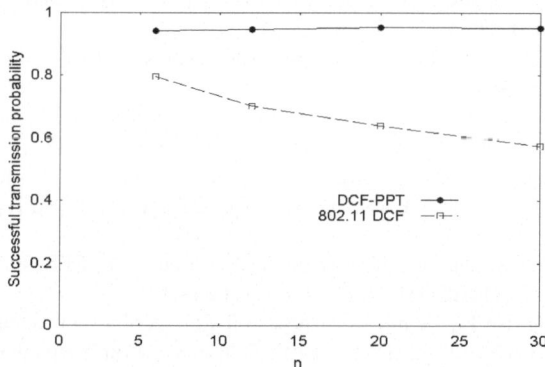

Fig. 5. The successful transmission probability of DCF-PPT and 802.11 DCF

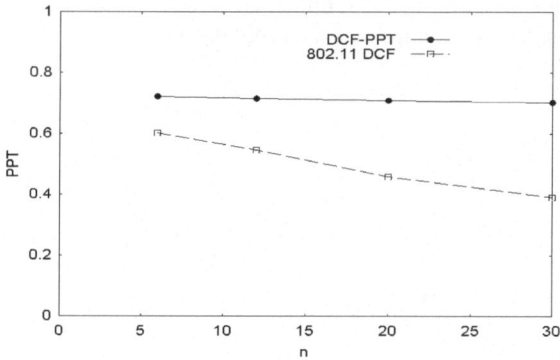

Fig. 6. The successful transmission probability of DCF-PPT and 802.11 DCF

Fig. 6 shows that the PPT of DCF-PPT is much higher than 802.11 DCF, and it does not decrease obviously when the number of stations increases.

4 Conclusion

In this paper, we define a novel performance parameter for 802.11 DCF, which binds successful transmission probability and saturation throughput together. The analysis is given to maximize PPT.

The performance of DCF-PPT is simulated with different stations on terms of saturation throughput, successful transmission probability and PPT. The simulation results indicate that DCF-PPT can largely increase the PPT and successful transmission probability in the condition that the saturation throughput is not decreased, comparing to 802.11 DCF.

References

1. IEEE standard for wireless LAN medium access control (MAC) and physical layer (PHY) specifications, 1999 Edition.
2. G.Bianchi. IEEE802.11 – Saturation throughput analysis. IEEE Communication Letters, Vol.2, (1998) 318 - 320.
3. G.Bianchi. Performance analysis of the IEEE 802.11 distributed coordination function, IEEE Journal on Selected Areas in Commu. , 18(3), (2000) 535-547.
4. Haitao Wu, Yong Peng, Keping Long and et.al.. Performance of Reliable Transport Protocol over IEEE 802.11 Wireless LAN:Analysis and Enhancement. IEEE INFOCOM, Vol.2, (2002) 599-607.
5. Fengji Ye, Su Yi, Sikdar, B.. Improving Spatial Reuse of IEEE 802.11 Based Ad Hoc Networks. IEEE GLOBECOM. Vol. 2, (2003) 1013 - 1017
6. Chonggang Wang, Bo Li, Lemin Li. A new collision resolution mechanism to enhance the performance of IEEE 802.11 DCF. IEEE Transactions on Vehicular Technology. 3(4), (2004) 1235-1246.
7. WU HaiTao, LIN Yu, CHENG ShiDuan, PENG Yong and LONG KePing. IEEE 802.11 Distributed Coordination Function: Enhancement and Analysis. Journal of Computer Science and Technology. 18(5), (2003) 607-614
8. The networks simulator ns-2, http:// www.isi.edu/nsnam/

An Energy*Delay Efficient Routing Scheme for Wireless Sensor Networks

Trong Thua Huynh and Choong Seon Hong

Computer Engineering Department, Kyung Hee Univerity,
1, Seocheon, Giheung, Yongin, Gyeonggi 449-701, Korea
htthua@networking.khu.ac.kr, cshong@khu.ac.kr

Abstract. Wireless sensor networks are composed of a large number of sensors densely deployed in inhospitable physical environments. How to disseminate information energy efficiently throughout such a network is still a challenge. Although energy efficiency is a key concern in wireless sensor networks, it often introduces additional delay. In this work, we first propose an Energy*Delay efficient routing scheme called C^2E^2S (Cluster and Chain based Energy*Delay Efficient Routing Scheme) for wireless sensor networks. This scheme is a combination of cluster-based and chain-based approaches. Next, we propose (1) an Energy*Delay-aware routing algorithm for sensors within each k-hop cluster, (2) an Energy-efficient chain construction algorithm for clusterheads. We also consider the network lifetime as an important factor as opposed to other approaches. The simulation results show that C^2E^2S consumes less energy, balances the energy and delay metrics, as well as extends the network lifetime compared with other approaches[1]

1 Introduction

In wireless sensor networks (WSN), where sensors are deployed densely in inhospitable environments, the proximate nodes will sense the identical data. Data aggregation from many of correlative data will reduce a large amount of data traffic on network, avoid information overload, produce a more accurate signal and require less energy than sending all the unprocessed data throughout the network. In various literatures, clustering approach is addressed as a routing method using the data aggregation feature effectively. LEACH [1] is one of the first cluster-based approaches in WSNs. Later, there are many protocols inspired from the idea proposed in LEACH. Works in [9],[11] involved the multi-hop approach into clusters for a larger set of sensors covering a wider area of interest. Many clustering algorithms in various contexts have also been proposed in these literatures, however, most of these algorithms are heuristic in nature and their aim is to generate the minimum number of clusters such that a node in any cluster is at the most d hops away from clusterhead. In our context, generating

---

[1] This research was partially supported by University ITRC Project. CS Hong is the corresponding author.

J. Dalmau and G. Hasegawa (Eds.): MMNS 2005, LNCS 3754, pp. 11–22, 2005.

the minimum number of clusters might not ensure minimum energy usage. In [7], authors have proposed a distributed, randomized clustering algorithm to organize the sensors in clusters. They consider the WSN in which the sensors are distributed as per a homogeneous spatial Poisson process. We use the results of their paper to support to our scheme.

The network lifetime can be defined as the time lasted until the last node in the network depletes its energy. Energy consumption in a sensor node can be due to many factors such as sensing event (data), transmitting or receiving data, processing data, listening to the media (avoid the conflict), communication overhead, etc. Considering the sensor's energy dissipation model in [1], the energy used to send q bits a distance d from one node to another node is given by $E_{tx} = (\alpha_1 + \alpha_2 d^n)*q$. Where α_1 is energy dissipated in transmitter electronics per bit, α_2 is energy dissipated in transmitter amplifier. For relatively short distances, the propagation loss can be modeled as inversely proportional to d^2, whereas for long distances, the propagation loss can be modeled as inversely proportional to d^4. Power control can be used to invert this loss by setting the power amplifier to ensure a certain power at the receiver. Obviously, energy consumption in a sensor will be significant if it transmits data to the node that is at long distance. This is one of the reasons that we suggest the k-hop cluster approach. Another reason is that the single-hop cluster approach is suitable only for networks with a small number of nodes. It is not scalable for a larger set of sensors covering a wider area of interest since the sensors are typically not capable of long-haul communication. Moreover, the energy dissipation is uneven in the single-hop cluster approach. In order to improve the energy efficiency, the chain-based approach has been proposed in [3]. In this approach, each node communicates only with a close neighbor and takes turns transmitting to the base station (BS), thus reducing the amount of energy spent per round. However, while chain-based protocols are more energy efficient than cluster-based protocols, they suffer from high delay and poor data fusion capacity.

Motivated by above mentioned issues, in this paper, we propose an energy-delay tradeoff routing scheme: a combination of cluster-based and chain-based approaches for WSNs. Plus, we propose an Energy*Delay-aware routing algorithm and an Energy-efficient chain construction algorithm for sensors within each k-hop cluster. The remainder of the paper is organized as follows: Section 2 mentions about related work. Section 3 and 4 describe the proposed scheme and its operation respectively. Intra-cluster routing algorithm is addressed in section 5 while inter-clusterheads routing is presented in section 6. We present the performance evaluation in section 7. Finally, we conclude the paper in section 8.

2   Related Work

Many WSN protocols have been developed for increasing energy efficiency in recent years. A clustering architecture based on the distributed algorithm for WSNs is provided in [1], where sensor nodes elect themselves as clusterheads with some probability based on residual energy of sensors for each round.

Although this approach has advantages to using the distributed cluster formation algorithm, it may produce poor clusters throughout the network. In addition, this approach allows only 1-hop clusters to be formed. This limits the capability of protocol. Then, authors improved clustering algorithm by using a center cluster algorithm. In this approach, the BS will control almost all operations in the network including computing and determining optimal clusters. In general, the clusters formed by BS are better than those formed using the distributed algorithm. However, this kind of approach suffers a large number of communication overheads between sensors and BS. Our approach is based on BS. However, to reduce the communication overheads, we propose a modified BS-based approach which will be described in sections 3 and 4.

Clustering architecture introduced in [4] provides two threshold parameters (hard, soft) in order to reduce number of transmission in the networks. The main drawbacks of the two approaches are the overhead and complexity of forming clusters in multi-levels and implementing threshold-based functions. Younis et al. have addressed hierarchical routing architecture in [10] based on 3-layer model. Clusters are formed by a lot of factors such as communication range, number and type of sensor nodes and geographical location, that can base on GPS [8] or other techniques. However, communication from clusterheads to the BS is still direct communication. Besides, authors only focused on the issue of network management within the cluster, particularly energy-aware routing. In [2], authors have provided a protocol called HEED. This approach selects well-distributed cluster-heads using information about residual energy and a second parameter such as node proximity to its neighbors or node degree. Authors have presented simulation results in order to prove the energy efficiency compared with other protocols (such as LEACH and its improvements). However, the clustering algorithm in HEED is still heuristic. Besides, HEED also assumes that communication from clusterheads to the BS is 1 hop away. This limits the capability of protocol, especially in large networks.

The approach proposed in [3] to improve the energy efficiency is chain-based approach. In this approach, each node communicates only with a close neighbor and takes turns transmitting to the BS, thus reducing the amount of energy spent per round. However, while chain-based protocols are more energy efficient than cluster-based protocols, they suffer from high delay and poor data fusion capacity. An Energy-Latency tradeoff approach in WSNs has been proposed in [6]. Authors studied the problem of scheduling packet transmission for data gathering in WSNs. They focus on the energy-latency tradeoffs using techniques such as modulation scaling. Although optimal algorithms based on dynamic programming have been proposed, they suffer an exponential complexity.

3   The Proposed Scheme (C^2E^2S)

A proposed network scheme for the WSNs is shown in figure 1. In this scheme, sensors in the WSN are distributed as a homogeneous spatial Poisson process of rate in a square area of side a. The computation of the optimal probability p

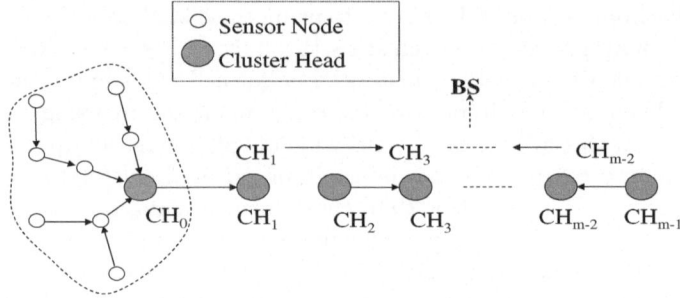

Fig. 1. A combination scheme of cluster and chain based approaches for the WSNs

to becoming a clusterhead and the maximum number of hops k allowed from a sensor to its clusterhead is beyond the scope of this paper. We use the results in [7] to obtain the optimal parameters for our scheme. According to this paper, we determine the maximum number of hops k as follows:

$$k = \lceil \frac{1}{r} \sqrt{\frac{-0.917 \ln(\alpha/7)}{p\lambda}} \rceil \qquad (1)$$

Where:
p : optimal probability of becoming a clusterhead
r : transmission range.
α : constant, ($\alpha = 0.001$ used in simulation).

Sensors are distributed into m k-hop clusters using these parameters. Each cluster has a clusterhead that aggregates all data sent to it by all its members. After that, m clusterheads form l binary chains. Each chain divides each communication round into log m/l levels. Each node transmits data to the closest neighbor in a given level. Only those nodes that receive data can rise to the next level. Finally, leader for each chain sends data to the BS. By then one transmission round completes. In this approach, each intermediate node performs data aggregation.

In this scheme, cluster and chain formation can either be computed in a centralized manner by the BS and broadcast to all nodes or accomplished by the sensor nodes themselves. To produce the better clusters and chains as well as to remove the strong assumption that all sensors have global knowledge of the network, we use the BS-based approach. However, the centralized approach suffers from very high communication overhead. To deal with this, we propose a passive approach (called passive-BS-based approach) in which each sensor node, upon sending a data packet, piggybacks related information. Upon a data packet reception, the BS extracts this information in order to apply for cluster and chain formation. The data packet format is depicted in figure 2. INFO part is a trio (Node ID, Node Energy, Number of bits). The BS bases on this trio in order to compute the residual energy for each node. For example, the trio (100, 1.5, 2500) describes that node 100 has 1.5 joules residual energy and sends 2500 bits data to the BS.

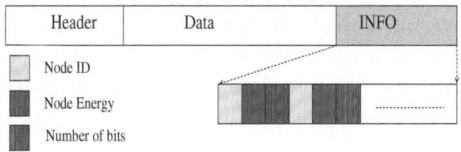

Fig. 2. Data Packet Format. The INFO includes information about ID, Energy, Number of bits of nodes that packet passed.

In this scheme, we assume the sensors are quasi-stationary. Each tiny sensor has a sensing module, a computing module, memory and wireless communication module. The BS has adequate energy to communicate with all sensor nodes in the network. Sensors are left unattended after deployment. They can use power control to vary the amount of transmit power to reduce the possibility of interfering with nearby cluster and its own energy dissipation.

4 C^2E^2S Operation

In C^2E^2S, network lifetime is divided into rounds. Each round begins with cluster and chain formation phase followed by data transmission phase. In each frame of data transmission phase, each sensor node is assigned its own time slot to transmit data to clusterhead. By turn, each clusterhead is also assigned its own slots to communicate with the nearest clusterhead based on chain construction. A detail description is depicted in the figure 3.

Using passive-BS-based approach, C^2E^2S distinguishes between the first round and the remaining rounds. In the first round, all sensors must send information about their location and current energy level to the BS directly. The BS uses this information and cluster and chain formation algorithms to choose clusterheads, to distribute remaining sensor nodes into associated clusters, and to construct l binary chains among clusterheads. In subsequent rounds, to form clusters and chain, the sensor nodes do not need to resend the information about location and residual energy to the BS anymore. Instead of this, information will be extracted from the INFO part in the data packets received from clusterheads in the previous round. The last packet from each node at the end of each round

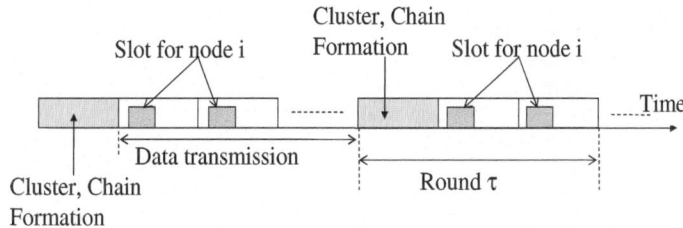

Fig. 3. Network lifetime for C^2E^2S

is the only one that carries information about residual energy level and number of transmitted bits of that node. The other packets carry data normally. Clusterheads receive data packets from other sensor nodes, perform data integration then send data packet to the BS following binary chains.

5   Intra-cluster Routing

The experiments were conducted for sensor networks of different intensity λ. For each network intensity, we used (1) to calculate the maximum number of hops k allowed from a sensor to its clusterhead. Results are given in Table 1.

Table 1. Maximum number of hops within each cluster for different network size (r=1)

Network size (number of sensors)	Intensity (λ)	Maximum number of hops (k)
1000	10	4
1500	15	3
2000	20	3
2500	25	3
3000	30	3
3500	35	3
4000	40	3

\# E_i :energy of node i;
\# $d(i,CH_j)$: distance from sensor i to clusterhead within cluster j
\# C_j : Cluster j   \# m : the number of clusters
\#z : the number of sensors within each cluster
\#$I_1 \leftarrow \{\}$: set of nodes that sense data, relay data from J_1, J_2 to clusterhead;
\#$J_1 \leftarrow \{\}$: set of nodes that sense data, relay data from K to I_1;
\#$I_2 \leftarrow \{\}$; $J_2 \leftarrow \{\}$; $K \leftarrow \{\}$: sets of sensing nodes;
\#J : union of J_1 with J_2.   \#I : union of I_1 with I_2.

1. $CAD = \dfrac{\sum\limits_{i=1}^{z} d(i,CH_j)}{z}$ $\forall i \in C_j, 0 \le j \le m-1$ /*average distance from sensors to associated clusterhead*/

2. $CAE = \dfrac{\sum\limits_{i=1}^{z} E_i}{z}$ $\forall i \in C_j, 0 \le j \le m-1$ //average energy for each cluster;

3. If $(d(i,CH_j) < CAD)$ then
If $(E_i \ge CAE)$ then $I_1 \leftarrow I_1 \cup i$;
Else $I_2 \leftarrow I_2 \cup i$;
4. Else If $(d(i,CH_j) \ge CAD$ and $d(i,CH_j) < 2*CAD)$ then
        If $(E_i \ge CAE)$ then $J_1 \leftarrow J_1 \cup i$;
        Else $J_2 \leftarrow J_2 \cup i$;
5. Else $K \leftarrow K \cup i$;
6. $I \leftarrow I_1 \cup I_2$; $J \leftarrow J_1 \cup J_2$

Fig. 4. Algorithm - partition sensors into 3 sets of nodes I, J, K

From results calculated in Table 1, obviously, 3-hop (at most) cluster is the best choice for the large sensor networks. Plus, the more hops are used, the higher latency is required. Hence, in this section, we propose an Energy*Delay-aware routing algorithm for sensors within each 3-hop cluster instead of k-hop cluster. This reduces significantly the complexity of algorithm compared with other approaches [10, 11]. The 3-hop routing algorithm within each cluster consists of 2 steps as follows:

1. Sensors within each cluster (except the clusterhead) are partitioned into three sets: I, J, K. The detailed algorithm is described in figure 4.
2. Using the Shortest Path Algorithm to determine the best route from these sets of node to clusterhead.

In step 2, we apply the Shortest Path Algorithm to determine the best route from clusterhead to $J(J_1 \cup J_2)$, K using the set nodes I_1, J_1 respectively.

Our intra-cluster routing problem can be considered as determining the shortest route (least cost) from one node to a set of nodes. We use Dijkstra's algorithm [5] to disseminate data from sensors to clusterhead with the link cost C_{ij} for the link between the nodes i and j defined as follows:

$$C_{ij} = \sum C_k (k = 1...4) \tag{2}$$

Where:

$C_1 = c_1 * d^2(i,j)$: data communication cost (energy) from node i to node j where c_1 is a weighting constant. This parameter reflects the cost of the wireless transmission power. Where d(i,j) is distance between the nodes i and j.

$C_2 = c_2 * d(i,j)$: delay cost because of propagation between the nodes i and j where c_2 is a constant which describes the speed of wireless transmission.

$C_3 = c_3 * E(j)$. This parameter reflects cost of energy, c_3 is a constant. Where E(j) is residual energy of node j.

$C_4 = c_4 * Z(j)$. Where c_4 is a constant, Z(j): number of connections to node j.

6   Inter-clusterheads Routing

In this section, we provide an Energy-efficient chain construction algorithm for clusterheads. The operation starts with one clusterhead, the farthest clusterhead from the BS. This node works as the head of the chain. Then, the non-chain node, the one that is closest to the head of the chain, will be appended into the chain. Besides, the BS also takes part in chain construction procedure in order to decide when a chain should be ended. This procedure repeats until all clusterheads are in the chains. The detailed algorithm is described in figure 5. The complexity of this algorithm is O(n^2). This algorithm ensures that clusterheads will communicate with the closest neighbor. Based on the radio energy dissipation model in [1], the receiving cost only depends on packet size, while the transmission energy depends on the distance between two nodes along a chain. As a result, that communication with the closest node is synonymous with consuming the least energy.

```
# CHAIN: chain
#HEAD: the head node in the chain
#d(i,j): distance from node i to node j
1. N: set of clusterheads;
2. HEAD ← The farthest clusterhead from BS, ∀ all nodes ∈ N;
3. N' ← N – {HEAD}; CHAIN ← {HEAD}; EndOfChain ← False;
4. While (N' ≠ ∅)
    key[i] ← min[d(HEAD,i)];    ∀ i ∈ N';  /* select a clusterhead
                                            i that is closest to the HEAD*/
    If key[i] < d(HEAD,BS);              //BS: base station
        HEAD ← i;
    Else {
        HEAD ← BS;
        EndOfChain ← True;
    }
    Append(CHAIN, HEAD);           // append HEAD at the end of CHAIN
    If (EndOfChain ← True)  Exit();  // end of While(N' ≠ ∅); a chain is
constructed
5. N ← N – N';
6. If (N≠ ∅)    Goto 2;        // construct another chain
7. Else      Stop;            // chains are constructed.
```

Fig. 5. Chain construction Algorithm for clusterheads

7 Performance Evaluation

In this section, we analyze the performance evaluated against LEACH-C, H-PEGASIS (Hierarchical PEGASIS), and HEED protocols in terms of communication overhead, the number of communication rounds (network lifetime), total amount of energy dissipated in the system over time, network delay and Energy*Delay metric using a simulator based on SENSE [12].

7.1 Simulation Setup

Our sensor field spans an area of $100x100m^2$ wherein 2000 sensors are scattered randomly with the BS location at (75,125). A node is considered "dead" if its energy level reaches 0. For a node in the sensing state, packets are generated

Table 2. Simulation Parameters

Parameter	Value
Network size	100x100
Number of sensors	2000
Base station location	(75,125)
Packet generating rate	1 packet/sec
E_{elec}	50nJ/bit
ε_{fs}	10pJ/bit/m^2
Initial energy (for each node)	2 Joule
Data packet size	500 bytes
Header size	25 bytes
Info packet size	25 bytes
Cluster Info packet size	50 bytes

at a constant rate of 1 packet/sec. For the purpose of our simulation experiments, the values for the parameters c_k in the link cost C_{ij} (given by (2)) are initially picked based on sub-optimal heuristics for best possible performance. The communication environment is contention and error free; hence, sensors do not have to retransmit any data. To compute energy consumption for each transaction sending and receiving, we use the radio energy dissipation model in [1]. The energy used to transmit q-bit data a distance d for each sensor node is: $E_{Tx}(q,d) = qE_{elec} + q\varepsilon_{fs}d^2$. The energy used to receive data for each node is: $E_{Rx}(q) = qE_{elec}$. Where E_{elec} is the electronics energy, ε_{fs} is power loss of free space. In these experiments, each node begins with 2 joule of energy and an unlimited amount of data to be sent to the BS. Table 2 summarizes parameters used in our simulation.

7.2   Simulation Results

For the first experiment, comparing the efficiency of network lifetime between the existing protocols and C^2E^2S, we studied the number of communication rounds as number of dead nodes increase and the total energy dissipated upon number of communication rounds. The graph in figure 6.a compares the network lifetime among LEACH-C, H-PEGASIS, HEED and C2E2S. In C^2E^2S, sensor nodes consume energy more evenly than other approaches. Although k-hop cluster approach in C^2E^2S suffers slightly higher delay, it balances energy dissipation between sensor nodes. Thus, number of communication rounds increase significantly. Compared with LEACH-C and HEED, C^2E^2S balances energy consumption between clusterheads. Compared with H-PEGASIS, C^2E^2S reduces a large number of identical data bits between sensors in the same cluster. Figure 6.b shows the amount of energy dissipated after a number of communication rounds. C^2E^2S is able to keep its energy dissipated gradually thus prolonging network lifetime.

For the second experiment, we first evaluate network delay metric. Next, to calculate the Energy*Delay, we multiply the total delay with total dissipated energy over time for each protocol. The graph in figure 7.a shows that the network delay in LEACH-C is the highest while C^2E^2S offers the lowest delay. However, when the number of dead nodes increases a lot, the network delay in C^2E^2S is

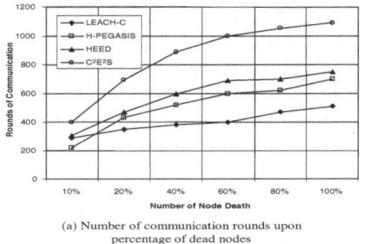

(a) Number of communication rounds upon
percentage of dead nodes

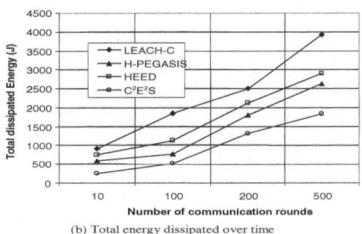

(b) Total energy dissipated over time

Fig. 6. Comparing the efficiency of network lifetime among protocols

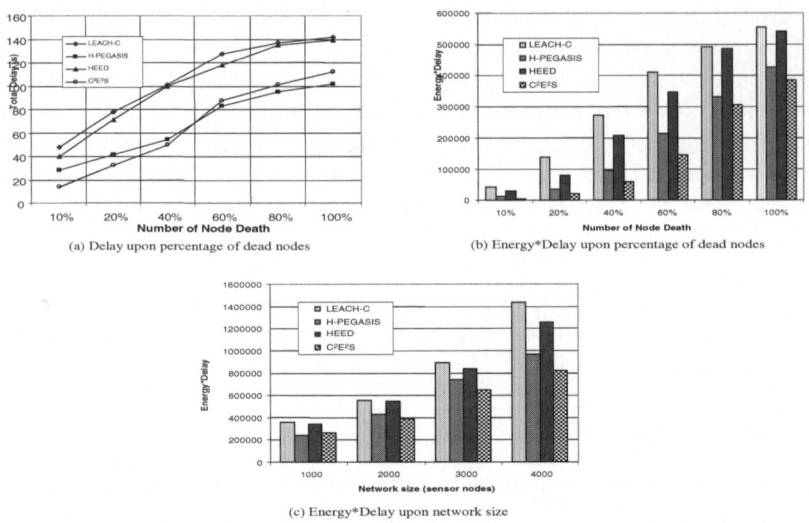

(a) Delay upon percentage of dead nodes   (b) Energy*Delay upon percentage of dead nodes

(c) Energy*Delay upon network size

Fig. 7. Comparing the efficiency of Energy*Delay metric among protocols

slightly higher than H-PAGESIS. Regardless of this, C^2E^2S saves much more energy than H-PEGASIS. Thus, Energy*Delay metric in C^2E^2S is always lower than H-PEGASIS. As shown in figure 7.b, this metric is also lower than in both LEACH-C and HEED (cluster-based approaches).

Besides, to indicate the effectiveness of our scheme in terms of Energy*Delay metric for large sensor networks, we ran several simulations with different network sizes (from 1000 to 4000 sensors). Figure 7.c shows that when network size increase, the effectiveness of Energy*Delay metric in our scheme also increases significantly. For 1000 sensor nodes, C^2E^2S is slight higher than H-PEGASIS. However, for more than 2000 sensor networks, Energy*Delay in C^2E^2S is lower than other protocols. Hence, we can say that, C^2E^2S is a very Energy*Delay efficient scheme for large WSNs.

In the last experiment, we studied the communication overhead as total number of header bits transferred from sensors to the BS. In our approach, node's information is piggybacked by data packets. Thus, it reduces a large number

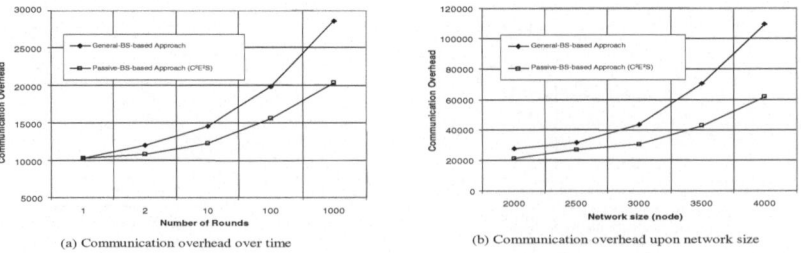

(a) Communication overhead over time   (b) Communication overhead upon network size

Fig. 8. Communication overhead for Gen-BS-based and Passive-BS-based approaches

of communication overheads broadcasting through the network using general BS-based approaches (we call Gen-BS-based approach). Figure 8.a shows that the number of communication overheads is equal in the first round for both the approaches. However, from the second round, the number of communication overheads increases gradually in C^2E^2S, while Gen-BS-based approach (LEACH-C, HEED) increase very fast.

The effectiveness of C^2E^2S is seen more clearly as there are several simulations run for a large number of sensor nodes. Yet again, we compare two approaches for different network sizes (from 2000 to 4000 sensors). Result in figure 8.b shows that the number of communication overheads increases very fast in Gen-BS-based approach, while it increases gradually as number of senor nodes increases.

8   Conclusion

Motivated by delay- awareness energy efficiency, in this paper, we have presented an Energy*Delay routing scheme (called C^2E^2S) for WSNs. We also have proposed two algorithms in order to balance the energy and delay metrics for all sensors in the network, extend lifetime of network and reduce the number of communication overheads in the network. One of these algorithms is Energy*Delay routing algorithm. This algorithm is applied within 3-hop cluster in order to balance energy*delay for sensors within each cluster. Another algorithm is Energy-efficient chain construction algorithm. This algorithm is applied for clustedheads to construct energy-efficient chains from clusterheads to the BS. Simulation results demonstrate that C^2E^2S consistently performs well with respect to Energy*Delay-based metric, network lifetime, and communication overhead compared with other approaches. As a future work, we need study on energy*delay optimal routing to improve the goodness of our scheme.

References

1. W. R. Heinzelman, A. Chandrakasan, H. Balakrishnan, "An Application-Specific Protocol Architecture for Wireless Microsensor Networks", in IEEE Transactions on Wireless Communications, October 2002.
2. O. Younis, S. Fahmy, "HEED: A Hybrid, Energy-Efficient Distributed Clustering Approach for Ad hoc Sensor Networks", in IEEE Transactions on Mobile Computing, October 2004.
3. S. Lindsey, el al., "Data Gathering Algorithms in Sensor Networks using Energy Metrics", in IEEE Transactions on Parallel and Distributed Systems 2002.
4. A. Manjeshwar, D. P. Agrawal, "APTEEN: A Hybrid Protocol for Efficient Routing and Comprehensive Information Retrieval in WSNs", in the Proceedings of IEEE IPDPS 2002.
5. F. Zhan, C. Noon, "Shortest Path Algorithms: An Evaluation Using Real Road Networks", Transportation Science, 1996.
6. Y. Yu, B. Krishnamachari, V. K. Prasanna, "Energy-Latency Tradeoffs for Data Gathering in Wireless Sensor Network", in Proceedings of IEEE INFOCOM 2004.

7. S. Bandyopadhyay and Ed. J. Coyle, "An Energy Efficient Hierarchical Clustering Algorithm for Wireless Sensor Networks", in Proceedings of IEEE INFOCOM 2003.
8. US Naval Observatory (USNO) GPS Operations, http://tycho.usno.navy.mil/gps.html.
9. K. Dasgupta, K. Kalpakis, P. Namjoshi, "An Efficient Clustering-based Heuristic for Data Gathering and Aggregation in Sensor Networks", in Proceedings of WCNC 2003.
10. M. Younis, M. Youssef, K. Arisha, "Energy-Aware Routing in Cluster-Based Sensor Networks", in the Proceedings of IEEE MASCOTS'02, October 2002.
11. Alan D. Amis, Ravi Prakash, Thai H.P. Vuong, Dung T. Huynh, "Max-Min D-Cluster Formation in Wireless Adhoc Networks", in Proceedings of IEEE INFO-COM 2000.
12. Gang Chen, et al., "SENSE - Sensor Network Simulator and Emulator", http://www.cs.rpi.edu/ cheng3/sense/.

Adaptive Supporting Prioritized Soft Handoff Calls for Power-Controlled DS-CDMA Cellular Networks

Wen Chen[1], Feiyu Lei[1], Weinong Wang[1], and Xi Chen[2]

[1] Network Information Center, Computer Science & Engineering Dept.,
Shanghai Jiao Tong University, 1954 Huashan Road, Shanghai 200030, China
wen.chenwen@gmail.com, {fylei, wnwang}@sjtu.edu.cn
[2] Computer Center, China ShipBuilding Industry Corporation,
No.701 Research and Development Institute, Wuhan Hubei 430070, China
cx040504@gmail.com

Abstract. We present feedback control techniques to intelligently support priorities of soft handoff calls during call admission control (CAC) in power-controlled DS-CDMA multicellular networks. We design a classic proportional controller to dynamically solve resource management problems, which arise during run-time adaptation, via continuously monitoring real-time system performance to adjust system parameters accordingly. Performance evaluation reveals that the solution not only has excellent stability behavior, but also meets zero steady state error and settling time requirements.

1 Introduction

It is well known that rejection of a handoff request causes forced termination of an ongoing service and wasting wireless resources due to retransmission. Therefore, the dropping of a handoff call is generally considered more serious than blocking of a new call. A basic approach to reduce handoff probability is to give handoff calls priority over new calls. In 2G TDMA/FDMA wireless networks, the popular guard channels (GC) [1] scheme and its numerous variants [2] exclusively reserve a fixed number of channels for handoff calls to make it. But the fundamental premise of the fixed GC schemes [3] is that the network behavior can be made to be deterministic through extensive a priori knowledge about network parameters. Therefore, they perform poorly in unpredictable dynamic systems.

Currently, emerging mobile wireless network such as DS-CDMA cellular networks are characterized by significant uncertainties in mobile user population and system resource state (i.e. soft capacity, soft handoff). Then, any solution for reducing handoff dropping in DS-CDMA systems must be highly adaptive for adherence to the desired system performance requirements, and cannot rely on the assumptions of traffic or mobility patterns. Feedback control theory can just be the theoretical basis for the design of adaptation-based architectures that handle QoS-aware services for current wireless networks with parametric, structural and environmental uncertainties.

J. Dalmau and G. Hasegawa (Eds.): MMNS 2005, LNCS 3754, pp. 23–34, 2005.

Although several recent studies [4][5] have been conducted concerning the forced-termination of calls due to soft handoff failure in DS-CDMA networks, the adaptation mechanisms are not considered at all. And that some adaptive QoS schemes such as [6] realize the adaptive control only by a predefined fixed stepwise way, which cannot react to the system changes efficiently.

In this paper, we propose a radically different approach to adaptively reduce soft handoff failure probability in DS-CDMA cellular networks based on feedback control theory. The main contribution of this paper is that adaptive system performance optimization and feedback control techniques are combined for modeling the unpredictability of the environment, handling imprecise or incomplete knowledge, reacting to overload and unexpected failures, and achieving the required performance levels. Our contribution can be summarized as follows:

- Formulating the reducing handoff dropping problem as a feedback control loop. And we choose to use a P(Proportional) control function to adjust some system parameter adaptively according to the real-time change of network performance, not as previous stepwise way (such as [6]). And that we use the Root Locus method to tune the controller so as to satisfy the performance specs.
- Through comparing real-time soft handoff failure probability with new call blocking probability in the controller, we not only characterize real-time system performance variances accurately but also achieve a satisfied tradeoff between them.
- Using system identification to design a mathematical model that describes the dynamic behavior of CAC process in a cellular network.
- Achieving the desired network performance with traffic conditions and user mobility that are unknown a priori.

2   Reference CDMA Cellular Network

We consider a multicellular network with spread signal bandwidth of WHz. We only focus on the uplink since it is generally accepted that it has inferior performance over the downlink.

2.1   Traffic Classes

We consider cellular networks that support both voice and data services. Assumed that there are $K(K \geq 1)$ different traffic classes with different QoS requirements. Namely, each class specifies their own transmission rate, activity factor, desired SIR requirement, and maximum power limit that can be received at the base station. We assume that traffic from the same service class has the same QoS requirements. We define a mapping $\sigma : Z^+ \rightarrow \{1, \cdots, K\}$ to indicate that the nth connection is from the service class $\sigma(n)$, where Z^+ denotes the set of nonnegative integers. Also, call requests are classified into soft handoff call and new call requests. In this paper, we give higher priority to soft handoff calls than new calls within the same class.

2.2   Uplink Capacity in Power Controlled Multicellular Networks

As the uplink is more critical to total capacity than downlink [7], we consider only the uplink capacity of a reference cell in a multicellular DS-CDMA network. Let N be the number of connections served by BS currently. The power received at the base station from the user (mobile station, MS) of the nth connection is denoted by S_n, $n = 1, \cdots, N$. In an SIR-based power-controlled DS-CDMA network [8], the maximum received power at BS is determined by maximum power limit H_k for connections from service class $k = \sigma(n)$, then

$$0 < S_n \leq H_k, \quad \forall n = \{1, \cdots, N\}. \tag{1}$$

The maximum power limits H_k, $k = 1, \cdots, K$, principally depend on [8] the maximum power p_k that can be transmitted by a MS of class-k and the expected value of path loss for class-k $E_k[L]$ from the cell boundary to the base station. Then, we can choose $H_k = p_k E_k[L]$, $k = 1, \cdots, K$. In this paper, the cases when $S_n > H_{\sigma(n)}$ for some received call n, BS will reject the call since otherwise either some MS (mobile station) would be required to transmit more power than they can possibly do or the acceptance of the new call will severely damage the QoS of existing connections.

Let α_k be the activity factor of a Class-k user, the bit-energy-to-interference ratio E_b/N_o for the nth connection at the BS can be expressed in terms of the received power of various connections existing in the considered cell (intra-cell) and the surrounding cells (inter-cell) as [8]:

$$\left(\frac{E_b}{N_o}\right)_n = \frac{S_n W}{R_{\sigma(n)}\left(\sum_{i=1, i \neq n}^{N} \alpha_{\sigma(i)} S_i + I_n^{\text{other}} + \eta_n\right)}, \tag{2}$$

where S_i is the power level of the ith connection received at the base station, $R_{\sigma(n)}$ is the data rate of service class $\sigma(n)$, I_n^{other} is the total interference from neighboring cells, η_n is the background(or thermal) noise. In [8], it had been shown that the total interference from neighboring cells, I_n^{other}, can be reckoned by

$$I_n^{\text{other}} = f \sum_{i=1, i \neq n}^{N} \alpha_{\sigma(i)} S_i, \tag{3}$$

where f is called the inter-cell interference factor with a typical value of 0.55 [8]. The value of f may not always be constant and can be updated properly to reflect changes in traffic conditions and distributions.

The soft capacity of CDMA systems is limited by the level of multiaccess interference measured by the SIR. In general, since SIR drops and the probability of packet error increases as the number of users increases, it appears reasonable to maintain SIR above set thresholds γ_k, $k = 1, \cdots, K$ by limiting the number of users. For example, the QoS requirement for voice users with a maximum bit error rate of 10^{-3} can be satisfied by the power control mechanism setting γ at a required value of $7dB$ [8]. Then we must hold $(E_b/N_o)_n \geq \gamma_{\sigma(n)}$ for all current calls to maintain BER (bit error rate) below a certain limit as the following inequality:

$$\frac{S_n W}{R_{\sigma(n)} \gamma_{\sigma(n)}} \geq (1+f) \sum_{i=0, i \neq n}^{N} \alpha_{\sigma(i)} S_i + \eta_n, \quad \forall n \in \{1, \cdots, N\}. \tag{4}$$

2.3 The Scheme for Assign Priority to Soft Handoff Requests

In general, handoff calls are payed more attention than new calls and we have to give priority to handoff calls [4][5][8]. The main idea of the present approach is as follows [8], we can choose a fixed threshold $T_k < H_k$, $k = 1, \cdots, K$, for new calls of class-k to allow higher priority for handoff calls of class-k. Thus, BS would admit less new calls in the case $T_k < H_k$ than in the case $T_k = H_k$. The call admission policy is given as follows:

1. if a new call marked by connection-$(N+1)$ arrives,then
   if $S_{N+1} \leq T_{\sigma(N+1)}$ and inequality(4) is satisfied $\forall n = \{1, 2, \cdots, N, N+1\}$,
      accept the call;
   otherwise, reject the call;
2. if a soft-handoff call marked by connection-$(N+1)$ arrives,then
   if $S_{N+1} \leq H_{\sigma(N+1)}$ and inequality(4) is satisfied $\forall n = \{1, 2, \cdots, N, N+1\}$,
      accept the soft-handoff call;
   otherwise, reject the soft-handoff call.

In the above algorithm, new call thresholds T_k, $k = 1, \cdots, K$ are key design parameters which effect the new call blocking probability and handoff failure probability at first hand. With highly variable conditions, any solution for reducing handoff dropping probability in a system must be highly adaptive. In our scheme, the main contribution is that we apply feedback control theory to adjust the thresholds T_k adaptively, so as to achieve satisfactory network performance and response to the system's real-time dynamic. In the next section, we will introduce the development of the feedback controller.

2.4 Network Performance Parameters

In this paper, we basically consider two performance measures in each service class, i.e. new call blocking probability of class-k $P_{k,b}$ and soft handoff call failure probability of class-k $P_{k,h}$. According to [5][9], we evaluate the network performance by grade of service (GoS), which is defined as

$$GoS_k = P_{k,b} + \omega P_{k,h}, \quad \text{for } k = \{1, \cdots, K\}, \tag{5}$$

where ω is a weighting factor to put greater importance on soft handoff call dropping probability and is set to 10 in most work [5][9]. Since the system capacity depends on the QoS difference between the two performance measures, it has been shown [5] that for a given service class, the system capacity is maximal when the new call blocking probability is equal to the weighted soft handoff failure probability. And in every monitoring period, defined the time interval $[t_{m-1}, t_m]$ as the mth monitoring period, we compute the two performance measures for each class.

3 Our Feedback Control Approach

In the next-generation wireless network, the resource requirements and the arrival state of service requests occur over time, so it is even more difficult to model because none of them is known a priori. These problems call for mechanisms that can control them effectively, without depending on detailed insight into their internal structure or on precise models of their behavior. Whereas feedback control strategy can be applied for behavior optimization in unpredictable or poorly modelled environments.

In our feedback control architecture, we define a set of control related variable for each service class $k = 1, \cdots, K$ in the following:

◇ Controlled Variable $\triangle P_k$: $\triangle P_k = \omega P_{k,\mathrm{h}} - P_{k,\mathrm{b}}$. It means network performance output, which is measured and controlled. This way can balance the two performance measures simply and efficiently.
◇ Set Point: 0. It represents that system capacity arrives maximal when the new call blocking probability is equal to the weighted soft handoff failure probability [5].
◇ Error E_k: $E_k = 0 - \triangle P_k = -\triangle P_k$. It shows the difference between the set point and the current value of the controlled variable.
◇ Manipulated Variable $\triangle T_k$: It is the quantity of the new call power threshold that is adjusted by the controller.

And a feedback loop of our architecture [12] is 1) the system periodically monitors and compares the controlled variable to the set point to determine the error; 2) the controller computes the required control with the control function of the system based on the error; 3) the actuators changes the value of the manipulated variable to control the system.

Note that for each service class, there is an independent feedback loop with the identical design process. For convenience, we will only discuss the whole design process for some service class k, $k = 1, \cdots, K$, in later development.

4 Threshold Feedback Loop Design

We utilize feedback control theory and methodology [10] to design an adaptive new call power threshold adjuster for each service class with proven performance guarantees. The corresponding design methodology includes

1. Choosing P control as the basic controller model for each class-k to compute the change to the power threshold of class-k $\triangle T_k$;
2. Using system identification to design the open-loop system model;
3. Tuning the control parameters and meeting performance specs requirements of adaptive system with Root Locus methods;

4.1   P Controller

We choose P control as the basic feedback control techniques in adaptive threshold adjustment for the following reasons [11][12]. The rationale for using a P controller instead of a more sophisticated Controller, such as PID (Proportional-Integral-Derivative) Controller, is that the controlled system includes an integrator in the adjustment of the new call power threshold (see the following (8)) such that zero steady state error can be achieved without an I (Integral) term in the Controller. The D (Derivative) term is not appropriate for controlling real-time systems because Derivative control may amplify the noise in new call blocking probability and soft handoff failure probability due to random workloads [10].

A basic form P control formula for controlling the change of the new call power threshold for some service class-k in our scheme is

$$\triangle T_k(t) = C_{k,P} E_k(t), \tag{6}$$

where $C_{k,P}$ is a tunable parameter (see Sect. 6). At each sampling instant m, P controller periodically monitors the difference between new call blocking probability and weighted soft handoff probability for each class, and computes the manipulated variable $\triangle T_k(m)$ with the following control formula:

$$\triangle T_k(m) = -C_{k,P} \triangle P_k(m), \tag{7}$$

If $\triangle T_k(m) > 0$, the new call power threshold of class-k should be increased. Otherwise, the new call power threshold of class-k should be decreased. Namely,

$$T_k(m) = T_k(m-1) + \triangle T_k(m). \tag{8}$$

In our work, the controller's tuning process needs to base on a linear model of the controlled system. It will be addressed in the following.

4.2   The Open-Loop System Model

As a basis for the analytical design of a controller, we must establish a dynamic model to describe the mathematical relationship between the input and the output of a system. Here, the input of the open-loop model is the change to the new call power threshold of class-k $\triangle T_k(m)$. The output of the model (i.e. the controlled variable) is the difference between the new call blocking probability and soft handoff probability of class-k $\triangle P_k(m)$. However, modeling computing systems with unknown dynamics has been a major barrier for applying feedback control in adaptive resource management of such system. As system identification methodology [11] provides a practical solution for solving such modeling problems, we utilize it to establish a linear model for the controlled system with differential or difference equations.

Model Structure. We observe that the output of an open-loop network model depends on previous input and outputs of the model. Then, the reference cellular network of some service class-k is modelled as a nth order difference equation with some unknown parameters,

$$\triangle P_k(m) = \sum_{j=1}^{n} a_{k,j} \triangle P_k(m-j) + \sum_{j=1}^{n} b_{k,j} \triangle T_k(m-j). \tag{9}$$

There are $2n$ parameters $\{a_{k,j}, b_{k,j} | 1 \leq j \leq n\}$ that need to be decided in an nth order model of service class-k. Next, we will apply least squares estimator to solve the problem.

Least Squares Estimator. Least-squares estimator [13] can estimate unknown parameters by recursion formula, if only a system is modelled to be the following standard structure,

$$y(m) = \Phi^T(m)\Theta(m) + e(m), \tag{10}$$

where $\Phi^T(m)$ denotes the input-output observation vector, $\Theta(m)$ denotes the unknown parameters vector, $e(m)$ represents noise. White noise input has been commonly used for system identification [13]. The estimator is invoked periodically at every sampling instant. At the mth sampling instant, according to the above (10), we define the vectors $\Phi_k(m)$ and $\Theta_k(m)$ for service class-k:

$$\Phi_k(m) = (\triangle P_k(m-1) \cdots \triangle P_k(m-n) \triangle T_k(m-1) \cdots \triangle T_k(m-n))^T,$$
$$\Theta_k(m) = (a_{k,1} \cdots a_{k,n} \, b_{k,1} \cdots b_{k,n})^T.$$

Let $\boldsymbol{R}(m)$ be a square matrix whose initial value is set to a diagonal matrix with the diagonal elements set to 10. The recursion formulas of the estimator's equations for class-k at sampling instant m are [13]:

$$\gamma_k(m) = [1 + \Phi_k^T(m)\boldsymbol{R}(m-1)\Phi_k(m)]^{-1} \tag{11}$$

$$\Theta_k(m) = \Theta_k(m-1) + \gamma_k(m)\boldsymbol{R}(m-1)\Phi_k(m)[\triangle P_k(m) - \atop \Phi_k^T(m)\Theta_k(m-1)] \tag{12}$$

$$\boldsymbol{R}(m) = \boldsymbol{R}(m-1) - \gamma_k(m)\boldsymbol{R}(m-1)\Phi_k(m)\Phi_k^T(m)\boldsymbol{R}(m-1). \tag{13}$$

At sampling instant m, we substitute the current estimates $\Theta_k(m)$ (reckoned by (12)) into (9), the estimator "predicts" a value of the model output $\triangle \hat{P}_k(m)$. The estimate error is $\triangle P_k(m) - \triangle \hat{P}_k(m)$. The objective of the least squares estimator is iteratively update the parameter estimates at each sampling instant so as to minimize $\sum_{0 \leq i \leq m} (\triangle P_k(m) - \triangle \hat{P}_k(m))^2$.

Our experimental results (Sect. 5) establish a second order difference equation of class-k to approximate the input-output relation of the dynamic open-loop model,

$$\triangle P_k(m) = a_{k,1}\triangle P_k(m-1) + a_{k,2}\triangle P_k(m-2) + b_{k,1}\triangle T_k(m-1) + b_{k,2}\triangle T_k(m-2). \tag{14}$$

4.3   The Closed-Loop Feedback Design

In this section, we obtain the transfer function of the closed-loop system model to analyze the system dynamic. First, we convert the open-loop controlled system model for class-k in (14) to a transfer function $G_{k,\mathrm{O}}(z)$ in z-domain:

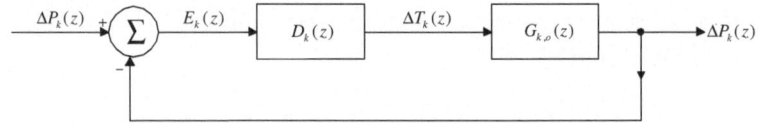

Fig. 1. New call power threshold of class-k feedback control loop

$$G_{k,\text{o}}(z) = \frac{\triangle P_k(z)}{\triangle T_k(z)} = \frac{b_{k,1}z + b_{k,2}}{z^2 - a_{k,1}z - a_{k,2}}. \tag{15}$$

Second, the transfer function of the class-k P controller in z-domain is also given by

$$D_k(z) = C_{k,P}. \tag{16}$$

Thus, given the open-loop model and the controller model, we achieve the transfer function $G_{k,\text{c}}(z)$ of the closed-loop model:

$$G_{k,\text{c}}(z) = \frac{D_k(z)G_{k,\text{o}}(z)}{1 + D_k(z)G_{k,\text{o}}(z)} = \frac{C_{k,P}(b_{k,1}z + b_{k,2})}{z^2 + (b_{k,1}C_{k,P} - a_{k,1})z + (b_{k,2}C_{k,P} - a_{k,2})}. \tag{17}$$

In summary, we present the block diagram of the adaptive new call power threshold of class-k feedback control system in Fig.1.

4.4   Performance Specs

To design adaptive systems, it is necessary to devise specifications for the adaptive process itself. The following metrics [10] of a closed-loop system are used to describe the quality of adaptation:

- **Stability:** BIBO (bounded-input bounded-output) stability, which means that the system output is always bounded for bounded references, is satisfied to avoid uncontrollable performance degradation in a system. In the context of our system, this means stability is a necessary condition to prevent the controlled variables $\triangle P_1$ from severe deviations with reference values 0. For example, although $P_{1,\text{b}}$ and $P_{1,\text{h}}$ exceed some limit values to make the link availability low, the controlled variable $\triangle P_1$ unexpectedly reaches the set point. To satisfy the stability, it avoids the situation happening.
- **Setting time T_s:** T_s is the time it takes the output to converge to within 2% of the reference and enter steady state. It represents the efficiency of the controller. We assume that our system requires the settling time $T_s < 10sec$.
- **Steady state error:** For a closed-loop system, the steady state error represents the accuracy of the basic controller in achieving the desired performance. And zero steady state error means our closed-loop controller can bring performance parameters to their set points in steady state with zero error.

5 System Identification Experiment

We first conduct simulation studies for a network with single class of service (e.g., voice). And the value of threshold T_1 (assumed that k=1 denotes voice class) changes in the range of $0.75 \cdot 10^{-14}$W to $1.0 \cdot 10^{-14}$W as the parameters used in [8]. We use the System Identification Toolbox of MATLAB to run the system identification experiments to respectively estimate a first order, a second order, a third order and a forth order model. Figure 2 demonstrates that the estimated first order model has larger prediction error than the second order model, while an estimated third/forth model does not tangibly improve the modeling accuracy. Hence the second order model is chosen as the best comprise between accuracy and complexity. The corresponding estimation parameters are $(a_{1,1}, a_{1,2}, b_{1,1}, b_{1,2}) = (0.6209, -0.06977, 3.813e010, -2.645e007)$.

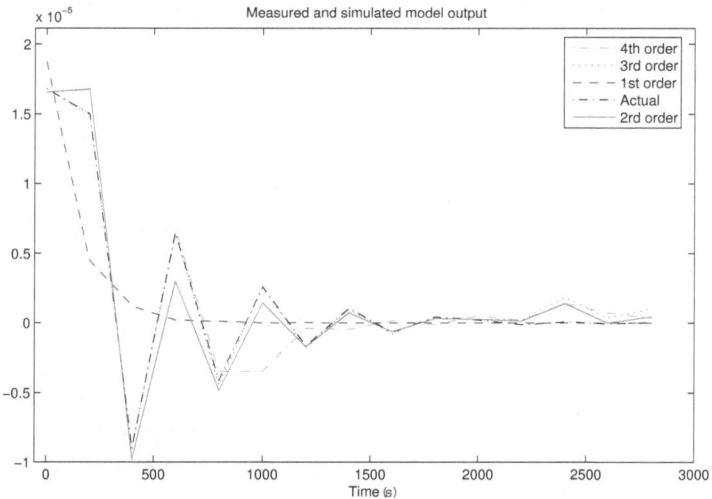

Fig. 2. System Identification Results of voice class

We can conduct estimation for cellular network with two or more than classes of services using the same way, for each class has a completely dependent controller and model with only relatively different network parameters (see [8]). Similarly, the following turning process of the controller for voice class also gives a demonstration.

6 Control Tuning and Performance Analysis

According to control theory, the performance profile of a system depends on the poles of its closed-loop transfer function. We can place the pole at the desired location by choosing the right vale for the control parameter $C_{1,P}$ (voice class) to achieve desired performance spec.

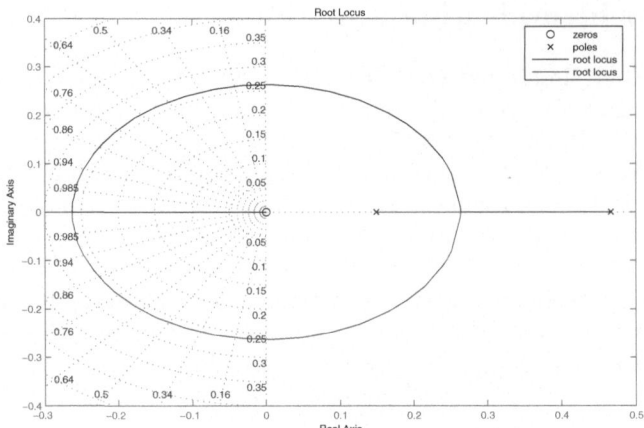

Fig. 3. Root Locus of the Closed-Loop Model

The Root Locus is a graphical technique that plots the traces of poles of a closed-loop system on the $z-$plane (or $s-$plane) as its controller parameters change. We use the Root Locus tool of MATLAB to tune the control parameter $C_{1,P}$ so that the performance specs can be satisfied. For the closed-loop model (17)(based on the estimated model parameters above), the traces of its closed-loop poles are illustrated on the $z-$plane in Fig.3. The closed-loop poles are placed at

$$l_1 = 0.4721, \quad l_2 = 0.1478 \tag{18}$$

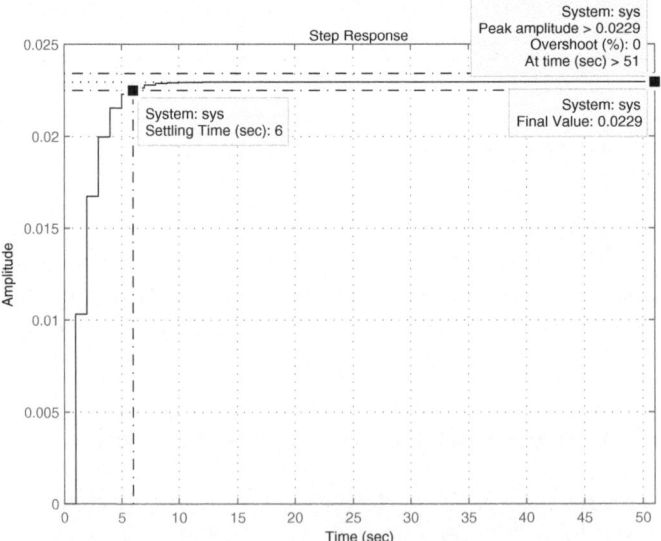

Fig. 4. Step Response of the Closed-Loop Model

by setting the controller parameter to

$$C_{1,P} = 2.7097e - 014. \tag{19}$$

Hence, our closed-loop system obtains the following performance profile:

- **Stability:** The closed-loop system with the power threshold controller(based on the parameters in (19)) guarantees BIBO stability because the real roots of all the closed-loop poles are in the unit circle, i.e. $|l_j| < 1 (j = 1, 2)$ (see (18) and Fig.3).
- **Setting time** T_s: From Fig.4, we observe that the controller achieves a settling time of $6sec$, lower than the required settling time ($10sec$).
- **Steady state error:** In our design, the controller achieves zero steady state error, i.e. $E_s \approx 0$ (see Fig.4). This means the closed-loop system can guarantee the desired performance in steady state.

In brief, the performance specs of our closed-loop system are proved to be satisfied. It demonstrates our adaptive architecture achieves robust QoS guarantee even when the environment varies considerably.

7   Conclusion

We have developed an novel adaptive new call power threshold adjustment algorithm based on feedback control theory. We have shown that the algorithm is stable and meets desired network performance. The algorithm is based both on a novel analytical model and employing standard feedback control design techniques using that model. This would be a new paradigm for adaptive QoS control in uncertain environments.

References

1. D. Hong and S.S. Rappaport. Traffic model and performance analysis for cellular mobile radio telephone systems with prioritized and no-protection handoff procedure. *IEEE Transactions on Vehicular Technology*, 35(3):77–92, 1986.
2. H. Chen, S. Kumar, and C.-C. Jay Kuo. Differentiated qos aware priority handoff in cell-based multimedia wireless network. *IST/SPIE's 12th International Symposium, Electronic Imaging*, January 2000.
3. Hossain Monir and Hassan Mahbub. Adaptive resource management in mobile wireless networks using feedback control theory. *Telecommunication Systems*, 25(3-4):401–415, 2004.
4. Wha Sook Jeon and Dong Geun Jeong. Call admission control for cdma mobile communications systems supporting multimedia services. *IEEE transactions on wireless communications*, 1(4):649–659, October 2002.
5. Jin Weon Chang and Dan Keun Sung. Adaptive channel reservation scheme for soft handoff in ds-cdma cellular systems. *IEEE transactions on vehicular technology*, 50(2):341–353, March 2001.

6. Christoph Linderman, Marco Lohman, and Axel Thümmler. Adaptive call admission control for qos revenue optimization in cdma cellular networks. *IEEE Transcations on vehicular technology*, 10:457–472, 2004.
7. Mi-Sun Do, Youngjun Park, and Jai-Yong Lee. Channel assignment with qos guarantees for multiclass multicode cdma system. *IEEE Transactions on Vehicular Technology*, 51(5):935–948, September 2002.
8. Derong Liu, Yi Zhang, and Sanqing Hu. Call admission policies based on calculated power control setpoints in sir-based power-controlled ds-cdma cellular networks. *Wireless Network*, 10:473–483, 2004.
9. Sungmoon M. Shin, Cheol-Hye Cho, and Dan Keun Sung. Interference-based channel assignment for ds-cdma cellular systems. *IEEE Transcations on vehicular technology*, 48(1), January 1999.
10. Chenyang Lu, Tarek F. Abdelzaher, John A. Stankovic, and Sang Hyuk Son. A feedback control approach for guaranteeing relative delays in web servers. *IEEE Real Time Technology and Applications Symposium*, pages 51–62, 2001.
11. Gene F. Franklin, J. David Powell, and Abbas Emami-Naeini. Feedback control of dynamic systems (4rd ed.). 2004.
12. J. Stankovic, C. Lu, S. Son, and G. Tao. The case for feedback control real-time scheduling. *EuroMicro Conference on Real-Time Systems*, June 1999.
13. FK.J Astrom and Wittenmark B. Adaptive control (2nd ed.). 1995.

Performance Bounds for Mobile Cellular Networks with Handover Prediction

Jose Manuel Gimenez-Guzman, Jorge Martinez-Bauset, and Vicent Pla

Departamento de Comunicaciones, Universidad Politecnica de Valencia , UPV
ETSIT Camino de Vera s/n, 46022, Valencia, Spain
jogiguz@doctor.upv.es, {jmartinez, vpla}@dcom.upv.es

Abstract. We determine the gain that can be achieved by incorporating movement prediction information in the session admission control process in mobile cellular networks. The gain is obtained by evaluating the performance of optimal policies achieved with and without the predictive information, while taking into account possible prediction errors. We evaluate the impact of predicting only incoming handovers, only outgoing or both types together. The prediction agent is able to determine the handover instants both stochastically and deterministically. Two different approaches to compute the optimal admission policy were studied: dynamic programming and reinforcement learning. Numerical results show significant performance gains when the predictive information is used in the admission process, and that higher gains are obtained when deterministic handover instants can be determined.

1 Introduction

Session Admission Control (SAC) is a key aspect in the design and operation of mobile cellular networks that provide QoS guarantees. Terminal mobility makes it very difficult to guarantee that the resources available at the time of session setup will be available in the cells visited during the session lifetime, unless a SAC policy is exerted. The design of the SAC system must take into account not only packet level issues (like delay, jitter or losses) but also session level issues (like loss probabilities of both session setup and handover requests). This paper explores the second type of issues from a novel optimization approach that exploits the availability of movement prediction information. To the best of our knowledge, applying optimization techniques to this type of problem has not been sufficiently explored. The results provided define theoretical limits for the gains that can be expected if handover prediction is used, which could not be established by deploying heuristic SAC approaches.

In systems that do not have predictive information available, both heuristic and optimization approaches have been proposed to improve the performance of the SAC at the session level. A optimization approach without using predictive information has been studied in [1,2,3,4]. In systems that have predictive information available, most of the proposed approaches to improve performance are heuristic, see for example [5,6] and references therein.

J. Dalmau and G. Hasegawa (Eds.): MMNS 2005, LNCS 3754, pp. 35–46, 2005.

Our work has been motivated in part by the study in [5]. Briefly, the authors propose a sophisticated movement prediction system and a SAC scheme that taking advantage of movement prediction information is able to improve system performance. One of the novelties of the proposal is that the SAC scheme takes into consideration not only incoming handovers to a cell but also the outgoing ones. The authors justify it by arguing that considering only the incoming ones would led to reserve more resources than required, given that during the time elapsed since the incoming handover is predicted and resources are reserved until it effectively occurs, outgoing handovers might have provided additional free resources, making the reservation unnecessary.

This paper can be considered an extension of the work presented in [7], incorporating new contributions. One of them is the comparative performance evaluation of incorporating different types of predictive information to the SAC optimization process, like only incoming, only outgoing and both types of handovers together. In [7] only the incoming handover prediction was studied. Another contribution is the evaluation of the impact that predicting deterministically the future handover instants have on the system performance. In [7] only stochastic prediction was modeled.

In a previous study [7] we considered a scenario with several service types and no qualitative differences were found between single and multiservice cases. On the other hand, the higher complexity of multiservice scenarios could hide the insight into the performance implications of using handover prediction information, which is the focus of this paper.

The rest of the paper is structured as follows. In Section 2 we describe the models of the system and the two prediction agents deployed. The two optimization approaches are presented in Section 3. A numerical evaluation comparing the performance obtained when using different types of information and when handovers instants are deterministically or stochastically predicted is provided in Section 4. Finally, a summary of the paper and some concluding remarks are given in Section 5.

2   Model Description

We consider a single cell system and its neighborhood, where the cell has a total of C resource units, being the physical meaning of a unit of resources dependent on the specific technological implementation of the radio interface. Only one service is offered but new and handover session arrivals are distinguished, making a total of two arrival types.

For mathematical tractability we make the common assumptions. New and handover sessions arrive according to a Poisson process with rates λ_n and λ_h respectively. The duration of a session and the cell residence time are exponentially distributed with rates μ_s and μ_r respectively, hence the resource holding time in a cell is also exponentially distributed with rate $\mu = \mu_s + \mu_r$. Without loss of generality, we will assume that each session consumes one unit of resource and that only one session is active per MT.

We used a model of the prediction agent, given that the focus of our study was not the design of it.

2.1 Prediction Agent for Incoming Handovers

An active MT entering the cell neighborhood is labeled by the prediction agent for incoming handovers (IPA) as "probably producing a handover" (H) or the opposite (NH), according to some of its characteristics (position, trajectory, velocity, historic profile,...) and/or some other information (road map, hour of the day,...). After an exponentially distributed time, the actual destiny of the MT becomes definitive and either a handover into the cell occurs or not (for instance because the session ends or the MT moves to another cell) as shown in Fig. 1(a). The SAC system is aware of the number of MTs labeled as H at any time.

The model of the classifier is shown in Fig. 1(b) where the square (with a surface equal to one) represents the population of active MTs to be classified. The shaded area represents the fraction of MTs (S_H) that will ultimately move into the cell, while the white area represents the rest of active MTs. Notice that part of the MTs that will move into the cell can finish their active sessions before doing so. The classifier sets a threshold (represented by a vertical dashed line) to discriminate between those MTs that will likely produce a handover and those that will not. The fraction of MTs falling on the left side of the threshold ($\hat{S}_H$) are labeled as H and those on the right side as NH. There exists an uncertainty zone, of width U, which produces classification errors: the white area on the left of the threshold ($\hat{S}_H^e$) and the shaded area on the right of the threshold ($\hat{S}_{NH}^e$). The parameter x represents the relative position of the classifier threshold within the uncertainty zone. Although for simplicity we use a linear model for the uncertainty zone it would be rather straightforward to consider a different model.

As shown in Fig. 1(a), the model of the IPA is characterized by three parameters: the average sojourn time of the MT in the predicted stage μ_p^{-1}, the probability p of producing a handover if labeled as H and the probability q of producing a handover if labeled as NH. Note that $1 - p$ and q model the

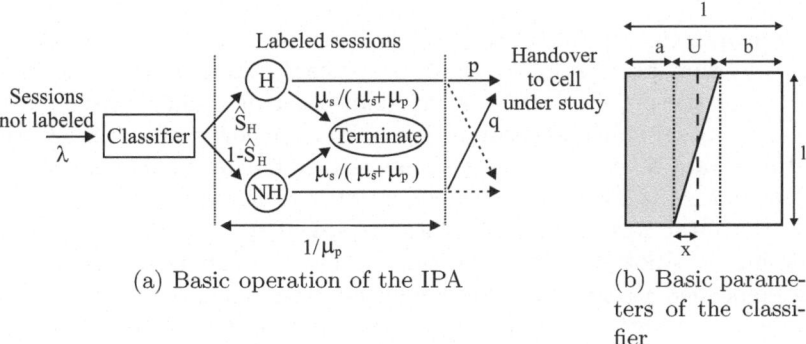

(a) Basic operation of the IPA

(b) Basic parameters of the classifier

Fig. 1. IPA and classifier models

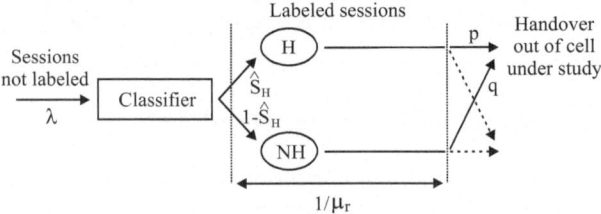

Fig. 2. Basic operation of the OPA

false-positive and non-detection probabilities and in general $q \neq 1 - p$. It can be shown that

$$1 - p = \frac{\hat{S}_H^e}{\hat{S}_H} = \frac{x^2}{(U(2S_H - U + 2x))}; \quad q = \frac{\hat{S}_{NH}^e}{(1 - \hat{S}_H)} = \frac{(U - x)^2}{(U(2 - 2S_H + U - 2x))} \tag{1}$$

2.2   Prediction Agent for Outgoing Handovers

The model of the prediction agent for outgoing handovers (OPA) is shown in Fig. 2. The OPA labels active sessions in the cell as H if they will produce a handover or as NH otherwise. The classification is performed for both handover sessions that enter the cell and new sessions that initiate in the cell, and are carried out by a classifier which model is the same as the one used in the IPA. The time elapsed since the session is labeled until the actual destiny of the MT becomes definitive is the cell residence time that, as defined, is exponentially distributed with rate μ_r. The fraction of sessions that effectively execute an outgoing handover is given by $S_H = \mu_r/(\mu_s + \mu_r)$. The OPA model is characterized by only two parameters $1 - p$ and q, which meaning is the same as in the IPA model. Note that $1 - p$ and q can be related to the classifier parameters by the expressions in (1).

3   Optimizing the SAC Policy

We formulate the optimization problem as an infinite-horizon finite-state Markov decision process under the average cost criterion, which is more appropriate for the problem under study than other discounted cost approaches. When the system starts at state $\boldsymbol{x}$ and follows policy π then the average expected cost rate over time t, as $t \to \infty$, is denoted by $\gamma^\pi(\boldsymbol{x})$ and defined as: $\gamma^\pi(\boldsymbol{x}) = \lim_{t \to \infty} \frac{1}{t} E\left[w^\pi(\boldsymbol{x}, t)\right]$, where $w^\pi(\boldsymbol{x}, t)$ is a random variable that expresses the total cost incurred in the interval $[0, t]$. For the systems we are considering, it is not difficult to see that for every deterministic stationary policy the embedded Markov chain has a unichain transition probability matrix, and therefore the average expected cost rate does not vary with the initial state [8]. We call it the "cost" of the policy π, denote it by γ^π and consider the problem of finding the policy π^* that minimizes γ^π, which we name the optimal policy.

In our model the cost structure is chosen so that the average expected cost represents a weighted sum of the loss rates, i.e. $\gamma^\pi = \omega_n P_n \lambda_n + \omega_h P_h \lambda_h$, where ω_n (ω_h) is the cost incurred when the loss of a new (handover) request occurs and P_n (P_h) is the loss probability of new (handover) requests. In general, $\omega_n < \omega_h$ since the loss of a handover request is less desirable than the loss of a new session setup request.

Two different optimization approaches have been used to find the optimal SAC policy: a dynamic programming (DP) approach and an automatic learning approach based on the theory of Reinforcement Learning (RL) [9]. DP gives an exact solution and allows to evaluate the theoretical limits of incorporating handover prediction in the SAC system, whereas RL tackles more efficiently the curse of dimensionality. In both approaches handover sessions have priority over new sessions and they are accepted as long as resources are available.

3.1 Dynamic Programming

We apply DP to the scenario that only considers the incoming handovers, in which case the system state space is $S := \{\boldsymbol{x} = (i,j) : 0 \le i \le C; \ 0 \le j \le C_p\}$, where i is the number of active sessions in the cell , j is the number of MTs labeled as H in the cell neighborhood and C_p is the maximum number of MT that can be labeled as H at a given time. We use a large value for C_p so that it has no practical impact in our results. At each state $(i,j), i < C$, the set of possible actions is defined by $A := \{a : a = 0,1\}$, being $a = 0$ the action that rejects an incoming new session and $a = 1$ the action that accepts an incoming new session. The system can be described as a continuous-time Markov chain which state transition diagram is shown in Fig. 3, where $\lambda'_h = q\lambda(1 - \hat{S}_H)\mu_p/(\mu_p + \mu_s)$ denotes the average arrival rate of unpredicted handovers. It is converted to a *discrete time Markov chain* (DTMC) by applying uniformization. It can be shown that $\Gamma = C_p(\mu_p + \mu_s) + C(\mu_r + \mu_s) + \lambda + \lambda_n$ is an uniform upper-bound

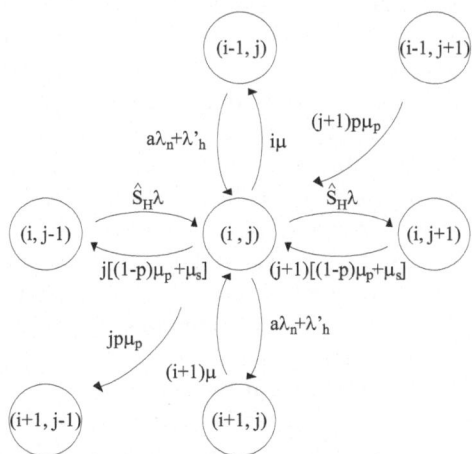

Fig. 3. State transition diagram

for the outgoing rate of all the states, being λ the input rate to the classifier. If $r_{xy}(a)$ denotes the transition rate from state x to state y when action a is taken at state x, then the transition probabilities of the resulting DTMC are given by $p_{xy}(a) = r_{xy}(a)/\Gamma$ $(y \neq x)$ and $p_{xx}(a) = 1 - \sum_{y \in S} p_{xy}(a)$. We define the incurred cost rate at state x when action a is selected by $c(x, a)$, which can take any of the following values: 0 $(i < C,\ a = 1)$, $\omega_n \lambda_n$ $(i < C,\ a = 0)$ or $\omega_n \lambda_n + \omega_h(\lambda'_h + jp\mu_p)$ $(i = C,\ a = 0)$.

If we denote by $h(x)$ the relative cost rate of state x under policy π, then we can write

$$h(x) = c(x, \pi(x)) - \gamma^\pi + \sum_y p_{xy}(\pi(x))h(y) \qquad \forall x \qquad (2)$$

from which we can obtain the average cost and the relative costs $h(x)$ up to an undetermined constant. Thus we arbitrarily set $h(0,0) = 0$ and then solve the linear system of equations (2) to obtain γ^π and $h(x)$, $\forall x$. Having obtained the average and relative costs under policy π an improved policy π' can be calculated as

$$\pi'(x) = \arg\min_{a=0,1} \left\{ c(x, a) - \gamma^\pi + \sum_y p_{xy}(a)h(y) \right\}$$

so that the following relation holds $\gamma^{\pi'} \leq \gamma^\pi$. Moreover, if the equality holds then $\pi' = \pi = \pi^*$, where π^* denotes the optimal policy, i.e. $\gamma^{\pi^*} \leq \gamma^\pi$ $\forall \pi$.

We repeat iteratively the solution of system (2) and the policy improvement until we obtain a policy which does not change after improvement. This process is called *Policy Iteration* [8, Section 8.6] and it leads to the average optimal policy in a finite — and typically small — number of iterations.

3.2   Reinforcement Learning

We formulate the optimization problem as an infinite-horizon finite-state semi-Markov decision process (SMDP) under the average cost criterion. The decision epochs correspond only to the time instants at which new session arrivals occur, given no decisions are taken for handover arrivals. Only arrival events are relevant to the optimization process because no actions are taken at session departures. The state space for the scenario that only considers the incoming handovers is defined as $S := \{x = (x_0, x_{in}) : x_0 \leq C; x_{in} \leq C_p\}$, where x_0 and x_{in} represent, respectively, the number of resource units occupied by sessions in the cell and by sessions in the neighborhood which are labeled as H. The state space for the scenario that only considers the outgoing handovers is defined as $S := \{x = (x_0, x_{out}) : x_0, x_{out} \leq C\}$, where x_{out} represents the number of resource units occupied by sessions in the cell labeled as H. The state space for the scenario that considers both the incoming and outgoing handovers is defined as $S := \{x = (x_0, x_{in}, x_{out}) : x_0, x_{out} \leq C; x_{in} \leq C_p\}$. At each decision epoch the system has to select an action from the set $A := \{0, 1\}$.

The cost structure is defined as follows. At any decision epoch, the cost incurred by accepting a new session request is zero and by rejecting it is ω_n. Further accrual of cost occurs when the system has to reject handover requests between two decision epochs, incurring a cost of ω_h per rejection.

The Bellman optimality recurrence equations for a SMDP under the average cost criterion can be written as

$$h^*(\boldsymbol{x}, a) = \min_{a \in A_x} \{ w(\boldsymbol{x}, a) - \gamma^* \tau(\boldsymbol{x}, a) + \sum_{\boldsymbol{x} \in S} p_{\boldsymbol{xy}}(a) \min_{a' \in A_y} h^*(\boldsymbol{y}, a') \}$$

where $h^*(\boldsymbol{x}, a)$ is the average expected relative cost of taking the optimal action a in state $\boldsymbol{x}$ and then continuing indefinitely by choosing actions optimally, $w(\boldsymbol{x}, a)$ is the average cost of taking action a in state $\boldsymbol{x}$, $\tau(\boldsymbol{x}, a)$ is the average sojourn time in state $\boldsymbol{x}$ under action a and $p_{\boldsymbol{xy}}(a)$ is the probability of moving from state $\boldsymbol{x}$ to state $\boldsymbol{y}$ under action $a = \pi(\boldsymbol{x})$. The greedy policy π^* defined by selecting actions that minimize the right-hand side of the above equation is gain-optimal [10].

In systems where the number of states can be large, RL tackles more efficiently the curse of dimensionality and offers the important advantage of being a model-free method, i.e. transition probabilities and average costs are not needed in advance. We deploy the SMART algorithm [10], which estimates $h^*(\boldsymbol{x}, a)$ by simulation using a temporal difference method (TD(0)). If at the $(m-1)^{th}$ decision epoch the system is in state $\boldsymbol{x}$, action a is taken and the system is found in state $\boldsymbol{y}$ at the mth decision epoch then we update the relative state-action values as follows: $h_{new}(\boldsymbol{x}, a) = (1 - \alpha_m)h_{old}(\boldsymbol{x}, a) + \alpha_m \{w_m(\boldsymbol{x}, a, \boldsymbol{y}) - \gamma_m \tau_m(\boldsymbol{x}, a, \boldsymbol{y}) + \min_{a' \in A_y} h_{old}(\boldsymbol{y}, a')\}$, where $w_m(\boldsymbol{x}, a, \boldsymbol{y})$ is the actual cumulative cost incurred between the two successive decision epochs, $\tau_m(\boldsymbol{x}, a, \boldsymbol{y})$ is the actual sojourn time between the decision epochs, α_m is the learning rate parameter at the mth decision epoch and γ_m is the average cost rate estimated as: $\gamma_m = \sum_{k=1}^{m} w_k(\boldsymbol{x}_{(k)}, a_{(k)}, \boldsymbol{y}_{(k)}) / \sum_{k=1}^{m} \tau_k(\boldsymbol{x}_{(k)}, a_{(k)}, \boldsymbol{y}_{(k)})$.

4   Numerical Evaluation

We evaluated the performance gain when introducing prediction by the ratio $\gamma_{wp}^\pi / \gamma_p^\pi$, where γ_p^π (γ_{wp}^π) is the average expected cost rate of a policy that is optimal in a system with (without) prediction. We assume a circular-shaped cell of radio r and a holed-disk-shaped neighborhood with inner (outer) radio $1.0r$ ($1.5r$).

The values of the parameters that define the scenario are: $C = 10$ and $C_p = 60$, $N_h = \mu_r / \mu_s = 1$, $\mu_r / \mu_p = 0.5$, $\lambda_n = 2$, $\mu = \mu_s + \mu_r = 1$, $S_H = 0.4$, $x = U/2$, $w_n = 1$, and $w_h = 20$. The value of the input rate to the PA λ is chosen so that the system is in statistical equilibrium, i.e. the rate at which handover sessions enter the cell is equal to the rate at which handover sessions exit the cell. It can be easily shown that for our scenario $\lambda = (1 - P_n)(1 - P_{ft})\lambda_n(N_h + \mu_r / \mu_p)(1 / S_H)$, where $P_{ft} = P_h / (P_h + \mu_s / \mu_r)$ is the probability of forced termination. Note that in our numerical experiments the values of the arrival rates are chosen to achieve realistic operating values for $P_n (\approx 10^{-2})$ and $P_{ft} (\approx 10^{-3})$. For such values, we make the approximation $\lambda \approx 0.989 \lambda_n(N_h + \mu_r / \mu_p)(1 / S_H)$.

For the RL simulations, the ratio of arrival rates of new sessions to the cell neighborhood (ng) and to the cell (nc) is made equal to the ratio of their surfaces,

$\lambda_{ng} = 1.25\lambda_{nc}$. The ratio of handover arrival rates to the cell neighborhood from the outside of the system (ho) and from the cell (hc) is made equal to ratio of their perimeters, $\lambda_{ho} = 1.5\lambda_{hc}$. Using the flow equilibrium property, we can write $\lambda_{hc} = (1 - P_n)(1 - P_{ft})(\mu_r/\mu_s)\lambda_{nc} \approx 0.989(\mu_r/\mu_s)\lambda_{nc}$. With regard to the RL algorithm, we use a constant learning rate $\alpha_m = 0.01$ but the exploration rate p_m is decayed to zero by using the following rule $p_m = p_0/(1 + u)$, where $u = m^2/(\varphi + m)$. We used $\varphi = 1.0 \cdot 10^{11}$ and $p_0 = 0.1$. The exploration of the state space is a common RL technique used to accept non-improving solutions in order to avoid being trapped at local minima.

Figure 4 shows the gain when introducing prediction for different values of the uncertainty U. When using RL, for each value of U we run 10 simulations with different seeds and display the averages. As observed, using incoming handover prediction induces a gain and that gain decreases as the prediction uncertainty (U) increases.

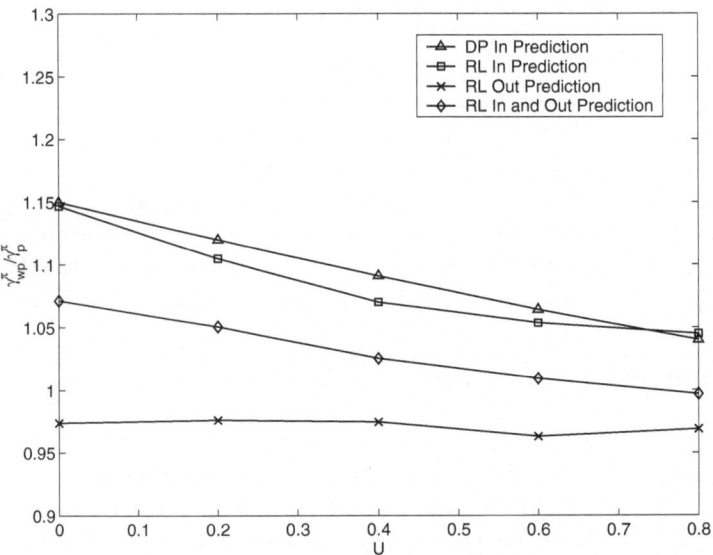

Fig. 4. Performance gain when using stochastic handover prediction

From Fig. 4 it is clear that the knowledge of the number of resources that will become available is not relevant for the determination of optimum SAC policies, being even independent of the degree of uncertainty. It can also be observed that the optimization algorithm founds slightly worse solutions when using information related to the outgoing handovers ($\gamma_{wp}^{\pi}/\gamma_p^{\pi} < 1$). This is probably due to the difficulty that the algorithm has to find good solutions in a bigger space state. This observation seems to be corroborated when comparing the results obtained using only the incoming handover information and using both the incoming and outgoing handover information together. As shown, the solutions found in the second case are slightly worse than the ones found in the first one.

4.1 Deterministic Prediction

The prediction agents described in Sections 2.1 and 2.2 predict the time instants at which handovers will occur only stochastically. In this section we evaluate the impact on performance that more precise knowledge of the future handover time instants have. Intuitively, it seems obvious that handovers taking place in a near future would be more relevant for the SAC process than those occurring in an undetermined far future. More precisely, in this section both the IPA and OPA operate as before but they label the sessions T time units before handovers take place, i.e. the component x_{in} (x_{out}) of the different state spaces represent the number of incoming (outgoing) handovers that will take place in less than T time units. A similar approach is used in [5], where authors predict the incoming and outgoing handovers that will take place in a time window of fixed size.

For the performance evaluation, the same scenarios, parameters and methodology described before in this same Section where used, except that we set the uncertainty to a constant value $U = 0.2$, which we consider it might be a practical value. Figure 5 shows the variation of the gain for different values of T. As observed, there exists an optimum value for T, which is close to the mean time between call arrivals (λ^{-1}), although it will probably depend on other system parameters as well. As T goes beyond its optimum value, the gain decreases, probably because the temporal information becomes less significant for the SAC decision process. As expected, when $T \rightarrow \infty$ the gain is identical to the one in the stochastic prediction case because the labeling of sessions occur at the same time instants, i.e. when handover sessions enter the cell or new sessions are initiated in the cell. When T is lower than its optimum value the gain also decreases, probably because the system has not enough time to react. When $T = 0$ the gain is null because there is no prediction at all.

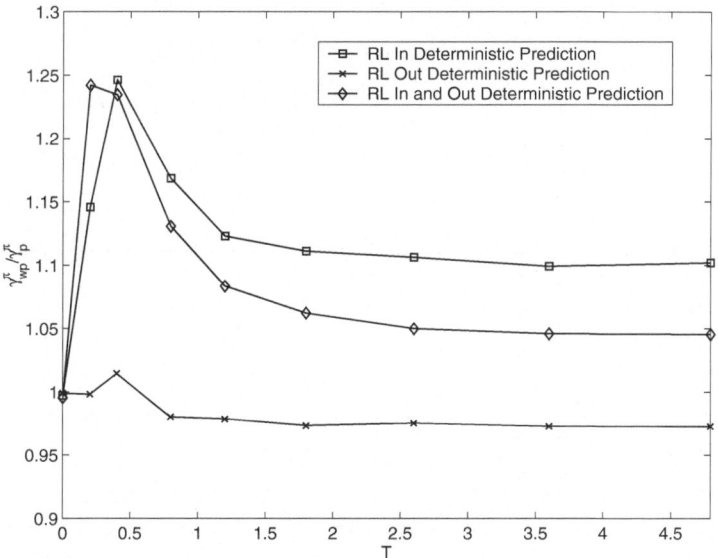

Fig. 5. Performance gain when using deterministic handover prediction

Figure 5 shows that the information provided by the OPA is again not relevant for the optimization process. For values of T close to its optimum the gain is similar when using incoming handover prediction or incoming and outgoing prediction together, and it is significantly higher than when stochastic time prediction is used.

In an earlier version of the IPA we were providing the optimization process with state information of the neighboring cells and obtained that the gain was not significant, possibly because the information was not sufficiently specific. The authors in [11] reached the same conclusion but using a genetic algorithm to find near-optimal policies. In the version described in this paper, we are providing the optimization process with state information of a sufficiently close neighborhood, obtaining significant gains. For the design of the OPA we were faced with the same dilemma but in this case we decided not to use more specific information. Defining a holed-disk-shaped neighborhood with outer (inner) radio r ($<$ r) for the outgoing handovers and an exponentially distributed sojourn time in it, would had open the possibility of having terminals that could go in and out of this area, making the cell residence time not exponential. This would had made the models with the IPA and with the OPA not comparable. Besides, providing the optimization process with more specific information of the outgoing handovers does not help to improve the performance either, as observed in Fig. 5.

Finally it is worth noting that the main challenge in the design of efficient bandwidth reservation techniques for mobile cellular networks is to balance two conflicting requirements: reserving enough resources to achieve a low forced termination probability and keeping the resource utilization high by not blocking too many new setup requests. Figure 6, which shows the utilization gain for different values of U, justifies the efficiency of our optimization approach. It

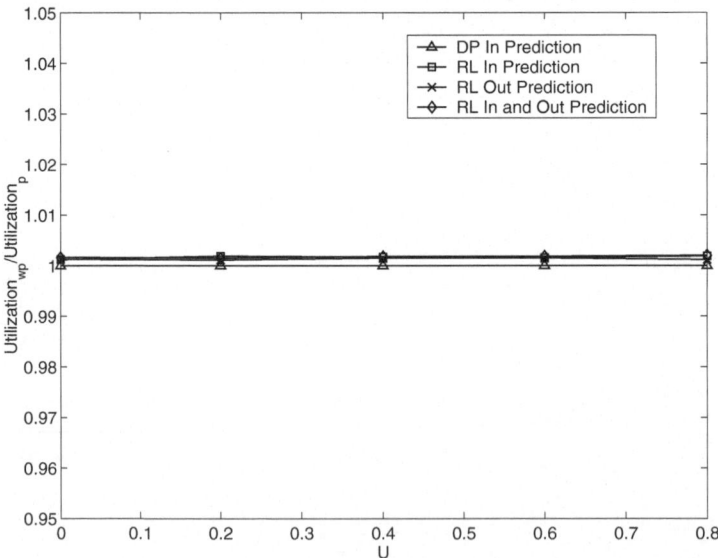

Fig. 6. Utilization gain when using stochastic handover prediction

has also been verified that the resource utilization obtained when deterministic time prediction is deployed is identical to the utilization achieved when the SAC policy is optimized without using predictive information.

As a conclusion, it looks clear that when using optimization techniques to determine the optimum policy, the information related to outgoing handovers is not relevant. This result would seem to contradict the conclusions in [5], but there the predictive information is integrated in the reservation scheme by means of heuristics and therefore their approximation and ours are not comparable.

5   Conclusions

In this paper we evaluate the performance gain that can be expected when the SAC optimization process is provided with information related to incoming, outgoing and incoming and outgoing handovers together, in a mobile cellular network scenario. The prediction information is provided by two types of prediction agents that label active mobile terminals in the cell or its neighborhood which will probably execute a handover. The prediction agents also provide information about the future time instants at which handovers will occur, being this information either stochastic or deterministic. The optimization problem is formulated as a Markov or semi-Markov decision process, for which different solving methods can be used. In this case we deployed dynamic programming and reinforcement learning. A general model of the prediction agents has been considered and as such it cannot be used to obtain concrete results for specific systems nor evaluate the added complexity of deploying a particular prediction method in operational systems. Nevertheless, the generality of the prediction model together with the optimization-based approach permit to obtain bounds for the gain of specific prediction schemes used in conjunction with SAC.

Numerical results show that the information related to the incoming handovers is more relevant than the one related to the outgoing handovers in the optimization framework deployed. Additional performance gain can be obtained when more specific information is provided about the handover time instants, i.e. when their prediction is deterministic instead of stochastic. The gain obtained has been as high as 25% in the studied scenario even when the prediction uncertainty is 20%.

In a future work we will study reinforcement learning algorithms different from SMART, which hopefully will be able to find better solutions in less time, even with more complex state spaces. Another aspect that deserves a closer study is the identification of the parameters that affect the optimum value of T and the study of its sensitivity.

Acknowledgments

This work has been supported by the Spanish Ministry of Education and Science (30% PGE, 70% FEDER) under projects TIC2003-08272 and TEC2004-06437-C05-01, and by the Universidad Politécnica de Valencia under "Programa de Incentivo a la Investigación".

References

1. R. Ramjee, R. Nagarajan, and D. Towsley, "On optimal call admission control in cellular networks," Wireless Networks Journal (WINET), vol. 3, no. 1, pp. 29–41, 1997.
2. N. Bartolini, "Handoff and optimal channel assignment in wireless networks," Mobile Networks and Applications (MONET), vol. 6, no. 6, pp. 511–524, 2001.
3. N. Bartolini and I. Chlamtac, "Call admission control in wireless multimedia networks," in Proceedings of IEEE PIMRC, 2002.
4. V. Pla and V. Casares-Giner, "Optimal admission control policies in multiservice cellular networks," in Proceedings of the International Network Optimization Conference (INOC), 2003, pp. 466–471.
5. W.-S. Soh and H. S. Kim, "Dynamic bandwidth reservation in cellular networks using road topology based mobility prediction," in Proceedings of IEEE INFOCOM, 2004.
6. Roland Zander and Johan M Karlsson, "Predictive and Adaptive Resource Reservation (PARR) for Cellular Networks," International Journal of Wireless Information Networks, vol. 11, no. 3, pp. 161-171, 2004.
7. V. Pla, J. M. Giménez-Guzmán, J. Martínez and V. Casares-Giner, "Optimal admission control using handover prediction in mobile cellular networks," in Proceedings of the 2nd International Working Conference on Performance Modelling and Evaluation of Heterogeneous Networks (HET-NETs '04), 2004.
8. M. L. Puterman, Markov Decision Processes: Discrete Stochastic Dynamic Programming. John Wiley & Sons, 1994.
9. R. Sutton and A. G. Barto, Reinforcement Learning. Cambridge, Massachusetts: The MIT press, 1998.
10. T. K. Das, A. Gosavi, S. Mahadevan, and N. Marchalleck, "Solving semi-markov decision problems using average reward reinforcement learning," Management Science, vol. 45, no. 4, pp. 560–574, 1999.
11. C. Yener, A. Rose, "Genetic algorithms applied to cellular call admission: local policies," IEEE Transaction on Vehicular Technology, vol. 46, no. 1, pp. 72–79, 1997.

Adaptive Trunk Reservation Policies in Multiservice Mobile Wireless Networks

David Garcia-Roger, M.ª Jose Domenech-Benlloch,
Jorge Martinez-Bauset, and Vicent Pla

Departamento de Comunicaciones, Universidad Politecnica de Valencia,
UPV ETSIT Camino de Vera s/n,
46022, Valencia, Spain
{dagarro, mdoben}@doctor.upv.es
{jmartinez, vpla}@dcom.upv.es

Abstract. We propose a novel adaptive reservation scheme designed to operate in association with the well-known Multiple Guard Channel (MGC) admission control policy. The scheme adjusts the MGC configuration parameters by continuously tracking the Quality of Service (QoS) perceived by users, adapting to any mix of aggregated traffic and enforcing a differentiated treatment among services during underload and overload episodes. The performance evaluation study confirms that the QoS objective is met with an excellent precision and that it converges rapidly to new operating conditions. These features along with its simplicity make our scheme superior to previous proposals and justify that it can satisfactorily deal with the non-stationary nature of an operating network.

1 Introduction

Session Admission Control (SAC) is a key mechanism in the design and operation of multiservice mobile cellular networks that guarantee a certain degree of Quality of Service (QoS). The mobility of terminals make it very difficult to insure that the resources available at session setup will also be available along the session lifetime, as the terminal moves from one cell to another. The design of SAC policies must take into consideration not only packet related parameters like maximum delay, jitter or losses, but also session related parameters like setup request blocking probabilities and forced termination probabilities.

For stationary multiservice scenarios, different SAC policies have been evaluated in [1], where it was found that trunk reservation policies like *Multiple Guard Channel* (MGC) and *Multiple Fractional Guard Channel* (MFGC) outperform those policies which stationary state probability distributions have a product-form solution. More precisely, it was found in [1] that for the scenarios studied the performance of the MFGC policy is very close to the performance of the optimal policy and that the performance of both the MGC and MFGC policies tend to the optimal as the number of resources increase beyond a few tens.

J. Dalmau and G. Hasegawa (Eds.): MMNS 2005, LNCS 3754, pp. 47–58, 2005.

In [1] the performance is evaluated by obtaining the maximum aggregated call rate that can be offered to the system, which we call the *system capacity*, while guaranteeing a given QoS objective. The QoS objective is defined in terms of upper bound for the blocking probabilities of both new session and handover requests. It was also found in [1] that the performance of trunk reservation policies is quite sensitive to errors in the setting of their configuration parameters, defining their values the action (accept/reject) that must be taken in each system state when a new session or handover request arrives.

For the class of SAC policies considered in [1] the system capacity is a function of two parameter sets: those that describe the system as a Markov process and those that specify the QoS objective. Two approaches are commonly proposed to design a SAC policy. First, consider the parameters of the first set as stationary and therefore design a static SAC policy for the worst scenario. Second, consider them as non-stationary and either estimate them periodically or use historical information of traffic patterns.

In this paper we study a novel adaptive strategy that operates in coordination with the MGC policy. Although for simplicity we only provide implementations for the scheme when operating with the MGC policy, it can be readily extended to operate with the MFGC policy. Our scheme adapts the configuration of the MGC policy according to the QoS perceived by users. The main advantage of our adaptive scheme is its ability to adapt to changes in the traffic profile and enforce a differentiated treatment among services during underload and overload episodes. In the latter case, this differentiated treatment guarantees that higher priority services will be able to meet their QoS objective possibly at the expense of lower priority services.

Recently, different SAC adaptive schemes have been proposed for mobile cellular networks. In these proposals the configuration of the SAC policy is adapted periodically according to estimates of traffic or QoS parameters. Two relevant examples of this approach in a single service scenario are [2] and [3]. A four parameter algorithm based on estimates of the blocking probability perceived by handover requests is proposed in [2] to adjust the number of guard channels. A two hour period is defined during which the system accumulates information to compute the estimates. This period is too long to capture the dynamics of operating mobile cellular networks. Besides, the value of the parameters proposed in [2] do not work properly when some traffic profiles are offered [3], (i.e. QoS objectives are not met). A two parameter probability-based adaptive algorithm, somewhat similar to that of *Random Early Detection* (RED), is proposed in [3] to overcome these shortcomings. Its main advantage is that it reduces the new requests blocking probability, once the steady state has been reached, and therefore higher resource utilization is achieved. Nevertheless, its convergence period is still of the order of hours. The scheme we propose is also probability-based like in [3] but it has a considerably lower convergence period and can be applied to single service and multiservice scenarios.

Adaptive SAC mechanisms have also been studied, for example in [4,5,6], both in single service and multiservice scenarios, but in a context which is somewhat different to the one of this paper. There, the adjustment of the SAC policy configuration is based on estimates of the handover arrival rates derived from the current number of ongoing calls in neighboring cells and mobility patterns. It is expected that the performance of our scheme would improve when provided with such predictive information but this is left for further study.

Our SAC adaptive scheme differs from previous proposals in: 1) it does not rely on measurement intervals to estimate the value of system parameters but tracks the QoS perceived by users and performs a continuous adaptation of the configuration parameters of the SAC policy; 2) the possibility of identifying several arrival streams as protected (with an operator defined order of priorities) and one as *best-effort*, being it useful to concentrate on it the penalty that unavoidably occurs during overloads; and 3) the high precision in the fulfillment of the QoS objective.

The remaining of the paper is structured as follows. Section 2 describes the model of the system and defines the relevant SAC policies. Section 3 illustrates the fundamentals of the adaptive scheme, introducing the policy adjustment strategy and how multiple services are handled. Section 4 describes the detailed operation of the scheme. Section 5 presents the performance evaluation of the scheme in different scenarios, both under stationary and non-stationary traffic conditions. Finally, Section 6 concludes the paper.

2   System Model and Relevant SAC Policies

We consider the homogeneous case where all cells are statistically identical and independent. Consequently the global performance of the system can be analyzed focusing on a single cell. Nevertheless, the proposed scheme could also be deployed in non-homogeneous scenarios. In each cell a set of R different classes of users contend for C resource units, where the meaning of a unit of resource depends on the specific implementation of the radio interface. For each service, new and handover arrival requests are distinguished, which defines $2R$ arrival streams.

Abusing from the Poisson process definition, we say that for any class r, $1 \leq r \leq R$, new requests arrive according to a Poisson process with time-varying rate $\lambda_r^n(t)$ and request c_r resource units per session. The duration of a service r session is exponentially distributed with rate μ_r^s. The cell residence (dwell) time of a service r session is exponentially distributed with rate μ_r^d. Hence, the resource holding time for a service r session in a cell is exponentially distributed with rate $\mu_r = \mu_r^s + \mu_r^d$. We consider that handover requests arrive according to a Poisson process with time-varying rate $\lambda_r^h(t)$. Although our scheme does not require any relationship between $\lambda_r^h(t)$ and $\lambda_r^n(t)$, for simplicity we will suppose that $\lambda_r^h(t)$ it is a known fraction of $\lambda_r^n(t)$. We use exponential random variables for two reasons. First, for simplicity. Second, although it has been shown that the random variables of interest are not exponential, deploying them allows to obtain values of the performance parameters of interest which are good approximations. Besides, the operation of the proposed scheme is independent of the distribution of the random variables.

Table 1. Definition of the scenarios under study

	A	B	C	D	E
c_1	1	1	1	1	1
c_2	2	4	2	2	2
f_1	0.8	0.8	0.2	0.8	0.8
f_2	0.2	0.2	0.8	0.2	0.2
$B_1^n\%$	5	5	5	1	1
$B_2^n\%$	1	1	1	2	1

	A,B,C,D,E
$B_r^h\%$	$0.1B_r^n$
λ_r^n	$f_r\lambda$
λ_r^h	$0.5\lambda_r^n$
μ_1	1
μ_2	3

We denote by P_i, $1 \leq i \leq 2R$, the perceived blocking probabilities for each of the $2R$ arrival streams, by $P_r^n = P_i$ the blocking probabilities for new requests and by $P_r^h = P_{R+i}$ the handover blocking probabilities. The QoS objective is expressed as upper bounds for the blocking probabilities, denoting by B_r^n (B_r^h) the bound for new (handover) requests. Let the system state vector be $n \equiv (n_1, n_2, \ldots, n_{2R-1}, n_{2R})$, where n_i is the number of sessions in progress in the cell initiated as arrival stream i requests. We denote by $c(n) = \sum_{i=1}^{2R} n_i c_i$ the number of busy resource units in state n.

The definition of the SAC policies of interest is as follows: 1) Complete-Sharing (CS). A request is admitted provided there are enough free resource units available in the system; 2) Multiple Guard Channel (MGC). One parameter is associated with each arrival stream i, $l_i \in \mathbb{N}$. When an arrival of stream i happens in state n, it is accepted if $c(n) + c_i \leq l_i$ and blocked otherwise. Therefore, l_i is the amount of resources that stream i has access to and increasing (decreasing) it reduces (augments) P_i.

The performance evaluation of the adaptive scheme is carried out for five different scenarios (A, B, C, D and E) that are defined in Table 1, being the QoS parameters B_i expressed as percentage values. The parameters in Table 1 have been selected to explore possible trends in the numerical results, i.e., taking scenario A as a reference, scenario B represents the case where the ratio c_1/c_2 is smaller, scenario C where f_1/f_2 is smaller, scenario D where B_1/B_2 is smaller and scenario E where B_1 and B_2 are equal. Note that the aggregated arrival rate of new requests is defined as $\lambda = \sum_{r=1}^{R} \lambda_r^n$, where $\lambda_r^n = f_i\lambda$. The system capacity is the maximum λ (λ_{max}) that can be offered to the system while meeting the QoS objective.

3   Fundamentals of the Adaptive Scheme

Most of the proposed adaptive schemes deploy a reservation strategy based on *guard channels*, increasing its number when the QoS objective is not met.

The extension of this heuristic to a multiservice scenario would consider that adjusting the configuration parameter l_i only affects the QoS perceived by s_i (P_i) but has no effect on the QoS perceived by the other arrival streams. As an example, Fig. 1 shows the dependency of P_1^n and P_2^h with l_1^n and l_2^h, respectively, while the other configuration parameters are kept constant at their optimum values. It has been obtained in scenario A with $C - 10$ resource units, when deploying the MGC policy and when offering an arrival rate equal to the system capacity. As shown, the correctness of the heuristic is not justified (observe P_2^h) although it might work in some cases (observe P_1^n).

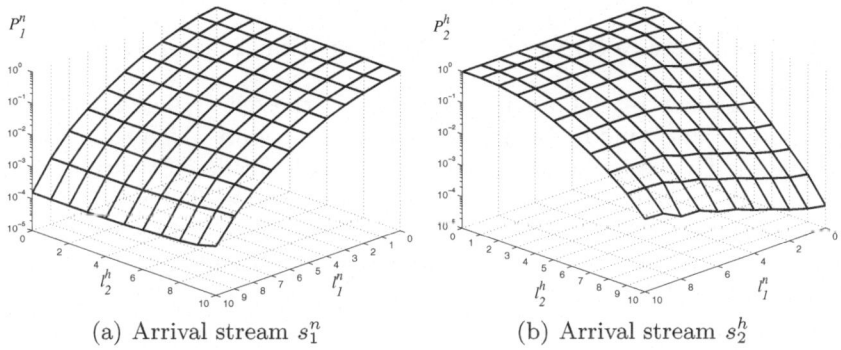

(a) Arrival stream s_1^n (b) Arrival stream s_2^h

Fig. 1. Dependency of the blocking probability with the configuration parameters

Our scheme has been designed to handle this difficulty and to fulfill two key requirements that have an impact on its performance: one is to achieve a convergence period as short as possible and the other is to enforce a certain response during underload or overload episodes. For these purposes we classify the different arrival streams into two generic categories: i) those that the operator identifies as "protected" because they must meet specific QoS objectives; ii) one *Best-Effort Stream* (BES), with no specific QoS objective.

Additionally, the operator can define priorities at its convenience in order to protect more effectively some streams than other, i.e. handover requests. If we denote the generic stream i by s_i, $1 \le i \le 2R$, and we assume that the order of priorities required by the operator for the different streams is $\mathbf{s}^* = (s_{\pi_1}, s_{\pi_2}, \ldots, s_{\pi_{2R}})$, then the vector $\pi^* = (\pi_1, \ldots, \pi_i, \ldots, \pi_{2R})$, $\pi_i \in \mathbb{N}, 1 \le \pi_i \le 2R$, is called the "prioritization order", being s_{π_1} the *Highest-Priority Stream* (HPS) and $s_{\pi_{2R}}$ the *Lowest-Priority Stream* (LPS). We study two implementations, one in which the LPS is treated as a protected stream and one in which the LSP is the BES. For clarity in some cases we will denote by s_r^n (s_r^h) the arrival stream associated to new (handover) requests. In relation to the parameters that define the configuration of the MGC policy, we will denote by l_r^n (l_r^h) the configuration parameter associated to the arrival stream s_r^n (s_r^h) and by l_i the one associated to s_i.

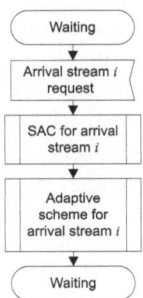

Fig. 2. Conceptual operation of the adaptive reservation scheme

3.1   Probabilistic Setting of the Configuration Parameters

A common characteristic of previous schemes like those in [2,3] and [4,5,6] is that
they require a time window (*update period*) at the end of which some estimates
are produced. The design of this update period must trade-off the time required
to adapt to new conditions for the precision of estimates. The adaptive scheme
we propose overcomes this limitation. The scheme tracks the QoS perceived by
each arrival stream and performs a continuous adaptation of the configuration
parameters of the SAC policy.

Let us assume that arrival processes are stationary and the system is in steady
state. If the QoS objective for s_i can be expressed as $B_i = b_i/o_i$, where $b_i, o_i \in \mathbb{N}$,
then it is expected that when $P_i = B_i$ the stream i will experience, in average,
b_i rejected requests and $o_i - b_i$ admitted requests, out of o_i offered requests.
It seems intuitive to think that the adaptive scheme should not change the
configuration parameters of those arrival streams meeting their QoS objective.
Therefore, assuming integer values for the configuration parameters, like those
of the MGC policy, we propose to perform a probabilistic adjustment each time
a request is processed, i.e. each time the system takes an admission or rejection
decision, by adding +1 or −1 to l_i, when it effectively occurs.

Figure 2 shows the general operation of the proposed scheme. As seen, when
a stream i request arrives, the SAC decides upon its admission or rejection and
this decision is used by the adaptive scheme to adjust the configuration of the
SAC policy.

4   Operation of the SAC Adaptive Scheme

Figure 3 shows the operation of the SAC subsystem and the adaptive scheme. In
our proposal, two arrival streams, the HPS and the BES, receive differentiated
treatment. On the one hand, a HPS request must be always admitted, if enough
free resources are available. On the other hand, no specific action is required to
adjust the QoS perceived by the BES, given that no QoS objective must be met.

As shown in Fig. 3(a), to admit an arrival stream i request it is first checked
that at least c_i free resource units are available. Note that once this is verified,

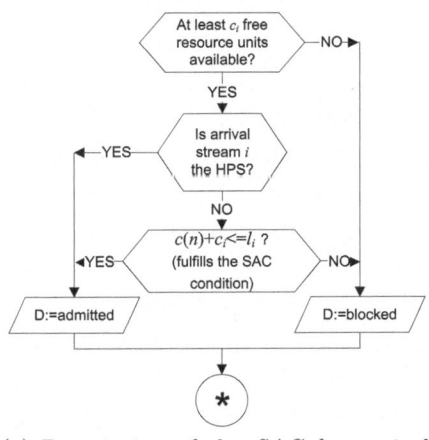
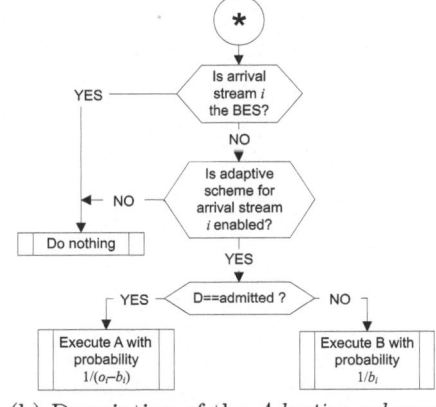

(a) Description of the *SAC for arrival stream i* block in Fig. 2.

(b) Description of the *Adaptive scheme for arrival stream i* block in Fig. 2.

Fig. 3. Operation of SAC policy and adaptive scheme

HPS requests are always admitted, while the rest of streams must also fulfill the admission condition imposed by the MGC policy. In general, the adaptive scheme is always operating (except for the BES), but meeting the QoS objective of higher priority streams could require to disable the operation of the adaptive schemes associated to lower priority streams, as explained below.

To be able to guarantee that the QoS objective is always met, particularly during overloads episodes or changes in the load profile (i.e. new f_i), the probabilistic adjustment described in Section 3.1 requires additional mechanisms. Two ways are possible to change the policy configuration when the QoS objective for stream i is not met. The direct way is to increase the configuration parameter l_i, but its maximum value is C, i.e. when $l_i = C$ full access to the resources is provided to stream i and setting $l_i > C$ does not provide additional benefits. In these cases, an indirect way to help stream i is to limit the access to resources of lower priority streams by reducing their associated configuration parameters.

As shown in Fig. 4(b), upon a rejection the adaptive scheme uses first the direct way and after exhausted it resorts to the indirect way, in which case the adaptive schemes of the lower priority streams must be conveniently disabled. Figure 4(a) shows the reverse procedure. Note that when stream π_k is allowed to access the resources, then the adaptive scheme of the π_{k-1} stream is enabled. When the LPS is the BES then its adaptive scheme is never enabled. Note also that we allow the values of the l_i parameters to go above C and below zero as a means to remember past adjustments.

The scheme described in this paper is a generalization of the one proposed in [8] because it incorporates two notable features. First, it provides the operator with full flexibility to define any prioritization order for the arrival streams and for selecting one of the two implementations proposed. Second, the penalty induced on the lower priority streams increases progressively to guarantee that the QoS objective of the higher priority streams is met.

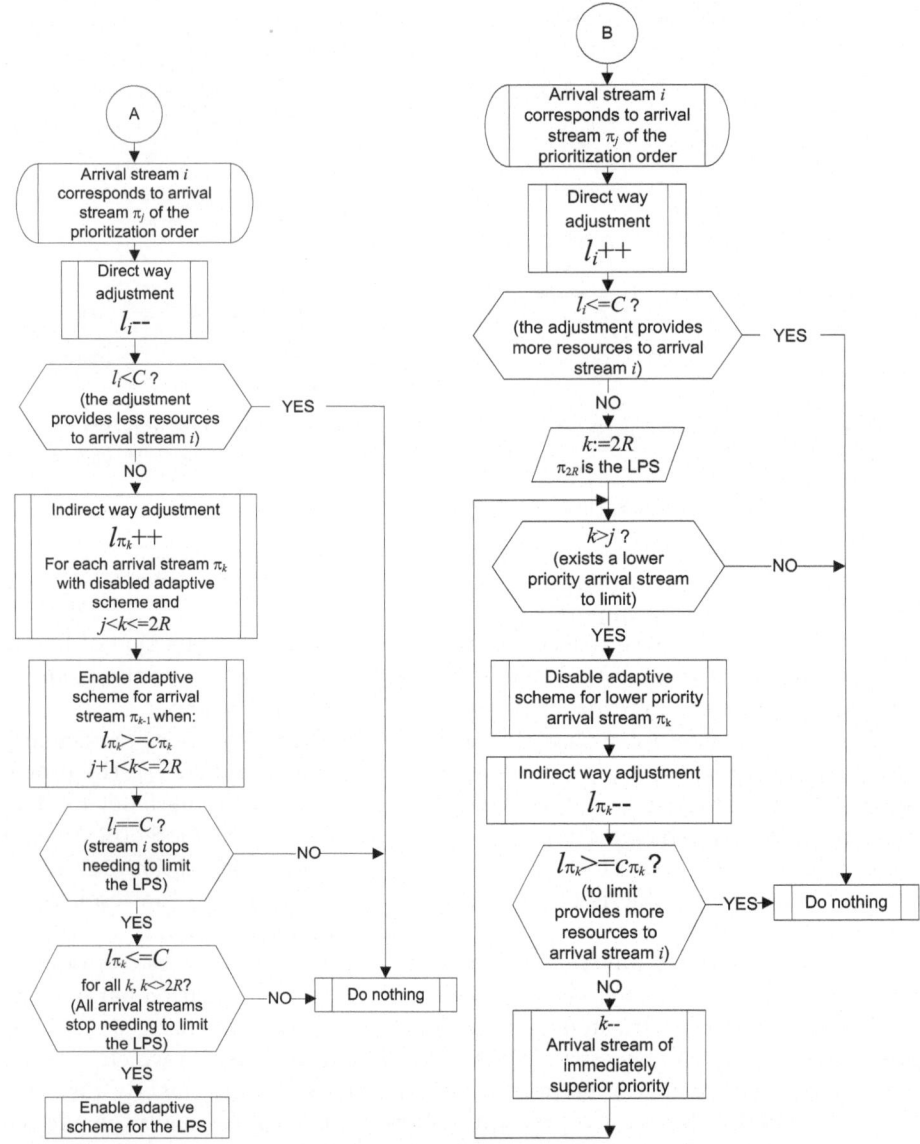

(a) Adjustment algorithm after an admission decision.

(b) Adjustment algorithm after a rejection decision.

Fig. 4. The adaptive algorithm

5   Performance Evaluation

The performance evaluation has been carried out using Möbius^{TM} [7], which is a software tool that supports *Stochastic Activity Networks* (SANs). Möbius^{TM}

allows to simulate the SANs that model the type of systems of interest in our study, and under certain conditions, even to numerically solve the associated continuous-time Markov chains.

For the five scenarios defined in Table 1, $\{A, B, C, D, E\}$, with $C = 10$ and with no adaptive scheme, the system capacity when deploying Complete Sharing is $\{1.54, 0.37, 1.37, 1.74, 1.54\}$, while when deploying the MGC policy is $\{1.89, 0.40, 1.52, 1.97, 1.74\}$. Refer to [1] for details on how to determine the system capacity. For all scenarios defined in Table 1 we assume the following prioritization order $\mathbf{s}^* = (s_2^h, s_1^h, s_2^n, s_1^n)$. We evaluate by simulation two implementations that differ in the treatment of the LPS (s_1^n), one in which it is a protected stream and one in which it is the BES.

5.1   Performance Under Stationary Traffic

Figure 5(a) and (b) show the ratio P_i/B_i for the four arrival streams in the five scenarios considered and for the two implementations of the adaptive scheme.

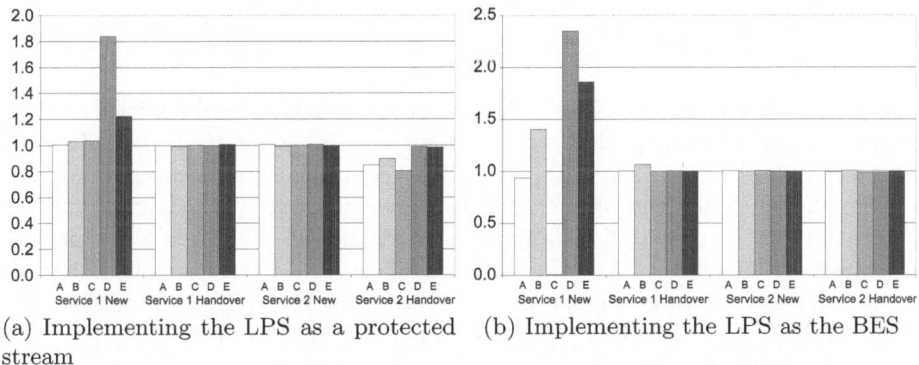

(a) Implementing the LPS as a protected stream

(b) Implementing the LPS as the BES

Fig. 5. P_i/B_i for a system with a stationary load equal to λ_{max}

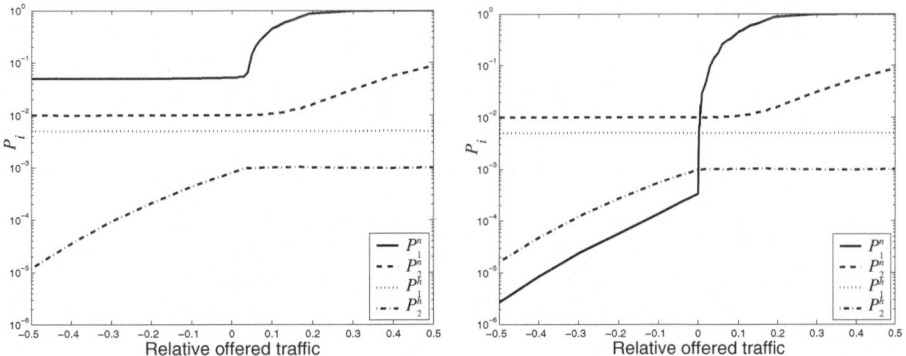

(a) Implementing the LPS as a protected stream.

(b) Implementing the LPS as the BES.

Fig. 6. P_i as a function of $(\lambda - \lambda_{max})/\lambda_{max}$ in stationary conditions

In all cases, an aggregated calling rate equal to the system capacity (λ_{max}) is offered.

Figure 6 provides additional information on the variation of performance for scenario C with $C = 10$ resource units. When the LPS is a protected stream (Fig. 6(a)) it does not benefit from the capacity surplus during underload episodes and it is the first to be penalized during overload episodes. On the other hand, when the LPS is the BES (Fig. 6(b)) it benefits during underload episodes and, as before, it is the first to be penalized during overload episodes. In both implementations, note that s_2^n is also penalized when keeping on penalizing the LPS would be ineffective. Note also that during underload episodes $P_i = B_i$ is held for protected streams and therefore the system is rejecting more requests than required, but some streams (HPS and BES) benefit from this extra capacity.

5.2   Performance Under Non-stationary Traffic

In this section we study the transient regime after a step-type traffic increase from $0.66\lambda_{max}$ to λ_{max} is applied to the system in scenario A when the LPS is a protected stream. Before the step increase is applied the system is in the steady state regime.

Figure 7 shows the transient behavior of the blocking probabilities. As observed, the convergence period is lower than 1000 s., which is 10 to 100 times lower than in previous proposals [2,3]. Note that the convergence period will be even shorter when the offered load is above the system capacity thanks to the increase in the probabilistic-adjustment actions rate, which is an additional advantage of the scheme. Additional mechanisms have been developed that allow to trade-off convergence speed for precision in the fulfillment of the QoS objective, but will not be discussed due to paper length limitations.

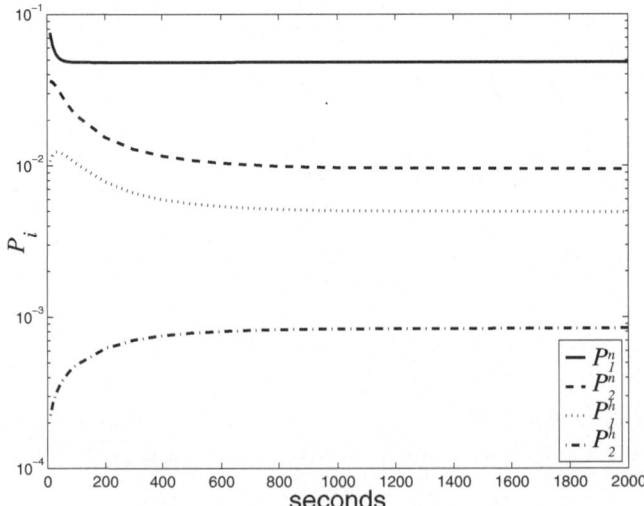

Fig. 7. Transient behavior of the blocking probabilities

6   Conclusions

We developed a novel adaptive reservation scheme that operates in coordination with the Multiple Guard Channel policy but that can be readily extended to operate with the Multiple Fractional Guard Channel policy. Three relevant features of our proposal are: its capability to handle multiple services, its ability to continuously track and adjust the QoS perceived by users and its simplicity. We provide two implementations of the scheme. First, when the LPS has a QoS objective defined, which obviously must be met when possible. Second, when the LPS is treated as a best-effort stream and therefore obtains an unpredictable QoS, which tends to be "good" during underload episodes but is "quite bad" as soon as the system enters the overload region.

The performance evaluation shows that the QoS objective is met with an excellent precision and that the convergence period, being around 1000 s., is 10 to 100 times shorter than in previous proposals. This confirms that our scheme can handle satisfactorily the non-stationarity of a real network.

Future work will include the evaluation of the scheme when operating with other SAC policies, for example those for which the stationary probability distribution has a product-form solution. Another interesting extension would be to base the adjustment of the configuration parameters not only on the decisions of the SAC subsystem but also on predictive information, like movement prediction.

Acknowledgments

This work has been supported by the Spanish Ministry of Education and Science (30%) and by the EU (FEDER 70%) under projects TIC2003-08272, TEC2004-06437-C05-01 and under contract AP-2004-3332, and by the Generalitat Valenciana under contract CTB/PRB/2002/267.

References

1. D. García, J. Martínez and V. Pla, "Admission Control Policies in Multiservice Cellular Networks: Optimum Configuration and Sensitivity," Wireless Systems and Mobility in Next Generation Internet, Gabriele Kotsis and Otto Spaniol (eds.), Lecture Notes in Computer Science, vol. 3427, pp.121-135, Springer-Verlag 2005.
2. Y. Zhang, D. Liu, "An adaptive algorithm for call admission control in wireless networks", Proceedings of the IEEE Global Communications Conference (GLOBECOM), pp. 3628-3632, San Antonio, (USA), Nov. 2001.
3. X.-P. Wang, J.-L. Zheng, W. Zeng, G.-D. Zhang, "A probability-based adaptive algorithm for call admission control in wireless network", Proceedings of the International Conference on Computer Networks and Mobile Computing (ICCNMC), pp. 197-204, Shanghai, (China), 20-23 Oct. 2003.
4. O. Yu, V. Leung, "Adaptive Resource Allocation for prioritized call admission over an ATM-based Wireless PCN", IEEE Journal on Selected Areas in Communications, pp. 1208-1224, vol. 15, Sept. 1997.

5. P. Ramanathan, K. M. Sivalingam, P. Agrawal, S. Kishore, "Dynamic Resource Allocation Schemes During Handoff for Mobile Multimedia Wireless Networks", Journal on Selected Areas in Communications, pp. 1270-1283, vol. 17, Jul. 1999.
6. O. Yu, S. Khanvilkar, "Dynamic adaptive QoS provisioning over GPRS wireless mobile links", Proceedings of the IEEE International Conference on Communications (ICC), pp. 1100-1104, vol. 2, New York, (USA), 28 Apr.- 2 May 2002.
7. Performability Engineering Research Group (PERFORM), Möbius^{TM}. User Manual. Version 1.6.0: http://www.perform.csl.uiuc.edu/mobius/manual/Mobius Manual_160.pdf.
8. D. Garcia-Roger, Mª Jose Domenech-Benlloch, J. Martinez-Bauset, V. Pla, "Adaptive Admission Control Scheme for Multiservice Mobile Cellular Networks", Proceedings of the 1st Conference on Next Generation Internet Networks (NGI2005), Roma, (Italy), 18-20 Apr. 2005.

Relevance-Based Adaptive Event Communication for Mobile Environments with Variable QoS Capabilities

Stephen Workman, Gerard Parr, Philip Morrow, and Darryl Charles

Faculty of Engineering, University of Ulster, Coleraine, BT52 1SA, Northern Ireland
{workman-s, gp.parr, pj.morrow, dk.charles}@ulster.ac.uk

Abstract. Recent trends in computing have been driving the demand for mobile multimedia applications, specifically distributed virtual environments (DVEs). These applications must deal with the variable resource availability of both connection and client device in order to achieve real-time event communication. Relevance-based event filtering is used to explore event stream adaptation in response to variable QoS. Results show that the performance gains from such adaptation are inconsistent due to the irregular nature of event communication. Increased reliability is proposed through dynamic consideration of the resource requirements of the various adapted event stream solutions.

1 Introduction

Recent trends in computing show increasing demand for mobile multimedia, specifically distributed virtual environments (DVEs) [1, 2]. Such multimedia applications take advantage of the mobility afforded by wireless networking and the pervasive nature of mobile devices. For example, in the Savannah Project [3] a DVE was used over mobile devices as part of an augmented reality game, to help educate children about lions and the savannah. For such virtual environments distributed over wireless networks, the tension between the real-time resource requirements and the inherent variable resource availability of both connection and client device must be managed by the server. Application layer adaptation of data has been suggested to overcome this resource variability with both general [4, 5] and event-based data communication [6]. This paper demonstrates how relevance-based event filtering as a method of data adaptation should take resource requirements of event type streams into consideration when adapting to the currently available device and connection resources.

2 Background and Existing Approaches

Real-time distributed applications in the wireless domain can be examined from two main viewpoints: communication and application [7]. The communication aspect deals with those issues pertaining to the transport of data across the network, while the application aspect deals with the encoding, decoding and use of data before and after transport.

The main resource requirement made of the communication aspect by DVEs is that data be transported in real-time. This requires a high quality of service (QoS)

J. Dalmau and G. Hasegawa (Eds.): MMNS 2005, LNCS 3754, pp. 59–70, 2005.
© IFIP International Federation for Information Processing 2005

requested from the network (high data throughput, low latency etc.) and the client (processing power, storage etc.). The 3rd Generation Partnership Project (3GPP) provides traffic classes for resource reservation in the sub-IP layers, including the "conversational" class meant for real-time transport [8]. Resource reservation is also provided in the IP layer through IntServ and DiffServ – in [9] the authors suggest the use of aggregated flows as the best way to provide the necessary QoS for event communication.

There are three main issues with the use of such reservation schemes in the mobile domain, however. Firstly, due to host mobility, QoS cannot be guaranteed for the life of the session due to connection handovers [10, 11]. Although delays incurred by handover can be reduced, e.g. [10], longer term disruptions can be caused if the new base station does not have the same resources as the old one, e.g. in the case of vertical handoffs [10-12]. Secondly, the resources set aside by a base station do not guarantee that the mobile node will be able to use them, since the QoS actually achieved is variable [12-15]. Trade-offs at the lower layers, in response to changing interference and fading, can reduce link throughput, resulting in lower bandwidth available to the application. Thirdly, there is no guarantee that traffic which crosses autonomous systems will have the same resources set aside as those at the edge, i.e. in the case of internetworking. Dynamic resource management is suggested in the network layer as a response to this resource variability [12].

Feedback of all such resource variability must be provided to the application layer. In session description protocol over session initiation protocol (SDP/SIP) [16, 17] resources are negotiated between peers during session setup, and re-negotiated during session run-time should conditions change. This capability to renegotiate without restarting a session allows the application layer to adapt to the variable network conditions inherent to mobile and wireless networking. Nonetheless, under SDP all the resources of the session need to be renegotiated, and not just those which have changed. The authors of [18] highlight the long delay in session renegotiation following a vertical handover while using SDP/SIP, while in [19] the End-to-End Negotiation Protocol (E2ENP) is provided as an alternative to SDP, where only relevant resources are re-negotiated.

The application layer must respond to variable network resource availability by changing the resource requirements of the pending traffic (i.e. events). All types of DVE contain client and server components [6], where the role of the server(s) is to maintain a consistent state of the virtual environment across all participating clients. In the mobile environment this role expands to take resource variability and connection heterogeneity into consideration. In [20] the authors suggest that the server deal with varying latencies through buffering real-time updates. This, however, doesn't deal with other variations in resources e.g. bandwidth. Event filtering methods can be used to cut down on the amount of data transmitted to certain clients in distributed virtual environments. Criteria for what is dropped can be based on spatial location in the gaming world, i.e. only transmitting data to players whose immediate environment is affected [21]. Interest in events can also be specified by clients, allowing them to choose event types which are relevant to them [21-23]. Another method suggests dropping obsolete events [6] i.e. events are dropped because their effect on the environment is contained in the effects of subsequent events. Methods can also be combined: the use of a two-tiered server network involving a separation of

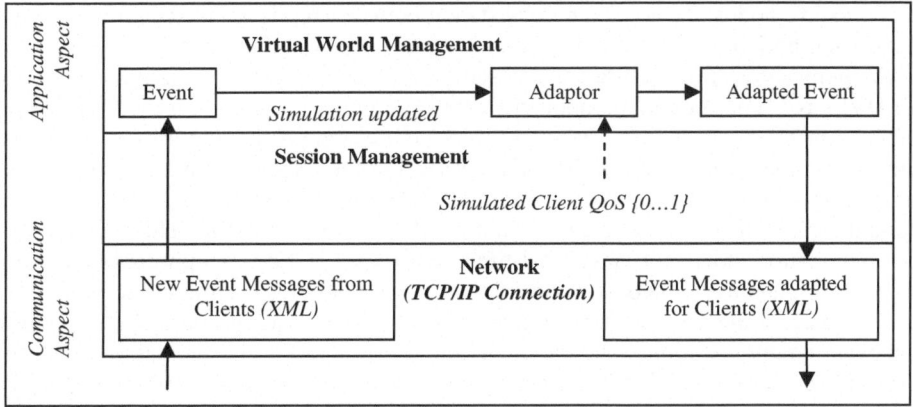

Fig. 1. Event flow between arrival on and departure from the server

relevance-filtering and bandwidth adaptation is suggested in [24]. In general, these filtering techniques try to reduce the resource requirements (specifically bandwidth) of the data that is to be sent across the network to the connected nodes, while maintaining a state consistency which is adequate for user interaction.

This paper demonstrates through simulation that event filtering based purely on location relevance does not take into consideration the effect that changing levels of activity in the virtual world can have on resource requirements. Adaptation which considers the resource requirements of the potential adapted event streams is proposed; the resources of the event stream are conditioned to match those resources which are available on the network and client.

3   Simulation Architecture

The aim of these simulations was to explore location-relevance filtering as a way to adapt event communication based on variable QoS. A two-player version of the classic arcade game Bomberman was chosen as an initial study of adaptive multipoint communication, as multiplayer games are typical of expected real-time mobile multimedia applications [1, 2]. Scalability testing and related issues are to be explored in future work. The rest of this section describes the current simulation test-bed, with particular emphasis given to the event communication model and the adaptation algorithm, in the context of the client/server architecture used.

3.1   Test-Bed Architecture

To understand the adaptation, it is important to understand the context of the game architecture. Virtual environments consist of a collection of virtual objects, as discussed in depth in [7]; Bomberman's virtual environment, or game world, is a 2D maze which is filled with piles of dirt and rocks. The aim of the game is to manoeuvre one's avatar around the dirt and rocks, laying bombs to clear paths through the dirt, with the ultimate goal of blowing up the other player's avatar and being the last alive. These objects are based on *SharedObjects*, from [7], since replicas of each exist at participating nodes. To maintain consistency between replicas, attribute changes are distributed between peers. This event processing is described in more detail later.

A client/server architecture was chosen for this implementation, as it the basis for all DVEs [6]. The internal components of this architecture, based on the OSI 7 layer model, are shown in Fig. 1. The game world is located on the application level, and identical copies are created on both the server and the clients when a session begins, i.e. during session setup the server establishes the initial state of the game world, and communicates this to the clients via an XML-based protocol. This part of the communication does not have real-time constraints. For the purposes of these simulations, adaptation is only performed on event messages leaving the server.

The state of the virtual world is maintained consistent across participating nodes, via event communication. When a client-side user interacts with the game world, the event is sent to the session layer where it is converted into XML and passed to the network layer for transmission to the server. On the server, the XML is parsed in the session layer, and passed up to the application layer, where it is assimilated into the server-side copy of the virtual world. After the simulation is updated, the event is passed to the adaptor (discussed in Section 3.2). Based on the client's simulated QoS obtained from the session layer, it is updated with events as is deemed necessary by the adaptor. Note that in the standard version of the game there is no adaptor.

The software was created using a combination of "off-the-shelf" and new components. Both the server and client were written in Java (J2SE and J2ME, respectively) using the NetBeans IDE due to Java's widespread use among mobile devices [25]. XML was used as the basis for the event communication protocol because of its suitability for use with an object-oriented model. The protocol also included basic session setup capabilities because of the lack of readily available support for SDP/SIP in J2ME. Existing Java TCP socket classes were used because of TCP's standard use in industry and as a basis for future studies involving variants which are more suitable to wireless communications.

3.2 Adaptation

The adaptation used changes how a client's copy of the game state is synchronised. This is based on the relevance of the events to be sent to the client, and the current QoS available to it, as in the algorithm outlined in figure 3. QoS availability was simulated and followed a sawtooth pattern, continuously cycling between poor and good service, in order to see how the adaptation functioned in response to varying QoS. QoS values ranged from 0 (i.e. minimum resources needed for gameplay) to 1 (i.e. optimal resources requiring no adaptation), with increments of 0.1 between.

This adaptation was based on the notion that events closer to an avatar are more relevant and should be given more priority in distribution (Figure 2) [21]. "Player movement" events were deemed to have absolute relevance, regardless of location, since knowledge of other players' locations is needed in order to play the game properly; thus these are added to the clients' queues without being adapted. Similarly, if a client has QoS of 1 all events are sent as it has enough resources to process this data. If the client's simulated QoS is between 1 and 0, however, the events are checked for relevance, based on their location relative to the client's avatar (figure 2 explains the notion of relevance based on location). The zone of influence varies in

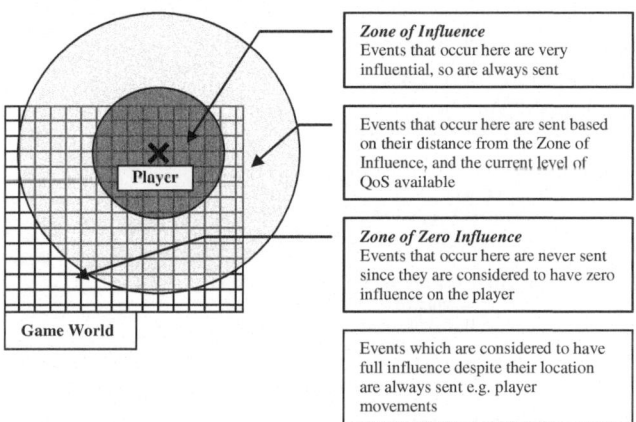

Fig. 2. Location based relevance filtering

size with the client's simulated QoS; in other words, with more resources available, the zone is bigger and more events are sent; whereas with fewer resources, the zone is reduced in size and more events are adapted. The basic size was varied in the simulations, as is explained further in the results section. It is important to note that since these are foundational simulations, the client event queues work purely on a first-come-first-served basis, and are not priority based. Further work is also to be conducted into the upper and lower thresholds of available QoS.

An adapted event is one whose message is incorporated into a simulation wide update message. Rather than sending multiple smaller event messages, those deemed less relevant by the algorithm discussed previously, are dropped. The server then sends an update message, i.e. the current game state as viewed by the server, after a certain time interval, which varies with the client's QoS. Thus, during a period of low QoS, instead of receiving many smaller event messages, the client receives one or a few larger update messages.

4   Results and Interpretation

Both the minimum size for the zone of influence, and the update interval were varied in the simulations to test the adaptation in a two-player environment. Baseline results were obtained from a standard version of the game, for comparison with the adaptive versions. Results were also verified using similar methods to those described in [26, 27].

4.1   Methodology

The simulations were carried out on a host platform; the J2ME Wireless Toolkit v2.2, using MIDP v.2.0 [25], emulated the mobile device environment for the client software on two Dell Optiplex GX270 (Pentium 4 CPU running at 3GHz, with 1GB of RAM) desktop computers connected via a 100 MBps switched Ethernet LAN. A third such machine ran the server software (using J2SE 1.4.2_04 [25]).

```
Event received from Client

Server-side simulation state updated

IF Event has preset relevance {
        Event posted on all Client queues
}
ELSE {
        FOR EACH Client {
                IF Client has QoS of 1 {
                        Event posted on this Client's queue
                }
                ELSE IF Client has QoS between 0 and 1{
                        Calculate size of zone of influence
                        IF Event occurs within zone of influence {
                                Event posted on this Client's queue
                        }
                        ELSE IF Event occurs in the zone of zero influence {
                                Event not sent
                                Client put on timer for state update
                        }
                }
                ELSE IF Client has QoS of 0 {
                        Event not sent
                        Client put on timer for state update
                }
        }
}
```

Fig. 3. Algorithm used to adapt events

Events were logged as and when they arrived and departed on all three nodes, along with their size, which client they pertained to, the time of arrival or departure, and the simulated QoS of the client at that time (NB: QoS values were recorded server-side only, since this is where their simulation occurred). The results used for analysis were based on the events sent and received from the perspective of the server, since this is where the adaptation took place. These results were verified by comparison of the recorded and captured logs, as well as comparison of logs from each node.

The two variables under scrutiny in these experiments were the basic size of the zone of influence, and the time interval between sending game state updates. Event streams, which are dependent on user activity, were controlled by being recorded and re-used under test conditions seen in table 1, including a standard game with no

Table 1. Values used in the experiments

Test	Update Timer (ms; 0...System Max.)	Zone of Influence (basic size and max. extension) (movement units; 0...$\sqrt{200}$(max. distance))
1	n/a (Standard version of game)	
2	1000	
3	2000	
4	3000	4
5	4000	
6	5000	
7		2
8		3
4 (not repeated)	3000	4
9		5
10		6

adaptation. These values were chosen to allow exploration of basic trends for future follow-up. Event logging, which was incorporated in the software, was validated by capturing the network traffic using Ethereal [28].

4.2 Results Analysis

Performance was measured based on the comparison of results from the adaptive version of the game with those from the standard version and with the simulated client-connection QoS values. Following this, logs of events sent by clients and received by the server were used to compare the performance of the adaptation using identical data.

Results for the standard version of the game ("Test 1" in figure 4) show almost identical traffic patterns for the two clients; there is no differentiation between clients. This is as expected, since without adaptation, all events are processed by the server and sent on to all clients, without distinction. The only significant difference between the two is seen at session start, which can be attributed to the simulation setup phase. This phase is not synchronised by event, so a difference is not unexpected, and does not affect the rest of the stream, which the server distributes on a per event basis, producing the similar streams as in the charts.

Results from the adaptive versions of the game (Figure 5) show that the event streams sent to each client are distinct. Over time, the amount of data that is sent to each client changes, as is seen in the charts with the variations in gradient. Thus, differentiation between clients is possible with this technique. Comparison with the simulated QoS, however, shows no correlation. Re-using the event streams sent from the client to the server shows how the different test conditions affect the adapted event streams sent from the server. Figure 6 shows a sample chart of the event streams produced using the same data set, under the four test conditions representing the extremes of the two variables – Tests 2 and 6 for update interval, and Tests 7 and 10 for zone of influence. Typical of the results, this chart shows that the zone of influence has a greater effect on the event streams than the update interval. Figure 7 shows a summary of the results, based on the overall data rate. Again, these charts suggest that the zone of influence has a greater affect on the data rates than the update interval does. Successful adaptation, however, would show a correlation between low simulated QoS and low data rates, but this is not the case.

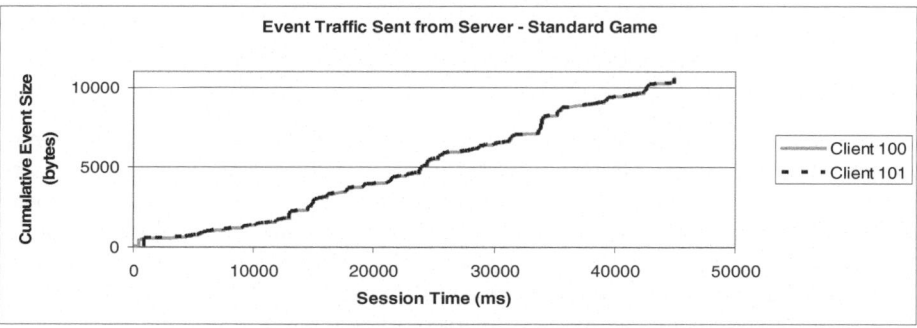

Fig. 4. Event traffic without adaptation

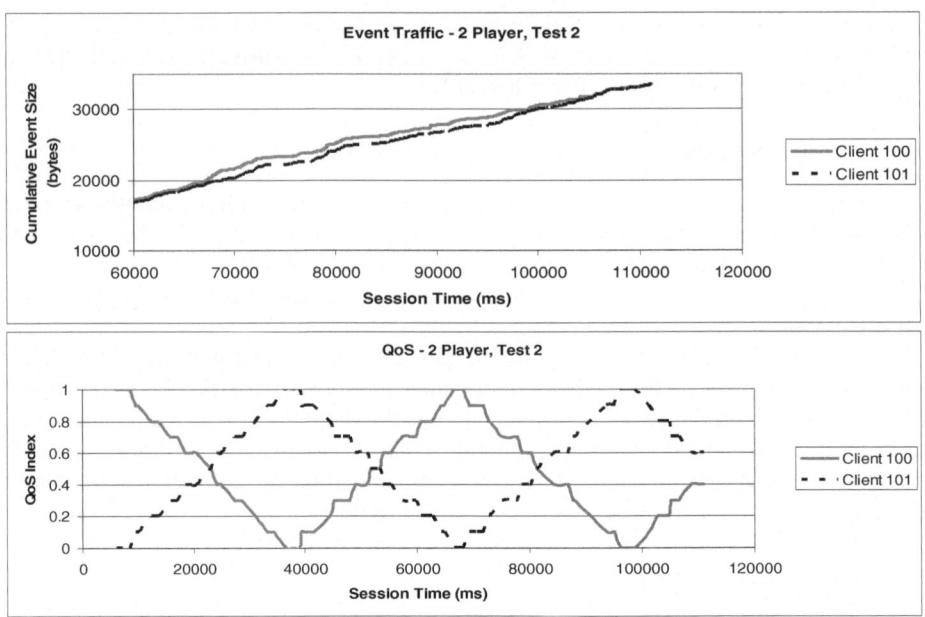

Fig. 5. Sample event traffic for adaptive game with simulated QoS

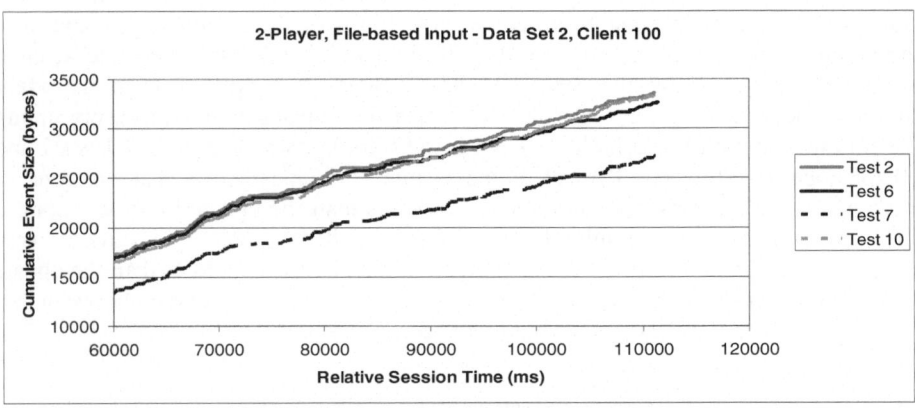

Fig. 6. Data set 2 under different test conditions

Because of the nature of the gameplay, the user follows the centre of activity around the game world. All events are initiated, directly or indirectly, by the users' intervention in the environment; furthermore, the users' avatars are likely to locate near each other, as the goal is to blow up the other's avatar. As such, the amount of activity outside the zone of influence is somewhat limited. This explains why larger zones of influence do not produce average data rates which are much different to those of a standard game, as the vast majority of events fall inside the zone and are thus sent to the client. An eleventh test condition was added to the simulations

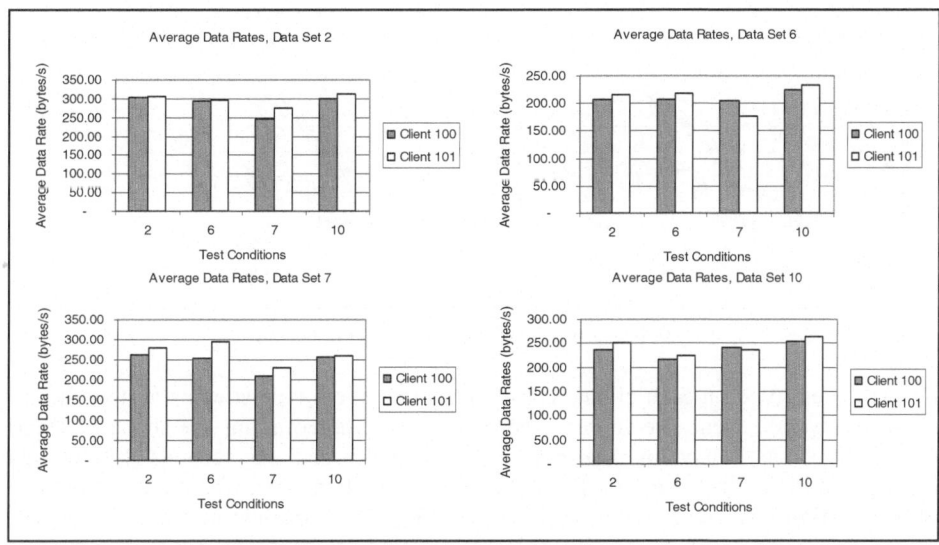

Fig. 7. Summary results for adaptive game

whereby the minimum size of the zone of influence and its maximum extension are no longer the same. In this test the variation in the size of the zone of influence is more closely tied to the QoS; where maximum QoS is available, the zone of influence covers the entire game world; when QoS is at a minimum, the zone of influence is reduced to the immediate vicinity of the player's avatar.

Overall, these results show better correlation with the simulated QoS than the previous test cases, but imperfections still remain. Figure 8 shows a sample chart of these results, showing a short session created by data set 6. This chart shows very similar traffic for the two clients for the first 13 seconds even though their QoS values are at opposite ranges of the scale, following the same pattern as seen in figure 5. Differences are clear between 13 and 16 seconds, but the event streams seem to return to similarity following this.

Examining the data streams for the adapted games shows the amount of activity within the zone of influence. Since events are sent directly if they fall within the zone, a large number of standard events would indicate a lot of activity within the zone, especially if the QoS were low. Figure 9 shows the individual traffic streams created

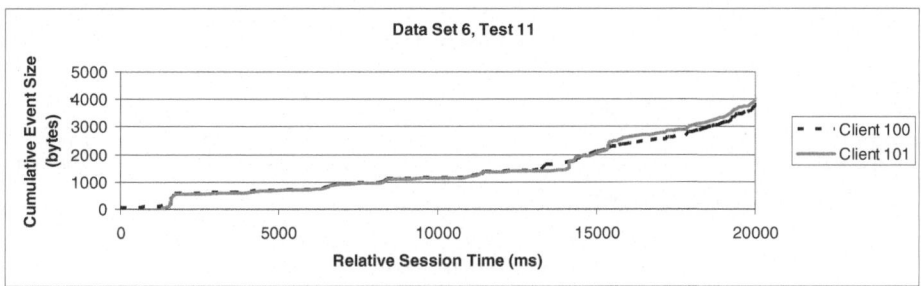

Fig. 8. Event streams for data set 6, test 11

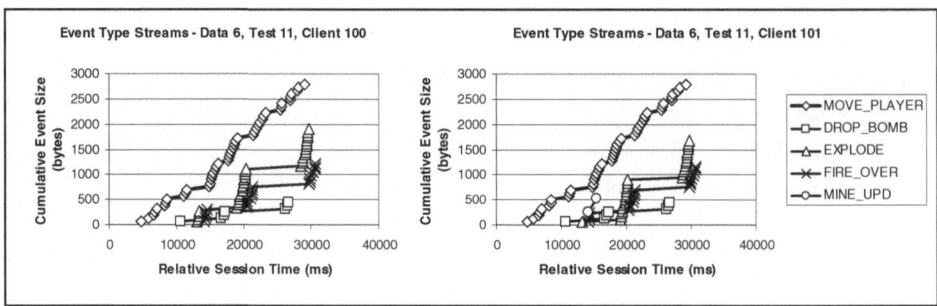

Fig. 9. Event type streams for data set 6, test 11

by each event type on each client. These individual event type streams go together to form the overall event streams as seen in Figure 8, determining the shape of these overall streams. Analyzing the period between 13 and 16 seconds which was highlighted in the discussion on figure 8, shows that client 100, which has almost full QoS (see figure 6), receives no update ("MINE_UPD") events; this is as expected, since the size of its zone of influence covers most of the game world. Client 101, however, receives two update events and standard events in this period, indicating activity both within and without its zone of influence; client 101's zone of influence is quite small as its QoS is also quite small. In this situation, client 101 would have benefited from a quick update sent immediately, and not put on a timer, which would have demanded less bandwidth, rather than the series of smaller "EXPLODE" events and update events which demanded quite a lot. If this had been the case, client 101's overall event stream would have had a smoother gradient at this time, rather than the larger jump. Figure 10 shows how this would look.

This example suggests a lack of consideration for the QoS requirements of the various streams. In the present algorithm, the zone of influence shrinks and grows depending on the QoS available; the user receives high detail over time nearby in the virtual world, and varying accuracy in the middle and long distances. Rather than reducing the number of events sent to the client to lower the overall QoS requirement, it may be possible to use a different event message which has smaller QoS requirements, as just discussed. Potential results could mean lower QoS requirements for the overall stream, while maintaining a higher number of events. To achieve this demands knowledge of the QoS requirements of the different event types; this will require further experimentation in the future.

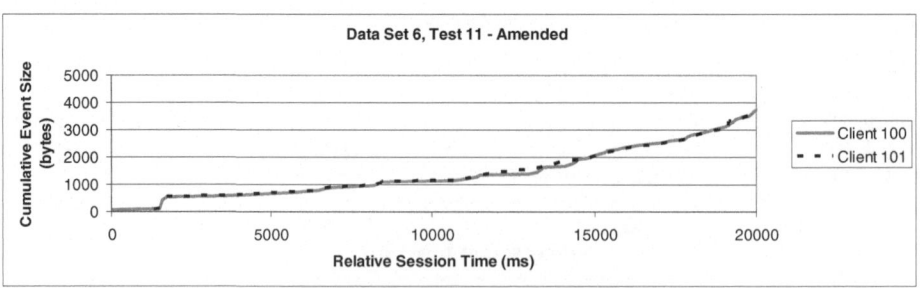

Fig. 10. Amended chart of data set 6

5   Conclusion and Future Work

This paper has presented an exploratory study of the use of data adaptation for the variable resource environment of wireless networking. Simulation suggests that in order for relevance-based adaptation to work optimally it must take the QoS requirements of the different event type streams into consideration. For DVEs, this means that there must be a method of describing events and event streams in terms of the resources they require, in order to provide a set of event stream solutions which have a range of QoS requirements. The decision of how best to adapt the basic event stream can then be based on such a set of solutions and the resources currently available. Issues involved in this continued work will examine how best to characterize QoS requirements using different metrics, as well as simulating the dynamic resource profile of wireless networking. Scalability and cost/efficiency analyses of the adaptation using different distribution architectures are also essential.

References

1. Ward, Mark. "Mobile games poised for take-off." BBC News. News, 2 May 2005. Available at http://news.bbc.co.uk/1/hi/technology/4498433.stm (17 May 2005).
2. Holden, Windsor. Juniper Research. White Paper, February 2005. Mobile Fun & Games - Second Edition
3. Facer, K, R Joiner, D Stanton, J Reid, R Hull, and D Kirk. "Savannah: mobile gaming and learning?" Journal of Computer Assisted Learning 20.6 (December 2004): 399-409.
4. Workman, SJH, G Parr, P Morrow, and D Charles. "Enabling Adaptive Multipoint Multimedia over Wireless IP Networks." Proceedings from PGNET 2004 (28-29 June 2004), 266-271.
5. Yan, Bo, and Kam W. Ng. "A Survey on the Techniques for the Transport of MPEG-4 over Wireless Networks." IEEE Transactions on Consumer Electronics 48.4 (November 2002): 863-873.
6. Ferretti, Stefano, and Marco Roccetti. "A novel obsolescence-based approach to event delivery synchronisation in multiplayer games." International Journal of Intelligent Games and Simulation 3.1 (March/April 2004): 7-19.
7. Matijasevic, Maja, Denis Gracanin, Kimon P. Valavanis, and Ignac Lovrek. "A Framework for Multiuser Distributed Virtual Environments." IEEE Transactions on Systems, Man and Cybernetics-Part B: Cybernetics 32.4 (August 2002): 416-429.
8. 3rd Generation Partnership Project (3GPP). Technical Specification Group Services and System Aspects. Technical Specification, March 2004. Quality of Service (QoS) concept and architecture (Release 6)
9. Busse, Marcel, Bernd Lamparter, Martin Mauve, and Wolfgang Effelsberg. "Lightweight QoS-Support for Networked Mobile Gaming." SIGCOMM'04 Workshops (30 August 2004).
10. Lo, Shou-Chih, Guanling Lee, Wen-Tsuen Chen, and Jen-Chi Liu. "Architecture for Mobility and QoS Support in All-IP Wireless Networks." 30 January 2003. IEEE Journal on Selected Areas in Communications 22.4 (May 2004): 691-705.
11. Moon, Bongko, and A. Hamid Aghvami. "Quality-of-Service Mechanisms in All-IP Wireless Access Networks." 1 June 2003. IEEE Journal on Selected Areas in Communications 22.5 (June 2004): 873-888.

12. Mirhakkak, Mohammad, Nancy Schult, and Duncan Thomson. "Dynamic Bandwidth Management and Adaptive Applications for a Variable Bandwidth Wireless Environment." December 2000. IEEE Journal on Selected areas in Communications 19.10 (October 2001): 1984-1997.

13. Mukhtar, Rami G., Stephen V. Hanly, and Lachlan L.H. Andrew. "Efficient Internet Traffic Delivery over Wireless Networks." IEEE Communications Magazine (December 2003), 46-53.

14. Fu, Zhengua, Xiaoquo Meng, and Songwu Lu. "A Transport Protocol for Supporting Multimedia Streaming in Mobile Ad Hoc Networks." 1 October 2002. IEEE Journal on Selected Areas in Communications 21.10 (December 2003): 1615-1626.

15. Akyildiz, Ian, Yucel Altunbasak, Faramarz Fekri, and Raghupathy Sivakumar. "AdaptNet: An Adaptive Protocol Suite for the Next-Generation Wireless Internet." IEEE Communications Magazine, Volume: 42, Issue: 3, March 2004, pp.128-136.

16. Handley, M., V. Jacobson, and C. Perkins. "SDP: Session Description Protocol." Internet Engineering Task Force. Stds. org, 27 October 2003. Available at http://www.ietf.org/internet-drafts/draft-ietf-mmusic-sdp-new-15.txt (9 February 2004).

17. Liscano, Ramiro, Allan Jost, Anand Dersingh, and Hao Hu. "Session-base Service Discovery in Peer-to-Peer Communications." Proceedings from CCECE 2004-CCGEI 2004, Niagara Falls (May 2004).

18. Pangalos, Paul A., Konstantinos Boukis, Louise Burness, Alan Brookland, Caroline Beauchamps, and AH Aghvami. "End-to-End SIP Based Real Time Application Adaptation During Unplanned Vertical Handovers." GLOBECOM '01. IEEE 6 (2529 November 2001): 3488-3493.

19. Guenkova-Luy, Teodora, Andreas J. Kassler, and Davide Mandato. "End-to-End Quality of Service Coordination for Mobile Multimedia Applications." 1 June 2003. IEEE Journal on Selected Areas on Communications 22.5 (June 2004): 889-903.

20. Diot, Christophe, and Laurent Gautier. "A Distributed Architecture for Multiplayer Interactive Applications on the Internet." IEEE Network 13.4 (July-August 1999).

21. Meier, René, and Vinny Cahill. "STEAM: Event-Based Middleware for Wireless Ad Hoc Networks." Proceedings of the 22nd International Conference on Distributed Computing Systems Workshops (ICDCSW'02) (2002).

22. Eugster, P.Th., P. Felber, R. Guerraoui, and S.B. Handurukande. "Event Systems: How to Have Your Cake and Eat It Too." Proceedings of the 22nd International Conference on Distributed Computing Systems Workshops (ICDCSW'02) (2002).

23. Hinze, Annika, and Sven Bittner. "Efficient Distribution-Based Event Filtering." Proceedings of the 22nd International Conference on Distributed Computing Systems Workshops (ICDCSW'02) (2002).

24. Aarhus, Lars, Knut Holmqvist, and Martin Kirkengen. "Generalized Two-Tier Relevance Filtering of Computer Game Update Events." NetGames 2002 (April 2002).

25. Sun Microsystems, Inc. "Java Technology." Sun Developer Network. 2005. Available at http://java.sun.com (17 May 2005).

26. Borella, Michael S. "Source Models of Network Game Traffic." Computer Communications 23.4 (February 2000): 403-410.

27. Färber, Johannes. "Traffic Modelling for Fast Action Network Games." Multimedia Tools and Applications 23 (2004): 31-46.

28. "Ethereal: A Network Protocol Analyzer". Available at http://www.ethereal.com/ (14 February 2005).

Seamless Network Mobility Management
for Realtime Service

Hee-Dong Park, Yong-Ha Kwon, Kang-Won Lee, Sung-Hyup Lee,
Young-Soo Choi, Yang Li, and You-Ze Cho

School of Electrical Engineering & Computer Science,
Kyungpook National University, Daegu, 702-701, Korea
yzcho@ee.knu.ac.kr

Abstract. A mobile network is a set of IP subnets connected to the Internet
through one or more mobile routers. When a mobile router moves into or out of a
subnet, it suffers from the same handover problems as a mobile node does in the
Mobile IP. A seamless handover scheme with dual mobile routers is proposed for
a large and fast moving network such as trains. Each of the dual mobile routers is
located at each end of the moving network for space diversity, but they perform a
handover as one logical mobile router. Since one of the two mobile routers can
continuously receive packets from its home agent, the proposed scheme can provide no service disruption time resulting in no packet losses during handovers.
Performance evaluation showed that the proposed scheme can provide excellent
performance for realtime service, compared with existing schemes.

1 Introduction

Mobile communication has become more popular due to the increased availability of
portable devices and advanced wireless technology. In addition, the need for broadband wireless Internet connectivity, even on fast moving vehicles such as trains, has
increased [1][2].

The IETF Working Group for network mobility (NEMO) is currently standardizing
basic support protocol for moving networks [3]. The nodes residing in a moving network are attached to a special gateway, so-called mobile router (MR), through which
they can reach the Internet. As like a mobile node (MN) in the Mobile IPv6, if a mobile router (MR) changes its location, then it registers its new care-of-address (CoA)
at its home agent (HA) with a binding update (BU). Through the MR-HA bidirectional tunnel, the nodes residing in a moving network can continuously send and receive packets without perceiving that the MR changed its point of attachment.

Recently, various multihoming issues have been presented in the NEMO Working
Group. The multihoming is necessary to provide constant access to the Internet and to
enhance the overall connectivity of hosts and mobile networks [4][5]. This requires
the use of several interfaces and technologies since the mobile network may be
moving in distant geographical locations where different access technologies are
provided. The additional benefits of the multihoming are fault tolerance/redundancy,
load sharing, and policy routing.

This paper proposes a seamless handover scheme with dual mobile routers for a
large moving network such as trains. Each of dual MRs is located at each end of the

J. Dalmau and G. Hasegawa (Eds.): MMNS 2005, LNCS 3754, pp. 71–81, 2005.

moving network for space diversity. One of the two MRs can continuously receive packets from its HA while the other is undergoing a handover. This can support a seamless handover providing with no service disruption or packet loss.

The remainder of this paper is organized as follows: In Section II, we discuss about handover for mobile networks. In Section III, we introduce a seamless handover scheme with dual MRs, and then in Section IV we evaluate the performance of the proposed scheme. Finally, we make a conclusion in Section V.

2 Handover for Mobile Networks

The NEMO basic handover consists of two components, L2 handover and L3 handover. The term L2 handover denotes network mobility that is handled by the MAC (medium access control) and its support for roaming at the link-layer level, while the L3 handover occurs at the IP (network) layer level. Usually, the L3 handover is not dependent on the L2 handover, although it must precede the L3 handover.

Fig. 1 shows the components of handover latency in the NEMO basic operation. The L2 handover at the link layer involves channel scanning, authentication, and MR-access router (AR) association. The total L2 handover latency is about 150 to 200 msec. The L3 handover at the IP layer involves movement detection, new CoA configuration, and binding updates, which lead to about a 2 to 3 second handover latency. The L3 handover latency can be reduced by link-layer triggering or pre-registration schemes [6]. However, this handover latency can cause a service disruption resulting in packet losses.

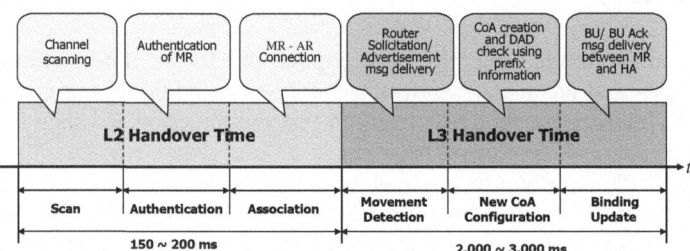

Fig. 1. Components of handover latency in the NEMO basic operation

Fig. 2 shows the L3 handover procedure in the NEMO basic operation based on Mobile IPv6. While an MR stays in an AR's coverage area, the MR receives periodic router advertisement messages from the AR. If the MR does not receive any messages from the AR during a predetermined time, it sends a router solicitation message to the AR to confirm its reachability. Nevertheless, if the AR does not respond, the MR detects its unreachability to that AR and sends router solicitation messages to new ARs for re-association. If a new AR replies with a neighbor advertisement message, the MR receives the prefix information from the AR and forms an association with the new AR by creating a CoA. Then, the MR sends a BU to its HA. After receiving the BU message, the HA replies with a binding ACK message and then can deliver data traffic from a correspondent node (CN) to the MR via the new AR.

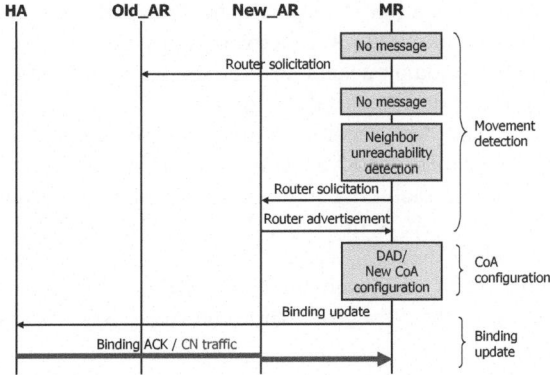

Fig. 2. The L3 handover procedure in the NEMO basic operation

3 Seamless Handover Scheme with Dual MRs

This section propose a seamless handover scheme with dual MRs for a large and fast moving network such as trains. Each of dual MRs, which associate with the same HA, is located at each end of the moving network for space diversity. One of the two MRs can continuously receive packets from its HA while the other is undergoing a handover.

3.1 Handover Procedure

The dual MRs, called as Head_MR and Tail_MR, are located respectively at each end of a train. Two MRs act as one logical MR, but the Tail_MR plays a major role in the L3 handover, thereby this gives the HA an illusion that only one MR exists in the mobile network.

Fig. 3 shows the handover procedure of the proposed scheme. When both MRs stay in the Old_AR's coverage area, the Tail_MR communicates through the Old_AR, while the Head_MR waits for an impending handover.

1. Phase 1: As the mobile network moves, the Head_MR reaches New_AR's coverage area prior to the Tail_MR and then performs a handover. After the Head_MR receives the prefix information from the New_AR and associates with the New_AR by creating a CoA, it sends a proxy BU message to its HA. The Proxy BU message contains the Head_MR's new CoA and the Tail_MR's home address (HoA), instead of the Head_MR's. This makes the HA to be under the illusion that the Tail_MR moves into the New_AR's coverage area. The Tail_MR, however, actually continues to send and receive packets in the Old_AR's coverage area, thus packet loss can be prevented. After receiving the proxy BU message, the HA updates the binding and delivers packets to the Head_MR through the New_AR. When the Head_MR receives a proxy BU ACK message from the HA, it enters into the data communication mode and sends a handover completion message to the Tail_MR. The Head_MR in the data communication mode can send and receive packets in the New_AR's coverage area.

2. Phase 2: When the Tail_MR stays in the Old_AR's coverage area and the Head_MR stays in the New_AR's coverage area respectively, the Head_MR can send and receive data packets through the New_AR, and the Tail_MR may receive data packets destined to the Old_AR.

3. Phase 3: If the Tail_MR receives a router advertisement message from the New_AR, it performs a handover. Unlike the Head_MR, the Tail_MR sends a general BU message including its own CoA and HoA through the New_AR. After receiving a BU ACK message, the Tail_MR can send and receive packets through the New_AR.

4. Phase 4: When both MRs stay in New_AR's coverage area, the Tail_MR communicates with the New_AR, while the Head_MR waits for an impending handover.

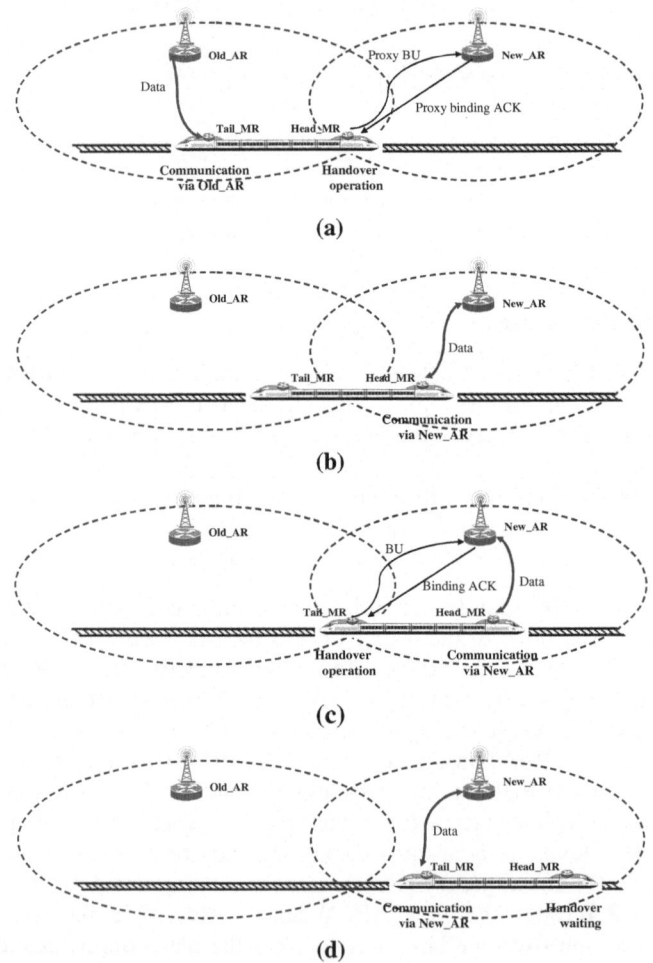

Fig. 3. Handover procedures of the proposed scheme (a) Phase 1, (b) Phase 2, (c) Phase 3, and (d) Phase 4

In the proposed scheme, the proxy BU and the proxy binding ACK messages are introduced. The formats of these messages, however, are the same as those of the general BU and binding ACK messages in the Mobile IPv6. The only difference between the proxy BU message and the general BU message is about the content of the messages. That is, the Head_MR inserts the Tail_MR's HoA into the Proxy BU message instead of its own HoA. Fig. 4 shows message flow diagram of the proposed scheme.

Table 1 shows the binding information maintained in the HA. With the binding information in this table, two MRs act as one logical MR during handovers.

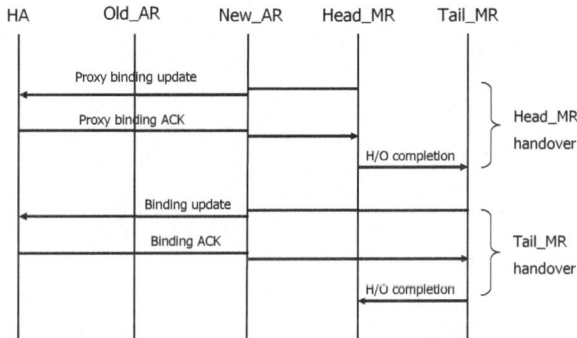

Fig. 4. Binding update messages for handover in the proposed scheme

Table 1. Binding information in the HA

Phases \ Binding	HoA	CoA
Phase 1	Tail_MR's HoA	Head_MR's New_CoA
Phase 2	Tail_MR's HoA	Head_MR's New_CoA
Phase 3	Tail_MR's HoA	Tail_MR's New_CoA
Phase 4	Tail_MR's HoA	Tail_MR's New_CoA

For outgoing packets to the Internet, the Tail_MR is configured as default router in the mobile network. When the Tail_MR can not communicate with the Old_AR, the Tail_MR will redirect or forward the received packets to the Head_MR.

3.2 Condition for Application

The proposed handover scheme exploits the difference between the handover execution time points of the Head_MR and the Tail_MR. In order to apply the proposed scheme for a moving network, the following condition should be satisfied:

$$\frac{d}{v} > T_{HO} \tag{1}$$

where d and v represent the distance between the two MRs and the speed of a moving network, respectively, and T_{HO} indicates the total handover latency during a handover.

Fig. 5 shows the relationship between the handover latency and the speed of a moving network for different distances between two MRs. The region under each curve indicates the range which satisfies the above condition (1). For example, an express train with 300 meters long, traveling at a speed of 300 km/hour, is large enough to apply the proposed handover scheme, even though the total handover latency is assumed to be 3 seconds.

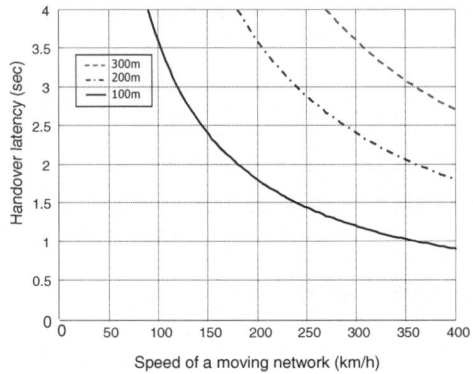

Fig. 5. The relationship between the handover latency and the speed of a moving network for different distances between two MRs

4 Performance Evaluation

This section compares the performance of the proposed handover scheme with the NEMO basic support protocol through analysis and simulation. Two critical performance criteria for realtime service are service disruption time and packet loss during handovers.

4.1 Analytical Results

Service Disruption Time. Service disruption time during a handover can be defined as the time between the reception of the last packet through the old AR until the first packet is received through the new AR. In this paper, we regard the service disruption

Table 2. Parameter definitions

Parameters	Definition
T_{HO}	Total handover latency
T_{MD}	Time required for movement detection
$T_{CoA\text{-}Conf}$	Time required for CoA configuration
T_{BU}	Time required for BU
τ	Router advertisement interval
$RTT_{MR\text{-}AR}$	Round-trip time between MR and AR
$RTT_{AR\text{-}HA}$	Round-trip time between AR and HA

time as the total handover latency, T_{HO}. Table 2 shows the parameters for performance evaluation.

As shown in Fig. 2, the total handover latency during a handover in the NEMO basic support protocol can be expressed as a sum of its components and signaling delays:

$$T_{HO} = T_{MD} + T_{CoA\text{-}Conf} + T_{BU}$$
$$= 2\tau + RTT_{MR\text{-}AR} + RTT_{MR\text{-}HA} \qquad (2)$$
$$= 2\tau + 2RTT_{MR\text{-}AR} + RTT_{AR\text{-}HA}$$

where the delays for encapsulation, decapsulation, and the new CoA creation are not taken into consideration. Generally, the L3 movement detection delay, T_{MD}, includes the L2 handover latency.

Each of dual MRs in the proposed scheme suffers from the same disruption in service during a handover as an MR does in the NEMO basic operation. However, in the proposed scheme, handovers of the Head_MR and the Tail_MR alternate each other, thereby the total service disruption time will be zero. Fig. 6 illustrates that one of the two MRs can continuously receive packets from its HA while the other is being engaged in a handover.

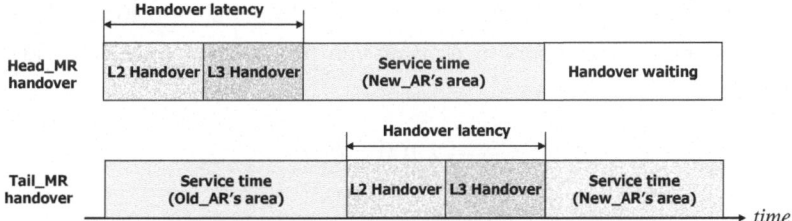

Fig. 6. Handover relationship between dual MRs

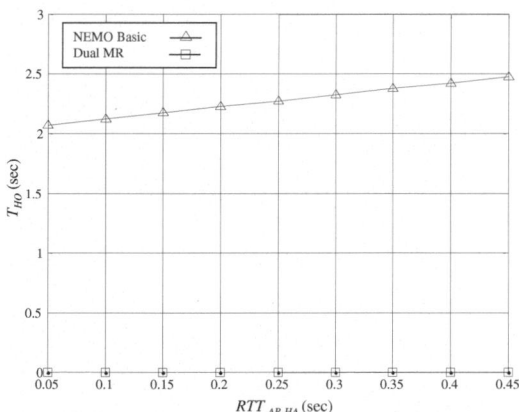

Fig. 7. Comparison of the service disruption time

Fig. 7 compares the service disruption time between the proposed scheme and the NEMO basic support protocol. We assume that the router advertisement interval is 1 second, the radius of AR cell coverage is 1 km, and RTT_{MR-AR} is 10 msec. As shown in this figure, the service disruption time of the NEMO basic is about 2 to 2.5 seconds, while the service disruption time of the proposed scheme is zero. This means that the proposed scheme can support a seamless network mobility for realtime service.

Packet Loss Ratio. Since packet loss does not occur during the time when the CN traffic travels from the HA to an MR after the completion of the BU, the packet loss period during a handover can be expressed as $T_{HO} - 0.5RTT_{MR-HA}$. Hence, using (2), the packet loss period can be given by:

$$T_{loss} = 2\tau + 1.5RTT_{MR-AR} + 0.5RTT_{AR-HA} \tag{3}$$

Also, the packet loss amount can be expressed as a product of the packet loss period and the bandwidth of the Internet link:

$$L = T_{loss} * BW \tag{4}$$

where L represents the packet loss amount, and BW represents the bandwidth of the Internet link. In the case of the proposed scheme, there is no packet loss during a handover because T_{loss} is zero.

Packet loss ratio (ρ_{loss}) is defined as the ratio of the number of lost packets during a handover to the total numbers of transmission packets in a cell. This can be also expressed as:

$$\rho_{loss} = \frac{T_{loss}}{T_{cell}} \times 100 \quad (\%) \tag{5}$$

where T_{cell} is the time it takes an MR to pass through a cell.

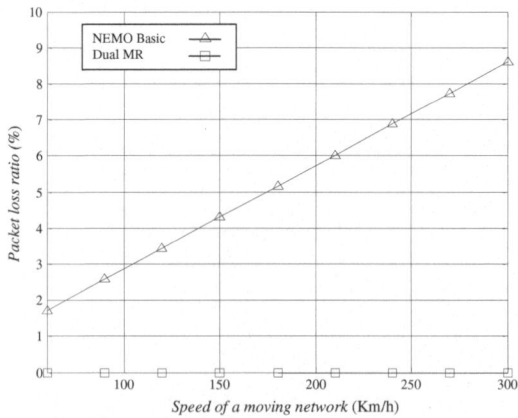

Fig. 8. Comparison of packet loss ratio

Fig. 8 shows the packet loss ratio according to the speed of a moving network. In this figure, RTT_{AR-HA} is assumed to be 100 msec. As shown in this figure, the packet loss ratio of the NEMO basic is proportional to the speed of a moving network, while the packet loss ratio of the proposed scheme will be zero regardless of the speed of the moving network.

4.2 Simulation Results

We compare the TCP/UDP goodput of the proposed scheme with those of the NEMO basic by simulation using NS-2.

Simulation Model. Fig. 9 shows the network model for simulation. We assume that the coverage area of an AR is 250 meters in radius, and the ARs are 400 meters apart each other. Therefore, there is 100 meters overlapping area between the adjacent ARs. The router advertisement interval is assumed to be 1 second. In our simulation we consider the IEEE 802.11b as the wireless LAN. The link characteristics, (the delay and the bandwidth), are shown beside each link in the Fig. 9. With regard to the MR, we only consider a linear movement pattern where the MR moves linearly from one AR to another at a constant speed. Also, the distance between the dual MRs is assumed to be 200 meters.

We have simulated for two traffic types: UDP and TCP. For UDP, the 512-byte packets were sent repeatedly at a constant rate of 20 packets per second from the CN to a mobile network node (MNN) residing in the train. For TCP, FTP traffic was generated with a full window.

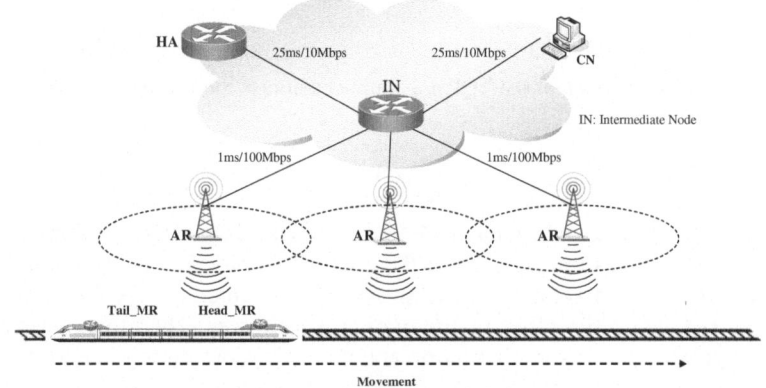

Fig. 9. Network model for simulation

Goodput. Fig. 10 and 11 compare the UDP and the TCP goodput behaviors between the proposed scheme and the NEMO basic, respectively. From these two figures, we note that the proposed scheme can provide a higher goodput in both cases of the UDP and the TCP, because the proposed scheme has no service disruption during handovers.

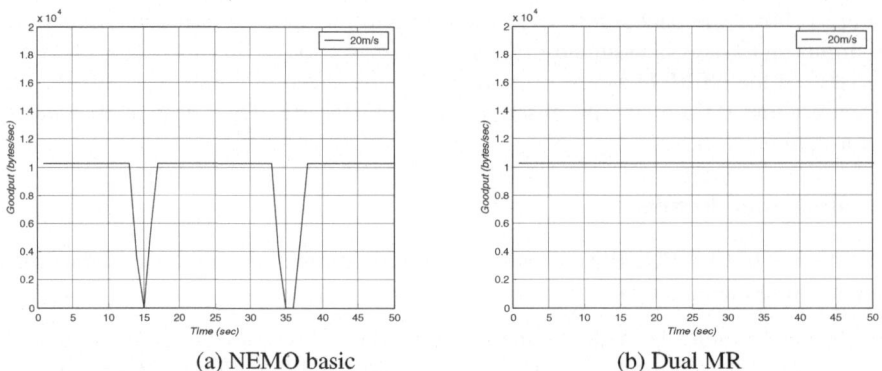

Fig. 10. Comparison of the UDP goodput behaviors at the speed of 20 m/sec

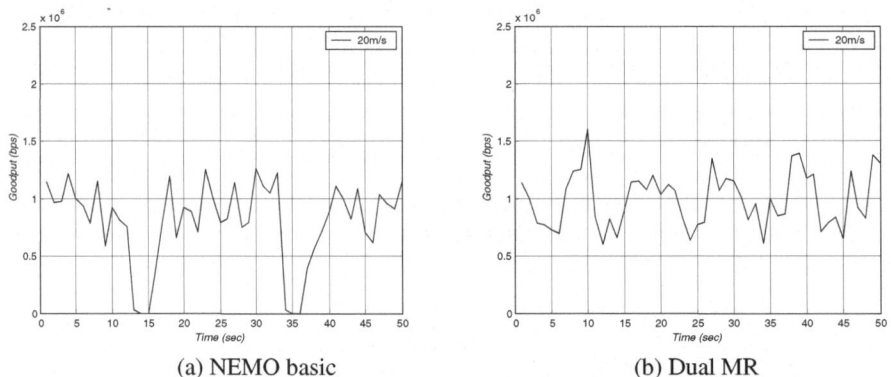

Fig. 11. Comparison of the TCP goodput behaviors at the speed of 20 m/sec

5 Conclusion

This paper proposed a seamless handover scheme with dual MRs for a large and fast moving network such as trains. Each of the dual MRs is located at each end of a mobile network for space diversity. One of the two MRs can continuously receive packets from its HA while the other is undergoing a handover. Therefore, the proposed scheme can provide no service disruption and no packet loss during handovers, which is very useful for realtime service. Performance evaluation showed that the proposed scheme can provide excellent performance for realtime service, compared with the NEMO basic support protocol.

The additional advantages of the proposed scheme are as follows: no modification requirements for existing network entities except MRs, support for load balancing and fault tolerance in special cases, and applicability to non-overlapping networks as well as overlapping networks. However, the proposed scheme has some overhead in comparison with NEMO basic support. The overhead involves the cost to maintain dual MRs with additional signaling messages.

Acknowledgements. This work was supported in part by the KOSEF (contract #: R01-2003-000-10155-0), the ITRC of the Ministry of Information and Communication (MIC), Korea, and the BK21 project.

References

1. Eun Kyoung Paik and Yanghee Choi, "Seamless mobility support for mobile networks on vehicles across heterogeneous wireless access networks," *Proc. of IEEE VTC 2003-Spring*, Apr. 2003.
2. X. Liang, F.L.C. Ong, P.M.L. Chan, R.E. Sheriff, and P. Conforto, "Mobile internet access for high-speed trains via heterogeneous networks," *Proc. of IEEE PIMRC 2003*, Sept. 2003.
3. V. Devarapalli, "Nemo basic support protocol," *Internet draft*, <draft-ietf-nemo-basic-support-01.txt>, Sept. 2003.
4. C. Ng, J. Charbon, E. K. Paik and T. Ernst, "Analysis of multihoming in network mobility support," *Internet Draft*, Feb. 2005.
5. N. Montavont, T. Ernst, and T. Noel, "Multihoming in nested mobile network-ing," *SAINT 2004 Workshops*, Jan. 2004.
6. M. Ronai, K. Fodor, and R. Tonjes, "IPv6 moving network testbed with micro-mobility support," *Proc. of IST Mobile and Wireless Communications Summit 2004*, June 2004.

Setup and Maintenance of Overlay Networks for Multimedia Services in Mobile Environments

Eskindir Asmare, Stefan Schmid, and Marcus Brunner

Network Laboratories, NEC Europe Ltd., 69115 Heidelberg, Germany
eskindir@kth.se, {schmid, brunner}@netlab.nec.de

Abstract. A Service-specific Overlay Network (SSON) is a virtualization concept proposed for customized media delivery in the Ambient Networks architecture [1]. The service specific media delivery network has to be constructed dynamically without prior knowledge of the underlying physical network. This process must consider unique properties, such as routing the media flow through strategic locations that provide special media processing capabilities (for example, media transcoding, caching and synchronization) inside the network. In today's dynamic and mobile network environments establishing an optimal SSON with a reasonable time and message/traffic complexity is challenging. This paper proposes a pattern-based methodology to establish the SSONs. This scheme enables setting up SSONs on demand without prior knowledge of the network topology and where the media processing capabilities are located in the underlying network. A new pattern referred to as *path-directed* search pattern is devised and applied to search for potential overlay nodes and to configure their media processing functions accordingly. The scheme is implemented on a pattern simulation tool and the result shows that SSONs of high quality can be built with a reasonable time and message/traffic complexity.

1 Introduction

A Service-Specific Overlay Network (SSON) is an overlay network solution developed for media delivery in particular. Media delivery in mobile networks has some additional challenges, since the nodes are not fixed, the topology is not stable, and processing of media data within the network makes sense as bandwidth on the wireless links is still limited and expensive.

Establishing service-specific overlay networks involves discovering network-side nodes that support the required media processing capabilities, deciding which nodes should be included in the overlay network and finally configuring the overlay nodes. Traditionally the list of nodes and their processing capabilities (services) are stored in a registry, which is queried during the overlay network setup to selected suitable nodes. However, the use of a registry for this information has serious limitations. One problem is that in dynamic networks, keeping an up-to-date registry is difficult and costly. Nodes with special services can join and leave the network with a high frequency.

Even if it was possible to keep an up-to-date registry of special service nodes, scalability will be a problem in big networks. The single point of failure that will be intro-

J. Dalmau and G. Hasegawa (Eds.): MMNS 2005, LNCS 3754, pp. 82–95, 2005.

duced by the registry and the administrative overhead are also problems worth mentioning. Automated node selection and configuration are also difficult tasks when establishing service-specific overlay networks across dynamic network infrastructures.

The objective of this work is to develop a concept and implementation of a provisioning and maintenance system for service-specific overlay networks. In this system, any node will be able to initiate a service discovery process, perform selection, and initiate configuration of the selected nodes. The proposed solution is a decentralized network management system that is based on a pattern-based paradigm [2]. By using patterns, the service discovery (i.e. the search for potential overlay nodes with the required media processing capabilities) and configuration of the selected overlay nodes is decentralized.

The problem is formulated as follows: Given any source node and a set of destinations, the system must setup an appropriate SSON based on an overlay network specification. The specification will state the number and type of media processing functions required between the source and each destination node as well as the preferred position of the functions with respect to the source and destination. The service provided by a node is referred to as a function. In this work we mainly focus on media processing functions like caching, transcoding, and synchronization. However, the setup and maintenance system works also for any other type of overlay network.

The paper is organized as follows: first we give some background on the overall SMART architecture for overlay networks and the pattern-based management paradigm; second, the related work section studies various related overlay deployment systems. Then, the overlay provisioning system is described, and its scalability properties are evaluated through simulation. Finally, the paper discusses the results and concludes.

2 Background

2.1 SMART Architecture for Mobile Overlays

In today's Internet technologies, there is no common control layer which controls and manages the different resources and technologies of heterogeneous networks. The Ambient Networks architecture [1] defines the Ambient Control Space (ACS), which is a common control layer to all resources and technologies in networks. One function of the ACS is Media Delivery. The Smart Multimedia Routing and Transport Architecture (SMART) [14] aspires for guiding media flow through specialized network nodes to make use of their ability to cache, transcoded or synchronize multimedia data as appropriate. To achieve this functionality, SMART makes use of overlay networks. It defines the Overlay Control Space (OCS), which will take care of selecting the necessary media processing nodes and establishing an end-to- end overlay network for media delivery. This overlay network is referred as Service Specific Overlay Network (SSON). Fig. 1 below shows the draft architecture for SMART [14], and how the service-specific overlay networks are used.

Some of the nodes in the physical network support special services which are used to enhance media delivery. These nodes are referred to as Media Ports (MP). The source of the media flow is referred as a Media Server (MS) and the receivers are referred as Media Clients (MC).

The SSON is an overlay network whose nodes are the Media Server, Media Ports and Media Clients. Specifically for mobile environments, certain network side multimedia processing functionality is helpful to get the best possible service to the mobile terminal. This paper proposes a scheme for dynamically establishing the media delivery SSONs by using a pattern-based network management paradigm [2].

2.2 Pattern-Based Management

Pattern-based management [2] is an approach to distributed management that aims at overcoming the limitations of centralized management. Its goal is to build scalable, robust and adaptable management systems.

Pattern-based applications map network-wide operations into local operations that will be performed by managed nodes. These operations are distributed using communications patterns, which create an execution graph. In the case of monitoring tasks, local operations typically include the collection of statistics and the incremental aggregation of the collected data. This aggregation is done in a parallel, asynchronous fashion across the network, whereby all nodes contribute to the computation. From the perspective of a network manager, a pattern provides the means to "diffuse" or spread the computational process over a large set of nodes.

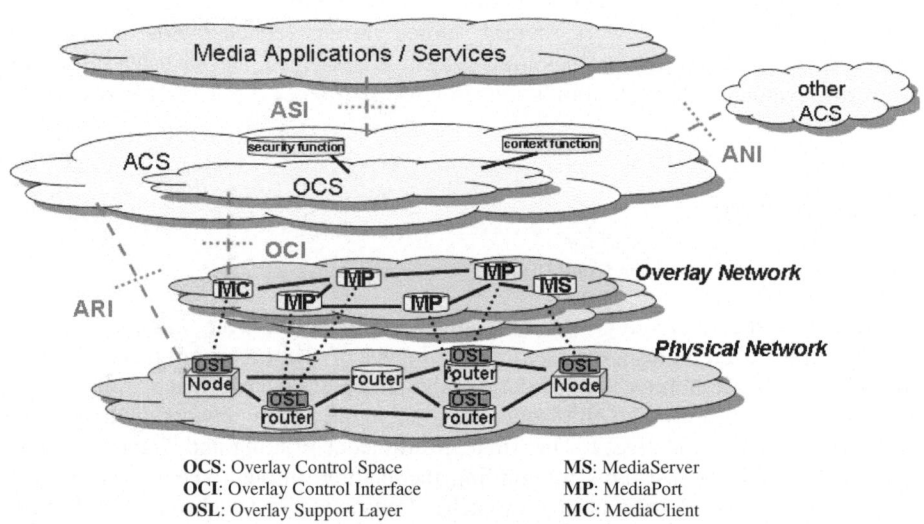

OCS: Overlay Control Space   MS: MediaServer
OCI: Overlay Control Interface   MP: MediaPort
OSL: Overlay Support Layer   MC: MediaClient

Fig. 1. The SMART SSON Architecture

The main benefits of pattern-based management are that it (i) separates the semantics of the task from the details of the distributed execution, (ii) enables building scalable management systems, (iii) facilitates management in dynamic environments, and (iv) does not require "a priori" knowledge of the network topology. Specifically the properties (iii) and (iv) are of major importance for mobile networks.

Previous work on pattern-based management [13] has identified a particularly useful pattern called the echo pattern. The defining characteristic of the echo pattern is its two-phase operation. In the expansion phase, the flow of control emanates from a node attached to the management station. A spanning tree is created to contact all managed nodes and request them to perform local management operations. After executing the local operation, the contraction phase starts. During this second phase, each node sends the result of the operations to its parent in the tree. The parent aggregates its result with its children's and forwards the aggregate to its parent. The global operation terminates when the root of the tree has received and aggregated the results from all its children.

The echo pattern dynamically adapts to changes in the network topology. It does not require global network information and thus scales well in very large networks like the Internet. Its time complexity increases linearly with the network diameter. The work presented in this paper improves the state-of-the-art of pattern-based management by proposing new patterns suitable for advanced overlay-network-management.

3 Related Work

Various structured peer-to-peer overlay network establishment schemes have been proposed recently. Also, several research activities have studied topology aware overlay construction. The overlay network proposed in this paper is different from the above networks in the way potential overlay node are discovered and the network graph is constructed. The network graph construction scheme is not the focus of this paper.

Touch et al. [8] define a Virtual Internet as a network of IP-tunneled links interconnecting virtual routers and virtual hosts providing full Internet capabilities at a virtual layer. One implementation of the Virtual Internet concept is the X-Bone [10].

Moreover, Bossardt et al. [9] have proposed a pattern based service deployment scheme for active networks, and Brunner et al. [15] have proposed a Virtual Active Network concept for dynamic service deployment, where the overlay setup is performed by a centralized management system in an operator environment.

The MBone [11] is a network layer overlay network running on top of the Internet. It is composed of networks that support multicasting. The purpose of this overlay network is to support audio/video multicasting.

Tapestry [4], Pastry [5], CAN (Content Addressable Network) [6] and Chord [7]: Although their implementation varies, these four application layer overlays pursue the same goal, namely to implement a Distributed Hash Table (DHT). The overlay is viewed as a distributed database. Because nodes are interconnected in a well defined manner the DHT based overlays are sometimes referred to as structured overlays.

4 Set-Up and Maintenance of Overlay Networks for Multimedia Services in Mobile Environments

The setup and maintenance of overlay networks is typically not seen a big problem in fixed networks. However, in mobile and wireless network environments, topologies and network characteristics dynamically change all the time, making the setup and maintenance a tricky problem. Additionally, the concept of overlay networks is a means of implementing service-specific routing, caching, and adaptation functionality. The service-specific overlay networks are tailored towards the specific requirements of a media delivery service, and with it, the topology of the overlay network is also dependent on the service running within an overlay network.

In the following, we assume a specific type of overlay for the transport of multimedia data as described above in the SMART Architecture [14]. We assume that multimedia processing engines are specialized network elements (potentially running on dedicated hardware). The multimedia flows must be forced to pass through those nodes, potentially in a certain order, to improve the end-to-end media service. So, only a relatively small set of nodes in the network is capable of running these expensive multimedia processing functions. We call those nodes the potential overlay nodes.

The proposed system consists of the following functions: (1) detecting potential overlay nodes, (2) selecting suitable nodes, (3) setting up the overlay network, (4) adding client nodes to the overlay network, and (5) maintaining the overlay in order to adapt to the changing network context, and user or service requirements.

Even though we implemented all the functions based on the pattern-based approach, only the detection of potential overlay nodes and the clients joining an overlay are in the focus of this paper. The selection of suitable nodes is a matter of an optimization algorithm for service-specific requirements, such as using the cheapest overlay network, the overlay with the least number of hops, or an overlay network that is load-balanced, etc. The setup of the overlay is straight forward, once the nodes are known; they only need to be configured accordingly. The addressing and routing within the overlay are an orthogonal problem.

Concerning the detection of potential overlay nodes, we assume overlay nodes storing the required overlay node parameters locally in a standard format. For instance, a node stores the set of functions it can perform, for how many media flows this node can perform each function, and the cost for each function. (These are the primary parameters, depending on the service and future capabilities further parameters might be of relevance.)

Detecting potential overlay nodes involves probing each node for the required functionalities for the multimedia service, the available resources, and the cost. This means only nodes capable of hosting a virtual node with a certain function are found in that process. There are various ways to perform this search. Using a directory based approach, the node capabilities and resources would register with a well-known directory service. Clients/nodes that want to find a suitable resource or function will then query the directory service. The downside of this approach is that it is expensive to keep the directory up-to-date in the case of highly dynamic and/or mobile environments. For example, when the availability or other necessary information about a resource or function changes frequently, or when the node providing the service is mobile, the update messages needed to keep the directory service up-to-date would increases rapidly. Moreover, such directory-based services are typically not able to take the topological location of a resource or service into account, which prevents selecting resources based on the proximity of the end-to-end communication path.

We show that the pattern-based paradigm is a nice tool for discovering network-side functions/resources. A pattern will determine which nodes should be probed. The pattern will also initiate the probing process as well as the gathering of information. Different patterns can be used for this purpose. The most basic one is the echo pattern (see the section above for a detailed description). The echo pattern starts from the requesting node and then expands towards the leaves (or any defined boundary) of the network. On the way back, when the pattern contracts towards the initiating node, it aggregates the results of the discovery. This serves the purpose of both detection of the network topology as well as discovery of potential overlay nodes. But, irrespective of the number of destination nodes in the overlay network, the echo pattern will flood the probing request throughout the whole network. A Time-to-Live (TTL) can be used for the flooding in case only local resources/services are of interest.

A more suitable pattern is the path-directed search pattern proposed here. The basic idea of this pattern is to limit the scope of the search to a configurable area along the end-to-end path between the communicating peers. The search pattern uses a parameter that defines the "distance" (e.g. in number of hops, delay, or any other measure, etc.) from the routing path that should be searched. This distance is also referred to as 'sideway expansion'. Depending on the type of resource or function that is searched, this parameter can be changed.

Our pattern assumes to know the source of a multimedia service and a number of destinations, or regions where one or more receivers of the multimedia services are located. The path-directed search pattern starts from the source node and expands along the end-to-end routing path towards the destination nodes with a sideway expansion of a given distance (e.g. based on the number of hops, delay, etc.). After visiting the nodes defined by the pattern scope, the pattern contracts towards the source node gathering the requested information (depending on the resources/service we are looking for). The sideway expansion parameter of the pattern controls the scope of the search and thus limits the number of nodes probed during the detection. Above all, it allows the discovery of network-side resources along a close approximation of the routing path.

Fig. 2 shows a simple logical sequence of the pattern execution with sideway expansion of 1 hop on a small grid network. The pattern starts on the start node (Src). The state when the start node has sent an explorer to the next hop is called initialization state. Every hop along the routing path towards the destination (Dest) sends explorers to the next hop as well as sideways to all neighboring nodes (because the sideway expansion is greater than zero). The sideway expansion limits the reach of the explorers that are sent sideways. When the pattern reaches its sideway limit, it will start the contraction phase (back to the parent node along the routing path that started the sideway expansion). Nodes that have completed the pattern, but do not fulfill the requirements are colored blue (dark). Two of the nodes in the example are potential overlay nodes (PONs); this is indicated with the color pink (less dark). When parent nodes receive the results of their child nodes (contraction), they will start aggregating the information. Nodes in this state are shown with the color yellow (light gray). Finally, when the destination node (Dest) is reached, the pattern starts contraction from the destination towards the source.

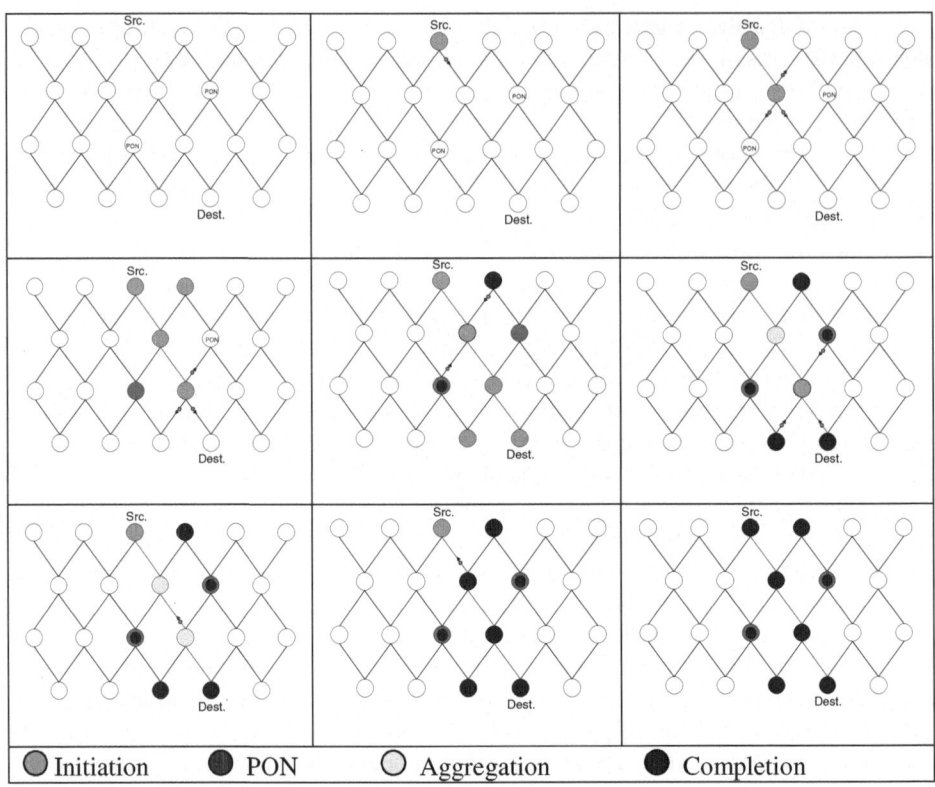

Fig. 2. Path-directed Search Pattern Execution

Fig. 3 depicts a scenario that illustrates the path-directed search scenario in a larger setting (as shown in the SIMPSON pattern simulator). The source node is node 110 and the destination nodes are nodes 209, 200, 11 and 20. The tested nodes are colored (dark). The potential overlay nodes are colored pink (light gray). The path-directed pattern assumes that the path from source towards the destination is known (according to traditional IP routing on all the nodes), but the multimedia processing functions are not necessarily directly on the path – they can be located anywhere 'along' the path. The path-directed search pattern is ideal to find appropriate network functions/resources (i.e. potential overlay nodes) along the end-to-end routing path from the source to the destination on-demand. I.e. whenever a particular network function/resource is required, the path-directed search pattern can be used to discover such functionality/resources.

The access of a new client to a given overlay for the first time is another problem, where patterns can help to reduce the amount of messages. Again, the echo pattern can be used with a certain diameter to search overlay nodes within a certain region around the client's network location. The path-directed search is helpful if the client knows the source, for example, the URL/DNS name of the source. In that case, the client can start searching towards the source with side way expansion in order to find another overlay node which might not be on the path, but nearby. If it finds an overlay of the desired type, a virtual link can be established and the client is then attached to the overlay. However, the point of attachment and the service received at the attachment point might be suboptimal. Therefore, the overlay topology and services should be regularly reconsidered. Overlay adaptation might also be triggered by the addition of a new client, but there we need to take into account the number of clients potentially attaching per time unit in order to find a scalable solution. This implics that the parameters are service specific and depend on the purpose and scale of the overlay network.

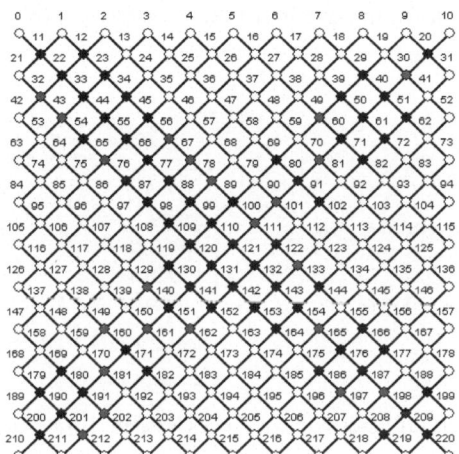

Fig. 3. The path-directed search pattern with sideway expansion of 1 hop

5   Evaluation of the Path Directed Search Pattern

The efficiency of the proposed pattern based scheme for the setup and adaptation of service-specific overlay networks are evaluated using the SIMple Pattern Simulator fOr Networks (SIMPSON) [3]. SIMPSON is a discrete event simulator used for implementing, testing, and evaluating pattern based systems.

Grid topologies with a node degree of 4 (except the nodes at the edges of the network) were used in the simulations. The protocol and operating system delay, propagation delay per hop, processing time on the nodes, and message size were taken to be 4ms, 5ms, 0.5s and 1024 bytes respectively. These values are justified to be reasonable estimates for the Internet in [12]. The link speed was taken as 10Mbs.

5.1   Single Destination

A set of simulations have been performed to observe the message complexity and the total number of nodes visited in a single destination scenario. The parameters used in the simulation were as follows: The simulation was done in the grid topology for different radiuses starting from radius = 5 hops to radius = 35 hops where the radius is the number of hops from the center of the grid topology to a corner. The number of nodes is given as $(r)^2 + (r+1)^2$ where r is the radius of the grid.

For each sideway value, the simulation was run 100 times with the middle node as the source and a randomly chosen node as a destination for each pass. The results of this simulation are illustrated below. Larger sideway expansion values were not used for smaller radiuses because they would visit all the nodes.

The percentage of visited nodes is computed out of the total number of nodes. The message complexity is plotted as compared to a pattern which will make a full search, i.e., probe all nodes. The echo pattern was used for the full search.

Both graphs show that the path-directed search pattern uses around 1 to 10 percent of the number of messages and visits only about 1-10 percent of the nodes. The impact of this enhancement for the quality of the overlay, by not visiting all the nodes, is shown below.

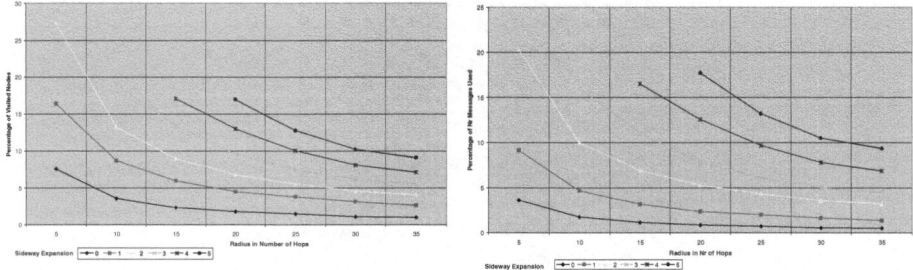

Fig. 4. Single Destination: (a) Percentage of Nodes Visited; (b) Percentage of Messages Used Compared to Full Search

5.2 Multiple Destinations

This simulation was performed to study the behavior of the pattern in a multi destination scenario. Again a grid topology with radius of 30 hops (1861 nodes) was used and the number of destinations was varied from 5 to 25 in steps of 5. For each number of destinations, 100 sets of randomly selected destination positions were used and for each position the simulation was run for sideway expansions of 0 to 5 inclusive. The results of the simulation are shown below.

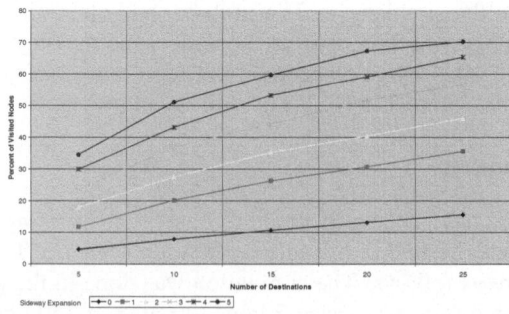

Fig. 5. Multiple Destinations: Percent of Visited Nodes

5.3 Quality of the Service Specific Overlay Network

This set of simulations has been performed in order to evaluate the performance of the pattern for service-specific overlay network construction. When selecting overlay nodes, we consider the price of using the required function on that node and the distance of that node from the source and/or the destination. As described earlier the requirement specifies the type and number of functions needed in the path from source-to-destination as well as their preferred position (as near-to-source, middle, near-to-destination). The optimization is performed by using a weighted cost function. The following cost function was used in the simulations:

$$Cost = 0.5 \times price + (0.5 \times src \times dist_{src} + 0.5 \times dest \times dist_{dest} + 0.25 \times med \times dist_{src} + 0.25 \times med \times dist_{dest})$$
$$\times \max(price)/\max(dist);$$

whereby $src = 0.9$, $dest = 0.1$, $med = 0$, when the requirement is 'near-to-source'; $src = 0.1$, $dest = 0.9$, $med = 0$, when the requirement is 'near-to-destination'; and $src = 0$, $dest = 0$, $med = 0.25$, when the requirement is 'in-the-middle'.

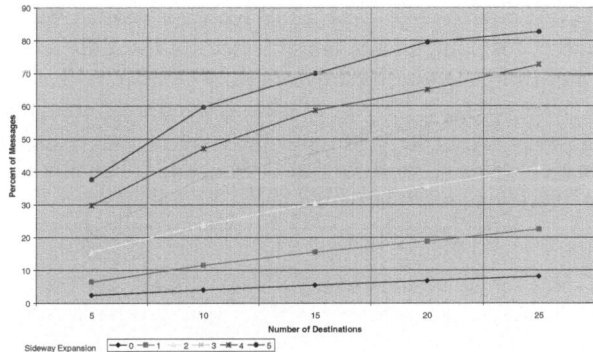

Fig. 6. Multiple Destinations: Percent of Messages Used Compared to Full Search

To make the result of this cost function meaningful, the distance is linked with the price. We assume that traversing the maximum distance will cost us as much as paying the maximum price. The maximum distance $\max(dist)$ is the maximum of the maximum distance from the source and the maximum distance from the destination of potential overlay nodes. It is computed after the pattern completed the search. The price of each function ranges from 1 to 100 price units.

The above cost function gives the cost of each detected potential overlay node and the nodes with the least cost will be selected for each function. As a measure of performance, in constructing a service-specific overlay network using patterns, the quality of an overlay node is defined as follows: $Quality = \max(price)/Cost$. Because we have set the maximum price to be 100, our formula reduces to $Quality = 100/Cost$.

The cost is a superposition of the price of using the node and the node's distance from the source and destination computed with weight based on the requirement. If a node has smaller cost then it will have higher quality. Also we define the quality of an overlay network as the average of the quality of its overlay nodes. We will later use this definition to interpret the result of the simulation. The following overlay specification was used in the simulation:

An overlay network of the least price with one transcoder (f1) preferably near to the source, two cache machines (f2) preferably in the middle and another transcoder (f3) preferably near to the destination.

A grid topology of radius 30 hops (1861 nodes) was used. The source node was the center node and the destinations were the 4 corner nodes. The potential overlay node density was varied from 25 nodes to 200 nodes in steps of 25. For each density, a random placement with randomly chosen prices for each node was generated. Then the placement was randomly shuffled 100 times and for each placement the simulation was run for the sideway values of 0 to 5 inclusive.

The simulation was also run for sideway value of 31 to determine the quality for full coverage In this case only the cost of the selected nodes was registered. The other parameters are taken from a simulation of the echo pattern for the same radius. Except for technical simplicity for batch processing, the number of potential nodes detected in this case is the same as running the echo pattern and it could have been done that way also.

The quality of the overlay network constructed using the path directed pattern as compared to the one constructed using a full search is plotted below. The quantities used for full search, for comparison, are obtained by using the echo pattern to probe all nodes in search for potential overlay nodes. The quantities shown are hence the best that can be achieved both number of message and time complexity wise as far as full coverage is concerned. This is because the echo pattern is the efficient way both message and time complexity wise for full coverage [2]. The plot of the quality of the service-specific overlay network is shown below in Fig. 7.

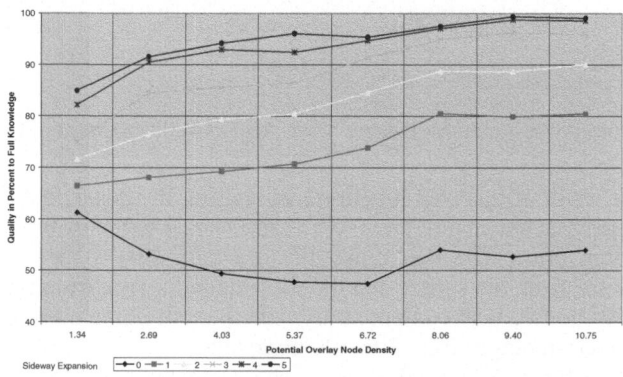

Fig. 7. Quality of SSONs

6 Discussion

The evaluation of the path-directed search pattern with respect to the number of nodes visited, as well as the message and time complexity gives an insight of the performance of the path-directed search pattern. We measured the percentage of the number of nodes visited in the single-destination pattern as compared to a pattern, which makes a full search. The regressions of the curves show that the percentages of the number of nodes are proportional to the inverse of the radius of the network with a correlation coefficient of greater than 0.99. This evaluation depicts one of the main advantages of the path-directed pattern. Because the search is made only along the end-to-end routing path, the number of visited nodes does not considerably increase with the size of the network.

It is worth noting that the perfect inverse relation is in part accounted to the characteristics of the simulated networks. The number of nodes in the grid network is $(r)^2 + (r+1)^2$ where r is the radius of the network, and in a pattern which makes a full search, all the nodes will be visited. Hence the number of visited nodes in a full search is $O(r^2)$.

On the other hand, for a specified sideway expansion value, the number of nodes visited in the path-directed pattern is only directly proportional to the radius of the network, i.e., $O(r)$. The percentage of number of nodes visited in the single destination pattern as compared to a pattern which will make a full search will then be inversely proportional to the radius of the network.

The message complexity has the same property as the number of visited nodes. Because the message is generated by each visited node, the lesser the number of nodes visited the lesser the number of messages exchanged.

The time complexity of the pattern (not shown in a graph) increases linearly with the radius of the network. The time complexity increases only slightly with the increase in sideway expansion. This behavior is due to the parallel processing nature of the pattern. It has been proved analytically, in [12], that the echo pattern has a time complexity which is directly proportional to the radius of the network. Time-complexity-wise, the path-directed search pattern obeys the same rule.

The multiple-destinations pattern evaluation shows that using higher sideway expansion values results in a considerably higher number of visited nodes. For instance, when the number of destinations is greater than 20, more than half of the nodes in the network will be visited for sideway expansions of greater than 4 hops.

The quality of the service-specific overlay network with respect to the stretch introduced by the overlay and the price incurred are studied in a multiple destination scenario. The result shows that even with densities of potential overlay nodes as small as 1%, the quality of the network constructed using the pattern-based system can be more than 50% of the quality achievable if the overlay was constructed based on full information about the network.

The quality with larger densities of potential overlay nodes is comparable with the maximum possible quality. For instance, with 95% confidence, the average quality achieved with a sideway expansion of 2 hops and a potential overlay node density of greater than 7% is greater than 80%. The average quality will be even greater than 90% for this density with sideway expansion greater than 2 hops.

However, choosing the sideway expansion without prior knowledge of the density is not possible, but can be learnt while using the pattern several times from the same location (source). Given a certain estimated density, and an optimality goal, the algorithm can derive an approximation for the sideway expansion using the numbers in Fig. 7. Note that the numbers are based on a certain topology and might not be easily extendable to any topology.

The issue of load balancing has not been further studied in this paper, but the choice of overlay nodes given a set of potential overlay nodes is an algorithm, where the load could be taken into account. So far we take only the availability of the resource and the price into account. Additionally, we can model the load by a flexible load-based pricing model on the nodes, and then our algorithm would immediately converge to a load balanced network.

7   Conclusion

The analysis of the pattern–based management approach and the evaluation of the path-directed search pattern in particular show that one can construct a service-specific overlay network of high quality on demand, with only a small traffic/message overhead. Its ability to construct the overlay network without prior knowledge of the existing physical network topology and the available network functions/resources makes the pattern-based approach most valuable.

There are still some issues to be addressed in using the path-directed pattern for service-specific overlay network construction. One open issue is security in the search, configuration, and reconfiguration process. Introducing authentication and authorization mechanisms is important to prevent an unauthorized node from initiating a search pattern, sending false configuration information, or requesting a false reconfiguration.

Additional further work includes the use of the approach across administrative boundaries, the porting of the pattern to a real pattern system like Weaver [13], and studying the possibility to run the optimization algorithm decentralized including appropriate management patterns.

Acknowledgment

This work is a product of the *Ambient Networks* project supported in part by the European Commission under its *Sixth Framework Programme*. The views and conclusions contained herein are those of the authors and should not be interpreted as necessarily representing the official policies or endorsements, either expressed or implied, of the *Ambient Networks* project or the European Commission.

References

[1] N. Niebert, A. Schieder, H. Abramowicz, G. Malmgren, J. Sachs, U. Horn, C. Prehofer, H. Karl, *"Ambient Networks: An Architecture for Communication Networks Beyond 3G"*, IEEE Wireless Communications, vol. 11, no. 2, Apr 2004, pp 14- 22.

[2] K. Lim, C. Adam, R. Stadler, *"Decentralizing Network Management"*, IEEE electronic Transactions on Network and Service Management (eTNSM), Vol 1(2), 2004.

[3] *"SIMPSON – a SIMple Pattern Simulator fOr Networks"*, http://comet.ctr.columbia.edu/adm/software.htm.

[4] B. Y. Zhao, LinHuang, Jeremy Stribling, S. C. Rhea, A. D. Joseph, J. D. Kubiatowicz, *"Tapestry: A Resilient Global-scale Overlay for Service Deployment"*, IEEE Journal on Selected Areas in Communications, 2004.

[5] Rowstron, P. Druschel, "Pastry: Scalable, Decentralized Object Location, and Routing for Large-Scale Peer-to-Peer Systems", International Conference on Distributed Systems Platforms(Middleware), pages 329- 350, Heidelberg, Germany, Nov 2001.

[6] S. Ratnasamy, P. Francis, M. Handley, R. Karp, S. Shenker, *"A scalable content address-able network"*, in Proceedings of ACM SIGCOMM, 2001.

[7] I. Stoica, R. Morris, D. Karger, F. Kaashoek, H. Balakrishnan, *"Chord: A scalable peer-to-peer lookup service for internet applications"*, in Proceedings of SIGCOMM, 2001.

[8] J. D. Touch, Y. Wang, L. Eggert, *"Virtual Internets"*, USC/Information Science Institute, Jul. 1, 2002.

[9] M. Bossardt, A. Mühlemann, R. Zürcher, B. Plattner, *"Pattern Based Service Deployment for Active Networks"*, in Proceedings of the Second International Workshop on Active Network Technologies and Applications, ANTA, Osaka, Japan, May 2003.

[10] J. Touch, S. Hotz, *"The X-Bone"*, In Proceedings of the third Global Internet Mini-Conference, Sydney, Australia, Nov. 1998, pp. 75-83.

[11] H. Eriksson, *"MBONE: The Multicast Backbone"*, ACM Communications of the ACM 37, Aug. 1994, pp. 54-60.

[12] K. S. Lim, R. Stadler, *"A Navigation Pattern for Scalable Internet Management"*, Seventh IFIP/IEEE International Symposium on Integrated Network Management (IM 2001), Seattle, USA, May 2001, pp. 405-420.

[13] K.S. Lim and R. Stadler; "Weaver: realizing a scalable management paradigm on commodity routers", 8th IFIP/IEEE International Symposium on Integrated Network Management, 24-28 March 2003, Colorado Springs, Colorado, March 2003, pp:409 – 424.

[14] S. Schmid, F. Hartung, M. Kampmann, St. Herborn, "SMART: Intelligent Multimedia Routing and Adaptation based on Service Specific Overlay Networks." To appear in Proc. of Eurescom Summit 2005, Heidelberg, Germany, 27–29 April, 2005.

[15] M. Brunner, B. Plattner, R. Stadler, "Service Creation and Management in Active Telecom Environments", Communications of the ACM, March 2001.

Multicast Tree Construction with QoS Guaranties

O. Moussaoui[1], A. Ksentini[1], M. Naïmi[1], and A. Gueroui[2]

[1] LICP EA 2175, Université de Cergy-Pontoise- 2 Av Adolphe Chauvin 95302,
Cergy-Pontoise, France
{omar.moussaoui, adlen.ksentini, mohamed.naimi}
@dept-info.u-cergy.fr
[2] PRiSM CNRS, Université de Versailles- 45, Av des Etats-Unis 78035,
Versailles, France
mogue@prism.uvsq.fr

Abstract. Multimedia applications, such as videoconferences, require an efficient management of the Quality of Service (QoS) and consist of a great number of participants which requires the use of multicast routing protocol. Unlike unicast protocol, multicast protocol handles a great number of users while minimizing both network overhead and bandwidth consumption. However, combining multicast routing and QoS guarantee is a hard challenging task, known as the delay and delay variation multicast problem. This problem is considered as an NP-complete problem, and is resolved only by heuristic solutions. In this paper, we propose a scalable multicast algorithm that tackle the delay and delay variation by exploiting the Hierarchic Tree construction concepts. In fact, the proposal algorithm guarantees QoS by: (i) reducing the network charge; (ii) decreasing the multicast delay variation. We compare the performance of our algorithm against the DDVCA (Delay and Delay Variation Constraint Algorithm) scheme and demonstrate lower multicast delay variation and efficient bandwidth utilization while maintaining lower time complexity.

1 Introduction

The demand for multimedia that combines audio, video and data streams over a network is quickly increasing. Among the most popular real-time interactive applications, videoconferences and games require a considerable amount of bandwidth and a great number of participants. In this context multicast is regarded as a promising solution for group multimedia applications. In fact, multicast is a bandwidth-conserving technology that reduces traffic by simultaneously delivering a single stream of information to thousands of corporate recipients or groups. Multicast delivers source traffic to multiple receivers without adding any additional burden on the source or the receivers while using the least network bandwidth of any competing technology. Multicast packets are replicated in the network through routers enabled with multicast protocol and other supporting multicast protocols resulting in the most efficient delivery of data to multiple receivers possible. All alternatives require the source to send more than one copy of the data. Some even require the source to send an individual copy to each receiver. If there are thousands of receivers, even low-bandwidth applications benefit from using multicast. High-bandwidth applications, such as H.264 video, may require a large portion of the available network bandwidth for a single stream [1]. In these

J. Dalmau and G. Hasegawa (Eds.): MMNS 2005, LNCS 3754, pp. 96–108, 2005.
© IFIP International Federation for Information Processing 2005

applications, the only way to send to more than one receiver simultaneously is by using multicast. Several protocols were proposed in the literature [2], [3], [4], [5] aiming to propose a multicast protocol. However, the majority of them are not scalable, which means not adaptable to the networks of great dimension like Internet. By limiting the deployment of these protocols, the Internet is becoming the unavoidable network. Furthermore, these protocols work as best effort protocols [6], so they cannot handle sensitive traffics such as video conference and real time game. Indeed, these applications require that all the destination nodes must receive the same data simultaneously; otherwise the communication may lose the feeling of an interactive face-to-face discussion. Thus it is important to sustain good QoS support while proposing a scalable multicast protocol. This constraint is related to the multicast Delay and delay-Bounded Multicast Tree (DVBMT) problem [7]. Although this problem is considered as *NP-complete* hard problem, there are some heuristics that are proposed as a possible solution [7], [8].

In this paper we tackle the DVBMT problem by proposing a novel scalable multicast algorithm, which produces multicast tree while maintaining a good sustained QoS. The main idea is to combine a hierarchic tree construction with efficient multicast grouping concepts. Firstly, like [9], we decompose the multicast group into local groups based on delay constraint and user's station capacity. This allows us to have several groups with a reduced intra group delays. Afterwards, we select a server that minimizes the delay variation with the others selected nodes from each group. From the server's set obtained, we choose a core nodes or rendezvous points. Finally, we use both the hierarchical trees and the core nodes to connect these multicast group members. Thus, we solve the DVBMT problem by decomposing the problem into two parts: *(i)* end to end delays which is solved by constructing local group with minimum delays; *(ii)* multicast delay variation solved by joining the hierarchic tree construction with the core nodes concepts.

The rest of the paper is organized as follows: In section 2, we give an overview of QoS and multicast protocols. Section 3 presents details of the proposed algorithm. Then, in section 4, we evaluate the proposed scheme by simulation model. Section 5 concludes this paper.

2   Multicast and QoS Overview

Algorithms for the tree construction in multicast protocols can be categorized as follows: Source-Based Algorithms (SBA) and Core-Based Algorithms (CBA) [10].

SBA constructs a specific tree where the tree's root is the source node and the leaves are the multicast group's components. SBA is currently used as the tree construction algorithm for Distance Vector Multicast Routing Protocol (DVMRP) [2], Protocol Independent Multicast Dense Mode (PIM-DM) [3], and Multicast Open Shortest Path First (MOSPF) [4].

CBA is used in the context of many-to-many multicasts. Actually, the core-based algorithm selects a core node as multicast tree's root. Afterwards, a tree rooted at the core node is constructed to span all members in the multicast group. Therefore it is very important to select the best core node as much as possible. Thus messages generated at the source are sent to the core node, and they are distributed to destinations through this core node. Multicast protocols using CBA as a tree construction algorithm include Protocol Independent Multicast Sparse Mode (PIM-SM) [5] and the Core-Based Tree (CBT) protocol [11]. The core-based algorithms are highly suitable for sparse groups and scalable for large networks. They provide excellent bandwidth conservation for receivers.

In addition to the need of scalability, group based multimedia applications also demand stringent QoS requirements such as bounded end-to-end delay, multicast delay variation and the efficient use of the bandwidth. The multicast end-to-end delay stands for an upper bound of all end-to-end delays associated with the paths from the source node to each of the destination nodes. The purpose of setting this parameter is to limit the time for message transmissions in the network. If the end-to-end delay exceeds the upper bound, the message will be counted useless. The multicast delay variation is the difference of the maximum end-to-end delay and the minimum end-to-end delay among the paths from the source node to all the destination nodes has to be kept within. Enabling this parameter allows all the destination nodes to receive the same data simultaneously as much as possible. The issue first defined and discussed in [7] is to minimize multicast delay variation under multicast end-to-end delay constraint. In fact, the authors tackle the DVBMT problem by proposing a heuristic solution called Delay Variation Multicast Algorithm (DVMA). DVMA constructs at first the tree by considering only the end-to-end delay constraints. Afterwards, the tree is enhanced by considering the multicast delay variation constraint. At the end, DVMA's algorithm returns a feasible tree, which minimizes the end-to-end delays and optimizes the multicast delay variation. Nevertheless, the main weakness of DVMA is time complexity. Actually, DVMA exhibits a high time complexity about $O(plmn^4)$, where in the worst case, the maximum value that p and l can take is equal to the maximum number of paths of the tree, m is the size of the multicast group M, and n is the number of nodes in the network. Accordingly, this time complexity does not fit in modern high-speed computer network environment. Delay and Delay Variation Constraint Algorithm (DDVCA) presented in [8] aims to solve the DVBMT problem by proposing another heuristic solution with lower time complexity than DVMA. DDVCA's algorithm is based on the Core Based Tree (CBT). In fact the authors propose to build the multicast tree around one core node, which is selected as the node with the minimum delay variation with all the others nodes present in the multicast group. Thus it has been shown that DDVCA outperforms DVMA in terms of the multicast delay variation of the constructed tree. Furthermore, DDVCA shows lower time complexity than DVMA, which is equal to $O(mn^2)$. Nonetheless, if we consider the network utilization, we see that DDVCA exhibits high network charge around the core node. In fact, all the multicast session's packets transit through the core node, which leads to network congestion in the neighboring of the core node. Furthermore, when packets arrive to the core node from the sender, this last one resends these packets to the leaves using a unicast routing protocol. Therefore, DDVCA looses the benefits of using a multicast routing protocol.

To overcome these limitations, we propose an algorithm which allows efficient communication between the multicast group's members by supporting QoS constraints. The proposed algorithm solves the DVBMT problem by constructing a hierarchical tree based on delay and multicast delay variation. Firstly, we decompose the multicast members into a disjoint local groups based on their localization and their response to application QoS requirement. Thus we obtain local groups with minimum intra-group delay. Afterwards, from each group a server is selected, where the server is the node that minimizes the multicast delay variation with the others group's node. At this point we have the first level of the hierarchical tree. Secondly, we select a core node from the server sets, and this core node is the server which minimizes the multi-cast delay variation with the others selected server. Here we are able to construct the second level of the hierarchical tree. In fact, based on this core node we build the autonomous domain (AD). The first AD contains a set of groups, where the delay from the core node to each group's server is less than a predefined threshold. From the server sets that not belong to the first AD, we elect another core node. This second core node is the server that minimizes the delay with the first core node. Through this second core node we create another AD. Thus we redo the procedure of AD creation until we incorporate all the local groups into different AD. At the end, we construct a hierarchical tree with core-based algorithms. However, unlike DDVCA where the tree construction is based only on one core node, we extend this construction of the tree on several core nodes. This allows us to share out the network charge around different core node, leading to minimize the bandwidth consumption. Further we limit the use of the unicast mechanism only at the intra local group communications.

3   Description of the Proposed Algorithm

To illustrate the proposed algorithm, we will use directed graph $G = (V, E)$ to denote a network, where V is a set of nodes or routers and E is a set of directed links, respectively. Each link $(i, j) \in E$ is associated with delay d_{ij}. The delay of a link is the sum of the perceived queuing delay, transmission delay, and propagation delay over that link. Here we note a path as sequence of nodes $u, i, j, ..., k, v$, where $(u, i), (i, j), ..., (k, v) \in E$. Let $P(u, v) = \{(u, i), (i, j), ..., (k, v)\}$ denotes the path from node u to node v, so a simple path is a path where all its elements are distinct. At this point a multicast group $M \subseteq G$ is constituted by m processes (participants) distributed geo-graphically on the Internet network. Moreover, these processes participate at the same multimedia application such as videoconferencing. Note that, communication be-tween two processes m_i and m_j can take different path.

3.1   Local Groups' Construction

Considering the high number of participants in multicast group M, it appears essential to divide them into local groups according to their concentration in the various areas of the Internet. This decomposition allows to: *(i)* efficiently use the bandwidth; *(ii)* reduce the consumption of resources; *(iii)* optimize the delay; *(iiii)* ensure communi-cations between processes.

At first we begin by constructing the neighboring sets NS_i for each process m_i according to two conditions: the round-trip delay and packets Time to Live (TTL). Actually, each m_i sends a request packet along its multicast groups by using the Internet Protocol (IP) multicast addresses. In the current IP multicast architecture, a globally unique class D is allocated to each group to identify the set of destination hosts belonging to the group. Through the responses obtained from the multicast group, m_i selects the process m_j to include into the NS_i by checking if the TTL_{ij} from m_i to m_j (decremented hop by hop) is not null and the Round-Trip Delay RTD_{ij} between m_i and m_j is less than a given threshold of delay $SupD$ (1). In other word, the path from m_i to m_j is the shortest in terms of delay. According to this selection, we divide the multicast group onto a set of NS_i with low intra-communication delays.

$$NS_i = \left\{ m_j \in M \ / \ RTD_{ij} \prec SupD \ \& \ \&TTL_{ij} \succ 0 \right\} \tag{1}$$

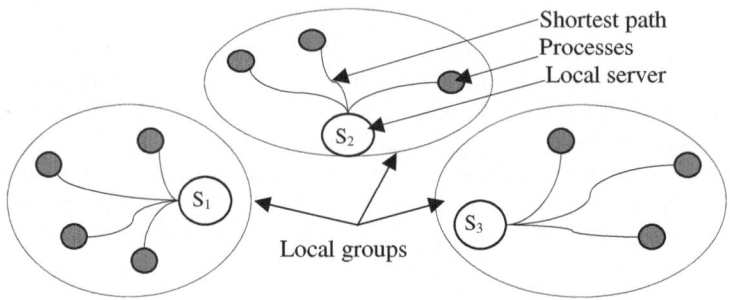

Fig. 1. Construction of local groups

At this point, each m_i has its own NS_i. However, this is insufficient if we consider the different process' capacities in terms of media unit processing time and the generated rate of media units, noted mpt_i and σ_i, respectively. In this context we must refine the NS_i in order to take the process's capacities into account. To this end, each m_i carries out evaluations on its capabilities of processing and buffering of media units, in order to choose the m_j which will constitute its new enhanced NS_i. Here we note this enhanced NS_i, by the transit group TG_i. Thus each m_i elects the m_j process that composes its transit group according to both (2) and (3). In fact these two constraints allow that m_i selects the other process in respect to its capabilities to handle data flow coming from its neighbors. Thus a process m_i must be able to: *(i)* process all media units generated in the same time by its neighbors in a time duration not exceeding the time allocated to the processing of media units; *(ii)* store all media units coming on different paths between m_i and its neighboring processes.

$$\left[\sum_{m_j \in NS_i} \sigma_j \right] * mpt_i < 1 \tag{2}$$

$$\sum_{m_j \in NS_i} B_{ij}(C_{ij}) < B_i \tag{3}$$

Where B_i represents the maximum buffer space available at the process m_i, and B_{ij} denotes the buffer size at m_i and C_{ij} is the path between m_i and m_j. Therefore, since m_i founds that neither (2) nor (3) are feasible when adding another m_j to the TG_i, the process stops and the TG_i is finalized.

Once transit groups are built, each process knows the members of its own set and the paths that connect it to them. However, some processes can belong to several transit groups at the same time. To solve this problem, a mechanism must take place to remove useless connections. Each process must broadcast its transit group to its neighbors. Once these packets are received, each receiver m_i selects the maximum of the processes existing simultaneously in these groups of transit ($LG_i = \bigcap_{j \in TG_i} TG_j$). If a process belongs to several local groups, then this process is placed into the smallest LG_i in size. This allows to equally balancing the process number in these groups.

Thus, the multicast group M is divided into local sub-groups (Figure 1). Each element of M belongs to only one local group. After that a local server and a secondary server are elected to represent each local group. In other terms, a process

---

Let $G=(V, E)$ a computer network and $M=\{m_1, m_2, ..., m_m\}$ a set of participants in group multicast M.

Begin

1. for each process $m_i \in M$ do //construct a neighboring set NS$_i$ of m_i

2. $NS_i = \left\{ m_j \in M \,/\, RTD_{ij} \prec SupD \;\& \;\&TTL_{ij} \succ 0 \right\}$

3. end of for each $m_i \in M$ loop

4. for each process $m_i \in M$ do //construct a transit group TG_i of m_i

5. $\sigma = 0, B = 0$ //σ and B are temporaries variables

6. for each process $m_j \in NS_i$ do

7. $\sigma = \sigma + \sigma_j, B = B + B_{ij}$

8. if $\sigma * mpt_i \prec 1$ and $B \prec B_i$ then $TG_i = TG_i \cup \{m_j\}$

9. end of for each $m_j \in NS_i$ loop

10. end of for each $m_i \in M$ loop

11. for each process $m_i \in M$ do // construction of local groups

12. $LG_i = \bigcap_{j \in TG_i} TG_j$

13. end of for each $m_i \in M$ loop

14. for each local group LG_i do // election of local servers

15. elect local server S_i and secondary server SS_i

16. $\Gamma = \Gamma \cup \{S_i\}$ and $k=k+1$

17. end of for each local group LG_i loop

18. for each local server $S_i \in \Gamma$ do

19. for each $m_j \in LG_i$ do

20. S_i joins m_j by the path which has a minimum round-trip delay.

21. end of for each $m_j \in LG_i$ Loop

22. end of for each local server $S_i \in \Gamma$

End of the algorithm

Fig. 2. Algorithm of local groups' construction

communicates with the other participants of the multicast group only through the server of its local group. The local and secondary servers are the processes that minimize the multicast delays with the others process, meanwhile these servers must have the maximum processing capacity. Note that, the principal role of the secondary server is to replace the local server if this last leaves the multicast group or it crashes (break down). For completeness, we draw in Figure 2 the local group algorithm construction.

3.2 Multicast Tree Construction Between Servers

Let us consider k local groups are built and each group has its local server (Figure 1). Here $\Gamma = \{S_1, S_2, ..., S_k\}$ is the set of these local servers distributed in different networks. It is important to note that the number of these servers can be very high and several sources can belong to the same multicast group. Accordingly, it is necessary to build a multicast tree which links these servers while reducing the multicast group's participants. In this context, like DDVCA, we propose the use of core-based tree. However, we based the tree construction on several core nodes instead of one, aiming to avoid congestion problem. These core nodes are selected from Γ, by considering the servers which minimize the multicast delay variation with the others Γ's servers.

Table 1. Packets and data structures employed

Type	Arguments	function
INIT	$adrS_i$: address of the local server S_i TTL: Time to Live $adrM$: address of the group multicast	initialization packet
ACK	$adrS_j$: address of the sender S_j $adrS_i$: address of the receiver S_i	acknowledgement packet
SUCC	$adrS_i$: address of the new indicated core node S_i $adrCN_j$: address of the core node predecessor of S_i $\$$: set of local servers which do not yet belong to any autonomous domains of core nodes already created MAT: matrix allowing to store the minimum delay between the elements of $\$$ and core nodes in the multicast tree	successor packet

Initially, each local server broadcasts hop by hop an initialization packet *INIT* (Table 1) at the multicast group *M* address. All members of *M* that are not servers delete the received packet, while the other nodes (server S_i) carry out the following operation:

- Response to the sender server S_j with an acknowledge packet *ACK*.
- Compute the minimum delay $d_{\min}(S_i, S_j)$ between it and S_j by using Dijkstra's algorithm [12].
- Memorize the address of S_j and the value of delay $d_{\min}(S_i, S_j)$.

Finally, each server S_i calculates its multicast delay variation through:

$$\delta_{S_i} = \max\left\{\left|d_{\min}(S_i, S_j) - d_{\min}(S_i, S_k)\right| / \forall S_j, S_k \in \Gamma, j \neq k\right\} \qquad (4)$$

From this point each server exchanges the multicast delays variations values with the other local servers. Thus the server that minimizes the multicast delay variation will be elected as the first core node and noted CN_1 ($\delta_{CN_1} = \min\{\delta_{S_i} / S_i \in \Gamma\}$).

Afterwards, the first core node CN_1 builds its Autonomous Domain AD_1 by selecting all local servers of Γ that are accessible through a delay time lower than a given threshold of delay D (the threshold D is selected by taking account of the network extent). These allow us to build an Autonomous Domain with a minimum intra-delay communications.

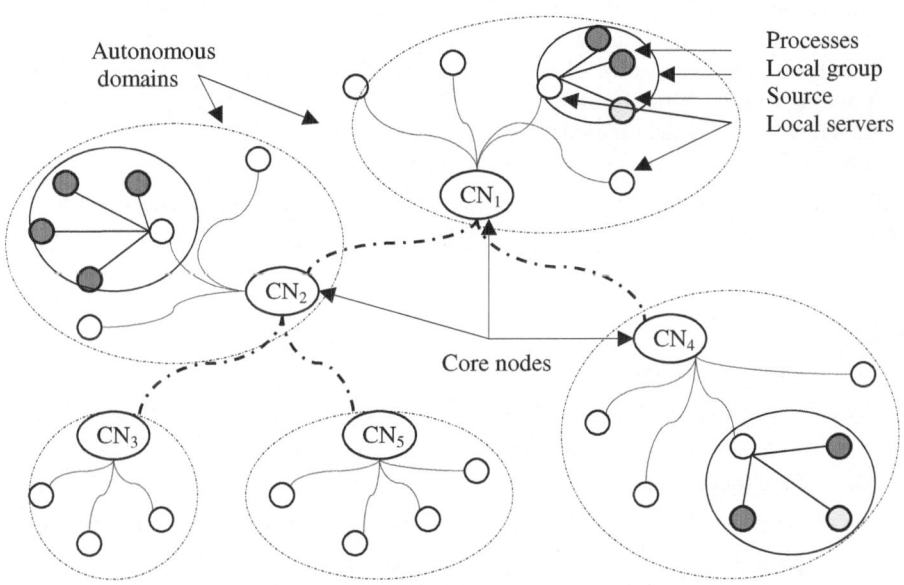

Fig. 3. Hierarchical structure of multicast group

Table 2. Delays between core nodes and servers of \$

	S_i	S_j	...
CN_1	$d_{\min}(CN_1, S_i)$	$d_{\min}(CN_1, S_j)$	
CN_2	$d_{\min}(CN_2, S_i)$	$d_{\min}(CN_k, S_i)$	
...			

Here, all the other servers that are not in CN_1's domain will be stored in \$ such as AD_1: \$ = $\Gamma \setminus AD_1$. Then, CN_1 stores the minimum delay between it and all servers of \$ in the matrix MAT (Table 2). After that CN_1's AD is built, and CN_1 gives the relay to another server in order to build the next AD. This is made by sending a $SUCC$ packet to the nearest server S_i belonging to \$. In other words, S_i is the server which minimizes the delay with CN_1 ($d_{\min}(CN_1, S_i)$). Finally, CN_1 joins the members of its autonomous domain AD_1 via the shortest path tree while the root is CN_1.

Meanwhile, when a local server S_i receives a *SUCC* packet from CN_1, this means that S_i is promoted as new core node noted CN_2. Accordingly S_i carries out the following operations:

- Select all servers of $ (the set of servers which are not in the domain of CN_1) having a delay smaller or equal to the threshold D and put them into its autonomous domain AD_2: $AD_2 = \left\{ S_i \in \$ / d_{\min}(CN_2, S_i) \prec D \right\}$.
- Remove from $ the selected servers: $\$ = \$ \backslash AD_2$.
- Remove the columns of the matrix *MAT* corresponding to the elements of its domain.
- Add a line into *MAT* to store the minimum delay between it and all servers of $: which do not belong to any domain.
- Search the smallest value of delays in *MAT* and take the pair (CN_p, S_q) corresponding to this value. In other terms, CN_2 selects the server Sq which minimizes the delay with already created core nodes (CN_1 or CN_2).
- Send a *SUCC* packet to the new core node S_q noted CN_3.

Finally, CN_2 joins its domain members and the predecessor core node CN_1 via the shortest path tree where the root is CN_2. Once the new core node CN_3 receives the

---

Let $\Gamma = \{S_1, S_2, ..., S_k\}$ be a set of elected local servers.
Begin

1. for each local server $S_i \in \Gamma$ do

2. $d_{\min}(S_i, S_j)$ = the minimum delay between S_i and S_j, where $S_j \in \Gamma$ (the minimum delay is computed by Dijikstra' Algorithm)

3. end of for each local server $S_i \in \Gamma$ loop

4. for each local server $S_i \in \Gamma$ do   //calculate the multicast delay variation of S_i

5. $\delta_{S_i} = \max \left\{ \left| d_{\min}(S_i, S_j) - d_{\min}(S_i, S_k) \right| / \forall S_j, S_k \in \Gamma, j \neq k \right\}$

6. end of for each local server $S_i \in \Gamma$ loop

7. $NewCN \leftarrow S_i$, where $\delta_{S_i} = \min \left\{ \delta_{S_j} / S_j \in \Gamma \right\}$ // the server which has a minimal multicast delay variation represents the first core node

8. $\$ \leftarrow \Gamma$, $Predecessor \leftarrow NewCN$ and $SetCN \leftarrow \emptyset$

9. while $\$ \neq \emptyset$ do

10. $CN_i \leftarrow NewCN$, $SetCN \leftarrow SetCN \cup \{CN_i\}$, $Pred(CN_i) \leftarrow Predecessor$

11. $AD_i = \left\{ S_j \in \Gamma / d_{\min}(CN_i, S_j) \prec D \right\}$ //CN_i builds its autonomous domain

12. CN_i joins member of its domain AD_i and its predecessor $Pred(CN_i)$ by the shortest path tree which root is CN_i

13. $\$ \leftarrow \$ \backslash AD_i$, removes AD_i from columns of *MAT* and adds line corresponding to $\left\{ d_{\min}(CN_i, S_i) / S_i \in \$ \right\}$ in *MAT*

14. $NewCN \leftarrow S_q$ and $Predecessor \leftarrow CN_p$, where $d_{\min}(CN_p, S_q) = \min \left\{ MAT(CN_j, S_k) / S_k \in \$, CN_j \in SetCN \right\}$

15. end of while loop
End of the algorithm

Fig. 4. Algorithm for multicast tree construction between local servers

packet *SUCC*, it makes the same thing as CN_2. Note that the AD building process is ended when $ is empty or in other words, until all servers are connected to the multicast tree (Figure 3). For completeness we draw in Figure 4 the multicast tree construction algorithm.

3.3 The Time Complexity of the Algorithm

In order to determine the complexity of the proposed algorithm, we consider the following lemma:

Lemma. The worst case complexity of the algorithm is $O[(k+1)n^2]$, where k is the number of selected local servers and n is the number of nodes in the network.

Proof. The proposed algorithm time complexity is the sum of the time complexity of building the local groups (Figure 2) and the time complexity of building the multicast tree between the servers (Figure 4). On the one hand, the time complexity of building the local groups is in the worst case $O(m^2)$, where m is the participants' number in the group multicast M. In fact, the time complexity of constructing a neighbouring set NS_i of process m_i (Figure 2, line 2) is $O(m)$. Given that our algorithm executes the loop from line 1 to line 3 once for each process m_i belonging to M. ($m_i \in M$), the time complexity of lines 1-3, therefore, is $O(m^2)$. Here, the transit groups are constructed from line 4 to line 10, so during one iteration of the outer loop (4-10), the lines 7 and 8 are executed at most m times ($\forall m_i \in M, |NS_i| \prec m$). Accordingly, the time complexity of lines 4-10 is $O(m^2)$. Further the loop from line 11 to line 13 constructs local groups. Since the time $O(m)$ is required at most in line 12 ($|TG_i| << m$), then the time complexity of lines 11-13 is $O(m^2)$. From this point the number of iterations required to elect local and secondary servers for each local group LG_i is $|LG_i|$. If one consider that $m= |LG_1| + |LG_2| + \dots + |LG_k|$, then the time complexity of lines 14-17 is $O(m)$. Finally, the time complexity of loop from line 18 to line 22 is $O(km)$. Since m is much higher than k ($m>>k$), then the time complexity of constructing local groups is $3*O(m^2) + O(km) + O(m)= O(m^2)$.

On the other hand, it is easily observed that the execution time of the multicast tree construction algorithm (Figure 4) is mainly spent on the loop between lines 1 and 3, namely on calculating the minimum delay between local servers. The time complexity of computing these minimum delays by Dijkstra's Algorithm is $O(n^2)$ [12]. Given that the proposed algorithm executes the loop from line 1 to line 3 once for each local server, the time complexity of lines 1-3, therefore, is $O(kn^2)$, where k is the number of elected local servers. Line 4 through line 6 compute the multicast delay variation for each local server $S_i \in \Gamma$, so if we consider that the time $O(k)$ is required in line 5, then the time complexity of lines 4-6 is $O(k^2)$. The design of the local server which has a minimal multicast delay variation as a first core node is in line 7. Thus, the time complexity required for execute line 7 is $O(k)$. Here, the loop from line 9 to line 15 connects all the local servers to the multicast tree. Line 11 requires k iteration to construct an autonomous domain AD_i for each selected core node CN_i. In line 12 the selected core node CN_i joins members of its domain AD_i and its core node predecessor $Pred(CN_i)$, within a number of iterations less than k ($|AD_i| + 1 < k$). Further line 14 selects the new core node from the set of servers which are not belonging to any created autonomous domain through k^2 times. Thereby, since the loop between lines 9 and 15 is executed at most k times, then overall time complexity of lines 9-15 is $O(k^3)$. Finally, the time complexity of constructing multicast tree between servers is $O(kn^2) + O(k^2) + O(k) + O(k^3) = O(kn^2)$, because n is much higher than k ($n>>k$).

At this point by considering that $O(m^2) + O(k\ n^2) = O[(k+1)n^2]$, because the number of destinations nodes m is lower than the number of nodes in the network n, the overall time complexity of the proposed algorithm is $O[(k+1)n^2]$. Since $k<<m$, then our algorithm shows lower time complexity than DDVCA, which is equal to $O(mn^2)$.

4 Simulations and Analysis

In order to evaluate the advantages of the proposed scheme, we have constructed a set of simulation using ns-2 (Network Simulator) [13]. We compare the proposed algorithm with DDVCA. The simulations focus on the protocols' abilities to maintain low multicast delay variation while minimizing the bandwidth consumption. During the simulation, we deliberately change the network topology by changing the network's size (500 and 1000 stations) in order to evaluate the ability of the proposed scheme to suit different network configuration. Further, the destination nodes in the multicast group represent 50% of the network size, while 10 source nodes are chosen randomly. Each run consists of 100 second, where each source generates 20 (media units/s). Note that the media unit size is 500 bytes. For completeness the scheduling of multimedia flows' diffusion is shown in Table 3.

Table 3. Scheduling of diffusion multimedia stream

Sources	1	2	3	4	5	6	7	8	9	10
Begin (s)	0	10	20	30	40	50	60	70	80	90
End (s)	100	100	100	100	100	100	100	100	100	100

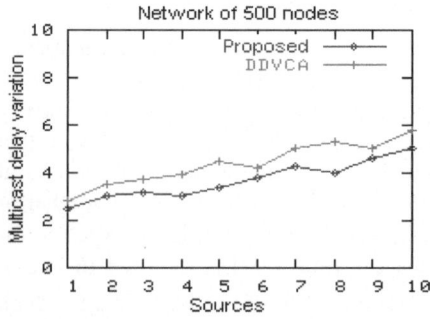
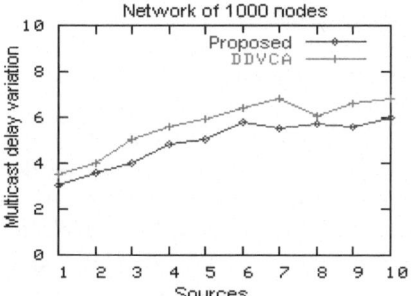

Fig. 5. Multicast delay variation's average 500 stations

Fig. 6. Multicast delay variation's average 1000 stations

Figures 5 and 6 represent the multicast delay variation average when using 500 and 1000 stations, respectively. It's clearly seen that our mechanism outperforms the DDVCA mechanism in both situations. This is expected as our algorithm constructs both the local group and the autonomous domain according to the multicast delay variation constraint. In contrast DDVCA takes this constraint into account only through the choice of the core node. Furthermore, it is important to note that our scheme's gain in multicast delay variation over DDVCA is roughly 1 sec, which is very high if we consider the case where the flows represent a video-based session. In fact, this translates into a high jitter entailing devastating consequences on the perceived video quality at the receiver.

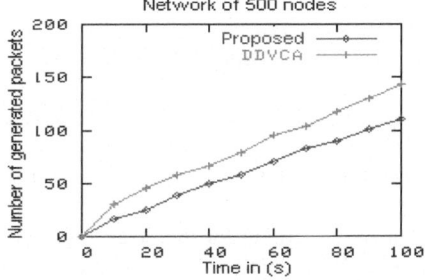
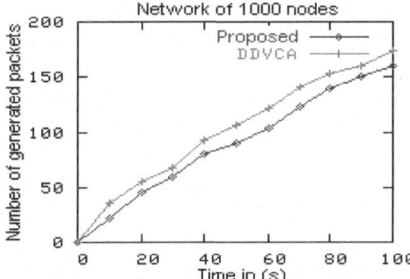

Fig. 7. Bandwidth consumption 500 stations   **Fig. 8.** Bandwidth consumption 1000 stations

Figures 7 and 8 show the bandwidth consumption of both the proposed scheme and DDVCA. Note that these graphs are obtained by computing periodically (10 s) the packets' number generated by both the proposed scheme and DDVCA. Actually, DDVCA uses more bandwidth than the proposed scheme. This is caused by the fact that DDVCA avoids using the unicast packets only between the senders and the core node. In contrary, the proposed scheme uses the unicast packets only in the intra-local group communication. Indeed, the unicast packets increase the bandwidth consumption.

Additionally, to see the influence of the multicast group's size, we have increased the number of nodes in the network (1000 stations). As indicated, it is easy to notice that the proposed algorithm is always better than the DDVCA.

5   Conclusion

In this paper we have proposed a novel multicast tree construction in order to solve the so called delay and multicast delay variation problem. The proposed scheme offers an improved ability to minimize the multicast delay variation as well as the bandwidth consumption while having a lower time complexity.

Simulations have shown that the proposed mechanism achieves numerous performance gains over the DDVCA. In addition to minimize the multicast delay variation, the proposed scheme improves efficiently the bandwidth utilization by minimizing the packets' number in the network. Furthermore, the proposed algorithm exhibits a time complexity lower than DDVCA, $O(mn^2)$ and $O[(k+1)n^2]$ respectively $(k << m)$. Our future works will focus on the implementation of our algorithm in real network configuration. Furthermore, we will also extend our proposal with a QoS management-based such as Diffserv.

References

1. A. Ksentini et al. "Novel Architecture for reliable H.26L video transmission over IEEE 802.11e", *Proc. IEEE PIMRC'05*, Barcelona, Spain.
2. D. Weitzman, C. Partridge, "Distance Vector Multicast Routing Protocol", *RFC 1075*, November 1998.
3. S. Deering et al., "Protocol Independent Multicast-Dense Mode (PIM-DM): Protocol Specification", *RFC 2365*, July 1998.
4. J. Moy, "Multicast Extension to OSPF", *RFC 1584*, Mars 1994.
5. D. Estrin et al., "Protocol Independent Multicast-Sparse Mode (PIM-SM): Protocol Specification", *IETF RFC 2362*, June 1998.
6. A. Striegel and G. Manimaran, "Survey of QoS Multicasting Issues", *IEEE Communications Magazine*, June 2002, pp. 82-87.
7. G. N. Rouskas, I. Baldine, "Multicast routing with end-to-end delay and delay variation constraints", *IEEE JSAC*, April 1997, pp. 346-356.
8. P.-R Sheu, S.-T. Chen, "A fast and efficient heuristic algorithm for the delay and delay variation bound multicast tree problem", *Information Networking, Proc. ICOIN-15*, January 2001, pp. 611-618.
9. A. Benslimane, O. Moussaoui, "A scalable Multicast Protocol with QoS guarantees", *Proc. of IEEE/IFIP Net-Con'2003*. Muscat, Oman. October 2003.
10. B. Wang and J. C. Hou, "Multicast Routing and its QoS Extension: Problems, Algorithms, and Protocols", *IEEE Networks*, January/ February 2000.
11. A. Ballardie, "Core Based Trees (CBT Version 2) Multicast Routing: protocol specification," *IETF RFC 2189*, September 1997.
12. E. W. Dijkstra, A note on two problems in connection with graphs, *Numeric Mathematic*, vol. 1, 1959, pp. 269-271.
13. Network Simulator 2, ns-2, http://www.isi.edu/nsnam.

A Semi-reliable Multicast Protocol for Distributed Multimedia Applications in Large Scale Networks

Christiane Montenegro Bortoleto[1], Lau Cheuk Lung[1], Frank A. Siqueira[2], Alysson Neves Bessani[3], and Joni da Silva Fraga[3]

[1] Pontifícia Univ. Católica do Paraná, Programa de Pós-Graduação em Informática Aplicada
{cbortoleto, lau}@ppgia.pucpr.br
[2] Universidade Federal de Santa Catarina, Departamento de Informática e Estatística
frank@inf.ufsc.br
[3] Universidade Federal de Santa Catarina, Departamento de Automação e Sistemas
{neves, fraga}@das.ufsc.br

Abstract. This paper proposes a semi-reliable multicast protocol that aims to increase the quality of video streams transmitted in large-scale systems without overloading the video source and the communications network. This protocol, which is based on the IP multicast protocol and the MPEG standard, evaluates the necessity of retransmitting lost packets taking into account the capacity of the corresponding MPEG frames to improve the quality of the video stream. The proposed protocol relies on the neighboring receivers for retransmitting lost packets, resulting in much faster recovery, which is vital in order to receive retransmitted packets in time to be exhibited. Besides, this strategy avoids overloading the video source, making it more scalable than the traditional approach of retransmitting from the source.

1 Introduction

Real-time multimedia applications have been widely developed in many platforms and topologies. Internet and intranet structures employ more and more integrated networking services, where applications with different characteristics are executed using the same communication infrastructure and service models. However, the ordinary communication infrastructure is risky to the quality of multimedia content due to the implementation of transmission policies, routing algorithms, packet discard strategies and due to the complexity of media data formats. Networking infrastructures need mechanisms to improve and guarantee the performance of these applications. Physical limitations - e.g. router overload caused by directing and retransmitting datagrams - may lead to the loss of information required by real-time and multimedia applications, affecting negatively their behavior.

Distributed multimedia applications have singular requirements that are not found in other kinds of distributed applications. In videoconferences through the Internet, for example, the communication support is the main cause of low performance. An audio/video stream requires data to be received at the right moment and can handle some data loss. If a packet arrives too late it does not contribute to the exhibition, meaning that, for the viewer, the effect would be the same as if the packet had never

J. Dalmau and G. Hasegawa (Eds.): MMNS 2005, LNCS 3754, pp. 109–120, 2005.

arrived. An acceptable amount of data loss in the audio/video stream can be handled without causing a significant loss of quality noticeable for the viewer.

In the literature, there is a substantial amount of work on best-effort multicast for distributed multimedia applications and reliable multicast for applications that demand reliable message delivery (i.e. fault tolerant applications). Between those two approaches lie the semi-reliable multicast protocols, which represent a more recent category of group communication protocols that are still maturing [12; 9; 11; 13]. Semi-reliable multicast is a communication paradigm in which data are classified, usually by the application, before being transmitted, establishing different importance or priority levels for error recovery (retransmission).

This paper presents a semi-reliable multicast protocol which was designed to be more efficient and scalable than reliable protocols. This protocol was designed to be used by distributed multimedia applications based on groups (i.e. digital video multicast). Through simulations, it is shown that this protocol is more efficient for use in large scale networks. The protocol is specified for video streaming multicast applications which use encoders that provide some kind of frame hierarchy, such as the MPEG standard, allowing the establishment of priority levels for frame recovery.

It is important to emphasize that the proposed protocol is not intended to be employed as a complete multicast protocol for media transfer. In this paper, we propose and study the impact of a data recovery technique that can be combined with other protocols found in the literature in order to provide semi-reliable media delivery.

This paper presents in section 2 the main characteristics of the MPEG standard. Section 3 describes the concept of semi-reliable multicast. The proposed protocol is presented in section 4. In section 5, experimental data is shown. Section 6 presents related proposals and, finally, section 7 presents the final conclusions and perspectives for future work.

2   The MPEG Standard

The most widely adopted standards for video compression belong to the MPEG (Motion Picture Experts Group) family [5]. There are different standards, such as MPEG-2, for example, which requires transfer rates from 3 Mbps to 100 Mbps. The MPEG-2 compression algorithm is based on pixel correlation and translational movement correlation between consecutive frames. It takes into account that the pictures in an image sequence are very similar, except for disjoints due to movement, so it is possible do code a frame through calculating the movement vector related to the previous frame [13]. The output stream consists of three types of frames:

- I-frames (Intra-coded): complete images individually coded;
- P-frames (Predictive): coded frames with prediction related to the previous frame;
- B-frames (Bidirectional): differences between the previous and the next frames.

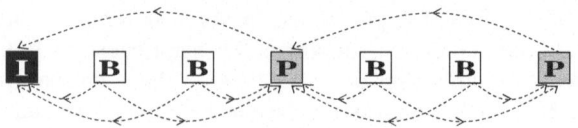

Fig. 1. IPB-frame Relation

The I frames are inserted in the output stream at a specific rate, with P and B frames between them. The I frames do not depend on other frames to be decoded, but they are necessary on P and B frame decoding. P-frames are needed on B frame decoding and they are based on forward prediction using the previous frame as reference, which can be a P or I frame. The P frame has a past movement reference vector, used as reference to the previous frame in the same position of the present one. B frames are based on backward prediction using the previous and the following frames, which can be I or P type. B frames have a forward movement vector, used as reference the next frame on the same position of the present one. This coding method makes some frames more important than others. If an I frame is lost during transmission, it will not be possible to decode the B and P frames that arrive before the next I frame. The relation between frames in an MPEG stream is shown in Fig. 1. Each GOP (Group Of Pictures) contains one I frame. A GOP is a set of frames where each one has the picture header and its present data. The GOP sequence is an N-sized sequence of frames between two consecutive I frames.

3   Semi-reliable Multicast

Semi-reliable multicast is a communication abstraction where not every packet is necessarily retransmitted when requested; only the most important packets for the application are given higher priority to be recovered. It means that the reliable delivery for a given set of packets which will be sent in a receiver group is granted only to a subset (i.e., the packets with higher priority). Reliable delivery means that a multicast packet has to be delivered to every correct receiver (agreement property [7]). This guarantee can be obtained through an error correction mechanism (i.e. packet retransmission). For other packets (with lower priority), transmission errors will only be corrected if the network conditions allow it. If the conditions are not favorable, the delivery is based on best-effort, where the agreement property can be infringed.

Packets to be multicast can be classified according to a hierarchy, based on some application semantic [11] or some rule from the semi-reliable multicast protocol itself, establishing importance or priority levels for error correction (selective retransmission [12, 9]). Error correction is made according to this property and to network state parameters (i.e. traffic, congestion, delay, and so on).

3.1   Semi-reliable Multicast for Distributed Multimedia Applications

Multimedia information transmission has a fixed rate and frames have to be received and rendered in the receiver with a similar rate to keep the original meaning of the sequence. Thus, each unit of information sent must be received within a certain time bound. Besides, the data loss ratio (which includes data delivered after the moment it was supposed to be rendered) should also be kept within the boundaries defined by the application. So, the quality of service (QoS) issue includes finding the boundaries through the networks for transmission errors and jitter.

A traditional reliable multicast tool is not appropriate for multimedia multicast for many reasons. The retransmission strategy with timeout achieves reliability through latency increase. Multimedia applications can tolerate errors due to lost and corrupted packets as long as they are kept within an acceptable limit. Thus, a multimedia transport protocol demands semi-reliable delivery where delay is more relevant than delivering every packet of the set. Other kinds of applications can use semi-reliable multicast for performance improvement. In [11], the author describes distributed multiplayer games as an example where obsolete messages can be eliminated without damaging the final result.

4 The Proposed Protocol

The proposed protocol uses the frame hierarchy defined in the MPEG standard for semi-reliable multicast through classifying MPEG frames and encapsulating them in UDP packets. Once having the frames classified, error correction (lost packets retransmission) can be made by the sender (source) or by the receivers, according to the lost frame type (I, P or B) and to some network parameters (traffic, reception rate, congestion, etc). The idea is that every I frame is reliably delivered and P and B frames, specially the first one, are retransmitted (if a loss occurs) depending on the conditions of the transmission environment. The proposed protocol is based on ideas from ReMIOP [4] and some concepts presented in [10].

In order to develop this protocol, the following assumptions were made:

- The environment presents no guarantees for message delivery.
- Neither the source nor the receivers know the members of the multicast group.
- The source sends one frame (I, P or B) per packet.
- Each packet carries information about: the sequence number of the frame it contains, the type of frame it contains and the type of the last eight frames sent.
- Both source and receivers are able to send messages to and receive messages from the multicast group.

The algorithm presented next describes the procedure to receive and send messages using the proposed protocol. In this algorithm it is assumed that when the sender detects a lost packet it is able to know what kind of MPEG frame it was carrying.

4.1 Protocol Description

Frames (packets) are multicast directly to the group, without previous knowledge of its members. Receivers put all received packets in a buffer and deliver them to the application (lines 5-8). In line 6 the receiver cancels any possible retransmission request for the received message. Then, receivers detect a packet loss (line 12) through the search for blanks in the sequence of received packets, which is expressed by a sequence number. When a loss is detected, the receiver evaluates if it is necessary to request retransmission through a NACK message (lines 13, 18 and 19). This evaluation is based on application QoS needs and network parameters. Application QoS considers relevance of the lost frames for media reproduction in the receiver and the usability of the lost frame by the time the retransmitted packet arrives at the receiver. Network parameters consider packet loss rate, congestion and acceptable delay.

If a lost frame is considered relevant (lines 16-19) retransmission is requested through a NACK message which is multicast to the group (line 21). If the is not relevant, the receiver ignores the lost packet. Any process (sender or receiver) which receives a NACK and has the requested frame, evaluates again the parameters (lines 33 and 36) and, if that is the case, multicasts it again to the group (line 38). Note that this QoS parameter evaluation for selective retransmission is made just for packets containing P and B-frames. Lost packets containing I frames are always retransmitted (lines 13-15 and 30-32).

```
1.  //RECEIVER'S ALGORITHM
2.  WHEN receives(m)
3.     IF m.type = DATA {if receives a data message}
4.        frame = m.type_of_frame
5.        IF search_buffer(m.sender, m) == NULL
6.           cancels_booked(NACKm) {cancels NACK for m}
7.           adds_to_buffer(m.sender, m)
8.           delivers(m) {delivers the message}
9.        ELSE
10.          cancels_booked(m) {cancels m retransmission}
11.       END-IF
12.       IF there is a missing message {recovery}
13.          IF frame == "I"
14.             wait(random(Tnack))
15.                     multicast(NACKm)
16.          ELSE IF still_relevant(frame)
17.             loss_rate = get_loss_rate()
18.          IF (frame == "P" AND loss_rate < 40%) OR
19.             (frame == "B" AND loss_rate < 20%)
20.                     wait(random(Tnack))
21.                     multicast(NACKm)
22.             END-IF
23.          END-IF
24.       END-IF
25.    ELSE IF m.type == NACK {retransmission request}
26.       FOR EVERY mn ∈ m.nacked
27.          cancels_booked(NACKmn) {cancels NACK for mn}
28.          mT = search_buffer(m.sender, mn)
29.          IF mT ≠ NULL
30.             IF mT.frame == "I"
31.                wait(random(Trepair))
32.                multicast(mT)
33.                   ELSE
34.                      loss_rate = get_loss_rate()
35.             IF(frame =="P" AND loss_rate< 40%) OR
36.                (frame =="B" AND loss_rate< 20%)
37.                wait(random(Trepair))
38.                multicast(mT)
39.                END-IF
40.             END-IF
41.          END-IF
42.       END-FOR
43.    END-IF
44. END-WHEN
```

4.2 Retransmissions

The proposed protocol is based on the principle of retransmission made by the receiver, where the receivers share the responsibility of helping their peers to recover their losses [6]. To analyze the decision parameters, it was defined that the maximum loss rate to require retransmission or to retransmit packets is 20% for packets containing B-frames and 40% for packets containing P-frames (lines 8-19 and 35-36).

The loss rate at each receiver is calculated based on a sample sequence – a window with the N last multicast packets. The protocol counts, for every window, the number of missing packets based on the sequence numbers. So, the get_loss_rate function (lines 17 and 34) calculates de percentage of lost packets for every N multicast packets.

The frame relevance is verified by the still_relevant function (line 16), which checks if the missing frame is still valid, i.e., if the moment for the packet to be shown by the application has not passed yet.

To avoid NACK or retransmission explosions the protocol employs a wait function that interrupts the execution during a random interval (whose superior limits are Tnack and Trepair respectively). When a receiver Ri is about to send a NACK, it waits for a random time Tnack (lines 14 and 20). If during this period Ri receives a NACK from another receiver Rj requesting the same packet, Ri cancels its NACK (line 27). In a similar way, when Ri receives a NACK and has the requested packet, it waits for a random time Trepair before multicasting this packet (lines 32 and 38). But if within this period Ri receives the requested packet, Ri cancels the retransmission (line 10).

4.3 Exhibition Buffer and Retransmission Buffer

An important issue related to the implementation of the proposed protocol is the exhibition buffer management in the receiver to deal appropriately with indirect losses, i.e. the discard of B and P frames that occurs due to the loss of an I-frame. Two classes were created to store received packets: WaitElement and WaitWindow. The WaitElement class represents a set of received packets where the first one contains an I-frame - i.e. a GOP - preceded by two control fields: the I-frame sequence number of that set and a flag that indicates if the I-frame is in the auxiliary buffer that stores the packets of that set. Fig. 2 illustrates this class.

The WaitWindow class represents a buffer that stores WaitElement objects. Packets that get to the receiver are put in the corresponding WaitElement, according to their sequence numbers. WaitElement objects are stored in the WaitWindow of the receiver, ordered by the sequence number of the corresponding I-Frame. Fig. 3 shows an example of WaitWindow object for a given frame sequence with some missing frames.

For each received packet containing an I-frame, a new instance of WaitElement is created and added to the WaitWindow object in the correct position, according to its sequence number. For packets containing P or B-frames, the WaitWindow object is searched for the WaitElement containing the I-frame that precedes the present frame. When it is found, the packet is added to the auxiliary buffer in the right position.

If the loss of a packet containing an I-frame is detected, an instance of WaitElement is created with the sequence number of the missing packet and then its flag is set to false, indicating that the I-frame is not inside the auxiliary buffer. Thus, if it comes

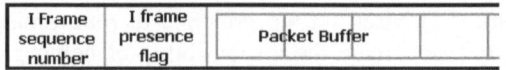

Fig. 2. WaitElement Class

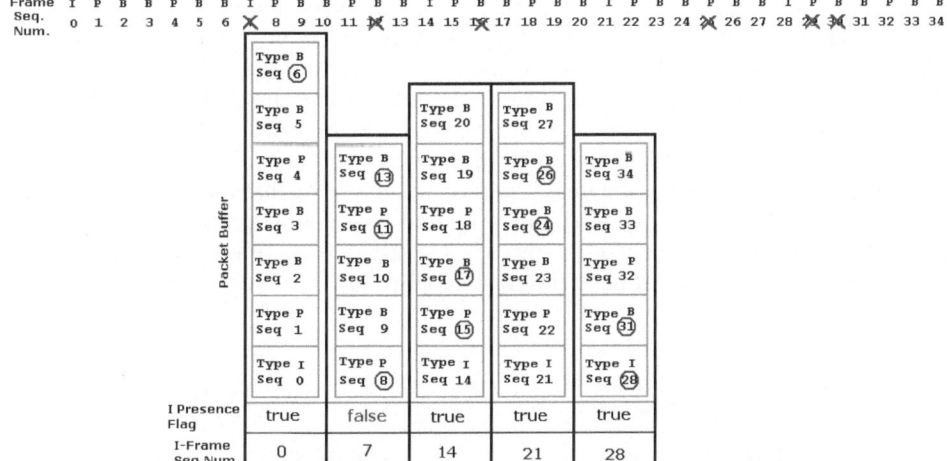

Frame	I	P	B	B	P	B	B	I	P	B	B	P	B	B	I	P	B	B	P	B	B	I	P	B	B	P	B	B	I	P	B	B	P	B	B
Seq. Num.	0	1	2	3	4	5	6	X	8	9	10	11	X	13	14	15	X	17	18	19	20	21	22	23	24	X	26	27	28	X	X	31	32	33	34

Packet Buffer

Type B seq ⑥			
Type B seq 5		Type B seq 20	Type B seq 27	
Type P seq 4	Type B seq ⑬	Type B seq 19	Type B seq ㉖	Type B seq 34
Type B seq 3	Type P seq ⑪	Type P seq 18	Type B seq ㉔	Type B seq 33
Type B seq 2	Type B seq 10	Type B seq ⑰	Type B seq 23	Type P seq 32
Type P seq 1	Type B seq 9	Type P seq ⑮	Type P seq 22	Type B seq ㉛
Type I seq 0	Type P seq ⑧	Type I seq 14	Type I seq 21	Type I seq ㉘

I Presence Flag	true	false	true	true	true
I-Frame Seq.Num.	0	7	14	21	28

Fig. 3. WaitWindow Object

the time to show that set of frames before the I-frame arrives, the whole set is discarded and the next set containing an I-frame goes to the exhibition buffer.

This algorithm allows that by the time the frames are sent to the exhibition buffer they have already been reordered and that discards have been made. Retransmission also takes place employing the frames kept in the WaitWindow object, occurring until the time the frames are sent to the application for being rendered. Using this structure, each receiver must have one entity to take care of the frame sending to the application. This is done by passing the frames from the WaitWindow to the exhibition buffer, which will be read by the application.

Each receiver has a retransmission buffer that stores the last received packets (frames). The packets in the exhibition buffer are also used by the receiver to answer retransmission requests (NACKs). This buffer has limited size and older packets are discarded when the limit is achieved by the FIFO (First In First Out) method.

5 Simulations and Results

In order to evaluate the proposed protocol, we have simulated its behavior using the Simmcast [3] network simulator. In these testes, comparisons were made between the proposed protocol, an ordinary multicast protocol, a NACK-sending multicast protocol and a reliable multicast protocol in terms of error correction, recovering time, receiver overload and video quality factor [10]. The topology adopted for the simulations, which was chosen with the intent of showing the adequacy of the proposed protocol for large scale networks, is illustrated by Fig. 4.

Simulations were performed using the same conditions for all four protocols. The adopted parameters are (section 4.2): N=50, Trepair = Tnack = 200ms.

In terms of lost packets recovery, the proposed protocol has presented an average of 81.7% of recovery against 2% of the multicast with NACK (simple retransmission) and 89% of the reliable multicast. The best performance from the proposed protocol and the reliable multicast can be credited, among other features, to the receiver-based retransmission. The reliable multicast has achieved a better rate because it tries to recover every single packet, no matter the temporal relevance of the packet for the application. The recovering averages for each type of frame are shown in Table 1.

It is convenient to compare the performance of the proposed protocol with the performance of the reliable multicast protocol in terms of discards. The results are shown in Table 2. Based on these figures, it is possible to notice that the reliable multicast protocol recovers more frames than the proposed protocol but great part of recovered data is discarded. It means that the proposed protocol is more efficient, once the recovered packets are more often useful to the application by the time they arrive.

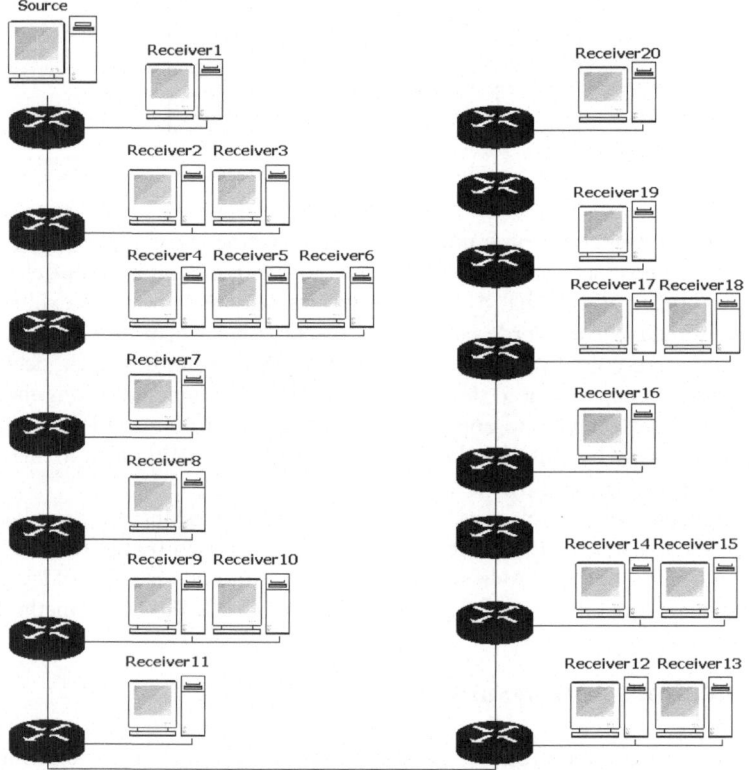

Fig. 4. Topology used in simulations

Table 1. Recovery per frame type

	% of recovered frames		
	I	**P**	**B**
Proposed Protocol	81.7	82.9	61.7
Multicast with NACK	1.0	2.1	3.4
Reliable Multicast	97.0	100.0	71.0

Table 2. Discards

	% of discarded frames		
	I	P	B
Proposed Protocol	45,4	33,0	24,8
Reliable Multicast	78,0	50,6	48,1

Another important result observed in the simulation is that the majority (93%) of recovered packets for the proposed protocol come from other receivers, instead of the source. This causes an improved performance in recovering time. For the topology shown in Fig. 4, the proposed protocol had an average recovery time of 95ms against 140ms of the reliable multicast and 962ms of the simple retransmission multicast.

A very satisfactory result obtained with the proposed protocol was the NACK suppression: an average of 39% of the NACKs were suppressed. The results show that the rate increases when the receiver is more distant from the source, as shown in Fig.5. This happens because the receivers that are closer to the source detect the losses more quickly and send their NACKs before the more distant receivers.

The reception rate obtained by the proposed protocol is shown is Fig.6. This feature varies according to the distance from the source.

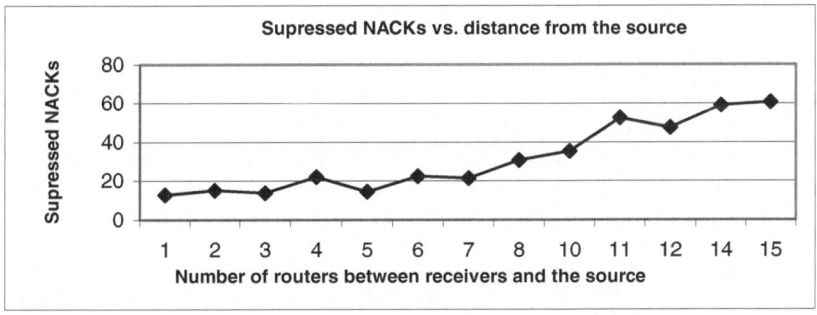

Fig. 5. Suppressed NACKs vs. distance from the source

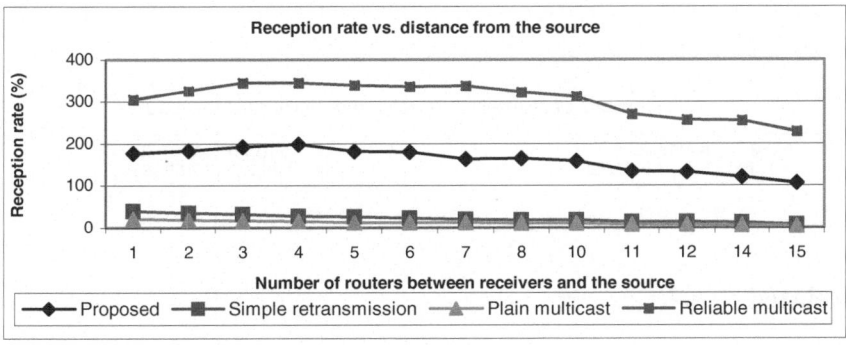

Fig. 6. Reception rate

Another parameter used in the evaluation was the Video Quality Factor (q), defined in [10]. This parameter consists in a metric based on the GOP structure to evaluate video quality. The formula, showed in equations 1 and 2, takes into account direct and indirect losses. Direct losses are the ones caused by losing the frame itself. Indirect losses are caused by the loss of another frame; for example, a P or B frame which cannot be exhibited because there is an I frame missing. It is important to highlight that this metric claims to evaluate video flow information transport, not video quality from the point of view of the observer.

$$q = \frac{a_I * x_I + a_P * x_P + a_B * x_B}{a_I * N_{TI} + a_P * N_{TP} + a_B * N_{TB}}, 0 \leq q \leq 1 \tag{1}$$

where:

j: Represents the frame type (I, P or B)
x_j: Represents the number of j-frames received and exhibited
N_{Tj}:   Represents the total number of j-frames in a GOP
a_j: Represents the relative coefficient (j-frames in the GOP)

and

$$a_j = \frac{N_{Ij}}{N_{II} * N_{TI} + N_{IP} * N_{TP} + N_{IB} * N_{TB}} \tag{2}$$

where

N_{Ij}: Represents direct and indirect losses caused by the loss of the j-frame.

The proposed protocol, as shown in Fig.7, has presented a better performance compared to all the other tested protocols, despite not recovering as many frames as the reliable multicast protocol. This result was obtained due to the selective discard of packets containing less relevant frames.

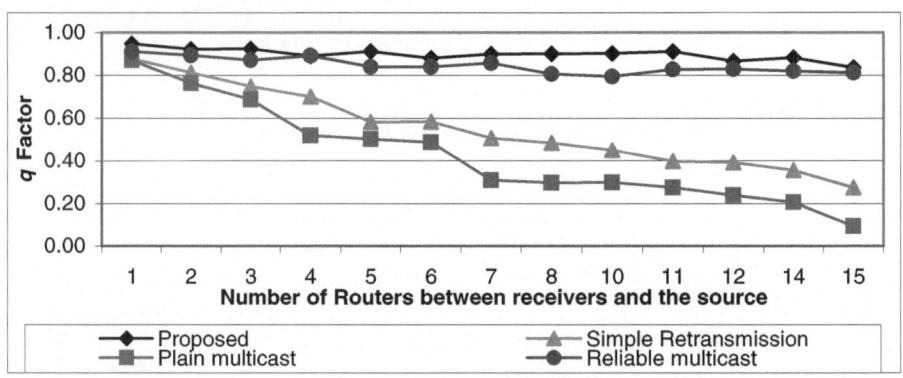

Fig. 7. q Factor vs. distance from the source

6   Related Work

It is possible to find in the technical literature papers proposing a few semi-reliable multicast protocols. The WAIT protocol [9], for example, is designed to adjust itself to different quality requirements of a multimedia session and to reduce the network load, providing an improved quality of service for applications exchanging data through the Internet without relying on routers to do so. The problem with this approach is that, in order to form a group, the receivers must have information about the topology of the network, which reduces the scalability of the protocol.

SRP [12] (Selective Retransmission Protocol) uses a specific decision algorithm for each application to determine if a retransmission request for a lost packet should be answered or not, adjusting the loss and latency levels according to the application. Just a percentage of the lost data is retransmitted. The amount of retransmission depends on QoS factors including total losses, latency RTT (round trip time), network congestion and quality required by the user.

An approach based on semantically reliable multicast protocols is presented in [11]. The proposed model for a reliable multicast protocol eliminates obsolete messages to sustain a higher throughput. The idea is that message obsolescence is only used to avoid network congestion. When the buffer occupancy gets beyond the established limit, the protocol searches for obsolete messages in the buffer and purges them. When the buffer occupancy gets back to normal, the protocol gets reliable again. Both source and receiver can purge obsolete messages from their local buffers. The results show that this protocol can improve the throughput stability even with limited performance receivers.

PRTP (Partially Reliable Transport Protocol) [13] presents a partially reliable service that does not insist on recovering every error. Instead, it recovers part of lost data and improves packet delivery, allowing applications to exchange a controlled amount of loss for better throughput. This implies that the application itself must define a minimum reliability. When the parameter level of reliability is above the limit, the receiver does not ask for retransmission and sends a positive ACK. If a packet is lost, the receiver checks if the reliability level is above the limit. If it is, the receiver sends an ACK.

Yavatkar and Manoj have proposed a quasi-reliable multicast transport protocol for transmitting multimedia information in large scale [14]. The authors state that, due to the nature of multimedia communication, the protocol must use forward error correction to avoid delays inherent to flow-based and error control techniques.

SRM (Scalable Reliable Multicast) [6] is a reliable multicast protocol in which the retransmission system of the proposed protocol is based. In this protocol, every time a loss is detected, a NACK is sent to the whole multicast group and any member having the packet can retransmit it. To avoid duplicated NACKs or packets, the node establishes a random time before sending them. If the node receives the packet or NACK it was about to send, it cancels the sending process.

PRMP (Polling-based Reliable Multicast Protocol) [1] is a reliable multicast protocol with a source-based recovery mechanism. This protocol tries to solve the problem of limited scalability through an election-based mechanism that avoids implosion. Receivers are chosen in carefully planned moments in a way that, despite different RTT sets, the feedback packet rate at the source does not exceed source or network capacity.

These protocols are complete solutions, with congestion and flow control mechanisms. The proposed protocol is a simpler idea which experiments the concepts of receiver-based retransmission combined with selective discards. In a near future, we intend to provide a complete protocol with congestion and flow control mechanisms.

7 Conclusion

This paper presented a protocol to improve video data delivery through the network. Based on MPEG standard and multicast technology, this protocol guarantees reliable delivery of all video frames or part of them. Its good performance is obtained by a receiver based retransmission method that uses selective discard of lost packets according to the relevance of MPEG frames contained in them.

In comparison to ordinary multicast and NACK sending multicast, it is possible to notice that the proposed protocol is more efficient in large scale networks and it has better results for receivers that are at a bigger distance from the source.

References

1. Barcellos, Marinho P. (1998). "PRMP: A Scaleable Polling-based Reliable Multicast protocol". Ph.D. Thesis, Dept. of Computing Science, Univ. of Newcastle, October 1998.
2. Marinho P. Barcellos, Valter Roesler (2000), "M&M: Multicast e Multimídia", SBC/JAI2000 - XX Congresso da Sociedade Brasileira de Computação - pp.203-244. July 2000.
3. Barcellos, Marinho et al. (2001). "Simmcast: a Simulation Tool for Multicast Protocol Evaluation". XI Simpósio Brasileiro de Redes de Computadores, Florianópolis, 2001.
4. Bessani, Alysson N., Lung, Lau C., Fraga, Joni da S. (2003). "ReMIOP: Design and Implementation of a reliable multicast mechanism in CORBA" technical report. LCMI-UFSC.
5. Chiariglione, Leonardo (2000). "Short MPEG-2 Description", April 2000. Available at http://mpeg.telecomitalialab.com/standards/mpeg-2/mpeg-2.htm.
6. Floyd, S. et al (1995) "A reliable multicast framework for light-weight sessions and application level framing". Proc. of the ACM SIGCOMM 95, August 1995, p.342-356
7. Hadzilacos, V. and Toueg, S. (1994). "A modular approach to the specification and implementation of fault-tolerant broadcasts". Technical report, Department of Computer Science, Cornell University, New York - USA.
8. Liao, T (1998). "Light-weight reliable multicast protocol". http://webcanal.inria.fr/lrmp/.
9. Mane, Pravin. (2000) "WAIT: Selective Loss Recovery For Multimedia Multicast", MSc Thesis - Computer Science Department, WPI. May 2000.
10. Martins, R. F. Leite, C. A., Farines, J-M (2003), "Toward Quality Evaluation and Improvement of a MPEG Vídeo Stream". Proc. of the 3th IEEE Latin American Network Operations and Management Symposium - LANOMS'03, Foz do Iguaçu, Brazil, 2003.
11. Pereira, Jose et al (2003) "Semantically Reliable Multicast: Definition, Implementation, and Performance Evaluation". IEEE Transactions on Computers, vol.52, no.2, p150-165, 2003.
12. Piecuch, Mike et al. (2000) "A Selective Retransmission Protocol for Multimedia on the Internet". Proc. of SPIE Int. Symp. on Multimedia Systems and Applications. Nov. 2000.
13. Schneyer, S., Garcia, J., Brunstrom, A., Asplund, K. (1999) PRTP: "A Partially Reliable Transport Protocol for Multimedia Applications", Proceedings Int. Symp. on Intelligent Multimedia and Distance Education (ISIMADE), Baden-Baden, Germany, August 1999.
14. Yavatkar, Rajendra e Manoj, Leelanivas (1993) "Optimistic Strategies for Large-Scale Dissemination of Multimedia Information", First of the ACM Int. Conf. on Multimedia '93.

MDFM: Multi-domain Fault Management
for Internet Services*

Xiaohui Huang, Shihong Zou, Wendong Wang, and Shiduan Cheng

State Key Lab of Networking and Switching,
Beijing University of Posts and Telecommunications
Beijing, P.R. China, 100876
{hxiaohui, zoush, wdwang, chsd}@bupt.edu.cn

Abstract. New requirements of service-oriented fault management are analyzed
and a framework MDFM (Multi-Domain Fault Manager) is proposed in this paper to solve the service fault localization problem in multi-domain context. Different from current solutions, our approach decomposes SLS (Service Level
Specification) based on network capability, and monitor service performance in
each domain along the end-to-end path. As a result, MDFM can localize the approximate domain rapidly on which the root cause resides, therefore causative
region is narrowed down and computation cost for fault analysis is reduced.
Faults on both server and client sides are considered in MDFM. A prototype has
been implemented to prove the feasibility and efficiency of our service fault
management framework.

1 Introduction and Motivation

As Internet migrates gradually to a Service Oriented Architecture (SOA), Service
Providers (SP) find out that Internet service has the potential to bring great profits.
Thus various Internet services appear, such as Video on Demand, IP TV, VoIP and
other multimedia services. In order to maintain regular customers and attract new
users, it's necessary for SPs to provide QoS (Quality of Service) for their services.

Fault management is crucial for service QoS guarantee. Service unavailability or
performance degradation may cause SLA violation. Therefore, SP desires for a service fault management mechanism, which can perform fault localization and adopt
countermeasures as quickly as possible to reduce the service down time and performance degradation period.

In general, an Internet service scenario comprises three parts: server/server farm,
client and the network. Consequently, service unavailability or performance degradation may be caused by the faults in the server side, client side or network. Service-
oriented fault management should take all these aspects into account, and justify who
will be responsible for the service failure.

Current Internet services are un-managed or managed by SPs in a non-standard and
proprietary way [6]. The private service management can merely deal with the intra-

---

*This work was supported by the National Basic Research Program of China (Grant No.
2003CB314806 and 2006CB701306), the National Natural Science Foundation of China (No.
90204003 and 60472067) and the National 863 Program of China (No.2003AA121220).

J. Dalmau and G. Hasegawa (Eds.): MMNS 2005, LNCS 3754, pp. 121–132, 2005.

net failures due to the lack of network related information. With regard to the network part, present network is divided into several domains (or Autonomous Systems, AS) and belongs to different Network Providers (NPs). End users reside in different geographical regions and most modern services may delegate parts of capabilities to other services distributed in the network. Therefore, service traffic may span several domains.

Multi-domain environment incurs a number of problems for fault management: Different NPs have proprietary network fault management systems without open interfaces for others to retrieve precise information. Thus a certain network element failure is only visible for the NP who governs the corresponding domain, though the failure may propagate to other domains and incur a number of alarms there. Intuitively, fault analysis should be performed in all domains to locate the root cause. However, such method is time-consuming. Before a fault analysis process is initiated, it is necessary to narrow down the causative region so as to shorten the time and improve the accuracy of fault diagnosis.

Therefore, it is necessary to build a universal fault management framework capable of end-to-end fault diagnosis for commercial operation of Internet services in multi-domain context.

Kong et al [6] suggested that the approaches taken in telecommunication industry offer a sound framework for defining Internet service management. However, there are still significant differences between service fault management and traditional network fault management:

- Stable Scenario vs. Dynamic Scenario: Network fault management considers network elements, thus it has a relatively stable view of the network. However, services face the dynamic management scenarios. Due to the distribution of service subscribers and the frequently changing routing information, different services traverse dissimilar network nodes and links, thus have diverse network topologies and management scenarios, which is also mentioned in [1].
- Whole View vs. Partial View: Network fault management has a whole view of all the failures in the network. While in service fault management, failures outside the end-to-end path of the service ought not to be observed by the service manager, even if they affect the service performance.
- Different Alarm Types: Network element malfunction is the major alarm type in traditional network fault management. But in SOA, performance degradation is also a symptom which needs to initiate a fault diagnosis process.
- Different Layers involved: In traditional network fault management, fault diagnosis is focused on lower layers (physical and data link layers). But the fault diagnosis in SOA reaches through to application layer.

In order to fulfill the new requirements of service-oriented fault management, MDFM (Multi-Domain Fault Manager) is proposed in this paper, providing a sound framework for multi-domain service fault management. By SLS (Service Level Specification) decomposition and monitoring, causative region is narrowed down rapidly to a certain domain. In addition, MDFM takes both the end systems and the network into account. A prototype is implemented and proves that MDFM can locate the root cause quickly to prevent service performance from degradation.

The rest of the paper is organized as follows: Section 2 gives a brief overview of current research work related to service fault management. We elaborate on MDFM in section 3. The prototype of MDFM along with the experiment results is presented in section 4. The whole paper is concluded in section 5 with the future work.

2 Related Work

Most solutions from Industry focus on the service fault management inside SP's intranet region. It may attribute to the absence of network related information. HP (Hewlett Packard) laboratory brought forward a series of solutions for Internet service fault management: Darst and Ramanathan [7] proposed a methodology and measurement instrumentation for managing the end-to-end ISP service performance. Caswell and Ramanathan [8] proposed to use service model for Internet Service health management. Bayesian network is employed by Alexandre et al [9] to assess the overall health of the service and to detect anomalies. Besides HP, IBM releases his business service management product, Tivoli [10], which can perform event correlation across multiple environments to identify the root cause of the problem. These solutions concentrate on the service management of SP's intranet, servers, applications and infrastructure components. They are insufficient because they fall short of addressing the network impact on services. In practical situation, faults of network elements along the end to end path have a great impact on services' performance.

In academia, the focus is on service fault localization algorithms and methodology. Andreas and his partners propose service oriented event correlation in [5] and demonstrate its importance in service fault management. However, reference [5] also merely focuses on intra-provider resource, and service fault management is performed within SP's intranet region.

Steinder and Sethi [2] point out that end-to-end service fault localization is a necessity for service management. In [3], a belief network is used as a probabilistic fault propagation model (FPM), and Bayesian reasoning technique is applied to perform fault localization. Steinder and Sethi extend their previous work in [4] and propose a distributed fault-localization technique to solve the end-to-end service fault localization in multi-domain environment. By contrast with aforementioned solutions, network faults are the major concern of [4] and no failures on the server side or the client side are considered. Furthermore, as pointed out by Steinder, accurate propagation patterns and relationships among network events are difficult to be obtained and maintained. Thus in [4], fault localization must be performed in all domains to find out the most likely hypothesis, which is time-consuming and inefficient in practical management system.

3 Multi-domain Fault Manager – MDFM

In the following we present our Multi-Domain Fault Manager (MDFM), which can fulfill the requirements of service fault management and solve the fault localization problem in multi-domain context. The framework of MDFM (Multi-Domain Fault Manager) is illustrated in Fig. 1, comprising Agents on both the server and the client side, and Fault Analyzer corresponding to each domain (composed of Alarm Collector, SLS Monitor and Fault Diagnostic Toolkit). SLS Decomposer and Monitoring Task Generator depicted in Fig. 2 are outside the Fault Analyzer, yet provide fundamental support for service fault diagnosis, thus they are also regarded as important parts of MDFM.

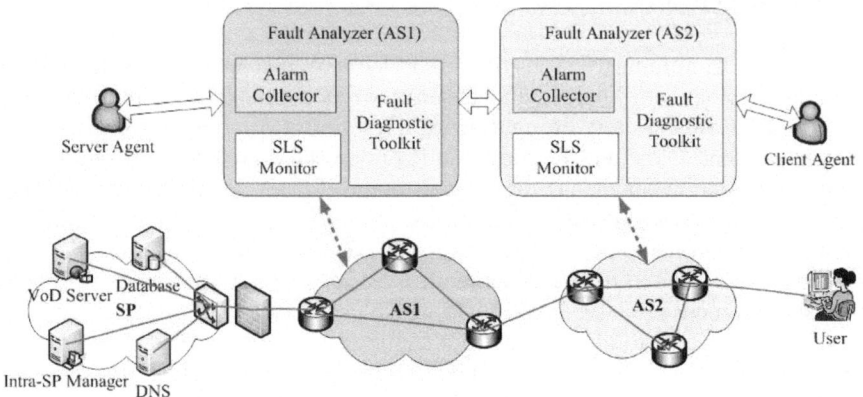

Fig. 1. MDFM Framework

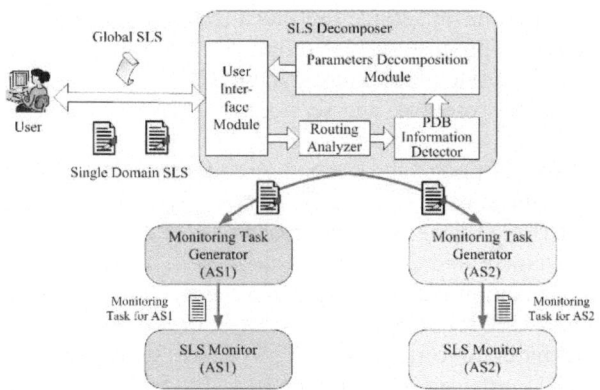

Fig. 2. SLS Decomposer

MDFM is a portion of our QoS provisioning architecture, QoSJava [13], which can provide an end-to-end QoS for users in IP network with heterogeneous QoS mechanisms and network devices. MDFM is responsible for finding out the root cause of service unavailability or performance degradation, and remedying the situation as quickly as possible to guarantee the QoS commitment. User's QoS requirement is specified in an SLS (Service Level Specification), which is the technical part of SLA (Service Level Agreement). If the subscribed SLS is admitted, monitoring tasks are generated and network devices are configured. When a service failure is reported to Alarm Collector, Agents and Fault Analyzers of all domains along the end-to-end path cooperate to find out the root cause. The capability of each component and the whole process of fault localization are described below.

3.1 Agents on Server Side and Client Side

Internet service is hosted in a server or server farm. Faults may occur in server side, including hardware malfunction, unavailable sub services, excess resource utilization resulted from huge amount of request attempts and so on. All these factors may cause service unavailability or performance degradation on the server side. In these cases, SP bears responsibility for SLA violation.

Users use their computers to obtain services. Service provisioning on the client side needs proper functioning of all layers in the protocol stack. Thus Service performance perceived by an end user is also affected by the performance of his computer. When the user executes too many programs, which devour CPU and memory resource, the speed of the computer is lowered down, and the service performance may degrade subsequently. Sometimes the client side has a narrowband connection, but the user subscribes a broadband service. Yet the user may still complain to SP about the service, though actually he is accountable for it.

Therefore, status of both sides needs to be monitored. Agents resided on both sides collect this information, including CPU usage, memory consumption, and number of open files or run state of a process or a thread. Status of the service can be gained by mapping processes and threads to applications [11]. Agent is an entity which reports service status about the server farm or client host. Our framework places no restriction on agent's implementation. In fact, SP can build up his own service management system for internal service fault management, and only needs to provide interfaces for our Fault Analyzer to collect the information of service status. Therefore, current solutions of HP, IBM and other enterprises can be integrated into MDFM. In our prototype, agent seems like a task manager of Windows with extended capabilities.

3.2 SLS Decomposer

When subscribing a service, user needs to sign a SLA with the SP. SLS is the technical part of SLA. User's QoS requirements of Internet service is depicted in SLS in terms of technical parameters quantifying network capabilities. Modern Internet service may delegate some capabilities to other services. In this case, service provisioning involves multiple SPs, which makes the situation complicated. In fact, the service which delegate capabilities can also be regarded as a service subscriber. Thus the scenario is divided into several sub-scenarios consisting of a single SP and a single customer. SLS is signed between each SP-customer pair. We focus on the sub-scenario and call the end-to-end SLS as a global SLS, its formal definition is given by the following tuple:

$$QoSReq \triangleq (SrcIP, DesIP, BW, Class, Delay, LossRate, Jitter, StartTime, EndTime)$$
$$GlobalSLS \in QoSReq$$

The parameters contained in the tuple can be extended as needed. At present, the following items are defined: Source IP Address ($SrcIP$), Destination IP Address ($DesIP$), Bandwidth required (BW), Traffic class of the service ($Class$), End-to-end delay (*Delay*), End-to-end packet loss rate (*LossRate*), End-to-end jitter (*Jitter*), the time when the contract begins to take effect (*StartTime*), and the time when the contract begins to expire (*EndTime*).

Global SLS may traverse several network domains with different capabilities. Thus we propose a PDB (Per-Domain Behavior) based SLS decomposition technique in [14]. PDB [12] is a term from Diffserv and is used here as a representation of network capability, such as delay, packet loss rate and jitter between edge-router pairs in a certain domain. PDB information can be obtained from monitoring statistics. Based on the PDB information, *GlobalSLS* is decomposed into several SLSs corresponding to each domain along the end-to-end path, which are called single domain SLS. For example, the end-to-end path crosses m domains, then *GlobalSLS* is decomposed into m single domain SLSs, $SLS_i \in QoSReq$ $(i = 1, 2, ...m)$, in which SLS_i corresponds to domain i.

If domain i has sufficient resource, SLS_i will be admitted by domain i. *GlobalSLS* is admitted iff all SLS_i in the end-to-end path is admitted. Thus far, user's QoS requirement is divided among network domains according to their network capabilities and each domain is responsible for fulfilling its commitment.

3.3 Monitoring Task Generator

If a global SLS is admitted, Monitoring Task Generators (MTG) will generate corresponding monitoring tasks for all single domain SLSs in the end-to-end path. Because different network domains may adopt heterogeneous QoS mechanisms and equipped with diverse network devices, which lead to different monitoring methods, MTG generates monitoring task for a domain according to its QoS mechanism. *TaskGen* is a function mapping a single domain SLS SLS_i to a monitoring task T_i to be performed in domain i. A monitoring task generation process for DiffServ domain is described as follows, and the parameters' semantics are listed in Table 1:

Table 1. Semantic of parameters

Item	Description
Address	The tuple represents the monitoring location
SrcIP	IP of Ingress router to be monitored
SrcPort	Port of Ingress router to be monitored
DesIP	IP of Egress router to be monitored
DesPort	Port of Egress router to be monitored
Class	Class of the service
Gold	Gold service, similar as EF traffic class in DiffServ
Silver	Silver service, similar as AF traffic class in DiffServ
Bronze	Bronze service, similar as BE traffic class in DiffServ
MonTime	The tuple represents monitoring task's schedule
StartTime	Start time of the monitoring task
EndTime	End time of the monitoring task
Interval	Interval of collecting monitoring data
Param	The tuple represents monitoring task detail
Throughput	Throughput between Ingress router and Egress router
Delay	Packet delay between Ingress router and Egress router
Jitter	Packet jitter between Ingress router and Egress router
LossRate	Packet loss rate between Ingress router and Egress router

$TaskGen : SLS_i \rightarrow T_i$

$T_i \triangleq (Address, Class, MonTime, Param)$ $Address \triangleq (SrcIP, SrcPort, DesIP, DesPort)$

$Class \triangleq Gold \mid Silver \mid Bronze$ $MonTime \triangleq (StartTime, EndTime, Interval)$

$Param \triangleq (Throughput, Delay, Jitter, LossRate)$

As presented in Fig. 2, SLS monitoring tasks will be deployed in SLS Monitors of all domains along the end-to-end path. SLS Monitor in a certain domain is responsible for measuring the performance of the SLS portion resided on that domain.

3.4 SLS Monitor

SLS Monitor in each domain monitors the single domain SLS admitted by that domain. Fig. 3 depicted the detail structure of SLS Monitor. Network Element Monitor employs the measurement approaches built on routers to surveil the network elements in the domain, such as Netflow and SAA provided by Cisco routers. Network Element Monitor stores the data in Monitoring Database. SLS Analyzer, comprising SLS Data Collector, SLS Data Aggregator and SLS Performance Checker, relies on these statistics to assess the service performance and to determine if the SLS is violated. Since the edge router pair is specified in the single domain SLS, SLS Monitor depends on Routing Analyzer to find out the intra-domain edge-to-edge path for the managed service. In practical network, the route between domains is relatively stable, thus we assume that in SLS's period of validity, the single domain SLS traverse the same edge router pairs. For example, single domain SLS SLS_i situated in domain i has ingress edge router $srcER_i$ and egress edge router $desER_i$ for domain i. Routing Analyzer finds out the path for SLS_i in domain i, say $path_i = (srcER_i, R_{i1}, R_{i2}, ..., R_{in}, desER_i)$. The SLS monitoring workflow and the analysis approach are anatomized in our previous work [15].

By SLS Monitor, the approximate causative domain can be localized rapidly. When an alarm is reported to the Alarm Collector indicating a failure happened to the managed service, the monitoring statistics of its related single domain SLSs provides the information about the probable root cause location. If the delay or loss rate between two edge routers in domain i is abnormally high, and other SLS monitors reports normal status, then the root cause occur in domain i with a high probability. In our implementation, the Policy Server provides policies for the delay bound and the loss rate bound in several network load conditions. For instance, in the medium load condition, the delay bound and the loss rate bound are $delay_m$ and $loss_m$, the monitored delay and loss rate in domain i is d_i and l_i. If a SLS traverse domain $i = 1...m$ and reports anomalies, the delay and loss rate in domain $i \in [1, m]$, $d_i - delay_m > \varepsilon_1$ or $l_i - loss_m > \varepsilon_2$, and the delay and loss rate of other domains are within the constraint, then the probability of root cause in domain i is very high.

Network Element Monitor may also report anomalies for SLS Monitor such as link failure, node failure or link utilization threshold is reached. In this case, SLS Monitor analyzes which services are affected by the failure and tries to take countermeasures to prevent the services' performance from deteriorating. For instance, demand Network Management System to initiate a traffic engineering process to change the routing of the service traffic.

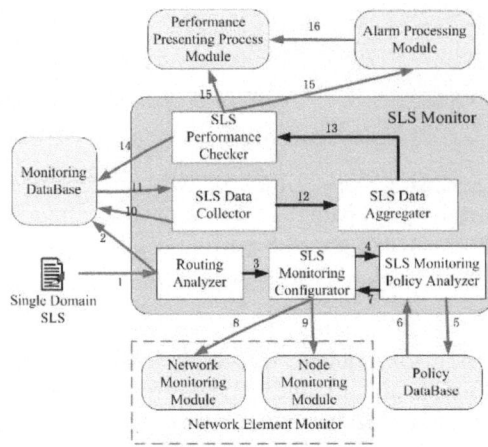

Fig. 3. SLS Monitor

3.5 Alarm Collector

Alarm Collector (AC) is analogous to a complaint department. Service failure alarms are reported to AC indicating faults or congestion happened. Event correlation [5] is used to compress the number of alarms. Then the typical alarms are sent to Fault Diagnostic Toolkit and initiate a fault diagnosis process. In our prototype, alarms are classified into Performance Alarm (PA) and Network Element Alarm (NEA). Performance Alarms are relevant to service performance, such as server is not reachable, server access is too slow, images of the movie cannot be recognized and etc. Network Element Alarms are similar to the alarms of traditional network management system indicating a certain network element failure is observed. Since NEAs have a great impact on service performance, they will be forwarded to SLS Monitor to determine which services are influenced and to take countermeasures, as is called Impact Analysis in [5].

3.6 Fault Diagnostic Toolkit

Fault Diagnostic Toolkit (FDT) starts a fault diagnosis process when alarms are reported. As mentioned in section 2, service unavailability or performance degradation has several probable causes, from server side, client side or the network. Therefore, the fault diagnosis in FDT consists of the following steps:

Server Side Analysis: Obtain the status of server or server farm from the Agent on the server side. If the server side is in a normal condition, go to client side analysis. Otherwise, inform the SP to cope with the service failure.

Client Side Analysis: Get the service status information from the Agent on the client side. If user's computer turns out to be highly occupied or other errors happen on the client side, the user should bear the responsibility. In this case, FDT will inform the user about the faults and guide him to retrieve services of good performance. If nothing is abnormal on client side, go to network analysis.

Network Analysis: Analysis of this stage means that the root cause may happen in the network. FDT retrieves the Global SLS corresponding to the alarm, and delivers it to SLS Monitor. Cooperating with SLS Monitors in other domains along the end-to-end path, SLS Monitor retrieve monitoring data of each single domain SLS. FDT relies on these statistics to determine the approximate root cause position. If an abnormally high delay or packet loss rate is observed in the monitoring statistics of a certain single domain SLS, say SLS_i, the root cause occur in domain i with a high probability. Thus a fault analysis process is initiated in domain i. The network elements along the intra-domain path of SLS_i in domain i, say $path_i = (srcER_i, R_{i1}, R_{i2}, ..., R_{in}, desER_i)$, are likely to be out of order. Sometimes service failure is not caused by these network elements, but by fault propagation from other network portions. Current fault localization techniques can be employed to cope with this case. Thanks to SLS Monitor, the causative region is narrowed down quickly and the accuracy of fault localization is increased.

Though in the initial phase FDT retrieves the Global SLS and the status of each domain in the e2e path, it consumes a little resource because the action only relates to information retrieval, and the fault localization algorithm, the most time-consuming part is not performed. Fault localization is started only after the causative domain in narrowed down. Moreover, each domain is monitored separately and the fault localization is done in a few domains instead of the whole network, thus MDFM is scalable in large network.

4   Implementation

A prototype of MDFM is implemented in a National 863 project of China. As a vital part, MDFM is responsible for localizing the root cause and taking countermeasures rapidly when service failures or performance degradation happens, as a result the user-perceived service down-time is reduced and the service quality is guaranteed. The tesbed is presented in Fig. 4, consisting of five domains with heterogeneous QoS mechanisms and network devices of different vendors. More than 20 routers are deployed in the testbed, and some of them are omitted in Fig. 4 to improve visibility. Fault Analyzer is deployed in each domain.

When Video Conference (Netmeeting) service is ongoing, interface 172.16.12.0 is manually disabled and enabled several times to simulate a link malfunction. To produce a congestion situation and cause performance degradation, we use RouterTest instrument manufactured by Agilent and Iperf [16], an open source bandwidth management tool as traffic generators. Iperf injects packets in router 11.11.11.11 and congest link/interface 172.16.12.0. And Routertest generates 256kb UDP packets in the rate of 171.24Mb/s, flooding link 172.16.4.0.

Fig. 5 presents Fault Analyzer's front-end for network administrators to browse the alarms generated by service failures. Detail content of a Performance Alarm is given in Fig. 6, including the alarm type (PA/NEA), subtype (bandwidth_rate/ drop_rate/link_down/...), status (active/cleared/unknown), level (critical/major/minor /warning/ Information) and etc. Bandwidth Usage, CPU usage and packet loss rate of interface 172.16.4.0 in congestion situation is presented in Fig. 7. The administrator doesn't need to handle the alarms manually. Instead, FDT performs fault diagnosis automatically.

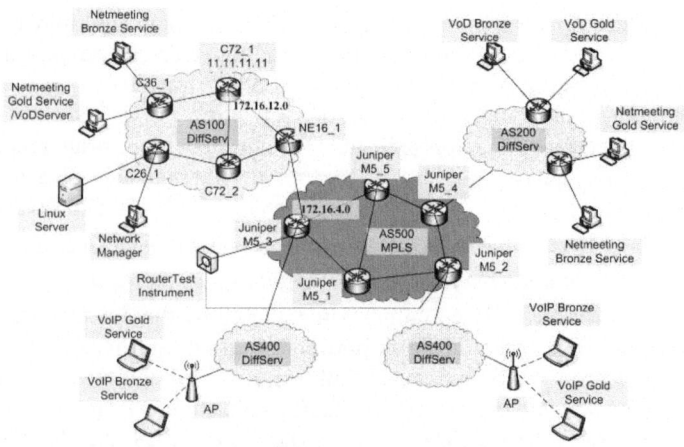

Fig. 4. Testbed

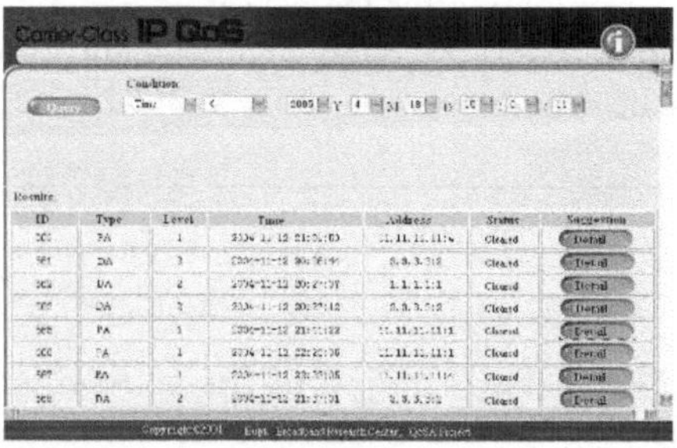

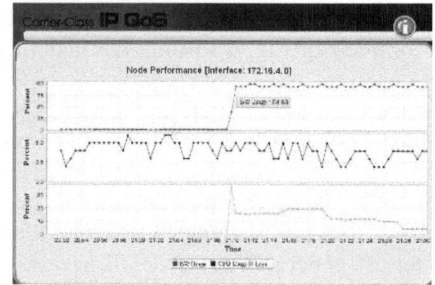

Fig. 5. Fault Analyzer (Alarms Browser)

Alarm ID	565
Alarm Type	PA
SubType	bandwidth_rate
Alarm Level	critical
Source	11.11.11.11:1
Threshold	0.90
Current Value	1.00
Time	2004-11-12 21:11:22
Device Type	
Repeat Times	1
Status	cleared

Fig. 6. A Performance Alarm Example

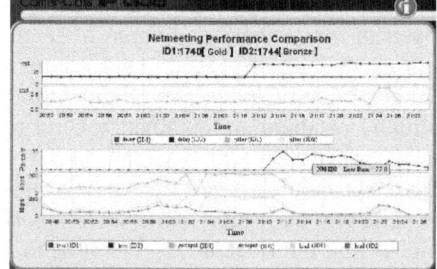

Fig. 7. Interface Usage in Congestion

Fig. 8. Netmeeting SLS Monitoring Result

Fig. 8 depicts the performance of Netmeeting service in Gold and Bronze aggregate when congestion happens. Fault management is performed for Gold service but not for Bronze service. From top to bottom, the five diagrams illustrate delay, jitter, packet loss rate, goodput, and network element load. Before the background traffic is generated, their performances are almost the same. But after the traffic is injected to the network, performance alarm of Gold service is reported to MDFM. Based on the SLS monitoring statistics, Fault Analyzer narrows down the causative regions to $AS100$ and $AS500$, and finds out that the root cause is link congestion. Then Fault Analyzer takes immediate countermeasures, demanding the network management system to redirect the service traffic to non-congested links. We can see from the curves that the performance of Gold Service is much better than that of Bronze Service. In addition, the artificial interface malfunction will cause fluctuations in the curve of Bronze service (especially in packet loss rate), but the curve of Gold service is comparatively smooth.

Experiments are also conducted for other services such as VoIP and VOD. The results are omitted here due to space constraint. On the whole, our fault analyzer can locate the root cause and take countermeasures quickly, as a result prevents service performance degradation when service failure occurs.

5 Conclusion

Due to the characteristics of Internet service, service fault management has new requirements. We analyze the challenges and propose a multi-domain service fault management framework MDFM in this paper. By SLS decomposition and monitoring based on network capability, root cause analysis of the service failure is focused rapidly on a certain domain, solving the problem of uncertain fault propagation probabilities among domains. In addition, our framework takes both the end systems and network failures into account. A prototype of MDFM is implemented and proves the feasibility and efficiency of our fault management framework.

Security is a necessity for commercial management system. In our future work, security mechanisms will be added to MDFM such as encryption, digital signature and access control to prevent illegal access of the Fault Analyzer. And Agents' abilities will be extended to find out the end-systems' failures.

References

1. Yemini, S.A., Kliger, S., Mozes, E., Yemini, Y., Ohsie, D.: High speed and robust event correlation, Communications Magazine, IEEE Volume 34, Issue 5, May 1996 Page(s): 82 - 90
2. M. Steinder and A. S. Sethi: The present and future of event correlation: A need for end-to-end service fault localization, World Multi-Conf. Systemics, Cybernetics, and Informatics (SCI), Orlando, FL, 2001
3. M. Steinder and A. S. Sethi: Probabilistic Fault Localization in Communication Systems Using Belief Networks, IEEE/ACM Transactions on Networking, Vol.12, No. 5, October 2004
4. M. Steinder and A.S. Sethi: Multi-Domain Diagnosis of End-to-End Service Failures in Hierarchically Routed Networks, Lecture Notes in Computer Science Vol. LNCS-3042, (2004), pp. 1036-1046, Heidelberg: Springer-Verlag.
5. Andreas Hanemann, Martin Sailer, David Schmitz: Assured Service Quality by Improved Fault Management - Service-Oriented Event Correlation, Proceedings of the 2nd international conference on Service oriented computing, November 2004

6. Qinzheng Kong, Chen, G., Hussain, R.Y.: A Management Framework for Internet Services, Network Operations and Management Symposium, 1998. NOMS 98., IEEE , Volume: 1 , 15-20 Feb. 1998 Pages:21 - 30 vol.1
7. Darst, C., Ramanathan, S.: Measurement and Management of Internet Services, Integrated Network Management, 1999. Proceedings of the Sixth IFIP/IEEE International Symposium on Distributed Management for the Networked Millennium, 24-28 May 1999, Pages:125 - 140
8. Deborah Caswell, Srinivas Ramanathan: Using Service Models for Management of Internet Services, IEEE Journal on Selected Areas in Communications, Volume: 18 , Issue: 5, Pages:686 – 701, May 2000
9. Alexandre Bronstein, Joydip Das, etc, Self-Aware Services: Using Bayesian Networks for Detecting Anomalies in Internet-based Services, Technical Report HPL-2001-23 (R.1), HP Laboratories Palo Alto, "www.hpl.hp.com/techreports/2001/HPL-2001- 23R1.ps", 2001
10. IBM Redbook, Business Service Management Best Practices, http://IBM.com/redbooks
11. Rainer Hauck, Igor Radisic: Service Oriented Application Management-Do Current Techniques Meet The Requirements?, New Developments in Distributed Applications and Interoperable Systems: 3rd IFIP International Working Conference (DAIS2001)
12. K. Nichols and B. Carpenter: Definition of Differentiated Services Per Domain Behaviors and Rules for their Specification, RFC 3086, April 2001
13. Xiaohui Huang, Yu Lin, Wendong Wang, Xirong Que, Shiduan Cheng, Li Jiao, Yidong Cui: QoSjava: An Open and Scalable Architecture Decoupling QoS Requirements from QoS Techniques, draft-bupt-qosjava-arch-02.txt, http://www.ietf.org/internet-drafts/ draft-bupt-qosjava-arch-02.txt
14. Xiaohui Huang, Yu Lin, Wendong Wang, Shiduan Cheng: PDB-Based SLS Decomposition in Heterogeneous IP Network, Proceedings of 2004 IEEE International Workshop on IP Operations & Management.
15. Junfeng Xiao, Yidong Cui, Wendong Wang, Shiduan Cheng: A Service Level Specification (SLS) Monitoring System in Multiple Services IP Network, High technology Letters, ISSN 1002-0470, published by Executive Office of the Journal, Institute of Scientific and Technical Information of China, to appear.
16. Iperf, University of Illinois, "http://dast.nlanr.net/Projects/Iperf/"

Real-Time Audio Quality Evaluation for Adaptive Multimedia Protocols

Lopamudra Roychoudhuri and Ehab S. Al-Shaer

School of Computer Science, Telecommunications and Information Systems, DePaul University, 243 S. Wabash Ave., Chicago, IL-60604, U.S.A

Abstract. The quality of audio in IP telephony is significantly influenced by the impact of packet loss rate, burstiness and distribution on a specific audio compression technique. In this paper, we propose a novel statistical-based on-line audio quality assessment framework, Audio Genome, that can deduce the audio quality of an on-going Internet audio for many different codecs under any network loss condition at real-time. Our approach is superior to proposed learning-based techniques in terms of computational speed and ease of deployment. Our extensive evaluation experiments, that include large simulation scenarios, show that our approach is accurate and viable for adaptive real-time audio mechanisms. Finally, we show a deployment of Audio Genome as an integral part of an adaptive rate control mechanism.

1 Introduction

Audio codecs have a diverse range of compression degrees and underlying technologies. The main factors that significantly influence the evaluation of audio quality in IP telephony thus include codec type, loss rate, loss burst, inter-loss gap, delay, and recency [1] [2] [4]. ITU specifies E-Model [5] to deduce relative impairments to voice quality. However, it is a real challenge to establish a framework that derives audio quality on-line considering all of these factors. Such a framework can be highly beneficial for quality monitoring of an ongoing VoIP communication, and can be part of adaptive multi-codec audio control mechanisms that switch and mix codecs according to changing bandwidth and delay conditions to maintain optimal quality.

Audio quality of any speech processing system is generally described in terms of MOS (Mean Opinion Score) [10], the formal subjective measure of received speech quality, which is a real number between 1 and 5, where 1 is bad and 5 is excellent. In contrast to subjective testing, objective testing schemes, such as PESQ (Perceptual Evaluation of Speech Quality [12]) are automated and repeatable speech testing schemes that take into account the subjective nature of human perception. ITU-specified E-model [5][6][7][11] provides a computational model to derive relative impairments to voice quality and to estimate subjective MOS. But ITU provides no analytic methods that can directly measure the impairment due to *random loss* conditions of bursts and inter-loss gaps.

J. Dalmau and G. Hasegawa (Eds.): MMNS 2005, LNCS 3754, pp. 133–144, 2005.

The objective of Audio Genome is to provide a statistical framework that first quantifies the effects of packet loss on various codecs by considering loss bursts, inter-loss gaps and various loss rates. We establish the audio quality as a set of functions that are derived from sufficient data generated from a large set of simulation experiments considering various codecs and a wide range of loss scenarios. Interpolation is used as the modelling technique to accurately characterize the curves representing the audio quality for codecs under any loss scenario. The resulting repository of quality information is used real-time that can assess the expected audio quality for an ongoing communication. Audio Genome, being a statistical approach, guarantees speed, accuracy and less overhead in terms of computation and data storage.

Many researchers have attempted to establish audio quality prediction models based on packet loss [2][3][13], but their work is not as comprehensive and complete as ours. Other researchers have used of neural networks [14][19] in order to provide an ongoing quality based on a set of codecs under various loss rates and distribution. Compared to these methods, our work is of lower complexity and computational delay, that can be directly applied to adaptive multimedia control mechanisms, and is also designed simple enough for easy deployment in hand-held devices. We provide a model of such an application, where Audio Genome is used to deduce the quality score for the current loss conditions in order for an adaptive multi-codec audio mechanism to take proper rate control actions.

Subsequent sections are organized as follows. Section 2 contains the related work. In section 3 we present the Audio Genome Approach. We describe the evaluation and experiment results in section 4, an application of Audio Genome in section 5, and conclusion and future work in section 6.

2   Related Work

ITU-specified E-model describes a computational model to derive relative impairments to voice quality and to estimate subjective MOS. ITU provides the measure of equipment impairment I_e for many codecs under no loss condition [11] and a limited number of codecs under very limited loss condition scenarios [7]. In addition, ITU framework does not directly consider random loss conditions of bursts and inter-loss gaps in measuring the impairment I_e. Ideally, we would like to be able to express I_e values for various codecs in fully analytic form as a function of packet loss and burstiness. However, at this point not enough subjective measurements and their specifics are available by ITU or in the literature.

Many authors have presented extensions to E-model. Cole and Rosenblath [3] described a method for monitoring VoIP applications based upon E-model, where they used curve fitting of ITU-published I_e values for selected codecs for various loss percentages. However, since they pointed out that ITU does not show a complete description of algorithms to generate loss data, they were unable to provide a complete framework of codec quality assessment, as in the case of our Audio Genome approach. In [13], the authors addressed the problem of predicting the quality of telephone speech and classified quality prediction models based on E-Model. But they did not provide a comprehensive study of impairments due to packet loss. VQMon [2] is a non-intrusive passive monitoring system for VoIP using an extended E-model incorporating packet loss and recency effect. It derives I_e values dynamically by solving the Markov model using probabilities of loss from the observed loss. However, VQMon uses a limited "burstiness" model that, for example, does not distinguish between "burst" situation when 3 packets are lost consecutively vs. 3 packets are lost with a gap of 1 or more packets in between each loss pair, these two scenarios producing completely different quality results. A different approach has been taken by training a neural network with MOS for a set of codecs under various loss rates and distribution [14][19]. This approach is less attractive to us because of complexity in training and computational delay, which can be a problem in practical deployment of an online quality assessment mechanism.

Audio Genome attempts to bridge this gap by providing a comprehensive framework for on-line audio assessment that is easy to deploy and can be extended to many codecs. Watson and Sasse [20] have conducted extensive subjective evaluation of audio quality under packet loss compensation in multimedia conference systems. We use PESQ instead, since subjective testing is time-consuming, cumbersome, error-prone and non-repeatable.

3   The Audio Genome Approach

The Audio Genome approach can be described as follows.

o *Generation of audio clips with packet loss scenarios:* We choose a periodic drop framework: we use a wide set of fixed inter-loss gaps (from 300 down to 2 packets) causing increasing degrees of packet loss, with a set of fixed loss burst lengths (1-4 packets) for a large number of short audio clips (9-12 sec) made by female and male voices. For a set of chosen codecs, we drop packets from audio clips using the periodic drop framework.

o *MOS evaluation and observations:* Using PESQ, we compare 'pure' and 'poisoned' audio clips to deduce MOS scores under loss. We also observe the characteristics and behavior of each codec under various packet loss conditions.

o *Validation of collected data:* We compare the results of representative clips with subjective testing and show that what we get analytically is close to subjective test MOS.

o *Codec Quality Function Derivation:* We deduce codec quality functions for the collected data under loss using Interpolation.

o *Online prediction of audio quality:* We use interpolation functions determined in the previous step to deduce the MOS for the ongoing transmission. We use weighted aggregation schemes that calculate MOS values for observed inter-loss gaps and burst sizes, and produce a combined MOS for the session so far.

3.1   Audio Clip Generation with Loss Scenarios

Experiment Codec Set. We choose G.711, as the standard audio compression technique or 'codec', a waveform PCM-16 (16 bit Pulse Code Modulation) coder of bitrate 128kbs [8] with the best quality. In addition, we choose multiple codecs of varied bitrates and underlying technology (Table 1) representing complex coding methods, such as Analysis By Synthesis (ABS) and Codebook Excited Linear Prediction (CELP). Apart from these codecs, G.722.2 (AMR-WB) is a fairly new Adaptive Multi-Rate Wideband codec with multiple bitrates [9] with not much testing results available. We choose 6 out of 9 bitrates of G.722.2 to evaluate how the different bitrates of the codec behave under degrees of packet loss in relation to each other. We measure the audio quality of each codec under no loss (Table 1 column 4) or the 'Pure' MOS, to create a referee for our measurements.

Experiment Methodology. Fig. 1 depicts the packet loss simulation framework. Each original PCM-16 audio clip is encoded and decoded with every codec to create a 'pure' image with no loss, and is compared with the original clip to deduce the 'Pure' MOS. To create the 'Poisoned' clips, we drop packets during encoding with each combination of gap and burst, and decode back to PCM-16. In the Packet Loss Simulator we use a wide combination of fixed inter-loss gaps from 300 down to 2 packets and a set of fixed loss burst lengths of 1, 2, 3 and 4 packets (the most occurring burst sizes as observed in the Internet [1]). We

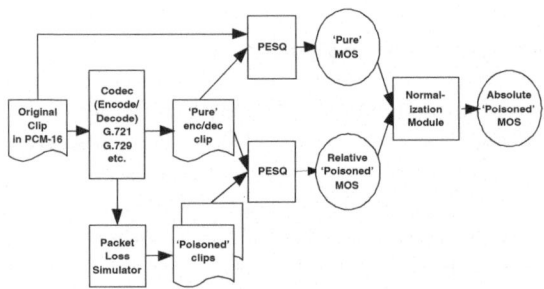

Fig. 1. Packet Loss Simulation Framework

Table 1. Audio Codecs used in Experiments

codec	Underlying technology	Bitrate kb/s	Measured MOS
G.711	waveform PCM 16 kHz	128	4.5
G.721	waveform ADPCM	32	3.04
G.729	ABS CS-ACELP	8	3.646
G.723.1	ABS MP-MLQ	5.3	3.485
GSM FR 06.10	ABS RPE-LTP	13	2.721
G.722.2			
mode (8)	ACELP	23.85	3.469
mode (6)	ACELP	19.85	3.392
mode (5)	ACELP	18.25	3.326
mode (3)	ACELP	14.25	3.1165
mode (1)	ACELP	8.85	2.718
mode (0)	ACELP	6.6	2.421

achieve a wide range of loss rates from 0.3% to 66.7% for the sake of completeness, though loss rates greater than 30% are too high for any meaningful result. We choose fixed inter-loss gaps and burst sizes in order to measure the effect of packet loss on each codec in a precise and controlled manner. We compare the 'Pure' and the 'Poisoned' images using PESQ to deduce the 'Poisoned' MOS. Since the 'Pure' image is an encoded-decoded clip, the comparison produces a quality score relative to the codec score under no loss. The absolute quality is obtained by normalizing the relative quality with the ratio of measured codec 'Pure' MOS (Table 1 column 4) and 4.5, the PCM MOS under no loss, as a scaling factor in the Normalization process.

We choose a total of 24 short PCM-16 audio clips, created by sequentially truncating 4 larger clips, about 1 minute each, spoken by 2 males and 2 females, into 6 short segments of 9-12 seconds, as prescribed by PESQ [12]. The periodic drop experiment is run using every clip for each codec, and the MOS for each gap-burst combination is taken as the average of the MOS for all clips under the same degree and distribution of loss. For each codec, the Data Collection step produces four tables of data, one for each burst size, containing the MOS scores for all possible gaps of 2 to 300 packets. For example, a part of the table for G.722.2 burst size 1 is $\{(x, y)\} = \{..(13, 1.94), (17, 2.32), (25, 2.58), (33, 2.74)..\}$, where x is Inter-loss gap and y is the corresponding measured MOS.

3.2   MOS Evaluation and Observations

We observe that the quality patterns vary from codec to codec under similar loss distribution scenarios. The codecs exhibit some inherent differences in their quality degradation patterns. Fig. 2(a) and (b) and Fig. 3(a) show that the quality curves for bursts of 2, 3 and 4 are close to each other for G.721, G.723.1 and GSM, at a lower level than burst of 1. Thus for these codecs, bursts of 2, 3 and 4 have comparable detrimental effects on quality. This is counter-intuitive, since the common expectation may be that the quality degrades somewhat linearly with increasing burst sizes. Fig. 3(b) shows that G.729, on the other hand, has four distinct levels of quality degradation for 4 burst sizes. In Fig. 3(a) we see that GSM in particular, reacts to bursts comparatively more than others, the burst-of-1 curve being at a significantly higher level than other burst curves, but

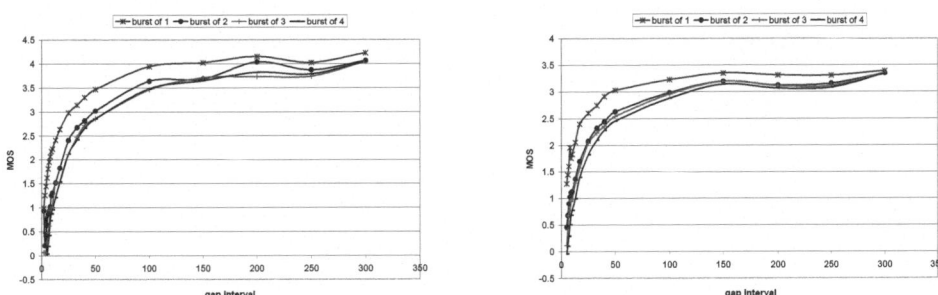

Fig. 2. Observed MOS (a) G.721, (b) G.723.1

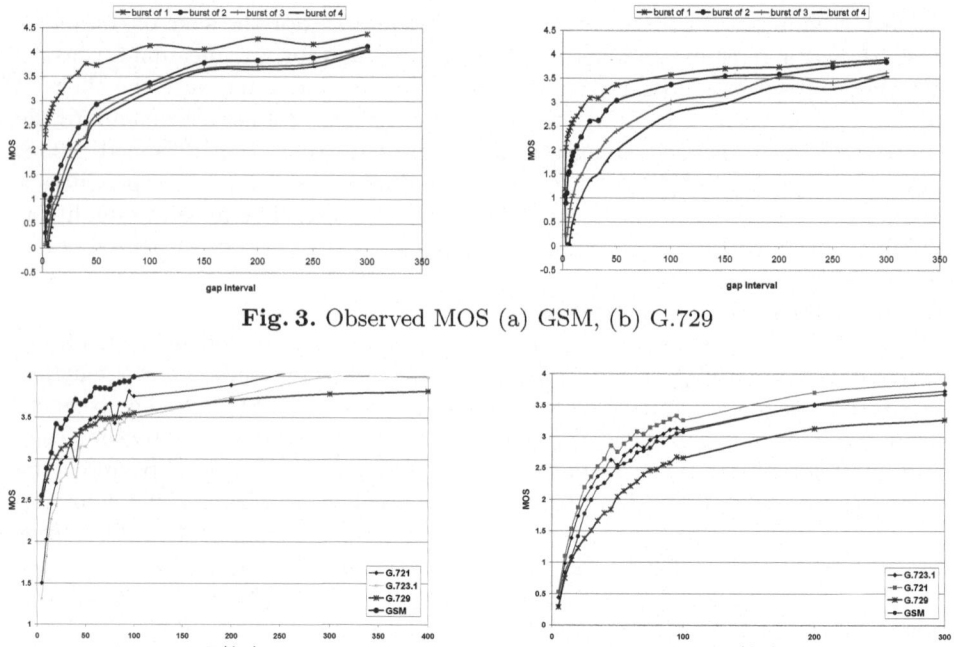

Fig. 3. Observed MOS (a) GSM, (b) G.729

Fig. 4. Comparison of codecs (a) single loss, (b) loss bursts of 4

still manages to maintain consistently better quality than other codecs under all loss conditions. In Fig. 4(a), GSM performs as the best codec in high loss range. G.729 starts well in high loss conditions (2.45 at gap 5, i.e. 20% loss), but performs much worse than others under low loss. Fig. 4(b) shows that all codecs perform worse under high loss bursts than single loss, especially G.729 deteriorates much worse in comparison to others.

For G.722.2, surprisingly, all bitrates show comparable, almost identical quality degradation patterns under all loss scenarios. In Fig. 5(a) we take the average of all observations as the dataset for G.722.2 as a whole codec. This significantly reduces the data that need to be stored for this codec, even though it can be used with multiple bitrates.

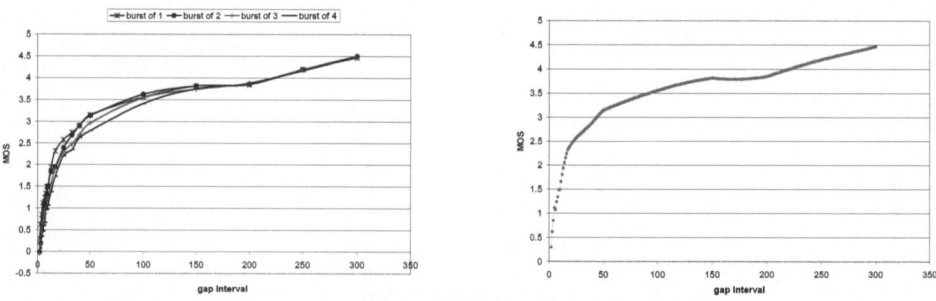

Fig. 5. G.722.2 (a) Observed MOS, (b) Interpolation of degree 2 for burst of 1

3.3   Codec Quality Function Derivation Using Interpolation

We use Newton's General Interpolation Formula with Divided Difference (Eqn. 1) [18] of degrees 1 and 2 to interpolate a MOS score from the scores for the preceding and the succeeding gaps, where x_0 is the preceding gap, y_0 is the corresponding MOS, and $x_1, ..x_n$ are the succeeding gaps.

$$
\begin{aligned}
y = y_0 &+ (x - x_0) * \delta(x_0, x_1) + (x - x_0) * (x - x_1) * \delta(x_0, x_1, x_2) + ... \\
&+ (x - x_0) * (x - x_1) * ...(x - x_{n-1}) * \delta(x_0, x_1, x_2, ...x_n) \\
&+ (x - x_0) * (x - x_1) * ...(x - x_n) * \delta(x, x_0, x_1, x_2, ...x_n)
\end{aligned}
\tag{1}
$$

For example, the MOS for G.722.2 burst size 1 and inter-loss gap of 21 is estimated to be 2.45, interpolating between the values at gap length 17 and 25 using Eqn. 1 of degree 2. In Figure 5(b) the Interpolation data of degree 2, computed between each pair of data points from 2 to 300, fit the observed data for G.722.2 burst-of-1 (Fig. 5(a)) fairly well.

3.4   On-line Prediction of Audio Quality

We use the interpolation audio quality functions determined in the previous step to deduce the MOS for the ongoing transmission. The process can be described in the following steps:

(i) *Loss Pattern Identification*: First, we monitor the loss for the session to keep track of the loss distribution and degree of burstiness observed so far, in terms of single, burst of 2, burst of 3, burst of ≥ 4, and inter-loss gaps preceding loss bursts, in a series of (gap,burst) pairs. This will be input to determine the quality (MOS) so far.

(ii) *Real-time deduction of MOS*: We use the packet loss pattern observed so far to derive the individual MOS values for gaps and bursts using interpolation functions, and combine them to deduce an aggregate MOS for evaluation of the ongoing session so far.

To find the MOS for each individual (gap,burst) pair as follows, we use interpolation for each observed (gap, burst) combination, where we select the stored codec table for the particular burst size, and interpolate the MOS values stored for gaps preceding and succeeding the observed gap to derive the intermediate MOS. We deduce the aggregate MOS score by combining the individual MOS scores using weighted aggregation schemes described next.

Weighted Aggregation Schemes - We first attempt to deduce the aggregate MOS by calculating the average of the individual (gap, burst) MOS values. However, PESQ dampens the effects of individual segment disturbances, after treating each occurrence of packet loss as a disturbance [12]. We mimic the dampening by accentuating the effects of larger inter-loss gaps, as they are analogous to lack of disturbance. We give higher importance to larger gaps to increase their effects on the overall calculated quality. We increase the accentuation in a weighted average scheme, where we give larger weights to better individual MOS

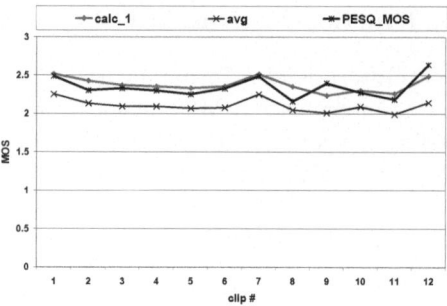

Fig. 6. Comparing Computed and PESQ MOS: G.729

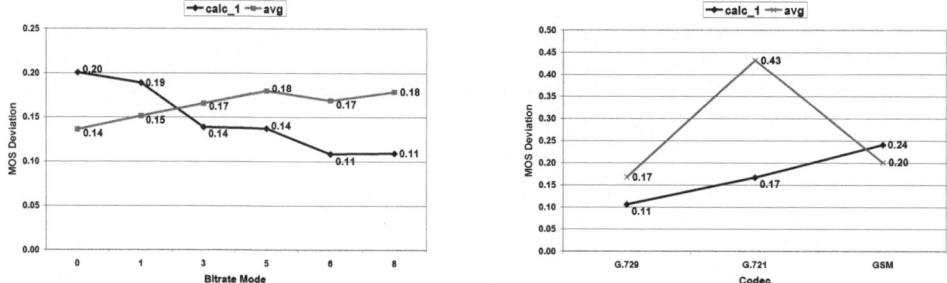

Fig. 7. Accuracy of Aggregate schemes (a) G.722.2 all modes, (b) G.729, G.721 & GSM

values due to bigger gaps, by using a factor of the gap value as the weight. The weighted average schemes avg and $calc\_1$ are computed as follows:

$$avg = (\sum_{i=1}^{P} MOS_i)/P \qquad calc\_1 = \sum_{i=1}^{P} (gap_i/10) * MOS_i$$

where P is the number of (gap,burst) pairs observed so far.

In order to evaluate the aggregation schemes and to derive a unified MOS deduction scheme for each codec, we conducted random packet drop experiments ranging in a wide degree of packet loss ratio (2% to 30%) and burst degree (single burst to burst of 4). Fig. 6 is an example of a randomized test on G.729 for 12 clips with 9-12% loss per clip. It shows a comparison of MOS scores derived using the aggregation schemes, compared with PESQ MOS. Since the goal is to assess the quality degradation during transmission, our aim is to deduce the aggregation scheme for each codec that will predict MOS closest to the PESQ MOS under all loss circumstances. We see that PESQ MOS matches $calc\_1$ closer than avg in Fig. 6. We define the MOS deviation as the deviation between the PESQ MOS and the predicted MOS to determine the measure of the prediction accuracy, as follows:

$$MOSdev = (\sum_{i=1}^{M}(|MOS\_PESQ_i - MOS\_pred_i|))/M \qquad (2)$$

where M is the set of clips in an experiment set. We calculate the error percentage as $MOSdev/4.5$, since 4.5 is the best score possible.

Figure 7 depicts the similarities and the differences of the behavior of the aggregation schemes on different codecs. Figs. 7(a) and (b) show the overall comparison of the aggregation schemes for all codecs. For most of the codecs $calc\_1$ stands out to be the best, except for GSM and G.722.2 modes 0 and 1, all 3 of which have avg as the preferred scheme. It is worth noting that the low bitrate modes 0 and 1 of G.722.2 exhibit a behavior different from the rest of the modes, even though all the modes were very close in quality under periodic loss scheme at the Data Collection phase. Table 2 column 2 depicts the aggregation schemes of highest accuracy for each codec under test. We use this set of schemes in the Audio Genome framework for evaluation in the next section.

4   Evaluation Results

The purpose of the evaluation experiments is to assess the accuracy of the Audio Genome framework under various ranges of packet loss scenarios. Fig 8 depicts the experimental framework we use to evaluate the accuracy of Audio Genome. In the Packet Loss Simulator we conducted sets of random packet drop experiments ranging in a wide degree of packet loss ratio (2% to 40%) and burst degree and distribution. We appended small audio clips spoken by the same person in sequence to create incrementally larger 6 clips for each speaker and poisoned them randomly in order to consider the recency factor [4] of disturbance in PESQ scoring. For each of the 6 small clips as well as 6 extended clips for 4 speakers, 5 loss-degree groups, 3 testing schemes, i.e. a total of 720 clips per codec (a total of 6480 clips), we performed the following: (i) Extract the sequence of (gap, burst) pair data from each "poisoned" clip, (ii) Evaluate MOS_PESQ using PESQ, (iii) Deduce MOS_pred from Audio Genome, (iv) Evaluate the accuracy by computing the MOS deviation $MOSdev$ (eqn. 2) in Evaluation Module.

We calculated $MOSdev$ for all experiment sets and computed the accuracy of Genome under various loss degree and burstiness scenario. We observed that Audio Genome shows good accuracy for the appended clips in particular, which shows that it accommodates PESQ recency factor very well. We present the aggregate and an overall accuracy result of Genome for each codec in Table 2.

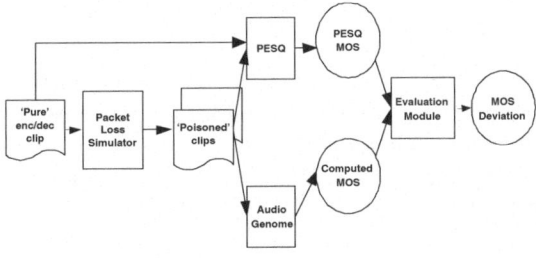

Fig. 8. Evaluation Experiment Framework

Table 2. Test Codec Set: Genome Accuracy

Codec	Overall Scheme	$MeanMOSdev$	Error %	Std Dev
G.729	$calc\_1$	0.11	2.4%	0.07
G.721	$calc\_1$	0.17	3.8%	0.09
GSM	avg	0.20	4.4%	0.11
G.722.2 0	avg	0.14	3.1%	0.12
G.722.2 1	avg	0.13	2.9%	0.12
G.722.2 3	$calc\_1$	0.13	2.9%	0.12
G.722.2 5	$calc\_1$	0.12	2.7%	0.10
G.722.2 6	$calc\_1$	0.11	2.4%	0.12
G.722.2 8	$calc\_1$	0.11	2.4%	0.09

Though the loss rate and degree is varied considerably over the experiments, the mean MOS deviation of Audio Genome for every codec is observed to be in a low range with low error percentage and standard deviation. Hence Audio Genome shows high accuracy under a wide range of loss scenarios.

5   An Application of Audio Genome: A Rate-Quality Optimization Mechanism

We present an example application, where Audio Genome is used to deduce the quality score for the current loss conditions in order for an adaptive multi-codec audio mechanism to take proper rate control actions. The objective of the Rate-Quality Optimization problem is to derive a codec combination set that will maximize the audio quality of the ongoing connection under the current constraints of available bandwidth, end-to-end delay and packet loss. The solution of the optimization problem is a combination ratio of codecs and/or bitrates that ensures the highest possible audio quality under current network conditions.

Problem Formulation. Maximize the audio quality under the constraint of available bandwidth and link delay.
Maximize $z = c_1x_1 + c_2x_2 + \ldots + c_nx_n$
subject to

$b_1x_1 + b_2x_2 + \ldots + b_nx_n \le B$ $d_1x_1 + d_2x_2 + \ldots + d_nx_n \le D$

$c_1x_1 + c_2x_2 + \ldots + c_nx_n \le 4.3$ $c_1x_1 + c_2x_2 + \ldots + c_nx_n \ge 3.5$

$x_1 + x_2 + \ldots + x_n = 1$ $x_i \ge 0, i = 1 \ldots n$

where

$x_1, x_2, \ldots x_n$ = percentage of each codec (type+bitrate) in the transmission mix
$c_1, c_2, \ldots c_n$ = MOS score for each codec under current loss
$b_1, b_2, \ldots b_n$ = bit rate of each codec
$d_1, d_2, \ldots d_n$ = (packet size in bytes)*(encode/decode delay for 1 byte)
B = available bandwidth, $D = 400$ - link OWD.

The rationale behind the constraints is as follows. *Constraint of Available Bandwidth:*The total bandwidth consumption by the codecs, expressed as the sum of the products of bitrate and percentage of each codec, should not exceed the available bandwidth. *Constraint of Delay:*The total codec delay, expressed as the sum of products of encode/decode delay and percentage of each codec, should not exceed the difference of the maximum allowable M2E delay (400ms) and the link OWD. *Constraint of Quality:*The quality sum cannot exceed the maximum quality value 4.3 (the MOS of G.711 under no loss), and should be greater than or equal to 3.5 (lower bound of acceptable speech quality). The objective function is the audio quality to be maximized, and is expressed in terms of the sum of the product of codec percentage and the codec quality score under current loss condition, as determined by Audio Genome.

6   Conclusion and Future Work

This paper presents a novel statistics-based real-time audio quality assessment framework, Audio Genome, that can deduce the audio quality of an on-going Internet audio for many different codecs under any network loss condition. We first provide an extensive experimental framework with 5 codecs G.721, G.729, G.723.1, GSM and 6 bitrate modes of G.722.2, where we quantify the effect of packet loss on the audio quality objectively by considering a wide range of loss bursts, inter-loss gaps and loss rates using interpolation as the modelling technique. For an ongoing communication, we evaluate 2 aggregation schemes to compare the predicted MOS with observed PESQ MOS. We derive a unified set of aggregation schemes for the codecs under test as the Audio Genome Model. We evaluate Audio Genome by conducting a set of extensive random loss experiments with loss degrees ranging from 2% to 40% and a wide range of packet burst distribution. For all codecs, under all loss scenarios, Audio Genome shows good accuracy: 96%-98% in average and never less than 91%. Audio Genome, being a statistical approach, guarantees speed, accuracy and less overhead in terms of computation and data storage. The framework being well-defined and repeatable, can be easily extended with any other codec. As an application, we provide a model of an adaptive multi-codec audio control mechanism that uses Audio Genome to perform rate control and maintain optimal quality.

As a future work, we plan to use multiple regression analysis for modelling the audio quality-packet loss relationships. We also plan to implement an adaptive multi-codec audio control mechanism with Audio Genome as an integral component. We intend to use Audio Genome to provide real-time feedback to end-to-end Internet audio transport protocols in order to increase the reliability and quality of the audio session.

References

1. Bolot,J., Vega-Garcia,A.: Control Mechanisms for Packet Audio in the Internet. IEEE Infocom, San Francisco (1996) 232-239
2. Clark, A.D.: "Modeling the Effects of Burst Packet Loss and Recency on Subjective Voice Quality." IPTel April (2001)

3. Cole,R.G., Rosenbluth,J.H.: Voice over IP Performance Monitoring. ACM SIG-COMM (2001)
4. Cox, R., Perkins, R.: Results of a Subjective Listening Test for G.711 with Frame Erasure Concealment. Committee contribution T1A1.7/99-016 (1999)
5. ITU-T Recommendation G.107 (12/98). "The E-Model, a computational model for use in transmission planning."
6. ITU-T Recommendation G.108 (09/99). "Application of the E-model: A planning guide."
7. ITU-T Recommendation G.113 (02/96). "Transmission impairments."
8. ITU-T Recommendation G.711 (11/88). "Pulse code modulation (PCM) of voice frequencies."
9. ITU-T Recommendation G.722.2 (11/02). "Wideband coding of speech at around 16 kbit/s using Adaptive Multi-Rate Wideband (AMR-WB)."
10. ITU-T Recommendation P.800 (08/96). "Methods for subjective determination of transmission quality."
11. ITU-T Recommendation P.833 (02/01). "Methodology for derivation of equipment impairment factors from subjective listening-only tests."
12. ITU-T Recommendation P.862 (02/01). "Perceptual evaluation of speech quality (PESQ), an objective method for end-to-end speech quality assessment of narrowband telephone networks and speech codecs."
13. Moeller, S., Raake, R.: Telephone speech quality prediction: towards network planning and monitoring models for modern network scenarios. Speech Communication, Vol. 38, Issue 1, pp. 47-75 (2002)
14. Mohamed,S., Cervantes-Perez,F., Afifi,H.: Integrating Network Measurements and Speech Quality Subjective Scores for Control Purposes. IEEE Infocom, Anchorage, Alaska, (2001)
15. Roychoudhuri,L., Al-Shaer,E., Hamed,H., Brewster,G.B.: Audio Transmission over the Internet: Experiments and Observations. IEEE International Conference on Communications (ICC), Anchorage, Alaska (2003)
16. Roychoudhuri,L., Al-Shaer,E., Hamed,H., Brewster,G.B.: Experiments on Audio Transmission over the Internet. Technical Report, April (2002). http://www.mnlab.cs.depaul.edu/ lroychou/techrep.pdf
17. SAS Institute Inc. http://www.sas.com/
18. Scarborough, J.B.: Numerical Mathematical Analysis, 6th Ed., Johns Hopkins University Press (1966)
19. Sun L. and Ifeachor E. C.: Perceived Speech Quality Prediction for Voice over IP-based Networks. IEEE International Conference on Communications (IEEE ICC'02), New York, NY (2002) pp.2573-2577
20. Watson A. and Sasse M. A.: Evaluating Audio and Video Quality in Low-Cost Multimedia Conferencing Systems. Interacting with Computers Vol. 8 No. 3 (1996), pp. 255-275

Policy Based Charging in Multimedia Networks

Brian Lee[1] and Donal O'Mahony[2]

[1] Ericsson Systems Expertise, Athlone, Ireland
Brian.A.Lee@ericsson.com
[2] Trinity College, Dublin 2, Ireland
Donal.Omahony@cs.tcd.ie

Abstract. The telecommunications landscape is undergoing a period of dramatic change. A near term next generation network (NGN) is emerging characterized by a rich set of services and a dynamic and competitive marketplace where innovation and time to market will be critical success factors. Changing consumer-provider relationships, competitive pressures and new e-commerce technologies will accelerate the use of real time payment and prepayment techniques. This will increase the demand for real-time processing of charging data. Powerful, new, charging support systems will be needed to enable real time charging of these new services. Policy based management appears to offer potential solutions.

1 Introduction

Current approaches to IP service charging systems development are an evolution of the traditional PSTN approach to charging. While these systems represent an advance on the state of the art they remain based on the "call data record", (CDR), paradigm and will not provide the scalability and flexibility needed for NGN charging. A more radical approach is needed which pushes elements of the charging process, e.g. rating, down into the network layer and allows for a more distributed and scalable charging system. The central theme of this paper is that the use of programmable networking technologies, specifically *active networking* and *policy management*, can provide a distributed charging system solution which meets the above demands.

Section II examines the evolving NGN and identifies the key issues characterizing its growth and identifies the main challenges it poses for charging and billing systems. Section III reviews the current charging approaches taken in the industry today and identifies why they will not provide the solutions that are needed in the emerging NGN. Section IV introduces the PEACH (Policy Execution Environment for Accounting and Charging) charging system and describes the main features of the system. Chapter V describes the some examples of the usage of PEACH. Section VI surveys the state of the art.

2 The Next Generation Network

The flux in the telecom industry caused by the ongoing technological and marketplace evolution has given rise to a diverse and complex public communications network. Older technologies are gradually being replaced as and when market economics judge

J. Dalmau and G. Hasegawa (Eds.): MMNS 2005, LNCS 3754, pp. 145–155, 2005.
© IFIP International Federation for Information Processing 2005

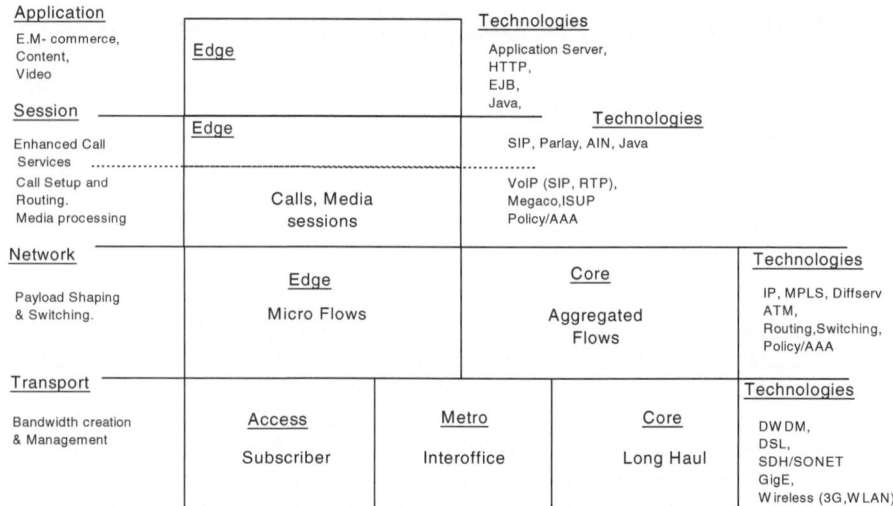

Fig. 1. NGN Reference Network

such updates to be viable. Newer technologies are continually being absorbed into the network. While the rate of change varies in different places, the network *is* nonetheless changing and .a next Generation Network (NGN) is emerging. Technology diversity, a service rich marketplace and fierce competition amongst a wide variety of service providers will characterize this network. The NGN will be complex in all respects. Figure 1 below presents a reference model, after [1] that places the various aspects of the NGN in context.

2.1 Networks and Services

The NGN in reality consists of a network of networks. Access networks enable end-users to gain entry to a service rich edge network. Access networks are based on technologies such as PSTN/ISDN, DSL, cable GSM , UMTS, wireless LAN based on 802.11 and wireless MAN based on 802.16 The emerging wireless network is sometimes termed "fourth generation" (4G) or "Beyond 3G", [2].

The network layer offers connectivity and routing services i.e. users can transfer information to, or between, addressable entities. The NGN network layer will be a *multiservice* network based on IP. This means that the network will provide better service guarantees, or quality-of-service (QoS), to some traffic flows to meet the transmission needs of real-time traffic flows. In order to allow this model to scale it is necessary to maintain flow state only in *edge* networks and to allow the high speed *core* of the network to be state-free.

The multiservice IP network serves as the platform for the provision of a large number of value added end-user services in the session and application layers. The HTTP like semantics of SIP (Session Initiation Protocol) means that the NGN concept of a session is much broader than the usual "telephony call" meaning of the word.

This allows the possibility to create a wide variety of session based services e.g. multiparty gaming while the inclusion of media, enabled by RTP (Real Time Transport Protocol), extends the service creation process even further to enable services based on a combination of media types.

2.2 Service Marketplace

As observed earlier each layer of the network offers services to layers above. The relationship between each layer is essentially client-server and the lower layers are in general unaware of the existence of upper layer services. One consequence of the layering of services and the diversity of network types is the emergence of a variety of service provider types. Examples include wireless ISP's (WISP), mobile Virtual Network Operators (MVNO's), who lease network capacity from large cellular operators and handle subscriber management and billing, and communication ASPs (CASP's) offering enhanced communication services using enhanced service API's. Competitive pressures will lead to specialisation and new business models based on wholesale and partnering relationship between service providers will emerge.

3 Pricing and Billing

A wide variety of pricing schemes is likely to be applied to multimedia services in the NGN. Competition will force service providers to differentiate themselves and they will want to experiment with different pricing models. Current approaches to pricing for Internet access are predominantly based around the *flat rate* model. In an examination of pricing models and cost structures for ISP's, Leida, [3], notes that service providers lose money for the provision of basic access with flat rate charging and that these losses are exacerbated when providing multimedia services. He concludes that some form of usage based pricing may be needed to recover costs and make profits.

Current approaches to usage-based charging are based heavily based on the processing of 'call detail records' (CDR), i.e.. records of usage generated by the network. In legacy approaches to billing these records are normally extracted from the network for processing in a billing centre. There, the CDRs are 'rated' to determine the charge to be associated with the users network session. Invoices are then prepared and dispatched for payment. These approaches are evolving in modern networks in a number of ways. Firstly the volume of CDR's is growing greatly as networks become more complex and more distributed in nature e.g. it is estimated that GPRS networks may generate up to forty times as much charging data as GSM networks, [4]. Secondly the complexity of services e.g. IP based QoS, will demand that billing systems become real time based and that some services become rated in real time in order to avoid fraud. Thirdly there is a continued movement toward the use of prepaid billing, a trend that is anticipated to increase as e-commerce technologies enable more dynamic business models.

These trends are placing new demands on charging and billing systems and leading toward an 'unbundling' of billing systems. Mediation systems are becoming more widespread and more complex in term of functionality as aggregation and correlation of multiple charging records becomes necessary to gain a view over a single user session. Rating engines are being extracted from the billing systems and deployed nearer the network, in some cases as adjuncts to the mediation systems. At the cutting edge specialized hardware engines are being deployed in layer 4-7 stateful inspection switches to rate IP encapsulated traffic, [5]. In the NGN a number of factors will drive the evolution of charging systems including

- The need to be able to rapidly create and deploy new pricing models
- The need to process charging data in real time
- The need to deal with very large amounts of charging data
- The need to be adaptable to new services and network elements

While current trends in charging system architecture are encouraging we do not believe that these approaches will provide the solutions needed. Today's systems are too tightly bound to the use of CDR's and we believe that over the longer term this will prove untenable. Neither will prepaid architectures scale in their current form as the billing system must maintain state for every session and this gives rise to large volume of traffic in a multimedia, multi-layered service network.

To overcome these limitations we propose a distributed charging system in which some elements of the charging /billing system are pushed into the network layer. In particular we propose that the rating engine be collocated with the data metering function. This will greatly reduce the amount of charging data that will need to be moved around the network and will remove the need for CDR's altogether in most cases. This represents a new architectural approach to provide the flexibility and scalability for real-time charging of complex network services. Rather than bringing the data to the processing logic we are bringing the processing logic to the data.

4   Charging Framework

The framework described here is called PEACH (Policy Execution Environment for Accounting and Charging) and is based on complementary fields of programmable networking research viz. *active networking* and *policy based management*.

Active networks are intended to allow programmability at the packet level, [6]. In addition to data, packets traversing an IP network may carry programs that can be executed in active node "execution environments", (EE), thereby introducing new features or services into a network. An EE provides the resources and support that agents need in order to execute, communicate and migrate through the network.

Policy management is a general term that describes how the resources and services of the network are allocated and managed in order to meet the strategic and business needs of the service provider. *Policies* formulate and express these goals in context specific terms e.g. security policies, QoS policies, routing policies, traffic management and indeed charging and accounting policies. A policy is defined as an aggregation of *policy rules* [7]. A policy rule is composed of a set of conditions and a set of actions. The use of rule based policies to manage and control has been spurred recently by the work on QoS policy management in the IETF [8].

The key features of PEACH include

- An architecture for interactive session-based NGN charging.
- A language and programming model for charging policy definition
- An execution environment for policy evaluation and communication

4.1 Charging Reference Model

PEACH defines a functional model for multi-layer charging based on well defined logical nodes. See Fig. 2. The model allows PEACH to cater for charging for any multimedia service session, whether in a single layer, or bundled across multiple

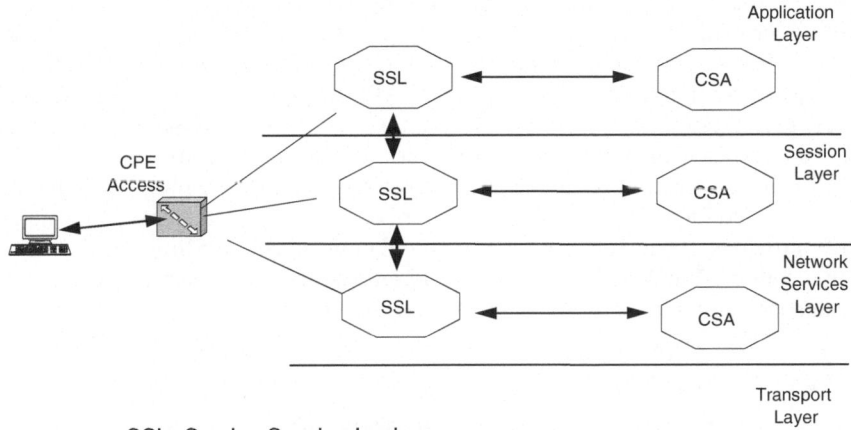

SSL- Service Session Logic

CSA - Charging Session Agent

Fig. 2. Charging Reference Model

Layers. The multi-layer aspect is a crucial feature of the reference model as it recognizes the reality of the evolving NGN as described in section II i.e. the model allows for separate pricing models to be applied at each network layer.

The model is predicated on the notion of a session. For example a VoIP SIP session may use a number of different RTP media sessions and the lifetime of the SIP session may vary considerably from the RTP sessions. The user-session is represented in the model by the Service Session Logic (SSL) entity that controls the set-up and removal of the session. A Charging Session Agent handles the charging for the session. This is decomposed into the three sub-nodes viz. the charge coordination point (CCP), charge analysis point (CAP) and the charge execution point (CEP). The CCP interacts the with the service logic and coordinates all the charging entities involved in the session. The CAP decides which pricing model should be applied and where in the network charging should apply. The CEP applies the actual pricing model in real time i.e. rates the call in real time.

4.2 Policy Language

PEACH provides a programming language, APPLE (Accounting Policy Programming Language), to define charging policies and charging agent task logic. APPLE provides two constructs to encapsulate program content. A *Rule* defines a specific policy for a particular charging situation. A *Module* defines active task logic for charging agents. It encapsulates state and co-ordinates with other modules to provide dynamic charging services. The charging model functional entities introduced above, (viz. CAP, CCP and CCP), are implemented in APPLE as modules. Rules represent static polices and capture business goals and pricing models. They are not standalone executable elements and must be invoked from within a module though rules may invoke other rules. Typically a charging policy is implemented as a chain of rules where the primary, or root rule, is triggered from within a module.

APPLE provides a form of *service composition* typical of programming network languages, [6], i.e. the languages provides hooks to incorporate service components which may be written in other languages into APPLE programs. APPLE distinguishes between *policy parameters* and *policy components*. Policy parameters are charging scheme data types while policy components are service components.

APPLE is a procedural language and can be regarded as a scripting language i.e. it is an interpreted language. As well as standard control flow statements (if, switch etc) APPLE provides statements for data manipulation, event handling and inter-node communication. Modules and rules place and retrieve data on a shared space and from external sources by means of the language statements

```
inp( policy parameter1, ... policy_parameterN);
outp(policy_parameter1, ...policy_parameterN);
```

Rules invoke each other by means of the call statement:-

```
call policy_rule;
```

Modules exchange information between each other by means of the statements

```
send(node-address, application, message,
policy_parameter1... policy_parameterN);

inputEvent{ event1 ->{}; ..eventN->{});
```

A message that is sent from node A is received as an event in node B. PEACH also provides support for code mobility: -

```
move(dest_url, module_name);
start(dest_url, module_name);
```

APPLE separates the act of migrating a code module from the act of activating the module. This gives greater flexibility to the charging architecture as it allows different nodes to initiate each action. APPLE also support the activation of user defined logic by means of:-

```
action(policy_component.called_method,
policy_parameter1..policy_parameterN);
```

```
Module AnalyseCharging {

   // message receiver info.
   application=" aChargingCoordinator";
   message="chargeResults";
   ccpl lrl="bilbo.bagend.shire:39001/ccp";

   // do analysis
   call IpQ_getEFcsch;

   // get results and return info to caller
   inp(chargingScheme);
   send(ccpUrl, application,  message,
        chargingScheme);

   // wait for next message and process
   inputEvent{
           close-> {
                   action(Logger.write, application);
                   exit(); // clean up and die
               }
       }
} //end module
```

```
Rule IpQ_getEFcsch{

   inp(originForCharging);

   switch(originForCharging)
   {
       between(1,10) :
           chargingScheme =#flat_rate;
       between(11,20) :
           chargingScheme=#no_charge;
       between(21,100) :
           chargingScheme=#EF_time_volume;
       in (101,102,103,104):
           chargingScheme=#EF_volume;
       gt 500:
           chargingScheme=#no_charge;
       default:
           chargingScheme =#flat_rate;
   }

   call CheckToD;
   meter="ipQosMeter";
   outp(chargingScheme,meter);

} // end IpQ_AnalyseEF
```

Fig. 3. APPLE Rule and Module example

A simplified example of a module and an associated rule are shown below. In this example a Charge Analysis Point (CAP) node has received a message from a charge coordination point (CCP) requesting analysis for a service session (in this case for the use of a particular IP QoS i.e. Expedited Forwarding) It invokes a rule to determine the type of charging to apply, returns this to the caller and then waits for any further messages.

4.3 Context Support

A context is a PEACH concept that defines a service category for which charging policies and modules may be specified. A PEACH node can support multiple simultaneous contexts. A context defines a family of policy parameters, policy rules and modules and policy (service) components. These elements are defined in an XML context configuration file.

A simplifying assumption in PEACH is that it is necessary only to manipulate primitive data rather than structured data. There are no entities or relationships visible in APPLE rules or modules and thus an information model of charging domain entities is not needed. The context mechanism enables the basic data type vocabulary to be defined and thereby removes the need for a complex object oriented schema.

Policy components must be provided in order to retrieve policy parameter data from external sources. Policy parameters may, in principle, be drawn from arbitrary sources and the PEACH context designer has complete freedom to extract data from any suitable source. This in turn puts the onus on the context designer to provide the appropriate policy component. Each context has an associated policy protocol. The policy protocol is used to transfer data between nodes. Many contexts can use the same policy protocol. PEACH is designed to support different policy protocols. This is done in order to be able to adapt PEACH to multiple network technologies. The data objects in the policy protocol are referred to as *protocol objects*. Policy protocols must support delivery of the data to an agent or handler at the destination node.

There are a number of directions in which future development of PEACH could occur. So far we have concentrated only on the language and policy evaluation. Since PEACH is liable to be used by marketing/commercial then a graphical "user friendly" toolset is needed to facilitate rapid creation of policies. APPLE is intended for deployment on network nodes but there is no conceptual reason why it could not be deployed on handsets. However a more efficient implementation of the language would be needed. This might entail a more efficient interpreter or the APPLE could be compiled to Java or other languages. Finally since there are a number of existing approaches to policy management it could be useful to examine if APPLE could be integrated into a broader policy context e.g. DEN-ng, [7].

PEACH is implemented as a prototype in JAVA.

5   Application to Multimedia Services

One of the main drivers in the design of PEACH has been the capability to enable charging for composite, or "bundled" end-user service i.e. services which may be composed of a number of network services, each of which may have different charging schemes[1]. Network multimedia services are typically bundled services e.g. SIP based VoIP. The use of PEACH to carry out charging of SIP based VoIP has been investigated - cf. Fig. 4 below:

This is based on the use of the QSIP implementation of SIP, [9] and using the implementation of Diffserv on Linux, including the BBTP bandwidth broker infrastructure, [10]. Figure 4 show the interaction between the service session logic (SSL from Figure 2) in each layer i.e. QSIP server and bandwidth broker, and the PEACH charging nodes in each layer viz. charging control point (CCP), charging analysis point (CAP) and charging execution point, (CEP). The charging nodes have been deployed in a variety of configurations on different hosts during this case study. QSIP contains non-standard extension to SIP to enable reservation of network resources. Minor Modifications have been made to both BBTP and QSIP in order to integrate them with PEACH.

The sequence of activities is :

1. The QSIP server receives a request to set up a VoIP session and creates a CCP to handle the charging . The CCP in turn invokes the CAP to determine which type of charging to apply. In the case where real time charging is to apply the CAP instantiates a charging algorithm in the CEP. The CCP returns a "charging_origin" token to the QSIP server to be passed to the Diffserv charging via the bandwidth broker (BB).

---

[1] Different service providers may indeed provide them.

2. The QSIP server then invokes the bandwidth broker to reserve resources in the network for the RTP session . The BB invokes creates a CCP and the charging process is repeated on the network layer. The token is passed to the charging analysis. If real-time charging is to occur then a module is instantiated in the CEP.

3. When all analysis is complete the VoIP session proceeds and charging is carried out in the CEP's. The calculated costs are periodically output to a charge accumulation point (not shown) which could be any of a range of options from a display of charge to a real-time payment system. When the session terminates all agents are removed.

Communication between the QSIP client and the PEACH entities is by means of a 'request-reply' protocol called PRR (PEACH request/reply). PRR is also used for communication between the PEACH entities. PEACH is architected so that any request/reply protocol maybe used.

Charging in each layer takes places independently of each other though the choice of charging scheme is influenced by the charging_origin token. Further the scenario above illustrates a fully distributed PEACH system which is unlikely to be the case in a deployed system for efficiency reasons. PEACH is designed to allow arbitrary distribution but does no mandate it. The architecture described above can be applied to many different types of NGN service and has been implemented also for transfer of MP3 files across a Diffserv network.

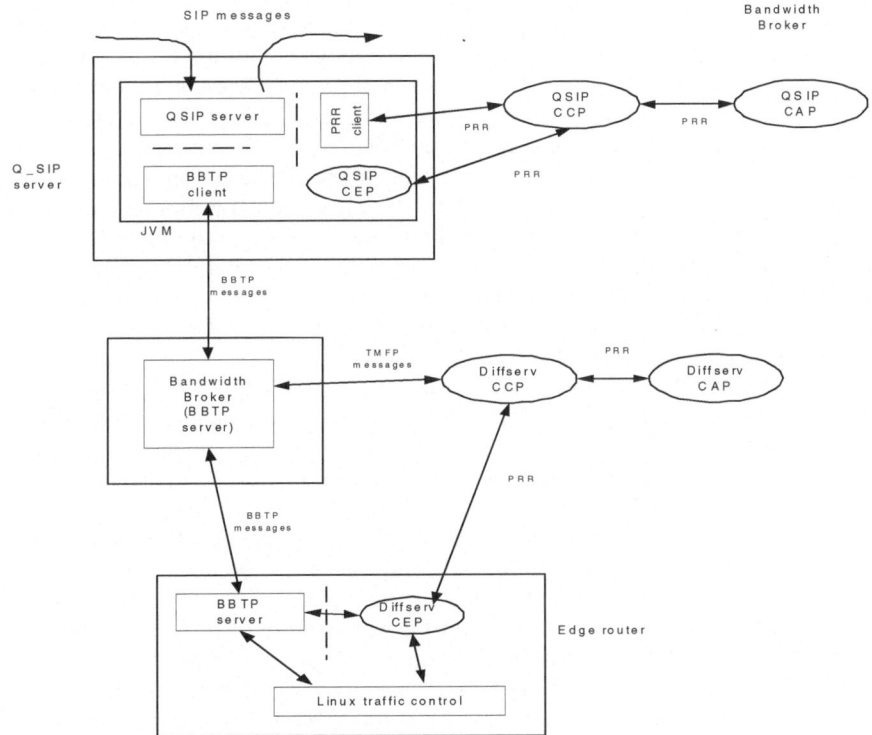

Fig. 4. QSIP VoIP charging

6 Related Work

Travostino, [11] describes an "Active IP Accounting Co-processor Environment" (AIACE) which embeds a dedicated accounting processor in network nodes to perform real time processing of accounting data. Real time processing will allow, prepaid billing, fraud detection, per-flow accounting etc. AIACE allows accounting "plug-ins" to be dynamically loaded onto the coprocessor. Plug-ins represent specific accounting functions or applications and are akin to active applications in the active network architecture. As presented AIACE is primarily an architectural approach and no information is given on how policies are defined or how "plug-ins" are deployed and activated. It is thus difficult to gauge how flexible AIACE is for particular service scenarios. AIACE in its current form is therefore unlikely to provide the flexibility and support for a competitive NGN marketplace.

Briscoe et al. [12], describe an approach to accounting based on "active tariffs". This proposes to push all accounting and charging on to end-customers hosts. Charging is on a per packet basis and tariffs, which are active Java objects, are disseminated to end-users via multicast, a multicast group corresponding to a particular network service. PEACH is intended to provide a flexible, extensible and scalable solution to real time charging in a multi-provider NGN and while Briscoe is also concerned to provide flexibility, his major goal is to use the charging/pricing system for traffic management by means of dynamic pricing. PEACH is a more general and suitable solution for real-time NGN service charging.

Carle, [13], describes a billing architecture that is policy based at all levels and provides the architectural adaptability and policy flexibility to incorporate new technologies. However Carle's work does not provide enough to meet real time charging needs. It is primarily a description of an architecture. No detail is given on how charging schemes can be created or modified.

Bellavista et al., [14], describe a charging approach based on the use of mobile agents, specifically to meet the challenges brought about by mobility in the NGN. Their proposal uses a couple of mobile agents, a configuration agent (CA) and a gathering agent (GA). The CA moves with the user and has responsibility to configure charging related parameters but also to configure any service specific elements that may be needed e.g. media transcoders. When the session is finished a GA is sent along the path to collect charging data that are then transferred to the billing system so that charges may be calculated. This approach addresses only the issue of mobility and does not address the overall issues of charging in the NGN.

Policy management is an active area of research and a number of approaches to policy specification and enforcement have been put forward. Perhaps the best known is Ponder, [15], DEN-Ng, [7] and the IETF QoS policy model ,[8].

Ponder is a declarative language which can be used to specify a broad range of policy types. Ponder also offers facilities for policy grouping and policies can be compiled to standard computer languages such as Java by provision of a suitable compiler back-end. Although Ponder allows for formulation of a wide variety of policies it is not suitable for the problem of real time charging. Charging policies require data comparisons to be quickly and easily made, something Ponder is not designed for. Further Ponder was not designed to be stateful and though it can be event driven it does not naturally lend itself to a stateful event loop charging session controller.

DEN-ng is primarily an architectural approach to policy based network management to facilitate the definition and deployment of a range of related policies. DEN-ng defines a "policy continuum" which represents the communications network as a number of layers with more abstract layers at the upper levels, e.g. service layer, and more device specific layers at the bottom. DEN-ng recognizes the need for a variety of formalisms to express policies. In terms of the DEN-ng policy continuum APPLE is located at the system or network layer..

References

1. Clavenna S. and Heywood P., "Optical Taxonomy", lightreading.com. http://www. lightreading.com/document.asp?site=lightreading&doc_id=3780&page_number=1
2. O'Mahony D. and Doyle L, "Beyond 3G: 4G IP-Based Mobile Networks" in *Wireless IP: Building the Mobile Internet* ed. Dixit S., Arctech House, Norwood, MA 2003 Chap. 6 pp 71-86.
3. Leida. B.A," A Cost Model of Internet Service Providers: Implications for Internet Telephony and Yield Management" , M. Sc. Massachusetts Institute of Technology, Feb 1998.
4. Sur A, "Technical Tutorial: Mediation Device Requirements for GPRS", *Billing World*, vol. 7 no. 6 June 2001, pp 100-107
5. "Encharge ", www.p-cube.com/products/encharge
6. Calvert K.L. et al. "Directions in Active Network".*IEEE Network* Oct. 1998
7. Strassner J., "Policy Based Network Management- Solutions for the Next Generation", ", Morgan-Kaufmann, Amsterdam 2003
8. Moore B. et al., "Policy Core Information Model – Version 1 Specification", IETF RFC 3060 Feb. 2001, www.ietf.org
9. Salsano S. and Vetriani L., "QoS and Policy Control by means of COPS to support SIP based Applications" *IEEE Network* Mar/Apr 2002
10. "Bandwidth Broker Transfer Protocol" Revision 0.3, British Columbia Institute of Technology, Group for Advanced Information Technology, Nov. 1998
11. Travostino F., "Towards an Active IP Accounting Infrastructure",., *Proc. 3rd IEEE Conference on Open Architectures and Network Programming, OPENARCH 2000*, Tel Aviv, Israel, March 2000
12. Briscoe B. et al., "Lightweight Policing and Charging for Packet Networks,". , *Proc. IEEE 3rd Conference on Open Architectures and Network Programming, OPENARCH 2000* Tel Aviv, Israel, March 2000
13. Carle G. et al. "Policy Based Accounting", IRTF Internet Draft Feb 2002, <draft-irtf-aaaarch-pol-acct-04.txt>
14. Bellavista P, Corradi A and Vecchi S, "Mobile Agents for Usage-based Accounting in Wireless Ubiquitous Networks", WOA2002 University of Milan-Bicocca, November 2002.
15. Sloman S. and Lupu E., "Security and Management Policy Specification", IEEE *Network* March 2002

Application-Level Middleware to Proactively Manage Handoff in Wireless Internet Multimedia

Paolo Bellavista, Antonio Corradi, and Luca Foschini

Dip. Elettronica, Informatica e Sistemistica, Università di Bologna,
Viale Risorgimento 2, 40136 Bologna, Italy
{pbellavista, acorradi, lfoschini}@deis.unibo.it

Abstract. New deployment scenarios tend to consider the requirement of session continuity for service provisioning, especially multimedia streaming, to limited heterogeneous portable devices roaming among wireless localities. In particular, multimedia streaming should not experience any interruption while clients roam in wired-wireless integrated networks based on the standard best-effort Internet. The paper proposes an application-level middleware approach to proactively overcome Wi-Fi handoff and maintain multimedia session continuity in the wireless Internet by exploiting mobile proxies running on the wired network. Mobile middleware proxies locally support resource-limited clients, avoid packet losses during handoffs, pre-fetch local buffers with multimedia contents before handoff occurrence, and possibly reconfigure/renegotiate ongoing sessions after handoffs. Experimental results show that, notwithstanding the application-level implementation, mobile proxies can avoid streaming discontinuities with good efficiency in wireless-wired integrated networks even if their pro-activity is based on simple and lightweight handoff prediction techniques.

1 Introduction

A more and more common deployment scenario is the *Wireless Internet* (WI), where wireless solutions enhance the accessibility to the traditional wired Internet and to its services via IEEE 802.11 Access Points (APs) that work as bridges between fixed hosts and wireless devices [1, 2]. The popularity of personal portable devices and the increasing availability of WI APs are suggesting the provisioning of distributed services to a wide variety of mobile terminals, even with heterogeneous and limited resources. Even if device and network capabilities are growing, the development of WI applications is still a very challenging task, in particular when dealing with continuous services, i.e., applications that distribute time-continuous flows with Quality of Service (QoS) requirements, such as in the case of audio/video streaming [3].

One of the most challenging issues in supporting WI continuous services is the avoidance of flow interruptions when clients roam from one wireless locality to another, e.g., during handoffs between different AP coverage areas. We distinguish two types of datalink handoff: i) hard handoff, where the destination cell AP takes over from the origin cell AP reactively in a relay mode, by minimizing signaling overhead, but by increasing latency and packet losses; and ii) soft handoff that proactively activates the new data path to the destination AP before client disconnection from the

J. Dalmau and G. Hasegawa (Eds.): MMNS 2005, LNCS 3754, pp. 156–167, 2005.

origin cell [4]. The Wi-Fi standard specification adopts hard handoff, thus complicating the development and deployment of continuous services [5].

All the above issues call for novel middlewares aimed at providing session continuity to multimedia services and capable of operating service management operations to fit the dynamic properties of deployment environments, in particular to overcome handoff-specific continuity issues. The paper proposes an innovative mobile middleware integrated with an original lightweight mechanism for Wi-Fi handoff prediction. One of the paper core claims is the opportunity of working at the application level to dynamically handle handoffs in WI multimedia: only middleware infrastructures that can access application-level information (characteristics of exchanged multimedia flows, user preferences, installed software, ...) can effectively take over client/server responsibility of application components and can perform the challenging operations of handoff handling on their behalf, thus facilitating the design and implementation of WI multimedia applications. In addition, we claim the suitability of middleware solutions based on mobile proxies that work as intermediate entities to assist and support client devices in scarcity of resources: this architecture guideline permits to introduce proxies whenever in need over the service path, to flexibly handle and adapt multimedia flow delivery without leaving the whole management burden to client/server end-nodes; mobile proxies can predict client handoff in advance and migrate to follow client movements, by exploiting pre-fetched data to sustain streaming until the completion of needed flow re-directions.

The paper describes a proactive handoff management solution integrated with our Mobile agent-based Ubiquitous multimedia Middleware (MUM)[1], an application-level proxy-based infrastructure to support both streaming quality adaptation and session continuity, independently of WI client roaming [6]. On the one hand, MUM performs quality of service management by exploiting mobile middleware proxies dynamically distributed to intermediate nodes along the activated service paths between clients and servers. On the other hand, MUM provides session continuity by predicting client movements and by proactively activating service path reconfiguration to accelerate application-level handoff. The paper also presents a thorough evaluation of the handoff management performance of the MUM middleware in a wide-scale simulated deployment environment, by taking into consideration the different handoff situations, i.e., micro/macro/global handoffs, as described in the following. The reported experimental results show that, notwithstanding the portable Java-based implementation, MUM prediction-based handoff management avoids streaming interruptions in most common deployment scenarios.

2   Design Guidelines for Handoff Management Infrastructures

We claim the need for application-level middlewares based on the introduction of mobile proxies to ease the design and implementation of WI continuous services by providing flexible solutions to crucial mobility issues, e.g., application-specific caching and filtering, QoS management, and interoperable session control (see also the

---

[1] Additional information, experimental results, and the prototype code of the MUM middleware are available at `http://lia.deis.unibo.it/Research/MUM/`.

related work section) [7, 8]. Let us introduce some of the benefits that application-level support solutions can provide with an example. Consider two users, Alice and Bob, who have subscribed for the same video broadcasting service to watch daily news while commuting by bus. The video broadcasting service is delivered through a 4G network composed by Wi-Fi hotspots, deployed at the bus station and at bus stops, and by a UMTS infrastructure deployed over the traversed city districts. Bob accesses the service from his full-fledged laptop and has subscribed for gold quality, i.e., maximum resolution and best possible network QoS, while Alice exploits a Personal Digital Assistant (PDA) and has subscribed for a bronze quality level (small frame size and no QoS guarantees at all). One day, Alice and Bob are sitting on the same bus when a vertical handoff between the Wi-Fi and the UMTS networks occurs due to the bus leaving the Wi-Fi enabled station: application-level middlewares can react to the discontinuity in available bandwidth by properly adapting provisioning depending on the differentiated profiles of Alice and Bob: Bob's video frames should become smaller while he continues to access the broadcasting service; Alice should have her service downscaled to only-audio streaming.

We claim that middlewares should relieve client/server application components from the above, possibly complex, handoff handling operations. Moreover, handoff management should be realized at the application layer since only this abstraction level offers the needed flexibility and expressiveness. Let us state that lower-layer handoff management solutions could neither take service-dependent decisions nor perform management operations selectively, e.g., only for WI multimedia.

In addition, handoff management middlewares should be aware of the runtime characteristics of provisioning environments: for instance, Wi-Fi implements hard handoff, while other networks, as UMTS, implement soft handoff (during handoffs, UMTS clients can receive packets from both the old and the new AP); by focusing on Wi-Fi networks, handoff duration greatly depends on client card implementation [9]. The application level is the most suitable to provide middleware supports with full context awareness [10]. Moreover, handoff management can benefit from multimedia flow tailoring to fit provision-time changing characteristics of execution environments: when Alice and Bob roam from the Wi-Fi network to the UMTS one, the handoff management middleware should degrade the broadcast QoS to fit UMTS bandwidth. We claim that middleware components should mediate and manage service adaptation: only an infrastructure at the application-level can properly exploit applicative protocols such as RealTime Protocol (RTP), Session Initiation Protocol (SIP), and RealTime Streaming Protocol (RTSP), to adjust service provisioning by acting as a mediator between clients and servers [7, 11].

Moreover, we claim that handoff management should exploit the introduction of mobile proxies. The current Internet is already populated by several kinds of proxies (for caching, authentication, re-directing, ...) and we claim that proxy-based architectures will spread more and more in the future as the most suitable design choice in the WI era. The exploitation of intermediate proxies is an effective alternative to designing and implementing fat clients/servers, specialized for peculiar characteristics of the provisioning environment. Proxy-based architectures can act as the middleware glue to extend client/server capabilities with new facilities, as in the addressed case of proactive handoff management, which should otherwise be replicated for each specific application, with higher development and deployment costs.

In particular, by focusing on WI multimedia, we claim the suitability of middleware proxies running on nodes along the path between clients and servers, and of dynamically injecting the management logic necessary for handoff handling and continuous service adaptation. Proxy-based middleware solutions can enhance the traditional client-to-server interaction model by decoupling the two endpoints with the insertion of an active service path [6]. Active service paths show their effectiveness when there is the need for runtime reconfiguration of only limited path segments and for decentralizing management operations to intermediate nodes traversed by service flows, thus improving scalability [12, 13]. In open and dynamic scenarios, it is crucial to build active paths only where and when needed, depending on the location of client requests and on client mobility during service sessions. To this purpose we claim the need for innovative code mobility techniques to dynamically migrate, install, and discard middleware proxy components at provision time, thus avoiding unnecessary static pre-installation; mobile agents are an effective technology to enable the dynamic mobility of support components depending on application requirements [14].

By concentrating on WI multimedia streaming, mobile proxy-based solutions can also reduce client-to-server signaling when handoffs occur. Continuous services usually adopt connection-less protocols such as UDP, and manage data re-transmissions directly at the application level to react to high jitter and packet losses. In the fixed Internet, the deriving flow-control signaling is fairly limited and present only during network congestions/failures. On the contrary, Wi-Fi hard handoff causes relevant packet losses and is perceived as a network failure at the application level; in traditional multimedia systems, that may produce non-negligible client-to-server signaling and wrong perceptions of client situations at server side. For instance, Internet radios degrade the provided QoS level by switching to lower quality flows, while Video on Demand (VoD) services require client re-buffering after a handoff-driven congestion, thus interrupting flow visualization for the duration of client re-buffering. Middleware proxies located at wired network edges close to their served wireless clients can split the direct client/server connection and significantly reduce both signaling traffic on the service path and QoS degradation at client. It is crucial to have mobile proxies that can follow client roaming at provision time to maintain co-locality with their supported devices during service sessions.

3   Proxy-Based Proactive Handoff Management

The section first introduces the different handoff types managed by the MUM middleware, and then focuses on the architecture of the proactive session handoff facility.

3.1 Handoff Types and Countermeasures for Multimedia Continuity

The WI consists of several networks that usually cover a large geographical area, each of them consisting of several sub-networks. It is possible to distinguish three types of handoff: micro, macro, and global handoff [4].

Micro handoff (intra-subnet handoff) relates to clients that roam between two different Wi-Fi cells without changing IP addresses, i.e., before and after handoff clients are attached to the same subnets. Nonetheless, given that Wi-Fi handoff is hard, micro handoff may produce packet losses when clients switch from origin to target APs. In particular, it includes three main phases: handoff detection, target AP search, and AP re-association [15]. The last phase is the fastest (usually a few ms) and is almost constant for different vendors [9]; the other two phases are longer and vendor-dependent, since IEEE 802.11 only specifies the mechanisms to implement them, by leaving unspecified their combination and durations. For instance, in a testbed composed by Cisco APs and Cisco/Orinoco Wi-Fi cards, different implementations of IEEE 802.11b probing algorithm largely influence AP search duration (about 400ms for Cisco and 60ms for Orinoco cards) [9]; the handoff discovery phase, i.e., the client decision to start or not a new AP search, is the longest and less standardized process, and may last from 1000ms to 1600ms depending on card implementation [15]. Therefore, the total micro handoff duration may even reach 2s, thus being incompatible with the jitter/packet loss requirements of usual WI continuous services.

Macro handoff (intra-domain handoff) refers to clients that move between two Wi-Fi cells attached to different IP subnets and includes network-layer handoff, i.e., client IP address change. In particular, macro handoff duration exceeds micro handoff of the time needed to get new IP addresses at target subnets. Widespread solutions for wired networks, such as Dynamic Host Configuration Protocol (DHCP), requires some seconds to complete address re-configuration and do not fit WI continuous services.

Global handoff (inter-domain handoff), instead, regards mobile clients that roam between two Wi-Fi cells attached to different Internet domains. This requires not only address change, but also some additional time to perform authentication, authorization, and accounting operations, usually necessary when entering a new access domain. Moreover, domain change could also require session re-configuration: for instance, in the new domain there could be a new server, functionally equivalent to the one used in the origin domain, with better QoS and/or lower pricing.

Client-side data buffering is a common solution in streaming over wired networks to smooth possible congestions and packet losses along client-to-server paths. Nonetheless, we claim the unsuitability of traditional buffering, i.e., only pre-fetching chunks of multimedia flows at clients, to support multimedia continuity during Wi-Fi handoffs. In fact, macro and global handoffs require service path reconfiguration to redirect provisioned flows to new client addresses and service reconfiguration time can be long (client-to-server roundtrip time, redirection request processing time at server, ...), thus imposing too heavy data buffering at clients. Moreover, if reconfiguration time is longer than handoff, all data transmitted by the server to client old addresses are wasted and must be re-sent, while they could be locally moved from the last client location to the new one until data redirection is completed. In addition, even in the case that client-side buffers could store enough data to sustain streaming continuity, long disconnection periods (up to 2s) could produce misleading signaling to the server and QoS degradation. Finally, when providing WI live streaming, it is not possible to command server flow rewinding and, consequently, long handoff durations necessarily produce streaming gaps as long as the difference between Wi-Fi disconnection time and client-side buffer duration. In any case, let us point out that WI client-side buffers should be as limited as possible since most clients are expected to have limited memory/storage capabilities.

3.2 MUM Proxies for Proactive Handoff Management

The architecture of the MUM infrastructure to dynamically activate intermediate nodes for quality control and adaptation of WI multimedia streaming has already been presented elsewhere [6]; in the following, the paper originally focuses on MUM proactive management of Wi Fi micro, macro, and global handoff. MUM grants service continuity by performing proactive handoff management at the application level, with WI-multimedia-specific protocols that aim at minimizing server signaling and client requests for flow redirection. MUM provides a proxy-based middleware support for micro, macro, and global handoffs by splitting client-server direct interaction and managing handoff at intermediate nodes. In addition, MUM employs an original two-level buffering technique to store data flows at both clients and proxies. Two-level buffering interacts with our lightweight Wi-Fi handoff prediction technique (Received Signal Strength Indication-Grey Model - RSSI-GM) that distinguishes which type of handoff is likely to occur with an appropriate advance time depending on the handoff type; the extensive presentation of our RSSI-GM solution is in [16]. MUM proxies interwork with lightweight MUM client stubs, which are the only middleware components executing on client devices and in charge of transparently interfacing to even legacy multimedia players and of executing the RSSI-GM prediction algorithm.

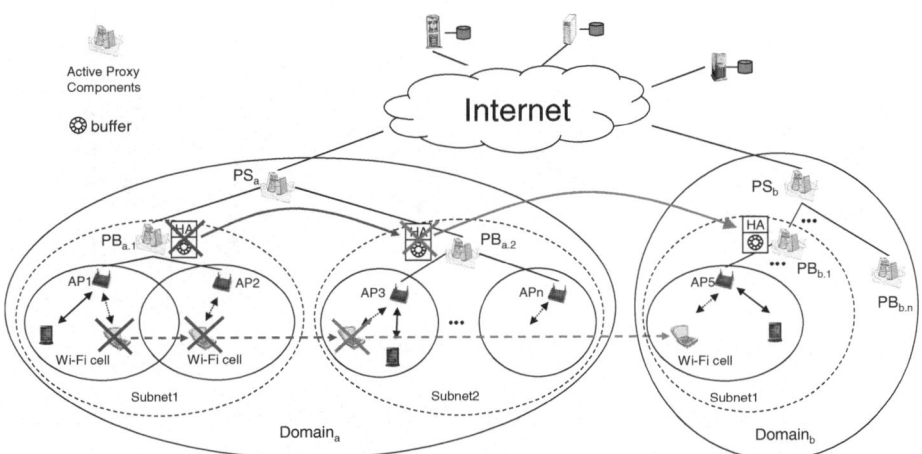

Fig. 1. MUM Handoff Management Architecture

In addition to client-side buffering, MUM originally proposes to exploit a second level of buffering proxies that use the storage resources of workstations on the wired network. Second-level buffers receive and store incoming flows during client disconnection, thus avoiding service interruptions, frame losses, and server re-transmissions. They are capable of promptly filling up client buffers at reconnection after handoff; they help in enabling streaming continuity also for clients with very limited memory resources; they interact with MUM handoff predictor to proactively increase their size only when handoffs are likely to occur. Besides, even in normal situations (far from handoffs) second-level buffers can improve visualization quality: they enable local retransmissions to client-side buffers in the case of packet losses due to the fragile connectivity of last wireless hops. In addition, second-level buffers hosted on the wired network can widen the accessibility of multimedia services by alleviating power consumption on limited clients [17]. MUM devices also continue to host first-level buffers with limited size, as commonly employed to improve user-perceived quality, by smoothing network jitter effects: client-side buffers are crucial to provide multimedia frames to local players in the time interval of client disconnection during handoffs.

With a finer level of detail, MUM supports handoff management by activating a mobile proxy (the Handoff Agent – HA) at the Proxy Buffer (PB) node in the service path between client and server (see Figure 1). MUM automatically instantiates a new HA, implemented as a mobile agent, when a client starts a streaming session: once activated, HA performs proactive handoff operations and manages second-level buffering for its client for the whole session duration, by executing in its proximity and migrating to follow it in the case of subnet/domain change.

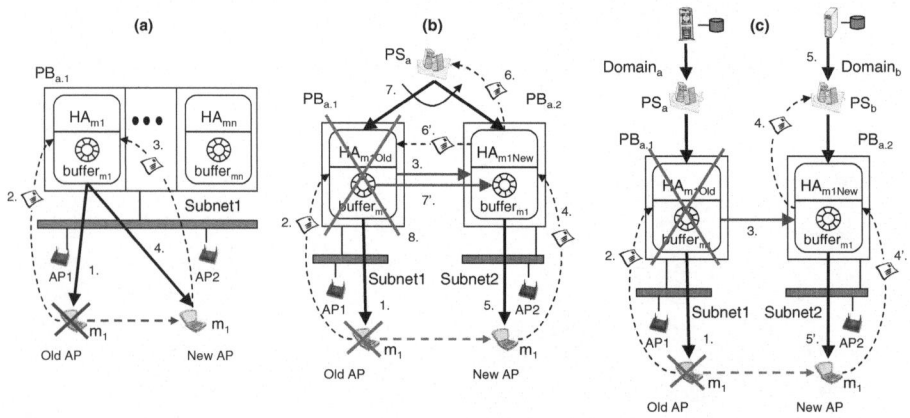

Fig. 2. Micro (a), macro (b), and global (c) handoff procedures

MUM micro handoff management starts when RSSI-GM foresees a client handoff. Triggered by handoff prediction notification (step 2 in Figure 2a), HA increases the size of its second-level buffer to store all data arriving from the server during micro handoff disconnection; second-level buffer size depends on micro handoff duration and, consequently, on several parameters related to client Wi-Fi card implementation. When the client is disconnected from its origin AP and not yet re-connected at the destination one, HA continues to buffer incoming streams as in normal conditions, while the player uses client-side buffered frames to sustain multimedia rendering. After reattachment at destination, the client stub notifies HA, thus causing the retransmission of lost frames (steps 3 and 4 in Figure 2a). Let us note that PB hosts HAs for all clients currently connected to the same subnet.

Macro handoff extends micro handoff with client address change, as shown in Figure 2b. By following the design principles of Section 2.2, MUM locally manages service reconfiguration and distributes handoff management load by exploiting code mobility. Local reconfiguration is made possible by introducing an indirection point (the Proxy Switch – PS) in the client-to-server service path: PS works as an application-level router that forwards the multimedia flow to the HA current location. MUM micro and macro handoff management operations proceeds in the same way until handoff prediction. At the notification of a macro handoff, the old HA enlarges its second-level buffer, clones itself, sends its clone (new HA) with a copy of the current second-level buffer to the new PB (step 3 in Figure 2b), and continues filling up its buffer. Once attached to the new subnet and obtained a new IP address, the client stub triggers the retransmission of un-received multimedia frames due to temporary disconnection (step 4). As a consequence, the new HA starts refilling client buffer (step 5), commands PS to redirect the flow to itself (step 6), and asks the old HA for the multimedia data received after its migration (by indicating the last frame in the new second-level buffer, step 6'). After sending that data, the old HA terminates (steps 7' and 8); the new HA, instead, reconstructs the flow by merging data from old HA and PS, and forwards the merged stream to the stub. Let us note that the protocol requires no PS-side buffering and produces no signaling/transmissions unless clients connect to new subnets. Finally, to avoid DHCP long latency, MUM adopts Dynamic Registration and Configuration Protocol for IP address re-assignment [18].

If compared with macro handoff, the additional complexity of global handoff is the possibility and suitability of performing also non-local service path reconfiguration, possibly up to the server node. First of all, adding another indirection point would activate a new PS within the wired Internet core, while MUM aims at deploying its middleware components only at wired-wireless network edges. In addition, MUM has the goal of keeping separated different administration domains, to distribute proxy management responsibilities and to facilitate resource accounting. Global and macro handoffs proceed in the same way as far as the old HA sends its clone towards the new PB. Then, in global handoffs, while the new HA waits for its client, it immediately starts the server re-connection operations to reduce as much as possible reconfiguration time (step 4 in Figure 2c). After client reattachment (step 4'), the new HA refills client buffer while it continues waiting for the flow from the server to merge it with second-level buffer data, as in the case of macro handoff. Let us note that global handoff only requires minimum management between the two domains: similarly to [19], the only system management operation needed is to set logical correspondences between APs in reciprocal visibility at domain boundaries and PB host names, to enable the correct migration of HAs to their destination nodes.

4   Experimental Results

To thoroughly evaluate the effectiveness of the MUM handoff management infrastructure, it is necessary to test the MUM prototype in a wide-scale deployment scenario, i.e., a WI testbed composed by several domains, several subnets, dozens of Wi-Fi APs, and hundreds of served roaming clients. Such a large testbed is difficult to deploy and would require a large number of available mobile users to accomplish valuable experiments; therefore, as many other research proposals in the WI area, we have decided to exploit a simulator to feed the MUM prototype with realistic data about client roaming in a modeled wide-scale deployment scenario. Several wired-network simulators are available, from both academy and industry; some of them also include wireless network modeling but, to the best of our knowledge, none addresses the specific problems of simulating different Wi-Fi card behaviors during handoff and of feeding pluggable software prototypes with simulation-generated handoff data. Thus, we have decided to develop a simple simulator that models user mobility and traversed tracks, calculates the RSSI values of mobile clients, feeds the MUM predictor with those values, and mimics physical/datalink/network-layer behaviors by temporary interrupting streaming transmission during handoffs. The considered WI testbed consists of 2 Internet domains and 6 subnets with 48 Wi-Fi cells; a mix of 600 wireless clients equipped with Cisco and Orinoco cards randomly move with variable speed between 0,6m/s and 1,5m/s; RSSI fluctuation has a 3dB standard deviation.

MUM components are implemented in Java and exploit the portable SUN Java Media Framework (JMF) for RTP-based video streaming and RTCP-based monitoring; in the experiments, we have provisioned H263-encoded VoD flows (frame size=176x144 pixels, and frame rate 8fps). Experimental results obtained in previous work have shown that HA migration and activation at new PBs takes less than 400ms; DRCP lasts about 100ms; macro handoff flow re-direction and merging require about 500ms; global handoff flow reconfiguration requires 340ms for PS interposition and 100ms for RTP streaming activation (with a JMF server); we assume 250ms as roundtrip time [6]. In other words, handoff duration is between 440ms and 1500ms for micro handoff, about 1900ms for macro handoff, and about 2300ms for global handoff.

Among the different experimental results that can provide significant indications about middleware performance, the paper originally focuses on evaluating the impact of handoff prediction on proactive buffer management and, consequently, on the maintenance of streaming continuity. To this purpose, we have measured four primary performance indicators: $Efficiency$ = (PHO/PH)*100, $Error$ = (NPH/PH)*100, $Effectiveness$ = (SH/PHO)*100, and $Continuity$ = (CV/SH)*100. Predicted Handoffs (PH) is the number of handoffs foreseen by MUM predictor; Predicted Handoffs Occurred (PHO) is the number of PH corresponding to actual handoffs in the simulated environment; Non-Predicted Handoffs (NPH) is the number of actual handoffs occurred without an associated correct prediction; Successful Handoffs (SH) are PH occurred when the second-level buffer is correctly sized (for micro handoffs) or when new HA activation terminates before client re-attachment to target APs (for macro and global handoffs); and Continuous Visualizations (CV) represent how many times new HAs have completed merging operations before the termination of buffers from old PBs (this performance figure only applies to macro and global handoffs).

As reported in Table 1, Efficiency and Error experimental results show that short-term predictions are more challenging for the MUM middleware than long-term ones. That primarily depends on the characteristics of RSSI-GM prediction, which exploits past RSSI values to estimate future client position, and MUM stubs can maintain longer past RSSI sequences for global handoff prediction. Long-term predictions, however, have shown a higher standard deviation, i.e., the exact handoff time of global handoff is harder to predict. In general, Efficiency and Error are strictly related to required prediction advance time, while Effectiveness and Continuity mainly depend on correct second-level buffer sizing and prediction standard deviation. For instance, when early predictions occur, clients re-attach before the completion of the MUM handoff procedure, thus decreasing Effectiveness and Continuity.

Table 1. Micro, macro, and global handoff performance indicators

	Efficiency	Error	Effectiveness	Continuity
Micro	90	10	99	–
Macro	93	8	98	99
Global	99	3	97	95

Micro handoff presents the worst Efficiency indicator, while Effectiveness is high, thus pointing out that MUM correctly dimensions second-level buffers in this case. Macro handoff limits useless HA migrations to 7% and achieves a good Error; Effectiveness is still high, i.e., almost all HA activations terminate before client re-attachment; Continuity is compromised only by sporadic late predictions. Finally, global handoff longer duration improves both Efficiency and Error; however, high standard deviation on predictions reduces Effectiveness and Continuity. Micro hand-off Efficiency improvements are possible by anticipating handoff predictions and consequently paying an earlier second-level buffer enlargement, thus trading between Efficiency and storage overhead at proxies. Let us note that high standard deviation on predictions risks to produce cases of too late predictions, which also require second-level buffer refresh (at new locations) to renew obsolete data (sent in the meanwhile to clients at old locations). To overcome the problem, in global and micro handoff predictions, MUM commands HAs to continuously refresh the current and new second-level buffers until clients re-attach; in addition, MUM refreshes the buffers stored at new PBs until client re-attachments, and new HAs command PSs to forward flows to both old and new second-level buffers.

5   Related Work

The distribution of both traditional and multimedia services over the WI is introducing novel significant challenges. By focusing on handoff management, several research proposals have worked at the datalink and network layers of the OSI stack: [20] and [4] survey a number of micro, macro, and global mobility management proposals that tend to minimize handoff delays and packet losses in the context of Mobile IP. These general-purpose approaches suffer from the portability limitations typical of solutions at datalink/network layers and address handoff issues uniformly for any service developed on top of them, thus making impossible differentiated strategies for different application domains.

By concentrating on the few application-level approaches already available in the literature, [11] proposes to deploy a proxy-based infrastructure for service continuity in the specific case of macro handoffs by exploiting standard Linux tools to forward multimedia flows. More recently, the same researchers have enhanced their solution via SIP: the guideline is to employ multicast in a local domain and movement prediction to reduce packet losses during SIP session re-directions [7]. Their solution does not require ad-hoc infrastructures at client domains; however, it needs complex network management functionality, assumes a collaborative secure deployment environment, and does not include original handoff prediction mechanisms.

Proxy Intelligent Modules for Adapting Traffic Efficiently (PRIMATE) proposes a proxy-based infrastructure to support micro, macro, and global handoff [8]. PRIMATE proxies are typically deployed at Wi-Fi APs, but can also install at border gateways connecting local networks to the rest of the Internet: similarly to MUM, they locally manage service reconfiguration without server intervention and predict client movements to adapt proxy-based buffering. However, PRIMATE prediction technique is centralized, scarcely scalable, and requires dedicated hardware; in addition, PRIMATE exploits kernel-level client modifications (data interceptors) that should be statically installed at each participant [21]. Another similar research proposal is [22], which describes a proxy-based mobile agent middleware for multimedia streaming: it proposes to employ proxies, called Virtual Servers, to assist roaming users but, differently from MUM, its proxies do not support proactive buffer movement and can be deployed only in intra-domain, ad-hoc, and statically installed network environments with specialized custom APs.

6   Conclusions and On-Going Work

Middleware proxies working over the fixed network on behalf of their resource-constrained clients are demonstrating their suitability and effectiveness in the WI, especially when integrated with Wi-Fi handoff prediction. In particular, handoff prediction can help in realizing novel proactive proxy-based infrastructures that perform adaptive second-level buffering to eliminate/smooth the different discontinuity issues intrinsic to micro, macro, and global handoffs. The MUM research work is showing that it is possible to preserve WI multimedia streaming continuity, even to limited client devices, by adopting an application-level middleware approach that is portable and dynamically deployable over the standard WI.

The promising experimental results of the MUM prototype, both in the presented wide-scale simulated environment and in small WI deployment scenarios in our campus, are encouraging further research. In particular, we are extending our solution to support vertical handoff towards Bluetooth connectivity and to enforce different Service Level Agreements when client roam to highly populated congested Wi-Fi cells.

Acknowledgements

Work supported by MIUR FIRB WEB-MINDS and CNR Strategic IS-MANET Projects.

References

1. M.S. Corson et al.: Mobile and Wireless Internet Services: Putting the Pieces Together. IEEE Communications, Vol. 39, No. 6 (2001)
2. W. Stallings: Wireless Communications and Networks. Pearson Education (2001)
3. P. Ramanathan et al.: Dynamic Resource Allocation Schemes during Handoff for Mobile Multimedia Wireless Networks. IEEE Journal on Selected Areas in Communications, Vol. 17, No. 7 (1999)

4. D. Saha et al.: Mobility Support in IP: a Survey of Related Protocols. IEEE Network, Vol. 18, No. 6 (2004)
5. T. Kuang, C. Williamson: Hierarchical Analysis of RealMedia Streaming Traffic on an IEEE 802.11b Wireless LAN. Elsevier Computer Communications, Vol. 27, No. 6 (2004)
6. P. Bellavista et al.: MUM: a Middleware for the Provisioning of Continuous Services to Mobile Users. IEEE ISCC (2004)
7. A. Dutta et al.: Fast-handoff Schemes for Application Layer Mobility Management. IEEE PIMRC (2004)
8. J. Chan et al.: A Framework for Mobile Wireless Networks with an Adaptive QoS Capability, MoMuC (1998)
9. A. Mishra et al.: An Empirical Analysis of the IEEE 802.11 MAC Layer Handoff Process. ACM Computer Communication Review, Vol. 33, No. 2 (2003)
10. Debian: Tools for Linux Wireless Extensions, http://packages.debian.org/stable/net/wireless-tools.html
11. P. Hsieh et al.: Application Layer Mobility Proxy for Real-time Communications. 3G Wireless and Beyond (2003)
12. R. Braden et al.: Resource ReSerVation Protocol (RSVP). IETF RFC 2205 (1997)
13. J. Rosenberg et al.: SIP: Session Initiation Protocol. IETF RFC 3261 (2002)
14. P. Bellavista et al.: Application-level QoS Control and Adaptation for Video on Demand. IEEE Internet Computing, Vol. 7, No. 6 (2003)
15. H. Velayos, G. Karlsson: Techniques to Reduce IEEE 802.11b Handoff Time. IEEE ICC, (2004)
16. P. Bellavista et al.: Mobility Prediction for Mobile Agent-based Service Continuity in the Wireless Internet. IEEE MATA (2004)
17. G. Anastasi et al.: A Power-Aware Multimedia Streaming Protocol for Mobile Users. IEEE ICPS (2005)
18. A. Dutta et al.: Implementing a Testbed for Mobile Multimedia. IEEE GLOBECOM (2001)
19. J. Hillebrand et al.: Quality-of-service Signaling for Next-generation IP-based Mobile Networks. IEEE Communications Magazine (2004)
20. A.T. Campbell et al.: Comparison of IP Micromobility Protocols. IEEE Wireless Communications, Vol. 9, No.1 (2002)
21. J. Chan et al.: A QoS Adaptive Mobility Prediction Scheme for Wireless Networks. IEEE GLOBECOM (1998)
22. D. Bruneo et al.: VOD Services for Mobile Wireless Devices. IEEE ISCC (2003)

A Voice over IP Quality Monitoring Architecture

Leandro C.G. Lustosa, Paulo H. de A. Rodrigues, Fabio David,
and Douglas G. Quinellato

Laboratório de Voz Sobre IP, Núcleo de Computação Eletrônica,
Universidade Federal do Rio de Janeiro (NCE/UFRJ),[*]
Caixa Postal 2324, 20001-970, Rio de Janeiro, RJ, Brasil
{leandro, aguiar, fabio, douglasq}@nce.ufrj.br
http://www.voip.nce.ufrj.br

Abstract. A voice over IP quality monitoring architecture based on the development of the VQuality library is described. VQuality implements the E-model and its extensions for objective voice quality measurement. The library also supports generation of a customized voice quality CDR with extensions that permit transfer of call quality parameters measured over different instants of time, besides interacting with a RADIUS server for data collection. The framework is exemplified in the context of the fone@RNP VoIP service and VoIP clients incorporating the new functionality are shown.

1 Introduction

Voice over IP communication systems have been proliferating and represent a viable technological solution for voice provisioning. Aligned with this tendency, the Brazilian Education and Research Network (RNP) started to offer a VoIP service over its backbone. The service, named fone@RNP, is based on a heterogeneous (H.323 and SIP) VoIP architecture, which supports voice calls among institutional PBXs, call establishment with the public service telephony network (PSTN), and interaction with other international academic and research H.323 and SIP initiatives.

The environment of a fone@RNP institution partner is composed of servers (H.323 GnuGK [1] or SIP Proxy SER [2]) for VoIP client registration and location. Client authentication is done consulting an LDAP directory [3] via RADIUS [4] and call statistics accounting records are stored in an SQL database. An optional gateway can be used for interconnection with PBX, as shown in Fig. 1. Cisco routers and Asterisk [5] are used as PBX gateways, while Asterisk is also used as an H.323/SIP signaling gateway. Since E.164 addressing is directly supported by the H.323 architecture, SIP servers route E.164 calls to H.323 server, if the call is not destined to the local gateway, which means not destined to the institutional PBX or local PSTN. There is an extensive use of IP clients, like Openphone for H.323 [6] and X-Lite for SIP [7].

Voice call quality statistics represent valuable information for system performance management, helping to validate admission control schemes and changes in network QoS configuration, besides enabling faulty service behavior detection and establishing parameters for monitoring user satisfaction.

---

[*] Partially supported by RNP Advanced VoIP Working Group. Paulo H. de A. Rodrigues is also a professor in the Computer Science Department/IM at UFRJ.

J. Dalmau and G. Hasegawa (Eds.): MMNS 2005, LNCS 3754, pp. 168–178, 2005.
© IFIP International Federation for Information Processing 2005

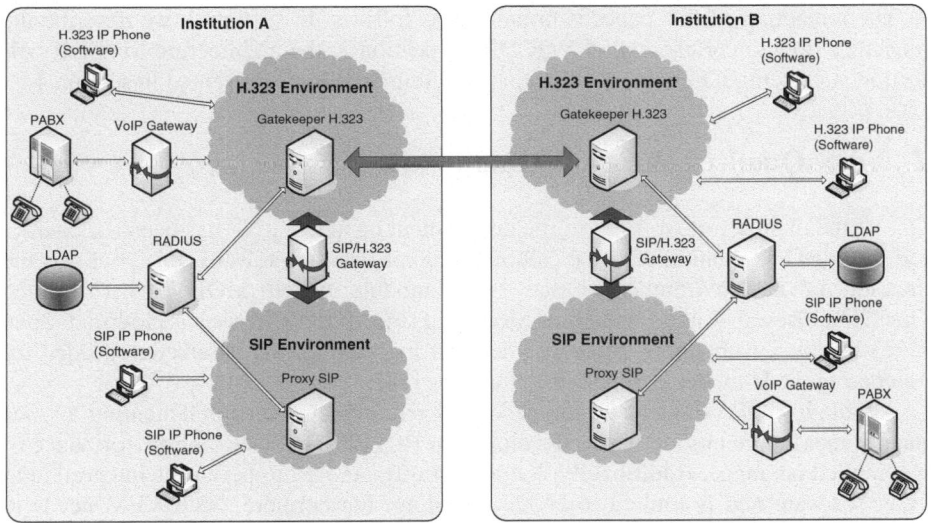

Fig. 1. fone@RNP service architecture

As shown in Fig. 1, accounting is performed with collection of call detailed records (CDR) generated by servers and gateways. However, only Cisco gateways give some call completion quality indication. Calls between clients (IP telephones or softphones) have no quality indication and the overall collected statistics are insufficient for precise system characterization.

CESNET, the Czech education and research network, has also implemented a CDR accounting and monitoring structure using RADIUS and gateways [8]. In [9], the *Enterprise Call Analysis System* (ECAS) architecture is presented, also based on the analysis and collection of gateway CDRs. These and similar architectures suffer from the same limitation of not taking in account the quality of calls between VoIP clients.

In [10], to monitor the call quality offered by a network, distributed SNMP agents periodically generate simulated calls and collect packet losses, delay and jitter. This solution does not address the collection of user calls statistics and the sampling procedure may not reflect the real network impact on voice calls. In [11], as in many commercial products [12,13,14], a passive monitoring solution is used. Probes able of capturing and analyzing voice flows are strategically placed in the network and generate quality reports. This active scheme is not always successful, because secure communication may block packet interpretation and analysis, or the point to point voice traffic nature may force packets to be routed away from the probes.

An alternate solution is been pursued in the fone@RNP service, in order to enable a more extensive and trustable quality accounting. A library, called Voice Quality (VQuality lib), capable of voice quality evaluation and quality CDR (VQCDR) generation, was developed and is being incorporated to softphones. This library implements the E-model [15] and its extensions [16,17]. Due to the use of the extended E-model, the generated voice quality indicators are extremely detailed and closer to human perception than those indicators generated by present VoIP gateways [18,19].

The remaining of this paper is organized as follows. In section 2, we describe the VQuality lib and corresponding VQCDR. In section 3, the architecture for CDR collection is presented. Finally, conclusions and future work are presented in section 4.

2 Voice Quality Library (VQuality Lib)

One of the main efforts to support the deployment of fone@RNP has been the characterization and evaluation of voice call quality. Our first step towards this goal was the creation of an environment based on a module called MOBVEM (Modified OpenH323 Based Voice Evaluation Module) [16]. MOBVEM uses a modified Open H323 library for obtaining voice call detailed log with all the parameters needed for computing the E-model [15] and its extensions [17].

Although MOBVEM has all the necessary requirements for implementing a voice quality measurement tool, it was developed in Perl [20] and lacks the performance of a compiled language. Additionally, it does not offer an API to permit its integration to other software and is limited to H.323 signaling. Furthermore, MOBVEM needs to simultaneously analyze the logs generated by both ends of a call to estimate RTT, making real-time voice quality determination unfeasible, when one of the ends of a call is a client that does not use the modified OpenH323 library.

To overcome MOBVEM limitations, VQuality library was developed. It is written in C++ and inherits the calculation of the extended E-model. Moreover, besides its superior performance, VQuality is flexible, extensible, portable, and its computation of received voice quality is independent of the other side of the call.

VQuality was developed under the oriented object paradigm and conceived for easy addition of new evaluation models or VoIP signaling protocols. Portability is achieved with a standard C/C++, except for TCP sockets and threads, which are implemented differently in each OS. We have implemented our own TCP sockets function, compatible with Windows and Unix systems. For thread handling, we use the Pthreads-win32 library [21], which allows code compilation based on Pthreads API, standard for Unix OS. The result is a code which is compilable in Linux, FreeBSD and Microsoft Windows, besides being portable to other architectures, if necessary.

A major challenge was to modify OpenH323 to make it full compliant with RTP and fill in all required fields. Integration of VQuality with OpenH323 lib permitted the creation of H.323 clients with VQCDR capability (see section 3.4).

3 Collection Architecture

One of the most important features of VQuality is its ability to send Voice Quality Call Detailed Record (VQCDR). At call completion, the library computes the quality of the received voice media, processes identification parameters for the call and involved terminals, and reports this information to a centralized entity, responsible for collecting CDRs. VQCDR is sent using TCP/port 80, by default. TCP assures reliable transfer and port 80 (HTTP) facilitates operation behind firewalls, which rarely block this port number. VQCDR format and attributes are shown in Table 1.

Table 1. VQCDR fields

# Field	Length (bytes)	Description
01 version	1 *	VQCDR version. Present version is 1.
02 signalingProtocol	1 *	Assigned: 0(II323), 1(SIP), 2 (MGCP).
03 IDSize	2 *	ID field length in bytes.
04 ID	0-65535	Call identification. In H.323 represents ConfID, while in SIP is Call-ID.
05 username	64 †	User identification.
06 model	1 *	Assigned: 0 (ITU-T E-model), 1(ETSI Extended E-model), 2 (UFRJ/UFAM Extended E-Model)
07 codec	1 *	Assigned: 0 (G.711), 1 (G.711 PLC), 2 (G.723.1 5.3kbps), 3 (G.723.1 6.3 kbps), 4 (G.726 16 kbps), 5(G.726 24 kbps), 6 (G.726 32 kbps), 7 (G.726 40kbps), 8 (G.728 16 kbps), 9 (G.729), 10 (G.729A), 11 (GSM FR (6.10)).
08 frameSize	4 *	Voice frame size in micro seconds.
09 framesPerPacket	1 *	Number of voice frames in IP packet.
10 IdEndOfCall	2 *	*Delay Impairment* (Id). Degradation indicator related to end to end delay and interactivity. Value times 100.
11 IeEndOfCall	2 *	*Equipment Impairment* (Ie. Degradation indicator related to high compression codecs, network packet losses and jitter buffer discards. Value times 100.
12 MOSEndOfCall	2 *	*Mean Opinion Score* (MOS) at call completion. Represents perceived human quality. Value times 100.
13 gapLossDensity	2 *	Loss density in isolated losses (gap). Value times 100.
14 burstLossDensity	2 *	Loss density in bursty losses (burst). Value times 100.
15 discardRate	2 *	Percentage of discarded packets in the jitter buffer. Value times 100.
16 lossRate	2 *	Percentage of loss packets. Value times 100.
17 RfactorEndOfCall	2 *	R factor at call completion (output from E-model). Value times 100.
18 duration	4 *	Call duration in seconds.
19 avgNetDelay	4 *	Network average delay in μ seconds. See note 1.
20 avgJitterBufferDelay	4 *	Jitter buffer average size in μ seconds. See note 2.
21 avgJitter	4 *	Average jitter in micro seconds. See note 3.
22 codecDelay	4 *	Coding and packetization delay in micro seconds.
23 packetsReceived	4 *	Total received packets.
24 packetsLost	4 *	Total lost packets.
25 packetsDiscarded	4 *	Total discarded packets in the jitter buffer.
26 mediaSource	256 †	Remote client address (IP or hostname), media sender.

27 mediaDestination	256 †	Local client address (IP or hostname), media receiver.
28 localAlias	64 †	Id of client emitting VQCDR. E.164 number or URI.
29 remoteAlias	64 †	Id of remote IP client. E.164 number or URI.
30 direction	1 *	Identification of call origin: 0 (called), 1 (calling)
31 appExtensionSize	1 *	Length of appExtension in bytes. 0 if field is absent.
32 appExtension	0-255 †	Application additional information.
33 VQLogSize	2 *	VQLog field length in bytes. 0 if field is absent.
34 VQLog	0-65535‡	Detailed quality log in VQLog format See sec. 3.5.

* Unsigned integer value (more significant byte first). ‡ Text file.
† ASCII coded text with delimitator (hex 00).

Note 1: Arithmetic average of the 16 last network delay calculations (netDelay).
Note 2: Arithmetic average of the 16 last jitter buffer delay calculations. If the length of the jitter buffer is not dynamic, this value is constant.
Note 3: Arithmetic average of the 16 last jitter variations in RTP format [22].

3.1 Voice Quality CDR Server (VQCDR Server)

The VQCDR Server is the central entity responsible for collecting VQCDRs, checking its legitimacy and sending them for storage. Server interacts with a database or application to check if VQCDR was generated by a valid user/client. VQCDR server architecture is composed of three modules, as shown in Fig. 2.

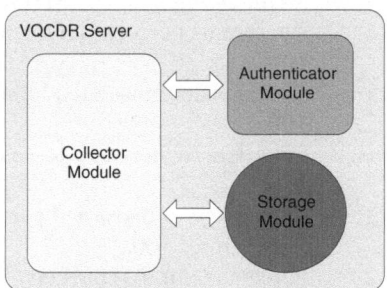

Fig. 2. VQCDR Server Architecture

Collector Module (CM): responsible for collecting and interpreting received VQCDR, and also responsible for activating the Authenticator Module (AM) and the Storage Module (SM).

Authenticator Module (AM): responsible for VQCDR validation. VQCDR Server can operate with zero or more AMs. For test or controlled environments, a simple IP address access list can be used to authenticate the VQCDR sender. However, in production environments, where a more sophisticated and flexible authentication procedure is required due to scalability reasons, use of an AM is more appropriate. When operating with SIP and H.323, for example, it may be necessary to access a specific

AM for each signaling protocol. In this case, CM has to be capable of selecting the right AM. The VQCDR protocol field can be handy for this purpose.

Storage Module (SM): responsible for storing the collected VQCDRs in a database. This database can be, for example, an SQL database or a RADIUS server.

For the H.323 fone@RNP service, we have implemented a VQCDR Server with an AM specific for the GnuGK gatekeeper and an SM based on RADIUS. VQCDR generation in SIP clients have not been implemented yet.

3.2 GnuGK Authenticator Module (GnuGK AM)

GnuGK AM uses GnuGK [1] remote management port for validating VQCDR originator (see Fig. 3-A). This port implements a communication channel which allows checking registered users and accessing user information in the system, such as: <u>user identification, registration IP</u> address (public IP address used by the user during registration) and <u>private IP</u> address (present if user is behind a NAT box [23]).

For the authentication procedure, AM checks username (user id) and mediaDestination (private IP address if user is behind a NAT box) fields in VQCDR and also the IP address of the packet received with CDR (registration IP address). In case user is behind a NAT box, VQCDR will be validated if and only if user identification, private IP and registration IP addresses match a GnuGk user active record.

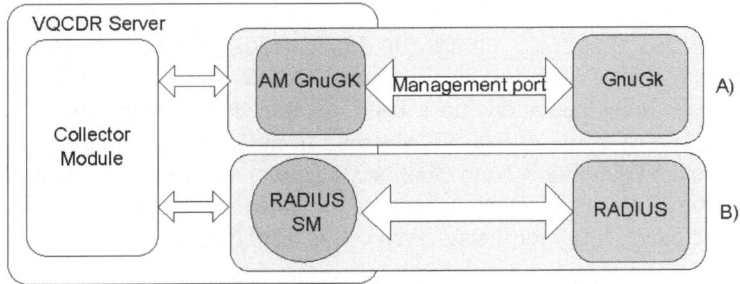

Fig. 3. GnuGK AM (A) and RADIUS SM (B)

3.3 RADIUS Storage Module (RADIUS SM)

RADIUS accounting offers a standard attribute set which is not enough to detail a voice call. However, RADIUS allows reporting extra attributes, application dependent, called VSAs (Vendor Specific Attributes). To use specific attributes, a Private Enterprise Number has to be solicited to IANA [24]. With this number, a vendor/application can define a data dictionary which allows RADIUS to interpret specific attributes. UFRJ VSAs were assigned data dictionary number 21715 by IANA.

SM interface with RADIUS (see Fig. 3-B) was implemented with use of the RadiusClient library [25], which is only available in Unix. In the future, this library will be modified to make it Windows compatible and allow running RADIUS SM on this OS. Our specific data dictionary is shown in Fig. 4.

# UFRJ Vendor Specific Attributes				discardRate	15	integer	ufrj
VENDOR ufrj 21715				lossRate	16	integer	ufrj
# VQCDR attributes				duration	18	integer	ufrj
signalingProtocol	1	string	ufrj	avgNetDelay	19	integer	ufrj
callStart	2	string	ufrj	avgJitterBufferDelay	20	integer	ufrj
callStop	3	string	ufrj	avgJitter	21	integer	ufrj
ID	4	string	ufrj	codecDelay	22	integer	ufrj
username	5	string	ufrj	packetsReceived	23	integer	ufrj
model	6	string	ufrj	packetsLost	24	integer	ufrj
codec	7	string	ufrj	packetsDiscarded	25	integer	ufrj
frameSize	8	integer	ufrj	mediaSource	26	string	ufrj
framesPerPacket	9	integer	ufrj	mediaDestination	27	string	ufrj
IdEndOfCall	10	integer	ufrj	localAlias	28	string	ufrj
IeEndOfCall	11	integer	ufrj	remoteAlias	29	string	ufrj
MOSEndOfCall	12	integer	ufrj	direction	30	string	ufrj
gapLossDensity	13	integer	ufrj	RFactorEndOfCall	31	integer	ufrj
burstLossDensity	14	integer	ufrj				
			1/2				2/2

Fig. 4. VQCDR RADIUS data dictionary

3.4 Modified H.323 Clients

Using a modified OpenH323 library, for implementing a full compliant RTP, and
VQuality lib, for voice quality evaluation and VQCDR generation, three clients based
on open source implementations have been developed: VQOpenphone, from Openphone, a graphics Windows client, VQMeeting, from Gnome Meeting [26], a graphics
Unix client and VQOhphone, from Ohphone, a textual multiplatform client (Windows
and Unix). Fig. 5 shows a VQOpenphone and VQMeeting clients at the end of a call.
In their status panel, MOS for the received call is displayed.

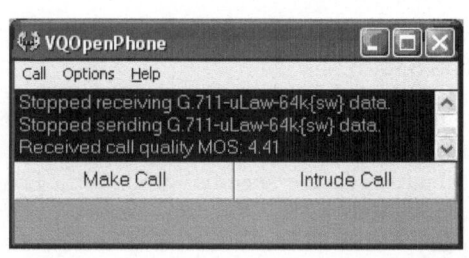 

Fig. 5. VQOpenphone and VQMeeting clients

3.5   Voice Quality Log (VQLog)

VQCDR quality indicators offer a receiver perspective call quality summary, very adequate for a large VoIP system supporting hundreds or thousands of calls a day. However, this information does not allow an analysis of quality variation over time, which may be needed in tests or in more detailed and specific experiments.

```
! Example of VQLog file
G.711-uLaw-64k 1 20.00 40.00
13:41:00.625 6 0 0.00 98.00 13 116 0.15 22.76 70.50 3.62
13:41:01.547 3 0 0.00 98.00 18 116 0.15 23.62 69.60 3.58
13:41:02.469 3 0 0.00 97.50 15 115 0.15 20.46 72.80 3.73
13:41:03.375 5 0 0.00 97.50 18 115 0.15 20.37 72.80 3.73
13:41:04.391 0 0 0.00 97.50 14 115 0.15 20.37 72.80 3.73
13:41:05.391 0 0 0.00 97.00 15 114 0.15 20.37 72.80 3.73
13:41:06.375 0 0 0.00 97.00 18 114 0.15 20.37 72.80 3.73
13:41:07.365 0 0 0.00 97.00 18 114 0.15 20.37 72.80 3.73
2 0.00 57.50 14.00 40.00 367 17 0 0.00 11.26 0.15 20.42 72.80 3.73
0 D41F4102AAF118109FED0040A70 leandro 3377 3354 1 10.10.1.1 10.10.2.1 8
```

Fig. 6. VQLog file example

Need for more detailed measurements and motivation for sharing reports among different applications based on VQuality produced the VQLog format, which allows sending of extra information besides VQCDR indicators. To enable the timely analysis of a call, a file with values of main quality variables at different instants of time is included and sent with VQCDR.

A VQLog file is coded in ASCII and must have one or more <u>codec identification lines</u>, one or more <u>quality indicators lines</u>, one <u>summary line</u> and a <u>call identification line</u>, necessarily in this order. Each line is formed by fields separated by blank spaces. During a call, one or more codecs can be used, needing one line for each. Each quality indicators line is associated with an instant of time, forcing sending many lines to characterize quality changes over time. A VQLog file example is shown in Fig. 6.

3.6   Voice Quality Plot (VQPlot)

VQPlot is an application which reads and plots VQLog information. Together with a client that uses VQuality, like VQOpenphone or VQMeeting, it becomes a very powerful analysis tool. At the end of a call, the user can run VQPlot. The application will automatically open the VQLog file and plot graphs showing the evolution of relevant parameters over time. These plots help to identify degradation factors for a call and its intensity. This analysis can help, for example, a technician give remote support to a user facing configuration problems with its network or personal computer.

Fig. 7 and Fig. 8 illustrate VQPlot output for a call originated from a VQOpenphone running on a laptop with a 802.11b wireless lan connection.

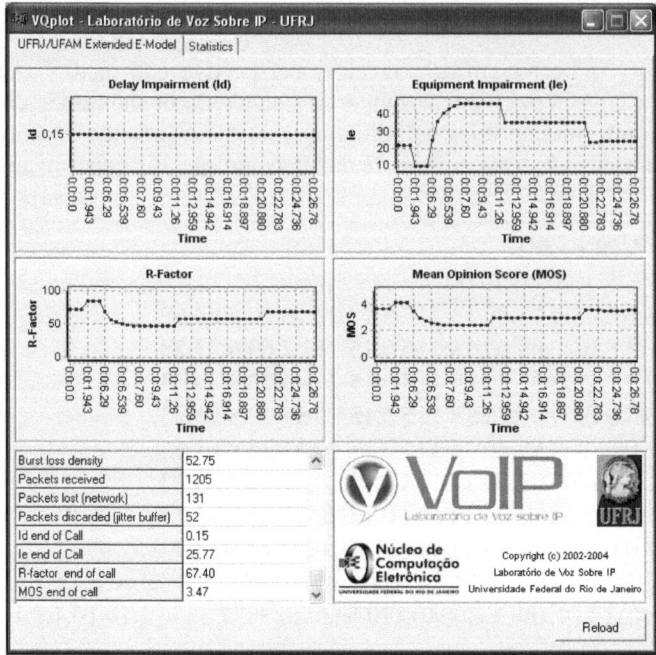

Fig. 7. Call quality over time

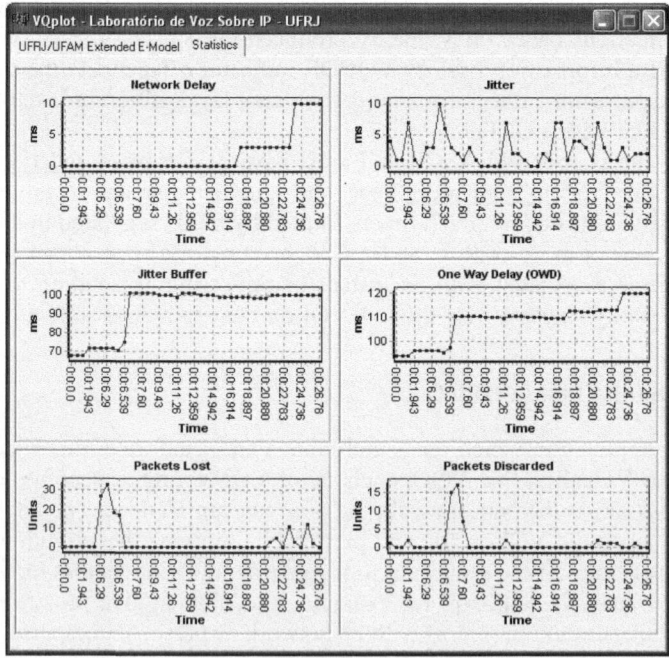

Fig. 8. Call statistics over time

3.7 Visualization Environment

All CDRs, generated by a server, a gateway or IP client (VQCDR), are sent to a RADIUS server and stored in an SQL database. Soon after, CDRs that refer to the same call are consolidated in one single record. A Web based interface (Fig. 9) generates reports such as: call distribution over a day, number of calls over a day period, call quality along a day, number of simultaneous calls, among others.

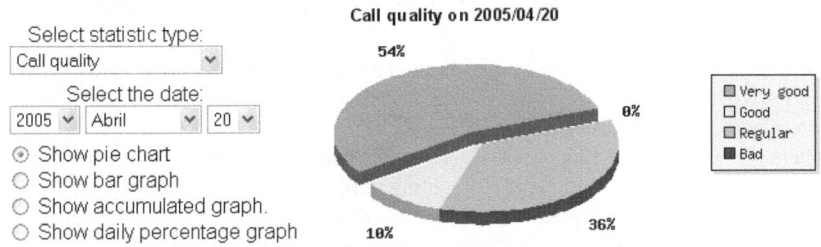

Fig. 9. Visualization Web environment for statistics reports

4 Conclusions and Future Work

In this paper, we presented a voice quality monitoring architecture which process voice quality CDRs (called VQCDR) generated by the VQuality library. VQuality implements objective voice quality evaluation based on the E-model and its extensions. This library, written in standard C/C++, is portable and supports different VoIP signaling protocols. Besides generating its VQCDR and sending it via RADIUS, it has extensions for sending complementary information as a textual file. An application called VQPlot is able to read this complementary information and plot graphs displaying parameter variation over time. Using VQuality and a modified OpenH323 lib, three clients, VQOpenphone, VQMeeting and VQOhphone, capable of generating voice quality CDRs, were developed.

One future step will seek the integration of VQuality lib into open source SIP client or in IP telephone under partnership with vendors. Another possible line of action would be the incorporation of VQuality to a simulation tool, as the Network Simulator [27], what could be helpful for the design and evaluation of complex VoIP systems.

When using VQCDRs and full compliant RTCP reports, it is possible to determine delays in each direction of a call. From the statistics database, as a future work, we could derive information about traffic asymmetry in the underlying network.

The lack of clients with the ability of measuring call quality should foster partnerships with vendors and providers, specially because of the increasing interest in VoIP and need for assuring and measuring user satisfaction.

References

1. OpenH323 Gatekeeper. The GNUGatekeeper: In://www.gnugk.org/. Accessed in May 2005
2. iptel.org SIP Server: SIP Express Router. In://www.iptel.org/ser. Accessed in May 2005

3. Hodges, J., Morgan, R.: Lightweight Directory Access Protocol (v3): Technical Specification . RFC 3377 (2002)
4. Rigney, C., Willens, S., Rubens, A., Simpson, W.: Remote Authentication Dial In User Service (RADIUS). RFC 2865 (2000)
5. Asterisk™ – The Open Source Linux PBX: In: //www.asterisk.org. Accessed in May 2005
6. OpenH323 Project: Available in http: //www.openh323.org/. Accessed in December. 2004
7. Xten X-Lite: Available in http://www.xten.com/. Accessed in May 2005
8. Ubik, S.: IP Telephony Accounting and WAN Deployment Experience. IPTEL 2001, USA (2001)
9. Lin, M., LO, C., e W., S.: Design and Implementation of an Enterprise Call Analysis System for VoIP Deployments. 2003 Australian Telecommunications, Networks and Applications Conference (ATNAC) (2003)
10. Huang, C., Chao, C., e Liu, A.: A Distributed Management Framework for H.323-Based VoIP System. Communications in Computing (CIC) 2003. USA, (2003)
11. Broom, S., Hollier, M.: Speech Quality Measurement Tools for Dynamic Network Management. Measurement of Speech and Audio Quality in Networks (MESAQIN) 2003 (2003)
12. Telchemy: SQmon - Service Quality Monitoring for Voice over IP. Available in: http://www.telchemy.com/sqmon.html. Accessed in May 2005
13. Empirix: Hammer XMS. Available in: http://www.empirix.com/Empirix/Network+ IP+Storage+Test/hammer+xms.html. Accessed in May 2005
14. Brix Networks: Advanced VoIP Test Suites. Available in: http://www.brixnet.com/ products/voip_testsuite.html. Accessed in May 2005
15. ITU-T Recommendation G.107: The E-Model, a computational model for use in transmission planning. Switzerland (2003)
16. Lustosa, L.C.G., Carvalho, L.S.G., Rodrigues, P.H.A., Mota, S. E.: Utilização do Modelo E para avaliação da qualidade da fala em sistemas de comunicação baseados em voz sobre IP, XXII Simpósio Brasileiro de Redes de Computadores. Brazil (2004)
17. ETSI TS 102 024-5 v4.1.1. Telecommunications and Internet Protocol Harmonization over Networks (TIPHON) Release 4: End-to-end Quality of Service in TIPHON systems; Part 5: Quality of Service (QoS) measurement methodologies. France (2003)
18. Cisco Syst., RADIUS VSA Voice Implementation Guide: In: //www.cisco.com/univercd/ cc/td/doc/product/access/acs_serv/vapp_dev/vsaig3.pdf. Accessed December 2004
19. Cisco Systems, Managing Voice Quality with Cisco Voice Manager (CVM) and Telemate: In: http://www.cisco.com/warp/public/788/AVVID/cvmtelemate.pdf. Accessed in Dec. 2004
20. The Perl Foundation. Perl Directory at Perl.org: In://www.perl.org/. Accessed in May 2005
21. PThreads-Win32. Open Source POSIX Threads for Win32: Available in http://sources.redhat.com/pthreads-win32/. Accessed in May 2005
22. Schulzrinne, H., Casnet, S., Frederick, R., Jacobson, V.: RTP: A Transport Protocol for Real-Time Applications. RFC 3550 (2003)
23. Srisuresh, P., Egevang, K.: Traditional IP Network Address Translator (Traditional NAT), RFC 3022 (2001)
24. Reynolds, J. e Postel, J.: Assigned Numbers, RFC 1700 (1994)
25. RadiusClient: Available in http://freshmeat.net/projects/radiusclient/. Accessed May 2005
26. Gnome Meeting: In://www.gnomemeeting.org/. Accessed in May 2005
27. The University Of Southern California: Network Simulator – ns2. Available in: http://www.isi.edu/nsnam/ns/. Accessed in May 2005

A Distributed Scheduling Scheme Providing QoS in Multimedia Ad Hoc Wireless Networks

Hyunho Yang

School of Electronic & Information Engineering, Kunsan National University,
San 68, Miryong-dong, Kunsan, Jeonbuk 573-701, Republic of Korea
hhyang@kunsan.ac.kr

Abstract. Providing Quality of Service(QoS) in distributed networks, such as multimedia ad hoc wireless network, also requires well defined scheduling schemes. However, due to the distributed nature of ad hoc networks, nodes may not be able to determine the next packet to transmit as in the centralized networks. Thus, it is a non-trivial issue to provide bounded delay guarantee, with fair share of resources. In this paper, we implement a scheduling scheme named delay guaranteed fair queueing (DGFQ) in a multimedia ad hoc wireless network with distributed manner. According to the performance evaluation results, both average and maximum delay could be controlled with varying *service differentiation coefficient*. In summary our new scheme can manages the delay performance of multimedia traffic in the distributed network environment.

Index terms: Fair queueing, Ad hoc network, Quality of Service (QoS), Multimedia network.

1 Introduction

The multimedia ad hoc wireless network is quite an attractive issue since it offers a flexible solution to enable delivery of multimedia services to mobile end users without fixed backbone networks. As a distributed network technology, it also required to provide a set of applications, e.g., both error-sensitive and delay-sensitive applications, over the bandwidth-constrained wireless medium. In practice, to implement those applications over the distributed networks aforementioned, the issue of providing fair and delay bounded channel access among multiple contending hosts over a scarce and shared wireless channel is essential.

Fair queueing has been a popular scheme to provide fair share of resources among nodes according to their application requirements in both wireline and packet cellular networking environments [1]-[6]. However, the problem of designing fully distributed, scalable, and efficient fair scheduling algorithms in the shared-channel ad hoc wireless network remains largely unaddressed. In essence, the unique characteristics of ad hoc wireless networks such as location-specific contention create spatial coupling effects among flows in the network graph, and the fundamental notion of fairness may require non-local computation among contending flows. Adding these features together, fair queueing in shared-channel

J. Dalmau and G. Hasegawa (Eds.): MMNS 2005, LNCS 3754, pp. 179–189, 2005.

multihop wireless environments is no longer a local property at each output link and has to exhibit global behaviors; this has to be achieved through distributed and localized decisions at each node.

In some related works the fair packet scheduling issues have addressed, in particular, on the aforementioned problems in ad hoc wireless networks,[7]-[9]. The focus of [7], [8] has been the problem formulation and an appropriate ideal centralized model for fair queueing in shared-channel multihop wireless networks. They also proposed a distributed fair scheduling implementation scheme, which merely approximate the centralized model. In [9], they devised distributed and localized solutions such that local schedulers self-coordinate their local interactions to achieve the desired global behavior. They also propose a suite of fully distributed and localized fair scheduling models that use local flow information and perform local computations only. Though the contributions stated above, [9] mainly addressed on the fairness of the overall throughput performance for the various usage scenarios without consideration of the QoS factors such as delay performance especially for the multimedia ad hoc wireless networks.

In [10], they propose a new fair queueing scheme i.e., delay guaranteed fair queueing (DGFQ), guaranteeing bounded delay for multimedia services. DGFQ scheme is basically a generalized process sharing(GPS) based fair queueing scheme with some modifications to guarantee bounded delay. In detail, the *service differentiation coefficient* was introduced to apply additional weight factor for the delay guaranteed (DG) class over non-delay guaranteed (NG) class. With this policy, DGFQ provides better delay performance for DG class at the same fairness guarantee without serious increase of computational complexity. However [10] has focused on the centralized network, rather than distributed one e.g., ad hoc wireless networks.

In this paper we implement the delay guaranteed fair queueing (DGFQ) in the multimedia ad hoc wireless network using the distributed fair queueing protocol to verify the controllability and adaptability of DFGQ on the bounded delay requirement in multimedia ad hoc wireless networks. Through the results of performance evaluation, we can conclude that DGFQ also performs well to control bounded delay in multimedia ad hoc wireless networks

The rest of the paper is organized as follows. Section 2 summarizes the delay guaranteed fair queueing (DGFQ). Section 3 describes the network model for ad hoc fair scheduling. In Section 4 we describe on distributed implementation of delay guaranteed fair queueing (DGFQ) in the multimedia ad hoc wireless network. Section 5 presents a simulation-based performance evaluation of the implementation, and, finally in Section 6 we conclude our work.

2   Delay Guaranteed Fair Queueing (DGFQ)

In delay guaranteed fair queueing (DGFQ)[10], two tags i.e., a start tag and a finish tag, are associated with each packet. Packets are scheduled in the increasing order of the start tags of the packets. Furthermore, $v(t)$ is defined as a virtual time function which calculates the start tag of the packet in service at time t.

Finally, in DGFQ scheme, there is a certain interval of time in which all flows are scheduled at least once, we call it *scheduling interval*.

All flows are classified into a number of classes according to their delay bound requirements. The simplest and basic classification is to make two classes, one for delay guaranteed (DG) flows and the rest for non delay guaranteed (NG) flows. In our scheme, we introduce the *service differentiation coefficient,* α $(0 < \alpha \le 1)$, to handle each flow class differently. By varying α, we can customize delay bound for individual flows i.e., adjust the relative service order of each flow in a scheduling interval.

The complete algorithm is defined as follows.

1. On the arrival of p_f^j, the jth packet of flow f, is stamped with start tag $S(p_f^j)$, computed as

$$S(p_f^j) = \max\{v[A(p_f^j)], F(p_f^{j-1})\} \quad j \ge 1 \tag{1}$$

   where $A(p_f^j)$ is the arrival time of packet p_f^j, $v[\cdot]$ is the virtual time function for the given arrival time and $F(p_f^j)$ is the finish tag of packet p_f^j.
   The finish tag of packet p_f^j is defined as

$$F(p_f^j) = S(p_f^j) + \alpha_f \frac{l_f^j}{\phi_f} \tag{2}$$

   where $F(p_f^0) = 0$, ϕ_f is the weight of flow f, l_f^j is the length of packet p_f^j, and α_f $(0 < \alpha_f \le 1)$ is the *service differentiation coefficient* for flow f. $\alpha_f=1$ for NG class or appropriate value for DG class.

2. Initially the system virtual time is 0. During a busy period, the system virtual time at time t, $v(t)$, is defined to be equal to the start tag of the packet in service at time t. At the end of a busy period, $v(t)$ is set to the maximum of finish tag assigned to any packets that have been serviced by then.

3. Packets are serviced in the increasing order of the start tags; ties are broken arbitrarily.

3   System Model

3.1   Network Model

In this paper, we consider a packet-switched multihop wireless network in which the wireless medium is shared among multiple contending users, i.e., a single physical channel with capacity C is available for wireless transmissions. Transmissions are locally broadcast and only receivers within the transmission range of a sender can receive its packets. Each link layer packet flow is a stream of packets being transmitted from the source to the destination, where the source and destination are neighboring nodes that are within transmission range of each other. Two flows are contending with each other if either the sender or the receiver of one flow is within the transmission range of the sender or the receiver of the other flows [11]. We make three assumptions [11]-[13]: (a) a collision occurs when a receiver is in the reception range of two simultaneously transmitting nodes, thus unable to cleanly receive signal from either of them, (b) a node cannot transmit and receive packets simultaneously, and (c) neighborhood is a commutative property; hence, flow contention is also commutative.

In addition, we do not consider non-collision-related channel errors. For simplicity of presentation, we only consider fixed packet size in this paper, which is a realistic assumption in typical wireless networks.

3.2   Flow Contention Graph

To visualize the contending flows in the network, we introduce the flow contention graph which precisely characterizes the spatial-domain, as well as the time-domain contention relationship among transmitting flows. In a flow graph, each vertex represents a backlogged flow, and an edge between two vertex denotes that those two flows are contending with each other. If two vertices are not connected, spatial reuse is possible because those two flows can transmit simultaneously.

As an example, Figure 1 shows the simple network consists of 8 nodes and 4 flows. The dashed lines in the node graph represents tow nodes are in the communication range. Each node in an ad hoc wireless network maintains information for flows within one-hop neighborhood in the flow contention graph. In Figure 1, one-hop neighborhood of flow $F1$ includes $F2, F3$. Therefore, for given flow f, it is required to maintain flow information for flows that are within the transmission range of either f's sender or its receiver. However, for any given node, our goal is to maintain flow information (e.g., service tags) for flows only within its one-hop neighborhood in the node graph, even though one hop neighborhood in a flow graph will translate to the two-hop neighborhood in the real node graph in practice. This means that no node needs to be aware of flow information at nodes that are more than one hop away in the node graph.

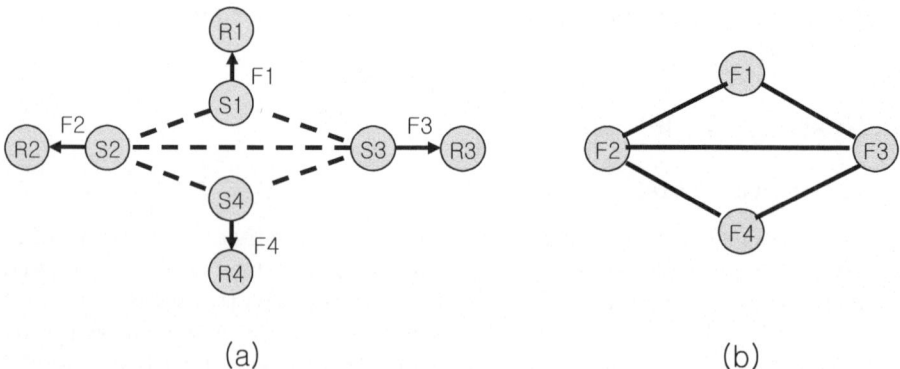

(a)   (b)

Fig. 1. Node graph and flow graph in location dependent contention (a) Original node topology graph (b) Flow graph

4   Distributed Implementation of DGFQ in Ad Hoc Wireless Networks

4.1   Basic Scheduling Operations

The detailed operations for distributed implementation of delay guaranteed fair queueing (DGFQ) in multimedia ad hoc wireless network consist of the following four parts:

- *Local state maintenance:* Each node n maintains a local table E_n, which records each flow's current service tag for all flows in its one-hop neighborhood of the flow graph. Each table entry has the form of $[f, T_f]$, where T_f is the current service tag of flow f, e.g., the most recent start tag of flow f.
- *Tagging operations:* Two tags, i.e., a start tag and a finish tag, are assigned for each arriving packet, using DGFQ algorithm described in Section **??**, for each flow f in the local table.
- *Scheduling loop:* After the tagging operation, at the sender node n of a flow f, the following procedure is performed, whenever the node n hears that the channel is clear,
  (a) if the flow f has the smallest service tag in the table E_n, of node n, transmit the head-of-line packet of flow f immediately;
  (b) otherwise, set the backoff timer B_f of flow f as

$$B_f = \sum_{g \in S} I(T_g(t) < T_f(t)),$$

  where g is a flow entry of table E_n and $I(x)$ denotes the indicator function, i.e., $I(x) = 1$, if $x > 0$; $I(x) = 0$, otherwise. Consequently, the value of B_f is equal to the number of flows in a table E_n which has smaller service tag than flow f.
  (c) if flow f's backoff timer expires, i.e., waits for B_f timeslots, and the channel is idle, transmit the head-of-line packet of flow f.

Table 1. Table updates between transmission of flows 1 and 4 (assume packet transmission time = 10)

	Table for F1	Table for F2	Table for F3	Table for F4
Before	F1: T1=1	F1: T1=1	F1: T1=1	F2: T2=2
F1 and F4	F2: T2=2	F2: T2=2	F2: T2=2	F3: T3=3
Transmit	F3: T3=3	F3: T3=3	F3: T3=3	F4: T4=4
		F4: T4=4	F4: T4=4	
	Backoff=0	Backoff=1	Backoff=2	Backoff=2
After	F1: T1=11	F1: T1=11	F1: T1=11	F2: T2=2
F1 and F4	F2: T2=2	F2: T2=2	F2: T2=2	F3: T3=3
Transmit	F3: T3=3	F3: T3=3	F3: T3=3	F4: T4=14
		F4: T4=14	F4: T4=14	
	Backoff=2	Backoff=0	Backoff=1	Backoff=2

- *Table updates:* whenever node n hears a new service tag T'_g for any flow g on its table E_n, it updates the table entry for flow g to $[g, T'_g]$. Whenever node n transmits a head-of-line packet for flow f, it updates flow f's service tag in the table entry.

We provide an illustrative example to show how the algorithm works. In the example, as shown in Figure 1, four flows are scheduled from the sender node to its respective receiver node and the dotted line denotes the two nodes are within the communication range. It is assumed that the initial virtual time $V = 0$, and the initial service tags for the four flows are $T_1 = 1$, $T_2 = 2$, $T_3 = 3$, $T_4 = 4$. The table maintained at each sender of the four flows and the backoff calculation and table updates before and after transmission of flows 1 and 4 are shown in Table 1. Flows F_1 and F_4 could transmit simultaneously because they are not neighboring flows (see Figure 1). After the transmission of F_1 and F_4, the service tags of two flows are increased by 10, the packet transmission time, and subsequently, the backoff value of each flow table updated to the number of other flows which have smaller service tag (T) value.

4.2   Protocol Description

In the distributed implementation protocol, each data transmission follows a basic sequence of RTS-CTS-DS-DATA-ACK handshake, and this message exchange is preceded by a backoff for certain number of timeslots. When a node has a packet to transmit, it waits for an appropriate number of timeslots before it initiates the RTS-CTS handshake. In particular, the node checks its local table and sets a backoff timer for flow f to be the number of flows with tags smaller than the tag of flow f. This way, the local minimum-tag flow backs off for zero minislot and contends for the channel immediately. If the backoff timer of f expires without overhearing any ongoing transmission, it starts RTS carrying B_f, the backoff time of flow f according to the table, to initiate the handshake. If the node overhears some ongoing transmission, it cancels its backoff timer and defers until the ongoing transmission completes; In the meantime, it updates its local table for the tag of the on-going neighboring transmitting flow. When other nodes hear a RTS, they defer for one CTS transmission time to permit the sender to receive a CTS reply. When a receiver receives a RTS, it checks its local table. If B_f is greater than or equal to the backoff value for flow f in the receiver's local table, it responds with CTS. Otherwise, the receiver simply drops RTS. This procedure is required for maintaining the table information at both sender and receiver nodes. Once a sender receives the CTS, it transmits DS. When hosts hear either a CTS or a DS message, they will defer until the DATA-ACK transmission completes.

In order to propagate a flow's service tag to all its one-hop neighbors in the node graph and reduce the chance of information loss due to collisions during this service tag information propagation, the tag T_f for flow f is attached in all four packets RTS, CTS, DS and ACK, i.e., the *old tag* in RTS and CTS packets, and *updated tag* in DS and ACK packet.

5   Performance Evaluation

5.1   Simulation Environment

We use simulations to evaluate the performance of our distributed implementation of DGFQ in multimedia ad hoc wireless networks. The following is the simulation environment used in this simulation.

The radio model is based on existing commercial wireless network with a radio transmission range of 250 meters and channel capacity of 2Mbit/sec which is typical capacity of current wireless mobile networks. Moreover, for the distributed implementation of DGFQ scheme, error free channel model is assumed to concentrate our evaluation work on the key features of proposed scheme, i.e., the controllability and adaptability of DGFQ scheme in distributed network environment such as multimedia ad hoc wireless networks to provide delay guaranteed service.

As the traffic source model, we choose the modified MPEG video source, described in [14]. Moreover, we assumed that all the sources have identical characteristics. In this video flow model, there are three types of frame, i.e., I, B and P frames. Each frame size is determined by a Lognormal distribution with a specified mean and standard deviation. A video source generates 24 frames per second.

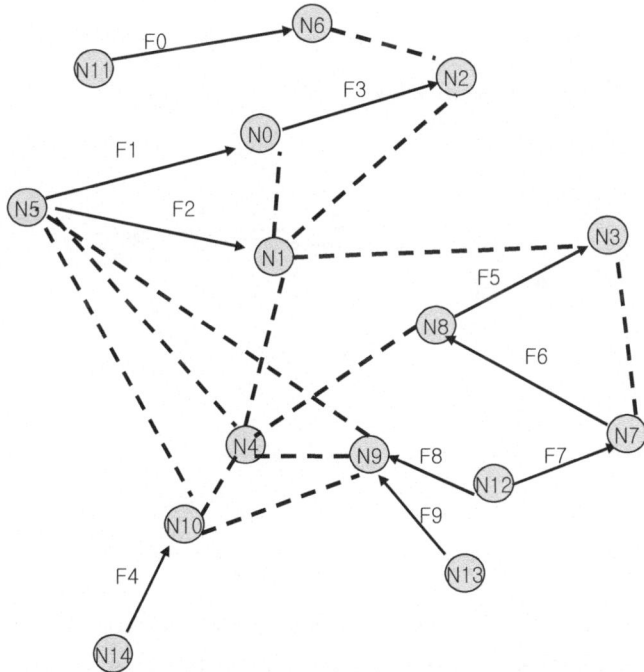

Fig. 2. Node graph of simulated multimedia ad hoc wireless network

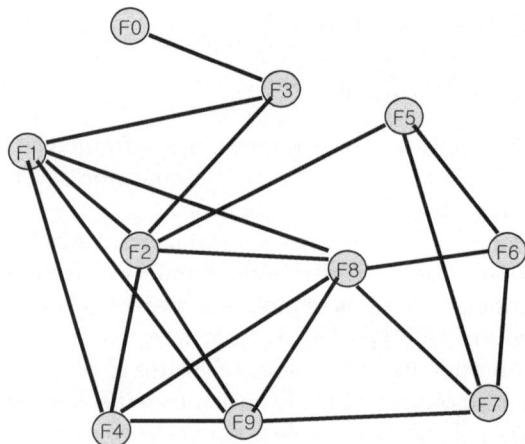

Fig. 3. Flow graph of simulated multimedia ad hoc wireless network

Further, we consider a wireless ad hoc network which includes 14 nodes transmitting 10 flows. Figures 2 and 3 show the node graph and flow graph of simulated network respectively. To testify the controllability of DGFQ for guaranteed
delay provision in distributed network environment, flow $F4$ is controlled with

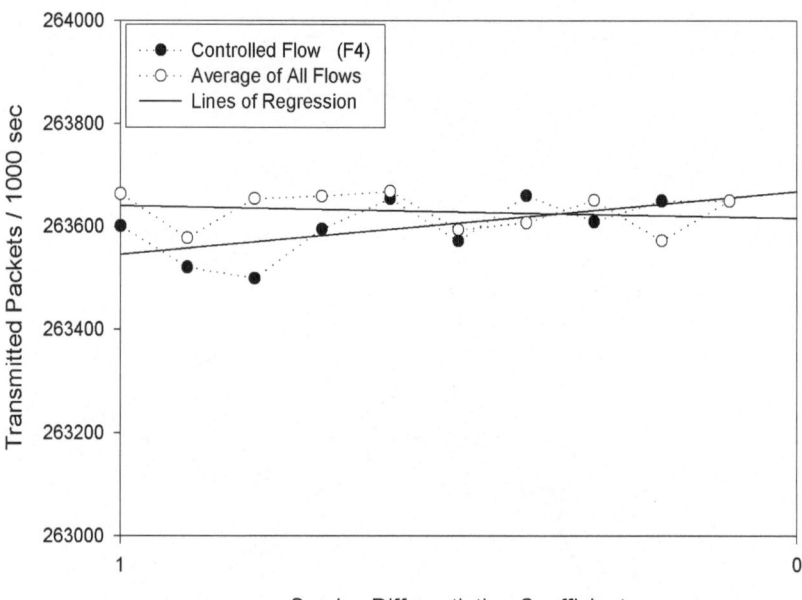

Fig. 4. Total transmitted packets with varying the value of *service differentiation coefficient* (α)

varying the value of α, *the service differentiation coefficient*, for the range of $0 < \alpha \leq 1$, while other flows are assumed to have α value of 1. Finally, the simulation results for flow $F4$ are compared with that of other contending flows and overall average.

Each simulation is run for 1000 seconds, and we selected average delay, maximum delay and throughput as the performance measures as in [10]. Detailed definitions and discussions for these measures are described in the following section.

5.2   Results and Discussions

Throughput. We used *throughput* as a fairness measure, which is total transmitted packets during the whole simulation duration, say, 1000 seconds. Figure 4 shows the throughput of flows with scattered points and their regression. Basically, as reported in [10], there is only a minor differences in throughput between flows either controlled ($F4$) or not (all other flows). In Figure 4, the white circle points and their regression line represents the average throughput of all flows and the black circle points and their regression line shows the throughput of the controlled flow ($F4$). Specifically, as shown in the figure, the difference is several hundred packets over more than 263,000 packets. The number of transmitted packets is inverse proportional to α, it is because α controls $F4$ with the share of channel in some extend, and, subsequently, it affects to the throughput of contending flows. It should also be noticed that it is possible to control individual flow with varying α.

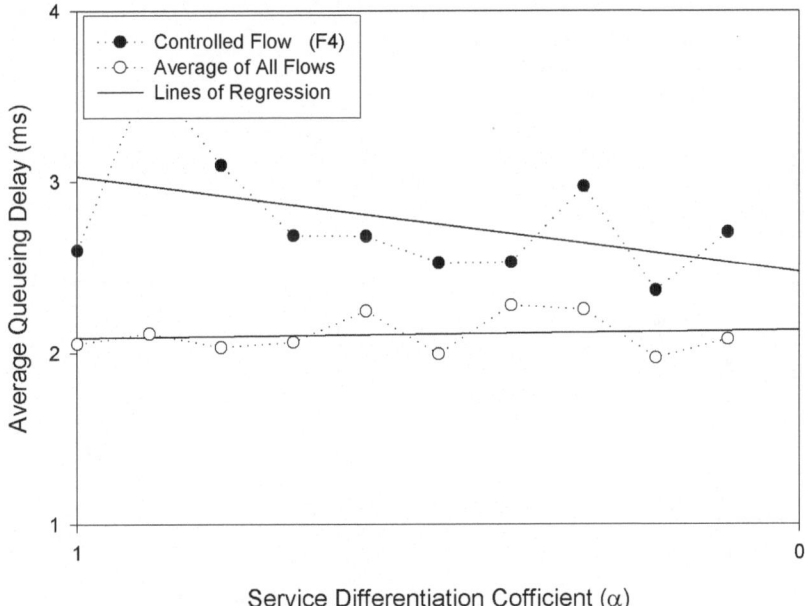

Fig. 5. Average delay with varying the value of *service differentiation coefficient* (α)

Average Delay. In our work *average delay* is defined as the average time interval between the arrival and departure of a packet for a certain time duration. As shown in the Figure 5, the *service differentiation coefficient* α is the key parameter to manage delay performance. In the figure, the white circle points and their regression line represents the overall average delay, averaged for all flows, and the black circle points and their regression line shows the average delay of the controlled flow ($F4$). With varying α we can control the average delay of flow $F4$. As shown in the figure, the control range of average delay could be 1ms. On the other hand, contrary to the throughput case discussed above, delay is proportional to α.

Maximum Delay. The *maximum delay* is another critical performance measure for real time multimedia flows. We define maximum delay as the maximum interval between the arrival and departure of a packet in the system in a certain duration of time, say, simulation duration. We can get the results simultaneously with average delay from the same simulation. As in the previous figures, in Figure 6, the white circle points and their regression line represents the overall maximum delay averaged for all flows, and the black circle points and their regression line shows the maximum delay of the controlled flow ($F4$). From the figure, the control range of maximum delay is about 10ms. We can conclude that maximum delay could also be controlled with α, which means DGFQ controls the maximum delay also in distributed networks.

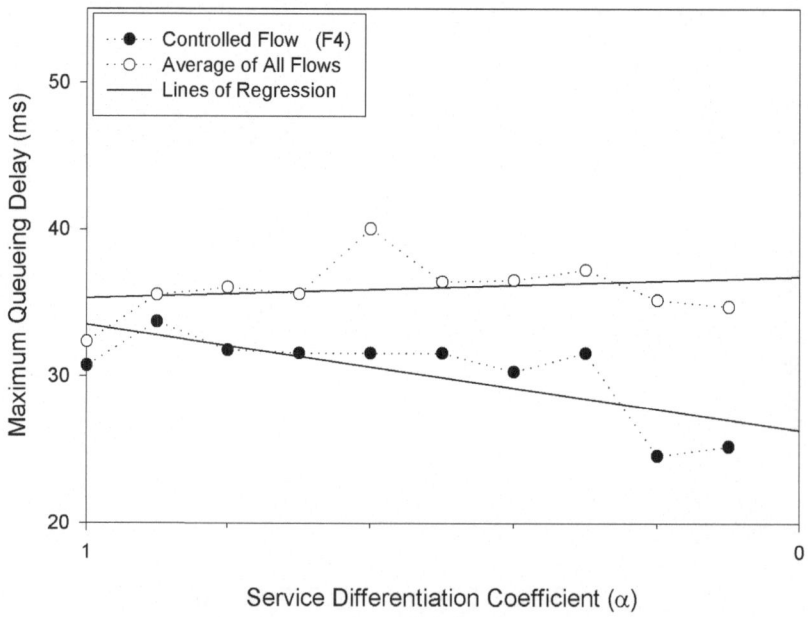

Fig. 6. Maximum delay with varying the value of *service differentiation coefficient* (α)

6   Conclusion

We implemented a delay guaranteed fair queueing(DGFQ) scheme, [10], distributively in the multimedia ad hoc wireless network environment. As far as throughput is concerned, there is only a minor differences between flows either controlled by *service differentiation coefficient* (α) or not. On the other hand, for delay performance, according to the simulation results, both average delay and maximum delay could be controlled by varying the value of α. In summary, it is clear that DGFQ can control the delay performance of multimedia traffic in the distributed network environment as well as centralized network.

We just consider about a limited network environment, i.e., stationary nodes with error-free wireless channel, which is too idealistic to apply our work in the practical systems. So, much more work should be done for the dynamic topology variation by mobile nodes in error-prone wireless channel case as a future work.

References

1. A. Parekh, "A generalized processor sharing approach to flow control in integrated services networks," *PhD Thesis*, MIT Laboratory for Information and Decision Systems, Technical Report LIDS-TR-2089, 1992.
2. J.C.R. Bennett and H. Zhang, "WF2Q: Worst-case fair weighted fair queueing," *IEEE INFOCOM'96*, 1996.
3. P. Goyal, H.M. Vin and H. Chen, "Start-time fair queueing: A scheduling algorithm for integrated service access," *ACM SIGCOMM'96*, August 1996.
4. M. Srivastava, C. Fragouli, and V. Sivaraman, "Controlled Multimedia Wireless Link Sharing via Enhanced Class-Based Queueing with Channel-State-Dependent Packet Scheduling," *IEEE INFOCOM'98*, March 1998.
5. S. Lu, V. Bharghavan and R. Srikant, "Fair scheduling in wireless packet networks," *IEEE/ACM Trans. Networking*, August 1999.
6. S. Lu, T. Nandagopal, and V. Bharghavan, "Fair scheduling in wireless packet networks," *ACM MOBICOM'98*, October 1998.
7. N. H. Vaidya, P. Bahl ann S. Gupta, "Distributed fair scheduling in a wireless LAN," *ACM MOBICOM'00*, August 2000.
8. H. Luo and S. Lu, "A topology-independent fair queueing model in ad hoc wireless networks," *IEEE ICNP'00*, November 2000.
9. H. Luo, P. Medvedev, J. Cheng and S. Lu, "A Self-Coordinating Approach to Distributed Fair Queueung in Ad Hoc Wireless Networks" ," *IEEE INFOCOM'91*, August 1991.
10. H. Yang and K. Kim, "Delay Guaranteed Fair Queueing (DGFQ) in Multimedia Packet Networks," *Proc. MMNS2003*, LNCS 2839, pp.170 - 182, Springer, September 2003.
11. V. Bharghavan, A. Demers, S. Shenker, and L. Zhang, "MACAW: A medium access protocol for wireless LANs, " *ACM SIGCOMM'94*, 1999.
12. J. Ju and V.O.K. Li, "An optimal topology-transparent scheduling method in multihop packet radio networks," *IEEE/ACM Trans. Networking*, 6(3), June 1998.
13. Z. Tang and J.J. Garacia-Luna-Aceves, "A protocol for topologydependent transmission scheduling in wireless networks," *WCNC'99*, September 1999.
14. S. Lee, K. Kim, A. Ahmad, "Delay and data rate decoupled fair queueing for wireless multimedia networks," *Proc. GLOBECOM '02*, 2002, vol. 1, pp.946-950.

End-to-End 'Data Connectivity' Management for Multimedia Networking

K. Ravindran

City College of CUNY and Graduate Center,
Department of Computer Science,
Convent Avenue at 138th Street,
New York, NY 10031, USA
ravi@cs.ccny.cuny.edu

Abstract. The paper describes a management-oriented model for cost-effective 'data connectivity' provisioning between the end-point entities of networked multimedia applications. The 'connectivity' service provider (SP) may maintain multiple policy-based protocol mechanisms that differ in the bandwidth allocation strategies exercised on transport networks and the extent of QoS guarantees enforced for application-level data flows. The required QoS is prescribed through a service interface, with the SP instantiating one of the policy modules with appropriate parameters to meet the QoS requirements. The model allows dynamic switching from one policy module to another, based on a *cost* associated with bandwidth usage by the network infrastructure for a given QoS offering. The management functions of SP monitor the changes and/or outages in network bandwidth in a dynamic setting, and map them onto connectivity costs incurred by the selected policy mechanism. To accommodate this end-to-end connectivity management, the SP employs an extended form of 'diffserv'-style traffic classification for flow aggregation purposes and 'intserv'-style resource control for bandwidth allocation purposes.

1 Introduction

The provisioning of end-to-end 'data connectivity' may be viewed as a service offered over the underlying network infrastructure. Thereupon, clients may build higher level multimedia-oriented services: such as image downloads, real-time video transport, and mining of time-sensitive data. The connectivity service provider (SP) may set up end-to-end paths between data aggregation points to carry the traffic — say, between New York and London. Individual clients may then exchange high volume information over these data paths for sports, business, and entertainment applications. The SP may possibly lease the bandwidth from infrastructure networks (such as telecom companies) for providing the session-level 'data connectivity' between end-points.

In providing 'data connectivity', the SP is faced with two conflicting goals: reducing the bandwidth costs incurred on the network infrastructure for data flows (to maximize the SP's revenues) and allocating enough bandwidth to meet the

J. Dalmau and G. Hasegawa (Eds.): MMNS 2005, LNCS 3754, pp. 190–203, 2005.

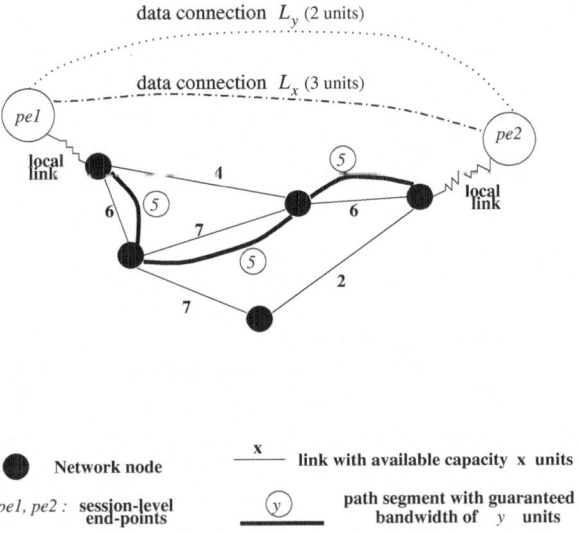

Fig. 1. Bandwidth-controlled connectivity

QOS needs of application sessions (to satisfy the end-user's utility). The SP needs to implement policy mechanisms and management tools that allow balancing these goals. In this paper, we identify a model of connectivity management that allows attaining the revenue and QoS objectives.

Figure 1 illustrates a session-level data path set up between two end-points pe_1 and pe_2. Each segment in the path may be a native communication link between the routers of an IP network or a TCP (or UDP) connection set up between the nodes of an overlay network. Or, the entire path between pe_1 and pe_2 may be a leased line with dedicated bandwidth. Regardless of the network infrastructure, the end-system treats the data path between pe_1 and pe_2 as a single object for the purpose of bandwidth management and admission control.

The SP may employ a control architecture based on *data flows* and *path guarantees* to exercise end-to-end QOS control. It involves:

- Maintaining multiple *diffserv*-type data paths between the end-points with parameterizable QoS differentiation between them;
- Admission control at the end-points with *intserv*-type bandwidth management over the data paths.

The admission control function in an end-system aggregates a large number of data flows with closely-similar QOS needs over a single path. The traffic correlations that exist among such flows allows reaping the statistical multiplexing gains in bandwidth. The path maintenance function in the end-system suitably apportions the available infrastructure bandwidth between the various paths that carry (aggregated) data flows with distinct QoS levels. This bandwidth apportionment allows the SP to enforce per-flow QoS guarantees.

Referring to Figure 1, the available bandwidth between pe_1 and pe_2 is 6 units. Out of this, 5 units are allocated to carry QoS-controlled data flows and the surplus 1 unit is allocated to carry, say, 'best-effort' traffic. The 5 units of bandwidth may in turn be split across two data connections, say, 3 units along L_x and 2 units along L_y to carry high resolution and low resolution video traffic respectively. Here, the SP-level control is about deciding how to estimate the bandwidth of 5 units needed for video traffic and how to split this bandwidth as 3 units and 2 units for L_x and L_y respectively.

The SP may use *policy* functions that prescribe how distinct the flow specs characterizing various data connections are and what cost the per-flow bandwidth usage on a data connection incurs. The SP may also dynamically switch from one policy to another, based on how the costs of bandwidth usage vary as the connection operating point changes (say, due to bandwidth outages in the underlying path). Our model allows installing a repertoire of policy functions at end-points and selecting a suitable policy to make the connectivity provisioning cost-optimal. The paper provides the functional mechanisms to realize the policy switching while sustaining a user-transparent QoS control. These mechanisms are based on our studies on different types multimedia data connections. Overall, our connectivity model can be incorporated into the 'telecommunications management' framework (TMN) that has been standardized for network services [1].

The paper is organized as follows. Section 2 describes a QOS-oriented view of 'data connectivity' and how 'data connections' are managed by the end-system in our model. Section 3 identifies the end-point mechanisms and infrastructure interfaces to support the model. Section 4 compares our approach with existing methods of connectivity control. Section 5 concludes the paper.

2   Our Model of End-to-End Connectivity Management

A session-level connectivity is based on setting up one or more 'data connections' between a pair of peer end-points. The set of links that provide the physical connectivity between end-points constitutes the 'infrastructure', and the available link capacities in a path connecting the end-points constitute the 'resource'. An admission control protocol exercises the bandwidth to sustain a certain QoS of data transfer over the connections.

In this section, we provide a management-oriented view of the end-to-end mechanisms that exercise bandwidth allocation control.

2.1   Management-Oriented View of Connectivity Protocols

A 'data connection' is characterized by QoS attributes: such as the sustainable rate of data flow, maximum allowed data loss, and end-to-end delay jitter on data [2,3]. The client application prescribes this QoS to the 'connectivity service' provider (SP) when requesting the setup of a 'data connection'. The internal functions of a SP's infrastructure that realize end-to-end data connectivity, such as packet scheduling strategies, are however hidden from the application.

A connectivity protocol $\mathcal{P}$ encapsulates the functionality to manage the end-to-end admission of data traffic and the required provisioning of infrastructure bandwidth. The QoS parameters q instantiate this functionality at run-time to control the extent of bandwidth allocation. The bandwidth expended b may be represented as: $b = \mathcal{R}(x_{\mathcal{P}})$, where $x_{\mathcal{P}}$ is the protocol-internal state that reflects the current operating point of the connection (such as queue sizes, window credits, etc). For instance, $\mathcal{R}$ may depict a mathematical formula for 'link utilization' achieved by a 'window-based data transfer' protocol, expressed in terms of the window sizes and link error rate. Such a functional representation allows a management module to maintain a handle on the bandwidth allocation exercised by $\mathcal{P}$ on 'data connections'.

2.2   Connectivity-Level Objects for Management Control

The management control is exercised on two types of session-level objects: 'data flow' and 'data connection'. A 'data flow' is a sequence of packets transported from the source to receiver entities, subject to a certain end-to-end QOS. A 'data connection' is set up over the transport path between source and receiver entities, with a prescribed amount of bandwidth allocation to carry a group of data flows with a closely-similar QOS characteristics. See Figure 2. A 'data connection' is the object granularity for bandwidth allocation purposes, whereas a 'data flow' is the object granularity for end-to-end admission control.

Given a bandwidth apportionment $b(r)$ for a data flow r, the amount of bandwidth usage $\sum_{\forall r} b(r)$ incurred by a 'data connection' C can be transcribed into a cost of transporting various data flows $\{r\}$ over C. This cost may depend

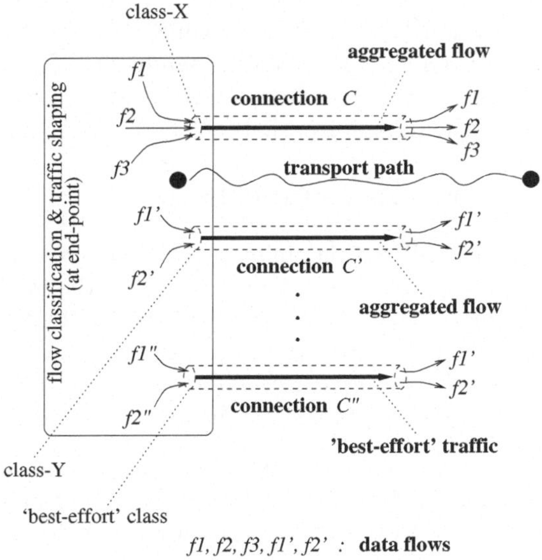

$f1, f2, f3, f1', f2'$: **data flows**

Fig. 2. 'Data connection' versus 'data flows'

on, say, the infrastructure-level tariffs incurred for bandwidth allocation[1]. The SP attempts to multiplex many data flows on a single connection to reap the gains arising from a statistical sharing of the bandwidth — and hence reduce the costs. This revenue-oriented incentive forms the basis for a dynamic control of connectivity mechanisms employed by the SP.

2.3 Application-Level Flow Specs

The connectivity protocol embodies a policy function $\mathcal{F}$ to map a data flow r to the bandwidth needs b at network elements in a data path. In one form, r may be given by a peak rate p, average rate A, loss tolerance limit Δ (specified as a fraction of the average rate in the range $[0.0, 1.0]$), delay tolerance limit $\mathcal{D}$, and auto-correlation parameter ζ of data traffic. Note that $\zeta \in (0.0, 1.0)$, with $\zeta \to 0.0^+$ indicating a totally random flow and $\zeta \to 1.0^-$ indicating a high degree of statistical dependence of the current peak rate on past peak rates. $\mathcal{F}$ maps a data flow r to bandwidth needs b such that $\mathcal{F}(r') > \mathcal{F}(r'')$ for $r' > r''$. See [4] for guidelines to prescribe the '>' relation on flow types f.

Consider a data flow r of type $f = (A, p, \zeta, \Delta, \mathcal{D})$ over a network element E, where $A < p$ and $\Delta > 0$. A policy function[2] $\mathcal{F}$ may employ *optimistic* bandwidth allocation on E by assuming that the peak rate of flow does not persist long enough to backlog packets at the input queue of E to a level where more than a fraction Δ of the packets will miss their deadlines prescribed by $\mathcal{D}$. Such an allocation will have: $[A - \Delta] < \mathcal{F}(r) < p$, with the actual allocation determined by $\mathcal{D}$, the duration of p relative to A (i.e, burstiness), ζ, and input queue length of E. If $\mathcal{F}$ and $\mathcal{F}'$ depict optimistic policies such that $\mathcal{F}(r) > \mathcal{F}'(r)$ for some $r \in \mathrm{FLOW\_SPECS}$, then $\mathcal{F}(r') > \mathcal{F}'(r')|_{\forall r' \in \mathrm{FLOW\_SPECS}}$.

Note that the flow type f may be viewed as a 'traffic class' in the DiffServ architecture. A connection $C(f)$ is then a 'DiffServ' path to carry data flows of type f. The apportionment of available bandwidth B on a network path across the various connections sharing this path corresponds to a 'proportional differentiation' in the scheduling of packets of these traffic classes [6].

2.4 Policy-Based Estimation of Bandwidth

$\mathcal{F}$ encapsulates a resource allocation policy realized at the end-points. Typically, an allocation may be somewhat less than supporting the peak rate p in a sustained manner, but more than the average rate A, with the constraint being that the packet loss over the observation interval T_{obs} is less than Δ. An example of allocation policy is to reserve 10% additional bandwidth relative to that necessary to sustain the average rate A. Typically, the scheduler should visit the

---

[1] The SP may possibly lease fiber-optic link-level connectivity between end-points from telecom companies (such as AT&T), and then control bandwidth allocation on this leased link to support session-level 'data connectivity' for customers.

[2] The (p, A, Δ, ζ) tuples may be viewed as prescribing distinct 'virtual link classes' (see [5] in this context). The admission controller then maps an application-generated data flow to one of these 'virtual links'.

packet queue of C for a portion $(\frac{b}{CAP(E)} - \Delta)$ of T_{obs}, where b is the effective bandwidth necessary for a no-loss transfer of packets over the link.

The resource encapsulation embodied in $\mathcal{F}$ allows different policy functions to be installed at the management interface points of a 'data connection'. Our focus here is not on the accuracy in estimating the bandwidth needs itself, but is on the signaling support for a reasonable estimate from the traffic-oriented QoS parameters. It may be noted that the IntServ-style bandwidth allocation embodied in our model is exercised only at the end-system[3].

2.5   Revenue Incentives of Flow Aggregation

One or more data flows may be multiplexed over a single connection C. The multiplexing may reap bandwidth gains due to statistical sharing of the bandwidth allocated for C across these flows. Typically, the SP may multiplex flows with similar QoS characteristics over C so that all packets of these flows get the same level of scheduling. For instance, multiple MPEG-2 video streams may require the same level of loss/delay tolerance [9], which makes the video packets schedulable with a single-level priority scheme. Such an aggregation allows incorporating the gains arising from a statistical sharing of connection bandwidth in the SP's revenue-oriented decisions.

In 'one-at-a-time' floor-controlled voice conferencing, the voice data bursts from various speakers may be spaced in time. This correlation in turn allows keeping the bandwidth allocation on C to just sustain a 64 *kbps* data rate for all the voice streams combined, that otherwise would be higher if allocations are done separately for each voice stream.

Consider a system of sensors that collect data pertaining to a common external phenomenon (e.g., multiple radars observing a plane flying over a terrain). The data collected by various sensors may exhibit a high degree of correlation in the traffic behaviors, since these data pertain to the same physical phenomenon. A traffic shaper at end-points can spread out the peak rates of sensor data in a controlled manner to achieve a steady but lower bandwidth consumption.

Thus, an aggregation of closely-similar data flows over C offers the potential for statistical multiplexing gains. Higher the number of flows multiplexed over C, more are the bandwidth gains. The gains however accrue at the expense of a certain amount of packet loss.

As can be seen, a 'data connection' offers the right granularity to enforce bandwidth allocation policies by the SP. A management perspective of the end-system mechanisms to control such 'connection' objects is described next.

3   End-System Protocol Mechanisms

The infrastructure mechanisms are built around 'packet scheduling' over data connections, weighted by their bandwidth allocations. The packet scheduler is

---

[3] The IntServ-type and DiffServ-type of functional elements in our end-system model are inspired by, but are different (both in context and scope) from, the IntServ and DiffServ architectures proposed by IETF for use in the core network elements [7,8].

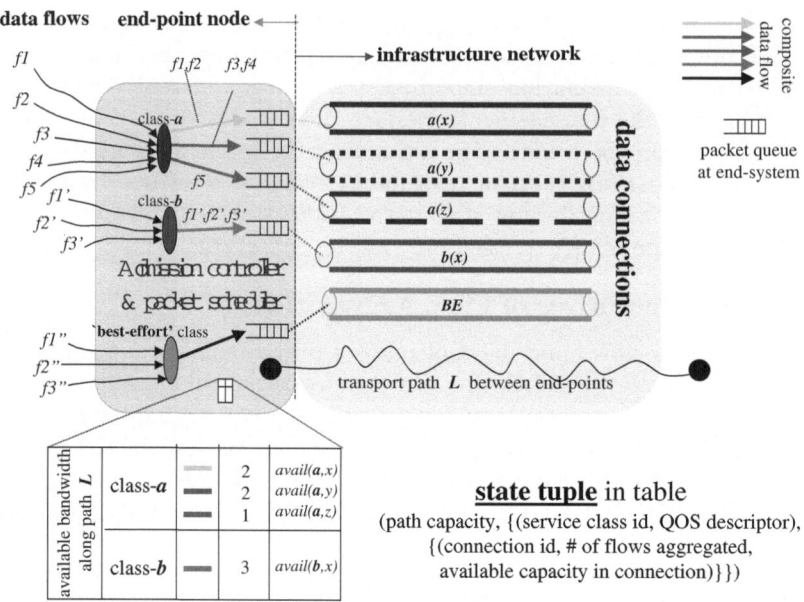

Fig. 3. State maintained at end-point nodes

a canonical end-point element that interfaces between the connectivity protocol $\mathcal{P}$ and the network infrastructure. There is however no per-flow state tracking at the infrastructure level[4].

3.1   State Information at End-Points

Aggregating multiple flows over a single connection C reduces the scheduling overhead, relative to setting up a separate connection for each data flow. Figure 3 illustrates the state information maintained at end-points to support flow aggregation. The key pieces of state information include the QoS specs that classifies the component flows, number of flows multiplexed, policy function to map QoS specs to bandwidth needs, and available bandwidth on a connection. Since this information is maintained at connection-level, the amount of per-flow state is reduced by $\mathcal{O}(n)$, where n is the number of flows aggregated over C. The only per-flow control activity incurred at the admission controller when flows are admitted or removed is to adjust the number of flows n and re-estimate the bandwidth needs using policy functions[5].

---

[4] We assume a FIFO based intra-connection scheduling across the component flows. This ensures the scalability of end-point mechanisms by avoiding the need for per-flow state-tracking.

[5] Flow aggregation in our model is primarily for revenue-oriented bandwidth management purposes (besides achieving scalability of protocol-level implementations of admission control). The per-flow guarantees experienced by end-to-end peer-entities is a by-product of this paradigm shift in bandwidth management.

To enable the aggregation of data flows, the session-level manager may assign a unique label $l(C)$ to bind the component flows together, whereupon the admission controller can multiplex them over C. Here, $l(C)$ is a session-level index to the grouping of data flows that are carried over C. In the example of sensor system, $l(C)$ may be the id referring to the external phenomenon from which the sensor data are collected. The session-level labeling of connections can be part of, say, a MPLS-based routing [10] over the path set up through the network.

3.2   Determination of Bandwidth Savings

A 'data connection' shared across many closely-similar flows entails a lower per-flow bandwidth allocation that is quantifiable, in comparison to a case of sharing the underlying network path across many disparate flows. The bandwidth allocation over a shared 'data connection' satisfies *weak additivity*, indicated as:

$$\mathcal{F}(r_i)|_{i=1,2,\cdots,n} < \mathcal{F}(r_1 \oplus r_2 \oplus \cdots \oplus r_n) \leq \mathcal{F}(r_1) + \mathcal{F}(r_2) + \cdots + \mathcal{F}(r_n),$$

where $\mathcal{F}(r_i) > A_i$ and '$\oplus$' is the aggregation operator. This relation captures the possible savings due to sharing of connection-level bandwidth across various flows, with the actual gains determined by the cross-correlation parameter associated with these flows. Such an end-point admission control procedure is illustrated below:

> **admit_flow**$(r_{i+1}, q, C)|_{i=1,2,\cdots}$ /* q: flow descriptor for connection C */
>   additional bandwidth $X := \mathcal{F}(r_1 \oplus \cdots \oplus r_i \oplus r_{i+1}) - \mathcal{F}(r_1 \oplus \cdots \oplus r_i)$;
>   if $(X < \text{availbw}(C))$ /* enough bandwidth is available */
>   admit new flow r_{i+1};
>   availbw$(C) := $ availbw(C) - X;
>   else
>   reject new flow r_{i+1}.

When there is no connection-level sharing, the inability to map the traffic correlation onto the packet scheduling exercised on various data flows forces the end-system to determine the bandwidth needs independently for each of the flows. So, the total allocation is $\sum_{i=1}^{n} \mathcal{F}(r_i)$. This in turn precludes bandwidth savings that may otherwise be feasible due to a shared allocation driven by traffic cross-correlation across the data flows.

In a general form, the per-flow bandwidth allocation may be given as:

$$\mathcal{R}_{bw}(n) = \frac{\mathcal{F}(r_1 \oplus r_2 \oplus \cdots \oplus r_n)}{n}.$$

The monotonicity condition that depicts the bandwidth sharing is: $\mathcal{R}_{bw}(n) < \mathcal{R}_{bw}(n')$ for $n > n'$. Figure 4 illustrates how a policy function $\mathcal{F}$ may

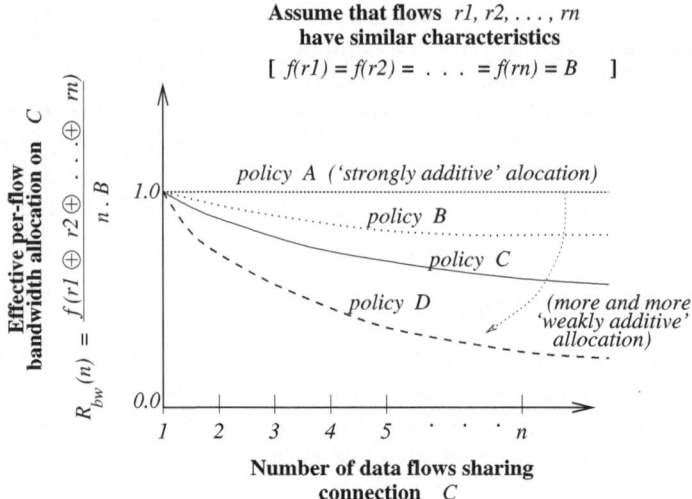

Fig. 4. Bandwidth allocation policies for shared connections (an empirical view)

capture these gains, so that it can be plugged in by the SP at appropriate control points[6].

3.3   Packet Delay and Loss Checks

Packet delay checks are made against flow-specific delay tolerances. However, a 'connection' is the object granularity seen at the scheduler level. The scheduler may use the connection id (cid) carried in packets to index them into appropriate queues and exercise packet scheduling therefrom. Since only flows with similar characteristics are multiplexed over a connection, delay checks at connection-level can provide information about packets meeting flow-specific delay tolerance parameter $\mathcal{D}$. The 'delay comparison' relation for a packet p is:

$$p.\text{timestamp} + \mathcal{D}(p.\text{cid}) \; > \; \text{current\_time} + T_{tx},$$

which qualifies p as meeting the deadline at receiver. Note that an excessively delayed packet is deemed as a lost packet for end-to-end control purposes. The tolerance parameters $\mathcal{D}$ and Δ are passed on to the admission controller through a signaling mechanism for use by the scheduler.

---

[6] It is not the mechanism of 'statistical multiplexing' that we focus in the paper. Rather, it is how we can quantitatively represent the policies that reap 'statistical multiplexing' gains, so that these gains can be factored into the flow admission decisions by the SP. In this light, how effective a statistical multiplexing scheme is and how good a quantitative representation of the multiplexing gains is are orthogonal aspects. The former pertains to a traffic engineering based protocol design, whereas the latter deals with how to incorporate the gains in a macroscopic policy function for use in revenue-based decisions.

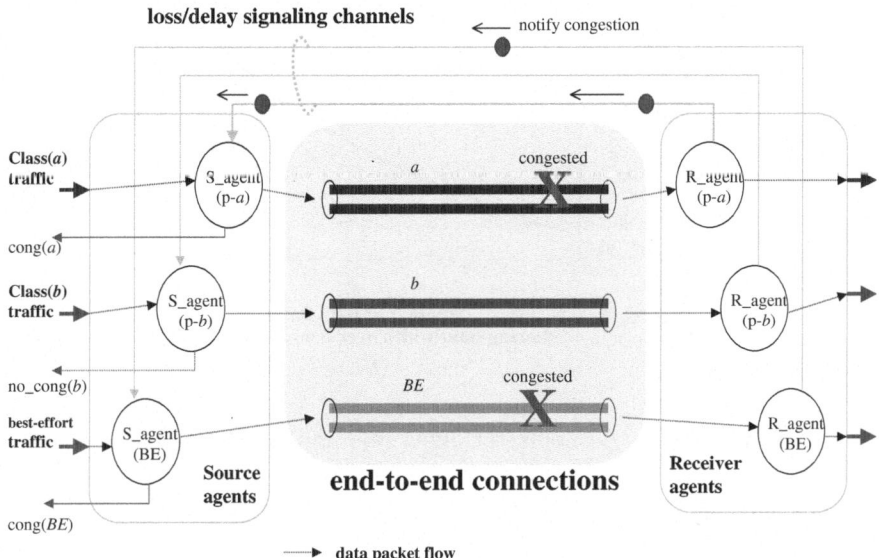

Fig. 5. Agent-based connection monitoring

Figure 5 shows an agent-based implementation of the monitor for packet loss and delays. Here, congestion on a data connection C may arise due to a possible inability of the admission controller to determine the allowed levels of flow multiplexing over C prior to actually admitting the flows. In our study, the signaling of packet loss from the agents at receiver end to the agents at source end is carried out using IETF RTCP. The signaling delay on a 4-hop network is measured about 30 $msec$.

3.4   Optimal Level of Multiplexing

The multiplexing of data flows over a connection C may affect client-level QoS due to excessive path sharing among data flows and sustained higher rates in many of them. Also, the intra-connection multiplexing and de-multiplexing overhead on packets — which is another form of cost (besides bandwidth cost) — increases with the number of flows multiplexed on C. Figure 6 shows this relationship in an empirical form. The work in [11] has shown that the queuing delay of packets is a monotonically increasing function of the number of flows n that feed packets into the queue. Thus, beyond a certain level of bandwidth sharing (say, for $n > n''$), the end-to-end delay of packets belonging to various flows may increase to a level where the client-prescribed loss tolerance limit Δ is not met. This packet loss behavior is depicted as:

$$\mathcal{R}_{loss}(n) = \frac{\sum_{i=1}^{n} p_i - \mathcal{F}(r_1 \oplus r_2 \oplus \cdots \oplus r_n)}{n},$$

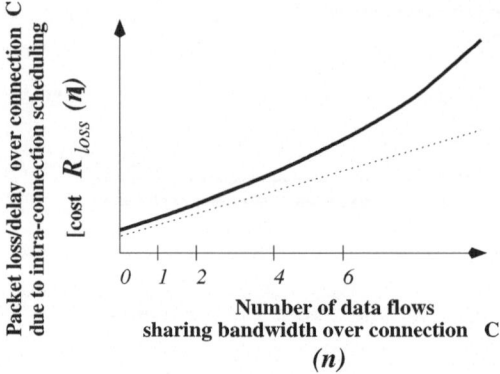

Fig. 6. Intra-connection scheduling costs (an empirical view)

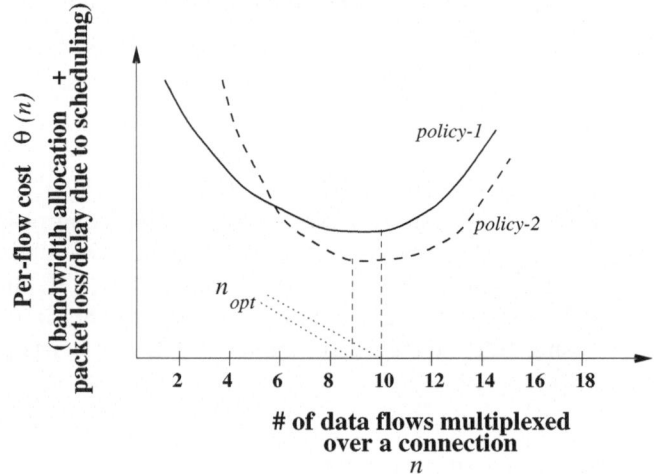

Fig. 7. Combined intra-connection bandwidth and scheduling costs

where p_i is the peak rate of flow r_i. The monotonicity condition is: $\mathcal{R}_{loss}(n) > \mathcal{R}_{loss}(n')$ for $n > n'$.

In general, the per-flow bandwidth cost $\mathcal{R}_{bw}(n)$ on a connection can be reduced by increasing the number of flows sharing this path. The lower bandwidth usage may however be counteracted by increased packet loss $\mathcal{R}_{loss}(n)$ arising from scheduling delays. Accordingly, the number of flows admitted in C should not exceed a threshold n_{opt} that may cause connection failures due to excessive packet loss. See Figure 7. To enable determination of this optimal point at run-time, the SP prescribes a cost function of the form:

$$\Theta(n) = a.\mathcal{R}_{bw}(n) + b.\mathcal{R}_{loss}(n)$$

for use by the admission controller, where a and b are normalization constants. Since there is no closed-form analytical relation between $\Theta(n)$ and n, the optimal value n_{opt} needs to be determined dynamically by measurements of packet loss experienced over C at run-time. That $\mathcal{R}_{BW}(n)$ and $\mathcal{R}_{loss}(n)$ exhibit monotonicity properties ensures that the $\Theta(n)$-versus-n relation has a single global minimum, and hence allows determining n_{opt} by an iterative search procedure.

With multiple policy functions available for the SP, empirically relating them in terms of cost allows the SP to dynamically switch from one policy to another. If $\mathcal{F}$ and $\mathcal{F}'$ depict policies such that $\mathcal{F}(r) > \mathcal{F}'(r)$ for some $r \in$ flow_specs, we then have: $n_{opt}(\mathcal{F}) > n_{opt}(\mathcal{F}')$. The SP thus determines the optimal assignment of groups of data flows to a set of distinct connections[7].

The cost analysis required for connectivity control may be based on separate empirical studies of various policy functions.

4   Related Works

There have been works that attempt to get the advantages of "IntServ" world, namely, flexibility and fair QoS support and that of "DiffServ" world, namely, robustness and scalability. We compare these works with our approach, with an emphasis on SP-level revenue incentives.

Techniques for flow aggregation and avoidance of per-flow tracking have been studied elsewhere: such as the 'dynamic packet state' based packet classification and scheduling by core routers [14] and the 'link-based fair aggregation' for class-based fair queue scheduling at the ingress and egress routers and for intra-class FIFO scheduling at the core routers [15]. Likewise, the admission control architecture in [16] allows the end-points probe the network for bandwidth availability and admit a group of flows only when there is no congestion in the network. Architecturally, these existing techniques for QoS control are based on two session-level objects: 'data flows' and 'bandwidth guaranteed data paths'.

In contrast, our model stipulates another object, namely, 'data connection', to embody the grouping of one or more closely-similar data flows. This in turn allows incorporating statistical multiplexing gains as part of a cost assignment policy to application-level flows. Referring to Figure 1, the 'data connections' L_x of 3 units bandwidth and L_y of 2 units bandwidth simply do not exist in the current models. Instead, only a single end-to-end path of 5 units bandwidth is visible to the session-level controller for multiplexing the various data flows. In this light, the 'data connection' objects in our model offer a better means of quantifying and estimating the bandwidth gains arising from statistical multiplexing of data flows to enable revenue-driven decision-making by the SP's.

In a larger sense, our connectivity model may provide a management dimension to the existing control architectures for end-point flow admissions.

---

[7] Methods to quantify network resource allocations (such as those described in [12,13]) can be incorporated in policy functions.

5   Conclusions

The paper described a model of session-level connectivity provisioning for use by multimedia networked applications. The model is based on creating a variety of diffserv-type of 'data connections' with QoS differentiation and apportioning the available bandwidth across these connections using intserv-type of end-point admission control. The model employs a policy-driven control of infrastructure bandwidth allocations, for cost-effective provisioning of data connectivity.

Our model allows dynamic switching from one policy function to another, based on a notion of cost associated with the infrastructure bandwidth usage, for a given level of QoS support. The strategy is to reduce the per-flow cost incurred by multiplexing many closely-similar data flows on a single connection. The multiplexing brings two benefits to the SP, without compromising the QoS needs of applications. First, it reduces the per-flow resource allocation due to the gains accrued from a statistical sharing of connection resources. Second, it amortizes the connection-level overhead across many flows. The level of cost reduction, and hence revenue accrual, can be controlled by the SP using a range of policy functions that take into account the QoS attributes of data flows.

Our model accommodates the above strategy through a management-oriented interface that allows the SP to maintain a repertoire of policy functions and choose one therefrom for providing an appropriate level of 'data connectivity' to the client applications. The paper described the functional mechanisms to monitor the end-to-end QOS and adjust the connection operating points to maximize the SP's revenue without compromising the user-level QoS needs.

Our study shows that the connectivity management model can be employed for QoS-sensitive multimedia networks in a scalable and flexible manner.

Acknowledgement

The author acknowledges **Dr. Xiliang Liu** for the discussions on how bandwidth estimation can be incorporated into a service-level management framework for 'data connections'.

References

1. M. Subramanian. Telecommunications Management Network. Chapter 11, Network Management: Principles and Practice, Addison-Wesley Publ. Co. (2000).
2. S. Keshav. Scheduling. Chapter 9, An Engineering Approach to Computer Networking, Addison-Wesley Publ. Co., (1996), 209-260.
3. A. S. Tanenbaum. Congestion Control, Quality of Service, Performance Issues. Chapters 5.3, 5.4, and 6.6, Computer Networks, Prentice-Hall Publ. Co., 4th ed. (2003).
4. J. Wroclawski. Specification of the Controlled-load Network Element Service. Internet RFC 2211 (1997).
5. S. Floyd and V. Jacobson. Link-sharing and Resource Management Models for Packet Networks. IEEE/ACM Transactions on Networking, vol.3, no.4 (1995).

6. C. Dovrolis and P. Ramanathan. Proportional Differentiated Services, Part-II: Loss Rate Differentiation and Packet Dropping. Intl. Workshop on Quality of Service, IWQoS'00, Pittsburgh, USA (2000).
7. S. Berson and S. Vincent. Aggregation Internet Integrated Services State. Internet RFC (1997).
8. K. Nichols, V. Jacobsen, and L. Zhang. Two-bit Differentiated Services Architecture for Internet. Internet RFC 2638 (1999).
9. L. Boroczky, A. Y. Ngai, and E. C. Westermann. Statistical Multiplexing Using MPEG-2 Video Encoders. IBM Technical Journal, vol.43, no.4 (1999).
10. U. Black. MPLS and Label Switching Networks. Prentice-Hall Publ. Co., 2nd ed. (2002).
11. R. Guerin and A. Orda. QoS Routing in Networks with Inaccurate Information: Theory and Algorithms. IEEE/ACM Transactions on Networking, vol.7, no.3 (1999).
12. H. M. Mason and H. R. Varian. Pricing Congestible Network Resources. IEEE Journal on Selected Areas in Communications, vol.13, no.7, (1995), 1141-1149.
13. J. Vicente, H. Cartmill, G. Maxson, S. Siegel, R. Fenger. Managing Enhanced Network Services: a Pragmatic View of Policy-Based Management. Intel Tech. Journal, Q1, (2000).
14. I. Stoica and H. Zhang. Providing Guaranteed Services Without Per-flow Management. Proc. ACM SIGCOMM'99, Cambridge, USA, (1999).
15. Y. Jiang. Link-based Fair Aggregation: a Simple Approach to Scalable Support of Per-Flow Service Guarantees. Tech. Report, Norwegian Inst. of Technology, Norway (2004).
16. L. Breslau, E. W. Knightly, S. Shenker, I. Stoica, and H. Zhang. End-point Admission Control: Architectural Issues and Performance. Proc. ACM SIGCOMM'00, Stockholm, Sweden, (2000).

Improving the SLA-Based Management of QoS for Secure Multimedia Services

Sandrine Duflos[1], Valérie C. Gay[2], Brigitte Kervella[1], and Eric Horlait[1]

[1] Laboratoire d'Informatique de Paris VI, 8, Rue du capitaine Scott, 75015 Paris, France
{sandrine.duflos, brigitte.kervella, eric.horlait}@lip6.fr
[2] UTS Faculty of IT, PO Box 123, Broadway NSW 2007, Sydney, Australia
Valerie.Gay@uts.edu.au

Abstract. This paper proposes to integrate security parameters into the Service Level Specification (SLS) template proposed in the Tequila project to improve SLA-based management of QoS [8], [21]. Integrating those parameters in the QoS part of the Service Level Agreement (SLA) specification is essential in particular for secure multimedia services since the QoS is negotiated when the multimedia service is deployed. Security mechanisms need to be negotiated at deployment time when sensible multimedia information is exchanged. In this paper we show that including security parameters in the SLA specification improves the SLA-based management of QoS and therefore the negotiation, deployment and use of the secure multimedia service. The parameters this paper proposes to integrate have the advantage to be understandable by both the end-users and service providers.

1 Introduction

Today, many multimedia services are available to end-users over the Internet. They allow the exchange of more or less sensitive information needing different levels of protection. These services have generally Quality of Service (QoS) requirements according to the medias used (audio, video, text, etc.) and also security requirements depending on the type of the service used and the sensibility of the data they exchanged. For example a personal electronic multimedia medical file exchange requires a high security protection whereas multimedia e-mail or videoconference services might not have the same security requirements.

The protection during the exchange is usually achieved using security mechanisms and protocols. However, adding security to a service increases the resource consumption and the delay of the exchange, and therefore decreases the quality of the service. The Centre for Information Systems Security Studies and Research (Monterey California) published studies on these issues [9], [24].

To provide the best possible QoS for secure services, we think that security needs to be negotiated and deployed at the same time than QoS since security processing consumes resources from both the end-user (EU) and the provider (e.g.: CPU, throughput, delay) and has therefore an impact on the QoS.

A SLA is a specific contract between a service provider (SP) and its customers [26]. It contains, on one hand, general information to identify the customer and the service to provide. On the other hand, it contains technical information to identify the

J. Dalmau and G. Hasegawa (Eds.): MMNS 2005, LNCS 3754, pp. 204–215, 2005.
© IFIP International Federation for Information Processing 2005

required quality for those services [26], [27]. This second (technical) part corresponds to the Service Level Specification (SLS). The integration of QoS in SLS is the subject of many projects and publications [5], [10], [2], [11], [12], [20], [13]. They are presented in sections 2.1 and 2.2. The SLA specifications used or defined in these projects are not explicitly considering security. We suggest to group QoS and security together for negotiation and deployment in the SLS.

Our proposal is to extend the SLS template defined by the members of the Tequila project using parameters to express security. The selection of these parameters is discussed in one of our previous publications [4]. The parameters have the advantage of being understandable by both EUs and SPs. Integration of such parameters would allow the improvement of SLA-based management of QoS with the generation of network policies that ensure the reservation of adequate amount of resources for both the security and QoS needs. In addition, integration of security parameters within the SLS would enable SPs to propose Security of Service (SoS) to their customers. This allows customers to get the level of security they require for their services, without needing to be experts in security and without necessary having the appropriated security mechanisms available on their host.

This paper gives in Section 2 a state of the art on SLS for QoS and SoS management. Section 3 describes how to insert selected SoS parameters in an existing SLS. Section 4 presents the mapping of SLS parameters onto network policies and Section 5 gives an example of mapping. Section 6 discusses issues on the influence of security mechanisms on network and service performance to improve SLA-based management of QoS and SoS. Section 7 concludes on open issues and perspectives of this work.

2   Service Level Specifications for QoS and Security Management

In this section we first describe existing work on SLS for QoS management. We then present existing work on security for SLS and finally we explain our choices to integrate security parameters in SLS.

2.1   Service Level Specifications for QoS Management

A lot of work deals with SLS for QoS management. We can mention various projects such as Aquila (Adaptive Resource Control for QoS Using an IP-based Layered Architecture) [5], [10], Cadenus (Creation and Deployment of End-User Services in Premium IP Networks) [2], Mescal (Management of End-to-end Quality of Service across the Internet At Large) [11], Sequin (Service Quality across Independently Managed Networks) [12] and Tequila (Traffic Engineering for Quality of Service in the Internet, at Large Scale) [20], [13].

The Aquila, Cadenus and Tequila consortia provide IP Premium services over the Internet [18]. These three projects have worked together to define an SLS template tailored to IP networks. The resulting SLS, the Tequila SLS consists of the four following units:

- The common unit, which contains general information identifying the context of the SLA (information about the provider, the customer, the service type, the time and the period of SLA applicability).

- The topology unit, which gives information on the points used by the service to access the provider domain, and the relationship of traffic generation and consumption amongst them.
- The QoS unit, which describes the traffic streams that are subject to the SLA and the nature and extent of service differentiation provided to them.
- The monitoring unit, which defines a set of parameters that need to be collected and reported to the customer in order to be compared with the SLA ones.
  Each unit is also divided in sub-units that are not detailed here.

This SLS template is in the process of being standardised through the IETF. The documents containing the drafts are [25], [21], [22], [8]. Furthermore, it is used in other projects such as Sequin or Mescal. The Sequin project handles the Tequila work to provide an SLS template for the IP Premium service between National Research and Education Networks and the trans-European research backbone GEANT [23]. The Mescal project, which builds on Tequila results, uses the Tequila SLS for inter-domain interactions. It aims at negotiating the QoS between Customer and SP and between two SPs, while the Tequila project focused mainly on Customer-SP interactions [19].

2.2 Service Level Specification for SoS Management

Little work has been conducted on security integration in SLS. The Arcade Project is one of the exceptions. It defines an SLS for IPsec [1], [28]. It proposes security parameters to integrate into SLS by succinctly defining a network level security SLS specific to a Linux implementation of the IPsec protocol [17]. Two categories of parameters are distinguished in this SLS: the *SLA-dependent* and the *SLA-independent* parameters. The *SLA-dependent parameters* are inherent to the SLA. The *SLA-independent* gather the parameters that can be reused in others SLAs, where a similar service is required. They consist of parameters that are used in the IPsec security association. Their objective is to map the SLS onto the IETF/DMTF IPsec Configuration Policy Information Model [14]. This SLS does not consider QoS.

2.3 Our Choices to Integrate Security in SLS

Of the studied projects none is considering both quality and security of service. The SLS defined in the Tequila project represents a complete specification for the IP service and is becoming a standard. However it is specific to QoS management and does not include security parameters despite the impact of security processing on the quality of the service. This SLS is a good base to add security parameters.

3 Extension of the Tequila SLS Template with Security Parameters

This section describes how we integrate the SoS parameters identified in [4] in the Tequila SLS template to improve the QoS management of secure services.

These parameters have the advantage of being interpretable by both EU and SPs. Two abstraction levels are therefore available: one abstract level that can be qualified, understandable by non expert EU and a precise level that can be quantified, interpretable by the expert EU and its SP to negotiate the service configuration and deployment. The identified qualitative parameters correspond to the common security services (confidentiality, authentication, integrity and non-repudiation) plus optional parameters derived from security protocols (security protocol, tunnelling and no-replay). To each qualitative parameter corresponds a set of quantitative values.

Supplying SoS is a quality guarantee for secure multimedia services. It is essential to consider security as a parameter to provide a good quality to the service. Also, security processing acts on the quality of the service. It increases resource consumption, induced delay and traffic load. Considering security as a QoS functionality makes it easier to take into account the impact of security on the QoS. It is also a logical placeholder since security and QoS are applied to the same traffic. Also, as the traffic is already described in the traffic descriptor sub-unit of QoS unit it avoids the useless repetition of the traffic description. This sub-unit contains combination of DiffServ Information, Source information, Destination Information and Application Information [8]. The Source, Destination and Application Information is necessary for security protocol configuration [17],[3].

To introduce SoS parameters in the SLS, we choose to add a new sub-unit to the QoS unit of the Tequila SLS template, the SoS parameters sub-unit, rather than adding a specific security unit. This sub-unit contains the common parameters plus the selected security protocol and the protocol options described in [4].

Fig. 1 presents the extension of the Tequila SLS QoS unit for security with quantitative guarantees. Only the two sub-units useful for SoS management are shown. The other QoS sub-units are outside the scope of this paper. The additional

Sub-Unit	Qualitative Parameters	Quantitative Parameters		Value
Traffic descriptor	Diffserv Information	DSCP		11101
	Source Information	Address	Type	IPV4 Address
			Value	190.20.1.1
	Destination Information	Address	Type	IPV4 Address
			Value	200.20.1.1
	Application Information	Protocol number		6
		Source port		1566
		Destination port		1566
SoS parameters	**Security protocol**	**Value**		ESP (or 50)
	Confidentiality	**Alg Name**		DES
		Alg Category		Block
		Alg Mode		CBC
		Alg Block size		64 bits
		Alg Key length		56 bits
		Alg round number		16
	Authentication	**Alg Type**		MAC
		Alg Name		HMAC
		Alg Key length		128 bits
	Integrity	**Hash function**		MD5
	Non-repudiation	**Value**		Off
	Tunnelling	**Source address**	**Type**	IPV4 Address
			Value	190.20.1.0
		Destination address	**Type**	IPV4 Address
			Value	200.20.1.1
	No-replay	**Sequence Number length**		32 bits

Fig. 1. In **bold:** proposed SoS parameters structure and example of quantitative SoS parameters

parameters are in bold. The first column presents the sub-unit. The second and third columns correspond respectively to the qualitative and associated quantitative parameters, and the fourth contains examples of associated selected values.

The negotiated values associated to the SoS parameters can be either qualitative or quantitative depending on the EU expertise. In the first case, a level, an on/off choice or a default value can be attributed to the parameters. In the second case, a subset of specific parameters is associated to the common ones except for the non-repudiation parameter which is 'on or off' depending on the type of authentication algorithm. Therefore, if non-repudiation is selected, the authentication algorithm must be a digital signature.

During the negotiation, it is possible not to select any of the security parameters or to use only part of it. For example, the required SoS can be confidentiality only. In this case, the common and optional parameters that are not selected can be qualitatively specified with the 'no', 'on' or 'off' value, or not specified at all. In the case where optional parameters are not specified, the options default values are attributed according to the security protocol selected.

In case quantitative values are attributed, as presented in Fig. 1, the SP can directly consider the SLS to configure security. However, in case of qualitative agreements, the SP must interpret the values. This interpretation is done through mapping tables such as Table 1, where a level corresponds to a set of algorithms to choose from. This choice is also possible with quantitative guarantees. Several alternatives can be associated to a particular SoS parameter.

Table 1. Example of a mapping table for confidentiality

Level	Name	Category	Mode	Block size	Key length	Round number	Security Protocol
High	AES	Block	CBC	128	128	9	ESP, TLS
	3DES	Block	CBC	64	192	48	ESP, TLS
	IDEA	Block	CBC	64	128	8	ESP, TLS
Medium	RC5	Block	CBC	64	128	16	ESP
	Blowfish	Block	CBC	64	128	16	ESP
Default	DES	Block	CBC	64	56	16	ESP, TLS
	RC2	Block	EBC	64	64	18	TLS
	DES	Block	EBC	64	56	16	TLS
No	NULL						

The SLS we propose is negotiated between a EU and its SP. The negotiated values are either qualitative or quantitative depending on the EU expertise. The quantitative parameters are derived from the SLS or obtained from the mapping tables that represent the SoS that can be provided by the SP. These parameters are used by the SP to configure its network. To do this, the SP must be able to translate the SLS into policies. These policies are then used to configure the SP network to provide the required security.

4 From SLS to Policies

The policies on which we map the SLS are described in a previous paper [7]. These policies are organised in a three levels hierarchy (service level, network level and element level policies). A service level policy is translated into a network level policy, which is also translated into several element level policies that are sent to the network elements where they are enforced.

Only SLS quantitative parameters are considered and mapped onto policies. The qualitative parameters must be previously translated in quantitative parameters through the mapping tables.

Therefore, the quantitative SLS is translated into the network level and then element level policies, as described in Table 2 and Table 3, where:

- **<Sec-Prot>** corresponds to the security protocol used (AH, ESP, TLS)
- **<C-Algo parameters>** represents the different confidentiality quantitative parameters. Several algorithms can be specified. In this case, the algorithm list is specified in braces. E.g.: {(AES, block, CBC, 128, 128, 9), (IDEA, block, CBC, 64, 128, 8), (3DES, block, 64, 192, 48)}. The NULL algorithm can be directly specified if confidentiality is not required.
- **<A-I-Algo parameters>** represents the different authentication and integrity quantitative parameters. The SLS non-repudiation parameter is not specified in the policy. It depends on the digital signature use as authentication algorithm and it is not necessary in the policy to configure network. As for confidentiality, several algorithms can be specified. Each list of parameters is described in brackets and the list of algorithms in braces. The NULL algorithm can also be directly specified if authentication and integrity not required.
- **<Tunnelling parameters>** corresponds to the type of the addresses and the IP source and destination addresses of the tunnel.
- **<Seq-Number Length>** refers to the sequence number length specified in the SLS.

Table 2. Network level policy

IF SourceIPaddress|UserIPaddresses = <SourceIPaddress|UserIPaddresses1..*> and SourcePortNo|UserportNo = <SourcePortNo|UserportNo> and DestinationIPAddress = DestinationIPAddress..(optional)> and DestinationPortNo = <DestinationPortNo (optional)>   THEN CONNECT with <QoSDirection> and <ConnectionType> from|among <SourceIPAddress!..*> at <SourcePortNo|UserPortNo> to <destinationIPAddress!..*(optional)> at DestinationPortNo1 (optional)> with <PhBtype> and **<Sec-Prot>** with **<C-Algo parameters>** and **<A-I-Algo parameters>** and **<Tunnelling parameters>** and **<Seq-Number Length>**

Table 3. Network level policy for dissemination to the network elements

IF SourceIPaddress|UserIPaddresses = <SourceIPaddress|UserIPaddresses1..*> and SourcePortNo|UserportNo = <SourcePortNo|UserportNo> and DestinationIPAddress = DestinationIPAddress..(optional)> and DestinationPortNo = <DestinationPortNo (optional)>   THEN SET at <InterfaceIPaddress> with <PhBtype> and **<Sec-Prot>** with **<C-Algo parameters>** and **<A-I-Algo parameters>** and **<Tunnelling parameters>** and **<Seq-Number Length>**

The element policy parameter *<InterfaceIPAddress>* represents the nodes where the policy must be enforced, i.e. the nodes crossed by the traffic for which the SLA is negotiated. This parameter can be directly deduced from the 'Topology unit' of the SLS, since this unit describes the SP domain access nodes.

5 SLS to Policy Mapping Example

In this section we are only interested in the SoS parameters mapping from SLS to policy. Consider a End-User (EU) who wishes to secure its video-conferencing service. S/he expresses her/his requirements in qualitative terms and requires a security with a medium confidentiality and a high integrity/authentication. Therefore, the non-repudiation parameter receives the 'off' value and the protocol options (tunnelling and no-replay) will receive their default value. As for security protocol parameter, it will be derived from the result of the qualitative to quantitative parameters mapping. The obtained security SLS is depicted in Fig. 2.

QoS Unit		
SoS parameters	Security protocol	*not defined yet*
	Confidentiality	Medium
	Authentication	High
	Integrity	High
	Non-repudiation	*Off*
	Tunnelling	*Off*
	No-replay	*On*

Fig. 2. The EU negotiated security SLS with qualitative guarantees

These qualitative parameters must be derived into quantitative ones to be interpreted to configure and manage the SP network. The mapping tables described in Tables 4 and Table 5 are used. The grey lines represent the quantitative values associated to the specified qualitative ones.

Table 4. Example of a mapping table for confidentiality

Level	Name	Categ	Mode	Block size	Key length	Key rounds	Security protocol
High	AES	Block	CBC	128	128	9	ESP, TLS
	3DES	Block	CBC	64	192	48	ESP, TLS
	IDEA	Block	CBC	64	128	8	ESP, TLS
Medium	RC5	Block	CBC	64	128	16	ESP
	Blowfish	Block	CBC	64	128	16	ESP
Default	DES	Block	CBC	64	56	16	ESP, TLS
	RC2	Block	CBC	64	40	18	TLS
	DES	Block	CBC	64	40	16	TLS
No	NULL						

Table 5. Example of a mapping table for authentication, integrity and non-repudiation

Level	N-R Value	Auth Type	Auth Name	Auth key length	Hash function	Security Protocol
High	off	MAC	HMAC	128	SHA-1	AH, ESP, TLS
	off	MAC	HMAC	128	RIPEMD_160	AH, ESP
Medium	off	MAC	HMAC	128	MD5	AH, ESP, TLS
Default	off	MAC	HMAC	128	MD5	AH, ESP, TLS
No	off		NULL		NULL	

These two tables are used to identify the algorithms associated to the negotiated security level. As for the column named 'Security protocol', it identifies the protocol that uses the algorithm.

We end up with the following alternatives. On one hand, the 'medium' level of confidentiality can be provided by the RC5 or Blowfish algorithms with ESP protocol. On the other hand, the 'high' importance of authentication/integrity can be provided by HMAC associated with the hash functions SHA-1 or RIPEMD-160, by using the AH, ESP or TLS protocols. The ESP protocol is therefore the only possibility since it is the only one proposing a 'medium' level of confidentiality.

The network level policy will be created from the new data. The policy conflict verification and resolution will need to be done but its description is out of the scope of this paper. This policy is then derived in two element level policies. The Tables 6 and 7 present these policies where the negotiated security parameters are in bold. In these Tables, the sequence number length is set to '32'. It corresponds to the IPsec default value of this parameter [4].

Table 6. Network level policy derived from the SLS parameters

IF UserIPaddress = *1.1.1.1, 2.2.2.2* and UserPortNo = *8000*
THEN CONNECT with *bi-directional* and *unicast* among *1.1.1.1, 2.2.2.2* at *8000* with *AF11*
and *ESP* with *{(RC5, block, CBC, 64, 128, 16), (Blowfish, block, CBC, 64, 128, 16)}*
and *{(HMAC, 128, SHA-1), (HMAC, 128, RIPEMD_160)}* and *off* and *32*

Table 7. Element level policies derived from the SLS parameters

IF SourceIPaddress = *1.1.1.1* and SourcePortNo = *8000* and DestinationIPAddress = *2.2.2.2* and DestinationPortNo=*8000* THEN SET at *1.1.1.0* with *AF11*
and *ESP* with *{(RC5, block, CBC, 64, 128, 16), (Blowfish, block, CBC, 64, 128, 16)}*
and *{(HMAC, 128, SHA-1), (HMAC, 128, RIPEMD_160)}* and *off* and *32*

IF SourceIPaddress = *2.2.2.2* and SourcePortNo = *8000* and DestinationIPAddress = *1.1.1.1* and DestinationPortNo=*8000* THEN SET at *2.2.2.0* with *AF11*
and *ESP* with *{(RC5, block, CBC, 64, 128, 16), (Blowfish, block, CBC, 64, 128, 16)}*
and *{(HMAC, 128, SHA-1), (HMAC, 128, RIPEMD_160)}* and *off* and *32*

The first policy in Table 7 is enforced by the network node 1.1.1.0 managing the IP address 1.1.1.1. The second policy is enforced at the network node 2.2.2.0 managing

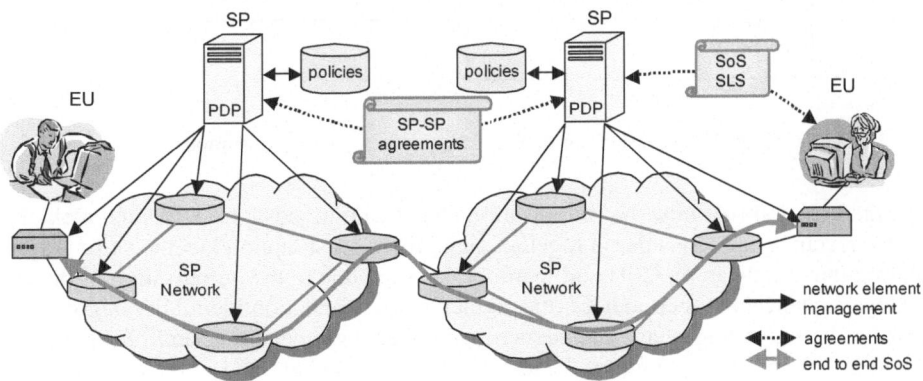

Fig. 3. End to end SoS with SLS enforcement

the IP address 2.2.2.2. These policies will secure the videoconferencing traffic between the IP addresses 1.1.1.1 and 2.2.2.2.

The network nodes where the policies are enforced can be edge routers of the SPs domains or device modems provided by SPs to the EUs. Those device modems are integrating security mechanisms and allow the SPs to provide end to end SoS to their customers. Fig 3. illustrates where SLSs can take place.

The mapping tables and policies presented in this section offer a choice among several SoS solutions, each having a different impact on the QoS.

6   Security Influence on Network and Service Performance

This section discusses the influence of security on network and service performance (in the context of our SLS for QoS and SoS). In our previous paper [4], we discussed how each SoS parameter affects the performance. The resources we studied are CPU, memory and bandwidth. For each resource two types of costs are distinguished: initialisation and streaming costs. The initialisation represents the initialisation phase of the security mechanism process (including the negotiation), and the streaming represents the data packet emission. In [4] we consider the resources (CPU, memory and bandwidth) and their associated costs with each SoS parameter specified in our SLS. We determine how each SoS parameter influences the different resources and therefore the importance of the impact. The figure 4 summarises this study with a down/top classification of resource consumption for our SoS parameters.

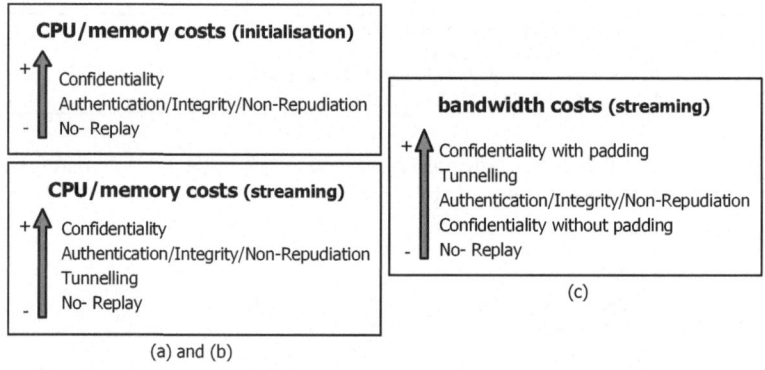

(a) and (b)

Fig. 4. Classification of SoS parameters resource consumption

Fig. 4 (a) and (b) show the initialisation and streaming costs for CPU and memory. These resources are considered together since their consumption has the same origin. During the initialisation, CPU and memory costs are due to the initialisation of the no-replay sequence number and of the authentication and confidentiality algorithms. During the streaming phase the sequence number incrementation and checking, the creation of a new (tunnel) header for each packet and the processes of authentication/integrity and confidentiality algorithms consume also these two resources. Fig. 4 (c) presents the bandwidth costs while streaming. Our classification depends on the amount of data transferred for each specific SoS parameter. For example, the sequence number exchanged to ensure the no-replay is a 32 bits value, whereas the size of the added header for tunnelling is at least 20 or 40 bytes for respectively IPv4 and IPv6, or more, the size of data when padding is added to enciphered data can reach 255 bytes. The initialisation bandwidth cost is not shown here. Only the protocol has an impact on it for its security context establishment (key generation, negotiation of used algorithms, etc.).

To determine the precise impact of the choice of the protocol on the bandwidth, we did run some tests that applied the IPsec protocols for different levels of security. We used the Ethereal tool [6], a network protocol analyser, to value bandwidth costs for a MPEG video and a DVD sequence. The multimedia sequences are read with VLC (Video LAN Client) on a laptop from a desktop running on Windows OS and are secured with the Windows OS IPsec Policy Tool. The data are exchanged over a LAN.

The Windows IPsec Policy Tool provides confidentiality using 3DES or DES algorithms. The SHA-1 and MD5 algorithms associated with HMAC are available for authentication and integrity services. To measure the bandwidth costs, we did test two times for both multimedia sequences (MPEG and DVD) with all possible combinations of security protocols and algorithms (i.e. AH with SHA-1, AH with MD5, ESP with SHA-1, ESP with MD5, ESP with 3DES, ESP with DES, ESP with SHA-1 and 3DES, ESP with SHA-1 and DES, ESP with MD5 and 3DES and ESP with MD5 and DES). We can notice that the quality of the multimedia sequence, the level of confidentiality and the level of authentication and integrity do not have an impact on the bandwidth costs. Only the choices of the security services and of the protocol do have an impact.

Table 8. Bandwidth costs for UDP and IPsec protocols

Protocol		Bandwidth cost during the initialisation (bytes)	Bandwidth cost while Streaming (bytes/packet)
UDP		*not relevant*	1358
AH	Authentication and integrity	1688	1382
ESP	Authentication and integrity	1712	1382
	Confidentiality	1712	1378
	Confidentiality, authentication and integrity	1712	1390

The table 8 depicts the increase bandwidth costs before and after the inclusion of security. The bandwidth cost during the initialisation phase is expressed in bytes because it consists in the security context establishment (key generation, negotiation of used algorithms, etc.) and the number of exchanged packets is limited (10 for IPsec). While streaming, it is expressed in bytes per packets because it corresponds to the protocol processing, which depends on the multimedia file. Table 8 shows that the bandwidth initialisation cost depends only on the protocol. ESP consumes more resources than AH. During the streaming phase the bandwidth consumption varies according to the chosen security services apart from the protocol. Confidentiality consumes less bandwidth than authentication and integrity, which consume fewer resources than confidentiality, authentication and integrity. This confirms our classification in Fig. 4 (c).

We are now extending our tests to the other resources (CPU and memory), and for each SoS parameter.

7 Conclusion and Future Work

This paper has proposed a solution to improve the SLA based management of QoS for secure distributed multimedia services. It used the Tequila project SLS definition as a basis and extends it with SoS parameters.

We identified the essential SoS parameter to integrate in the QoS part of an SLS. It consists of a set of network specific parameters useful for network security protocols configuration and to evaluate the impact on resource consumption and consequently on the QoS. We also highlighted the necessity for EUs to provide higher-level parameters to the SLS in order to express their SoS requirements in terms they do understand. Then, we described the mapping of SLS parameters on policies and give an example of this mapping. Finally we discussed the influence of security on the performance of services and networks. It is essential to consider it to improve the QoS management. Our SoS quantitative parameters are useful to evaluate this influence.

Including security parameters in the SLS allows SPs to propose end to end SoS to their customers. The SLS can be used by the modem devices provided by SPs to EUs. These devices can integrate security mechanisms that can be dynamically configured by the SP.

We are currently continuing our tests on the other resources consumptions for each SoS parameter. The objective is to determine and add parameters that are representative of the resource consumption into mapping tables. It can be useful to choose the most suitable algorithm and security protocol. It will improve the QoS management by adapting and optimising the resource consumption for security.

References

1. Arcade Project Home Page: http://www-rp.lip6.fr/arcade/ [last accessed on 1st Aug. 2005]
2. Cortese, G. et al: Cadenus: creation and deployment of end-user services in premium IP networks. IEEE Communications Magazine, Jan. 2003, pp 54-60.
3. Dierks, T. and E. Rescorla: The TLS Protocol Version 1.1. IETF Internet Draft, May 2005. <draft-ietf-tls-rfc2246-bis-11.txt>
4. Duflos, S., et al: Integration of Security Parameters in Service Level Specification to Improve QoS Management of Secure Distributed Multimedia Services. In Proc. of IEEE INA'05 Workshop, Taipei, IEEE Press, March 2005.
5. Engel, T., et al: AQUILA: adaptive resource control for QoS using an IP-based layered architecture. IEEE Communications Magazine, Jan. 2003, pp 46-53.
6. Ethereal home page: http://www.ethereal.com [last accessed on 1st Aug. 2005]
7. Gay, V. et al: Policy-Based Quality of Service and Security Management for Multimedia Services on IP networks in the RTIPA Project. In Proc. of IEEE MMNS'02, Santa Barbara, LNCS Springer-Verlag, Oct. 2002.
8. Goderis D., et al.: Attributes of a Service Level Specification (SLS) Template. Internet Draft, Oct. 2003. <draft-tequila-sls-03.txt>

9. Irvine, C., et al: Security as a Dimension of Quality of Security Service. In Proc. of the Active Middleware Services Workshop, San Francisco, CA, Aug. 2001, pp 87-93.
10. IST Aquila Project Home Page: http://www-st.inf.tu-dresden.de/aquila/ [last accessed on 1st Aug. 2005]
11. IST Mescal Project Home Page: http://www.mescal.org [last accessed on 1st Aug. 2005]
12. IST Sequin Project Home Page: http://archive.dante.net/sequin/ [last accessed on 1st Aug. 2005]
13. IST Tequila Project Home Page: http://www.ist-tequila.org [last accessed on 1st Aug. 2005]
14. Jason, J., et. al: IPsec Configuration Policy Information Model. RFC 3585, Aug. 2003.
15. Kent S.: IP Authentication Header. IETF Internet Draft, Mar. 2005. <draft-ietf-ipsec-rfc2402bis-11.txt>
16. Kent S.: IP Encapsulating Security Payload (ESP). IETF Internet Draft, Mar. 2005. <draft-ietf-ipsec-esp-v3-10.txt>
17. Kent, S., Atkinson, R.: Security Architecture for the Internet Protocol. RFC 2401, Nov. 1998.
18. Koch, B. et al: IST Premium IP Cluster. IST deliverable, Mar. 2003.
19. Morand, P. et al: Initial Specification of Protocols and Algorithms for Inter-domain SLS management and Traffic Engineering for QoS-based IP Service Delivery and their Test Requirements. Deliverable D1.2, IST Mescal Project, Nov. 2003.
20. Mykoniati, E. et al: Admission control for providing QoS in DiffServ IP networks: the TEQUILA approach. IEEE Communications Magazine, Jan. 2003, pp 38-44.
21. Rajan, R., et al: Service Level Specification for Inter-domain QoS Negotiation. Internet Draft, Nov. 2000. < draft-somefolks-sls-00.txt >
22. Salsano, S. et al: Definition and usage of SLSs in the AQUILA consortium. Internet Draft, Nov. 2000. <draft-salsano-aquila-sls-00.txt>
23. Sevasti, A., Campanella, M.: Service Level Agreements specification for IP Premium Service. Deliverable D2.1 - Addendum 2, IST Sequin Project, Oct. 2001.
24. Spyropoulou, E., et al: Managing Costs and Variability of Security Services. IEEE Symposium on Security and Privacy, Oakland, California, May 2001.
25. T'Joens, Y. et. al.: Service Level Specification and Usage Framework. Internet Draft, Oct. 2000. <draft-manyfolks-sls-framework-00.txt>
26. Verma, D.: Service Level Agreements on IP Networks. Proc. of the IEEE, vol 92, no. 9, Sept. 2004.
27. Westerinen, A. et al: Terminology for Policy-Based Management. RFC 3198, Nov. 2001.
28. Yilmaz, V. et al: Gestion et déploiement de services de sécurité dans un réseau basé sur des politiques (In English: Management and Deployment of Security Services over a Policy-based Network). SAR 2003 Conference, Nancy, France, June 2003.

Managing Bandwidth in Multimedia Applications Using a Market-Based Middleware

Johan Kristiansson, Jeremiah Scholl, and Peter Parnes

Department of Computer Science & Electrical Engineering,
Luleå University of Technology, 971 87 Luleå, Sweden
{Johan.Kristiansson, Jeremiah.Scholl, Peter.Parnes}@ltu.se

Abstract. [1] This paper presents an application-layer middleware that applies a microeconomic model to help multimedia applications utilize available bandwidth in a way that maximizes the user's net benefit. The key components are a bandwidth broker that puts the supply of available bandwidth on a virtual market residing inside the application, and utility functions for each media, which are used to calculate their relative gain to the user at each bandwidth level. Basic supply and demand principles are used where the broker raises a virtual price if the total demand from all media exceeds the available supply, or lowers the price if demand is lower than the available supply. The advantage of the middleware is that it allows problems related to network management (usually affecting the supply) and human computer interaction (usually affecting demand) to be researched and integrated separately into an application and combined to leverage bandwidth in the best possible way. As a proof of concept, a prototype has been built by integrating the middleware into Marratech Pro, a commercially available e-meeting application. The paper presents experimental results using this prototype.

1 Introduction

Distributed multimedia applications provide users with a variety of inherently dynamic media, each having bandwidth requirements that can rapidly change over time. While a significant amount of research has targeted the creation of specific media that can adapt to bandwidth fluctuations (e.g. layered video coding), a still relatively unsolved problem is how to obtain bandwidth from various networks during a multimedia session, and then share the bandwidth efficiently between the different media inside an application in order to provide the user with the optimal aggregated experience.

Solving this problem requires a large amount of interdisciplinary knowledge. First of all, in order to obtain bandwidth in the best way designers must be able to deal with an increasingly complex network infrastructure. For example, applications must be able to handle IP mobility and QoS requirements and also consider financial aspects when switching between different wireless networks. Secondly, since user-perceived performance depends critically on the way bandwidth is shared between various media,

---

[1] This work was done within the VITAL project, which is supported by the Objective 1 Norra Norrland - EU structural fund programme for Norra Norrland. Support was also provided by the Centre for Distance-spanning Technology (CDT).

J. Dalmau and G. Hasegawa (Eds.): MMNS 2005, LNCS 3754, pp. 216–227, 2005.

designers must also deal with human factors in order to calculate the relative worth of each media stream to the user. For example, it might be useful to allocate more bandwidth to "important" users in a multimedia conferencing session [3], [15], or to allocate less bandwidth to a video stream to make room for an audio stream.

This paper presents a middleware framework based on microeconomic principles of supply and demand to deal with bandwidth related issues in multimedia applications. The middleware consists of a virtual marketplace that functions as a management layer for deciding how to best obtain bandwidth and how to best consume bandwidth. The advantage of the middleware is that it allows the various solutions related to network management (usually affecting the supply) and the various solutions related to usability (usually affecting demand) to be researched and integrated separately into an application. Ultimately, this will allow various experts from fields such as human computer interaction and computer communications to combine their knowledge so that bandwidth can be obtained and divided between several media streams in the way that provides users with the most benefit.

The rest of the paper is organized as follows. Section 2 covers previous work done in the area. Section 3 gives a brief introduction to microeconomics in relation to the problem. Section 4 gives an overview the middleware, and in section 5 the middleware is evaluated using a prototype implemented into a commercially available e-meeting application called Marratech Pro. In section 6, a summary and conclusions are given followed by future work.

2 Related Work

A considerable amount of research has been carried out to provide QoS support in distributed multimedia systems [9,13,14]. In [13] K. Nahrstedt et al. give an overview of existing middleware systems that have been proposed to support applications in heterogeneous and ubiquitous computing environments. To name just a few efforts, Agilos (Agile QoS) [9] is designed to serve as a coordinator to control the adaptation behavior of all concurrent applications in an end system so that the overall system performance is maximized. Similarly, Q-RAM [14] proposes a method to allocate resources between applications so that the system utility is maximized under the constraint that each application can meet its minimum QoS requirement. In contrast to the middleware proposed in this paper, these middlewares are not based on the concept of a virtual marketplace and generally focus on sharing resources between applications running on the same machine, or in the same network, rather than utilizing available bandwidth in the best possible way between several media within the same application.

A variety of papers have been published that use microeconomics as resource management method for bandwidth in conjunction with real economies [4,11,12]. However, the mechanisms described are generally dependent on support from nodes within the network and/or on variable rate pricing schemes for bandwidth. Both of these requirements have drawbacks in that dependency on router support can make systems much more difficult to deploy and because there is a strong evidence that users find dynamic pricing to be unacceptable [4].

The work presented in this paper differs from previous work in that the middleware uses microeconomic theory in a novel way by applying it inside multimedia applications without assuming the existence of non flat-rate pricing schemes for bandwidth or additional support from nodes within the network. Instead, microeconomics is used in order to run a *virtual economy inside the application* in order to make it easy to combine various network services, such as IP-mobility and congestion control while maintaining the efficient use of resources and maximizing the benefit to the user.

The idea of a market-based middleware was briefly mentioned in a poster paper [7] previously published by the authors. However, this paper contains a more extensive description of the middleware as well as a proof of concept implementation used in several experiments presented in the paper.

3   Market-Based Bandwidth Management

Microeconomic theory deals with production, purchase and sales of commodities that are in limited supply [5]. In this context, the commodity on the market is bandwidth, and is traded by two key players: *consumers* and *suppliers*. Consumers attempt to optimize their gain by purchasing commodities (i.e. bandwidth) that give them the maximum gain at the lowest price, and suppliers try to sell commodities at the highest price they can get in order to maximize their own profit. This leads to a variable pricing system that works like an "invisible hand" in order to distribute and allocate resources efficiently despite the selfish actions of each player. Eventually, this price fluctuation will reach a state where the demand for goods at the going price equals the supply for goods at that price. When this state is reached, all resources are fully utilized and the market is said to be in *equilibrium* [5].

In practice, equilibrium prices can be difficult to calculate because demand and supply vary over time. The supply will for example vary depending on the type of connection in use, congestion, financial constraints set by the user, or because of wireless interference. The demand may vary due to a wide variety of factors unique to every application. For example, in an e-meeting application the demand for the video stream of a particular user may vary depending on communication patters such as who is the current speaker [15].

One way of solving this problem is to use a *tâtonnement process* [5] to adjust the price iteratively until an equilibrium price is obtained. In this way, producers decrease the price if their production is not sold and increase the price if demand exceeds the supply.

$$p_{n+1} = p_n \cdot \frac{d}{s} \qquad (1)$$

Equation (1) shows how the price is iteratively calculated based on supply and demand using the tâtonnement process, with p_n representing the current price, p_{n+1} next price, d the aggregate demand of all media, and s the current supply. As p_{n+1} is recalculated at discrete intervals of time, equation (1) will adjust the price towards a new equilibrium when either the demand or the supply changes. However, if the price is not recalculated fast enough, there is a risk that demand will not adjust to match the supply in time, which can either cause *over-demand* (over-utilization), or *under-demand* (under-utilization). In section 5 it is investigated how this affects the performance and the stability of the market.

4   Overview of the Middleware

Middlewares are designed to manage complexity and heterogeneity in distributed systems and are defined as a layer above the operating system but below the application. Figure 1, shows an overview of the proposed middleware, which operates on the market principles previously described. The key player in the virtual marketplace is the *Bandwidth Broker Agent (BBA)*, which acts as a go between connecting all the buyers and sellers. Thus, the BBA sells bandwidth to all the different media streams used in the application, while obtaining bandwidth from various networks. Note that the middleware is implemented in the application-layer and *does not require support* from the network infrastructure or other clients/servers.

Each media has its own *Bandwidth Consumer Agent (BCA)* acting as its representative on the market for purchasing bandwidth. By using an optimization method described in subsection 4.2, the BCA calculates the total amount of bandwidth that should be purchased in order to maximize the benefit to the user. The BCA also communicates information to the media it represents regarding bandwidth it has purchased so that the media can adapt accordingly. For example, based on this information a video encoder will be able to change the video quality, or the interval at which it encodes frames.

The *Network Agent (NA)* contributes to the market by obtaining the actual supply of bandwidth that will be sold by the BBA. The purpose of the NA is not to actually provide the bandwidth (e.g. requiring packets to be sent/received through the NA) but rather to make sure that the application is connected to the best available networks without explicitly requiring the user to manually configure the application or the operating system. Depending on services available to the application, the NA can be responsible for managing policy based routing, configuring mobility protocols, logging in to wireless networks, dealing with congestion control and so on.

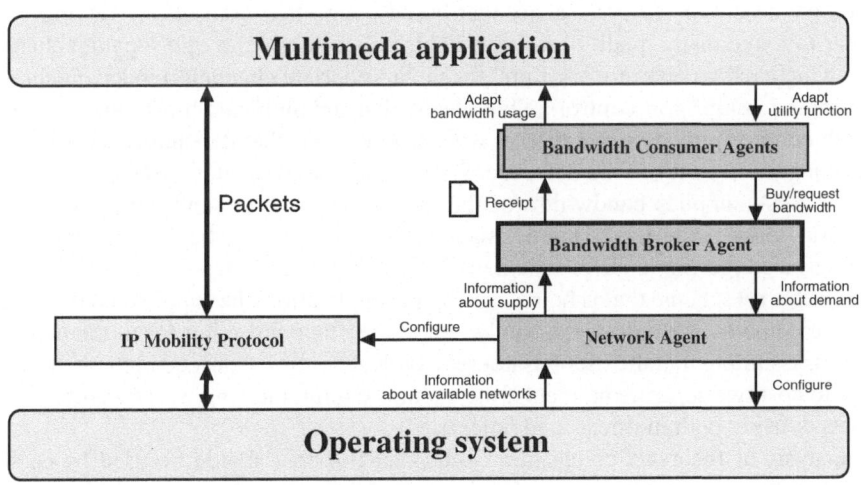

Fig. 1. Interaction between agents in the middleware

In addition, the NA periodically receives information about current demand levels from the BBA, which can be used to make decisions on how to best obtain future supply of bandwidth. For example, if the current network round-trip-time is too high to be useful for a particular media, the BCA will reject sales offers from the BBA on the grounds that the product (bandwidth) is of too low quality. The BBA will then forward this information to the NA allowing it to take appropriate action (such as looking for a new network provider) if possible. Once the operating system has been correctly set up, the NA passes information about the available bandwidth to the BBA so that it can be sold to the various BCA. How the supply is calculated is described more closely below.

4.1   Calculating the Supply

The total supply that the BBA can put onto the market is directly related to the amount of bandwidth available to the application and can be bounded by a variety of factors. Most often the supply will be equal to the *bottleneck bandwidth* to the other end-point, but for non-flat-rate connections it may also be bounded by budget controls set by the user. For example, if the user specifies a maximum burn-rate in $/s it would set an upper-bound on bandwidth supply.

K. Lai et al. [8] summarizes several techniques such as the *Pathchar* and the *Packet Pair algorithm* that can be used to accurately measure bandwidth. As the main usage of these algorithms is congestion control, it can be possible to let the NA obtain information about available bandwidth directly from the congestion control scheme instead of implementing an independent method for calculating the available network bandwidth.

However, due to the varying requirements for individual applications and media, there is no one-size-fits-all congestion control scheme that can be used by the NA. For multicast traffic the problem is a bit more complex than for unicast and has resulted in the creation of a wide variety of protocols. In general, these protocols follow one of two strategies, either relying on the sender to adapt its send rate in a way that serves the needs of the entire receiver set (sender-based congestion control), or relying on the sender to make many quality levels available concurrently through separate channels, allowing each receiver to "sign up" for the appropriate channel(s) independently (receiver-based congestion control). This means that for multicast traffic the type of bandwidth being supplied on the market will change somewhat depending on the underlying congestion control scheme in use. When using purely sender-based congestion control the BBA supplies bandwidth for the media that wish to send out packets on the network, whereas the BBA supplies bandwidth for packets to be received when a receiver-based congestion control scheme is in use. However, independently of which congestion control scheme that is being used by the application, the supplied bandwidth is always affected by the bottleneck bandwidth to the other end-point (or to the multicast group), assuming that the user has not set a budget control. Consequently, the BBA will have to host two separate markets if the client is communicating with two different end-points or using both multicast and unicast.

An analysis of the exact congestion control scheme that should be used by each individual application in order to calculate bandwidth is outside the scope of this paper. Instead, the proposed middleware is intended to help solve the orthogonal problem of how to leverage the available bandwidth in the way that gives the user the most benefit.

4.2 Calculating the Demand

In order for the BCA to decide how much bandwidth to buy given the price p per unit of bandwidth, it must calculate the relative gain the media can offer the user if allocated the amount of bandwidth x. This is done by creating utility functions for each media, m, where each utility function $u_m(x)$ maps the gain with different bandwidth levels. Since each media wants to provide the user with the maximum net benefit (also known as the consumer surplus, CS) at a given price level, it can calculate the amount of bandwidth x^{cs} to purchase by solving the problem, $CS = max[u_m(x^{cs}) - px^{cs}]$ as stated in [5]. The aggregate demand, d, is used to calculate the new price during each iteration in equation (1), and is calculated as the summation of the x^{cs} of each individual media.

Figure 2 shows the relationship between a utility function, $u(x)$, and the total price, px it will cost the media m to obtain x. If the utility function is differentiable, strictly increasing and strictly concave for all m, C. Courcoubetis et al. [5] show that the maximize CS for media m can be found by calculating the x^{cs}, where

$$u'_m(x^{cs}) = p \qquad (2)$$

Increasing concave utility functions are useful in this context since they give a fairly accurate model of media that are less sensitive to bandwidth changes when allocation reaches some maximum requirement [10]. Video is a good example of a media that falls into this category since human beings can only notice a difference in the frame rate up until about 25 frames-per-second and tend to be more sensitive to changes below 15 frames per second. They tend to gain much more for example when raising the frame rate from 1 to 6 frames per second than from 20 to 25 frames per second.

Allowing utility curves to dynamically change based on contextual information available to the application is also possible. This allows for a high degree of customization to serve users more optimally under changing conditions. For example, for multimedia conferencing it has been proposed that video streams of certain "important" users

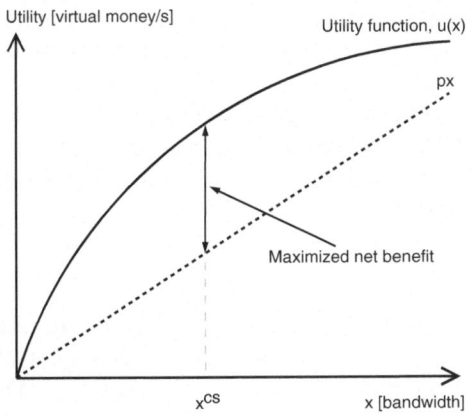

Fig. 2. A model for local optimization

should be prioritized by passing messages between clients in order to find out who is getting "attention" from the group [3,15]. This type of scheme can be integrated into the market-based system by having each client use the information contained in these messages in order to change the utility curve for its video stream when appropriate.

Creating accurate utility curves for real world use may be a fair challenge, and therefore it is not expected that in most situations the user will be given this responsibility in any explicit way. However, application designers with a fair amount of expertise about the operation and use of their application should be able to create fairly robust utility curves that serve the general needs of users. Nevertheless, one of the advantages of our middleware is that it allows this work to be done by usability specialists, without requiring them to tackle complex issues related to network management, as those can be contained completely within the NA.

5   Evaluation and Implementation

A proof of concept implementation has been built by incorporating the middleware into Marratech Pro [2], a commercially available e-meeting application that provides tools for synchronous interaction including audio, video, chat and a shared white-board. Marratech Pro supports data distribution using IP-multicast or distribution through a media gateway called the Marratech E-Meeting Portal, which can be used when IP-multicast is not available.

The prototype was tested by using two Marratech Pro clients. The first client (client A) used the prototype and was responsible for collecting data during the experiments. The second client (client B) did not adapt bandwidth usage based on the middleware, and was only used in order to change the level of incoming traffic on the link, as this directly affected the available supply as described in the next subsection. Both clients sent video traffic at all times during the experiments, with audio being used by client A at various intervals in order to investigate the effects it had on the system. In the two first experiments, a 100 Mbit local Ethernet network was used to evaluate how the middleware shared bandwidth between media. Client B sent approximately 25 kB/s video traffic in these experiments. In the third experiment, a commercial GPRS network was added to evaluate the BBA. In this case, Client B was configures to only send 3 kB/s video traffic.

Three computers were used during the experiments. The E-Meeting Portal was run on a Pentium III 1.2 GHz machine running Windows XP. Client A was an Intel P4 2.4 GHz machine running Windows XP and Client B was an AMD Athlon 1.2 GHz machine running Windows XP.

5.1   Implementation

The prototype was implemented in Java JDK 1.4 in order to make it easy to integrate into the Marratech source code. It followed the middleware as described in section 4 with the agents contained in figure 1 having the following characteristics.

The Bandwidth Broker Agent. The BBA used the tâtonnement process as described in section 3. In the current implementation it provides an API where different BCAs can register and receive call-backs when the price is updated. The total supply and demand are calculated by using an API provided by the NA, which will be discussed later in this subsection.

The Bandwidth Consumer Agent. When the price is recalculated each instance of the BCA receives a price update through a call-back. Current demand is calculated based on the price set by the BBA and is used to decide how much bandwidth the BCA should try to purchase. The following utility functions were used for calculating the demand during the experiments. For audio the utility function was

$$u_{audio}(x) = \begin{cases} 0 & x < x_{audio}^{min} \\ \infty & x \geq x_{audio}^{min} \end{cases},$$

where x_{audio}^{min} represents the minimum amount of bandwidth needed by the audio codec. This utility function was used in order to describe the audio media as something very unadaptive, which is the case with many codecs used today, for example GSM. In the experiments, a commercial audio codec called EG711 (GIPS) [1] was used, and x_{audio}^{min} was set to 12.2 kB/s.

The utility function for the video was modeled using the logarithmic function, $u_{video}(x) = ln(1 + x)$, which was used in order to create a basic concave function. In reality a more complex and accurate function will be more appropriate, but as the purpose of the experiments was to study the marketplace, an optimal utility function was not necessary. Thus, using equation 2, the demand function for bandwidth by the video media is calculated as $x_{video}(p)^{cs} = \frac{1}{p} - 1$.

During each price iteration, the BCA informed a bandwidth manager in Marratech Pro about the purchased bandwidth in order to adjust the video encoder to the bits-per-second corresponding to the purchased bandwidth.

The Network Agent. During the experiments the NA was responsible for calculating the supply. This was done by setting an upper-bound supply limit s_{limit} for each type of network, and then by calculating the supply s by subtracting the amount of incoming bandwidth obtained from the operating system from the s_{limit} (i.e. $s = s_{limit} - bw_{received}$). For the 100Mbit Ethernet network the s_{limit} was set to 100 kB/s and for the GPRS network it was set to 6 kB/s. Note that this allowed for large fluctuations in available supply by altering the amount of traffic sent out by the other end-point.

Mobility support was provided by using an UDP-socket extension called the Resilient Mobile Socket (RMS) [6]. In practice, it would be possible to use other protocols such as Mobile IP, but RMS was mainly chosen because we already had a working prototype based on RMS.

5.2   Experiment One: Bandwidth Sharing Between Multiple Media

Three experiments using the prototype were conducted. The first experiment was conducted to demonstrate that the prototype could effectively divide the available bandwidth between multiple media. This was done by utilizing all available bandwidth and varying the use of audio at client A in order to show that video would effectively back-off due to price increases in the market.

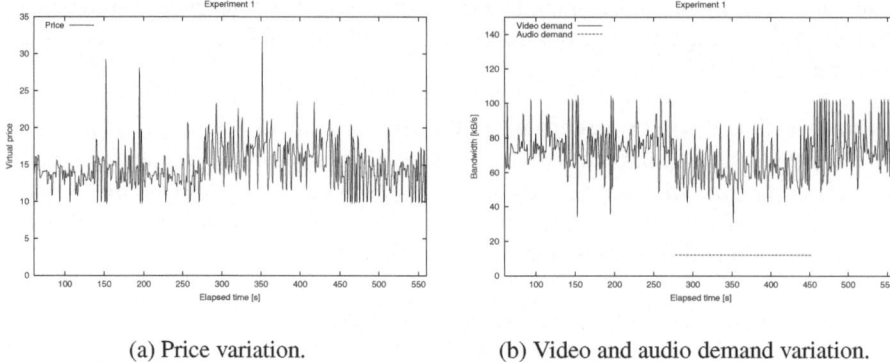

(a) Price variation.   (b) Video and audio demand variation.

Fig. 3. Results from experiment one. The figures show the effect of introducing a new media into the market. The price was recalculated every 100 ms, and the supply every 1200 ms.

Figure 3 shows results from this experiment. As shown in figure 3(a), the price goes up almost immediately when audio is sent. This results in a reduction of the demand for bandwidth by the video media, as shown in figure 3(b). This creates the ultimate effect of a reduction in the video bit-rate used by the video encoder, allowing bandwidth to be consumed by the audio encoder.

5.3 Experiment Two: Investigation into the Price and Supply Recalculation Rates

In order to investigate how the price and the supply recalculation rates affected the market, data was collected multiple times while sending video from each client during a period of 10 minutes. The price recalculation rate was studied by locking the supply recalculation rate to 500 ms and decrementing the price recalculation rate from a high value of 1000 ms to a low value of 20 ms. The supply recalculation rate was studied in a similar way with the price recalculation rate locked to 50 ms, instead of by locking the supply recalculation rate.

Table 1 shows the benefits of a higher price recalculation rate, in that it leads to a more efficient allocation of bandwidth, as determined by calculating the average over and under-demand. An explanation is that a higher price recalculation rate improved the response time, allowing the demand to more closely match variations in supply. A high supply recalculation rate on the other hand did not improve the performance as it resulted in more fluctuation in terms of over and under-demand, which can be seen in table 2. This problem can be explained by the fact that a high supply recalculation rate in combination with variable bit-rate video codecs (H.261) causes supply to vary rapidly, making it harder for the market to reach an equilibrium.

5.4 Experiment Three: Obtaining and Selling Bandwidth from Multiple Networks

The third experiment was conducted to demonstrate that the BBA could sell bandwidth obtained from more than one network. Another purpose was to investigate how the market reacted when there were large variations in supply caused by mobility. In the experiment, NA was configured to trigger a handover as soon as the LAN interface became available in Windows, and similarly trigger a handover to the GPRS interface if the LAN interface became disconnected. This was done by calling a handover function provided by RMS.

Table 1. The table shows the effects of varying the price recalculation rate. The supply recalculation was recalculated every 500 ms.

Price recalculation rate	Avg. over-demand	Avg. under-demand
20 ms	0.25 kB/s	0.25 kB/s
50 ms	1.14 kB/s	0.87 kB/s
100 ms	2.66 kB/s	2.59 kB/s
200 ms	4.09 kB/s	3.98 kB/s
400 ms	7.18 kB/s	7.10 kB/s
500 ms	7.86 kB/s	7.79 kB/s
800 ms	10.63 kB/s	10.53 kB/s
1000 ms	11.20 kB/s	11.07 kB/s

Table 2. The table shows the effects of varying the supply recalculation rate. The price recalculation was recalculated every 50 ms.

Supply recalculation rate	Avg. demand	Avg. supply	Avg. over-demand	Avg. under-demand
200 ms	97.57 kB/s	86.30 kB/s	11.63 kB/s	4.45 kB/s
400 ms	88.77 kB/s	80.20 kB/s	7.26 kB/s	3.64 kB/s
500 ms	76.51 kB/s	75.20 kB/s	6.87 kB/s	2.10 kB/s
600 ms	74.82 kB/s	74.80 kB/s	1.20 kB/s	1.17 kB/s
800 ms	74.97 kB/s	74.95 kB/s	1.06 kB/s	1.04 kB/s
1000 ms	73.57 kB/s	73.56 kB/s	0.96 kB/s	0.94 kB/s

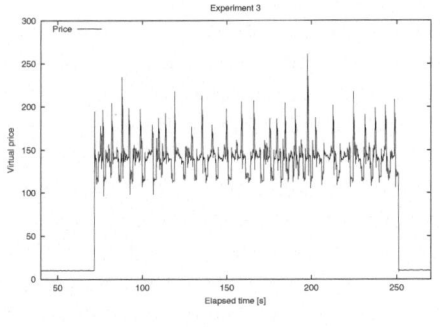

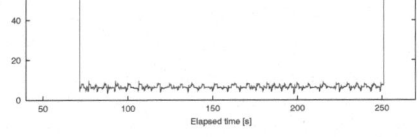

(a) Price variation. (b) Video and audio demand variation.

Fig. 4. Results from experiment three. The figures show the effect on the market when switching between networks with different bandwidth capacity. The price is recalculated every 100 ms and the supply every 600 ms.

Figure 4 shows the result from the experiments. As can be seen in the figure, the supply dramatically decreases from 100 kB/s to only 6 kB/s after switching to the GPRS network, which consequently caused the price to immediately rise and the video BCA to decrease its demand. Note that the price is less stable on the GPRS network compared with the Ethernet network, which can be explained by the fact that the incoming traffic (3 kB/s video data) relatively caused more variations in supply on the GPRS network than on the Ethernet network.

6   Discussion

This paper has presented a middleware framework based on microeconomic principles of supply and demand that deals with bandwidth issues inside a multimedia application. The key design principle that has been proposed is to view bandwidth as a universal commodity that can be consumed and produced by different components in the application. The advantage of this approach is that the system becomes more modular as each component can contribute to the equilibrium separately in the market. This makes it is possible to replace and upgrade each component in the middleware in a "plug and play" style without needing to redesign the whole application. For example, if a new component for mobility management is developed that can take advantage of several wireless base-stations simultaneously [6] it could be integrated into the middleware simply by upgrading the NA. Similarly, if a new method is developed that can better utilize bandwidth in video group communication softwares [15], it can be integrated simply by defining new utility functions in the BCA.

Ultimately, this makes it possible for usability researchers to develop more advanced applications that consume bandwidth in the best possible way without having to care about heterogeneity and complexity in the networks while networking researchers can develop more advanced networking components for obtaining bandwidth without having to consider specific application related issues. Although this is not a new idea in general, we believe that a middleware layer is needed to hide heterogeneity as both applications and networks are becoming more complex to manage.

Moreover, the paper has presented a proof of concept prototype based on the commercially available e-meeting application Marratech Pro. This prototype has been used in several exploratory experiments, which has shown that the middleware can be used in order to share bandwidth effectively between multiple media using the BBA as a single centralized supply point for managing bandwidth.

The experiments have shown that it is possible to allocate bandwidth close to an equilibrium allocation by using a high price recalculation rate and a low supply recalculation rate. However, as a high supply recalculation rate negatively affected the market, studying how a real congestion control scheme affects the performance is something that requires further investigations. Hence, for future work we plan to use a real congestion control scheme and study its implications on the market. In addition, we plan to investigate more effective utility functions for the various media contained in Marratech Pro, and integrate some other related prototypes developed by our research group into the system in order to make more sophisticated experiments.

References

1. Global IP Sound AB, 2005. Homepage: http://www.globalipsound.com/.
2. Marratech AB, 2005. Homepage: http://www.marratech.com.
3. E. Amir, S. McCanne, and R.H Katz. Receiver-driven Bandwidth Adaptation for Lightweight Sessions. In *ACM Multimedia*, pages 415–426, 1997.
4. B. Briscoe, V. Darlagiannis, O. Heckman, H. Oliver, V. Siris, D. Songhurst, and B. Stiller. A Market Managed Multi-Service Internet (M3I. *Computer Communications*, 26(4):404–414, 2003.
5. C. Courcoubetis and R. Weber. *Pricing Communication Networks;Economics, Technology and Modelling*. Wiley, 2003.
6. J. Kristiansson and P. Parnes. Application-layer Mobility support for Streaming Real-time Media. In *IEEE Wireless Communications and Networking Conference (WCNC'04)*, 2004.
7. Johan Kristiansson, Jeremiah Scholl, and Peter Parnes. Bridging the Gap between Multimedia Application and Heterogeneous Networks using a Market-based Middleware. In *IEEE International Symposium on a World of Wireless, Mobile and Multimedia Networks (WOW-MOM), Extended abstract*, 2005.
8. K. Lai and M. Baker. Measuring Bandwidth. In *INFOCOM*, pages 235–245, 1999.
9. B. Li. *Agilos: A Middleware Control Architecture for Application-Aware Quality of Service Adaptations*. PhD thesis, University of Illinois, USA, 2000.
10. Raymond R.F. Liao and A. T. Campbell. A Utility-Based Approach for Quantitative Adaptation in Wireless Packet Networks. *Wireless Networks*, 7(5):541–557, 2001.
11. J.K. MacKie-Mason and H.R. Varian. Pricing the Internet. In *The second International Conference on Telecommunication Systems Modelling and Analysis*, pages 378–393, 1994.
12. J.K. MacKie-Mason and H.R. Varian. Pricing Congestable Network Resources. *IEEE Journal on Selected Area in Communication*, 13(7):1141–1149, 1995.
13. K. Nahrstedt, D. Xu, D. Wichadakul, and B. Li. QoS-Aware Middleware for Ubiquitous and Heterogeneous Environments. *IEEE Communications Magazine*, 39(11):140–148, 2001.
14. R. Rajkumar, C. Lee, J. Lehoczky, and D. Siewiorek. A Resource Allocation Model for QoS Management. In *Proceedings of the IEEE Real-Time Systems Symposium*, 1997.
15. J. Scholl, S. Elf, and P. Parnes. User-interest Driven Video Adaptation for Collaborative Workspace Applications. In *International Workshop on Networked Group Communication NGC*, pages 3–12, 2003.

Static Weighted Load-Balancing for XML-Based Network Management Using JPVM

Mohammed H. Sqalli and Shaik Sirajuddin

Computer Engineering Department, King Fahd University of Petroleum & Minerals,
Dhahran, 31261, KSA
{sqalli, siraj}@ccse.kfupm.edu.sa

Abstract. SNMP-based network management is simple but lacks scalability and efficiency of processing the management data as the number of agents increases. XML-based network management is a new paradigm developed to overcome these limitations. One of the main challenges is how to distribute the management tasks to achieve efficiency and scalability. In this paper, we propose a framework using JPVM to distribute the management tasks among multiple gateways. We compare the performance of three approaches, namely the static weighted load balancing approach, the equal work non-weighted load balancing approach, and the single gateway approach. The first approach provides better communication time between the XML-based manager and the SNMP agents. It takes advantage of the XML, DOM, and Java servlets.

1   Introduction

The main goal of network management systems (NMS) is to ensure the quality of the services that networked elements provide. To achieve this, network managers must monitor, control, and secure the computing assets connected to the network. The Simple Network Management Protocol (SNMP) is currently the most widely used protocol for network management. SNMP is based on a centralized approach and confronted with two main limitations that are scalability and efficiency. A number of approaches have been proposed to overcome these limitations, including XML-based Network Management (XNM). One of the issues for an XNM system is to be able to support legacy SNMP agents, since they constitute the largest base of network management systems.

XML-based network management applies Extensible Markup Language (XML) technologies to network management. In XNM, the management information is defined using XML and the management data is exchanged in the form of an XML document and processed using the standard methods available for XML [1][2][3].

XML-based integrated network management architecture consists of an XML-based manager (XBM), an SNMP/XML gateway and SNMP agents [2]. In [4], we proposed a framework for extensions to an existing XML-based network management system, which can reduce the response time between the XBM and the SNMP agents. The extensions consist of new types of messages, including the multi-get-request and multi-set-request. These new types, for instance, allow a manager to send one or more requests to one or more agents bundled in one message. This framework decreases the overall traffic between the XBM and the XML/SNMP gateway.

J. Dalmau and G. Hasegawa (Eds.): MMNS 2005, LNCS 3754, pp. 228–241, 2005.
© IFIP International Federation for Information Processing 2005

In this paper, we present a new DOM-based approach to the proposed extended XNM, namely a static weighted load balancing approach that makes use of JPVM in XNM. We compare results obtained to the single gateway approaches and to the equal work non-weighted load balancing approach. The comparison of these approaches shows that the static weighted load balancing approach outperforms all the others and provides a savings in term of response time as the number of agents in the network increases.

The rest of the paper is organized as follows; first we will give a general overview of the XML-based network management. Then, we will discuss the current related work. We will then introduce the JPVM environment and describe the static weighted load balancing and the equal work non-weighted load balancing approaches with JPVM. The section that follows will include the experimental setup and results of comparing these approaches. The paper ends with a conclusion.

2 XML-Based Network Management

Extensible Markup Language (XML) is a Meta markup language, which was standardized by the World Wide Web Consortium (W3C) for document exchange in 1998[5]. We can define our own Structure of Management Information in a flexible form using either Document Type Definition (DTD) or XML Schema [6][7][8]. XML documents can be transmitted on the Internet using HTTP. XML offers many free APIs for accessing and manipulating the XML data. XML separates the contents of a document and the expression methods, i.e., the management data is stored in XML documents and the presentation or format of the management data is stored in Extensible Style Sheet Language (XSL) documents using Extensible Style Sheet Transformations (XSLT) representation. XML supports the exchange of management data over all the hardware and software that supports HTTP. XML needs low development cost, since all the APIs and development kits are freely available.

Fig. 1. shows one of the manager and agent combinations in XML-based network management [2]. It shows the approach that requires a translation from XML to SNMP through a gateway [1][2]. Since most network devices have legacy SNMP agents installed in them, this combination is simpler to implement in the current network environment, and is more appropriate for the current network management framework. In this paper, we only address this combination and we consider non-legacy network elements providing native XML interfaces outside the scope of this work. This combination, however, requires the development of an SNMP/XML gateway to exchange the messages between the XML-based network manager and SNMP agents.

XML-based network management can overcome many limitations of SNMP. For instance, an SNMP request can not exceed a maximum message length limit, but XML supports the transfer of large amount of data in a single document. This allows the transfer of multiple SNMP requests bundled in one message from the manager to the gateway. This message can also be summarized to decrease the amount of traffic to be exchanged between the manager and the gateway. This will result in less traffic at the manager side. The gateway will then expand the message received from the manager into multiple SNMP requests to be sent to multiple agents. With the use of multiple gateways, the processing time of multiple SNMP requests can also be reduced. All these advantages make XML a good candidate to solve the problems of scalability and efficiency of existing SNMP based NMS.

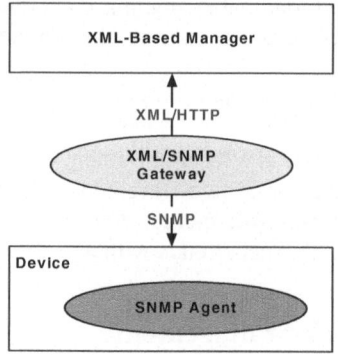

Fig. 1. An XML-based Network Management Architecture

3 Related Work

J.P. Martin-Flatin [3] proposed using XML for network management in his research work on web-based integrated network management architecture (WIMA). He proposed two SNMP-MIB-to-XML translation models. WIMA provides a way to exchange management information between a manager and an agent through HTTP. HTTP messages are structured with a Multipurpose Internet Mail Extensions (MIME) multipart. Each MIME part can be an XML document, a binary file, BER-encoded SNMP data, etc. By separating the communication and information models, WIMA allows management applications to transfer SNMP, common information model (CIM), or other management data. A WIMA-based research prototype, implemented push-based network management using Java technology.

F. Strauss [9] developed a library called "libsmi", which can be used to access SMI MIB information. It can even translate SNMP MIB to other languages, like JAVA, C, XML, etc. This library has tools to check, analyze, dump, convert, and compare MIB definitions. The tool used for this is called "smidump".

Network devices developed by Juniper Networks are equipped with the JUNOS Operating system, which supports JUNOScript [10]. The JUNOSciprt allows the client applications to connect to the Juniper network devices and exchange messages as XML document. The request and response are represented as DTDs and XML Schemas. The communication between the client and network devices is through RPC requests. An XML-based RPC consists of a request and the corresponding response. It is transmitted through a connection-oriented session using any transport protocols like SSH, TELNET, SSL or a serial console connection. Juniper Networks has already implemented a tool for mapping SNMP SMI information modules to the XML Schema. This tool is an extension of a previously implemented tool for converting SNMP SMI to CORBA-IDL. Currently Juniper

Networks is working on the implementation of an XML document adapter for SNMP MIB modules using Net-SNMP and XML-RPC libraries.

Jens Muller implemented an SNMP/XML gateway as Java Servlet that allows fetching of XML documents on the fly through HTTP. MIB portions can be addressed through XPath expressions encoded in the URLs to be retrieved. The gateway works as follows: when a MIB module to be dumped is passed to mibdump, an SNMP session is initiated, and then sequences of SNMP GetNext operations are issued to retrieve all objects of the MIB from the agent. Mibdump collects the retrieved data and the contents of this data are dumped in the form of an appropriate XML document with respect to the predefined XML Schema.

Today's network is equipped with legacy SNMP based agents, and it is difficult to manage legacy SNMP agents through an XML-based manager. Conversion of the XML-based request to an SNMP-based request through an XML/SNMP gateway provides the interaction between the XML-based manager and SNMP-based agents. For a validation of the algorithm, POSTECH implemented an XML-based SNMP MIB browser using this SNMP MIB to XML translator. This gateway is developed by POSTECH at their DPNM laboratory [1][2]. This gateway provides modules to manage networks equipped with SNMP agents [1]. The implementation of the gateway requires two types of translations: specification translations and interaction translations. The specification translation is concerned about the translation of the SNMP MIB to XML. POSTECH uses an automatic translation algorithm for SNMP MIB to XML. The interaction translation methods for XML/SNMP gateway are the process level interaction translation, the message level interaction translation, and the protocol level interaction translation.

In a previous paper [4], we proposed to extend the work of POSTECH & Juniper Networks. The framework proposed allows a manager to send requests to multiple agents using a single message. We defined new types of messages that could be sent by a manager, namely multi-get-request, multi-set-request, and response. These messages can be widely used in configuration management. The implementation for both multi-get-request and multi-set-request can be achieved through an HTTP-based interaction method and a SOAP-based interaction method. We described how a manager can send in one message either one request to multiple agents, multiple requests to one agent, or multiple requests to multiple agents. For the multi-set-request message, if an abnormal condition or an error occurs, some agents may not set the values requested. This will be reported to the gateway and the manager. However, our system does not automatically provide for a rollback mechanism to the previous state. This can be the subject of future work.

In this paper, we will compare the performance of our system using two different JPVM DOM-based approaches, namely a static weighted load balancing and equal work non-weighted load balancing approaches. We will also compare this to a single JPVM gateway approach.

4   System Architecture

Our framework is based on the XML/SNMP gateway architecture, which is shown in Fig. 2. Communication is between an XML-based Manager, an XML/SNMP Gateway, and SNMP Agents. In this paper, we present a static weighted JPVM-based approach for the implementation of the XML/SNMP gateway.

In this section we present the JPVM-based approach for XML-based Network Management. First, we present the single-DOM tree XML-based Network Management architecture. Then, we give a general background of the JPVM. Finally, we describe the proposed architecture and its implementation. We also present the algorithms for load balancing and our contribution to JPVM.

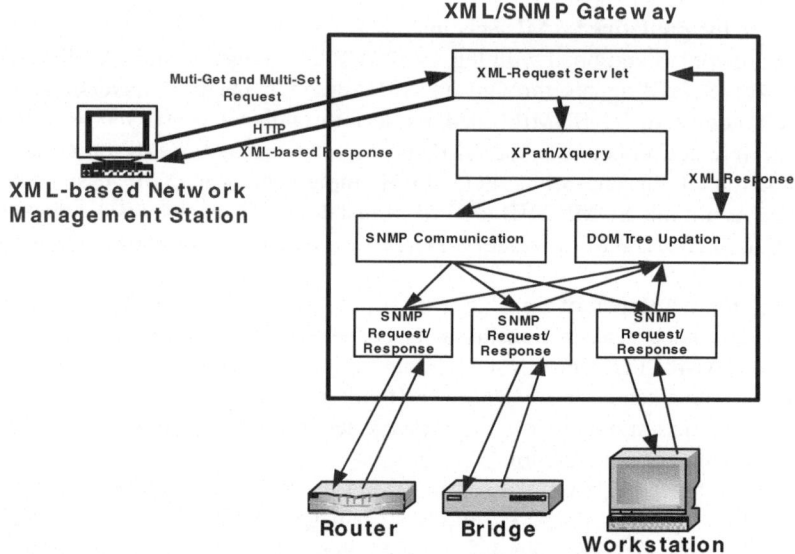

Fig. 2. Single-DOM Tree based Framework

4.1 Single DOM Tree-Based Approach

The proposed architecture for the single-DOM tree has three main components as shown in Fig. 2.:

- XML-based Network Management Station (XBM).
- XML/SNMP Gateway.
- SNMP agents.

The XML-based request is represented as an XML document. The XBM prepares and sends the XML-based request to the XML/SNMP gateway. The request is received by the XML request servlet, which retrieves the number of target agents present in the request. It extracts the Xpath component of the request and sends it to the Xpath/Xquery module, which parses the XML-based request document. Parsing extracts the target MIB object present in the XML-based request received from the XBM.

Using these target objects and the target hosts, the SNMP communication module will send the SNMP-based requests to the agents and receives the SNMP responses.

The DOM tree is updated with the received response values. The updated response DOM tree can be translated into any form according to the user requirements using the XSL style sheets. Here in our approach we apply the XML style sheet to convert the response DOM tree into an HTML format and it is transmitted over the HTTP protocol to the XBM. Another option would be to transmit the XML document to the XBM which will in turn convert it to an HTML document. This will provide more flexibility to the XBM to manipulate the response, at the expense of adding more processing overhead. Since our goal is to minimize the overhead of the manager, we have chosen the first option.

4.2 JPVM Background

Adam J. Ferrari introduced the Java Parallel Virtual Machine (JPVM) [11] library. The JPVM library is a software system for explicit message passing based on distributed memory MIMD parallel programming in Java. JPVM supports an interface similar to C and FORTRAN interfaces provided by the Parallel Virtual Machine (PVM) system. The JPVM system is easily accessible to the PVM programmers and has low investment target for migrating parallel applications to a Java platform. JPVM offers new features such as thread safety, and multiple communication end-points per task. JPVM has been implemented in Java and is highly portable among the platforms supporting any version of the Java Virtual Machine.

The JPVM system is quite similar to that of a PVM system. JPVM has an added advantage of the Java as a language for network parallel processing. In the case of PVM, we divide a task into a set of cooperative sequential tasks that are executed on a collection of hosts. Similarly, in the case of JPVM, one has to code the implementation part into Java. The task creation and message passing is provided by means of JPVM.

4.3 JPVM Interface

In this section we explore the JPVM interface that provides the task creation, and execution. The most important interface of the JPVM package is the *jpvmEnvironment* class. The instance of this class is used to connect and interact with the JPVM systems and other tasks executing within the system. An Object of this class represents the communication end-points within the system, and each communication point is identified by means of a unique *jpvmTaskId*. In PVM, each task has single a communication end-point (and a single task identifier), but JPVM allows programmer to maintain logically unlimited number of communication connections by allocating multiple instances of *jpvmEnvironment*.

First, we need to set the JPVM environment on all the hosts that we are interested to use for parallel communication. For this, we need to run the *jpvmDaemon* java program on all the hosts. By running *jpvmDaemon* threads, we just initiate the JPVM environment. These threads are not used until all the hosts know about their JPVM environment. Next, we need to start the Console on one of the *jpvmDaemon* running hosts. The console program can be started running the *jpvmConsole* java program. Then, we have to register or add the other *jpvmDaemon* hosts to the host running the console program. We add the hosts by giving the name and the port at which the *jpvmDaemon* started. This port is used during message passing between the JPVM hosts, and is the port through which the JPVM communication takes place.

4.4 JPVM Architecture

The proposed JPVM architecture is shown in Fig. 3. It has mainly 3 components, namely an XML-based Manager, JPVM gateways, and SNMP agents. All the JPVM gateways are configured to run daemon processes. There will be one JPVM gateway that will run the *jpvmConsole* in order to notify all the hosts one another's existence and this is called as the master JPVM gateway. The master JPVM gateway will communicate directly with the XML-based manager. The other JPVM gateways are known as slave JPVM gateways. These slave gateways communicate only with the master JPVM gateway. Hence, the JPVM-based network management is based on a master slave paradigm.

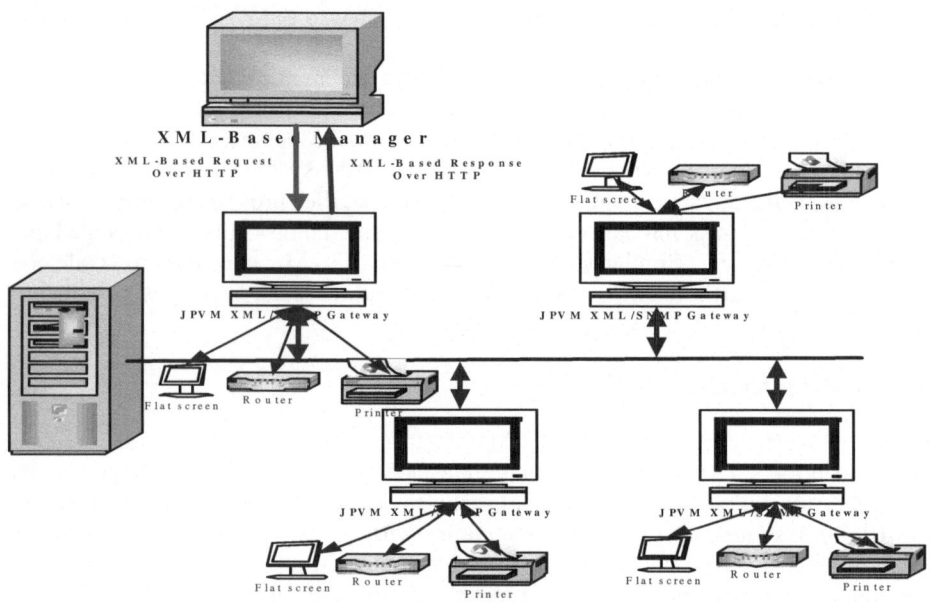

Fig. 3. JPVM Framework for Parallel XML-based Netwrok Management

4.5 Implementation of the Proposed Framework

The JPVM-based framework is implemented as a master-slave architecture, where a master JPVM is running at the web server. The master JPVM gateway receives the request from the XML-based manager. A *jpvmDaemon* program will be running on all the JPVM gateways. The master JPVM gateway is connected to a number of slave JPVM gateways, and will run the *jpvmconsole* program. The JPVM slave gateways have only the slave programs running on them for communication with the master JPVM and SNMP agents. The slave JPVM carries out the actual XML to SNMP translation and SNMP communication with the SNMP agents. The master JPVM status can be either working or not working. If the master has a working status, it can communicate with the SNMP agents after dividing the tasks.

4.6 JPVM Master Algorithm

The JPVM master gateway algorithm is presented in Fig. 4. The Master JPVM algorithm has three stages: initialization, waiting for the work, and termination. In the initialization stage, the master will start the JPVM environment, and create a pool of slave JPVM gateways. In the wait for request stage, the master will wait for the request from the XBM, and upon receiving the request it divides the work among the available pool of slave JPVM gateways, and dispatches the work to the slave JPVM gateways. It will wait for the response from all the slave JPVM gateways, and after receiving the response, it joins the responses into one response document. Then, it will apply XSL to the XML document before transmitting the response over HTTP protocol to XML-based manager. In the termination stage, the master JPVM will send the *stop* command to the slave JPVMs, and then exit from the JPVM environment.

Algorithm JPVM Master Gateway	Algorithm JPVM Slave Gateway

Begin
Initialization:
  Start the JPVM Environment
  Create Pool of JPVM Slave Gateways
  Initialize the JPVM _Spawn for each Slave
Wait For Request:
  Divide the work
  Send the work to each Slave JPVM gateways
  Get the result from all the Slave JPVM gateways
  Join the work
Termination:
  Send to each Slave the Stop command
  Exit from the JPVM Environment
End Master JPVM
	Begin
	  Start the JPVM Environment
	  Parse the RFC-1213
	  While (true)
	    Wait to receive the work from the Master
	    If (Stop)
	      Exit from the JPVM Environment
	    If (Work)
	      Get the XML-Document
	      Do the Work.
	  End While
	  Exit from the JPVM Environment
	End Slave

Fig. 4. Master and Slave JPVM Gateway Algorithms

4.7 Slave JPVM Algorithm

The slave JPVM algorithm is presented in Fig. 4. The slave JPVM gateway starts the JPVM environment and parses the RFC-1213 MIB objects during the master JPVM initialization stage. The slave JPVM will wait for the work from the master JPVM gateway. Once the work is received from the master, each slave JPVM performs Single DOM tree-based approach (converting the XML-request into SNMP requests, sending SNMP requests, receiving the SNMP responses, and updating the SNMP responses in the DOM tree). All the slave JPVM gateways will pass the XML response document to the master JPVM gateway. Then, all the slaves wait again for work from the master. This repeats until the master sends the terminate command to all the slave JPVM gateways.

4.8 Contributions to JPVM

JPVM supports basic data types like integer, long, string, character etc. The communication (message passing) between the different JPVMs is through these data types. XML-based network management requires communication by means of XML documents. JPVM does not support message passing of XML documents among the different JPVM. In order to support message passing of XML documents, we added new data types such as: XML document, NodeList, Node, and SnmpPdu to the current JPVM source code.

4.9 Static Weighted Load Balancing

In the equal work non-weighted load balancing approach, we assign equal work to all slave JPVM gateways (i.e., we divide the work based on the number of slave JPVM gateways present in the pool). This approach provides good performance only for a homogeneous network of workstations.

A second approach is the static weighted load-balancing algorithm in which we divide the work based on the processing speed of the workstations. In this approach, we assign a weight to the workstations depending on their processing speed. During the work assignment, a gateway will be assigned work according to its weight. The higher the weight the larger the amount assigned to the slave JPVM gateway.

The weights are assigned based on the base processor's processing speed as follows: First, each workstation is assigned the same number of agents that it will communicate with. The workstation that takes the longest time to finish the work is taken as the base processor. The weight of this workstation is set to 1, and the weight of any other workstation is obtained by dividing the base processor time by the amount of time taken by this workstation.

The second approach provides better results when we have a heterogeneous network of workstations. Results are shown later that support this statement.

5   Experiments and Results

5.1 Experimental Setup

In the experimental setup for the XML-based network management using JPVM, the master JVPM gateway is connected to a number of slave JVPM gateways. All the JPVM gateways are windows workstation and running on windows 2000 operating system. The master JPVM gateway has a TOMCAT 5.0 web server running on it. The same experimental setup has been used with homogenous and heterogeneous systems. In the case of homogeneous systems the slave JPVM gateways are of equal processing speed and in the other case they are of different processing speed. The experiments were conducted from our University campus, and all the SNMP agents are connected over 100Mbps access network connection and a Gigabit Ethernet backbone. Each experiment was conducted for 25 runs. The maximum number of agents used in our experiments is 200. The request/response messages are for the system group MIB objects from RFC-1213.

The time elapsed between issuing the XML-based request from the XBM to the XML/SNMP gateway and the time the response is received from the XML/SNMP gateway back to the XBM is termed as the response time. We have shown in [12] that most of the response time is consumed during the communication between the XML/SNMP gateway and the SNMP agents, that is the SNMP-STACK communication. For example, more than 90% of the time is consumed by the SNMP-STACK communication when the number of agents exceeds 50. Our goal is then to reduce the SNMP-STACK communication time. This was achieved through the distribution of the work among multiple gateways. In our experiments, we will however compare the overall response time to show the improvements achieved.

5.2 Results and Discussion

Table 1 shows the response time values for single gateways (i.e., 350-No-JPVM, 350-JPVM, 711-No-JPVM, and 711-JPVM), homogeneous systems, heterogeneous systems, and static weighted allocation as the number of agent increases.

Table 1. Response Time values for Homogenous, Heterogeneous, and Static Weighted

Agents	350-No-JPVM	350-JPVM	711-No-JPVM	711-JPVM	HOMO EqualWork	HETERO EqualWork	STATIC	STATIC (Agents assigned) 350	711
				Response Time				350	711
1	523.2	1221.8	609.4	737.0	1070.8	821.2	786.4	0	1
10	1528.6	2445.5	1131.5	1636.4	2160.7	1939.8	1551.1	3	7
20	3319.6	4534.6	2369.4	2834.2	2971.6	2692.9	2021.7	7	13
30	5717.9	7141.2	3575.5	4728.8	4256.0	3734.4	3304.4	10	20
50	11678.8	14061.2	6780.9	8233.8	6322.1	5370.6	5692.7	17	33
60	15779.5	18769.1	8949.7	10420.6	7849.9	6566.5	6936.2	20	40
90	31032.2	37661.0	18237.7	20030.8	13364.0	12238.7	11032.1	30	60
100	37481.5	45195.8	21733.8	24419.2	16435.4	14764.3	12724.9	33	67
110	44291.2	54004.7	25692.5	27860.2	18861.3	17302.0	13195.9	37	73
140	69174.2	80195.3	39770.3	41776.2	24561.4	21974.6	23042.4	47	93
150	78327.4	90753.5	42279.3	46507.0	26741.3	25396.4	25655.3	50	100
180	108866.2	129406.3	59818.3	66253.4	41106.2	37756.4	34308.4	60	120
190	123441.5	147638.4	65247.4	71603.0	44417.2	40355.1	37045.5	63	127
200	134577.5	153398.6	70516.2	76602.2	48740.3	44477.9	38905.3	67	133

Fig. 5. shows the response time for the homogeneous vs. heterogeneous systems for the system group MIB objects in the case of equal work assignment. The

experiment is conducted with two homogeneous systems and then with two heterogeneous systems. The homogeneous systems are of 350 MHz processing speed Intel Pentium II processors and the heterogeneous systems are a 350 MHz processing speed Intel Pentium II processor and a 711MHz processing speed Intel Pentium III processor. In both cases, the response time is mainly dependent on the slower processor that takes longer to finish the work; since equal work is assigned to the two processors, whether these are of the same speed or not. Since the slowest processor is the same in both cases, i.e., 350MHz, the equal work assignment provides similar response times as shown in Fig. 5. Hence, homogeneous systems are better to use because, in the case of heterogeneous systems, the higher speed processor will be underutilized.

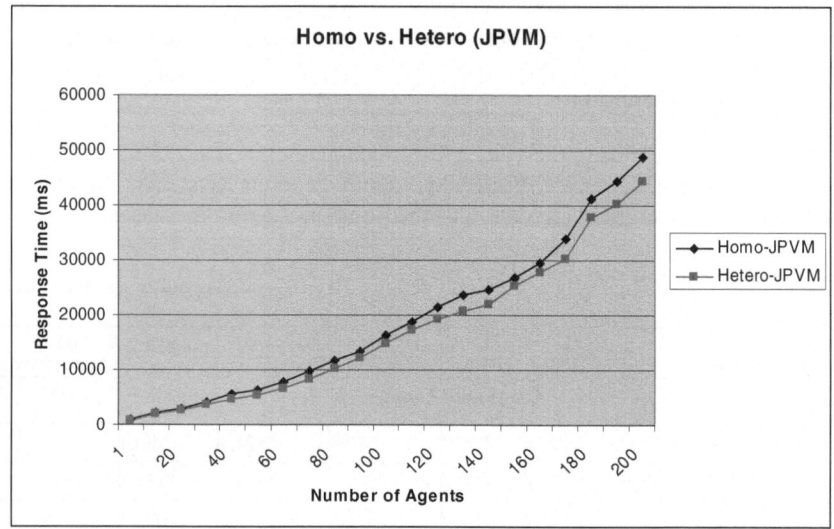

Fig. 5. Response Time for Homogeneous vs. Heterogeneous Systems

Fig. 6. shows the response time for heterogeneous systems vs. static weighted load balancing for the values in Table 1. Let us illustrate the difference between the results of the two approaches through the example of an XML-based request with 30 agents. In the case of heterogeneous systems, the response time is 3,734.4 ms, which is equal to requesting 15 agents by the slowest processor, i.e., 350 MHz processor. In the case of static weighted load balancing approach, the allocation of the work to each JPVM gateway is 10 and 20 respectively for the 350 MHz and the 711 MHz processors. In this case, the response time is 3,304.4 ms, which is equal to requesting 20 agents by the 711 MHz processor, i.e., 2,834.2 ms; in addition to the communication time for data packing and unpacking due to the use of two slave JPVM gateways. We can also observe in this case that the slower processor, i.e., 350 MHz processor, takes less time to request 10 agents, i.e., 2,445.5 ms; compared to the response time of the faster processor requesting 20 agents, i.e., 2,834.2 ms. Hence, the slower processor is underutilized in this case.

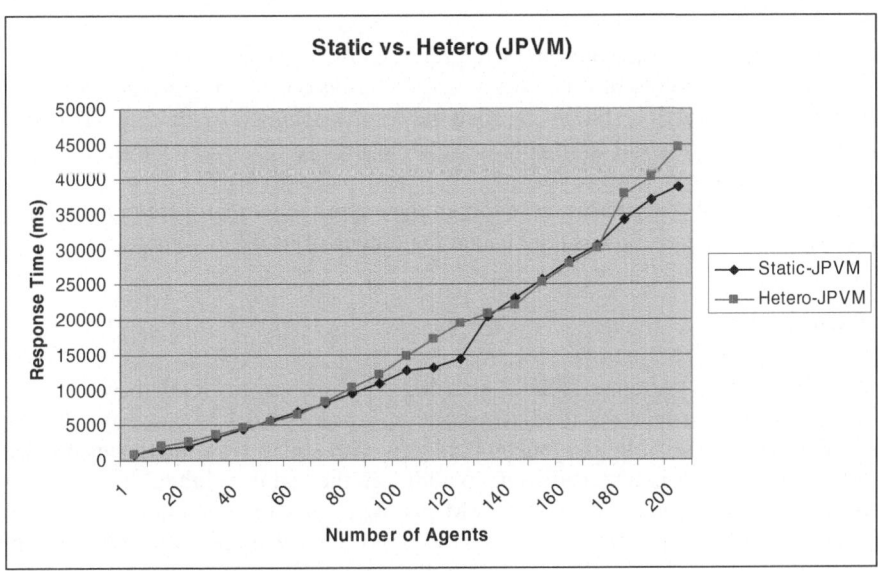

Fig. 6. Response Time for Heterogeneous Systems vs. Static Weighted Load Balancing

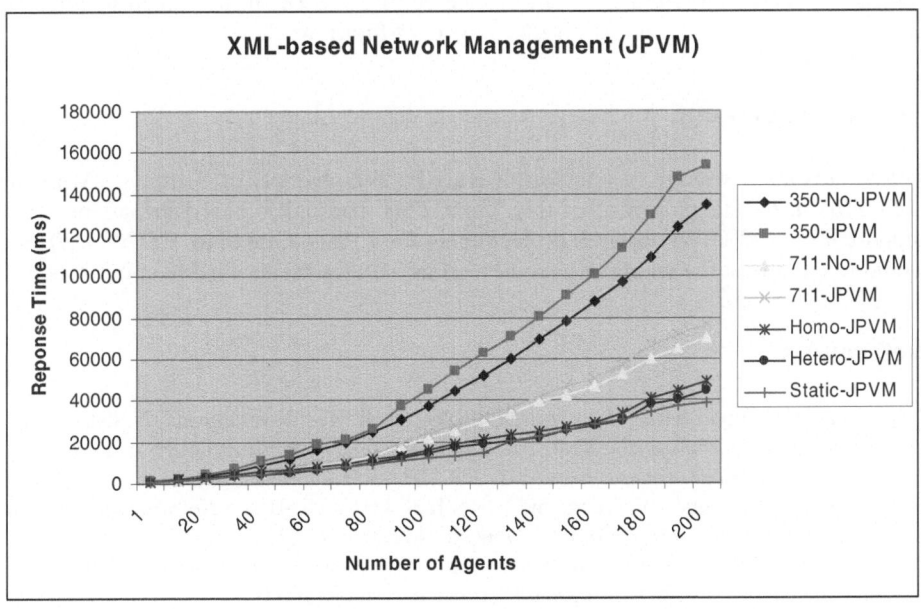

Fig. 7. Response Time for all experiments

The response time in the case of heterogeneous systems with equal work allocation will be almost the same as that of the slower processor. In this case, as the number of agents increases, the faster processor needs lesser time to finish the work and thus is underutilized. There will be better response time with the static weighted load balancing compared to the equal work approach as the number of agents increases.

The choice of weights in this work is solely based on the processing speed of the systems used. We may be able to improve the results obtained by finding a better way to assign weights to avoid as much as possible underutilized gateways. This is the subject of future work.

Fig. 7. shows the comparison between all the experiments that were performed. We can see that the static weighted load balancing outperforms all the others.

6 Conclusion

In this paper, we presented load balancing approaches to XML-based network management, to distribute the load across multiple parallel JPVM gateways. We have shown that in the case of heterogeneous systems with equal work, the faster processor completes earlier and is underutilized. In addition, the static weighted load balancing approach with heterogeneous slave JPVM gateways provides a better response time than the equal work non-weighted approach, and a much better one than all single gateway approaches. We found as well that in the case of static weighted load balancing approach, the response time is closer to that of the faster processor which takes more time to complete the work. This also led to the fact that the slower processor became underutilized. The weight setting can be further tuned to improve the results obtained, but this will be the subject of future work.

Acknowledgement

The authors acknowledge the support of King Fahd University of Petroleum Minerals (KFUPM) in the development of this work. This material is based in part on work supported by a KFUPM research project under Fast Track Grant No. FT/2004-20. We would like to thank the anonymous reviewers as well for their valuable comments.

References

[1] Jeong-Hyuk yoon, Hong-Taek Ju and James W.Hong, "Development of SNMP-XML translator and Gateway for XML-based integrated network management", *International journal of Network Management*, 2003, 259-276.

[2] Mi-Jung Choi, James W. Hong, and Hong-Taek Ju, "XML-Based Network Management for IP Networks", *ETRI Journal, Volume 25*, November 6, 2003.

[3] J.P.Martin-Flatin, "Web-Based Management of IP Networks and Systems", Wiley series in communications Networking and Distributed Systems, 2003.

[4] Sqalli H.M., and Sirajuddin S., "Extensions to XML based Network Management", International Conference on Information and Computer Sciences (ICICS-2004), Dhahran, KSA, November 2004.

[5] W3C, "Extensible Markup Language (XML) 1.0", *W3C Recommendation*, October 2000.

[6] W3C, "XML Schema Part0: Primer", *W3C Recommendation*, May 2001.

[7] W3C, "XML Schema Part1: Structures", *W3C Recommendation*, May 2001.

[8] W3C, "XML Schema Part2: Data Types", *W3C Recommendation,* May 2001.

[9] Straus, F. "A library to access SMI MIB information", http://www.ibr.cs.tubs.de/ projects/libsmi/

[10] Phil Shafer "XML-Based Network Management" – White Paper, *Juniper Networks, Inc.,* 2001, http://www.Juniper.net/solutions/literature/white_papers/200017.pdf

[11] Adam J.Ferrari, "JPVM: The Java Parallel Virtual Machine", http://www.cs.virginia.edu/ jpvm/

[12] Sirajuddin S., and Sqalli H.M., "Comparison of CSV and DOM Tree Approaches in XML-based Network Management", 12th International Conference on Telecommunications (ICT-2005), Cape Town, South Africa, May 3-6, 2005.

[13] Hyoun-Mi Choi, Mi-Jung Choi, James W.Hong, "XML-based Configuration Management for Distributed System", Proc. of 2003 Asia-Pacific Network Operations and Management Symposium (APNOMS 2003), Fukuoka, Japan, October 1-3, 2003, pp. 599-600.

[14] Mani Subramanian, "Network Management: Principles and Practice", Addison-Wesley, Hardcover, Published December 1999, 644 pages, ISBN 0201357429.

[15] W3C, "Document Object Model (DOM) Level 2 Core Specification", *W3C Recommendation*, November 2000.

[16] W3C, "Document Object Model (DOM) Level 2 Traversal and Range Specification", *W3C Recommenda-tion*, November 2000.

Application of OWL-S to Define Management Interfaces Based on Web Services

Jorge E. López de Vergara[1], Víctor A. Villagrá[2], and Julio Berrocal[2]

[1] Departamento de Ingeniería Informática, Universidad Autónoma de Madrid,
Escuela Politécnica Superior, Francisco Tomás y Valiente, 11, E 28049 Madrid, Spain
`jorge.lopez_vergara@uam.es`
[2] Departamento de Ingeniería de Sistemas Telemáticos, Universidad Politécnica de Madrid,
E.T.S.I. de Telecomunicación, Av. Complutense, s/n, E 28040 Madrid, Spain
`{villagra, berrocal}@dit.upm.es`

Abstract. Some network management trends are currently analysing the application of several generic technologies that include Web Services and Ontologies. Web Services can provide an interface to access to managed resources. On the other hand, ontologies provide a way to represent management information. Web Services interfaces can be defined using OWL-S, an ontology of services that semantically describes the set of operations a Web Service provides. This can be useful in configuration management, where each network resource defines the way it can be configured. This paper presents a proposal to describe with the OWL Service ontology the management interfaces based on Web Services. To illustrate this approach, an example is provided in which OWL-S is used to specify the processes needed to configure a resource.

1 Introduction

Network management has evolved in the last decade from proprietary interfaces to standard integrated management interfaces. These interfaces have been based on management specific protocols, such as SNMP or CMIP. This has helped to the development of management applications, among other reasons because it is easier to find a developer with knowledge on these standards than one who can code proprietary interfaces.

However, as stated in [1], the technology market has learnt that implementation costs can be reduced by using generic technologies independent of the application domain, and management applications have not been an exception: it is even easier to find a developer with general communication abilities than with specific network management skills. Nowadays, generic Internet technologies such as HTTP or XML are being adopted to manage network resources.

One of the most promising technologies in this scope is the one related to Web Services, given that they can provide a distributed processing environment with the advantage that they are based on well-known technologies, used broadly by developers. This is one of the reasons why Web Services is a key technology in the evolution of network management systems, solving the complexity problems of other similar approaches such as CORBA, also used to implement management interfaces.

J. Dalmau and G. Hasegawa (Eds.): MMNS 2005, LNCS 3754, pp. 242–253, 2005.

On the other side, one of the pillars of the network management is the definition of the information related to managed resources. Applying the same idea of using generic technologies, these definitions have evolved from using network management specific languages, such as SMI or GDMO, to other generic ones, such as XML schemas or lately, ontology languages such as OWL [2].

At this point, both technologies, Web Services and OWL, meet: it is possible to leverage semantic capabilities of the Web Ontology Language to define the interfaces of Web Services. Instead of using WSDL (Web Services Description Language) [3], the ontology of services known as OWL-S [4] can be used. This ontology can be used to define composite processes by following a well defined structure, formalizing the way in which a set of Web Services operations are invoked. If it is applied to network management, managed resources can semantically describe how they can be managed. In addition, the parameters of each operation can also be classes defined in the ontology that semantically describes the management information.

This article proposes the application of OWL-S to define management interfaces based on Web Services. For this, next sections show how to apply Web Services and Ontologies to network management. Then, OWL-S service ontology is presented, explaining how it can help in the definition of management interfaces. For it, an application example is provided. Conclusions finally remark most important ideas and future works.

2 Web Services in Network Management

A Web Service is a software system designed to support interoperable machine-to-machine interaction over a network, as described in [5]. The main difference with other systems that comply with this definition is that Web Services are an instantiation of the Service-Oriented Computing paradigm [6]. Web Services describe their interfaces with WSDL and their interactions are based on SOAP messages serialized in XML over HTTP. WSDL are XML documents that include definitions of data types, messages, port types or operations, bindings with transport protocols and services. SOAP messages are structured in an envelope with a header, used to transmit metadata, and a body, which is suitable to support RPC-like communications. Also, a third technology that is usually linked to Web Services is UDDI (Universal Description, Discovery and Integration), which allows a service to be registered and later be found by clients.

In the network management scope, several initiatives are related to Web Services:

- WBEM (Web Based Enterprise Management) [7] shares some common characteristics with Web Services: messages are serialized in XML over HTTP. However, WBEM was defined before Web Services, and although it makes use of these standards it defines its own syntax, being a management-specific technology. The Distributed Management Task Force is trying to solve this question, and currently has a workgroup to align WBEM with Web Services.
- OASIS consortium, one of the supporters of Web Services related technologies, has started several initiatives to use them in management, specifying what is known as MoWS (Management of Web Services) and MuWS (Management using Web Services) [8]. These specifications define an architecture and a set of XML

schemas with management parameters that extend the functionality initially provided by Web Services.

• Network Configuration Working Group (Netconf) of the IETF is currently defining a specification to configure network resources using XML messages defined in XML schemas [9]. In this case, they propose several application protocols for the communications, such as SSH, BEEP, and SOAP. This variety allows a better adoption of a future standard, but also reduces the application of Web Services features. It is interesting to notice that this specification is only focused on the interaction between a manager and a managed device, leaving the configuration information standardization as a future work, which is being studied by the Netconf Data Model (Netmod) Working Group.

• Several researchers have studied and compared the SNMP framework with Web Services applied to network management. Some of these works are related to the definition of WSDL interfaces based on SNMP MIBs [10, 11], being able to define coarse and fine grained methods to access MIB information. Other ones are focused on performance of Web Services when they are used to retrieve management information [12, 13, 14]. Results show that Web Services performance is comparable to SNMP when SOAP messages are compressed, so this factor should not be taken as a key factor to reject this technology for network management.

Although most of these approaches are related to interfacing network elements, Web Services can also be used in other more general management tasks. As a conclusion, Web Services can be one of the dominant technologies for network management in the near future to access and perform operations on managed resources.

3   Ontologies in Network Management

Other generic technology currently under review in the network management scope is the Semantic Web and its main component: ontologies. They are explicit and formal specifications of shared conceptualizations [15]: they provide the definition of a set of concepts, their taxonomy, interrelation and the rules that govern these concepts. The interesting point that differentiates ontology languages from management information definition languages is that their semantics has been formalized. Then, different ontology representations have been proposed to describe the management information, including OKBC [16], RDF-S [17] or description logics [18].

Prior works of the authors about ontologies in network management have also given some results:

• A framework can be established to compare different management information languages from an ontology viewpoint. All these languages have different levels of expressiveness, so the same resource can be defined in multiple ways depending on the used model. As ontologies provide the necessary constructs to represent the semantics of specified information, these constructs can be used to compare the semantic expressiveness of management information languages in a neutral way. Using this approach, management information description languages are analyzed and compared based on their semantic expressiveness in [19].

- Solutions applied to integrate different ontologies are not only syntactic translations of different languages: they also deal with the semantics of the information. A method to merge and map management information models of different domains (e.g. CIM schemas and SNMP MIBs) can be defined by applying ontology techniques [20], generating a mapping ontology that contains all the elements defined in both models and their mapping rules. These mapping rules can describe 1:1, 1:n and m:n correspondences.
- Several ontology definition languages can be found in the literature, being OWL [2] currently the most relevant one because of its adoption by the World Wide Web Consortium. Still, they have to be adapted to the management scope, as there are some constructs they do not include. In [21], the use of OWL has been proposed to specify management information, describing a set of mapping rules with constructions of management languages. Besides the mapping specification, other constructions that include all the components of the management information models are proposed to be included in OWL.
- Another advantage of ontologies is the ability of expressing behaviour of the defined information. For this, OWL provides the Semantic Web Rule Language (SWRL) [22], allowing the definition of horn clauses inside the ontology. A proposal to include behaviour rules in management information with this language is given in [23]. Thus, usual behaviour definitions included implicitly in the management information definitions and explicitly in policy definitions can then be expressed formally, and included with those definitions, which allows a manager reasoning and working with them.

Finally, this work provides an application of OWL-S, an ontology of services, to improve current approaches based on the use of Web Services for network management, as shown in next section.

4   OWL-S and Network Management

In this section, the benefits of using the ontology of services OWL-S to describe Web Service management interfaces are provided. For this, OWL-S is first described, and later its usefulness in network management is given.

4.1   OWL-S: An Ontology to Describe Services

OWL-S [4] is an upper ontology of services developed in the semantic web scope that aims at the automatic discovery, invocation, composition and interoperation of Web Services. It has been defined as a part of the DARPA Agent Markup Language program, and later submitted to the World Wide Web Consortium. OWL-S complements WSDL descriptions by supporting a richer semantics, including logical constraints between the input and output parameters of services. Moreover, WSDL documents can specify data types using XML Schema, whereas OWL-S uses OWL classes, which provides a better semantics. In this way, a software agent can select and operate with the Web Service that meets its needs to perform a task.

The ontology OWL-S is composed of several classes. The main class is the service. This service presents a service profile, is described by a service model, and supports a service grounding:

- The service profile provides the information needed to discover a service. It tells what the service does, so that an agent can determine if the service meets its needs.
- The service model tells a client how to use the service, detailing the semantic content of each request, including preconditions, results, and processes to be carried out by the service. These processes can be atomic or composite. Composite processes model the behaviour the client can perform by sending and receiving a set of messages following a set of control constructs (sequence, split, join, choice, if-then-else, iterate, repeat-while, repeat-until).
- The service grounding details how an agent can access a service, defining a mapping with a WSDL document of the Web Service: an atomic process is a WSDL operation, and inputs and outputs are WSDL messages.

One of the initial goals of OWL-S was the automatic monitoring of Web Service execution. This can be useful for the management of these services, where a user could know the state of a request (how long it is taking, exceptions appeared, etc.). However, this feature has not been included in any of the versions released so far.

4.2 Application to Network Management

Once OWL-S has been presented, some ideas can be applied in a Web Services management scenario which makes this ontology useful:

- Management information exchanged between managers and managed elements by means of Web Services can directly be instances of ontology classes, as proposed previously. Web Services can exchange OWL instances instead of XML schema datatypes. This can be useful to avoid several management information translations (SMI or MOF to XML schema, WSDL, OWL, etc.) if the manager can deal with ontology definitions.
- The definition of processes includes a set of preconditions and results that can be expressed as formal logic rules (in SWRL or other languages), specifying the behaviour of such processes. This can help managers to interact with managed resources in an easier way, behaving as described in those rules.
- The description of a service with OWL-S can be used to obtain in runtime how to manage a resource, as it includes both the definition of the needed processes and their mappings to Web Service operations. This can be important in a future scenario in which every resource (which can be devices, applications or services) defines its own management information, not only based on a set of variables, but also on a set of operations, self-describing its manageability. Then, a manager, based on this description can manage the resource easily, thanks to the formality of OWL-S.

Next section applies these ideas to a concrete management functional area: network configuration.

5   Application of OWL-S to Network Configuration

This section shows how OWL-S can be useful in network management, with an example of its application to the configuration of managed resources. It is very common that each network resource has its own configuration. In fact, current standardization efforts of the Netconf Working Group are only focused on the definition of a set of operations, but it is not included how to sequence them, and what information has to be provided, as they depend on each concrete resource. However, it is also very important to specify the way to perform that configuration to reduce the costs of implementing a management application.

Then, as stated before, OWL-S can be useful in this scope, as it can be used to describe how to perform the configuration of a network resource. With this information, a generic management application able of reading such ontologies could manage the configuration of resources based on Web Services, even if it does not know *a priori* how to do it, which can be very helpful in multimedia networks and services. Moreover, configuration information can be defined as a set of classes of a configuration ontology, leveraging existing definitions (for instance, CIM Setting classes), to be used as parameters of the configuration operations. Generic classes can be later specialized for each resource, partially solving the problem of specifying the configuration information. These configuration classes will be defined in OWL, allowing a complete integration with OWL-S, and with an ontology-based management system.

To illustrate these ideas, OWL-S has been applied to describe a network configuration service based on current Netconf works. Although this example is generic, it can be valid to understand how to use this ontology. In a real scenario, each resource will define its own configuration service, with its own preconditions, results processes, and mappings with related Web Service operations, in the same way this generic configuration service has been specified.

To describe in OWL-S this generic network configuration service, several instances of different classes of this ontology have to be defined so that they can semantically describe this service. To help in this work, OWL-S Editor [24] has been used, as shown in **Fig. 1**. This tool is integrated with Protégé [25], an open source ontology editor that in its last version is well integrated with the OWL knowledge model. All diagrams presented in this paper have been generated with this tool, taking the information introduced in the ontology editor.

Four main instances have been defined, as depicted in **Fig. 2**, using the classes presented before in section 0. The first instance is named *netconfService*, and it is an instance of *service:Service*. This is the main instance, which links with *netconfProfile*, *netconfGrounding*, and *netconfConfigurationProcess*. The instance *netconfProfile* represents the property *service:presents* of the *netconfService*, that is, the profile of the service with a general description of the Web Service, including required inputs and preconditions, as well as expected effects of the service. The instance *netconfGrounding* represents the property *service:supports* of the *netconfService*, the grounding of the service with the mappings of the ontology in a WSDL document. Finally, *netconfConfigurationProcess* is a composite process defined in the service model that defines the sequence of atomic processes to be performed when configuring the resource.

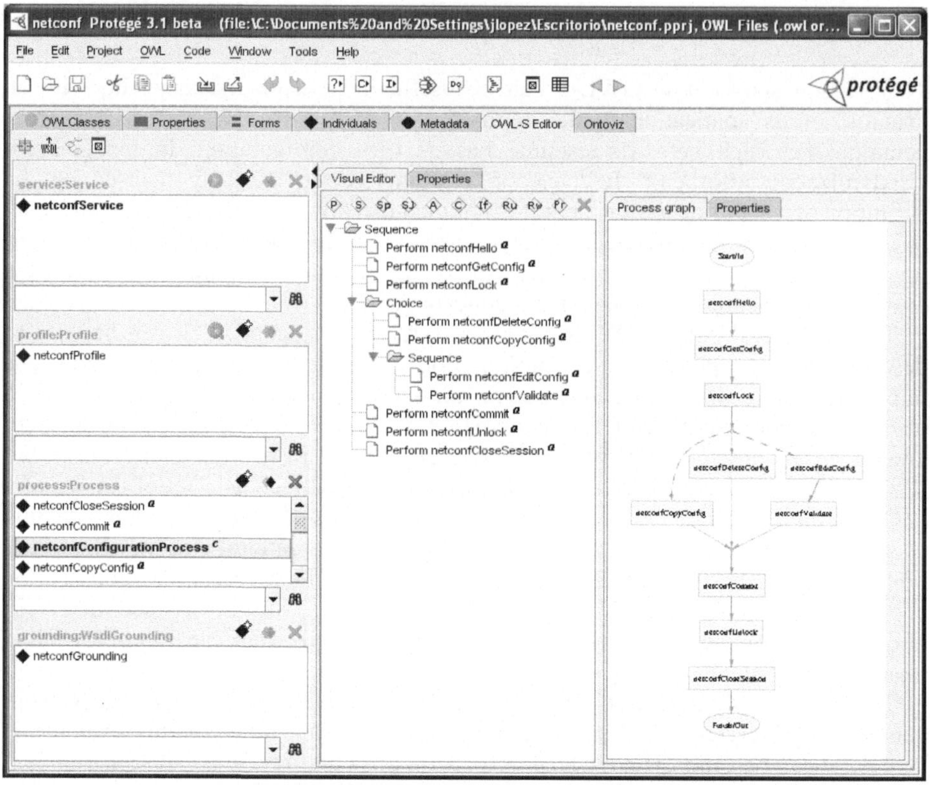

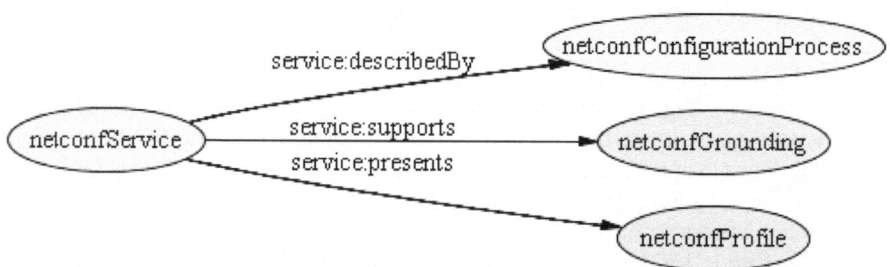

Fig. 1. Editing OWL-S ontology about network configuration with OWL-S editor

Fig. 2. Instances of OWL-S classes to describe the Network Configuration Service

The service model also includes several atomic process instances, as shown in **Fig. 3**, where they are linked to the class *process:AtomicProcess*. They are related to different NetConf operations [9]:

- Session maintenance: hello (*netconfHello*), close-session (*netconfCloseSession*)
- Configuration manipulation: get-config (*netconfGetConfig*), edit-config (*netconfEditConfig*), copy-config (*netconfCopyConfig*), delete-config (*netconfDeleteConfig*), validate (*netconfValidate*).

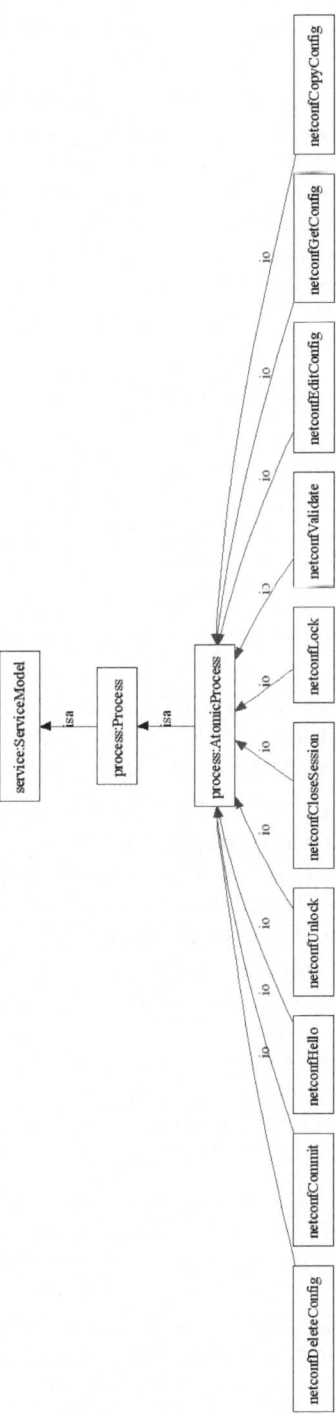

Fig. 3. Atomic process instances

- Transaction management: lock (*netconfLock*), commit (*netconfCommit*), unlock (*netconfUnlock*)

Each of these processes has its own input and output parameters, preconditions and results. For example, the process *netconfEditConfig* has as inputs a target datastore, a configuration subtree, and the kind of operation (merge, replace, create, delete). These parameters can be defined using OWL classes as parameter types. For instance, the *Datastore* class can be specialized in *Startup*, *Running* or *Candidate*, as shown in **Fig. 4**. A precondition for *netconfEditConfig* can logically express in SWRL the need of obtaining a lock on the edited configuration before performing this process.

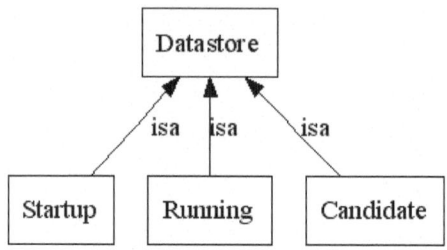

Fig. 4. Datastore class specialization

Then, the *netconfConfigurationProcess* can be composed of this set of atomic processes, defining a control flow similar to the one depicted in **Fig. 5**. In this case, the following sequence of processes has been defined:

1. The first process is a *netconfHello* to open the NetConf session.
2. Then, a *netconfGetConfig* is performed to obtain current configuration.
3. Next, there is a *netconfLock*, to lock it from other managers.
4. At this point, there is a choice with three different possibilities:
   - *netconfDeleteConfig*, to delete the configuration.
   - *netconfCopyConfig*, to copy the configuration.
   - The sequence *netconfEditConfig* and *netconfValidate*, to edit and validate the configuration.
5. Then, once one of the processes of this choice has been performed, the new configuration is committed with a *netconfCommit*.
6. Next, the configuration is unlocked with a *netconfUnlock*.
7. Finally, the session is closed with a *neconfCloseSession*.

This control flow could be enhanced by including if-then-else or repeat-while constructs, which would only let the flow continue if a logic expression is met (for instance, a SWRL expression stating that the configuration is committed only if it has been previously validated).

Once that the set of instances of OWL-S classes have been defined, a network resource can publish the ontology describing its configuration service, and an OWL-S-capable manager can configure it properly, by following the set of processes defined in the service model.

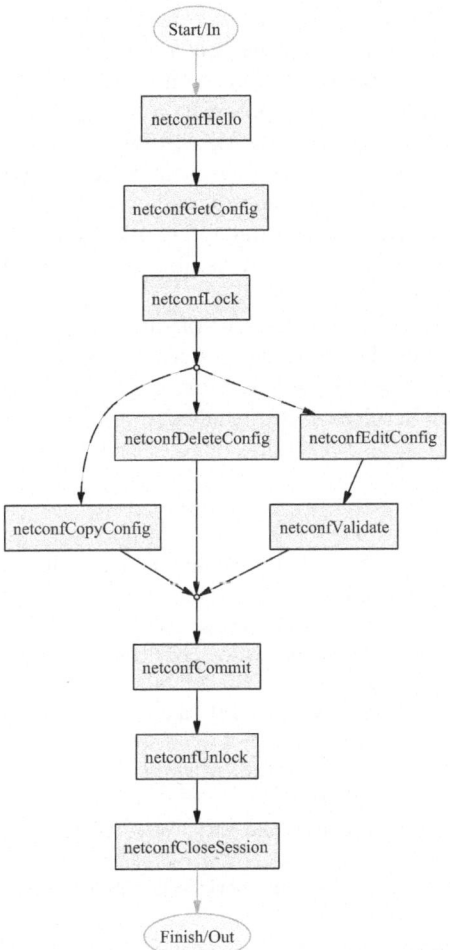

Fig. 5. Control flow of atomic processes conforming the *netconfConfigurationProcess*

6 Conclusions

Web Services provide a generic technology that is currently gaining momentum in the network management community. At the same time, other works have also proposed the use of ontology languages to describe the management information. OWL-S is an upper ontology of services defined to enrich the semantics of Web Services, being also applicable to management interfaces based on Web Services. This paper has presented a proposal that applies OWL-S in this scope.

The OWL-S ontology can be useful to self-describe how to manage a resource, which can be important if that resource does not use standard management information. In this case, a manager can download the OWL-S description of the management interface, and manage the resource by interpreting this description, which includes the definition of management information as a set of OWL classes, including logic rules describing preconditions and control expressions.

To check the feasibility of this approach, a set of OWL-S classes have been instantiated to describe a generic network configuration service. In this case, the service model included a set of atomic processes, based on the operations defined in the Network Configuration Working Group, and a composite process that represents the flow control of a manager configuring a network resource. As these resources are very different, it can be very useful to describe in such a way how a manager can perform the configuration.

Future works include the improvement of the defined information, containing logic expressions to better model the composite process, as well as the implementation of a manager able of interpreting these OWL-S ontologies and accessing to management interfaces based on Web Services with such descriptions.

References

1. J. Schönwälder, A. Pras, J.P. Martin-Flatin: On the Future of Internet Management Technologies. IEEE Communications Magazine, Vol. 41, Issue 10 (2003) 90-97
2. P.F. Patel-Schneider, P. Hayes, I. Horrocks: OWL Web Ontology Language Semantics and Abstract Syntax. W3C Recommendation (10 February 2004)
3. R. Chinnici, M. Gudgin, J.J. Moreau, J. Schlimmer, S. Weerawarana: Web Services Description Language (WSDL) Version 2.0 Part 1: Core Language. W3C Working Draft (3 August 2004)
4. D. Martin, editor: OWL-S: Semantic Markup for Web Services. W3C Member Submission (22 November 2004)
5. H. Haas, A. Brown: Web Services Glossary. W3C Working Group Note (11 February 2004)
6. M. P. Papazoglou, D. Georgakopoulos: Service-Oriented Computing. Communications of the ACM, Vol. 46, No. 10 (2003), 24-28
7. Distributed Management Task Force, Inc.: Specification for CIM Operations over HTTP, Version 1.1. DMTF Standard DSP0200 (2003)
8. OASIS Web Services Distributed Management (WSDM). http://www.oasis-open.org/committees/tc_home.php?wg_abbrev=wsdm
9. M.J. Choi, H.M. Choi, J.W. Hong, H.T. Ju: XML-Based Configuration Management for IP Network Devices. IEEE Communications Magazine, Vol. 42, Issue 7 (2004) 84-91
10. J. van Sloten, A. Pras, M. van Sinderen: On the standardisation of Web Service management operations. In: Proc. 10th Open European Summer School (EUNICE 2004) and IFIP WG 6.3 Workshop, Tampere, Finland (2004) 143-150
11. T. Drevers, R. van de Meent, A. Pras: Prototyping Web Services based Nework Monitoring. In: Proc. 10th Open European Summer School (EUNICE 2004) and IFIP WG 6.3 Workshop, Tampere, Finland (2004) 135-142
12. R. Neisse, R.L. Vianna, L.Z. Granville, M.J.B. Almeida, L.M.R. Tarouco: Implementation and Bandwidth Consumption Evaluation of SNMP to Web Services Gateways. In: Proc. 9th IEEE/IFIP Network Operations and Management Symposium (NOMS 2004), Vol.1, Seoul, Korea (2004) 715 - 728

13. G. Pavlou, P. Flegkas, S. Gouveris, A. Liotta: On Management Technologies and the Potential of Web Services. IEEE Communications Magazine, Vol. 42, Issue 7 (2004) 58-66
14. A. Pras, T. Drevers, R. van de Meent, D. Cuartel: Comparing the Performance of SNMP and Web Services-Based Management. eTransactions on Network and Service Management (Fall 2004)
15. R. Studer, V.R. Benjamins, D. Fensel: Knowledge Engineering: Principles and Methods. Data & Knowledge Engineering. 25. (1998) 161-197
16. E. Lavinal, T. Desprats, Y. Raynaud: A Conceptual Framework for Building CIM-Based Ontologies. In: Proceedings of the Eighth IFIP/IEEE International Symposium on Integrated Network Management (IM'2003), Colorado Springs, Colorado, U.S.A. (2003) 135-138
17. J. Shen, Y. Yang: RDF-Based Knowledge Models for Network Management. In: Proceedings of the Eighth IFIP/IEEE International Symposium on Integrated Network Management (IM'2003), Colorado Springs, Colorado, U.S.A. (2003) 123-126
18. G. Lanfranchi, P. Della Peruta, A. Perrone, D. Calvanese: Towards a new landscape of systems management in an autonomic computing environment. IBM Systems Journal, Vol. 42, No. 1 (2003) 119-128
19. J.E. López de Vergara, V.A. Villagrá, J.I. Asensio, J. Berrocal: Ontologies: Giving Semantics to Network Management Models. IEEE Network, Vol. 17, No. 3 (2003) 15-21
20. J.E. López de Vergara, V.A. Villagrá, J. Berrocal: Benefits of Using Ontologies in the Management of High Speed Networks. Lecture Notes in Computer Science, Vol. 3079, Springer-Verlag. (2004) 1007-1018
21. J.E. López de Vergara, V.A. Villagrá, Julio Berrocal: Applying the Web Ontology Language to management information definitions. IEEE Communications Magazine, Vol. 42, Issue 7, (2004) 68-74
22. I. Horrocks, P.F. Patel-Schneider, H. Boley, S. Tabet, B. Grosof, M. Dean: SWRL: A Semantic Web Rule Language Combining OWL and RuleML. W3C Member Submission (21 May 2004)
23. A. Guerrero, V.A. Villagrá, J.E. López de Vergara: Including management behavior defined with SWRL rules in an Ontology-based management framework. Proceedings of the 12th Annual Workshop of the HP Openview University Association, Porto, Portugal (2005)
24. D. Elenius, G. Denker, D. Martin, F. Gilham, J. Khouri, S. Sadaati, R. Senanayake: The OWL-S Editor – A Development Tool for Semantic Web Services. In: Proc. Second European Semantic Web Conference, Heraklion, Greece (2005)
25. N. F. Noy, M. Sintek, S. Decker, M. Crubézy, R. W. Fergerson, M. A. Musen: Creating Semantic Web Contents with Protégé-2000. IEEE Intelligent Systems, Vol. 16, Issue 2, (2001) 60-71

Web Services Based Configuration Management for IP Network Devices[*]

Sun-Mi Yoo[1], Hong-Taek Ju[2], and James Won-Ki Hong[1]

[1] Dept. of Computer Science and Engineering, POSTECH
{sunny81, jwkhong}@postech.ac.kr
[2] Dept. of Computer Engineering, Keimyung University
juht@kmu.ac.kr

Abstract. The tasks of operating and managing diverse network devices from multiple vendors are getting more difficult and complicated. For that reason, IETF Netconf Working Group has been standardizing network configuration management. The Netconf protocol is an output of that standardization and can be used to effectively manage various devices on a network. However, it is still problematic for the manager to discover and manage configurable parameters in various devices. This paper proposes a method that can quickly discover devices and their parameters as well as methods to manipulate the configuration information on them. We present the architecture for XCMS-WS which meets this mechanism. Using the Web Services technologies, we have develioed a more powerful and flexible system than our previous XCMS. For validation, we have applied XCMS-WS for the configuration management of NG-MON, a distributed, real-time Internet traffic monitoring and analysis system.

1 Introduction

The rapid pace of Internet evolution is currently witnessing the emergence of diverse network devices from multiple vendors. Current networks are complex and are composed of various network devices. Efficient network management systems are necessary to manage these networks and devices effectively. Most configuration management systems for network devices are inefficient, because they use CLI depending on the proprietary operating systems of the vendors. To solve these problems, XML [1] technologies have been applied to configuration management. A standardization process of configuration management for network devices is also in progress. The standardization uses XML technologies and is consisted of protocol message and communication protocol. The IETF Network Configuration Working Group (Netconf WG) [2] is responsible for this standardization work, which attempts to fulfill operational needs for the manager and agent on diverse network devices manufactured by different vendors and guarantees interoperability. The Netconf standard protocol helps to send and receive configuration information between managers and agents, and to manage various network devices of different vendors.

[*] This work was in part supported by the Electrical and Computer Engineering Division at POSTECH under the BK21 program of Ministry of Education, and the Program for the Training of Graduate Students in Regional Innovation of Ministry of Commerce, Industry and Energy of the Korean Government.

J. Dalmau and G. Hasegawa (Eds.): MMNS 2005, LNCS 3754, pp. 254–265, 2005.

Current networks are still hard to manage with only Netconf protocol in configuration information management. The network administrators need to perform various configuration tasks for the newly added devices. For such configuration tasks, they should input appropriate parameters to the manager. More efficient configuration tasks are possible if each device can register their parameters to UDDI [3] on their own and the manager find the device parameters accordingly. A set of parameters only needs to be changed while performing a number of similar configuration tasks on single or multiple devices. We used WSDL [5] to minimize any redundancy of the tasks. In this paper, we propose a configuration management system and mechanisms to solve this inefficiency issue. The Netconf agents register and the Netconf manager operates configuration management with reference to the information registered. This mechanism applies Web Services technologies [3], namely UDDI, WSDL, and SOAP [6] to configuration management.

We have previously developed an XML-based Configuration Management System (XCMS) [7] which was based on the sixth draft version of Netconf protocol [10]. We have developed XCMS-WS which has extended XCMS by applying the Web Services technologies and the latest draft version of Netconf protocol [5]. The XCMS-WS system designed based on the above mechanism can communicate between a manager and agents using the Netconf protocol, quickly and effectively find device agents and provide instructions for the operations of devices. XCMS-WS can send and receive messages between a manager and agents and more effectively manage configuration information using Web Service technologies. We have verified our proposed mechanism by applying it to the NG-MON system [8].

2   Related Work

In this section, we explain Web Services technologies and Netconf protocol. We also introduce related work on XML-based network management by others and describe earlier our work.

2.1 Web Services Technologies

Web Services provide standard means to interoperate between different software applications and to run on a variety of operating system and hardware platforms. A Web service describes a collection of operations that are network accessible through standardized XML messaging. Web services fulfill a specific task or a set of tasks. A Web Service can be published and discovered through UDDI. It can also interoperate as XML message over the internet protocol (SOAP).

Web Services technologies [9] consists of certain functional areas, XML messaging (e.g., SOAP), transport (e.g., HTTP, FTP and SMTP) and description of application interactions (e.g., WSDL) and discovery (e.g., UDDI). XML describes a class of data objects called XML documents. SOAP is a lightweight protocol for the exchange of information between peer entities in a decentralized, distributed environment. It is an XML-based protocol and defines the use of XML and HTTP to access services, objects, and servers in a platform-and language-independent manner. WSDL is an XML format for describing web services as a set of endpoints operating on messages. WSDL describes services starting with the messages that are exchanged between the service requester and the provider. UDDI specifications define methods to publish and discover information about web services offerings.

Web Service is divided into three roles: the service provider, the service requester, and the service registry. The objects are the service and the service description. Moreover the operations performed by the actors on these objects are published, found and bound. A service provider creates a Web Service, defines the services and then publishes the service with a service registry based on a UDDI specification. Once a Web Service is published, a service requester may find the service via the UDDI interface. The UDDI registry provides the service requester with a WSDL service description and a URL pointing to the service itself. The service requester may then use this information to bind it directly to the service and invoke it.

2.2 IETF Netconf Protocol Overview

The IETF Netconf WG was formed in May 2003. It has attempted to standardize a protocol suitable for configuration management of multiple heterogeneous network devices. It has been defining the Netconf protocol and transport mappings.

The Netconf protocol [10] uses XML for data encoding and a simple RPC-based mechanism to facilitate communication between a manager and agents. The Netconf protocol defines messages in a well-defined XML format to manage the configuration information easily and to provide interoperability among the devices from different vendors. The Netconf protocol obtains configuration information from an agent and in reference provides modified configuration management information using the RPC mechanism through a structured XML message.

The state of configuration information is divided into three phases: candidate, running, and startup. The 'running' is a complete configuration, which is currently active on the network device. The 'candidate' is a candidate configuration, which can be manipulated without impacting the device's current configuration. The 'startup' is a copied configuration from the 'running' state when the running configuration is reliable. Expressing management operations is not easy with only one transmission, data, and operation model because the environment of transmission of device information, management data, and management operation widely varies. Therefore, the transmission message is divided into 4 layers to satisfy the requirements of various environments [6]. Table 1 shows four layers defined in Netconf and examples of the contents in the layers.

Table 1. Netconf Protocol Layers

Layer	Contents
Application	Transmission protocol to provide a communication path between agent and manager: BEEP, SSH, SOAP over HTTP
RPC	A simple, transport-independent framing mechanism for encoding RPC.: <rpc>, <rpc-reply>, <rpc-error>
Operation	A set of base operations invoked as RPC methods with XML-encoded parameters.: <get-config>,<edit-config>,<copy-config>
Content	Configuration data

The Netconf protocol currently considers three separate application protocol bindings for transport: SSH [18], BEEP [19], and SOAP over HTTP [10]. The SOAP over HTTP transport mapping uses WSDL for binding services and its specification proposes standardized WSDL.

2.3 University of Twente Research on Web Services Based Management

Aiko Pras et. al have published several papers in which they suggested uses for Web services based management. As part of their research, the performance differences between SNMP and Web Services-based management have been investigated [16]. To compare performance, they investigated bandwidth usage, CPU time, memory requirements and round trip delay. To conduct tests, they implemented several Web services based prototypes and compared the performance of these prototype to various SNMP agents. That tests showed that there is a significant difference in the bandwidth requirements of SNMP and Web services. They concluded that SNMP is more efficient in cases where only a single object is retrieved but Web services is more efficient for larger number of objects. Web services management is more suitable for large scale networks such as an enterprise network.

2.4 XCMS

In our previous work, we had developed an XML-based configuration management system called XCMS which implemented the first draft IETF Netconf specification. XCMS proposed XPath which has been standardized since the fourth draft and used SOAP over HTTP as a transport mechanism. XCMS supports the fifth draft IETF Netconf protocol specification. In XCMS, a centralized manager controls the configuration information of network devices equipped with Netconf agents. XCMS works like Web Service with Netconf protocol. XCMS can manage configuration information of diverse devices. Yet, we found limitations of XCMS on networks where various network devices change dynamically. XCMS has difficulty when it searches for devices to operate configuration management and it uses configuration operations of unfamiliar devices. So, we have developed a new configuration management system called XCMS-WS by extending XCMS.

3   Proposed Method

We have mentioned the limitations of configuration management for network devices using only the Netconf protocol. Our proposed mechanism for solving these problems incorporates Web Services into configuration management.

3.1   Registration and Search for Configuration

The Netconf protocol allows managing various devices from diverse vendors. However, the discovery of necessary parameters for configuration tasks is not trivial. If the Netconf manager can find device parameters which are managed by Netconf protocol in a repository, it can more easily and efficiently manage the devices.

Netconf protocol uses WSDL and SOAP with the 'SOAP over HTTP' transport mapping [20]. But, that does not provide a registry function. We apply UDDI as a registry for configuration management. The UDDI structure in our system consists of four factors: businessEntity, businessService, bindingTemplate, and tModel. The businessEntity represents information about a business. Each businessEntity contains a unique identifier, the business name, a short description of the business, some basic contact information [12]. Each businessService entry contains a description of the service, a list of categories that describe the service, etc. The bindingTemplate provides technical description about how and where to access a specific service. A tModel includes descriptions and pointers to external technical specifications. XCMS-WS adapts the above structure; however the contents are different. businessService and bindingTemplate represent configuration parameters and the location of WSDL containing the descriptions of configuration parameters, respectively.

The Netconf manager sends out requests to discover parameters of network devices, which manage configuration information using the Netconf agent in the UDDI registry. The UDDI registry searches the business using a query on the structured data contained in a UDDI registry and then provides information of the business. This business is a set of parameters of the network device. This process brings business entry XML data into a Netconf manager. It finds the NETCONF_AGENT of businessService in the data and analyzes the entry list. The entry information includes the tModel instance info and the description of the Netconf agent service. The Netconf agent can be searched through the WSDL description which is pointed to by the overviewURL. The Netconf manager accesses the Netconf agent using information provided by the UDDI registry. Then, the manager operates configuration management to the device using the Netconf protocol with the parameters.

We use a private UDDI because private UDDI provides more valuable functions in a private setting. When using a public UDDI registry, it publishes local devices on the whole Internet creating some major security problems. However, a private UDDI registry is accessible by entities internal to an organization. This registry will be behind the organization's firewall and only accessible via the organization's intranet. The devices are managed by the administrator only. A private UDDI registry can also simplify organization's extranet operations.

3.2 WSDL for Netconf Agents

When a new network device is added or a network device's software changes, operations are updated on network. Sometimes, on a network consisting of many network devices, the configuration management work can be done perfectly after configuration information of several devices linked to the work is modified. Moreover, the work may be repeated many times. For instance, the operation which changes and reverts to a network configuration for network upgrade is often needed. In the case of repeated configuration management, it is better to describe the task. There exist many approaches for describing configuration management. We use WSDL for the configuration management task.

WSDL can be used as a task description. Its operations and messages are described abstractly, and it provides a concrete protocol and message format to define a concrete endpoint. The Netconf Manager connects to the Netconf agent in a network device which is going to operate configuration task. This process needs a description that provides all the details necessary to communicate between a Netconf manager and a Netconf agent. So, the Netconf WG proposes the standardization of WSDL used on Netconf protocol. And then a Netconf manager operates configuration information of a network device. For correct configuration management of the network device, the Netconf agent describes the message format, data types, operations and a location where the service called is binding in WSDL. The manager can perform configuration management by changing the parameters belonging to the WSDL defined tasks. Also, it would be more efficient to conduct multiple configuration tasks.

```
<message name="NetconfdRequest">
 <part name="req-msg" type="xsd:string" />
</message>
<message name="NetconfdResponse">
 <part name="rpl-msg" type="xsd:string" />
</message>
<portType name="NetconfdPortType">
  <operation name="Netconfd">
     <documentation>Service definition of function ns__Netconfd</documentation>
     <input message="tns:NetconfdRequest" />
     <output message="tns:NetconfdResponse" />
  </operation>
</portType>
<binding name="Netconfd" type="tns:NetconfdPortType">
  <SOAP:binding style="rpc" transport="http://schemas.xmlsoap.org/soap/http" />
     <operation name="Netconfd">
        <SOAP:operation soapAction="" />
        <input>
           <SOAP:body use="encoded" namespace="urn:Netconfd"
           encodingStyle="http://schemas.xmlsoap.org/soap/encoding/" />
        </input>
        <output>
           <SOAP:body use="encoded" namespace="urn:Netconfd"
           encodingStyle="http://schemas.xmlsoap.org/soap/encoding/" />
        </output>
     </operation>
  </binding>
<service name="Netconfd">
     <documentation>gSOAP 2.7.0d generated service definition</documentation>
     <port name="Netconfd" binding="tns:Netconfd">
        <SOAP:address location="http://141.223.82.6:5455" />
     </port>
</service>
```

Fig. 1. WSDL of NETCONF agent

Fig. 1 is a fragment of the WSDL used by a XCMS-WS agent. An XCMS-WS manager can operate configuration information of Netconf agents as calling a service daemon, 'Netconfd'. The manager can realize new information changed of the device as analyzing the WSDL and UDDI. The Netconf manager can recognize devices which are new installed or modify functions. And it can also know that devices software is changed or operations are updated. When the Netconf manager makes a request message for operating configuration task of a device, it can refer useless information from WSDL of the device. A Netconf agent operates configuration tasks based on request message from the Netconf manager.

4 Architecture for XCMS-WS

In this section, we present the design of XCMS-WS, XML-based Configuration Management System using Web Services. XCMS-WS consists of a manager, an agent and a private UDDI registry. Fig. 2 illustrates the detailed architecture of XCMS-WS, in which a centralized XML-based manager controls the configuration information of agents. A Netconf protocol request message is generated by the manager and sent to the agent. The agent analyzes this message and performs the configuration management function.

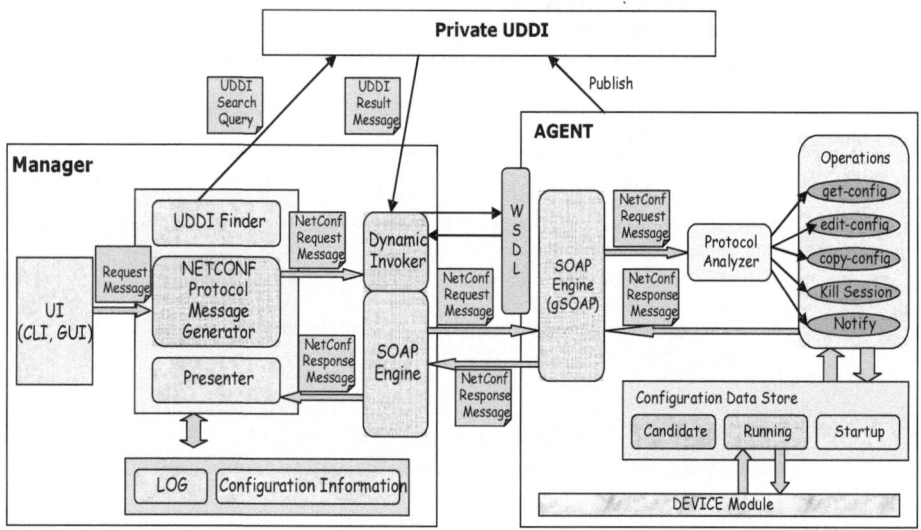

Fig. 2. Detailed Architecture of XCMS-WS Manager

A manager consists of five elements: UI, Protocol Message Generator, UDDI Finder, Dynamic Invoker, and SOAP Engine. The UI is used by the administrator to input request messages. A XCMS-WS manager provides CLI which is required essentially by Netconf standardization and also provides a GUI for the Web environment. In GUI, the administrator does not need to type the entire request message. A XCMS-WS manager semi-automatically creates a request message based on objects selected by the administrator using the GUI. The request message which is inputted by the administrator is translated into a Netconf protocol request message by the XML parser module of the manager. The XML parser module is a NETCONF Protocol Message Generator, which translates just an XML message to a Netconf request message using Netconf message formats. The Netconf protocol response messages are analyzed by the Presenter. Agents which can be managed by XCMS-WS are discovered and registered at the UDDI registry. The UDDI Finder module discovers device agents. If you get agent information from the UDDI Finder module, you can know the location of WSDL which is a description of the agent's service, and then you can do remote call through WSDL.

An agent is composed of the SOAP Engine module to deliver messages and the Protocol Analyzer module to parse messages. An agent also provides the service of processing the operation that is included in the configuration management message. There is a Configuration Data Store which stores data corresponding to 'candidate', 'running' and 'startup' as the configuration information model. One of these, 'running' synchronizes with real device modules and this information describes the present running state. Processing Netconf protocol messages through the SOAP engine needs architecture like a message-queue style architecture because of the delay in processing messages as they arrive at the agent. Using a message queue can solve message loss problems that can occur because of multiple requests from several managers and processing delays. It also provides architecture for synchronizing configuration information. The protocol interpreter is a very important module related to the Netconf protocol, it extracts operation names described as XML tag and parameters which are needed for operating from the requirement message. Operations are called from this extracted information. When an agent executes operations, each operation reads and modifies information stored in the configuration information stores. The operating results are loaded on a Netconf protocol message and are transmitted to manager.

The configuration information of agents must be managed automatically by a manager in network management. Managers and agents synchronize state information of agent through Private UDDI. If an address of an agent is changed and the agent changes its address at UDDI, managers can automatically provide a layout changing the address.

5   Implementation

We have implemented an XML-based configuration management system based on the XCMS-WS design presented in Section 4. The distributed system applying the architecture of XCMS-WS is NG-MON which is a passive network monitoring system with a clustered and pipelined architecture for load balancing and distribution. This section explains the XCMS-WS implementation environment and describes about the manager, the agent, and UDDI registry in detail.

5.1   Implementation Environment

The manager of the XCMS-WS is on a Pentium IV 2.4 GHz CPU and 500 MB RAM server running Redhat Linux 9. The platform of the agent is different depending on the platform of the device agent. The manager uses various XML technologies to provide Web-based user interfaces and an XMLDB. We resorted to Apache that provides APIs implemented with JAVA. XCMS-WS needs the following APIs: Xindice as an XMLDB and AXIS as SOAP engine to apply the SOAP/HTTP communication method between the manager and the agents. The manager and the agents must setup a Web server for HTTP communications. Following the user interface implementation with Java Server Page (JSP), the manager installs TOMCAT provided in Jakarta Apache.

The manager composes a Dynamic Invocation environment with using WSDL when placing a service call. We used WSIF [13] for the Dynamic Invocation environment. Consequently, the manager can make a service call only with WSDL which is described as a service agent. XCMS-WS can call dynamically using WSDL which is discovered at the UDDI Netconf agent.

The agent uses a parser based on C compiler and gSOAP [14]. If the device agent has few resources, as in an embedded system, it must sparse resources. The gSOAP provides the smallest and most efficient environment among the SOAP/HTTP sources based on C/C++ language. It also guarantees interoperation with other SOAP implementation and can transmit SOAP RPC message between a manager and an agent. The gSOAP generates a stub, a skeleton, and a WSDL file using the header file which declares RPC operations. We select the libxml [15] which is lightweight compare to existing XML parsers in the agent. This deployment provides DOM APIs which supports to select the specified node, update the selected node value, and read management information. The XCMS-WS uses a private UDDI registry in the WSDK [15] package provided by IBM. We selected the private UDDI for security reasons.

5.2 Verification

NG-MON [8] consists of five subsystems: a packet capture, a flow generator, a flow store, a traffic analyzer, and the presenter of analyzed data. Each subsystem of NG-MON runs on a Linux server with Pentium III 800 MHz CPU and 256 MB RAM.

XCMS-WS consists of a manager, agents and private UDDI. The UDDI registry is located between a manager and agents for searching devices to be configured. The XCMS-WS agent manages the NG-MON module. The NG-MON module loads configuration information files from the NG-MON subsystems to manage the configuration information of the NG-MON system on the XCMS-WS agent, which it synchronizes with real configuration information of the NG-MON system. The XCMS-WS manager sends a request message to the XCMS-WS agent and the XCMS-WS agent sends this message to the NG-MON module.

```xml
<?xml version="1.0"?>
<ng-mon ip="141.223.82.144">
          <admin name="DongHyun Kim"
email="dhkim03@postech.ac.kr"></admin>
          <database user="root" password="********"/>
          <packetcapture>
                    <device name="eth1"/>
                    ......
          </packetcapture>
          <flowgenerator interval="2">
                    <subsysip = "141.223.11.3"/>
                       <subsysip = "141.223.11.4"/>
          </flowgenerator>
          <flowstore>
                    <p2p file="p2p.xml"/>
          </flowstore>
</ng-mon>
```

Fig. 3. XML-based Structure of the Configuration Information

Fig. 3 is an XML-based structure of the configuration information of the NG-MON subsystems. The NG-MON module which manages the configuration information is loaded on the XCMS-WS agent in the NG-MON system. The manager then can manage the configuration information of the NG-MON.

The UDDI TREE of GUI connects to private UDDI registry with the administrator ID and shows the search results that are registered at UDDI. Using the Netconf protocol, we can easily select a list of manageable devices from all devices registered at the UDDI registry. While retrieving information registered at the UDDI registry

```
<?xml version="1.0" encoding="UTF-8"?>
<BusinessName bizID="DPNM">
  <Service serviceID="NETCONF_AGENT">
    <TModelInst devID="NETCONF_AGENT1"
            overViewDoc="http://141.223.82.6:8080/xcms-ws/Netconfd.wsdl"/>
    <TModelInst devID="NETCONF_AGENT2"
            overViewDoc="http://141.223.82.7:8080/xcms-ws/Netconfd.wsdl"/>
  </Service>
  <Service serviceID="SNMP_XML_GATEWAY">
    <TModelInst devID="SNMP_XML_GATEWAY"
    overViewDoc="http://141.223.82.6:8080/axis/services/SNMP_XML_GATEWAY?wsdl"/>
  </Service>
</BusinessName>
```

Fig. 4. UDDI Search Result

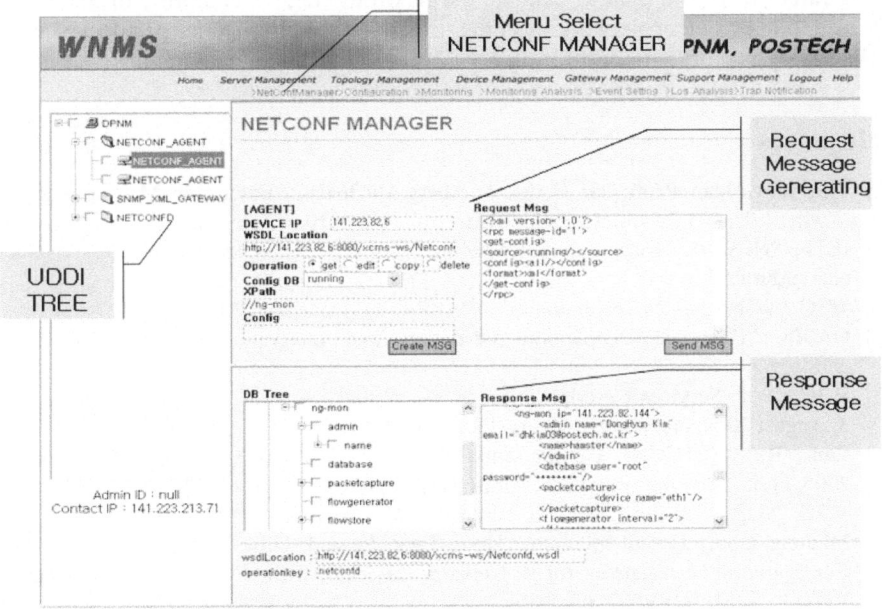

Fig. 5. Web-based user interface of XCMS-WS

into XCMS-WS, our system filters the necessary data and updates information automatically using the UDDI registry. Fig. 4 shows that two available devices including Netconf agent and a SNMP_XML_Gateway are registered at UDDI.

The Web-based user interface of XCMS-WS as shown in

Fig. provides the following functions: viewing, modifying and searching devices from UDDI registry, and creating and sending request messages for configuration task. Moreover, it shows responses from Netconf agents and configuration information DB tree of the device.

6 Concluding Remarks

In this paper, we have proposed a mechanism to manage configuration information more effectively using the Netconf protocol and Web Services technologies. Using UDDI helps a Netconf manager to quickly and intelligently recognize required parameters of network devices to operate configuration tasks. A Netconf manager finds a parameter description of a device to manage configuration from a private UDDI registry. Using WSDL configuration tasks can be done efficiently and repeatedly to operate configuration tasks of several devices.

We have presented the design and implementation of XCMS-WS, which is based on the mechanisms above. The XCMS-WS effectively manages the configuration information using Web Services technologies. It automatically modifies configuration information of the related devices using the Netconf protocol when the configuration information shared with other devices is modified. We applied the XCMS-WS to the configuration management system used for NG-MON.

For future work, we plan to validate the flexibility and extendibility of the XCMS-WS as applied to other network systems. Finally, we will conduct performance tests on XCMS-WS in order to optimize it for adaptation to embedded systems.

References

[1] Tim Bray, Jean Paoli and C. M. Sperberg-McQueen, "Extensible Markup Language (XML) 1.0", W3 Recommendation REC-xml-19980210, Feb. 1998.
[2] IETF, "Network Configuration (Netconf)", http://www.ietf.org/html.charters /Netconf-charter.html.
[3] W3C, "Web Services Technologies", WASP/D3.1, December 2002.
[4] OASIS, "Universal Description, Discovery and Integration (UDDI)", http://www. uddi.org/.
[5] W3C, "Web Services Description Language (WSDL) Version 2.0" W3C Working Draft 3, August 2004, http://www.w3.org/TR/wsdl20/.
[6] Enns, R., "NETCONF Configuration Protocol" draft-ietf-Netconf-prot-06, April 26, 2005, http://www.ietf.org/internet-drafts/draft-ietf-Netconf-prot-06.txt.
[7] W3C, "SOAP Version 1.2 Part 2: Adjuncts", W3C Working Draft, Dec. 2001.
[8] Mi-Jung Choi, Hyoun-Mi Choi, Hong-Taek Ju and James W. Hong, "XML-based Configuration Management for IP Network Devices", IEEE Communications Magazine, Vol. 41, No. 7, July 2004. pp. 84-91.

[9] Se-Hee Han, Myung-Sup Kim, Hong-Teak Ju and James W.Hong, "The Architecutre of NG-MON: A Passive Network Monitoring System", DSOM2002, Montreal, Canada, October, 2002, pp. 16-27.

[10] Goddard, T., "NETCONF over SOAP", draft-ietf-Netconf-soap-05, October 11, 2005, http://www.ietf.org/internet-drafts/draft-ietf-Netconf-soap-05.txt.

[11] Enns, R., "NETCONF Configuration Protocol", draft-ietf-Netconf-prot-06, October 27, 2005, http://www.ietf.org/internet-drafts/draft-ietf-Netconf-prot-06.txt.

[12] Simeon Semeonov, *Building Web Services with Java*, SAMS, 2001.

[13] Apache WebService project, WebService Invocation Frameworks "WSIF", http://ws.apache.org/wsif/.

[14] Robert A., "gSOAP: Generator Tools for Coding SOAP/XML Web Service and Client Applications in C and C++", http://www.cs.fsu.edu/~engelen /soap.htm/.

[15] IBM, "Web Services Development Kit (WSDK)", http://www-106.ibm.com/ developerworks/webservices/wsdk/.

[16] XMLSOFT, libxml, "The XML C parser and toolkit at Gnome", http://www.xmlsoft.org/.

[17] A. Pras, T. Drevers, R. v.d. Meent, D. Quartel, "Comparing the Performance of SNMP and Web Services-Based Management," IEEE eTNSM, V1, N2, Dec. 2004, pp. 1-11.

[18] Wasserman, M., "Using the NETCONF Configuration Protocol over Secure Shell (SSH)", April 9, 2005, http://www.ietf.org/internet-drafts/draft-ietf-Netconf-ssh-04.txt.

[19] Lear, E., Crozier, K., Enns, R., "BEEP Application Protocol Mapping for NETCONF", March 2005, http://www.ietf.org/internet-drafts/draft-ietf-netconf-beep-05.txt.

[20] Lear, E., Crozier, K., Enns, R., "BEEP Application Protocol Mapping for NETCONF", draft-lear-Netconfbeep-05, March 2005, http://www.ietf.org/internet-drafts/draft-ietf-netconf-beep-05.txt.

A Scalable Contents Distribution Service Using a Java Agent Application Framework

Kil-Hung Lee, Jae-Soo Kim, and Yong-Hyeon Shin

Dept. of Computer Science and Engineering, Seoul National Univ. of Tech.,
172 Gongnung-2dong, Nowon-gu, Seoul, 139-743, Korea
{Khlee, Jskim, Yshin}@Snut.ac.kr

Abstract. This paper presents a Java agent application framework and shows its example through the implementation of an agent application service. This framework comprised of agent, agent system, agent master and agent manager components. Each component is connected to others via an agent interface, and messages are passed through these interface points. By using this framework, it is possible to deploy a new agent application service with simple and efficient operation. Herein, we implemented the agent application service network using a Java agent application framework. Specifically, the implemented network was a contents distribution network using an agent service, and the network was both controlled and managed with the agent framework interface. In our test, the network service decreased network traffic while preserving reasonable quality through the adequate deployment and management of agent components.

1 Introduction

With the development of the Internet, many new and hitherto unimagined application services have been introduced through this revolutionary medium. To facilitate the actual use and embodiment of such services, innovative new approaches have been studied and many are now in the process of development. As an example, the peer-to-peer (P2P) method has strong merits given its scalability, and has the potential to serve as an applicable means of tackling errors more easily. Or consider distributed computing technology through the grid framework, which may serve to bring us closer to the time when these exciting application services can be used. Likewise, mobile agent technologies that can conduct critical operations at precise locations are of significant importance in the overall software technology and development progress [1].

An agent is an autonomous programming object that can perform by itself those functions that have been entrusted to it by the software user. This operational method is an innovative new way of implementing the traditional distributed computing system and constitutes a new computing paradigm. An agent can be characterized as autonomous, responsive to given conditions, and self-mobile with cooperative and learning properties. Through proper utilization of the functions of an agent, which can be used to operate in specific places at precise times, we can achieve reductions in network traffic and contribute to increased operational efficiencies.

These agent technologies may be applicable to e-commerce and information retrieval technology, to mention just two potential services: *Applications to*

J. Dalmau and G. Hasegawa (Eds.): MMNS 2005, LNCS 3754, pp. 266–276, 2005.
© IFIP International Federation for Information Processing 2005

communication infrastructures and *network management services* [2]-[4]. In [5], the agent technology was exploited to effectively monitor a large-scale network. Having reproduced itself and allocated various management functions by deployed distribution of these reproduced agents in the network, they reduced management traffic, shortened the response time, and provided the context wherein agents can safely operate even in periods of malfunction. In [6], a mobile agent was used to gather data through the Internet. After transferring to each server where the data is located, agents accumulate and collect the information gathered from their each visit. Such methods showed significant reductions in data traffic as well as much improvement in reducing response time when planned efficiently [7].

In this paper, a JAAF (Java Agent Application Framework) has been implemented to deploy the application service more effectively by using agents. The means to better define what agents are and their effective control and management, and new services utilizing these functionalities will be discussed. In Section 2, the standards and deployment status of the agent system will be examined. In Section 3, the agent application framework will be discussed. Thereafter, the implementation of a distribution network service using agents will be presented and the implemented service property further elaborated upon in Section 4. This paper will be closed with final remarks in Section 5.

2 Status of the Agent System

Since the early 1990s, software agents – also known as intelligent agents – have been the subject of a great deal of speculation and marketing hype. Agents can be classified into two major categories: *resident* and *mobile*. Resident agents are software agents that stay in the computer or system and perform their tasks there. For instance, many of the wizards in software programs are designed to carry out a very specific task while we are using the computer. Mobile agents are also software agents that can transport themselves across different system architectures and platforms.

The agency's core is the agent platform, a component model infrastructure that provides local services such as agent management, security, communication, persistence and naming. In the case of mobile agents, the agent platform also provides agent transport. Most agent systems provide additional services in the form of specialized agents that reside in some – possibly remote – agency. Some agent systems also include standard service agents, such as a broker, auctioneer, or community maker. These service agents augment the basic agent infrastructure. The agent platform and additional service agents can monitor and control message exchanges to detect any violation of the rules of engagement [8].

2.1 Agent Standards

As various kinds of agent technologies have been developed, OMG (Object Management Group) set up the standard for the MAF (Mobile Agent Facility) mobile technology [9]. This standard is based on the outer interface of CORBA (Common Object Request Broker Architecture) with regards to the mobile agent system. The agent standards for by OMG or FIPA (Foundation for Intelligent and Physical Agent) have been emphasizing the communication between agents and agent management as it relates to their creation and deletion. Developing ways to implement the necessary system needed for compatibility within the application environment, at the same time observing such standards, may take various forms depending on available options.

MAF is basically comprised of agents, place, agent system, and communication infrastructure. The agent system is a platform that supports the composition, interpretation, operation, and movement of agents. The place, which identifies logical location, is defined within this agent system and agents are located in specific places while operating the service by moving from place to place. The locations of agents include the place where agents are located and the address of the agent system.

A communication infrastructure is the basis for providing communication to agent systems, and provision of services such as RPC (Remote Procedure Call), naming services, and security are possible. However, since the naming service of CORBA does not need to be operated separately in order to support mobile agents, it alternately provides a naming service called MAFFinder for MAF exclusively and sends that interface to COBRA instead.

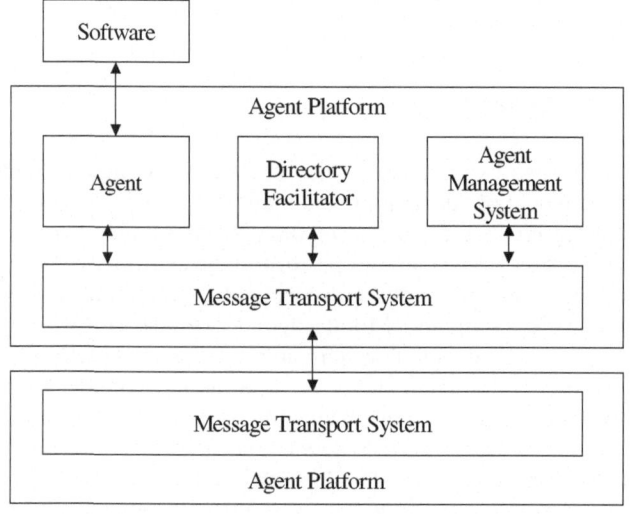

Fig. 1. Agent Management Reference Model

The purpose in setting up the FIPA standard was to help operations among applied agents by defining a common communication standard among agents in various computing environments. FIPA has been preparing five standards such as application, abstract structure, agent management, agent communication and agent message transmission. The agent management, stipulated in the FIPA, is concerned with the life cycle management of agents such as creation, registration, designating location, movement, or termination [10].

As shown in Fig. 1, FIPA agent management reference model consists of a DF (Directory Facilitator), AMS (Agent Management System), ACC (Agent Communication Channel) or MTS (Message Transport System). The DF provides agents with a

'Yellow Page' function. The AMS and ACC back up the communications among agents. The DF, AMS, and ACC form the group that defines functions and can be operated by individual agents or by all of the different agents.

2.2 Examples of Java Agent Development Systems

Although mobile agents can be developed with virtually any kind of programming, the development of a platform running on an independent language to serve as the interpreter when considering different operation environments. Developers often use distributed objects, active objects, and scriptable components to implement agents. To build agents, Java, Java-based component technologies, XML, and HTTP have been used. These technologies are simple to use, ubiquitous, heterogeneous, and platform-independent. Among such languages, Java is particularly ideal for use in developing mobile agents. Some currently available toolkits using the Java mobile agent system include IBM's Aglet, JADE (Java Agent DEvelopment Framework), and FIPA-OS (Open Source), to name a few.

Aglet, developed by IBM's Japan laboratory, is a Java-based workbench and is a system that combines agents and the applet [11]. The development of agent applications using the Aglet class provides a convenient means of mobile agent implementation while preserving a significant portion of necessary characteristics and functions. These functions include an unique name assigning function for the agent, an asynchronous and synchronous communication method among agents, an agent class loader that can bring the Java byte code of agent through the network, and an agent context that can obtain environmental information independently without regard for the agents' operating system environment.

JADE is a framework implemented entirely using the Java language [12]. The goal of JADE is to simplify the development of multi-agent systems while ensuring standard compliance through a comprehensive set of system services and agents in compliance with the FIPA specifications: naming service and yellow-page service, message transport and parsing service, and a library of FIPA interaction protocols ready to be used. The JADE Agent Platform complies with FIPA specifications and includes all those mandatory components that manage the platform, that is the ACC, the AMS, and the DF. All agent communication is performed through message passing, where FIPA ACL (Agent Communication Language) is the language to represent messages.

FIPA-OS is a component-based toolkit that makes it possible for fast development of agents while observing the FIPA standards [13]. FIPA-OS supports most standard specifications, and is continuously being improved upon through the management of an open source community project, and can also be regarded as the ideal choice for easy and fast development of agents that follow the FIPA specification. The Agent City Network consists of set of software systems (platforms) connected to the public Internet [14]. Each of these platforms hosts agent systems capable of communicating with the outside world using standard communication mechanisms. Each agent is in turn able to provide zero or more services which can be requested and accessed by other agents in the network. The network is completely open and anybody wishing to deploy a platform, agents or services is welcome to do so. All technologies used are based on consensual standards such as the FIPA standard or the emerging Semantic Web Ontology standard.

3 JAAF (Java Agent Application Framework)

Java Agent Application Framework is an agent development framework developed using Java language and consists of several components. Each component is a package of classes that has a role in agent application environment. Messages are exchanged between these components through the agent interface.

3.1 JAAF Components

The agent application framework component is composed of the agent, agent system, agent master system and agent manager. Fig. 2 shows the agent components.

Agent: An agent is a software component and a small program that is designed to fulfill certain service operations. The agent is a class implementing a service interface in Java, which defines the method necessary for both the operation and control of the service. The agent is sent to the agent system and performs certain tasks while also responding to various events. Agents can be divided into two types depending on the ways they are to be operated in JAAF: *RMIAgent* and *MSGAgent*. An *RMIAgent* is sent to its target place to conduct necessary operations and called its service function by the client. Fast deployment of services and the small one-time operation is easily implemented by using the *RMIAgent* service. A *MSGAgent* communicates with the client through the exchange of agent messages. The *MSGAgent* has the advantage of continuing one specific operation and sends messages when they are necessary without having to maintain the connection.

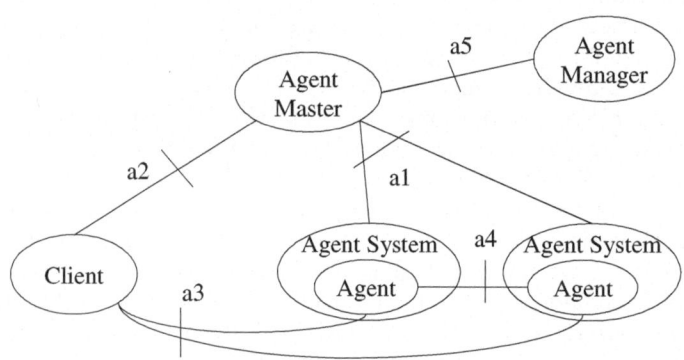

Fig. 2. Components and Interfaces of Java Agent Application Framework

Agent System: An agent system provides a place for the agent and controls the agent service. Agents are sent to the agent system through the *Service* message. The class loader in the agent system is in charge of loading the agent and can be operated through the following steps. First, confirm whether the *Service* message includes the code. Then, immediately create the object from the code and start the service. If the message does not have a service code, load the class from the user using the additional information in the *Service* message, that is, the code server *URL*. After receiving the service code, the agent system creates the object and provides the operation environment using services such as start, stop, restart, and termination. During the agent operation, the agent system delivers the receipt and transmission of messages and reports the agent state to the agent master.

Agent Master: An agent master controls the local agent system, intercedes with clients who are service users for the agent's service provided, and provides management interface to the agent manager. It connects between the client and the agent provider domain. It has available lists of the agent system and maintains the location and the status of the agent. It delivers the *Service* message to the appropriate agent system and returns the *Status* messages to the client. And, it relays the agent's *Inform* messages for cooperative operations between agents. The registry is the RMI (Remote Method Invocation) functional components, which is being used to expose the *RMIAgent* by itself to the client. The client can access the registry through the agent master and request the necessary service by obtaining the agent pointer. The registry is implemented as an internal function of the agent master.

Agent Manager: An agent manager can manage many agents with fewer complications by managing the agent master rather than directly controlling the agents. The agent master embodies the agent management information that is necessary to manage how agents behave. The agent manager can carry out monitoring activities by reading an MIB (Management Information Base) and service management functions by creating needed values. This scalable solution simplifies the agent management function efficiently.

Client: A client requests the service and gets the result and can offer the service codes through the agent master. The client can designate the agent system directly or help the agent master choose the appropriate agent to carry out the service. In the case of P2P applications, the agent system and the client can be combined and operated together.

3.2 JAAF Interfaces

In order to have effective control and management of the agent, we first need to define the interface. The definition of the agent interface is composed of the definitions of the exchanged messages. The standards of MAF and FIPA are reflected in the definition of the interface and each interface is represented in Fig. 2. The agent master performs the DF function for FIPA and the agent system carries out the MAF and AMS functions for FIPA. Messages are defined to perform functions similar to those of standard messages for FIPA.

a1: This interface refers to an interface between the agent master and the agent system. A *Register* message is sent from the agent system to the agent master to signal the commencement of services. This message includes the parameter values such as the agent's system identifiers for the agent system registration and place. An *Unregister* message is sent from the agent system to inform the end of the agent service. The abnormal ending process can be detected when the agent system is not responding in the form of a *Status* message after receiving the message from the agent master.

a2: This interface refers to an interface between the client and the agent master. If a client sends a *Lookup* message together with the information necessary for the service request, the agent master resends the *Status* message with the agent's system information suitable for the user's demand. The agent service request, as demanded by a client, is initiated by the *Service* message. The *Service* message includes the service name, program information, and the agent system information to be operated. A client can check the condition of the service through the *Status* message.

a3: This interface refers to an interface between an agent and a client. Through this interface, service conditions and results can be exchanged via *Report* message. Usually, agents notify the service status information through the agent master. If the agent system accepts the command of the client via the *Command* message, the values of current and final results are delivered to the client.

a4: This interface exists between the agents. When the agents need to communicate, they can exchange the *Inform* message immediately through the a5 interface. Since the agents do not know where other agents are located and can transfer at any time, information exchange among the agents is generally conducted through the agent master.

a5: This interface refers to an interface between the agent manager and the agent master. The message passing through the interface is a SNMP (Simple Network Management Protocol) message. A SNMP message is composed of five messages including *Get*, *GetNext*, *Set*, *Response* and *Trap*. The information in the message is the MIB (Management Information Base) information necessary for controlling and managing the agents and the agent master.

3.3 JAAF Application Deployment

A client is an agent service user, and others are an agent service provider. The service provided by the agent application framework operates by the following steps. In the initial stage, the agent master starts the service and waits for the agent system to register. The agent system registers in the agent master by opening its service port. When registered, the agent system submits the service profile. This profile includes information regarding the system construction and the ability of agent, including communication method, the maximum number of threads or available memory size, and also notes whether network communication functions are provided and whether file or DB service is offered. The client searches for an accessible agent system to use the available agent system and start a service by sending the *Service* message to the agent master. This search is done through the system profile and examines the location of agent the system, the level of service provided and the cost.

The client that requested the agent service can call out the necessary services and check the results by accessing its service through the registry and message service. Through the agent master, accessing for all agents as well as monitoring current operation locations and agents status is possible. The agent manager manages the agent and the agent system in the network through the managing MIB of the agent master. Service can be stopped and restarted by the client, agent master and agent manager. Information concerning the setting up the execution environments of the agent master is composed by the agent manager. The agent master is one of the points where it controls the agent in its own area. The agent manager can manage all of the various agents through the many agent masters within its allotted zone. This structure, through the thousands of agent systems and scores of agent masters, makes effective management possible. The agent MIB located in the lower part of the *iso.org.dod .internet.private.enterprise.snut.network.agent* of the complete MIB tree [15].

4   Agent Service Application Using JAAF

By applying the agent application, a contents distribution network was implemented and monitored. In order to understand the network, definition of service components such as contents distribution server, contents distribution agent, contents distribution manager and client need to be examined. This structure is implemented in the dynamic fashion through the distribution agent and distribution manager.

4.1   Contents Distribution Networks

The contents distribution network is comprised of 3 domains: *service provider, service network* and *agent manager domain.* The service network is a tree structure and the original contents server is located at its root. Several agents are directly connected to the server and this constitutes the first level distribution network. On its lower location, other agents are connected and result in the gradual expansion of the network. A contents client is connected to the contents agent that is either the nearest from its location or favorable to its quality of service (QoS). The contents client receives the contents by attaching himself to the leaf of the connected agent tree network. Fig. 3 shows these components and the functions of the components in the contents service model are as follows.

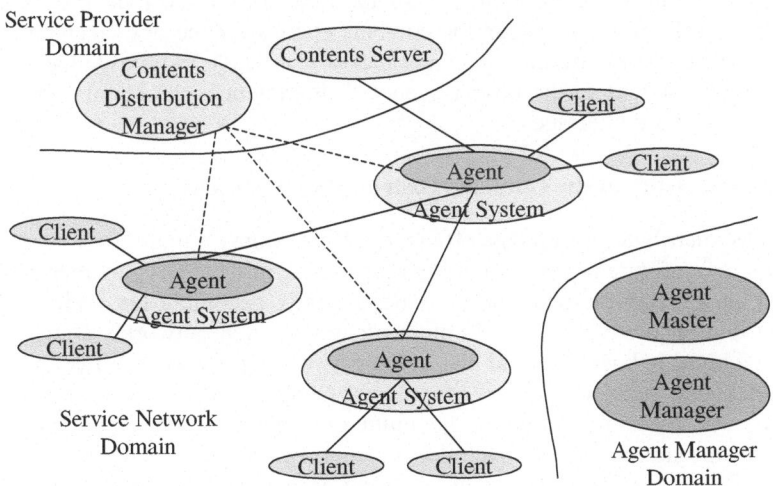

Fig. 3. The Components of the Contents Distribution Networks

Contents Server: The contents server is the root server that provides the information. The services provided by the contents server include broadcasting, video conferencing, real-time news services, and more. Methods of service provision can take various forms, including usage of stream, UDP datagram, and RTP service. In addition, depending on the types of services provided, there are various kinds of servers to be used, such as a push server where the client gathers information, and pull servers where the server provides information.

Contents Distribution Agent: A distribution agent takes the contents from the contents server and distributes them again to the client or other distribution agents. The distribution agents, depending on the contents types served, take different forms. Therefore, the agents locate themselves where the service providers want them to place and are served in a specific manner depending on the particular services and type of server. Like servers, agents also provide services with the contents client list and depending on the quality and forms of service, one or more threads are involved in the operations. An agent monitors the quality of service while at the same time providing services.

Contents Client: A client receives the contents from the agent distributor and sends it to users in the proper forms. In general, the communication handling and information handling portions constitute the client system.

Contents Distribution Manager: A contents distribution manager is the component that controls the data service between the server and the contents client. A con-tents distribution manager possesses all of the information regarding the server, distribution agent, and the client served, and manages the types of services provided by coordinating the distribution tree. In addition, the contents distribution manager is involved in the preparation of the list and the location of new agent through the service quality that is monitored and reported, and readjusts the distribution tree. The distribution manager, according to its location, locates the new agents into their proper position within the distribution tree. When the contents client near the new agents requests a contents service, the distribution manager makes it possible to provide the service by connecting new agents to the proper agents. This system is the client component in the agent framework interface.

4.2   Characteristics of the Contents Distribution Networks

IP Multicast distributes group data efficiently. But forming a multicast router network is difficult to configure in the current Internet architecture [16]. As an alternative to IP multicast, an overlay multicast network has recently become a hot topic [17]. Contents distribution network is one implementation of such networks. Delivery bandwidth is required in backbone and leaf of the network. Specially, bandwidth reduction in the backbone network is very important. Contents distribution network saves bandwidth with the same amount of the multicast router network in a backbone area.

The transmission property of the delivery network requires some increased delay and jitter. But in the Intranet case, its delivery property is not significant and shows reasonable results. Transmission delays are measured from a few milliseconds to some tens of milliseconds depending on the condition of the network and host load. As the transmission hop of the tree is increased, delays are proportionally increased. Despite of this delay extension, the missing of the packet and average errors are not to be dramatically increased. Between autonomous systems through the Internet, the trans-mission delay property had more than 1 second in average delay and an average jitter of several hundreds to thousands of milliseconds.

Thus, the service provided by the contents distribution network that is composed of agents, reduces the required bandwidth dramatically. The delays and the jitter in the Intranet are not subject to significant changes. In the Internet environments, the service quality can be degraded in its nature. So, if the agent possesses a scheme that minimizes the jitter, the property of the service can be improved upon. Deployment of the agent at proper location increases the effect of bandwidth reduction and controls the service quality effectively.

5 Conclusions and Future Works

In this paper we present an agent framework and agent application service using the developed platform. The Java agent application framework is designed with the simplicity, accessibility, and manageability properties in mind. By using this framework, we can deploy new agent application services faster and more efficiently. In addition, each component's access can be improved upon by defining interfaces and messages among components. Agents can be controlled and managed effectively through the services provided by the agent master and the agent manager.

For providing the reliable and satisfactory service to clients, further study should be devoted in two areas; QoS guaranteeing scheme and strengthening security measures. Also, ensuring proper communications with other systems or languages in different types of platform settings would be needed. For this, defining and implementing the gateway functions for other service framework could be required.

References

1. Vu Anh Pham and Ahmed Karmouch, "Moble Software Agents: An Overview", IEEE Communication Magazine., Vol. 36, No. 7, pp. 26-37, July 1998.
2. Alex L. G. Hayzelden and Rachel A. Bourne, Agent Technology for Communication Infrastructures, Weley, 2001.
3. R. Kawamura, R. Stadler, "Active Distributed Management for IP Networks", IEEE Communications Magazine, Vol. 38, No. 4, pp. 114-120, April 2000.
4. Ichro Satoh, "Building Reusable Mobile Agents for Network Management", IEEE Trans. on Systems, MAN, and Cybernetics-Part C: Applications and Reviews, Vol. 33, No. 3, pp. 350-357, Auguest 2003.
5. Antonio Liotta, George pavlou, and Graham Knight, "Exploiting Agent Mobility for Large-Scale Network Monitoring, IEEE Network", Vol. 16, No. 3, pp. 7-15, May/June 2002.
6. Manuel G. and Torsten. B., "Internet Service Monitoring with Mobile Agents", IEEE Network, Vol. 16, No. 3, pp. 22-29, May/June 2002.
7. Jin-Wook Baek and Heon-Young Yeom, "d-Agent: An Approach to Mobile Agent Planning for Distributed Information Retrieval", IEEE Transaction on Consumer Electronics, Vol. 49, No. 1, pp.115-122, Feb. 2003.
8. Dinverno, M., and M. Luck, eds., "Understanding Agent Systems", New York: Springer Verlag, 2001.

9. GMD FOKUS and IBM, Mobile Agent Facility Specification V1.0, Jan. 2000.
10. XC00023J, FIPA Agent Management Specification, 2002.12.6
11. Danny B. Lange and Mitsuru Oshima, Programming and Deploying Java Mobile Agent with Aglets, Addison Wesley, 1998.
12. F. Bellifemine, A. Poggi and G. Rimassa, "JADE – A FIPA-Compliant Agent Framework", Proc. Fourth Int'l Conf. Practical Applications of Intelligent Agent and Multi-Agent Sys-tems (PAAM '99), pp. 97-108, April 1999.
13. http://fipa-os.sourceforge.net
14. http://www.agentcities.org
15. Kil-Hung Lee, "A Study of Agent Management Scheme", Journal of Korea Computer Industry Education Society, Vol. 4, No. 3, pp. 191-198, March 2003.
16. J. Liebeherr, M. Nahas and W. Si, "Application-Layer Multicasting With Delaunay Triangulation Overlays", IEEE JSAC, Vol. 20, No. 8, pp. 1472-1488, Oct 2002.
17. M. Castro, M.B. Jones, H. Wang and et el, "An evaluation of scalable application-level multicast built using peer-to-peer overlays", IEEE INFOCOM 2003. Vol. 2, pp. 1510-1520, April 2003.

User-Centric Performance and Cost Analysis for Selecting Access Networks in Heterogeneous Overlay Systems

Bed P. Kafle[1], Eiji Kamioka[1,2], and Shigeki Yamada[1,2]

[1] Department of Informatics, The Graduate University for Advanced Studies,
2-1-2 Hitotsubashi, Chiyoda-ku, Tokyo 101-8340, Japan
kafle@grad.nii.ac.jp
[2] National Institute of Informatics,
2-1-2 Hitotsubashi, Chiyoda-ku, Tokyo 101-8340, Japan

Abstract. In recent years, a wide variety of wireless access networks that support multimedia services have been emerging with different characteristics. The service areas of many of these networks overlap so that a mobile user from an overlapped service area can access any network that supports the user's application. A mobile user can take advantage of the availability of such heterogeneous multimedia networks only when the user terminal is equipped with a mechanism that can select an optimal network for the application. This paper proposes a novel analytical framework of such a mechanism. For this purpose we define the user-centric performance and user-centric cost, and derive their expressions. The user-centric performance, which is also a measure of the user-perceived quality of service (QoS), relates the requirements of user applications with the parameters of network services. The user-centric cost is measured by the user's willingness to pay the price and allow for the consumption of the mobile terminal's resources for accessing the network services. Based on the performance and cost analyses, we describe a network selection mechanism and discuss its implementation issues. We then present an example system to numerically elaborate the functioning of the proposed mechanism.

1 Introduction

The next generation of mobile communication networks is expected to be a heterogeneous multimedia system widely comprising different radio access networks. Each access network may possess some advantages over the others in terms of network characteristics, such as bandwidth, coverage, cost, and reliability. To exploit these advantages, the heterogeneous system appears in an overlay form [1,2]; one access network (e.g. wireless LAN) overlapping the service area of the other access networks (e.g. 3G networks). In such an environment, a mobile host with multi-mode network interfaces should be capable of carrying out the following two functions: (1) selecting an optimal access network and (2) transferring connections from one access network to others when the previous one becomes

J. Dalmau and G. Hasegawa (Eds.): MMNS 2005, LNCS 3754, pp. 277–288, 2005.

sub-optimal or unavailable. This paper focuses on the first function, i.e. the selection of an optimal network. For this purpose, we (a) define user-centric performance, (b) define user-centric cost, and (c) present a mechanism for selecting an optimal network based on a performance-cost analysis.

There has been a lot of research on the evaluation of network-centric performance or network-level quality of service (QoS), which is concerned with optimizing the network characteristics. The network-centric evaluation indicates, for instance, that the larger the bandwidth, the better the network performs. However, it cannot answer the following question: how much large bandwidth and smaller latency or loss rate are appropriate for a user's application. To answer this question, we need to evaluate the user-centric performance. The user-centric performance, which is also a measure of the user-perceived QoS, relates user application requirements with the network service characteristics or quality. Note that a user requires network resources to be just sufficient enough to satisfy its application's requirements. Any extra resource beyond the requirement, may not give any additional benefit to the user. In such cases, users may not opt for a network that has the highest resources; they may rather select a network that provides the optimal performance at the lowest user-centric cost. The user-centric cost includes the price of network service as well as the resource consumption, such as the battery power of the mobile terminal. It is indisputable that a mechanism should exist that enables mobile users to carry out intelligent decisions for optimal network selection. Without such a mechanism, mobile users cannot get the benefits from the availability of different types of networks; instead they would be overloaded with choices.

There are only a few published research papers dealing with this issue from different aspects. Lee et al. [3] applied a software agent based approach in a personal router (PR) that lies between the user and network. The PR selects a suitable service for the user based on the network information and user preferences. The PR continuously gets feedback of the user's subjective evaluation in terms of quality and cost of service, and accordingly adjusts the user preference parameters. However, their paper does not provide any quantitative analysis of the relationship between the user's requirements and the network's information. Moreover, the subjective evaluation of a particular user cannot be universally valid to all users. Altmann et al. [4] explained a mechanism for enabling users to select a service from a fixed number of priority-level/price pairs provided by a single network. Their paper is more concerned with improving the efficiency of switching service levels when the observed network performance changes than evaluating the user-centric performances.

Complementing the above work, we develop and evaluate an analytical framework for selecting an optimal network in a heterogeneous wireless network environment. For this purpose, we define the user-centric performances and user-centric costs and derive their expressions. The user-centric performance is obtained by relating the network attributes with the requirements of the user applications. We take into consideration three types of attributes - bandwidth, latency, and delay - and derive the user-centric performance for three classes of applications - rigid, adaptive, and elastic. Similarly, we consider the price of the network service as well as the power consumption of the mobile terminal to estimate the user-centric cost. Based on the performance and cost analyses, we present a network selection mechanism and discuss its implementation issues.

This paper is organized as follows. In Section 2 we analyze the user-centric performances and user-centric costs. The implementation issues of the proposed network selection mechanism are described in Section 3. We present an example of the performance of the network selection mechanism in Section 4, and a summary and plan for future work in Section 5.

2   Performance and Cost Analyses

2.1   User-Centric Performance

We define the user-centric performance (UcPerf) as the degree of fulfillment of user requirements by the network characteristics. There are the following two issues associated with UcPerf analysis.

- *The relationship between the UcPerf and network characteristics*: how the UcPerf can be expressed as a function of the network characteristics. For instance, how the UcPerf increases as the bandwidth increases or delay decreases.
- *The combination of the UcPerf of the characteristics to get an overall UcPerf* how to combine the performance of each characteristic to get an overall UcPerf.

As a first step towards these issues, we define a UcPerf as a continuous function of network characteristics because the continuous functions are easier to generate and manipulate than other types of functions. We take the weighted sum of the UcPerf of the characteristics to get an overall UcPerf, because the weights enable us to control the contribution of the individual characteristic on the overall performance. Suppose that there are N wireless networks, each having some different characteristics from the others. Let $\varphi_x^a(x_k)$ be the UcPerf component of characteristic x (with value x_k) for an application a in a network k ($k \in N$). Then the overall UcPerf of the network, $UcPerf_k^a$, is given as:

$$UcPerf_k^a = \sum_F w_x \varphi_x^a(x_k), \qquad (1)$$

where w_x is the weighing factor for characteristic x and F is the set of network characteristics that are considered for evaluating the overall UcPerf.

We define $\varphi_x^a(x_k)$ as a continuous function whose value ranges between 0 and 1; 0 indicating the worst performance and 1 indicating the best performance. The value of the weighing factor w_x determines the contribution of the network characteristic x on the overall UcPerf. Considering $\sum_F w_x = 1$ guarantees $0 \leq UcPerf_k^a \leq 1$. The shape (or nature) of the $\varphi_x^a(x_k)$ function depends on both the application type and network characteristic under consideration. We take into consideration three types of applications: rigid, adaptive, and elastic. These applications correspond to the following service classes, respectively, defined in the 3GPP specifications [5].

1. Real-time conversational services: e.g. voice, video telephone, and video gaming, which require minimum bandwidths that must be met, very low delays and no losses - the loss recovery mechanism cannot be effective.
2. Real-time streaming services: e.g. multimedia, video on demand, and webcast, which require adaptive bandwidths, bounded delays and minimum losses.
3. Non real-time interactive and background services: e.g. web browsing, network gaming, database access, email, SMS, and downloading, which require flexible bandwidths, and tolerate delays and losses - the loss recovery mechanism can be used.

Similarly, although UcPerf depends on many networks characteristics, such as bandwidth, latency, loss rate, reliability, availability, coverage, and service provider's reputation, for simplicity, we take into consideration only the first three characteristics, i.e. bandwidth, delay, and loss rate, because these are the most commonly used network characteristics to assess network quality. Let $\varphi_b^a(b_k)$, $\varphi_l^a(l_k)$, and $\varphi_r^a(r_k)$ be the respective UcPerf components derived from bandwidth (b_k), latency (l_k), and loss rate (r_k) in a network k for an application a, where $a \in \{rigid, elastic, adaptive\}$. To define $\varphi_b^a(b_k)$, we take the bandwidth utility functions defined by Shenker [6], and Kafle et al. [7]. In addition, we provide novel definitions of $\varphi_l^a(l_k)$ and $\varphi_r^a(r_k)$ based on the specifications of applications as mentioned above.

Rigid application: The UcPerf curves of a rigid application are shown i Fig. 1(a). There can be different sets of functions that can generate these curves. One set of such functions is shown by Equations (2)-(4). As a rigid application requires a minimum amount of bandwidth (say B_{min}) to support it, its performance is zero when bandwidth is less than B_{min}. Similarly, it can tolerate a very low network latency of up to L_{max}^{rigid} without affecting performance. However, when the delay increases beyond L_{max}^{rigid}, the performance exponentially degrades at a rate of δ_l^{rigid}. Since these applications are loss intolerant, the performance exponentially decreases at a rate of δ_r^{rigid} as the loss increases.

$$\varphi_b^{rigid}(b_k) = \begin{cases} 0 & \text{for } b_k \leq B_{min} \\ 1 & \text{otherwise.} \end{cases} \tag{2}$$

$$\varphi_l^{rigid}(l_k) = \begin{cases} 1 & \text{for } l_k \leq L_{max}^{rigid} \\ e^{-(l_k - L_{max}^{rigid})\delta_l^{rigid}} & \text{otherwise.} \end{cases} \tag{3}$$

$$\varphi_r^{rigid}(r_k) = e^{-r_k \delta_r^{rigid}} \tag{4}$$

Adaptive application: The UcPerf curves of an adaptive application are shown in Fig. 1(b), and the corresponding functions are given by Equations (5)-(7). Adaptive applications adapt their data rate to the available bandwidth in the

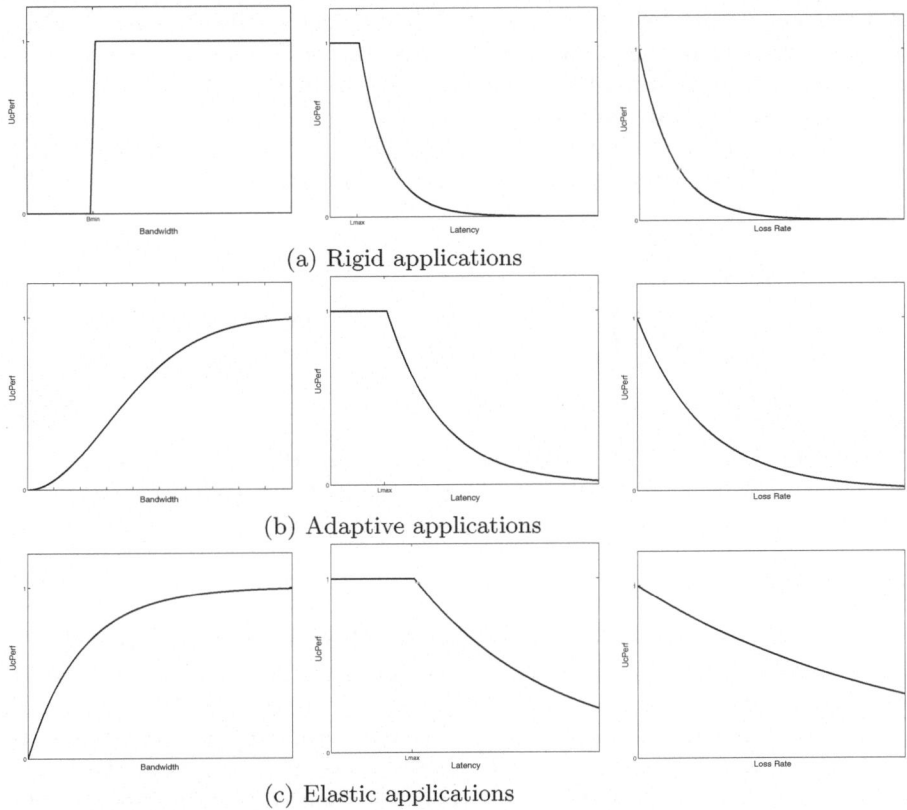

(a) Rigid applications

(b) Adaptive applications

(c) Elastic applications

Fig. 1. User-centric performances ($UcPerf$) of bandwidth, latency and loss rate of (a) rigid, (b) adaptive and (c) elastic applications

network and can tolerate occasional delay bound violations and packet losses. However, they have intrinsic bandwidth requirements, as they must maintain the data rate at some minimum level, below which performance suffers badly. This is accounted by a constant C_b in Eq. (5); the larger the value of C_b, the larger the bandwidth required for better performance. Similar to the rigid applications, the latency and loss rate performances of adaptive applications exponentially decrease at the rate of $\delta_l^{adaptive}$ and $\delta_r^{adaptive}$, respectively.

$$\varphi_b^{adaptive}(b_k) = e^{-\frac{b_k^2}{b_k + C_b}} \tag{5}$$

$$\varphi_l^{adaptive}(l_k) = \begin{cases} 1 & \text{for } l_k \leq L_{max}^{adaptive} \\ e^{-(l_k - L_{max}^{adaptive})\delta_l^{adaptive}} & \text{otherwise.} \end{cases} \tag{6}$$

$$\varphi_r^{adaptive}(r_k) = e^{-r_k \delta_r^{adaptive}} \tag{7}$$

Elastic application: The UcPerf curves of an elastic application are shown in Fig. 1(c), and the corresponding functions are given by Equations (8)-(10). Elastic applications follow the diminishing marginal rate of performance improvement as bandwidth increases [6]. This means, when the bandwidth is low, an increment in the bandwidth increases the performance higher than the same increment does when the bandwidth is high. In Eq. (8) $\delta_b^{elastic}$ is the performance increment rate, and B_{max} is the maximum bandwidth the application can utilize to improve its performance. Similarly, the performances of the latency and loss rate exponentially decrease at the rate of $\delta_l^{elastic}$ and $\delta_r^{elastic}$, respectively.

$$\varphi_b^{elastic}(b_k) = e^{-\frac{\delta_b^{elastic} b_k}{B_{max}}} \tag{8}$$

$$\varphi_l^{elastic}(l_k) = \begin{cases} 1 & \text{for } l_k \leq L_{max}^{elastic} \\ e^{-(l_k - L_{max}^{elastic})\delta_l^{elastic}} & \text{otherwise.} \end{cases} \tag{9}$$

$$\varphi_r^{elastic}(r_k) = e^{-r_k \delta_r^{elastic}} \tag{10}$$

Note that since the delay and loss tolerant capacities increase from the rigid to elastic applications, the following relations hold: $L_{max}^{rigid} \leq L_{max}^{adaptive} \leq L_{max}^{elastic}$, $\delta_l^{rigid} \geq \delta_l^{adaptive} \geq \delta_l^{elastic}$, and $\delta_r^{rigid} \geq \delta_r^{adaptive} \geq \delta_r^{elastic}$.

2.2   User-Centric Cost

We now derive the expressions of the user-centric costs (UcCost). We take into consideration two types of costs that a user can save: monetary cost and resource cost. The monetary cost includes the price that users have to pay, and the resource cost includes the resources of the user terminal that have to be used for accessing the network services. From the users' point of view, the battery power of a mobile terminal may be a precious resource that the users want to save. For instance, users with lower battery power prefer 3G networks to wireless LANs as the former consume less power. Similar to the UcPerf, the UcCost is a normalized cost whose value ranges from 0 to 1; a 0 indicates that the service cost is trivial, and an 1 indicates that the service cost is the highest of what users are willing to pay.

Let $\vartheta_p^k(p_k)$ and $\vartheta_e^k(e_k)$ be the UcCost components of the network service price and battery power (energy) consumption, respectively, in a network k for an application a. Then the overall UcCost of the network, $UcCost_k^a$, is given as:[1]

$$UcCost_k^a = w_p \vartheta_p^a(p_k) + w_e \vartheta_e^a(e_k), \tag{11}$$

where w_p and w_e are the weighing factors, such that $(w_p + w_e) = 1$.

To derive the $UcCost$, we use the well-known principle of the demand function of economics. The theory of economics states that the quantity of goods/services demanded (q) increases as the price (p) decreases [8]. As shown by the empirical results in [9,10], the demand function of a communication service is:

$$q = Ap^{-E}, \tag{12}$$

---

[1] Although we have assumed only two costs: network price and battery power consumption, our model can be extended to more costs cases by introducing additional weights and cost functions.

where A is the scaling constant that is equal to the value of q when p = 1, and E is the constant elasticity of demand for the given service. E is defined as the negative ratio of the relative change in demand to the relative change in price, that is:

$$E = -\frac{\Delta q/q}{\Delta p/p},$$ (13)

where Δq is the change in demand and Δp is the change in price. Since the demand increases (decreases) as prices decrease (increase), Δq and Δp have opposite signs. Therefore, the value of E is always positive. As estimated by France Telecom, the elasticity, E, for a voice service is 1.337 [10].

An important property of the constant elasticity in Equation (12) is that it creates a demand curve that has different slopes in different price regions. When the price is lower, small changes in price create larger changes in the quantity demanded. On the other hand, when the price is higher, even a large change in price creates only a small change in demand. The demand function can also be interpreted in terms of a utility function. A utility function measures the willingness of users to pay an amount of money for a service with a certain performance or QoS guarantee [11]. When the price is lower, users think that the utility of the service is higher than the price paid, so they demand more quantity. On the other hand, when the price is higher, the utility of the service becomes smaller than the price paid, so that users demand less quantity. Based on this assessment, we can express the utility function (u) of the service in terms of the amount of quantity demanded as: $u = q$ when $A = 1$, so that $0 \leq u \leq 1$. A high utility indicates that the user is more satisfied, hence the user-centric cost is low. Similarly, a low utility indicates that the user is less satisfied, hence the user-centric cost is high. Therefore, the user-centric cost of the price can simply be expressed as inversely proportional to the service utility. That is,

$$\vartheta_p^a(p) = \frac{C}{u},$$ (14)

where C is the proportionality constant. To keep the value of $\vartheta_p^a(p)$ within the range of 0 to 1, we take $C = q_{min}$, where q_{min} is the minimum amount of service demanded when the price is maximized (p_{max}). When we plot the utility and $\vartheta_p^a(p)$ on a y-axis, and the price on an x-axis, we get the curves shown in Fig. 2.

Now we define $\vartheta_e^a(e)$ as a function of the battery power consumption (e) of the mobile terminal. As there are no references available on how users behave for different levels of power consumption, for the sake of simplicity, we assume that $\vartheta_e^a(e)$ varies with the battery power consumption in the same way as $\vartheta_p^a(p)$ does with the price. This means, we suppose that the elasticity of power consumption is the same as that of the network service price.

We use UcPerf and UcCost to estimate the performance-cost ratio (PCR) as given by Eq. (15). The PCR is used as the decision metric to select an optimal access network (that has the maximum value of PCR).

$$PCR_k^a = UcPerf_k^a/UcCost_k^a \quad \text{for} k = 1, 2, 3, ..., N,$$ (15)

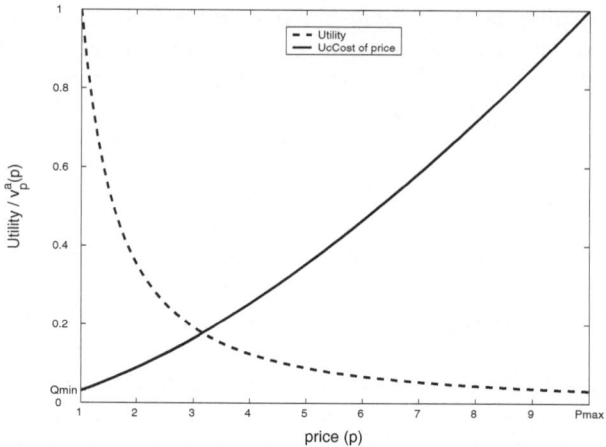

Fig. 2. Utility and UcCost of price $(\vartheta_p^a(p))$ versus network price

where N is the number of access networks available from the location of the mobile user.

3   Implementation Issues

The optimal network selection mechanism can be implemented as a module that comprises a number of profiles (Fig. 3). These profiles are described below.

Network profile: The network profile includes the values of network attributes, e.g. bandwidth, latency, loss rate, and prices. The mobile terminal can obtain these values either by monitoring all the available networks in its surrounding area or by consulting a single entity or network that can provide the attributes of all the networks, depending on the architecture of the heterogeneous system. The MIRAI architecture [2] suggests that in heterogeneous system, it is possible to have a basic access network, separate from other wireless networks, for using as a means for wireless access discovery, signaling, and other network management functions. If such a basic access network exists, it can be consulted to get the network characteristics of all access networks in the vicinity of the mobile user.

Application profile: The application profile maintains the values of parameters, such as B_{min}, L_{max}, δ_r, and δ_l, related to the application requirements. These parameters vary from application to application, even within the same type of applications. For instance, the minimum bandwidth requirement of a rigid application depends on whether the application is voice phone, videophone, or video gaming. These parameters of an application can be defined while the application is designed or developed, by observing the effect of the parameter changes on the application quality. These parameters are provided to the application profile when the application is installed in the mobile terminal. Alternatively, these parameter values can be supplied by an independent network

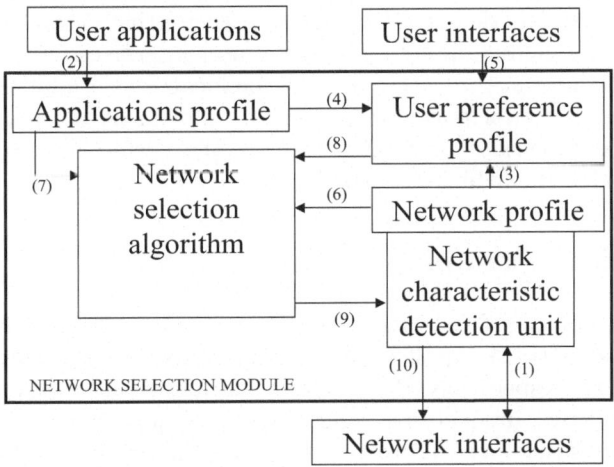

Fig. 3. Interactions among the components of the network selection module

entity similar to the DNS server of current Internet system providing the domain name to IP address mapping information.

User preference profile: The user preference profile maintains the values of the weighting factors used in the evaluations of the user-centric performance and cost. These factors give the notion of the relative importance of the components of $UcPerf$ and $UcCost$. For instance, if a user considers the network price is more important than the battery power consumption, it sets the values of w_p and w_w in such a way that $w_p > w_w$. The update of a user preference profile can be done by the users themselves through user interfaces or done automatically (by mobile terminals) by interacting with the application profile, network profile, and user and device contexts.

The components of the network selection module are shown in Fig. 3. In addition to the different profiles, the module includes the network selection algorithm and network characteristic detection unit. In this figure, arrows with numbers in parentheses show the interaction between the different components of the module. We describe these interactions one by one, starting from (1). The network characteristics detection unit probes the available networks in its surrounding area through network interfaces and stores the collected attributes of the networks in the network profile. The application profile interacts with the user applications to collect the application related parameters. The user preference profile consults the network profile, application profile, and user interfaces to maintain the up-to-date values of the user preference parameters based on the supported applications and available networks. The network selection algorithm gets the required information from the network profile, application profile, and user preference profile to compute the UcPerf and UcCost, which are used as the decision metrics to select the best access network. After determining the best access network for the given application, the network selection algorithm request the network characteristic detection unit to activate the relevant network interface card. As this module interacts with the user interfaces and applications as well as network interfaces, it can efficiently be located as a middleware between the application and transport layers. We will implement the proposed mechanism in an experimental system and evaluate the performance to validate the theoretical model in our future work.

4   Numerical Example

To evaluate the proposed network selection mechanism, we present an example system that has network, application, and user preference profiles as shown in Tables 1, 2, and 3, respectively. We took into consideration two wireless networks, N1 and N2, and two applications, rigid - voice and adaptive - webcast.

Table 1 shows the network profile containing the attribute values of the network characteristics. Network N1, such as a GSM network, has a smaller bandwidth support ($b = 10$ kbps) and network N2, such as a 3G network, has a higher bandwidth support ($b = 2$ Mbps). Network N2 has a higher bandwidth (b), a lower latency (l), and a lower loss rate (r), but has a higher price (p) and a higher power consumption (e) than network N1. The units of the service price can be in Japanese yen (or US dollors, etc.) per unit of connection time and/or data volume. As we assumed that both price-related and power consumption-related components of user-centric cost vary in the same way, the units of power consumption are chosen in such a way that the values of the power consumption and price become comparable. That means the units of price and power consumption are adjusted so that these values are close to each other. For instance, if the network service price is 10 Yen, and power consumption is 100 milliwatts,

Table 1. Network profile: attributes

Network (k)	b	l	r	p	e
N1	14kbps	0.12s	0.1%	10	10
N2	2000kbps	0.10s	0.1%	13	15

Table 2. Application profile: parameters

Application	B_{min}/C_b	L_{max}	δ_l	δ_r	E
voice	10kbps	0.1s	2.0	2.0	1.5
webcast	1000	1.0s	1.0	1.0	1.5

Table 3. User preference profile: parameters

Application	w_b	w_l	w_r	w_p	w_e	p_{max}	e_{max}
voice	0.6	0.3	0.3	0.8	0.2	20	20
webcast	0.6	0.3	0.3	0.8	0.2	20	20

Table 4. Decision metrics

Application	Network	UcPerf	UcCost	PCR
voice	N1	0.96	0.35	**2.70**
voice	N2	0.98	0.55	1.79
webcast	N1	0.49	0.35	1.38
webcast	N2	0.99	0.55	**1.80**

then the unit of power consumption is converted to a deciwatt so that the value of the power consumption becomes 10 deciwatts.

Table 2 shows the application profile. Here the elasticity (E) of both voice and webcast services are taken as 1.5. The minimum bandwidth (B_{min}) required to support the voice service is taken to be 10 kbps, and the constant C_b of the adaptive webcast application is taken as 1000. Similarly, Table 3 shows the user preference profile. We assumed that user preferences (weighing factors and the maximum amount of price and battery energy that the user can afford) are the same for both applications under consideration.

We evaluated the UcPerf and UcCost of these applications in networks N1 and N2 and listed them in Table 4. It shows that the UcPerfs of the voice application are comparable in both networks, whereas the UcCost is much higher in network N2 than in network N1, because of the higher price and power consumption in network N2. Therefore, the PCR in network N2 smaller than that in network N1. Thus, network N1 is better for the voice application. On the other hand, when we consider an adaptive webcast application, the UcPerf in network N1 is smaller than that in network N2, because the webcast application requires a higher bandwidth for better performance. In this case, the PCR in network N2 is higher than that in network N1, resulting in the selection of network N2 for the webcast application. The UcCosts are the same for both applications, as we have used the same user preference profile.

In our evaluation, not only the network performances, but also the network costs greatly affect the network selection decision. For instance, if the price of the second network (N2) is raised from 13 units to 17 units, keeping other parameters the same, the UcCost in N2 for the webcast application rises to 0.76 (from 0.55) and consequently the PCR falls to 1.31 (from 1.80). This change in price results in the selection of network N1, as its PCR (1.38) is higher than the PCR (1.31) of network N2.

5   Conclusion

We developed the theoretical framework of a mechanism that carries out optimal network selection decisions based on the user-centric performance and user-centric cost analyses. The user-centric performance is estimated by comparing the network attributes with the user application requirements. Similarly, we considered the price of the network service and the power consumption of the mobile terminal to estimate the user-centric cost. We presented a network selection mechanism and discussed the relevant issues. Through an example, we numerically illustrated the performance of the proposed mechanism. The limitation of this work is that we have assumed that a user activates only one application at a time and selects the best network for the application. Our model needs an extension to address the issues of selecting an optimal network for multiple applications running simultaneously.

In this work we concentrated on the theoretical work on selecting an optimal network when the user application is initiated. In future work, we will carry out a simulation experiment to strengthen the proposed network selection algorithm. We will also evaluate the computational and communicational overheads introduced by the proposed mechanism.

References

1. E. A. Brewer et al., "A network architecture for heterogeneous mobile computing," IEEE Personal Commun., pp.8-24, Oct. 1998.
2. G. Wu, M. Mizuno, and P. J. Havinga, "MIRAI architecture for heterogeneous networks," IEEE Commun. Mag., pp.126-134, Feb. 2002.
3. G. Lee, P. Faratin, S. Bauer, and J. Wroclawski, "A user-guided cognitive agent for network service selection in pervasive computing environments," IEEE PerCom 2004.
4. J. Altmann, H. Daanen, H. Oliver, and A. S.-B. Suarez, "How to market-manage a QoS network," IEEE InfoCom, 2002.
5. 3GPP TS 23.107, "Quality of service (QoS) concept and architecture," Version 6.1.0, April 2004.
6. S. Shenker, "Fundamental of design issues for the future Internet," IEEE J. Sel. Areas Commun., vol.13, no.7, pp.1176-1188, Sept. 1995.
7. V. P. Kafle, E. Kamioka, and S. Yamada, "Maximizing user satisfaction based on mobility in heterogeneous mobile multimedia communication networks," IEICE Trans. Commun., vol.E88-B no.7, pp.2709-2717, July 2005.
8. N. G. Markiw, Essential of Economics, Second Edition, South-western, Thomson Learning, 2001, pp.67-98.
9. S. G. Lanning, D. Mitra, Q. Wang and M. H. Wright, "Optimal planning for optical transport networks," Philosoph. Trans. Royal Soc. London A, vol.358, no.1773, pp.2183-2196, Aug. 2000.
10. M. Aldebert, M. Ivaldi, and C. Roucolle, "Telecommunication demand and pricing structure: an econometric analysis," Telecommunication System, Kluwer, vol.25, no.1-2, pp.89-115, 2004.
11. L. A. DaSilva, "Pricing for QoS-enabled networks: a survey," IEEE Commun. Surveys, http://www.comsoc.org /pubs/surveys, Second Quarter 2000.

On Using a CDN's Infrastructure to Improve File Transfer Among Peers[*]

Minh Tran and Wallapak Tavanapong

Department of Computer Science, Iowa State University, Ames, IA, 50011, USA
{ttminh, tavanapo}@cs.iastate.edu

Abstract. Content Distribution Network (CDN) technology has been proposed to deliver content from content nodes placed at strategic locations on the Internet. However, only companies or organizations, who can pay for the services of CDNs, have the privilege of using CDNs to distribute their content. Individual users (peers) have to resort to more economical peer-to-peer (P2P) technologies to distribute their content. Although P2P technologies have demonstrated tremendous successes, they have inherent problems such as the instability and the limited bandwidth of peers. In this paper, we propose a new approach to build bandwidth bounded data distribution trees inside a CDN so that external peers can leverage the power of a CDN's infrastructure for distributing their content. Our performance evaluation shows that, with some limited help from a CDN, the content distribution time among peers can be speeded up from 1.5 to 3 times.

1 Introduction

Content distribution networks (CDNs) have contributed significantly to transform the Internet into a successful content dissemination system. They have been proposed and deployed to primarily distribute content from companies and organizations (who are content producers/publishers such as CNN, Yahoo, etc.) to individual Internet users. A CDN operator deploys CDN nodes at *strategic and fixed* locations on the Internet to replicate data of content producers/publishers [1,2] (publishing content on a CDN is only available to some companies/organizations). Thus, current CDNs do not address the need of individual users (also known as peers[1]) to publish/distribute their own content. On the other hand, peer-to-peer (P2P) networks have emerged as an alternative approach for sharing content among thousands of peers on the Internet. This approach employs peers' resources (network bandwidth, storage space, and available time, etc.) to disseminate shared files. A P2P network is *flexible* because anyone could participate in the network. However, the resources of a P2P network are only as good as the aggregated resources of the contributing peers. Building on the CDN and P2P content distribution models, we investigate an integrated content distribution framework named *Synergetic Content Distribution* that takes advantage of both models. We shift from the

---

[*] This work is partially supported by National Science Foundation under Grant No. 0092914. Any opinions, findings, and conclusions or recommendation expressed in this paper are those of author(s) and do not necessarily reflect the views of the National Science Foundation.
[1] We hereafter use the term peers instead of individual users.

J. Dalmau and G. Hasegawa (Eds.): MMNS 2005, LNCS 3754, pp. 289–301, 2005.
© IFIP International Federation for Information Processing 2005

conventional wisdom by not considering CDN and P2P as two separate content delivery models. We instead see a potential for merging them so that peers help a CDN in delivering the CDN's content (that of big content producers/publishers) and the CDN in return helps peers to distribute peers' own content.

Three main challenges for the realization of our Synergetic Content Distribution framework are (i) designing a mechanism to help a CDN to recruit peers to become part of the CDN. The recruited peers collaborate with the CDN to deliver the CDN's content; (ii) designing a mechanism to help a CDN to open up its network efficiently and securely[2] so that peers can take advantage of the CDN's infrastructure in distributing peers' content[3]; and (iii) designing an incentive mechanism to entice peers to become part of a CDN and also to entice a CDN to open its distribution network to benefit peers. Because each of these challenges deserves its own study and requires a different technical solution, our methodology is to address these challenges separately while still considering each of them as an integral part of our Synergetic Content Distribution framework. The eventual deployment of our framework requires the presence of satisfactory solutions to all three challenges.

In this paper, we focus on addressing the second challenge discussed in the preceding paragraph. The idea of opening up a CDN so that peers can take advantage of the CDN's infrastructure will bring the power of having efficient and high quality content distribution to everyone (both companies/organizations and individual users). To the best of our knowledge this idea has not been documented in the literature. Our contributions in this paper are (i) a formulation of the problem of peers using a CDN's infrastructure to distribute their content. Our proposed solution to this problem is to build bandwidth bounded trees inside the CDN to allow peers to send/receive content. The bandwidth bounded trees provide peers with reliable and higher bandwidth than normal end-to-end direct connections among peers. They also prevent the CDN from using too much of its bandwidth for peers' traffic. (ii) a CDN-assisted peers' content delivery protocol; and (iii) an evaluation of our proposed approach showing that with some limited help from a CDN the content distribution time among peers can be speeded up from 1.5 to 3 times.

The rest of this paper is organized as follows. In Section 2, we present an overview of our Synergetic Content Distribution framework to give an idea of our overall research effort in content distribution. We then focus on one specific research problem and provide a solution in Section 3. We present the performance study and simulation results Section 4. In Section 5, we discuss related work. Finally, we conclude the paper in Section 6.

2   Overview of Our Synergetic Content Distribution Framework

In this section, we provide an overall picture of our current research directions in content distribution. We show how this paper relates to our other research directions. Our overall research goal in content distribution is to design and evaluate a Synergetic Content

---

[2] Not allowing peers to abuse or to pose a security concern for a CDN.

[3] We make a distinction between CDN's content belonging to the content producers/publishers and peers' content belonging to individual users.

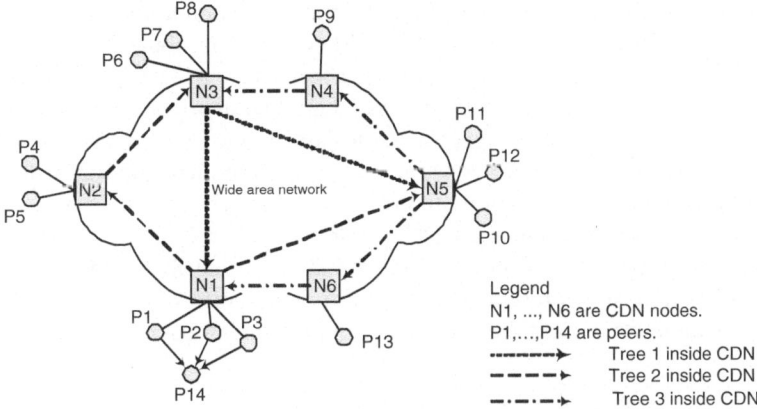

Fig. 1. Synergetic Content Distribution

Distribution framework that takes advantage of both the CDN and the P2P distribution models. Our motivation for this new framework comes from our observation that peers can help a CDN to deliver the CDN's content while a CDN can help peers in return to distribute peers' content. Distributing CDN's content and distributing peers' content differs in that CDN's content is always replicated on CDN nodes while peers' content are never replicated on CDN nodes. To achieve this research goal, we pursue three different, but closely related, research directions to be described briefly in the following.

The first research direction addresses the challenge of designing a mechanism to help a CDN to recruit peers to become a part of the CDN. Then, the CDN and the recruited peers collaborate to deliver the CDN's content. For example, in Figure 1 the CDN node N_1 recruits peers P_1, P_2, and P_3 so that they can collaborate to deliver the CDN's content to peer P_{14}. The benefit of this approach is to allow a CDN to be more dynamic by exploiting readily available resources of peers to deliver the CDN's content. Our approach improves the service latency of streaming content by 30% compared with an approach where a CDN does not exploit peers' resources to distribute CDN's content. We present this research direction in more details in [3].

The second research direction, **which is the main focus of this paper**, aims at designing a mechanism to allow a CDN to use its infrastructure to help peers in their content distribution[4]. An important issue is to limit the resources a CDN makes available to peers. Therefore, we propose that a CDN only contributes its resources to peers proportional to what it received from peers earlier when peers used their resources to deliver the CDN's content. For example, in Figure 1, the set of twelve peers $\{P_1, \ldots, P_{12}\}$ had contributed their resources to help the CDN earlier. Now, when they want to distribute content among themselves, the CDN creates three different bandwidth bounded trees rooted at CDN nodes N_1, N_3, and N_5, respectively. The peers transfer their content through these trees inside the CDN. We provide more details on this direction in Section 3.

---

[4] By peer content distribution we mean a peer (or some peers) wants to send an entire file (e.g., MP3 or movie file) to a group of other peers.

The third research direction, which is under investigation at the time of this writing, focuses on an incentive mechanism to entice peers to contribute their resources to a CDN and also to entice a CDN to provide peers accesses to its infrastructure. Our incentive mechanism builds on the fairness and the reciprocation principles. The mechanism strictly follows a policy to require peers to contribute first to build up their credit before being able to use the CDN to distribute their content. Another important element for our incentive mechanism is the ability to prevent malicious behavior. That is, we do not want peers to collaborate to cheat a CDN nor do we want a CDN to refuse to provide accesses to its infrastructure to good peers who already contributed their resources to the CDN. We have briefly presented our overall research effort in content distribution. In the next section, we discuss the main research problem of this paper and we propose a solution.

3   CDN-Assisted Peers' Content Delivery

3.1   System Model and Assumptions

We assume that the network topology of a CDN is known and stable. The CDN has network measurement features to maintain an accurate view of the bandwidth, delay, and other metrics of the links inside the CDN. Each CDN node is responsible for handling a network area consisting of a number of peers. For example, in Figure 1 CDN node N_1 is responsible for handling peers $\{P_1, P_2, P_3\}$. The bandwidth between any two CDN nodes is higher than the end-to-end bandwidth between two peers in the respective network areas that the two CDN nodes are responsible for. The bandwidth is not necessarily symmetric.

Peers run a P2P protocol that has the following key features. A centralized node provides a new peer with information about a subset of nearby peers and a nearby CDN node responsible for the network area. This can be achieved through a network positioning system such as [4]. A group of peers distribute content among themselves in sessions. At the beginning of a session only one peer (or only a few peers) is a seed (i.e., having the whole content other peers want). At the end of the session, all peers in the group have the whole content. Content is divided into data blocks of equal size. A peer uses parallel downloading to get different data blocks from different peers.

3.2   Delivering Peers' Content Through a CDN

There are two scenarios for content delivery among peers. First, if the content delivery involves only peers in the same network area of one CDN node, the CDN node may not help much the peers in improving (i.e., provide faster delivery or more reliable network connections) the delivery of content. Therefore, a natural solution in this scenario is to let the peers to deliver content directly among themselves without the involvement of the CDN. The peers use their default P2P protocol to transfer content. For example, in Figure 1 if only peers $\{P_1, P_2, P_3\}$ want to distribute content among themselves, N_1 may not help much. Second, if the content delivery involves peers in many different network areas handled by many CDN nodes, the CDN nodes can help to improve the transfer rate of content. Without such a help from the CDN, the peers would have to establish several end-to-end connections among themselves to transfer data. The quality (bandwidth and reliability) of these end-to-end connections is not as good as that of the connections among CDN nodes.

A good solution for our problem should (i) enable a fast exchange of data blocks through the CDN among multiple peers and (ii) limit the resources of CDN used in helping distributing peers' content. There are several methods for building a communication medium to achieve many-to-many communications such as using a mesh, a graph, or a tree. In our case, a mesh or a graph would not be the best choice because we do not need redundant links among CDN nodes to distribute peers' content. We choose tree for its simplicity. With regards to limiting the resources a CDN uses to help peers, one should limit the transfer rate (i.e., transfer bandwidth) because a CDN should not be overloaded with peers' content. Note that the primary goal of a CDN is to distribute CDN's content. The main idea of our solution is to build bandwidth bounded trees in the CDN as a common medium for peers to distribute their content. Each tree is rooted at one of the CDN nodes, where there are peers wishing to send data, and spans to the remaining CDN nodes, where there are peers wishing to receive data. A CDN commits to provide a better transfer rate than the maximum achievable transfer rate of most peers. This is done by first taking into account the outgoing bandwidth distribution of peers and the mean and mode of that bandwidth distribution. Then a CDN provides peers with a transfer rate in a range that is in between the mean and a factor improvement of the mode. We next present our formal problem formulation.

Problem Formulation. *Given a graph $G = (V, E)$ representing a content distribution network, where V is the set of all CDN nodes and E is the set of logical links connecting the CDN nodes. Let P be the set of peers who want to distribute content. Let V' be the set of the CDN nodes responsible for the network areas of peers in P. Set P can be categorized into $|V'|$ subsets of peers, each subset S_i ($i = 1 \ldots |V'|$) is handled by a CDN node $v_i \in V'$. Let B_i be the median of the set of outgoing access bandwidth in a subset of peers S_i. Let M_i be the mode of the set of outgoing access bandwidth in a subset of peers S_i. Let C_i be the growth factor that a subset of peers S_i provides to the CDN.* **The goal is to** *construct $|V'|$ trees such that each tree satisfies the following conditions: (1) each tree covers all vertexes in V'; (2) each tree is rooted at a vertex $v_i \in V'$. Vertex v_i is a CDN node handling a subset of peers S_i; and (3) each tree rooted at v_i has a bottleneck bandwidth of at least B_i, and a maximum bandwidth of $C_i \times M_i$.*

We propose the following BUILDTREES algorithm to solve our formal problem. The algorithm consists of $|V'|$ steps. Each step produces a tree that is rooted at a node $v_i \in V'$, covers all the other nodes in V', has a minimum bandwidth of B_i, and that has a maximum bandwidth of $C_i \times M_i$. At each step we choose to build a tree in a way that leaves as much bandwidth as possible for the remaining steps. This is an insight we learned from a recent work in fast replication of content in CDN [5]. However, their algorithm cannot be directly applied to solve our problem because they consider the problem of replicating data from *a single source* to multiple CDN nodes. We consider the problem of using a CDN to help many peers (i.e., *many sources*) to distribute content. Their algorithm builds multiple trees from a single source to *all* nodes in a CDN and it builds trees with the highest possible throughput. Whereas, our algorithm

---

Algorithm 1 Building bandwidth bounded trees in a CDN to distribute peers' content

```
 1: procedure BUILDTREES( G(V, E), V', set of B_i, set of M_i, and set of C_i )
 2:     TreesList ← ∅
 3:     Sort V' to rank vertex(es) responsible for seed(s) first, then the remaining vertexes in decreasing order of growth
        factor provided to the CDN.
 4:     for each vertex v_i ∈ V' in the sorted order do
 5:         Temporarily remove all edges (u, v) ∈ E whose current bandwidth bw_uv < B_i
 6:         Tree_i ← ∅
 7:         NodesInTree_i ← v_i
 8:         while NodesInTree_i ≠ V' do
 9:             for each vertex u ∈ NodesInTree_i do
10:                 Edge_u ← Find edge (u, j) with bw_uj ≥ (C_i × M_i) and with min{bw_uj − (C_i × M_i)}
11:                 RemainedBW_u ← BW_u − {Bandwidth of Edge_u}
12:             end for
13:             x ← Node j with max{RemainedBW_j}
14:             NodesInTree_i ← NodesInTree_i ∪ {destination of Edge_x}
15:             Tree_i ← Tree_i ∪ Edge_x
16:         end while
17:         for each edge (u, v) ∈ E and (u, v) ∈ Tree_i do
18:             bw_uv ← bw_uv − {bottleneck in Tree_i}
19:         end for
20:         TreesList ← TreesList ∪ Tree_i
21:         Restore temporarily remove edges for next vertex v_{i'}
22:     end for
23:     Return TreesList
24: end procedure
```

---

builds multiple trees for *multiple sources* (one tree for one source) and each tree reaches only *some* nodes in a CDN. Our algorithm does not build trees with the highest possible throughput, it only finds trees with a throughput being in a predetermined range (i.e., between the mean and the mode of outgoing bandwidth of peers).

We use the BUILDTREES algorithm to create one tree for each vertex v_i in V'. We start by sorting the vertexes (line 4) and proceed by this order of vertexes in the for loop (line 5). This method gives the set of peers that contributed the most to the CDN the highest chance of having the best links in CDN first. For constructing the tree rooted at each vertex, all edges that do not satisfy the minimum bandwidth requirement of B_i are temporarily removed (line 5). Note that this removal is only temporary for building the current tree. After a tree is constructed, the removed edges are restored so that they can be reconsidered in the next tree construction (line 21). We then add the root to the tree (line 7) and continuously add the remaining vertexes of V' until all of them are included (lines 8-16). The for loop (lines 9-12) is used to find an edge $Edge_u$, which is incident on each existing vertex u in the tree, that has the smallest bandwidth but still higher than $C_i \times M_i$. This guarantees the tree would be able to provide a bandwidth growth rate of C_i for the subset of peers S_i who already contributed to the CDN. The remaining available bandwidth $RemainedBW_u$ of node u is then calculated (line 11). Note that BW_u is the actual bandwidth that node u has at the time. Whereas, the $RemainedBW_u$ would be the new bandwidth that node u would have if $Edge_u$ was to be added to the tree. At the end of the for loop we have a set $\{RemainedBW_j\}$ of remaining available bandwidth of the nodes currently in the tree. We pick the node j that has the most remaining available bandwidth and assign it to variable x (line 12). We then add the corresponding neighbor of that node (chosen earlier in line 10) to the list of nodes in the tree (line 14). We next add the new edge to the tree. Finally, we reduce the bandwidth of edges in E that are also in the new tree by the bottleneck bandwidth of the new tree (line 18) and add the new tree to the list of trees (line 20).

We construct one tree per a CDN node in V', instead of following existing multiple trees approach in the literature [6,7,5], because the nodes in our tree are only CDN nodes (not peers). Once the tree is constructed it is stable, therefore, we do not need redundant trees. Moreover, we do not aim to use a CDN to achieve the fastest possible transfer of peers' content, therefore, we do not need multiple trees to get the highest throughput. We only want trees inside a CDN to provide higher bandwidth than the bandwidth of the end-to-end direct connections among peers. This is why we limit the bandwidth of a tree rooted at a CDN node to be within a specific range between the median (B_i) of the outgoing access bandwidth and at most C_i times of the mode (M_i) of the outgoing access bandwidth of the peers in the network area the CDN node (the root) is responsible for. Another reason that we construct one tree per CDN node in V' is because our incentive mechanism only allows a set of external peers to send data through a CDN for as long as they have enough credit. When the set of peers run out of credit, the corresponding tree rooted at the CDN responsible the set of peers will be deactivated. In other words, the tree is removed so that set of peers cannot use the CDN to send data anymore. Note that the peers can still receive data from other trees (which belong to other sets of peers who still have enough credit). This approach provides us more simplicity and more flexibility in enforcing our incentive mechanism compared to other more complicated tree building approaches.

3.3   CDN-Assisted Peers' Content Delivery Protocol

We assume that a group of peers, who want to use a CDN to distribute their content, already contributed their resources to the CDN. Now, the CDN is going to help the peers in return by increasing the transfer bandwidth of the content transfer among peers. The peers follow their P2P protocol to find out which content they want to distribute and which peers they want to distribute the content to. The peers also know which CDN node is responsible for the their network area (all these CDN nodes constitute the set V'). This information is handed over to one of the CDN nodes in V' who will run the BUILDTREES algorithm to construct the trees. Once the trees construction is completed, each CDN node in V' receives its tree information. The content distribution starts. Instead of sending data blocks to and receiving data blocks from other peers directly, as in the default P2P delivery protocol, each peer now sends to and receives from the CDN node responsible for the peer's network area.

When a CDN node receives a data block from a peer, it forwards the data block along the branches of the tree rooted at itself to other CDN nodes in the set V'. These CDN nodes are responsible for the network areas of the peers who interested in receiving the data block in question. Note that a peer may not be interested in some data blocks because it got them directly (without the help of the CDN) from other peers in its local network area. When a CDN node receives a data block from another CDN node, it forwards the data blocks to the peers that are participating in the content distribution in its network area. In addition, if the CDN node is not a leaf of a tree, it also replicates the data blocks and forward them to its children in the tree. Note that during content distribution, each data block traverses only one tree. A CDN node only replicate and forward data blocks of peers to other nodes down a tree, it does not cache nor store the data blocks of peers for later usage[5]. When a set of peers in a network area completely finishes a content distribution session (received all data blocks), the tree rooted at the CDN node handling that area is still kept to distribute data to the remaining unfinished peers. A tree rooted at a CDN node responsible for one area is destroyed only when either the peers in the network area do not have credits to send data anymore or there no data sending out on the tree for an extended amount of time. The latter case is possible when peers just leave after getting the content. Nevertheless, all trees are destroyed when all the peers finish.

4   Performance Study

In this section, we present the evaluation of our technique. We use a packet level simulator (ns-2 version 2.27) to compare our CDN-assisted peers' content delivery protocol to a default P2P delivery protocol. Some main features of the P2P protocol are (i) using parallel downloading of data blocks; (ii) allowing upload to at most five other peers at a time; and (iii) changing the corresponding peer often. The performance metric is the total time it takes so that all peers in the content distribution group finish receiving the content. We next discuss more details about our simulation setup.

4.1   Simulation Setup

Fig. 2 shows the network topology used in all the simulations. Due to the lack of actual topology information of a CDN, we adapt this topology from real cities in the United States with an assumption that a CDN operator would also want to deploy services in these geographical locations. The topology has 12 IP routers (R1-R12). The link propagation delays among these IP routers correspond relatively to their geographical distances. The bandwidth between a pair of IP router is symmetric (assuming a leased line connection) and is set at 1.5 Mbps. Each IP router connects to some peers via asymmetric connections. The maximum download bandwidth of a peer from an IP router is 700 Kbps while the maximum upload bandwidth of a peer to an IP router is only 200 Kbps (note that when there are a maximum of five concurrent receiving peers, each peer only gets 40 Kbps). This is a typical connection for DSL/Cable Internet users. Peers are assumed to have a 2-millisecond delay from the nearest IP router in our topology. We use 12, 24, and 36 peers in our simulations.

On top of this IP level topology, we build an overlay network of six CDN nodes (N1-N6) connecting to six IP routers as shown. Node N_1 is responsible for peers connecting to IP routers R_5, R_9, and R_{10}. Node N_2 is responsible for peers connecting to IP routers R_1 and R_3. Node N_3 is responsible for peers connecting to IP routers R_2, R_6, and R_7. Node N_4 is responsible for peers connecting to IP router R_8. Node N_5 is responsible for peers connecting to IP router R_4. Node N_6 is responsible for peers connecting to IP routers R_{11} and R_{12}. Each CDN node has a 10 Mbps symmetric bandwidth to its corresponding IP router. The maximum bandwidth between a pair of CDN

---

[5] This is a major constrast to using the CDN to distribute CDN's content.

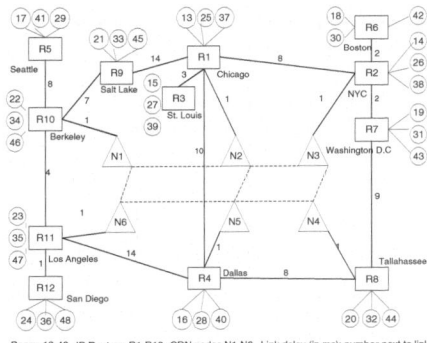

Fig. 2. Simulated network topology

nodes is 10 Mbps. However, at anytime *the CDN only gives at most 1 Mbps for distributing peers' content*. The propagation delay among CDN nodes are 2 milliseconds. In our CDN-assisted technique, the peers use the CDN overlay to transfer only data blocks. Other types of packet (protocol signals, requests, etc.) have to go through the IP level network. The default P2P protocol only uses the IP level network for both data and other types of packets.

In our simulations, a group of peers distribute files of medium size (50 MBytes) and large size (500 MBytes). At the beginning of the distribution, there are only two seeds (two peers that have the complete content). This is why in our figures the lines start out flat. At the end, all peers have the complete content. We also consider two different scenarios for peers' arrival. The first one is the flash crowd situation in which all peers suddenly want to download the content at once (all peers arrive at the same time). The second one is a normal situation in which peers' arrival time follows a Poisson distribution.

4.2   Simulation Results

We run ten simulations, each with a different random seed to obtain an average value of the completion time of each peer. The standard errors of the completion times of peers are small: with an average of 2 minutes for flash crowd situation and 5 minutes for normal situation.

Fig. 3 and Fig. 4 show the CDF of distribution completion time when we use 12 peers (peers numbered 13-24 in the topology) and 24 peers (peers numbered 13-48 in the topology), respectively, to distribute small objects. Our technique (CDN-assisted) provides a speed up of 1.5 to 2 times in terms of distribution completion time in both flash crowd and normal scenarios. This result is expected because the CDN in our technique allows the peers to use its infrastructure to transfer data blocks. Note that the CDN only devotes at most 1 Mbps of its bandwidth to peers's traffic. We observe that during a flash crowd situation, the performance gap between our technique the default P2P protocol is reduced. This is because there are many peers available within a short period of time, increasing the service capacity of the P2P network.

Fig. 5 and Fig. 6 show the CDF of distribution completion time when we use 12 peers (peers 13-24) and 24 peers (peers 13-48), respectively, to distribute large objects

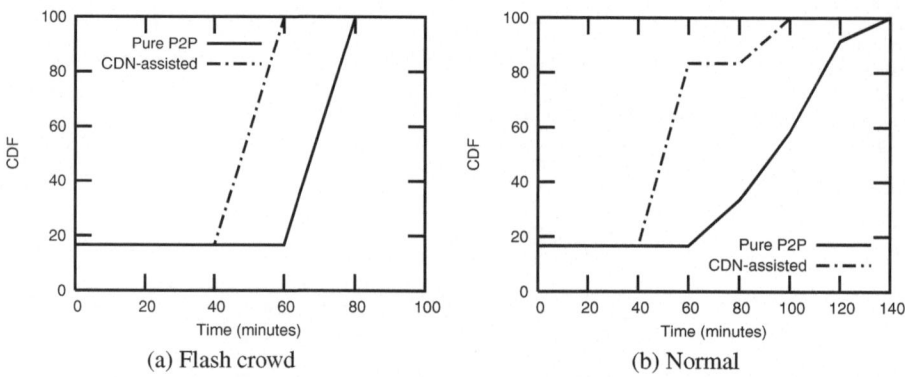

Fig. 3. CDF of distribution completion time, 50MB per object, 12 peers

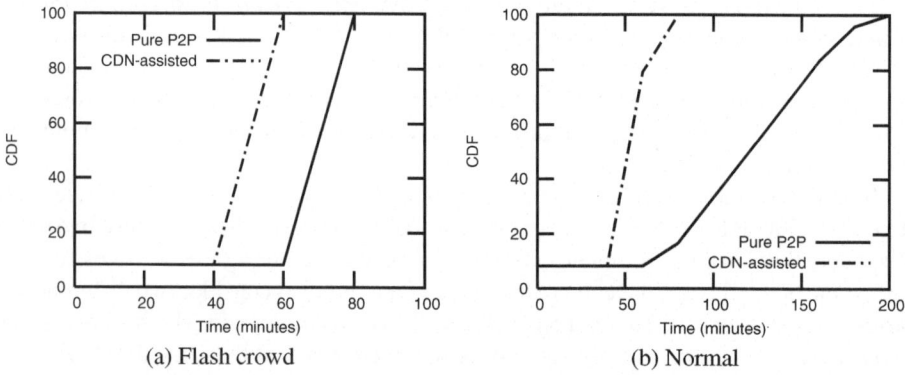

Fig. 4. CDF of distribution completion time, 50MB per object, 24 peers

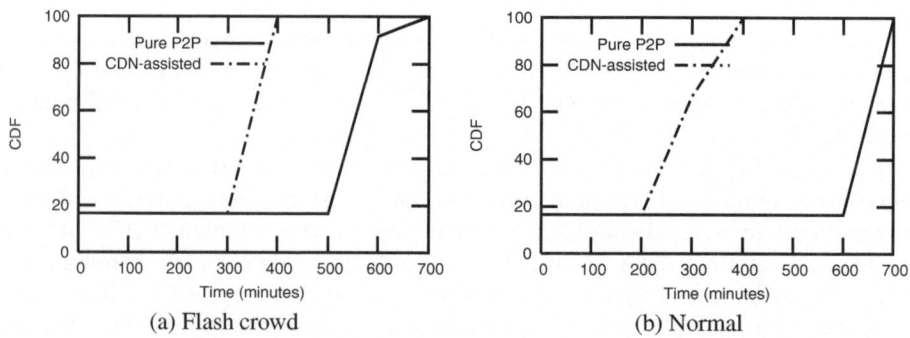

Fig. 5. CDF of distribution completion time, 500MB per object, 12 peers

of 500 MBytes each. Similarly, our technique offers a speed up of 1.5 to 3 times in terms of completion time in both flash crowd and normal scenarios. The result of simulations with 36 peers shows a similar conclusion; hence, it is omitted to save space.

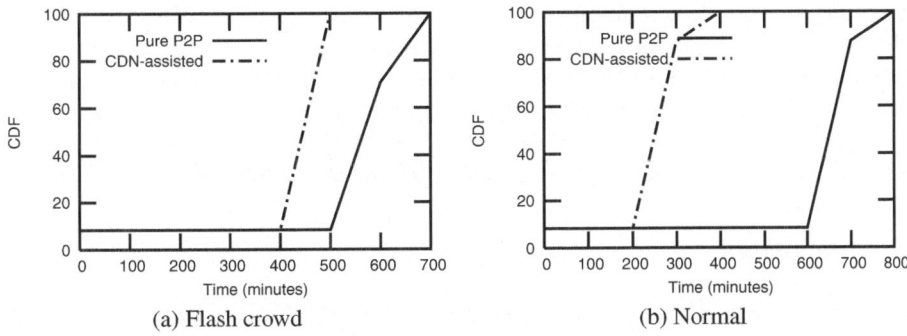

Fig. 6. CDF of distribution completion time, 500MB per object, 24 peers

5   Related Work

There have been previous research on using pure CDNs for distributing web content [8,1,9,10] and video content [11,12], but they did not consider the problem of using a CDN to help peers in exchanging their content, which is the main focus of this paper. There have also been some recent proposals on building pure P2P networks for video streaming [13,14,15]. These systems differ from our approach mainly because they rely on purely peer nodes to build a distribution tree. Although this is a perfectly cost-effective approach, it differs from our approach in that our approach has the availability and reliability provided by the CDN nodes. Our decision to use a CDN to help peers in content distribution is also strengthen by recent evidence that a purely P2P based streaming system needs some reliable nodes (some PlanetLab nodes in this case) to provide acceptable quality [16,17].

There are some existing hybrid approaches of using both CDN and P2P networks for distributing content, such as PROP [18] and that of Xu *et al.* [19]. PROP [18] uses arbitrary local peer nodes to assist a local proxy server in an enterprise video streaming environment. PROP uses peers belonging to structured P2P networks [20] and it relies on the distributed hash table of structured P2P networks to perform content location. Xu *et al.* [19] proposed a hybrid CDN and P2P video delivery system in which a CDN hands over the serving of requests to a set of serving peer nodes at a calculated hand-off time. After this hand-off time, the system practically becomes a pure P2P content delivery system because the CDN does not serve requests anymore. However, these approaches differ from our approach in this paper in that they only look at peers as potential helpers for distributing a CDN's content, but they do not consider using a CDN to help peers distributing their content. A similar idea, to that of PROP [18] of using local proxies (web caches) in conjunction with peers, is implemented as a modification [21] to the original eMule file sharing network to improve download for peers. However, this approach considers local proxies as stand alone nodes and requires local proxies to cache peers' content. Our approach leverages the collaboration of CDN nodes and does not require CDN nodes to cache peers' content.

Comparing with recent research efforts in large file transfer like SplitStream [6], Bullet [7], Slurpie [22], ROMA [23], SPIDER [5], and using network coding with peers [24], our problem/solution is different because we build trees inside a CDN to help external peers to distribute their content. Our method of opening up a CDN to allow the transfer of peers content, as discussed in this paper, is a part of our larger Synergetic Content Distribution framework in which we maintain a two-way collaborative relationship between a CDN and the peers so that everybody (both companies/organization and individual users) can distribute content easily and efficiently.

6 Conclusion

In this paper, we have proposed a new approach of using a CDN to help peers in transferring their content. Our main new idea is to open up a CDN's infrastructure through which many individual users can deliver their content. This approach is in a direct contrast with the common wisdom of keeping CDNs closed to a small group of big content producers/publishers (e.g., CNN, Yahoo). We have proposed and evaluated an algorithm to build trees within a CDN to be used as communication medium for external peers to distribute content. Our initial results have shown the potential of this approach. Our future work includes the implementation and evaluation of our approach on PlanetLab.

References

1. Qiu, L., Padmanabhan, V., Voelker, G.: On the placement of web server replicas. In: Proc. of the 20th IEEE INFOCOM, Anchorage, AK (2001) 1587–1596
2. Jamin, S., Jin, C., Kurc, A., Raz, D., Shavitt, Y.: Constrained mirror placement on the internet. In: Proc. of the 20th IEEE INFOCOM, Anchorage, AK (2001) 31–40
3. Tran, M., Tavanapong, W.: Peers-assisted dynamic content distribution networks. In: Proc. of the 30th IEEE Local Computer Networks Conference (LCN), Sydney, Australia (2005)
4. Ng, T., Zhang, H.: A network positioning system for the internet. In: Proc. of the USENIX Annual Technical Conference, Boston, MA (2004) 141–154
5. Ganguly, S., Saxena, A., Bhatnagar, S., Banerjee, S., Izmailov, R.: Fast replication in content distribution overlays. In: Proc. of the 24rd IEEE INFOCOM, Miami, FL (2005) –
6. Castro, M., Druschel, P., Kermarrec, A.M., Nandi, A., Rowston, A., Singh, A.: Splitstream: high-bandwidth multicast in cooperative environments. In: Proc. of the 19th ACM Symposium on Operating Systems Principles (SOSP), Bolton Landing, NY (2003) 298–313
7. Kostic, D., Rodriguez, A., Albrecht, J., Vahdat, A.: Bullet: high bandwidth data dissemination using an overlay mesh. In: Proc. of the 19th ACM Symposium on Operating Systems Principles (SOSP), Bolton Landing, NY (2003) 282–297
8. Michel, S., Nguyen, K., Rosenstein, A., Zhang, L., Floyd, S., Jacobson, V.: Adaptive web caching: towards a new global caching architecture. Computer Networks and ISDN Systems **22** (1998) 2169–2177
9. Kangasharju, J., Ross, K., Roberts, J.: Performance evaluation of redirection schemes in content distribution networks. Elsevier Computer Communications Journal **24** (2001) 207–214
10. Wang, L., Pai, V., Peterson, L.: The effectiveness of request redirection on cdn robustness. In: Proc. of the 5th Symposium on Operating Systems Design and Implementation (OSDI), Boston, MA (2002) 345–360
11. Apostolopoulos, J., Wong, T., Wee, S., Tan, D.: On multiple description streaming with content delivery networks. In: Proc. of the IEEE INFOCOM 2002, New York, NY (2002) 1736–1745

12. Chawathe, Y.: Scattercast: an adaptable broadcast distribution framework. ACM/Springer Multimedia Systems Journal, Special Issue on Multimedia Distribution **9** (2003) 104–118
13. Padmanabhan, V., Wang, H., Chou, P.: Resilient peer-to-peer streaming. In: Proc. of 11th IEEE International Conference on Network Protocols (ICNP 2003), Atlanta, GA (2003) 16–27
14. Hefeeda, M., Habib, A., Botev, B., Xu, D., Bhargava, B.: Promise: Peer-to-peer media streaming using collectcast. In: Proc. of ACM Multimedia 2003, Berkeley, CA (2003) 45–54
15. Guo, Y., Suh, K., Kurose, J., Towsley, D.: A peer-to-peer on-demand streaming service and its performance evaluation. In: Proc. of IEEE International Conference on Multimedia and Expo (ICME 2003), Baltimore, MD (2003) 649 –652
16. Chu, Y., Ganjam, A., Ng, T., Rao, S., Sripanidkulchai, K., Zhan, J., Zhang, H.: Early experience with an internet broadcast system based on overlay multicast. In: Proc. of the USENIX Annual Technical Conference, Boston, MA (2004) 155–170
17. Sripanidkulchai, K., Ganjam, A., Maggs, B., Zhang, H.: The feasibility of supporting large-scale live streaming applications with dynamic application end–points. In: Proc. of the ACM SIGCOMM, Portland, OR (2004) 107–120
18. Guo, L., Chen, S., Ren, S., Chen, X., Jiang, S.: PROP: A scalable and reliable p2p assisted proxy streaming system. In: Proc. of the 24th International Conference on Distributed Computing Systems (ICDCS), Tokyo, Japan (2004) 778–786
19. Xu, D., Chai, H., Rosenberg, C., Kulkarni, S.: Analysis of a hybrid architecture for cost-effective streaming media distribution. In: Proc. of the SPIE/ACM Multimedia Computing and Networking conference (MMCN), Santa Clara, CA (2003) 87–101
20. Ratnasamy, S., Francis, P., Handley, M., Karp, R., Schenker, S.: A scalable content-addressable network. In: Proc. of the ACM SIGCOMM, San Diego, CA (2001) 161–172
21. eMule Webcache Project: WebCache modifications for eMule. In: URL http://www.emule-mods.de/?mods=webcache. (Last accessed July 2005)
22. Sherwood, R., R.Braud, Bhattacharjee, B.: Slurpie: A cooperative bulk data transfer protocol. In: Proc. of the 23rd IEEE INFOCOM, Hongkong, China (2004) 941–951
23. Kwon, G., Byers, J.: Roma: reliable overlay multicast with loosely coupled tcp connections. In: Proc. of the 23rd IEEE INFOCOM, Hongkong, China (2004) 385–395
24. Gkantsidis, C., Rodriguez, P.: Network coding for large scale content distribution. In: Proc. of the 24rd IEEE INFOCOM, Miami, FL (2005) –

QoSJava: An End-to-End QoS Solution*

Xiaohui Huang, Yu Lin, Wendong Wang, and Shiduan Cheng

State Key Lab of Networking and Switching,
Beijing University of Posts and Telecommunications,
Beijing, P.R. China, 100876
{hxiaohui, linyu, wdwang, chsd}@bupt.edu.cn

Abstract. Incompatibility of different QoS (Quality of Service) mechanisms and heterogeneity of different vendors' network devices are the major obstacles for providing end-to-end QoS in IP network. Inspired by Java, we propose an end-to-end QoS solution in this paper, i.e. QoSJava, which decouples QoS requirements from network details. By QoS Mechanisms Adapter and Device Driver, which act as "Java Virtual Machine", QoSJava enables interoperation between different QoS mechanisms and cooperation of dissimilar network devices. A prototype of QoSJava has been implemented, and the experimental results prove that network devices can be configured automatically to provide an end-to-end QoS. Moreover, QoSJava is not only compatible with current QoS mechanisms and devices, but open to new QoS solutions and advanced devices in the future.

1 Introduction and Motivation

Today network becomes a necessity in most people's daily life. People use network to do shopping, watch movies, make phone calls, read news, play games and so on. And naturally, they require current network infrastructures to transform from providing mere connectivity to a wider range of tangible and flexible network services with QoS. However, current traffic of various services is carried by IP network, which only provides best effort transmission. Therefore, QoS provisioning in IP network has been a hot topic in recent years.

Many researchers concentrate on this problem and have proposed a great deal of solutions. Among them, IntServ [1], DiffServ [2] and MPLS [3] are well-known. Moreover, many projects brought forward innovative solutions. CADENUS [4], TEQUILA [5] and AQUILA [6], which are part of Euro Commission's IST (Information Society Technologies) projects, have implemented architectures to provide QoS in IP network. They are independent between each other and provide solutions for IP QoS.

However, none of the QoS solutions proposed is in use. The current network is still a best effort IP network. Though some network regions are equipped with routers with MPLS capabilities, to establish LSP for each micro-flow is impractical. End-to-end QoS is still far away from the ultimate goal.

---

*This work was supported by the National Basic Research Program of China (Grant No. 2003CB314806 and 2006CB701306), the National Natural Science Foundation of China (No. 90204003 and 60472067) and the National 863 Program of China (No.2003AA121220).

J. Dalmau and G. Hasegawa (Eds.): MMNS 2005, LNCS 3754, pp. 302–313, 2005.
© IFIP International Federation for Information Processing 2005

QoS will bring profits for Service Providers (SP) without any question. But why does the situation remain the same? When investigating the large scale network, the essential reason can be found out. Current network infrastructure is divided into several domains and belongs to different Network Providers (NP), who purchase network devices with diverse capabilities in light of their budget, and adopt different QoS mechanisms based on the devices. Noticeably, dissimilar QoS mechanisms are not compatible with each other. Thus all the aforementioned projects [4, 5, 6] assume that a unique QoS mechanism is deployed in the whole network, which makes them impractical in the real environment. Though mapping mechanisms enable the interoperation of two different QoS mechanisms [7, 8], we argue that developing mapping mechanisms between all QoS mechanism pairs is impractical, especially as more and more new QoS mechanisms appear in the future. In addition, devices of different vendors have disparate command sets. When QoS mechanisms need to be changed, instead of issuing an order to do batch modification, network administrator has to log in each router and modify the configuration one by one, which increases the operational cost. In a word, a major obstacle for providing end-to-end QoS in IP network is the heterogeneity of network devices and QoS mechanisms.

QoSJava is proposed in this paper to solve the problem. Our solution is named QoSJava only because the idea comes from Java. Providing e2e QoS in current network has some similarities with programming in distributed environment. Programming in distributed environment should consider the portability of the program and the heterogeneity of the runtime environment. Analogously, providing e2e QoS in heterogeneous IP network should adapts to various QoS mechanisms and devices. As we known, Java is a powerful language for distributed network environment. After compiled, Java programs run on Java Virtual Machine (JVM) implemented on a particular platform. JVM plays a central role in making Java portable. It provides a layer of abstraction between the compiled Java program and the underlying hardware platform and operating system. Thus Java can conceal the heterogeneity of runtime environment and gain great success.

Inspired by Java, we propose QoSJava and believe it is a desirable solution for QoS provisioning in IP network. Different from other QoS solutions [1-3, 4-6], QoSJava can provide QoS for heterogeneous IP network, without assuming that the network is deployed with the same QoS mechanism. QoSJava achieve this goal by QoS Mechanism Adapter plus Device Driver, which accomplish the similar functions as JVM. They provide an abstraction layer between the application and the heterogeneous environment. Analogous to Java, QoSJava firstly translates user's QoS requirement to a stream of "bytecodes", i.e. deployment task specification. After that, QoS Mechanisms Adapter translates the deployment task specification into a script of instructions. Then the script is fed into Device Drive, which interprets each instruction in the script into a series of commands corresponding to the network devices. Finally, the commands are executed on the devices and configuration is actually completed. Thus QoSJava can migrate to arbitrary networks with different QoS mechanisms and devices of different vendors, as a result provides an end-to-end QoS.

The rest of the paper is organized as follows: Section 2 describes the detail of QoSJava framework, especially the QoS Mechanism Adapter and Device Driver, which is the major contribution of this paper. The deployment of QoSJava is given in section 3. Then our implementation of QoSJava and the experimental results are presented in section 4. The paper is concluded in Section 5 with the future work.

2 QoSJava

The framework of QoSJava consists of two parts, the user part and the administrator part, as illustrated in Fig.1. The user part resides on the left of the dash, dealing with the whole process from user submitting QoS requirement to network devices being configured. The administrator part situates on the right side, which is for network administrator to initialize the network, monitor network performance and execute high level configuration task. QoS Mechanism Adapter and Device Driver traverse two parts, acting as the "Virtual Machine". In this paper, we focus on the user part, since it lays the foundation of end-to-end QoS provisioning.

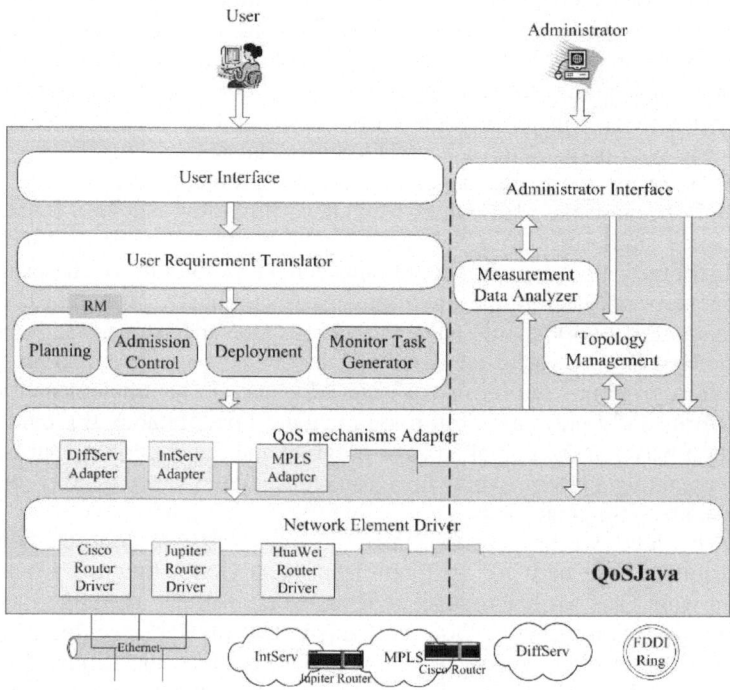

Fig. 1. QoSJava Architecture

2.1 User Interface

User Interface (UI) is the entrance for end users. As the front-end, UI is responsible for receiving user's requirement, delivering it to User Requirement Translator and returning the admission result to the user. In Java, the software function is coded in Java language. Similarly, in QoSJava, user's QoS requirement is expressed by QoS requirement description language, which can be SLA (Service Level Agreement), xml specification or any other standard format. The implementation of UI subjects to no constraints, so developer can choose any suitable technologies to realize it. SLA is adopted in our prototype to express user's requirement, and the UI is presented to end users as a web service.

2.2 User Requirement Translator

Not all end users are network experts, thus they always express their QoS requirements in a simple way. In addition, due to the different implementations of User Interface, various expression patterns exist. Therefore, a layer is needed to be inserted between User Interface and the execution logic to extract the technical parameters reflecting user's actual requirements, and denote them in a consolidated way. User Requirement Translator (URT) is such a layer in QoSJava. Based on the policies provided by Policy Server, URT analyzes user's expectation and educes the following tuple to describe a specific QoS requirement:

$$QoSReq \triangleq (SrcIP, DesIP, BW, Class, Delay, LossRate, Jitter, StartTime, EndTime)$$

$$q_{e2e} \in QoSReq$$

The parameters contained in the tuple can be extended as needed. At present, the following items are defined: Source IP Address ($SrcIP$), Destination IP Address ($DesIP$), Bandwidth required (BW), Traffic class of the service ($Class$), end-to-end delay ($Delay$), end-to-end packet loss rate ($LossRate$), end-to-end jitter ($Jitter$), the time when the contract begins to take effect ($StartTime$), and the time when the contract begins to expire ($EndTime$).

2.3 Resource Manager

Resource Manager (RM) has a logical view of its corresponding domain's physical network, including network topology, the state and the available resource of each network device. Compared to the whole network, a domain has fewer network devices, which makes the domain oriented resource management practical. RM obtains network information from a network management system developed by ourselves. After the information of network devices (mainly routers) is collected, RM does calculations for resource planning and management. RM maintains a resource database to record the resource information of the domain where it resides. According to the q_{e2e} tuple specifying user's QoS requirement, RM enforces admission control and generates corresponding monitoring tasks.

Routers are the most important components of IP network, hence router resource gives a reflection of network resource. Router resource correlating to QoS can be abstracted into the following tuple:

$$Res \triangleq (RouterID, DomainID, RT, IfNum, If_1, If_2, ..., If_{IfNum})$$

$$\text{In which} \quad \bigvee_{i=1}^{IfNum} If_i \in If$$

$$If \triangleq (BW, Buffer, Priority, Bucket, NextHop)$$

Current tuple has the following items: Identity of Router ($RouterID$), which is one IP of the router. Identity of the domain where the router is situated ($DomainID$), Routing Table (RT), Number of the Interfaces in the router ($IfNum$), the detail of each router interface ($If_1, If_2, ..., If_{IfNum}$), Bandwidth of the interface (BW), Buffer size of the interface ($Buffer$), Scheduling priority ($Priority$), Bucket Size ($Bucket$), and the router to which the interface connects ($NextHop$).

Router information can be obtained from network management system. The items contained in tuple *Res* can be extended as needed, and corresponding interfaces should be added to network management system to retrieve the required information.

Based on the resource information collected, network planning is done at first. Planning is coarse-grained, which can improve resource utilization instead of reaching the optimal resource assignment. In fact, there is no solution for optimal resource utilization in Internet due to its complex traffic pattern. Planning calculates the resource matrixes for Gold, Silver and Bronze services, which are analogous to EF, AF and BE aggregates in DiffServ [2]. Resource matrixes set the stage for admission control process. The fundamental idea of planning is to locate the bottleneck of the network, and distribute its bandwidth to the aggregate flows which share the link. Please refer to [11] for the detail algorithm. The resource matrixes produced by planning are R^{Gold}, R^{Silver}, and R^{Bronze}. They are $n \times n$ matrixes, in which n is the number of edge routers in the domain. The semantic of the element in the matrix is explained below. Take $r_{i.j}^{Gold}$ in matrix R^{Gold} as an example, it represents the available resource for Gold Service between ER_i and ER_j. It is defined by the following tuple, among which *SrcER* and *DesER* are the IP addresses of Ingress edge router and Egress edge router separately. Other parameters have the same meaning as in tuple *QoSReq* and *If*.

$$r_{i.j}^{Gold} \triangleq (SrcER, DesER, BW, Class, Buffer, Priority, Bucket)$$

Since User's QoS requirement q_{e2e} may involve multiple domains adopting different QoS mechanisms, Admission Control component (AC) firstly decomposes q_{e2e} into several QoS requirements $q_i \in QoSReq$ ($i = 1, 2, ..., m$) based on domains' capabilities, and sends them to the AC of domain i ($i = 1, 2, ..., m$) for admission. m is the total number of domains along the end-to-end path, and q_i corresponds to domain i. The decomposition algorithm is presented in our previous work [10].

After decomposition, AC translates each QoS requirement q_i into resource requirement for domain i. Function f maps QoS requirement to resource requirement.

$$f : q_i \rightarrow r_i^{out}$$

In which $r_i^{out} \triangleq (SrcER, DesER, BW, Class, Buffer, Priority, Bucket)$

According to resource requirement r_i^{out} and the admission policies provided by the Policy Server, AC consults the resource database for corresponding resource matrix, and determines whether the user's requirement can be admitted. If resource of all domains along the end-to-end path is sufficient, admission is successful, or a failure notification will be returned with the failed reason to guide the user's renegotiation process.

If admission turns out to be successful, AC subtracts the resource assigned from the available resource database. A monitoring task T_i is also generated by Monitor Task Generator to perform QoS surveillance during the service operation time. The parameters of T_i are not given here for the space constraint, Please refer to [9].

After user's requirement is admitted and monitoring task is generated, Deployment component creates deployment task for lower layers. The deployment task specification is the "bytecode" of QoSJava, designating how much resource should be assigned for QoS provisioning and how to execute monitoring task for QoS guarantee. The specification can be written as an xml document. It can also be written as a configuration file with APIs (Application Program Interface) provided by lower layers. In our implementation, QoS Mechanisms Adapter provides a series of APIs for Deployment component. Deployment component can use these APIs to issue orders, such as resource assignment and monitoring task enforcement.

2.4 QoS Mechanisms Adapter

Different QoS mechanisms have dissimilar resource management patterns and QoS provisioning approaches. In IntServ, resource should be reserved in all routers along the end-to-end path. DiffServ classifies traffic at the edge and specifies packets' PHB, i.e. EF, AF and BE. As for MPLS, it establishes LSP and sticks labels to packets at the network entrance. In addition, dissimilar QoS mechanisms behave differently in traffic monitoring. The purpose of QoS Mechanisms Adapter (QMA) is to conceal their heterogeneity and provides a unified interface for Resource Manager.

QoS Mechanisms Adapter should perform at least two operations. One is to interpret resource assignment task r_i^{out}, and the other is to interpret monitoring task T_i.

Both r_i^{out} and T_i are designated in the Deployment Task Specification. Based on the QoS mechanism adopted in the domain, QMA translates the deployment task specification to a script containing a series of instructions provided by Device Driver. The adapting scheme is as follows:

$$QoSAdapter(r_i^{out}) = \begin{cases} Configuration\ of\ all\ Routers\ along\ the\ path & IntServ \\ Configuration\ of\ Edge\ Rounters & DiffServ \\ Establish\ LSP\ between\ Routers & MPLS \\ To\ be\ extended & other\ QoS\ mechanisms \end{cases} \quad (1)$$

$$QoSAdapter(T_i) = \begin{cases} Monitor\ all\ Routers\ along\ the\ Path & IntServ \\ Monitor\ Ingress\ Router\ and\ Egress\ Router & DiffServ \\ Monitor\ entrance\ and\ exit\ of\ LSP & MPLS \\ To\ be\ extended & Other\ QoS\ Mechanisms \end{cases} \quad (2)$$

In IntServ, QMA needs to translate the Deployment Task Specification into the configuration of all routers located in the domain along the end-to-end path. In DiffServ, QMA translates the specification to the configuration of Ingress router and Egress Router, designating traffic class (EF/AF/BE), queue priority, packet dropping scheme, and etc. In MPLS, the specification is translated into label distribution, LSP establishment and monitoring.

Formula (1) and (2) only give the semantics of QMA's result. In the implementation, the result produced by QMA is an execution script with instruction sequence. An instruction encapsulates a series of commands of network devices and can perform more advanced task than a single command. An execution script example is given below. It describes a scenario in which domain D_1 adopts IntServ. Thus in D_1, resource reservation and monitoring task deployment should be done in all routers along the end-to-end path.

[INTSERV_QOSCONFIG]

#ResvRes<Domain D_1 , IP of Router 1, r_i^{out} tuple>

#DeployMonTask<Domain D_1 , IP of Router1, T_i tuple>

...

#ResvRes<Domain D_1 , IP of Router N, r_i^{out} tuple>

#DeployMonTask<Domain D_1 , IP of Router N, T_i tuple>

When a new QoS mechanism appears, new adapting module can be added to QoSJava by extending current execution scripts or adding new execution scripts. Therefore new QoS mechanisms can merge into QoSJava without violating the existing QoS mechanisms. Thanks to QMA, variety of QoS mechanisms could be coexistent in the network to provide an end-to-end QoS.

2.5 Device Driver

While QoS Mechanisms Adapter conceals the heterogeneity of QoS mechanisms, Device Driver (DD) makes the difference of network devices transparent. Due to router vendors' different strategies, their products have disparate command sets. DD in our prototype can adapt to command sets of major router vendors including Cisco, Juniper and HuaWei.

DD provides instructions for QMA, and is responsible for interpreting each instruction into commands according to the devices' types in the domain. Instructions describe advanced tasks to be performed, such as resource reservation and monitoring task deployment. Completion of such tasks involves a sequence of commands to be executed in the router. Upper layer can issue high level orders using the instructions, and DD translates the order into a series of commands correspondingly. Thus DD can realize automatic configuration of network devices, and administrators don't have to manually modify routers' configuration one by one.

Our prototype provides more than 20 instructions, categorized into QoS provision, monitor task deployment, data collection, router configuration/control, and network management. The instructions for network management encapsulate SNMP commands. An instruction example which is interpreted to commands of Cisco Router (2600, 3600 and 7200 series) is given below.

```
#MODIFY_SERVICECLASS <19>
@TELNETCONN <1>
******
Enable
******
Config terminal
policy-map p-in-<19>
class <17>
police cir <10> bc <11> pir <12> be <13> conform-action set-
dscp-transmit <14> exceed-action drop
violate-action drop
@TELNETDISC
```

Note: <N> means the Nth formal parameter of the instruction.

When the script with this instruction (#MODIFY_SERVICECLASS) is executed by Device Driver, the instruction will be interpreted into a sequence of commands, completing the task of service class modification. First the API of telnet package provided by operating system is used to telnet to the router and establishes a connection (@TELNETCONN). Then password (******) is transmitted to the router. After authentication, administrator's priority would be upgraded using command "enable" and password needs to be input again. Service class is modified in succession. The command "police" sets the parameters including committed information rate (cir), confirm burst (bc), peak information rate (pir), exceed burst (be) and the dscp value attached to packets whose rates are less than cir (set-dscp-transmit). It also indicates that all packets whose rates are greater than cir will be dropped. When the task is completed, it disconnects from the router (@TELNETDISC). These commands will be executed in batch, avoiding administrator's interference.

3 Deployment of QoSJava

QoSJava is deployed in each domain of the network and communicates in a distributed manner. It can be hosted by server farm or just a computer with powerful computation capability. A deployment example is given in Fig. 2, in which QoSJava is hosted by server farm. Components of QoSJava are hosted in separate servers.

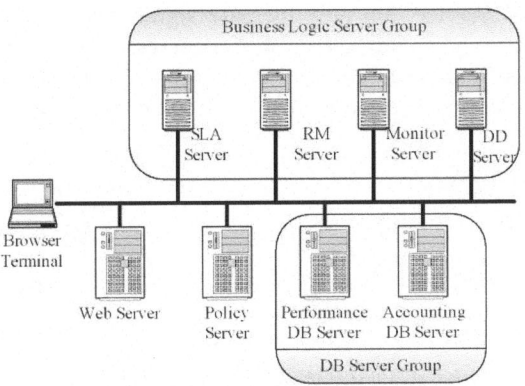

Fig. 2. QoSJava Deployment

4 Implementation and Experimental Results

A prototype of QoSJava is implemented in the National 863 project of China, whose purpose is to establish a carrier-class IP network and provide the QoS as in telecommunication network. QoSJava is the essential part of the project. Fig. 3 presents our testbed, which consists of five domains with different QoS mechanisms including DiffServ and MPLS, and consists of different network devices from Cisco, Juniper and HuaWei. We deploy more than 20 routers in the testbed. Some of them are omitted in Fig. 3 to improve visibility. A management system is also implemented as an affiliated system to monitor the performance perceived by end users [13].

In our experiment, user subscribes his SLA by a web page. Fig. 4 gives a demonstration when the user subscribes a VoIP Service. The technical parameters specified in SLA are translated into resource requirement and admitted by Admission Control component. Once the SLA is admitted, QoS mechanisms Adapter plus Device Driver configures the network devices according to the QoS mechanisms and devices series in the domain.

RouterTest instrument of Agilent and Iperf [12] are used as traffic generators. Routertest generates 256kb UDP packets at the rate of 171.24Mb/s, flooding link 172.16.4.0 to produce a congestion situation. Iperf [12] is an open source tool for network performance measurement. It injects packets in router 11.11.11.11 and congests link/interface 172.16.12.0. The link utilization of a router interface in congestion situation is illustrated in Fig. 5 in terms of CPU utilization, bandwidth utilization and packet loss rate.

Fig. 6 compares the performance of Audio service when the user subscribes to Gold Service and Bronze Service separately. Mobile nodes and correspondent nodes of VoIP service situate in WLANs (Wireless LAN) and connect to the testbed through APs (Access Point). In Fig. 6, from top to bottom, the five diagrams illustrate delay, jitter, packet loss rate, goodput, and network element load. The following statistics are obtained from the curves: packet loss rate is much less in Gold Service, approximate 2.6%, compared to 40% average loss rate in Bronze Service. The delay and jitter are very small in Gold Service, but they increase significantly in Bronze Service when congestion occurs. Some spikes appear in the curves of Gold Service because of the noise in the wireless link. The quality of voice is excellent in Gold Service. But when carried on Bronze Service aggregate, there is obvious incontinuity in the speech.

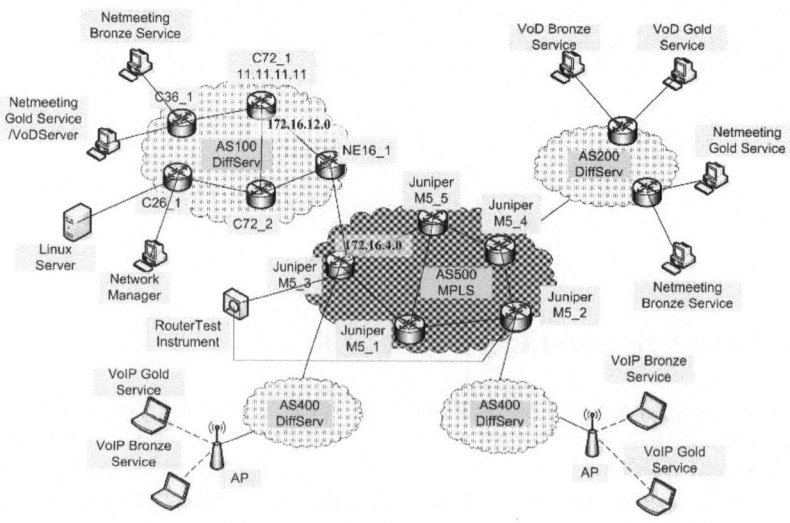

Fig. 3. Testbed

Fig. 4. User Interface for signing contract

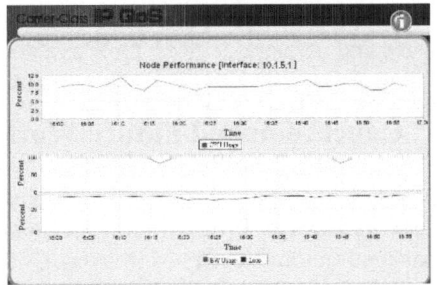

Fig. 5. Congestion Link Utilization

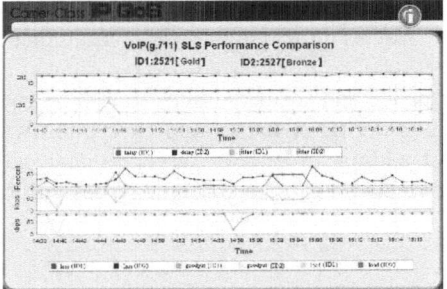

Fig. 6. Audio Performance Comparison

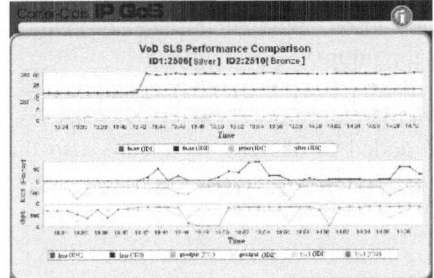

Fig. 7. Video Performance Comparison

Fig. 8. Video with QoS in congestion

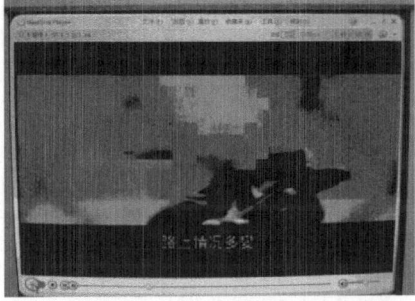

Fig. 9. Video without QoS in congestion

Fig. 7 depicts the performance of Video service in Silver and Bronze aggregate. Before the background traffic is generated, their performances are almost the same. But after the traffic is injected into the network, the curves show that the Video performance of Silver Service is much better than that of Bronze Service. Fig. 8 and 9 present the image of a movie, one with QoS (Silver Service) and the other without (Bronze Service). When congestion happens, the distinction of their performance is obvious. Experiments are also conducted for other services including video conference (Netmeeting), on-line games and ftp service. The results are omitted due to the space constraint.

The experiments prove that, even in the network with heterogeneous QoS mechanisms and network devices, QoSJava does deliver differentiated quality of service.

5 Conclusion and Future Work

QoSJava can conceal the heterogeneity of different QoS mechanisms and devices. Network devices from different vendors such as Cisco, Juniper and HuaWei can be managed automatically. Moreover, QoSJava is compatible with new QoS solutions and advanced devices. QoS is provided by software implementation and current network needs little modification. Therefore the network can evolve smoothly and legacy investments are preserved. QoSJava is an open and stable QoS management architecture. It is independent of the evolvement of network technology, QoS mechanism and application implementation. Consequently, it can adapt to new service requirements in the future.

When it is put into large scale use, performance and security issues should be considered carefully. Security mechanisms such as digital signature and encryption will be added to our prototype. We also think of adding an Access Server to deal with huge number of concurrent requests to improve the performance. These issues will be studied in the future work.

Acknowledgement

We would like to thank Xirong Que, Li Jiao, Yidong Cui, Huirong Tian, JunFeng Xiao for their intelligent idea. And we also want to thank all members of QoSA project for their hard work on QoSJava implementation.

References

1. Braden, R., Clark, D. and Shenker, S.: Integrated Services in the Internet Architecture: an Overview, Internet RFC 1633, June 1994
2. D. Grossman: New Terminology and Clarifications for Diffserv, RFC 3260, April 2002
3. E. Rosen, A. Viswanathan and R. Callon: Multiprotocol Label Switching Architecture, RFC3031, January 2001
4. CADENUS Project Consortium, Deliverable D1.2, End-user services in the Premium IP: Models, Architectures and Provisioning Scenarios, http://www.cadenus.org, November 2001
5. TEQUILA Project Consortium, Deliverable D1.1, Functional Architecture Definition and Top Level Design, http://www.ist-tequila.org, September 2000
6. AQUILA Project Consortium, Deliverable D1201, System Architecture and Specification for the first trial, http://www.ist-aquila.org, June 2000
7. Y. Bernet, P. Ford, R. Yavatkar, F. Baker, L. Zhang, M. Speer, R. Braden, B. Davie, J. Wroclawski, E. Felstaine: A Framework for Integrated Services Operation over Diffserv Networks, Internet RFC 2998, November 2000

8. F. Le Faucheur, L. Wu, B. Davie, S. Davari, P.Vaananen, R. Krishnan, P. Cheval, J. Heinanen: Multi-Protocol Label Switching Support of Differentiated Services, Internet RFC 3270, May 2002
9. Xiaohui Huang, Yu Lin, Wendong Wang, Xirong Que, Shiduan Cheng, Li Jiao, Yidong Cui: QoSjava: An Open and Scalable Architecture Decoupling QoS Requirements from QoS Techniques, draft-bupt-qosjava-arch-02.txt, http://www.ietf.org/internet-drafts/draft-bupt-qosjava-arch-02.txt
10. Xiaohui Huang, Yu Lin, Wendong Wang, Shiduan Cheng: PDB-Based SLS Decomposition in Heterogeneous IP Network, Proceedings of 2004 IEEE International Workshop on IP Operations & Management
11. Xiaohui Huang, Wendong Wang, Yu Lin, Shiduan Cheng: Resource Manager in Heterogeneous IP Network, Proceeding of International Conference on Communication and Information, 2005, to appear
12. Iperf, University of Illinois, http://dast.nlanr.net/Projects/Iperf/
13. Junfeng Xiao, Yidong Cui, Wendong Wang, Shiduan Cheng, A Service Level Specification (SLS) Monitoring System in Multiple Services IP Network, High technology Letters, ISSN 1002-0470, published by Executive Office of the Journal, Institute of Scientific and Technical Information of China, to appear.

Partial Video Replication for Peer-to-Peer Streaming

Sailaja Uppalapati and Ali Şaman Tosun

Department of Computer Science,
University of Texas at San Antonio,
San Antonio, TX 78249
{suppalap, tosun}@cs.utsa.edu

Abstract. Video streaming over peer-to-peer networks has attracted a lot of interest recently. However most of the research on streaming in peer-to-peer networks focused on schemes where all the clients have the whole movie. In this paper we propose schemes where clients store only partial movie after viewing the movie. We propose cooperative schemes where replication is done in a way that maximizes a global function and uncooperative schemes where each node makes replication decision independently. We evaluate both schemes using extensive simulation. Simulation results show that cooperative schemes perform better but they are harder to implement and maintain. Uncooperative schemes are simpler, based on a distributed algorithm but they suffer from lower performance.

1 Introduction

Peer-to-peer (P2P) is a new paradigm in which each peer stores the movie after streaming and act as a supplying peer by streaming the movie to other requesting peers thus serving both as a client and as a server. Combined storage of large number of peers allows users to locate a wide variety of multimedia content on the P2P network. The popularity of P2P networks and high number of peers on P2P networks with high-speed Internet connections have fueled interest to stream video over P2P networks. There are many challenges introduced when streaming is done using P2P paradigm as opposed to client-server paradigm which suffers from single point of failure, performance bottlenecks as media is centralized at the server.

Recently, streaming media from multiple sources has received a lot of attention. When all the nodes store the whole video, packets can be retrieved from the node which minimizes loss and delay [6]. The probability of packet loss in bursty environment is reduced by using FEC [7] where the source sends multiple redundant packets to the receiver. The receiver can reconstruct the original packets upon receiving a fraction of the total packets. PeerCast[3] streams live media using an overlay tree formed by clients and CoopNet [8] proposes a mechanisms for cooperation of clients to distribute streaming video when server is overloaded. A peer-to-peer media streaming model with an optimal media data assignment algorithm and a differentiated admission control protocol is proposed [14] assuming that all the peers store the whole video. A hybrid architecture that integrates Content Distribution Network(CDN) and P2P based media distribution given in [13]. CDN has a number of CDN servers deployed and the client can request media from the closest CDN server. Layered peer-to-peer streaming

J. Dalmau and G. Hasegawa (Eds.): MMNS 2005, LNCS 3754, pp. 314–325, 2005.

is proposed to handle asynchrony of user requests and heterogeneity of peer network bandwidth [2]. Administrative organization of peers to reduce control overhead in media streaming is proposed in [12]. Many P2P networks like CAN [9], CHORD [11] and Pastry [10] were proposed to perform peer lookups. Promise peer-to-peer system [4] supports peer lookup, peer-based aggregated streaming and dynamic adaptations to network and peer conditions. Gnustream [5] is a receiver-driven media streaming system built on top of Gnutella. Splitstream [1] distributes the forwarding load among all the nodes and accommodates peers with different bandwidth capacities by constructing a forest of interior-node-disjoint multicast trees.

All of the above techniques assumes that the whole movie is stored at all the peers and focussed on how to choose the peers based on their delay, loss and outgoing bandwidth. They didnot consider the case where peers have limited storage and may not be able to store the entire movie. If peers store partial video, a whole new set of challenges are introduced including the following

- How can a client determine whether a given set of peers are enough to stream the video?
- Given space for k segments, how can a peer determine the k segments that it stores?
- Should a peer cooperate with other peers to determine which segments it stores?
- How much control information needs to be exchanged to determine the supplying peers when a client requests a movie?

In this paper, we investigate the above issues. We propose two classes of schemes: cooperative and uncooperative. In cooperative schemes peers exchange information with each other and segments that are to be replicated are the ones that maximize the global utility function. In uncooperative schemes no information is exchanged between peers and each peer independently makes a decision on which segments it stores. We evaluate both schemes using extensive simulation. Cooperative schemes are complex to implement. However, they perform much better. Uncooperative schemes requires no coordination and are simpler to implement. This comes at the cost of lower streaming sessions that can be supported simultaneously. We also propose region-based cooperative scheme to reduce the overhead of cooperative schemes and to make them more scalable.

The rest of the paper is organized as follows: In section 2 we describe the cooperative and uncooperative schemes. We provide experimental results in section 3 and discuss pros and cons of each in section 4. Finally, we conclude with section 5.

2   Proposed Schemes

We assume the following to simplify the problem. Each movie consists of M segments labeled S_1 to S_M and each segment takes a weight between [0..1]. In the homogeneous case the weights of all the segments are equal. To simplify the problem we consider the homogeneous case. Each peer stores partial movie after streaming the whole movie. Partial storage is based on segments and each peer stores a subset of the segments. Peers are denoted by P_i and fraction of video stored at peer P_i is denoted by f_i. Each peer determines the value of f_i based on available disk space and outgoing bandwidth. If the consumption rate of the movie is B Mbps and outgoing bandwidth is $\frac{B}{4}$ Mbps then f_i should be $\leq \frac{1}{4}$. On the other hand, f_i should be set in such a way that storing f_i fraction of movie does not exceed the available disk space at the peer.

We assume the following in proposed schemes: peers can join and leave the peer-to-peer network, peers have limited storage and may not be able to store the whole video.

2.1 Uncooperative Schemes

Uncooperative schemes involves no communication between nodes to determine which segments to replicate. Since nodes may join and leave the peer-to-peer network at any time uncooperative schemes are interesting. In addition, uncooperative schemes are simpler.

In uncooperative schemes the peer P_i first determines the value of f_i and the picks a random number seed s_i. Let $rand(s_i, n)$ denote the nth random number generated by seed s_i. We assume that random numbers generated are in the range [0..1]. Peer P_i stores segment j if $rand(s_i, j) <= f_i$. As a result each segment is stored with probability f_i. So, expected number of segments stored is $f_i M$ where M is the number of segments.

When a peer sends a streaming request, each peer P_i responds with the pair (f_i, s_i). The peer needs to make a decision based on the pairs received. The peer chooses a subset of peers to stream the video. Ideally, the subset of peers selected should satisfy two constraints. Every segment should be stored by at least one peer and the set should be as small as possible. However, since storage decision is made probabilistically, it is not possible to guarantee that every segment be stored by at least one peer. Assume k peers given by $\{P_1, ..., P_k\}$. First fragment is not stored in these peers with probability $P_e = \prod_{i=1}^{i=k}(1 - f_i)$. So, no matter how many peers we have, there is a small probability that a fragment may not be available in them. In such cases, we request the missing fragment from the original source. Since source needs to handle too many requests, we want to limit the probability of contacting the source. We have a threshold and select peers in such a way that the expected number of segments that need to be retrieved from the source is less than the threshold.

Peer selection problem can be stated formally as follows:

Peer Selection Problem: *Consider a movie with M segments. Given a set of peers* $\{P_1, P_2, ..., P_N\}$ *with each peer having* (s_i, f_i). *Find the smallest subset* $\{P_1, ..., P_k\}$ *of peers such that* $M \prod_{i=1}^{i=k}(1 - f_i) \leq threshold$.

Peer selection problem can be solved efficiently by sorting the f_i's in decreasing order and by choosing the largest values until $M \prod_{i=1}^{i=k}(1 - f_i) \leq threshold$.

In uncooperative schemes, requesting client broadcasts a message to the peer-to-peer network (limited broadcast with increasing ranges) and receives the pair $((s_i, f_i))$ from each corresponding peer. It solves the peer selection problem and determines a set of peers. By using the information embedded in $((s_i, f_i))$ it can determine which peers store which segments. Peer i stores segment j if $rand(si, j) < f_i$ where $rand(a, b)$ is the bth random number generated with seed a. Control messages in uncooperative scheme are quite short and it is possible to use aggregation techniques to reduce the number of messages.

2.2   Cooperative Schemes

In cooperative schemes, the segments that are stored after streaming the video are chosen based on a global optimization criteria using the utility function. The segments that maximize the utility functions are chosen for storage.

We next discuss the desirable properties of utility function and then propose some functions that meet the properties. Users view the movie from the beginning till the end and it is better to replicate segments that are stored at fewer nodes. As the number of copies of a segment increases, the potential gain from one more copy decreases. Having 4 copies of a segment instead of 3 copies is great. However, there is no big difference in having 200 copies of a segment versus 199 copies of a segment in the network. Utility function is also independent for each movie since a client who streams and views a video can only store that video.

Utility function for movie m is denoted by U_m and utility of a movie is the sum of utilities of all the segments in the network. Utility of segment S_i is denoted by v_i. Therefore, utility function of movie m is given by

$$U_m = \sum_{k=1}^{M} v_k \tag{1}$$

As the number of copies of a segment increases, the utility value should increase but at a much slower rate. We use the following function for v_k.

$$v_k = \sum_{i=1}^{c_k} \frac{1}{i} \tag{2}$$

The *segment vector* $C_m = (c_1, c_2, ..., c_M)$ denotes the number of copies of each segment available in the network for movie m. c_i denotes the number of copies of ith segment available in the network. So, utility value for movie m is

$$U_m = \sum_{k=1}^{M} \sum_{i=1}^{c_a} \frac{1}{i} \tag{3}$$

In cooperative schemes, original source of the movie maintains the segment vector and each peer determines the segments to replicate according to the utility function. The segments that maximize the utility value are chosen for storage. Increasing the number of copies of segment i from c_i to c_{i+1} increases the utility value by $\frac{1}{c_i+1}$. Therefore, to maximize the utility value the segment that needs to be replicated should have the smallest value of c_i and the segment to replicate is determined by the equation $x = argmin_k \frac{1}{c_k}$. If multiple segments are to be replicated then the equation is solved again with updated segment vector C_m.

There are many challenges in implementation of cooperative schemes. The vector C_m needs to be computed and this computation requires input from all the peers who has the movie. When a peer leaves the network the vector C_m needs to be updated. When a node fails the vector C_m will not be accurate. To handle these problems proposed scheme assigns a leader to each movie. This leader maintains C_m and handles update and retrieval requests for C_m. When a node decides to leave the network, it sends a message to the leader. When a node starts a streaming session, it sends a message to the leader indicating its value of f_i and requesting the vector C_m. The leader can compute the segments that the peer will choose for replication by solving the replication equation. The leader updates the vector C_m accordingly.

Each node stores an *local vector* D_m whose entries are 0-1s and indicate whether segment i of movie m is stored by the peer or not. The leader stores the local vectors of all the clients in the system who partially replicate the movie. When a client requests the movie, the leader uses this information to find a subset of peers who can stream the video to the client. The subset of peers has to satisfy two conditions. First, each segment should be stored by at least one peer. Second, the set of peers should be as small as possible to reduce control message overhead and to improve utilization of our system. In proposed scheme, a peer can supply video to a single node at a given time (since f_i determined according to outgoing bandwidth). Therefore, minimizing set of supplying peers is required. Peer selection problem can be stated formally as follows:

Peer Selection Problem: *Given a set of peers $\{P_1, P_2, ..., P_N\}$ with each peer having local vector D_m. Find the smallest subset of peers such that each segment is available by at least one peer.*

Peer selection problem can be reduced to *set cover* problem and is NP-complete. Think of the segments stored at a peer as a subset and the problem is to find the smallest set of subsets that cover the whole set. We used the greedy heuristic given in figure 1 to solve the peer selection problem. In this algorithm X denotes the set of segments $\{1, 2, ..., M\}$ and F denotes a family of sets where the segments stored by each peer is an element of this family. Since this heuristic requires input from all the nodes, the leader solves the peer selection problem. When a node requests a movie, it sends a message to the leader. If the set of active nodes in the system can grant this request, the client and the supplying peers are contacted to inform what they need to do. Supplying peers are then placed on the inactive list for the duration of the streaming session.

The leader stores the local vector received from each client. In addition the leader maintains a status list. So, the amount of space required at the leader is $O(AM)$ where A is the number of nodes currently connected to the peer-to-peer network and partially store the movie, M is the number of segments in the movie. Storage requirement is reasonable and a typical machine can handle hundreds of thousands of clients.

Greedy heuristic of choosing the peer that has the maximum number of unselected segments has an approximation ratio of $H_P = \sum_{i=1}^{P} \frac{1}{i}$ where P is the largest set in F.

Greedy-Set-Cover(X,F)

```
01 U ← X
02 C ← ∅
03 while U ≠ ∅
04        select an S ∈ F that maximizes | S ∩ U |
05        U ← U-S
06        C ← C ∪ {S}
07 return C
```

Fig. 1. Greedy Set Cover Algorithm

This means that number of peers selected by greedy algorithm can be at most H_P times more than the number of peers in optimal solution. In our case the number of segments determines the approximation ratio. With M segments the approximation ratio is $H(M)$.

Since greedy algorithm will be executed whenever a client requests a movie, efficient implementation is crucial. It is possible to implement greedy set cover to run in $O(\sum_{S \in F} |S|)$ time. So, running time is proportional to the total number of segments stored in the network.

If the leader is able to find the set cover for a request, it sends the list of peers in the set cover and their local vectors to the requesting client. Requesting client contacts the peers and streams the video from them. It is possible that a segment is stored at multiple peers in the set cover, in this case the requesting client can pick a peer based on some other criteria such as delay or number of hops.

2.3   Region Based Cooperative Scheme

When the network grows a single leader may not be able to handle all the clients requests. To minimize the load on the leader we divide the network into regions with each region having a regional leader.

Splitting of a region means moving some of the nodes of region R to region R'. This is done only when both the regions R and R' can handle client requests independently otherwise we ignore the idea of splitting. To make the splitting decision we consider the distance between peers and the network conditions. The distance between peers is determined by the number of common segments that exists between the two peers. Since the number of common segments between peers may be large we normalize it by taking value between $a = 0$ and 1. The network conditions can be the delay and bandwidth of the network in consideration and let this value be between $b = 0$ and 1. Thus the cost of edge between peers is $a\alpha + b\beta$ where $\alpha + \beta = 1$, α and β are user defined parameters.

For splitting a region the following challenges are to be addressed.

– When the splitting of a region can be done?
– How to pick a leader for region R'?
– How to create balanced self-sufficient regions?

The splitting algorithm shown in figure 2 takes a region R and the parameters a and b. The Split-Region algorithm can be called if min count is greater than M' otherwise the region is too small to split. Here M' , D' are user defined parameters and min count is the minimum number of copies of fragment i in system. The line 8 selects the leader of region R' by choosing one node at random from the candidate set and line 9 moves the node to region R' from region R making it the leader of R' as it is closer to R'. The algorithm continues to move nodes from region R to region R' until the set cover for R' can be done or the number of nodes currently in R' is less than low-threshold. If the number of nodes in region R' is greater than high-threshold, a balanced split is not obtained so we abort the split test and merge the nodes of region R and R'. The low-threshold and high-threshold are used to obtain balanced self sufficient regions.

Split-Region(R,a,b)
01 p ← leader(R)
02 **for** each i ∈ R
03      $d_{i,p}$ = Compute-Distance(i,p)
04 C ← ∅
05 **for** each i ∈ R
06   **if** $d_{i,p} > D'$
07   C ← C ∪ {node i}
08 q ← Select-Leader(C)
09 R' ← {q}
10 **for** each i ∈ R
11      $d_{i,q}$ = Compute-Distance(i,q)
12   **if** $d_{i,p} > d_{i,q}$
13   R' ← R' ∪ {node i}
14   R ← R − {node i}
15 **if** SET-COVER(R') = False
16   **for** each i ∈ R
17            $d_{i,q}$ = Compute-Distance(i,q)
18   D = Sort $d_{i,q}$ in increasing order
19   **for** each i ∈ D
20   **if** SET-COVER(R') = False *or* num-of-nodes(R') < low-threshold
21   R' ← R' ∪ {node i}
22   R ← R − {node i}
23   **if** num-of-nodes(R') > high-threshold *or* SET-COVER(R) = False
24   Abort Split test
21 return

Fig. 2. Split Region Algorithm

3 Experimental Results

We simulated both cooperative and uncooperative schemes using extensive simulation. Simulation is written using csim. Initially only the source node has the movie and movie requests arrive according to poisson distribution. The simulation is done with three values of $\lambda = 0.001, 0.0001$ and 0.0003. Movie is divided into 100 segments and clients store some of the segments after streaming. The results were based on homogeneous case where all the segments are of equal weight, heterogeneous case is part of future work. 50% of the clients store 10-20 segments and the remaining 50% store 20-50 segments. 20% of the clients who join the network remain in the network till the end of simulation. Since the peers can set their fraction of video stored based on outgoing bandwidth, peers can supply video to at most one client at a given time. Since storing segments involve control overhead in addition to storage overhead, it is not feasible to store a few segments. In simulation, minimum number of segments stored at a node is 10 corresponding to 10% of movie. Similarly, missing a few segments is not feasible since the nodes need to be involved in peer-selection problem. We assume that nodes store at most 50 segments corresponding to 50% of the movie. Movie length is 120 minutes. We have two sets of results. In the first set, after streaming nodes stay in the network till the end of simulation. In the second set, 80% of the nodes stay in the network for 5-24 hours and 20% of nodes stay in the network till the end of the simulation. Simulation length is 1 month.

We use the following metrics to compare the performance of cooperative and uncooperative schemes.

- *min-max count:* Let n_i be the number of copies of segment i in the system. *Min* is given by $\min_{i=1}^{100} n_i$ and *max* is given by $\max_{i=1}^{100} n_i$. Ideally, we want the gap between *min* and *max* to be low.
- *utility value:* Value of utility function. Smooth curves in utility graph are desirable since they correspond to smooth transitions when peers leave the network.
- *number of supplying peers:* Average number of supplying peers involved in streaming sessions. Smaller number of supplying peers are desirable since streaming client needs to manage streaming session with all of them.
- *success-failure count:* Requesting peers resend their request every 5 minutes and leave the network if streaming is not feasible in 20 minutes. *success* denotes the number of streaming sessions successfully completed during the simulation and *failure* denotes the number of nodes that leave the network without streaming.

4 Discussion

The graphs for cooperative and uncooperative schemes are similar when all the nodes stay in the network till the end of simulation. They differ in case of 5-24hrs. So we mainly focus on graphs for 5-24hrs .

Figures 3 and 4 shows the increase in utility as more and more nodes join and the decrease in utility when the nodes leave. This decrease in utility is recovered by new nodes joining the network. In figure 3 uncooperative case between 0 to 5 days there is sudden raise and fall in utility. This is because threshold was initially set to 20 as the number of missing segments will be high. Later when we know that the peers have enough segments we set the threshold to a small value thereby limiting the probability of contacting the source. Min Max values are shown in figure 8 and figure 9. As expected the difference between min and max values are low in case of cooperative whereas in uncooperative, it is large due to the lack of coordination between nodes. Success and failure count shown in figures 5 and 6. Initially the number of streaming sessions is low

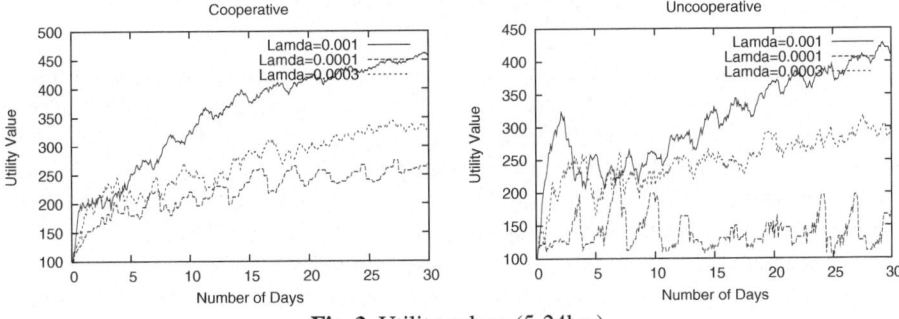

Fig. 3. Utility values (5-24hrs)

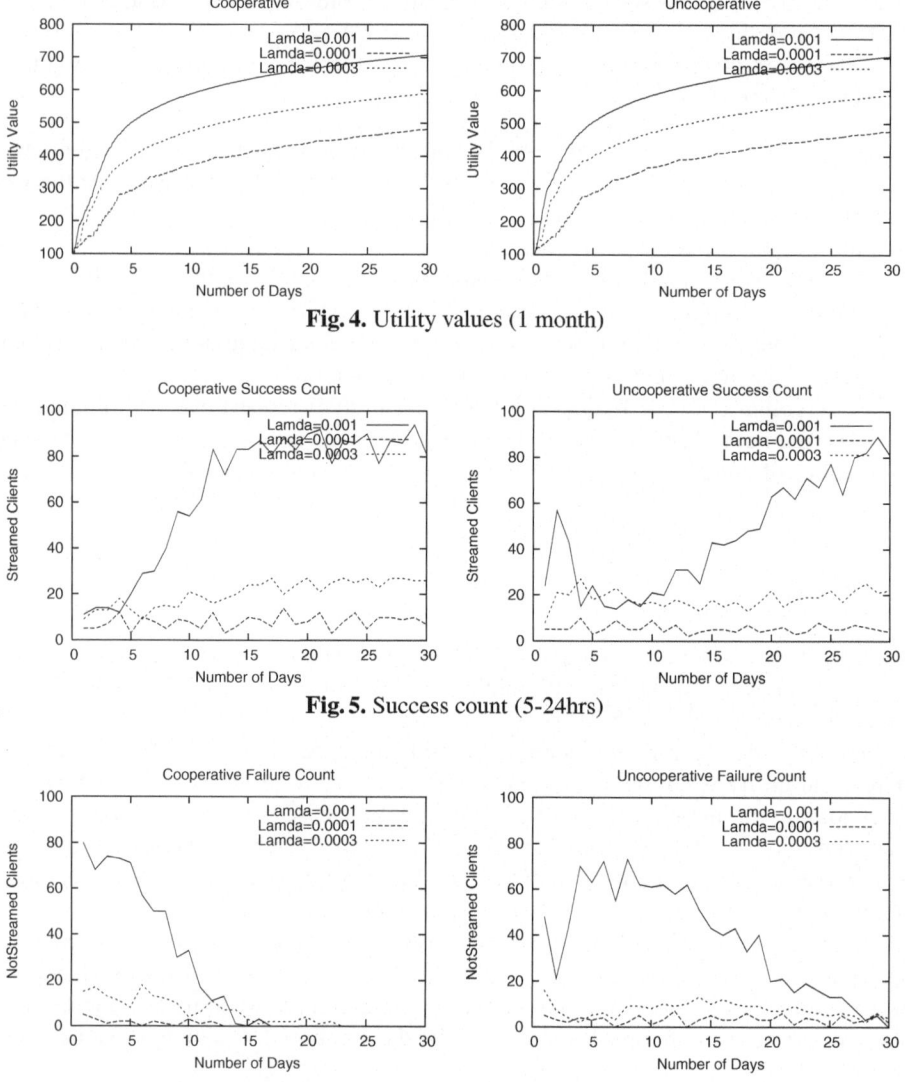

Fig. 4. Utility values (1 month)

Fig. 5. Success count (5-24hrs)

Fig. 6. Failure count (5-24hrs)

since only leader has the movie and many clients leave the network without getting the movie. As content is replicated success count increases and failure count decreases. In case of $\lambda = 0.0001$ and $\lambda = 0.0003$, the success and failure is not that significant since the arrival rate i.e. the rate at which the nodes join is low. By the time the new node join the network the existing nodes might leave and the new node is not able to do the streaming with the available nodes thus increasing the failure rate. In case of $\lambda = 0.001$ the success and the failure rate can be seen more significantly.

The supplying peers graphs shown in figure 7 indicates the average number of peers involved in streaming session. Graph shows sudden raises and falls. This is because

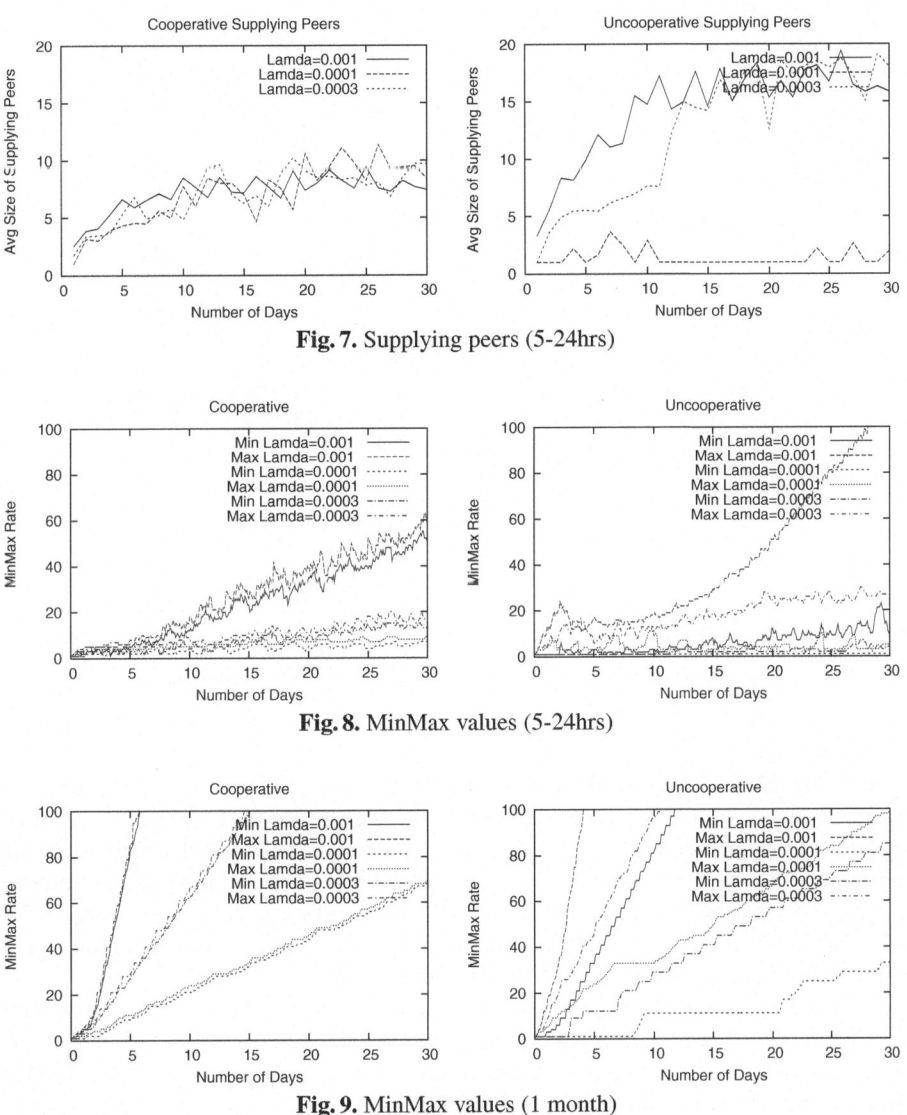

Fig. 7. Supplying peers (5-24hrs)

Fig. 8. MinMax values (5-24hrs)

Fig. 9. MinMax values (1 month)

when a new node joins the network to satisfy its streaming request the peers in the smallest set cover might be busy in streaming session with other nodes so its request is satisfied by the available peers forming a set cover. The peer size graphs shown in figure 10 specifies the average number of peers holding copies of a segment. Based on the network delay, bandwidth client can select the peer with high bandwidth and less delay. Multiple peers having a copy of a segment is 40% in cooperative case whereas in uncooperative it is 80%. This shows uncooperative scheme is better even though its supplying peer size is large. When $\lambda = 0.0001$, this is not true as the arrival rate is low. Most of the incoming clients will be streamed by the leader, since the existing clients may leave the network as their time expires.

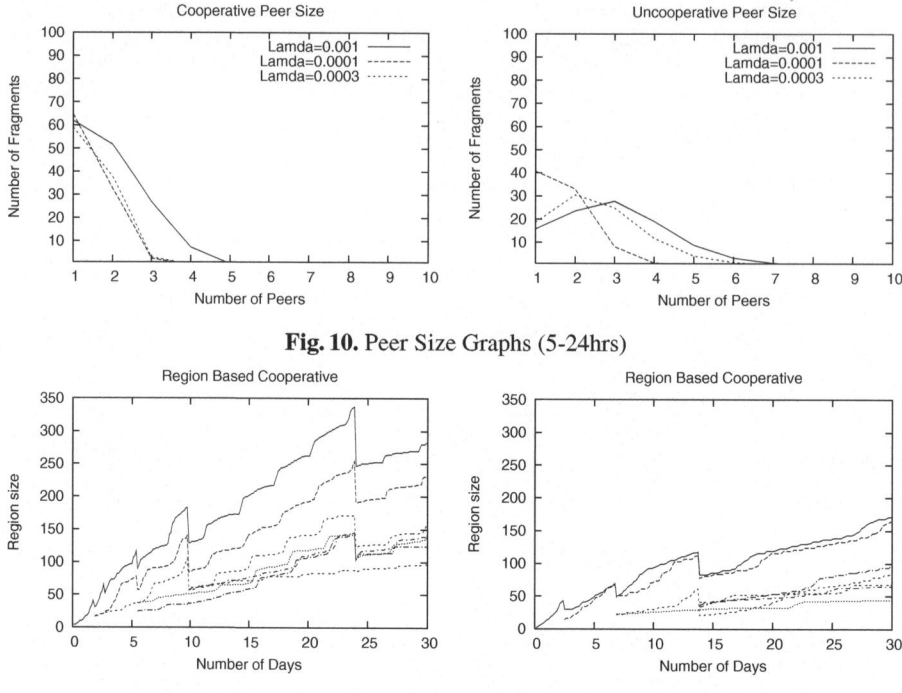

Fig. 10. Peer Size Graphs (5-24hrs)

Fig. 11. Region Graphs

In figure 11 the graph on left shows the region size when $\lambda = 0.001$ and graph on right is for $\lambda = 0.0003$. Each line in the graph corresponds to a region. From the graph we see whenever a region size decreases it indicates a split of that region causing a new region to start. In case of $\lambda = 0.001$, at the end of the simulation we obtained 14 regions with minimum region size of 144 nodes and maximum region size of 282 nodes. Similarly for $\lambda = 0.0003$, we obtained 6 regions with minimum region size of 44 nodes and maximum region size of 171 nodes.

Cooperative schemes perform better than uncooperative schemes in terms of number of streaming sessions that can be supported by the system. However, large scale implementation of cooperative schemes is not feasible since nodes selected for set-cover can be far away from each other. Centralized nature of cooperative schemes is also problematic since failure of leader will render the streaming impossible.

Uncooperative schemes perform reasonably and can be implemented in a distributed way using limited range broadcast on the peer-to-peer network. Having a larger set of supplying peers increases the possibility of more than one peer having a copy of a segment. The decision of which peer to choose can be made based on other decisions such as network delay and the number of hops.

5   Conclusion

In this paper, we investigate partial replication strategies for streaming video over peer-to-peer networks. Each client stores partial video after streaming depending on its available disk space and outgoing bandwidth. We propose cooperative schemes where the replication is done in a way to maximize the utility function and uncooperative shemes where the replication is done independent of what is stored at other nodes. Cooperative schemes perform much better than uncooperative schemes. However, cooperative schemes are more complex and requires execution of greedy set cover algorithm for each arriving request. Uncooperative schemes on the other can be implemented in a simple and distributed way. Future work includes investigation of hybrid schemes that combines the benefits of these two by using regional leaders or a hierarchy.

References

1. Miguel Castro, Peter Druschel, Anne-Marie Kermarrec, Animesh Nandi, Antony Rowston, and Atul Singh. Splitstream: High-bandwidth multicast in cooperative environments. In *SOSP'03*, October 2003.
2. Yi Cui and Klara Nahrstedt. Layered peer-to-peer streaming. In *NOSSDAV 2003*.
3. H. Deshpande, M Bavea, and H. Garcia-Mollina. Streaming live media over peers. Technical report, Stanford Database Group Technical Report (2002-21).
4. Mohamed Hefeeda, Ahsan Habib, Boyan Botev, Dongyan Xu, and Bharat Bhargava. Promise: Peer-to-peer media streaming using collectcast. In *ACM Multimedia 2003*.
5. Xuxian Jiang, Yu Dong, Dongyan Xu, and Bharat Bhargava. Gnustream: A p2p media streaming system prototype. In *IEEE International Conference on Multimedia and Expo (ICME 2003)*, 2003.
6. T. P. Nguyen and A Zakhor. Distributed video streaming over internet. In *SPIE/ACM MMCN 2002*.
7. Thinh Nguyen and Avideh Zakhor. Distributed video streaming with forward error correction. In *Packetvideo Workshop 2002*.
8. V.N. Padmanabhan, H. Wang, P. Chou, and K. Sripanidkulchai. Distributed streaming media content using cooperative networking. In *NOSSDAV 2002*.
9. S. Ratnasamy, P. Francis, M. Handley, R. Karp, and S. Shenker. A scalable content addressable network. In *ACM SIGCOMM*, August 2001.
10. Antony Rowstron and Peter Druschel. Pastry: Scalable, decentralized object location, and routing for large-scale peer-to-peer systems. In *IFIP/ACM International Conference on Distributed Systems Platforms (Middleware)*, pages 329–350, 2001.
11. I. Stoica, R. Morris, D. Karger, F. Kaashoek, and Balakrishnan H. Chord: A scalable peer-to-peer lookup service for internet applications. In *ACM SIGCOMM*, August 2001.
12. Duc Tran, Kien Hua, and Tai Do. A peer-to-peer architecture for media streaming. *Journal in Selected Areas in Communications, Special Issue on Advances in Service Overlay Networks*, 22(1):121–133, January 2004.
13. Dongya Xu, Heung-Keung Chai, Rosenberg Catherine, and Sunil Kulkarni. Analysis of a hybrid architecture for cost-effective streaming media. In *SPIE/ACM Conference on Multimedia Computing and Networking (MMCN 2003)*.
14. Dongyan Xu, Mohamed Hefeeda, Susanne Hambrusch, and Bharat Bhargava. On peer-to-peer media streaming. In *IEEE International Conference on Distributed Computing Systems (ICDCS 2002)*, July 2002.

Network-Adaptive QoS Control for Relative Service Differentiation-Aware Video Streaming

Gooyoun Hwang[1], Jitae Shin[2], and JongWon Kim[1]

[1] Networked Media Lab., Department of Information and Communications,
Gwangju Institute of Science and Technology (GIST), Gwangju, 500-712, Korea
{gyhwang, jongwon}@netmedia.gist.ac.kr
[2] School of Information and Communication Engineering,
Sungkyunkwan Univ., Suwon, 440-746, Korea
jtshin@ece.skku.ac.kr

Abstract. Emerging networked multimedia applications in the Internet require special supports from the underlying network such as real-time treatment, guaranteed service, and different levels of network service quality. However, the current Internet having the same-service-for-all paradigm is not suitable for these multimedia communications. In this paper, firstly we introduce a scalable and adaptive quality of service (QoS) mapping framework over the differentiated services (DiffServ, or DS) network. The framework is composed of the functionalities of proactive and reactive QoS mapping controls to provide reliable and consistent end-to-end service guarantee. On this framework, we propose a network-adaptive QoS control to have a feedback of instantaneous network fluctuation. The main idea of our proposal is to employ explicit congestion notification (ECN) mechanism in conjunction with the proactive QoS mapping control at the ingress of a DiffServ domain. It is possible not only that the status of network classes is notified to the end-host applications but also that a reactive QoS adjustment is triggered at the ingress side. Our simulation results illustrate how to enhance the QoS performance of streaming video in the under-provisioned network.

1 Introduction

Delivering networked multimedia services over the Internet, such as IP telephony, video-conferencing, and online TV broadcast, demand very stringent level of quality of service (QoS) guarantee. However, the current IP Internet is based on a simple service commitment, so called best-effort (BE) service, thus lacking the ability to support the QoS requirement from the multimedia applications. The differentiated services (DiffServ, or DS) model specified by the Internet Engineering Task Force (IETF) has been proposed as a more scalable and manageable architecture for network QoS provisioning [1]. In this model, resources are allocated differently not for individual packet flows but for aggregated traffic flows based on a set of bits (i.e., DSCP) and two other service models, premium service (PS) and assured service (AS), are currently defined to provide different level of forwarding assurance for IP packets at each node [1,3,4]. The PS

J. Dalmau and G. Hasegawa (Eds.): MMNS 2005, LNCS 3754, pp. 326–337, 2005.

is designed to provide a low-loss, low-latency, and assured bandwidth service (i.e., absolute service differentiation) [4]. It requires an admission control to prevent resource starvation of other service classes and thus trades off the flexibility for more guarantees. In contrast, the assured service provides a relative service differentiation among DS classes, in the sense that high-priority classes receives a better (or at least not worse) service than low-priority ones [3]. Since most of recent multimedia applications, which include streaming video as a special example, have become more and more resilient to occasional packet loss and delay fluctuation, the assured service of DiffServ networks seems a more attractive choice due to its simplicity and flexibility.

However, since the assured service only provides qualitative differentiation between a number of classes, service guarantee is limited. Recently, some research works have tried to strengthen the service guarantees that can be provided within the context of the relative service differentiation without sacrificing its scalability and simplicity. Probably the best-known approach is the proportional differentiated services (PDS) model [6,8], which quantifies the difference in the service by making the ratios of delays or loss rates of different classes roughly constant. This model can allow the network operator to control the quality spacing between a number of classes independent of the class load variations. Thus, we can focus on the PDS model for relative service differentiation-aware video streaming.

Within the DiffServ architecture, various types of video delivery scenarios have been proposed to integrate applications and networks for enhanced media streaming [5,7,10]. One possible scenario is to adaptively combine application requirements into appropriate network resource parameters such as end-to-end delay, jitter, packet loss, and bandwidth. Accordingly, an adaptive QoS mapping[1] mechanism depending on the network situation is required to support the end-to-end QoS guarantee dynamically to end systems and improve the network utilization. From this point of view, we presents a scalable and adaptive QoS mapping-control (shortly, control) framework, which consists of proactive QoS control and reactive QoS control in network class/flow-based granularity, over the DiffServ domain for service differentiation-aware video streaming. The QoS control framework is strongly coupled with a pricing or policy infrastructure of the corresponding domain to make higher classes more costly than lower ones. Given a certain cost constraint, the users/applications are supposed to find an optimal way based on the contracted QoS level.

Meanwhile, unstable network service situations caused by instantaneous class load fluctuations still occur even though the resource provisioning policy of underlying network is strictly managed. The unstable situations obstruct video applications to achieve their desired service requirements persistently. Since the end-to-end QoS perceived by applications mainly depend on the current network load condition, video applications should response to this fluctuation in

---

[1] The issue of *QoS mapping* occurs when we map prioritized and classified groups of some applications(or users or flows) based on their importance into different DS levels or network classes.

a proper way. Furthermore, the adjustment of proactive QoS control is needed when a video receiver is not satisfied with the received quality compared to its expectation. For these reasons, a network-adaptive QoS control is proposed to enhance relative service differentiation-aware video streaming in this paper. With the help of network feedback, the end-host video application can recognize the status of network classes and can now react in advance. Basically, the provided feedback information is incorporating latest status of underlying routers. By leveraging the end-to-end feedback (i.e., in tie with the required congestion control), the feedback is relayed to the sender in a similar way as the explicit congestion notification (ECN) [2]. The network feedback-based QoS control triggers the QoS mapping adjustment at the ingress of DiffServ networks. NS 2-based network simulation is performed to demonstrate the enhanced performance of the proposed QoS mapping control framework (i.e., more efficient and adaptive to network variation).

The remainder of this paper is organized as follows. Section 2 presents a scalable and adaptive QoS mapping framework as our future direction. In section 3, we propose the network-adaptive control to enhance relative differentiation-aware video streaming. Various sets of performance evaluation through computer simulations are presented in section 4. Finally, section 5 concludes this paper.

2   Scalable and Adaptive QoS Mapping Framework over the DiffServ Network

To provide reliable and effective end-to-end video streaming, this section presents a scalable and adaptive QoS mapping framework over the DiffServ networks. As illustrated in Fig. 1, the proposed QoS mapping framework can be divided into three QoS controls : (1) proactive QoS control for aggregated flows at the ingress point of the network, (2) reactive edge-to-edge QoS control between the borders of the network (e.g., edge router and/or media gateway), and (3) reactive

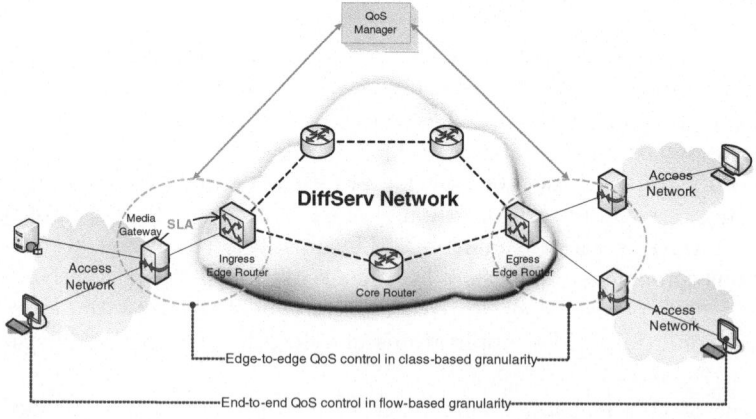

Fig. 1. Overview of scalable and adaptive QoS mapping framework

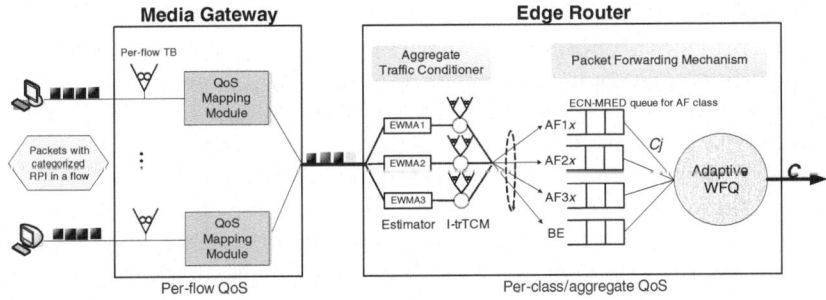

Fig. 2. Overall structures of media gateway and edge router

end-to-end QoS control. The former two controls are based on network-class QoS, while the last reactive control is based on flow QoS as a complementary role and fine-tuned for end-to-end QoS provisioning. A key assumption in this architecture is that if a user (or application) has absolute QoS requirements, he/she has to dynamically choose a class in which the observed QoS is acceptable. If the user is also interested in minimizing the cost of the session, he would choose the least expensive or minimum class that is acceptable.

For the end-to-end video streaming, sources within the access network send videos to the corresponding clients. The access network subscribes to DS services, and traffic is delivered to the clients through the DS domain. The access network has service level agreements (SLAs) [1] with the DS domain. In this framework, the video applications at the source assign a relative priority-based index (RPI) to each packet in terms of loss probability and delay as studied in [7] so that each packet can reflect its influence to the end-to-end video quality. The source then furnishes each packet with this prioritization information for a special edge node called media gateway (MG)[2] as shown in Fig. 2. Thus, the video streams from the sources are merged at the MG. In order to prevent the sources from violating their SLAs and protect resources from a selfish source, the MG exercises the traffic shaping on a per-flow basis through the token buckets (TBs) assigned for individual flows, as seen in Fig. 2. The packets violating this agreement are assigned with the lowest DS class (i.e., best-effort class).

The main function of the MG is to make a cost-efficient coordination between the prioritized packets (or flows) and the DS service classes, which we call *QoS mapping*. For the optimal QoS mapping of the relative prioritized packet on to the DS level, we just refer [7] and mention briefly due to page limitation. That is, for packets conforming to the TB, the MG assigns to each packet a DiffServ codepoint (DSCP) on the basis of the packet's RPI. Then, the MG forwards the packet streams to the edge router (ER) at the ingress of the DS network. The ER is composed of an aggregate traffic conditioner (ATC) and a packet forwarding mechanism [9]. The ATC is employed to observe the traffic

---

[2] The MG can be existed as an independent entity or combined with the edge router (ER) if necessary. The deployment issue of the MG is not fully investigated in this work yet.

conditioning agreement (TCA) with the DS domain and the packet forward mechanism provides proportionally relative QoS spacing between network service classes by using a joint buffer management (e.g., multiple random early detection (RED)) and a dynamic scheduler (e.g., adaptive WFQ). In the QoS mapping framework, the proactive QoS control is realized as discussed.

However, the network QoS of a DS domain may be time-varying due to traffic load fluctuation. Thus, the egress MG monitors the QoS performance of each class and notifies the ingress MG about the observed QoS level through a feedback channel or a QoS manager. Based on this feedback, the ingress MG decides whether to stay in the same class or switch to the higher or lower class in order to satisfy the specified QoS performance of a class in the SLA. In this paper, we put aside the reactive edge-to-edge QoS control out of scope (but under our further investigation). Finally, a proper network-aware feedback control (i.e., reactive flow-based QoS control), which can give the applications a guidance of network status, enables the fine-tuned refinement on top of coarse proactive QoS control. For this, a network-adaptive QoS control will be proposed in next section.

3   Proposed Network-Adaptive QoS Control

The intermediate routers in the DS domain have a better understanding of dynamic network fluctuation. Thus, in our opinion, a proper combination of congestion signalling from network and source reaction will be an effective solution to the instantaneous network fluctuation in the Internet. A feedback mechanism encompassing both network and end-systems can contribute to enhance the performance of video applications. Explicit congestion notification (ECN) for IP routers [2] has been proposed as a mean of giving more direct feedbacks of congestion information back to end-systems. By marking packets, the ECN does

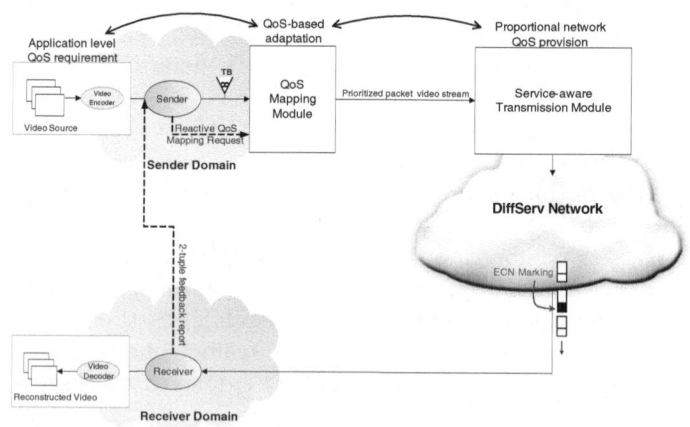

Fig. 3. Overview of network-adaptive QoS control

not waste the network bandwidth used to forward packets and detects incipient congestion in the network. Many researches have accomplished active queue management, e.g., RED or RED variants, with and without ECN support even in TCP networks. It is also possible for media applications using UDP protocol to react to ECN marks. This motivates us to design a network feedback-based

ECN marking at the routers

1. When a DS class queue of ECN-MRED router experiences congestion, the router sets the CE bit to indicate the onset of congestion to the end nodes.

Receiving end-system

1. Upon the receipt of a ECN-marked packet, the receiver checks its DS class $\tilde{q}$ and computes $\overline{C}_{recv}^{f}$ at that time.
2. Send a 2-tuple $\{\tilde{q}, \overline{C}_{recv}^{f}\}$ feedback information to the MG.

Reaction of the MG for reactive QoS control

1. Upon the receipt of a feedback report, the MG regards $\tilde{q}$ as a congested class and compares $\overline{C}_{recv}^{f}$ with $\overline{C}_{send}^{f}$.
2. The MG adjusts the mapping of source category k to DS level q based on the above comparison. That is, k involved in the expected congestion class is re-mapped to higher non-congested classes, for $\overline{C}_{recv}^{f} \leq \overline{C}_{send}^{f}$. Otherwise, k is reallocated to lower non-congested ones.
   - DS level: Let q be a DS level, where $1 \leq q \leq Q$ with the increasing order of network service quality and Q is the total number of DS levels.
   - RPI partitioning : Let $R_q^k(i)$ be a partition i among the RPI k category and be assigned into DS level q. Each k category has equal number of packets initially and is sorted in an increasing order, that is, $1 \leq k \leq K$, where K is the category with highest RPI values. Generally, the packets within the same k could be assigned into different q levels.
   - Proactive mapping: Each packet, whose RPI is k ($k \in R_q$), is mapped to q in order to meet the requested $\overline{C}_{send}^{f}$.
   - Reactive mapping: When a congestion feedback, i.e., ECN, from a class $\tilde{q}$ is received, $R_q^k(i)$ is distributed into $S_q(t)$ subset, where $S_q(t)$ is the number of non-congested DS levels at time t and $1 \leq j \leq S_q(t)$, which are higher levels than the level q for $\overline{C}_{recv}^{f} \leq \overline{C}_{send}^{f}$. Then, the packets belonged to $R_q^k(i)$ are re-mapped to DS level j.
3. This reactive control is operated in time of $[t_{ACK}, t_{ACK} + \Delta]$, where t_{ACK} and Δ denote the times of receiving feedback packet and a certain time interval, respectively.
   - Receiving a congestion feedback: The MG sets Δ to 0.1 (sec) and performs the reactive mapping during Δ.
   - Monitoring congestion: After the expiration of Δ, the MG returns back to the normal state and observes a congestion feedback during $2RTT$.
   - Increasing Δ: If a congestion feedback is received again within $2RTT$, the MG increases $\Delta = 2\Delta$ and goes to the reactive control state. Otherwise, $\Delta = 0.1$.

QoS control with the extension of ECN. The major idea of our feedback control is employing ECN mechanism in conjunction with the proactive QoS control at the ingress of a DiffServ domain. It is possible that not only the congestion status of network class is notified to the end-host video applications but also the reactive QoS mapping control is triggered in a faster manner.

Fig. 3 shows the outline of proposed network-adaptive QoS control on top of the scalable and adaptive QoS mapping framework. Routers in the DS domain are assumed to be ECN-enabled and equipped with multiple RED (MRED) queues. The CE (congestion experienced) bit on incoming packets is set when a DS class queue enters into an unstable state.

On the other hand, the ECN-aware receiver monitors the CE bit on each arrived i-th packet of a flow and calculates the received average cost of a flow, $\overline{C}^f_{recv}$, using the following equation.

$$\overline{C}^f_{recv} = \frac{\sum_{i=1}^{N^f} C_q(i)}{N^f}, \tag{1}$$

where N^f is total received packet numbers of flow f and $C_q(i)$ is unit cost of DS level q, which i-th packet is mapped to, predefined by the SLA. This observed value is considered as a barometer to interpret the degree of service degradation which the receiver experiences. When a ECN-marked packet is arrived, the receiver immediately sends a report of its DS level q and the average cost $\overline{C}^f_{recv}$ to the MG through the corresponding sender. Hence, the MG examines the feedback information and triggers the reactive QoS mapping control. The MG considers the DS level q of the report as a congested class and compares the received average cost $\overline{C}^f_{recv}$ with the requested average payment $\overline{C}^f_{send}$[3]. Then, on the basis of the feedback information, the categorized packet k belonging to the congested class is reassigned to non-congested classes appropriately. The overall algorithm of this feedback control is summarized in the box.

4   Simulation Results

In this section, we will demonstrate the performance evaluation to compare the two types of QoS mapping control, i.e., the proactive class-based QoS control (PQ-only) and our network feedback-based QoS control (PQ-NBF, that is PQ-only plus reactive flow-based QoS control). The overall simulation setup is illustrated in Fig. 4. The standard-based H.263+ encoding/decoding and the NS-2 network simulator are used to evaluate the end-to-end video performance.

While H.263+ encoder encodes video, mean-square-error (MSE) value of each group of block (GOB) is calculated and stored as a data file. Since each GOB is packetized into a separate packet in the simulation, priority will be assigned to each packet according to the relative loss importance of payload. Error patterns

---

[3] $\overline{C}^f_{send}$ is computed by the equation (1) when video packets of a flow are initially sent.

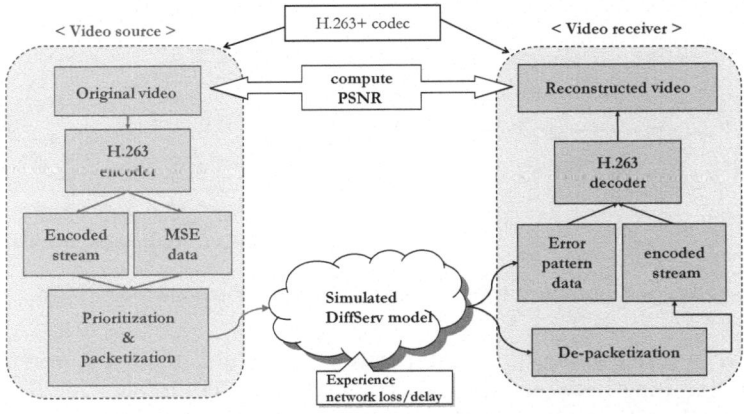

Fig. 4. Overall simulation diagram for H.263+ streaming video over a simulated Diff-Serv network

generated from results by the NS-2 simulations are used to decide whether the packet is lost or not. Then, at the receiver side, encoded bitstream is decoded with the error pattern file. Consequently, peak signal to noise ratio (PSNR) between original and reconstructed video is calculated to quantify how much video quality is degraded by the packet loss during transmission. The PSNR is computed as

$$PSNR_{n_{th}} = 10 \cdot log_{10} \frac{255^2}{\sum_{i \in frame} MSE_{(n,i)}} \tag{2}$$

where

$$MSE_{(n,i)} = \frac{1}{N} \sum_{n \in video} |\hat{R}_n^i(x,y) - R_n(x,y)|^2 \tag{3}$$

$MSE_{(n,i)}$ is the mean square error of n_{th} frame when i_{th} packet is lost. Using (x,y) as a 2-D coordinate of pixel in a frame, $\hat{R}_n^i(x,y)$ and $R_n(x,y)$ are the reconstructed n_{th} frames when i_{th} packet is lost and kept, respectively.

Fig. 5(a) shows the simplified simulation topology model, which is used to generate underlying network dynamics. One test video source and several background traffic sources are connected to the DS domain through the MG and communicate with one of different destination nodes. The link between the ER and the core router(CR) is the bottleneck link with a capacity of 3Mbps, where the video flow competes with other background UDP flows. In order to support the relative service differentiation, we assume that the DS domain provides three assured forwarding (AF) classes and that each class queue has three drop precedences [3]. That is, the DS level order from high to low is $\{AF_{11}, AF_{12}, AF_{13}; AF_{21}, AF_{22}, AF_{23}; AF_{31}, AF_{32}, AF_{33}; BE\}$. On the other hand, a video source (S_0) in Fig. 5(a) transmits a video stream from the video trace (*Foreman* sequence) with RPI. In the simulations, we use a reference QoS mapping for the video flow as follows: $k=0\sim1 \rightarrow BE$, $k=2\sim5\rightarrow AF_{32}$, $k=6\sim9\rightarrow AF_{31}$, $k=10\sim13\rightarrow AF_{22}$, $k=14\sim16\rightarrow AF_{21}$, $k=17\sim18\rightarrow AF_{12}$, and $k=19\rightarrow AF_{11}$, re-

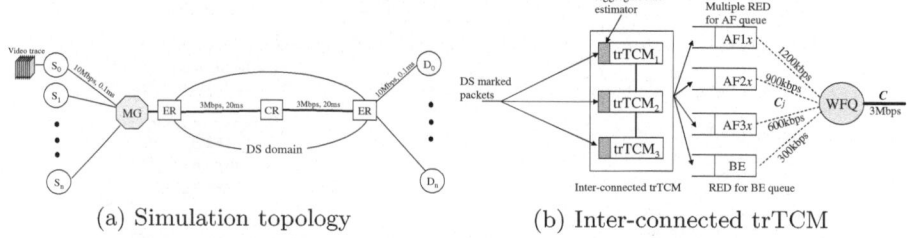

(a) Simulation topology   (b) Inter-connected trTCM

Fig. 5. Simulation topology model and inter-connected trTCM

spectively. In order to get a fair comparison, we do not differently use the reference QoS mapping between categorized packets and DS levels.

As described in Section 2, the ER is responsible for realizing the specialized traffic managements. An extended version of two-rate three-color-maker (trTCM), so called inter-connected trTCM, is adopted to monitor and mark all incoming traffics based on the TCA of SLA. The inter-connected trTCM measures the aggregated ingress rate for each class j. If the aggregated rate reaches the maximum assigned rate C_j for each class queue as presented in Fig. 5(b), the incoming packets into this queue are handed over randomly. Please refer [9] for the detailed description of the inter-connected trTCM. Queueing with MRED and WFQ, also shown in Fig. 5(b), is applied for the drop precedence of queue management and link sharing of scheduler. For our simulations, the routers in the DS domain use the MRED with the values of [50, 70, 0.01] for AF_{x1}, [30, 50, 0.02] for AF_{x2}, and [10, 30, 0.1] for AF_{x3}. Note that the notation $[x, y, z]$ represents minimum threshold, maximum threshold, and maximum drop probability, respectively, of the RED queue.

The main objective of the experiments is to investigate the effectiveness of our network feedback-based control. With this network-application feedback control mechanism, it is expected that the video applications can manage their flows more effectively, thereby achieving an enhanced QoS performance. In order to verify this expectation, each QoS control is simulated in different runs under the same network load conditions. To make a severe congestion period, the sending rates of AF_{2x} sources and AF_{3x} sources are adjusted in runtime from 10 to 20 (sec) alternately so that it corresponds to total provision level of 110%. For the sake of simplicity, the range of unit cost per packet in PQ-NBF is 9 to 0 and is associated with the same order of DS level.

Table 1. The end-to-end performance results of the QoS mapping controls

QoS mapping controls	End-to-end QoS Parameters			
	Achieved throughput (kbps)	Average loss rate (%)	Average delay (msec)	Average PSNR (dB)
PQ-only	391.446	7.672	73.608	29.797
PQ-NBF	406.518	1.387	61.727	33.378

Table 1 presents the end-to-end performance results of two QoS controls, i.e., PQ-only and PQ-NBF, in terms of achieved throughput, average loss rate, and average delay. It represents that the proposed feedback control effectively responses to the network congestion and has competitive advantage for video streaming. Based on the performance results of the achieved throughput and average packet loss rate, the PQ-NBF can achieve better resource utilization than the PQ-only. Furthermore, the delay and jitter performance can be improved significantly under the PQ-NBF, as shown in Fig. 6. This result is quite desirable because video clients feel much annoyed when the video packet does not arrive on time. Recall that the congestion period in the simulation starts at run time 10 sec. Additionally, the PQ-only cannot achieve better performance than the PQ-NBF. It means that a suitable feedback mechanism can assist video applications to adapt dynamically to underlying network and to stabilize the end-to-end QoS within an acceptable range.

Finally, to examine the perceptual quality of the H.263+ video, we play out the decoded video sequence at the receiver and measure the PSNR as an

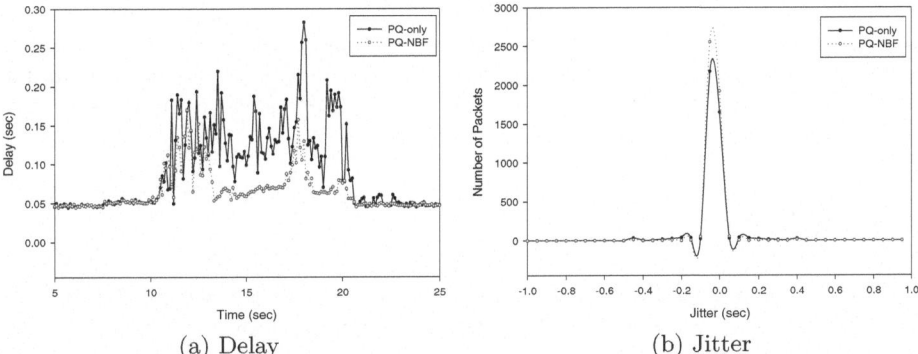

(a) Delay   (b) Jitter

Fig. 6. Performance comparison of the controls in terms of average delay and jitter

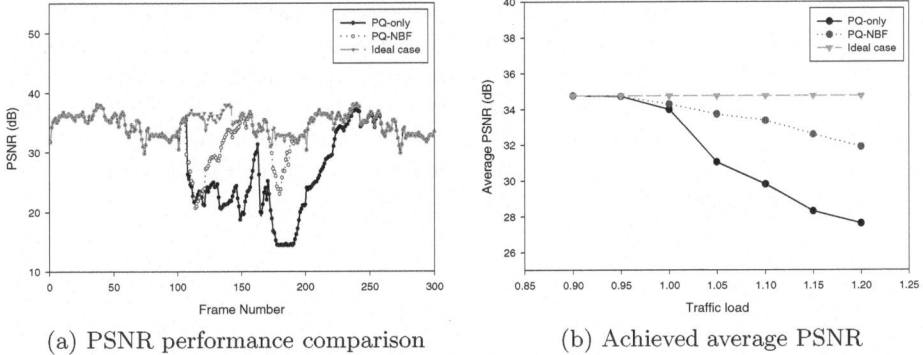

(a) PSNR performance comparison   (b) Achieved average PSNR

Fig. 7. PSNR performance comparison at 110% network load level and achieved average PSNR at different traffic loads

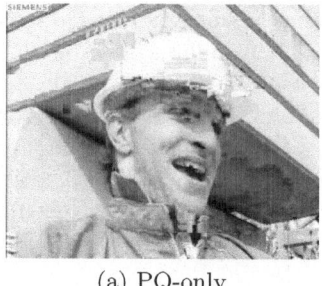
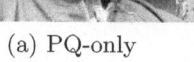

(a) PQ-only

(b) PQ-NBF

Fig. 8. Video quality comparison of a sample frame of the *Foreman* sequence at 110% network load level

objective quality metric, which calculates the difference between the original source video sequence and the received video sequence. Note that the average original PSNR for the video trace is about 34.76 *dB* (i.e., ideal case). Fig. 7(a) and Fig. 7(b) present PSNR performance comparison of different QoS controls and achieved average PNSR at different traffic loads . The objective PSNR quality measure of the PQ-NBF is better than that of the PQ-only over various under-provisioned situations. Also, the corresponding snap shots of a decoded video frame are shown in Fig. 8(a) and Fig. 8(b). The visual quality under the PQ-NBF can outperform in the average or instance sense over time-varying network load conditions.

5   Conclusion

In order to provide reliable and consistent end-to-end service guarantee, we present a scalable and adaptive QoS mapping framework over the DiffServ networks. The framework is composed of the functionalities of proactive QoS control and reactive QoS control. We investigate mainly network-adaptive reactive QoS control to obtain the QoS enhancement of a video streaming by proposing a network feedback mechanism on top of proactive class-based QoS control. The key point of this feedback control is interacting between network and end systems using the ECN mechanism. Through simulation experiments with video trace, we show that the proposed QoS control improves the quality of video streaming significantly in a DiffServ network. Future work would include the reactive edge-to-edge QoS control between network border entities to take care of the end-to-end video streaming over multiple DiffServ domains.

Acknowledgment

This work was supported in part by Korea Ministry of Education through the BK21 Program and in part by the Korea Institute of Industrial Technology Evaluation and Planning (ITEP) through the Incheon IT Promotion Agency.

References

1. S. Blake, D. Black, M. Carlson, E. Davies, Z. Wang, and W. Weiss, "An architecture for differentiated services,", IETF RFC 2475, Dec. 1998.
2. K. K. Ramakrishnan and S. Floyd, "A proposal to add explicit congestion notification (ECN) to IP,", IETF RFC 2481, Jan. 1999.
3. J. Heinanen, F. Baker, W. Weiss, and J. Wroclawski, "Assured forwarding PHB group,", IETF RFC 2597, June 1999.
4. K. Nichols, V. Jacobson, and L. Zhang, "A two-bit differentiated servicesarchitecture for the Internet,", IETF RFC 2638, July 1999.
5. Y. T. Hou, D. Wu, B. Li, T. Hamada, I. Ahmad, and H. J. Chao, "A differentiated services architecture for multimedia streaming in next generation Internet," *Computer Networks*, vol. 32, pp. 185-209, Feb. 2000.
6. C. Dovrolis, D. Stiliadis, and Parmesh Ramanathan, "Proportional Differentiated Services, Part II: Loss Rate Differentiation and Packet Dropping," in *Proc. of International Workshop on Quality of Service (IWQoS)*, Pittsburgh PA, June 2000.
7. J. Shin, J. Kim, and C.-C. J. Kuo, "Quality-of-Service mapping mechanism for packet video in differentiated services network," *IEEE Transaction on Multimedia*, vol. 3, no. 2, pp. 219-231, June 2001.
8. C. Dovrolis, D. Stiliadis, and P. Ramanathan, "Proportional differentiated services: delay differentiation and packet scheduling," *IEEE/ACM Transactions on Networking*, vol.10, no. 1, pp. 12-26, Feb. 2002.
9. J. Shin, "An analysis of aggregated traffic marking for multi-service networks," *IEICE Transactions on communications*, vol. E86-B, no.2, pp. 682-689, Feb. 2003.
10. S-R. Kang, Y. Zhang, M. Dai, and D. Loguinov, "Multi-layer active queue management and congestion control for scalable video streaming," in *Proc. IEEE ICDCS*, Mar. 2004.

QoS Management in Fixed Broadband Residential Gateways

C. Guerrero, J. Garcia, F. Valera, and A. Azcorra

University Carlos III of Madrid, Telematic Engineering Department,
Avda. de la Universidad, 30, E-28911 Leganés, Spain
{guerrero, jgr, fvalera, azcorra}@it.uc3m.es

Abstract. QoS management is nowadays a mandatory feature in current broadband residential gateways developments. The interconnection between different QoS domains has to be treated into different steps in order to provide a reliable end-to-end QoS solution. The scenario analyzed in this paper is the mapping between QoS requirements in residential users connected to a broadband access network across a multiservice broadband access gateway. Different approaches to provide QoS in the access network are discussed as well as their impact in the design of a residential gateway. An architecture of a gateway based on IMS (IP Multimedia Subsystem) as SIP-based signaling domain for multimedia services is presented with the corresponding adaptation to a broadband fixed access scenario according to Next Generation Networks (NGN) standardization. Finally, the implementation of a prototype of the QoS-enabled gateway, based on the Click! modular router [1], is described to demonstrate end-to-end QoS provisioning for multimedia services. This prototype allows us the demonstration of (1) an innovative way of extending gateway device functionalities using Click! and (2) the feasibility of residential gateway architecture proposed. The work presented in this paper has been developed within the framework of the 6th Framework Programme IST MUSE [2] project.

Keywords: NGN, SIP, IMS, fixed broadband, access network, residential gateway.

1 Introduction

Next Generation Networks (NGN) are considered multiservice networks based on packet switching technology, and basically using the IP protocol as the only available technology to provide end to end connectivity. During these last years the first elements for NGN networks have emerged: the 3GPP Release 6 has defined with the IP Multimedia Subsystem IMS [3] a first instantiation of the NGN architecture in the mobile field, which will be detailed in next releases. Another important example of a NGN architecture may be found in the scenario of a multiservice broadband fixed access network where the IST MUSE European project [2] is focused on.

The 3GPP IMS is rapidly becoming the de facto standard for real-time multimedia communications services. Although the IMS was originally specified for 3G generation mobile networks, it also provides excellent service deployment

J. Dalmau and G. Hasegawa (Eds.): MMNS 2005, LNCS 3754, pp. 338–349, 2005.

architecture for any fixed or wireless network, and all IP-based networks such as WiFi, corporate enterprise networks, residential LANs or the public Internet. IMS standard define open interfaces for session management, access control, mobility management, service control and billing. The use of SIP [4] as the main signaling protocol in IMS allows independent software developers to leverage a broad range of third party applications servers, media servers and SIP-enabled end user devices to create next generation services. There are many experiences of implementing IMS in mobile environments, but this work considers a contribution in using IMS principles and architecture in a fixed broadband access scenario, where some considerations and redesigns have to be performed in order to adapt the IMS model to this new scenario. Recently, ETSI-TISPAN [5] standardization work is focused on migrating IMS to a fixed access network scenario in the context of an overall NGN architecture. MUSE project is studying the possibility of using IMS adaptation from TISPAN standardization as an alternative for QoS provisioning model in the access network.

It is important not to forget the QoS viewpoint of the end-users. Their assumed business role is to pay for a certain service or application subscription (i.e. VoIP, video on demand or Internet browsing) instead of paying for a class of service (always on with guaranteed bandwidth rate). The way of charging them is expecting to be based on services usage instead of network usage and in order to allow this, resource availability has to be checked for every service application request, and not only during the subscription. Several models, considering key aspects like the entity that requests QoS needs or how the resources are provided and charged, are considered and discussed in section 2 that describes the standardization work in fixed broadband access networks in the framework of NGN.

These assumptions let us present in section 3 an innovative scenario with the deployment of an IMS infrastructure in a fixed broadband access network by mainly focusing on the residential gateway (RGW) that interconnects the residential end-users to the corresponding service providers. Finally, a prototype of this RGW lets us demonstrate the feasibility of supporting some QoS scenarios using an innovative Click! modular router platform approach. The conclusions of this experience of prototyping a RGW architecture based on a still open standardization process are presented in conjunction with future work in these topics.

2 Standardization in Fixed Broadband Access Networks

The main standardization body that is contributing to the definition and dissemination of today and future telecommunications networks for broadband fixed and mobile access is the ETSI-TISPAN in the framework of NGN, trying to facilitate the convergence of network and services supporting both users and services nomadism and mobility. NGN enable different business models across access, core network and service domain. SIP will be the call and control session protocol and 3GPP Release 6 IMS will be the base for NGN IMS. It enables any IP access to Core IMS and other subsystems from different domains (mobile, home and corporate). Internetworking towards circuit switched voice traditional services is considered too. Service providers use NGN architecture to offer real-time and non real-time communications services between peer-to-peer or client-server configurations.

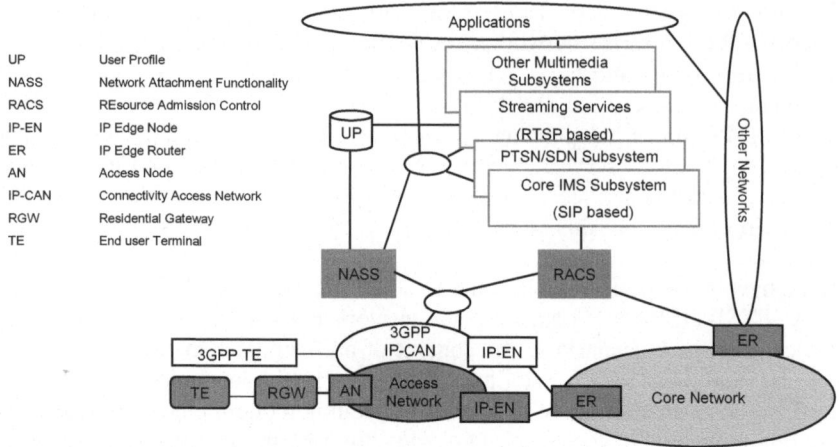

Fig. 1. TISPAN-NGN architecture in fixed-mobile broadband access

Fig. 1 shows an overview of TISPAN-NGN architecture in Release 1 [5] where new key network elements for the fixed scenarios are included: the Access Node (AN) that interconnects the customer premises network to the access network; the IP Edge Node (IP-EN) that terminates L2 connections; the Resource and Admission Control Subsystem (RACS) provides to applications a mechanism to request and reserve resources from the access network and the Network Attachment Subsystem (NASS) that provides authentication and autoconfiguration services.

To ensure QoS aware NGN service delivery, two architectures for dynamic QoS control are considered in the standardization process. The first one is the *guaranteed QoS* model, where the services are delivered with previously reserved resources. The RACS performs admission control in the access network throughput control and traffic policing. The other model is *relative QoS*, which implies traffic class differentiation (DiffServ) by means of separate queues dedicated to particular IP traffic classes and by performing priority scheduling between these queues in the IP-EN and the access network.

Support of other models like best effort networks or statically provisioned networks are not considered by RACS. The architecture supports both QoS control architectures – *guaranteed* and *relative* – allowing the access provider to select the most suitable QoS architecture for its needs. When QoS differentiation is used (*relative QoS*), DiffServ marking/remarking shall be performed at the IP-EN. DiffServ marking may be performed also by the RGW for uplink traffic, considering that the network operator controls the RGW in the customer premises network. For *guaranteed QoS control*, enforcement of QoS admission control decisions (throughput control and traffic policing) shall be performed in the IP-EN and the RGW. At this point it is important to remark that TISPAN-NGN standards do not consider the requirement to provision QoS control in the RGW and it is considered for further study [6], [7] and [8]. Another interesting issue considered in the standards is the resource reservation mechanisms. Two models are defined: the *proxied QoS reservation request with policy push* and the *CPE-request QoS reservation with policy pull.* The main difference between these two models is whether the end user terminal equipment (TE) (or the RGW on behalf of it) is capable or incapable of sending explicit QoS requests. In the *proxied QoS reservation request,* the TE does not support native QoS signalling mechanisms. When the end user invokes a specific service using a SIP based signalling, the RACS is the responsible for QoS authorization (policy control) and resource reservation. The TE, in the *CPE-request QoS reservation* model, is capable of sending QoS requests over dedicated signalling in the user plane. The RACS sends an authorization token to the TE through the signaling channel.

As a conclusion, it is important to emphasise that the current standard is still not mature enough in the QoS control from the end user side in the scenario of a fixed broadband access scenario and the design and implementation work of a RGW with QoS support is an innovative approach that demonstrates the possibility of implementing the architectures that are being currently standardized in a real scenario.

3 Residential Gateway Architecture

The QoS support in the RGW described here is being developed in the framework of MUSE project [2]. Next subsection describes the broadband access scenario considered in MUSE emphasizing some concepts like network entities, business roles and QoS models. A detailed description of the RGW QoS support in a set of scenarios considering some of the described QoS models is presented afterwards.

3.1 MUSE Broadband Access Scenario

MUSE project is designing the architecture of a multiservice broadband access network and it is studying the feasibility of TISPAN-NGN standardization for QoS solutions. Fig. 2 represents the broadband access scenario in MUSE where we can

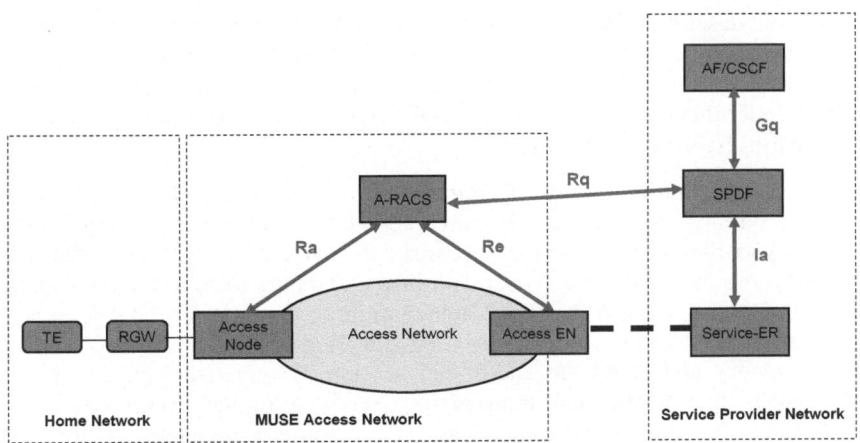

Fig. 2. MUSE broadband access scenario

identify the main roles involved in the architecture. There are three identified network segments: the *Home Network* where QoS provisioning is out of scope of both MUSE and TISPAN standardization. This segment is critical in end to end scenario and the RGW is the network element in which we are going to focus our work. The Access-RACS (A-RACS) in the *Access Network* segment plays an important role in QoS provisioning. It is remarkable that the interfaces ("Ra" and "Re") between A-RACS and AN and EN are still in standardization process (by TISPAN).

Other interfaces relevant from QoS provisioning viewpoint in the access network are "Rq", "Gq" and "Ia" that interconnects the *Service Provider Network* segment with the *Access Network* segment. The AF/CSCF (Application Function/Call and Session Control Function) is the element that offers the required resources to the applications. SPDF (Service Policing Decision Function) perform policy decisions based on policy set-up information obtained from the AF/CSCF via the "Gq" interface and authorizes QoS resources to the AF and edge routers (Service-ER and Access-EN) via "Rq" and "Ia" interfaces. Considering that the access network QoS model is TISPAN-NGN compliant according to Fig. 2, and that the standardization work is not focused on the RGW QoS support, we are going to define several scenarios in which QoS facilities are deployed in the RGW. Extensions to other possible QoS models that are not covered in TISPAN-NGN R1 standardization are being studying in MUSE project. Specifically, a *service oriented model* is considered as relevant in a fixed broadband scenario like MUSE one. In this model, the service provider is the responsible of requesting the resources to the access network provider, and in consequence, the responsible of configuring the RGW, or TE, without any specific QoS signaling flow at application level. Another QoS model in MUSE, that it is compliant with TISPAN-NGN models, is the *application signaling based model* where the end user is capable of sending standard SIP-based signaling to the service provider in order to request services using two different procedures depending on whether SIP requests support QoS information via SDP extensions or not [9].

3.2 QoS Management in the Residential Gateway

This section describes the RGW QoS support in the *application signaling based* model. The facilities provided by SIP-based signaling in order to extend services requests with QoS information and the massive use of this signaling protocol in TEs lets us consider this QoS model for the RGW architecture to be prototyped and tested. Two scenarios have been identified:

Scenario 1. *Signaling Relay Scenario (SRS)* where the RGW detects and transparently relays the end user SIP-based signaling to the corresponding IMS node (AF/CSCF) in the service provider network. In that case, the RGW transparently treats SIP flows as any other end user data flows, mapping them to the corresponding preconfigured QoS class in the RGW autoconfiguration phase. Fig. 3 represents this scenario where (1) the TE sends a SIP-based signaling to the AF/CSCF located in the service provider and starts the end-to-end session characteristics negotiation. The RGW detects that traffic and transparently sends it to the access network. (2) AF/CSCF by the "Gq" interface indicates the resources associated to the service requested in previous step to the SPDF/RACS.(3) and (4) the SPDF/RACS checks if the QoS characteristics negotiated by the end users can be delivered by the respective access network. This checking is based on several sources of information: view of all network resources (preconfigured and already in use) and the user profile and subscription information. If the access network cannot deliver the requested QoS, the involved SPDF can modify the QoS characteristics. After successful end-to-end negotiation, the SPDF/RACS authorizes the use of the resources for the session, configuring the QoS resources to the corresponding nodes in the access network completing the steps (4), (5) and (6) in the Fig. 3. Finally, the IP media flow is established considering the provisioned resources in all the network elements at each segment involved in the end to end communication.

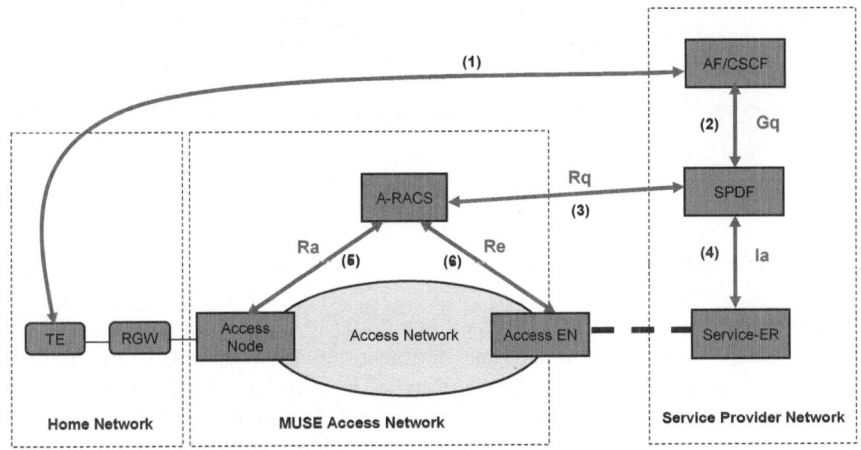

Fig. 3. Signaling Relay Scenario (SRS)

Scenario 2. *Signaling Proxy Scenario (SPS)* where the RGW supports SIP-based signaling on behalf of the TEs at home, by generating the signaling associated to upstream and downstream traffic and acting as a signaling proxy, requesting the corresponding QoS. The RGW is capable of identifying end user flows that do not correspond to any SIP-based terminal. In order to authorize this flow and to provide the resources in the access network, the RGW acts as a signaling proxy sending a SIP based signaling to the service provider. To harmonize the end-to-end QoS architecture, it could be useful to support a non-IMS terminal at home or even a SIP terminal but not full 3GPP/IMS compliant or without the QoS extensions in SDP needed for the QoS model negotiation. In all these cases, a signaling proxy has to be performed by the RGW but with differences depending on the TE SIP capabilities. Fig. 4 shows this scenario where a legacy terminal sends a session request (1a). The RGW detects that this particular request (without signaling or with SIP-based signaling without QoS extension) has to be proxied and acts on behalf of the TE sending the corresponding SIP-based signaling to the AF/CSCF (1b). Next steps are similar than in the previous scenario displayed in Fig. 3. Both scenarios have a strong performance overhead in the treatment of signaling messages in the RGW and it is important to measure the performance of a RGW prototype in the case of SIP-based signaling in comparison with user data messages. This prototype and the results are described in next section.

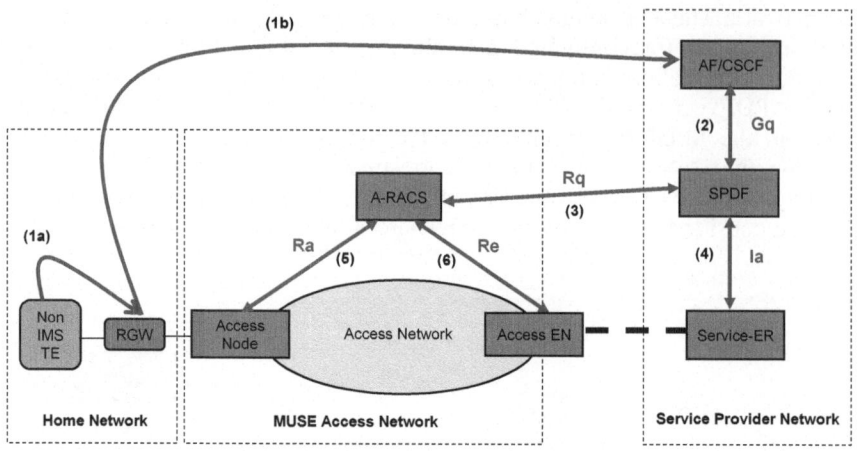

Fig. 4. Signaling Proxy Scenario (SPS)

4 The Prototype

The RGW scenarios previously described are going to be developed using the Click! modular router platform that let us demonstrate the capability for extending functionalities to the RGW node. The prototype described in this section is a starting point for analyzing a flexible platform so as to study and propose RGW architectures, mainly focusing on the QoS support within the framework of a fixed broadband access in the MUSE project.

Click! [1] is a modular software router developed by MIT, the ICSI and UCLA. A Click! router is an interconnected collection of modules called *elements* in the Click! terminology and an element is a C++ implementation of a specific functionality. There are elements to communicate devices, to modificate packets, to program dropping policies and packet scheduling. It is quite simple to construct a router with Click! since the only thing to do is to specify the elements connections using a specific Click! script language. Click! can be executed in two different modes: *User-level* and *Linux module*. In the *User-level*, the Click! is another application with their restrictions (see Fig. 5). A patch must be applied to the kernel sources in order to use the kernel mode. When the Click! is installed as a *Linux module*, the kernel chain is changed, so all incoming packets will enter to the Click! router first. The user can then fully control packets transmission from/to the kernel. Changing the routing table, and creating a virtual device, all packets can be force to go through Click!. Outgoing packets (packets from applications to the network) do not necessarily have to pass through the Click! router in case it is not needed (see Fig. 6).

Important Click! functionalities to be considered in order to select this platform are IPv4/IPv6 datagram processing, extensibility, maintenance, performance and network connections availability. Click! uses Linux drivers, so there are no practical problems with hardware compatibility since Linux has a big hardware compatibility list with network cards. As a negative point to be remarked, Click! has no elements to work

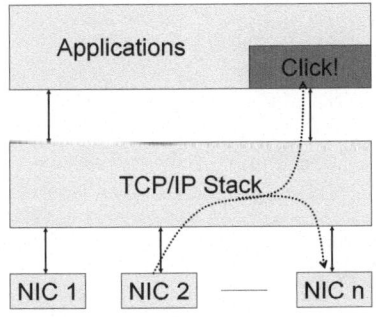

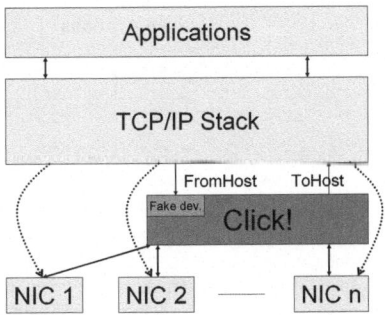

Fig. 5. Click at the user level   **Fig. 6.** Click as a Linux module

with MPLS, VLANs, VPLS, etc., so, it does not accomplish these functionalities nowadays and there seems to be working groups around it. Based on a previous study (comparing the use of iptables [10], netlink, libpcap [11] and Click!), we will use Click! to implement the RGW prototype. Click! is not a complete software so far, due to its lacks in IPv6 functionalities, the impossibility to work with the 2.6 new Linux kernel and it deficiencies to directly process layer 2 frames other than Ethernet frames but our idea is to create a first stage prototype using the Click! elements available now, and enhance it with new functionalities in a second stage.

4.1 The Hybrid Model

For the RGW prototype, software is required capable of capturing all packets at layer 2 level, modifying them, re-injecting them into the network, sending them to upper layers, etc., so it was decided to use the Click! modular router software (more precisely the 'Click' module). Although we chose Click!, it may not be mandatory or desirable to develop new applications at Linux kernel level because programming new applications at the kernel level is sometimes very difficult and the creation of new hardware and software network applications is also desirable, and they should be as independent as possible from low level packet facilities. To overcome these problems, it was decided to create a new *hybrid model* where neither pure Click! nor pure application level programs will be developed but a combination of these two ones. Fig. 7 depicts this *hybrid model* with three main boxes: **Click** is the Click! software router working at kernel level. It will receive every packet, wrap them inside a new UDP packet and forward them up to the Manager or Process application (this will be configured by the Manager). **The Manager** will receive fresh packets from the Click! module and process them. Depending on the packet characteristics, the Manager could configure the Click! module to forward the same kind of packets to a certain process. **Processes P1..Pn** are the user level applications developed to perform certain functions.

This model must be tested to assure that it can possibly be used and that it is not suffering any serious performance problem. When an application is programmed at the Click! module level the time a frame spends crossing the Linux kernel is saved. This is why the delay imposed by the Manager must be estimated to validate the

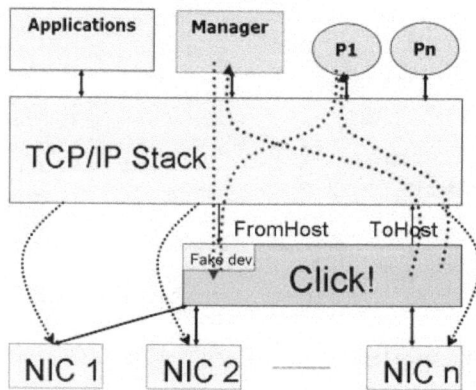

Fig. 7. Hybrid model

hybrid model. The main intention of the hybrid model is to help the programmer to develop RGW applications in an easy and fast way, but there are some issues that must be validated. In these tests, we try to measure the additional delay introduced by the hybrid model due to the transmission of the packet from the Click! layer to the application layer and back.

4.2   Delay Introduced by the Manager Application

This scenario tests whether the use of a user-level application called Manager does slow down frame management or not (should it really reduce the performance it could always be possible to manage the frames inside the Click! module, without passing them to the user level although the flexibility of the development at the application layer would be lost). For this test Click! has been installed in a computer with two different configurations. *Direct connection* where frames are encapsulated in an UDP packet by Click!, and then they are sent again directly to the same interface where they came from.

The other one is *Manager connection* where frames are also encapsulated in an UDP packet, but now they are sent to the Manager. This process can be carried out by a fake interface called *fake0* (for example). When the Manager receives a frame, it returns it to the source machine through Click!. In both cases, packets had the same size and were sent by the same source machine. In order to perform the test, a large number of streams of 1000 packets have been sent, with different sizes in each experiment. Information was collected by the source machine with a sniffer application (*Ethereal*). Table 1 shows the results obtained in these tests.

Table 1. Delay introduced due to the Hybrid Model

Packet size	Direct Connection	Manager Connection	Gap
100 bytes	120 µs	250 µs	+130 µs
540 bytes	200 µs	330 µs	+130 µs
1060 bytes	290 µs	430 µs	+140 µs
1440 bytes	365 µs	500 µs	+135 µs

Taking into account this result it can be concluded that the usage of the Manager increases the time around 130-140 µs, (this is a packet size independent result). Nevertheless, the Manager will not always directly resend packets, because sometimes it has to send packets to another user-level applications or Click! modules (through a fake interface for example). Then, time used for managing frames could be similar in both cases (Click! handling or Manager handling).

4.3 Supported Load in the Hybrid Model

The aim of this test is to probe the RGW load capacity when the hybrid model is used. Two PCs where connected to the *compact* device working as a RGW as showed in Fig. 8. The RGW implements the NAPT (Network Address and Protocol Translation) in three different ways:

- Linux using the iptables functionality. The Linux kernel must be configured to support the iptables module. To set the NAT table the command *iptables -t nat -A POSTROUTING -o eth1 -j MASQUERADE* must be invoked. It is also necessary to set the *ip_forwarding* behaviour.
- NAT functionality implemented at the Click! level. It is easy to create the NAT functionality using Click! elements.
- NAT functionality implemented at the application level (Manager). The Click! level wraps the received frame in an UDP packet and sends it to the TCP/IP stack using the ToHost Click element. The frame is received by the Manager at the application level which performs the NAT functionality sending the modified frame to the Click! level again.

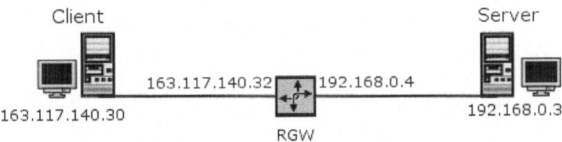

Fig. 8. Load testing scenario

Results are shown in Fig. 9 where the iptables values are omitted due to their similarity with Click ones. The most important comments extracted from these results are than there exists a maximum packet generation rate depending on the size of the packet. The client can not generate the nominal interface rate and this value decreases when packet size also decreases. If the Iperf program is launched using 1470 bytes as the packet size, the maximum rate is 95,1 Mbps. For packet lengths of 850 bytes, just 92,7 Mbps can be generated and this values is reduced to 75,1 Mbps for 200 bytes packets. The iptables and Click scenarios show similar results. In the Manager scenario, the results are similar to the other ones while 40 Mbps rate is not reached and packets size is above 850 bytes. For higher inputs or lower packet sizes, the performance decreases drastically. It is important to note that in the hybrid model (Manager scenario) just some packets will go up to the application level. Just signaling and fresh (not configured flows) packets must be processed by the Manager and we expect a lower rate than 40 Mbps for this kind of packets. Another important point is the packet size. Normally, data packets are bigger than 200 bytes, so we just must take care about the signaling packets. For example, for SIP messages the worst case is for INVITE (mean of 465 bytes) and OK messages (mean of 388 bytes). More complex SIP messages where the header is extended with SDP QoS information, the size of these messages are between 838 and 1024 bytes.

Another interesting test is to change de RGW device by a more powerful equipment than the compact one. The new device has a Pentium 4 2,4 GHz processor and 512 Mbytes of RAM (the same than the compact one). Fig. 10 depicts the results obtained in this new test where, as the previous one, the iptables results are omitted due to its similarity with the Click experiments. The results are notably better than the obtained with the compact device and it proves the importance of a powerful processor. In another model, where all frames were treated at the application level, a high performance device is firmly recommended. Nevertheless, in the Hybrid Model that we proposed, where just signaling and fresh frames are treated at the application level, the compact device is capable enough so as to process the estimated traffic.

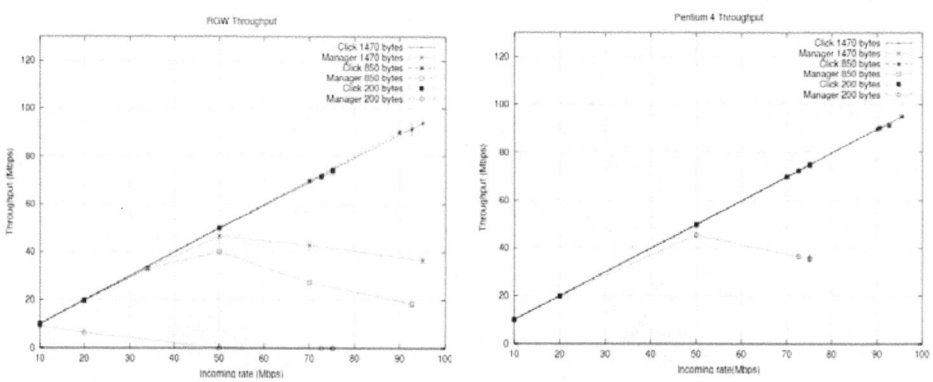

Fig. 9. RGW throughput   **Fig. 10.** Pentium 4 throughput

5   Conclusions

In this paper it is showed an innovative software architecture of a RGW node with support of QoS functionalities in a flexible and extensible way by using the Click! platform. Click! lets us to process traffic at different levels as it is described in several models and we are interested in treating the QoS signaling traffic (SIP-based) separately from data plane traffic. The differentiation of SIP traffic managed in Click! allows us to support dynamically QoS facilities in the RGW. Several QoS signaling scenarios have been proposed following the drafted TISPAN-NGN standardization in Release 1. This work contributes to offer an open testbed for probing their feasibility in an european broadband access scenario where the RGW is considered a critic node when end-to-end QoS is provided.

Future research will follow not only the standardization process but also the technological trends in segments like home and access networks where the RGW plays an important role in the mapping of QoS architectures.

Acknowledgements

This article has been partially granted by the European Commission through the IST-507295 Multi-Service Access Everywhere (MUSE) project.

References

[1]   The Click Modular Router Project. www.pdos.csail.mit.edu/click.
[2]   MUSE (Multi-Service Access Everywhere). IST European Project. www.ist-muse.org.
[3]   3GPP TS 23.228: IP Multimedia Subsystem, Stage 2, Release 6, January 2003.
[4]   J. Rosenberg, H. Schulzrinne, G. Camarillo, A. Johnston, J. Peterson, R. Sparks, M. Handley, and E. Shooler. IETF RFC 3261. SIP: Session Initiation Protocol. June 2002
[5]   DES/TISPAN-02007-NGN-R1 NGN Functional architecture for NGN Release 1
[6]   DES/TISPAN-02021-NGN-R1. NGN Functional Architecture; Network Attachment. Draft 2005.
[7]   DES/TISPAN-02020-NGN-R1. Functional Architecture; Resource and Admission Control Subsystem (RACS). Stable Draft 2005.
[8]   DTS/TISPAN-05002-NGN Interface Protocol Req. Definition; QoS Control in Access Networks. Draft 2005.
[9]   M. Handley and V. Jacobson. IETF RFC 2327. SDP: Session Description Protocol. April 1998.
[10] The netfilter/iptables project. http://www.netfilter.org/
[11] Lawrence Berkeley National Labs, libpcap, Network Research Group, URL: http://www.tcpdump.org/

Proactive Two-Tier Bandwidth Brokerage for On-Demand Policy-Based Resource Allocation in Stateless IP Networks

Kamel Haddadou[1], Yacine Ghamri-Doudane[2],
Samir Ghamri-Doudane[1], and Nazim Agoulmine[2]

[1] LIP6, Pierre & Marie Curie University, 8, rue du Capitaine Scott, 75015 Paris, France
Kamel.Haddadou@lip6.fr, Samir.Ghamri-Doudane@lip6.fr
[2] Networks and Multimedia Systems Research Group, IIE/University of Evry joint group,
18 allée Jean Rostand, 91025 Evry Cedex, France
Ghamri@iie.cnam.fr, Nazim.Agoulmine@iup.univ-evry.fr

Abstract. In order to improve the scalability of the IETF's PBM architecture, we previously proposed an extension to this architecture. The aim of our proposal was to facilitate the support of on-demand resource allocation in stateless IP networks. The proposed schema distribute part of the decision making process but keeps centralized the bandwidth brokerage operation as this latter uses a critical resources (traffic matrix). Our current work aims to render the PBM architecture completely distributed by designing a scalable scheme for bandwidth brokerage. To that end, we propose using a proactive two-tier scheme in order to improve the scalability of the resource management procedures. In this paper, we present the proposed scheme, its design features and the set of experimentations we realized in order to demonstrate its performances.

1 Introduction

A major challenge in emerging multi-service and QoS-enabled IP networks is to offer access to a wide range of services anytime and ideally anywhere. Both of network operators and end-users are willing to respectively offer and use these services with a large range of QoS-guarantees. To achieve this aim, efficient and dynamic control of network resources is submitted to be the key issues in the ongoing all-IP realm. To that end, we proposed in a previous work [1] a scalable on-demand policy based resource allocation framework.

The proposed framework is based on the combination of per-session QoS signaling and Policy-Based Management (PBM) [2]. It suggests distributing part of the decision making while keeping centralized the critical operations which use critical resources on the management system. In our previous work, we identified the bandwidth brokerage operation as the only one that uses critical resources (the traffic matrix). Indeed, two different resource requests initiated by different traffic sources may concern the same link in the network. This operation has then been maintained centralize. Moreover, the Bandwidth Broker (BB) has been designed in such a way that it avoids parallel access to the traffic matrix. The analytical and experimental

J. Dalmau and G. Hasegawa (Eds.): MMNS 2005, LNCS 3754, pp. 350–361, 2005.

results, we obtained when distributing some of the decision making operations in the PBM system [1], showed that our architecture is highly scalable compared to the PBM architecture proposed by the Internet Engineering Task Force (IETF) [3]. However, the system-throughput, that represents the rate of QoS request treated by the management system, has always an upper bound. We proved analytically that this upper bound is only due to the operations that remained centralization (i.e. the Bandwidth Broker). Indeed, we demonstrated analytically that the system-throughput is inversely proportional to the average computational time of the Bandwidth Broker element. The maximum number of active users in the network was also proven to be upper bounded.

In order to render our on-demand policy-based resource allocation framework completely insensitive to both the rate of requests and the number of active users, we suggest to instantiate several bandwidth brokers in the domain. We propose that each BB will be responsible of managing a part of the network resources. To do so, the idea is to manage network-resources using two granularity levels: a link-level and a path-level. A path is defined as the set of links between two edge-routers. Then, the idea behind instantiating multiple BBs is to allocate to each path a part of the resources of each of its links. Note however that in order to optimize network-resource usage, this part should not be static. Hence, we will have two hierarchical levels for bandwidth management:

1. A centralized Bandwidth Broker (cBB) aiming to manage link resources as a traffic matrix.
2. Multiple edge Bandwidth Brokers (eBBs) aiming to both: (i) realizing a per-session path-oriented admission control procedure, and (ii) proactively managing the amount of resources assigned to the subset of network-paths managed by the eBB. The proactive allocation/de-allocation of link-resources to paths is realized in order to automatically adapt path-resources according to the customers' resource-request distribution.

The idea of distributing the bandwidth allocation among multiple bandwidth brokers by using the two granularity levels (link-level and path-level) is not new. This idea was previously presented in [4]. In our work, we follow the same idea but we propose a different way to manage the bandwidth assignment to paths. Indeed, in order to minimize the delay to respond to a resource allocation request, we suggest to proactively increase (respectively decrease) the amount of resources assigned to a particular path depending on its actual usage. The objectives of this paper are to present, discuss the design feature, and realize a complete experimental evaluation of our Proactive Two Tier Bandwidth Brokerage (PTT-BB) Architecture.

The rest of this paper is organized as follows. IETF's PBM architecture and its scalability limitations are presented in Section 2. Then, we briefly review our previously proposed scalable on-demand policy-based resource allocation framework and its performances. In Section 4, we present the bandwidth brokerage operation and the problem statement. Following section presents the PTT-BB architecture and its components. The test-bed description and the empirical results targeting several testing scenarios are presented in Section 6. Finally, Section 7 concludes the paper.

2 Scalability Limitation of the IETF's PBM Architecture

The IETF Resource Allocation Protocol (RAP) Working Group has specified a complete framework for policy definition and administration [3]. This framework introduces a set of components to enable policy rules definition, saving and enforcing: the Policy Decision Point (PDP), the Policy Enforcement Point (PEP), and the Policy Repository. PEP components are policy decision enforcers located in network and system equipments. The PDP is the component responsible for high-level decision-making process. This process consists of retrieving and interpreting policies, and implementing the decision in the network through the set of PEPs. The policy repository contains policy rules that are used by the PDP.

In order to exchange policy information and/or decisions, the PDP interacts with the PEPs using one of the several protocols specified or extended for this purpose. Among them, the Common Open Policy Service (COPS) protocol [3] is the one which was specifically designed by the IETF to realize this interaction.

Initially, the COPS protocol was designed mainly for resource allocation in an Internet backbone. In order to make such allocation, two models within the COPS protocol were proposed: the Outsourcing model and the Provisioning model. In the former, policy-requests are triggered by particular events and forwarded to the PDP for policy-decisions. In contrary, in the provisioning model, policy-decisions are installed in the PEP prior to the arrival of the concerned flows. In both cases, the used policies are supposed deduced from static customer's contracts which are called Service Level Agreements (SLAs).

The main problem with the IETF PBM architecture is that it does not take into account the scalability problem. In fact, the client-server architecture as defined by the IETF is not scalable as it stands. In the case of a large network, the PDP become a bottleneck leading to serious problems while handling a potentially high number of policy requests. Hence, this architecture does not handle explicitly dynamic changes in the users' Service Level Agreements (SLA). The SLA is treated in a static manner and the customer should re-negotiate completely her/his SLA in the case of changes in her/his requirements. This lack of dynamicity is a curb to the development of punctual access and usage of services such as Voice over IP (VoIP) and Video on Demand (VoD). This is also harmful for the optimization of network-resource usage.

3 Scalable On-Demand Policy-Based Resource Allocation

It appears nowadays that management systems following the PBM architecture are neither responding to operators' scalability issues nor to customers needs. In fact, customers are willing to dynamically request network-resources depending on their instantaneous needs and without having to contract a SLA for long period of time. However, from the operator perspective, the integration of dynamic resource allocation to the existing IETF's PBM architecture is not feasible in a large scale.

In order to overcome these limitations, we proposed in a previous work [1] a novel solution for on-demand policy-based resource allocation in IP networks. This solution aims to distribute the decision making operations among several distributed PDPs. Therefore, the PBM architecture has been decomposed into a set of functional components. The idea of this decomposition is to identify which components represent critical sections in the decision-making process. Once this phase achieved, the solution consists on proposing a new instantiation model where non-critical components are distributed according to none functional requirements (such as performance objectives, network size, etc.). Hence, the impact of critical operations on the overall management system performances is minimized. To maintain the consistency of the decision-making process, critical operations are kept centralized. These operations are identified as those operations that need to access to critical resources (shared information, common databases, etc.) in the system.

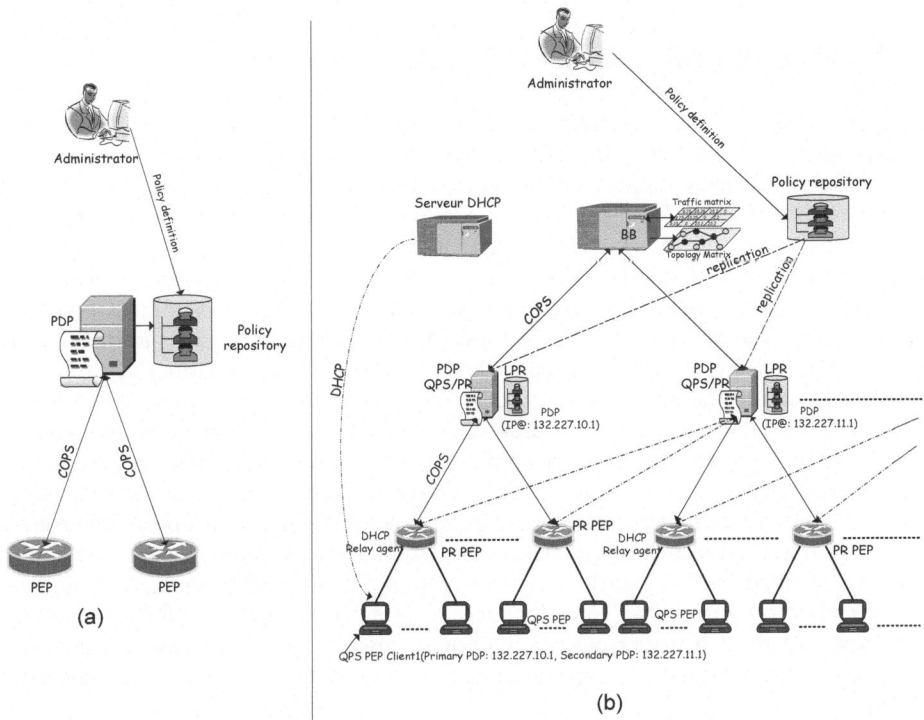

Fig. 1. Policy-based Management: (a) the IETF framework, and (b) our framework

The critical operations identified in our framework are identified as those related to the bandwidth brokerage. All other operations related to decision making appeared as replicable. Based on these statements verified in our previous work [1], we propose to keep centralized the Bandwidth Brokerage while distributing all other functional components. Fig. 1 presents in details our framework (Fig. 1(b)) and shows its differences with the IETF's PBM framework (Fig. 1(a)).

As our objective is to demonstrate its scalability features, we both realized a complete implementation and a detailed analytical analysis of our proposed framework. The practical experiments highlighted the scalability property of our approach. These experiments also permitted to identify the effect of each component of the framework on the overall performance of the management system. The obtained practical results demonstrated that the overall-system delay is always below the ITU-T recommended signaling-delay limit [5] and that the system throughput is higher than the 200 req/s as recommended by the ITU-T [6]. However, the system throughput has an upper bound. The analytical study confirmed that the bottleneck of such framework is the bandwidth broker. Undeniably, we demonstrated throughout our analytical model that the system throughput is inversely proportional to the average computational time of the BB element. This parameter is recognized as having a major influence on the size of a domain (number of customers). Hence, we concluded that the performances of the BB element will always drive the performance of the framework we proposed.

4 Bandwidth Brokerage and Problem Statement

Bandwidth Brokers uses generally traffic matrices in order to store and manage network resource usage. Let's first explain how these traffic matrices are organized. In fact, the traffic matrix representation depends on the network technology used, such as the use of the Multi-Protocol Label Switching (MPLS). In our work, we are interested in the most general case for traffic matrix representation. As proposed in [4], a traffic matrix of a particular administrative domain contains several management information bases (MIBs). Among them, one can find a topology information base and a link-QoS information base. The topology information base helps to identify the set of links forming a particular path while the link-QoS information base contains information about the available resources within each link. Using these two specific MIBs, the BB element can achieve admission control and update the amount of available resources on all path-links accordingly. The admission control procedure involves checking each link on the path to verify whether or not it has sufficient resources to satisfy a particular resource request. The traffic matrix is updated whenever a new resource allocation is granted or a resource release is achieved. The traffic matrix described here is clearly a critical section. It can not be accessed simultaneously by several requests as some inconsistent states can appear leading to deadlock situations. As the BB in our on-demand policy-based resource allocation framework uses this operational mode, it appeared as the bottleneck of the overall management system.

One solution to overcome this limitation is to instantiate several bandwidth brokers in the domain. In this case, each BB will be responsible for managing a part of the network resources. In order to avoid conflicts between BB, the idea is to allocate distinct parts of link-resources to the various bandwidth brokers. The authors in [4] have proposed an interesting approach to achieve this. They proposed to use a hierarchical scheme for link-resource distribution over multiple BBs. In this scheme, a centralized Bandwidth Broker (cBB) is in charge of managing link-resources while a set of edge Bandwidth Brokers (eBBs) are responsible for managing the resources assigned to a mutually exclusive subset of paths. As a link can be shared by multiple paths, then the cBB will be in charge of allocating/de-allocating the link-bandwidth to paths. This is realized on an on-demand basis. Hence, the cBB is in charge of link-based resource management and has a micro view of the resource management problem when eBBs are in charge of path-based resource management and has a macro view of the resource management problem.

In our work we will use the same concept of hierarchical bandwidth brokerage. We will however implement this concept differently to achieve better performances.

5 PTT-BB: Proactive Two Tier Bandwidth Brokerage

The proposal in [4] is to virtually divide the bandwidth of each link into *quotas*. Quotas are allocated/de-allocated to paths on an on-demand basis with one quota at a time. Hence, in the case where a particular path is unable to handle an arriving resource request then the corresponding eBB requests the cBB to increase the bandwidth allocated to the corresponding path (quota request). Note also that when an eBB has a quota in excess for a particular path it returns it to the cBB (quota release). If the quota request is granted by the cBB, the eBB accepts the resource request (normal mode). Otherwise (critical mode), two different behavior models are considered: a *non-lossy-path* model and a *lossy-path* model. In the former the cBB keep a part of link-resources shared and centralizes its management. Consequently, when the quota request is not granted by the cBB, the eBB forwards the per-session resource request to the cBB which tries to satisfy it thanks to the shared resource part. Contrarily to this first model, in the *lossy-path* model when a quota request fails, the eBB simply rejects the per-session resource request, instead of passing it to the cBB. In this latter model, the cBB distributes all link-resources to paths and does not maintain a shared part. It then only performs quota management.

Even if the resource usage is not optimized when using the lossy-path model, this latter clearly decreases the processing overhead of the cBB. This is very important as the cBB is the bottleneck of the bandwidth management system. The scalability of the system remains however highly limited by the fact that a quota request is sent to the cBB each time a resource request targeting a critical path is received by the eBB. Indeed, from our previous experience [1], we argue that the quota request rate that can be handled by the cBB is upper bounded. In fact, the cBB can be analytically modeled as a single server queue (as it processes quota-requests sequentially). Let's assume that the cBB service law is approximated by an exponential distribution with a mean of μB. Then, the maximum quota request rate that can be handled by the cBB within the critical mode can be computed using the formula: $1/\mu B$. Furthermore, this assumes that no quota releases are generated towards the cBB for the mean time. Otherwise, the maximum quota request rate will be smaller. We can then conclude that in large scale networks and when the resource usage is very high (i.e. several paths are running under the critical mode), the resource request rate can be very high and therefore the cBB will not be able to manage all the quota-requests. For these reasons, we propose to use a proactive scheme for quota management rather than the on-demand quota management scheme introduced in [4].

In the scheme we propose, quota requests are set-up proactively once the available resources for a particular path are below a certain threshold (T_{REQ}). Similarly, quota releases are triggered proactively once the available resources for a particular path are above a certain threshold (T_{REL}). Quota requests and releases can only be achieved in periodical cut-off times. As the quota request rate that can be handled by the cBB is upper bounded, the periodical cut-off times should be chosen in accordance to the number of eBB and to the processing capabilities of the cBB. In addition to the fact that our proposal have a better scalability features than the one proposed in [4], it also minimizes the time needed for handling resource allocation request. Indeed, if there are not sufficient resources on the corresponding path once a resource request is received, this latter is immediately rejected by the eBB without referring to the cBB.

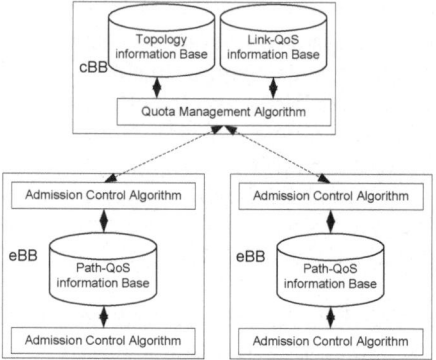

Fig. 2. PTT-BB Architecture

Following the description of the basic design features of our Proactive Two Tier Bandwidth Brokerage (PTT-BB) architecture, let's now give a more formal and detailed description. Fig. 2 highlights the set of functional components of PTT-BB. Hence, as introduced before, we use a hierarchical scheme composed of a centralized Bandwidth Broker (cBB) and a set of edge Bandwidth Brokers (eBB). The cBB uses a topology information base and a link-QoS information base in order to realize per-path quota allocation/de-allocation. The quota management algorithm is depicted in Fig. 4. Each eBB is assigned a mutually exclusive subset of paths which it stores within a path-QoS information base. Each eBB performs two different resource management operations: the Proactive Path-Bandwidth Adaptation (PPBA) algorithm and the path-oriented admission control algorithm. Fig. 5 and Fig. 6 present in details these two algorithms. Fig. 3 outlines the notations used in the different algorithms.

As depicted in Fig. 6, the PPBA algorithm periodically checks the resource availability of all the paths managed by the eBB. If the available resources level is under a fixed threshold T_{REQ} (respectively above a fixed threshold T_{REL}) for a particular path then the PPBA algorithm requests the cBB to increase (respectively decrease) the amount of resources allocated to this one. In both cases, the eBB asks the cBB to increase (respectively decrease) its path-resource availability in order to reach $T_{REQ}+N*Quota$, respectively $T_{REL}-N*Quota$. This is undertaken in order to always maintain the resource availability level between the following values $[T_{REQ}, T_{REL}]$ for each path. Note that an appropriate choice of T_{REQ}, T_{REL} and N permits to optimize the resource usage while minimizing the call blocking probability in the network. However, the optimization of these parameters is outside the scope of this paper and will be the subject of a future work.

- Req (s,d).Bw and Rel (s,d).Bw : resource allocation and release requests of Bw between two edge routers identified by their interface addresses s and d.
- Q_{BW} : bandwidth unit (or quota) size in bits per second.
- P(s,d) : path allowing to handling the communications between two addresses s and d.
- P(s,d).A_{BW} : Available bandwidth along the path P(s,d).
- P(s,d).Q : the number of quotas allocated to the path P(s,d)
- L(i,j) : link between two routers identified by their interface addresses I and j.
- L(i,j).A_{BW} : Available bandwidth along the link L(i,j).
- PTT-BB.Time : Adaptation Time Interval

Fig. 3. Notations

```
1:   If Message[i] == msg(Req, P(s,d), ReqQuota) {
2:          If all L(i,j) ∈ P(s,d)) verify (L(i,j).ABW>ReqQuots
3:               For each link L(i,j) ∈ P(s,d)
4:                    L(i,j).ABW - ReqQuota;
5:                    Msg (Req, P(s,d), granted);}
6:   If Message[i] == msg(Rel, P(s,d), ReqQuota) {
7:          For each link L(i,j) ∈ P(s,d)
8:               L(i,j).ABW + ReqQuota;}
```

Fig. 4. Quota management algorithm.

```
1:   Arrival of a Req (s,d).Bw
2:   If  (Req (s,d).Bw < P(s,d).ABW) {
3:          P(s,d).ABW = P(s,d).ABW - Req (s,d).Bw;
4:          Accept Req (s,d).Bw;}
5:   Else Reject  Req (s,d).Bw;
6:
7:   Arrival of a Rel (s,d).Bw
8:   P(s,d).ABW = P(s,d).ABW + Rel (s,d).Bw;
```

Fig. 5. Path oriented admission control algorithm

```
1:   While (true) {
2:          For each path P(s,d).Bw in eBB {
3:               NbQuota = P(s,d).ABW / QBW;
4:               If (NbQuota < TREQ)
a.                    Msg.add (Req, P(s,d), (TREQ – NbQuota)+N*QBW);
5:               If (NbQuota > TREL)
a.                    Msg.add (Rel, P(s,d), (NbQuota – TREL)+N*QBW); }
6:          Send (Message)
7:          Sleep (PTT-BB.Time); }
```

Fig. 6. Proactive path-bandwidth adaptation (PPBA) algorithm

6   Performance Evaluation

In order to analyse the performances of our PTT-BB, a test-bed has been implemented and a set of intensive experimentations have been carried out. The objective of these experiments is to compare the performances of PTT-BB to those obtained using a single BB. Both these solutions have been implemented and integrated to the test-bed. Two performance parameters are analyzed: the call blocking probability and the scalability gain.

6.1 Call Blocking Probability

The experimentations have been carried out using two different topologies (Fig. 7). These topologies are referred to as the peer-to-peer topology (Fig. 7.a) and the chain topology (Fig. 7.b). In the case of PTT-BB and for each topology, the paths to manage have been distributed among the 3 eBBs used in our test-bed.

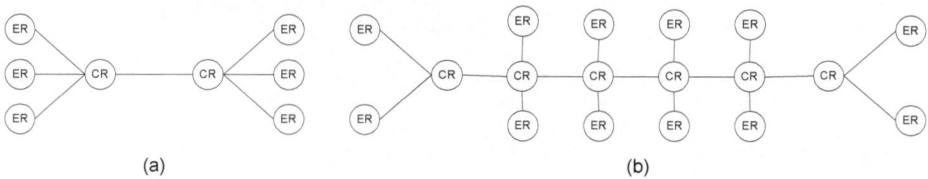

(a)   (b)

Fig. 7. Experimentation topologies: (a) the peer-to-peer topology, and (b) the chain topology

Resource-requests are generated by a Poisson process with a rate λ equal to 300 requests/s. Each session lifetime is exponentially distributed and its average duration is $\mu^{l} = 30$ (in seconds). Session throughputs are chosen randomly in the interval [0.5Mbps, 1.2Mbps]. Note that each link capacity is set to 1 Gbps. The path is also chosen randomly according to the topology. These values have been chosen in order to simulate a highly load network. Several experimentations have been carried out by changing one of the two parameters: the adaptation time interval and the bandwidth unit (or Quota) size. Each experimentation-duration is 200s.

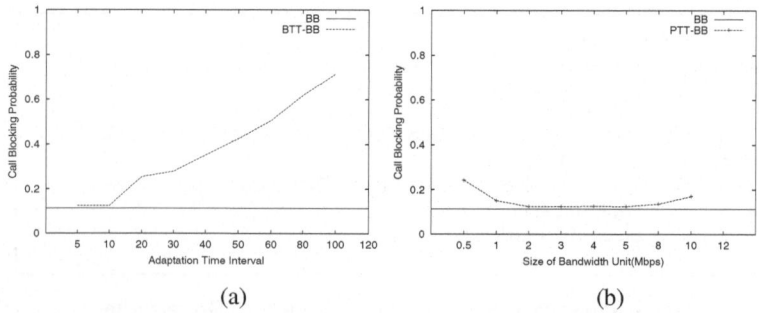

(a)   (b)

Fig. 8. Call blocking probability, in the peer-to-peer topology, as a function of: (a) adaptation time interval, and (b) quota size

In all our experimentations, T_{REQ}, T_{REL} and N were chosen as being multiple of the bandwidth unit (*Quota*) size. Hence, T_{REQ} was chosen equal to *5*Quota*, T_{REL} to *10*Quota* and N to *2*Quota*.

The obtained results throughout the experimentations carried out using the peer-to-peer topology are depicted in Fig. 8. Those obtained using the chain topology are depicted in Fig. 9. Both curves depicted in Fig. 8 (respectively Fig. 9) shows the evolution of the call blocking probability while changing the adaptation time interval and the bandwidth unit (or quota) size. In the former the quota size is set to 5Mbps while in the latter the adaptation time interval is set to 10s. The evolution of the call blocking probability for PTT-BB is also compared to the one obtained with a single BB.

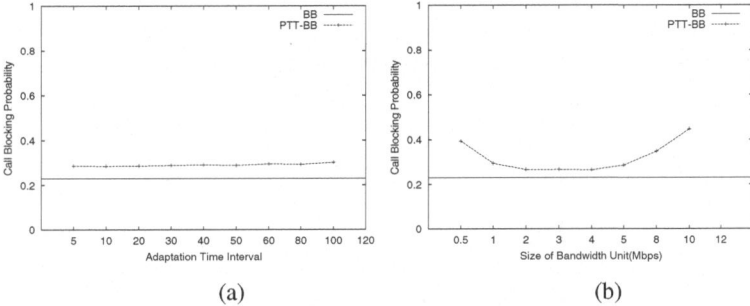

(a)   (b)

Fig. 9. Call blocking probability, in the chain topology, as a function of: (a) adaptation time interval, and (b) quota size

From Fig. 8.a we can see that the call blocking probability obtained with PTT-BB is slightly higher than the one obtained with a single BB for adaptation time interval less than 10s. Even if 10s corresponds already to a low adaptation frequency (as the cBB can support even higher loads), we have also performed experimentations for a higher adaptation time intervals (i.e. lower adaptation frequencies). With the decrease of the adaptation frequency, we have noticed an important increase in the call blocking probability. This is not surprising, as the request rate to be handled by PTT-BB is very high and the evolution of the bandwidth allocation to paths is very slow. Consequently, the resources allocated to a path are rapidly consumed and the number of unsatisfied requests becomes significant. This is mainly due to the fact that the number of paths in the peer-to-peer topology is very small (30 paths). Thus, the per path request rate is very high. In parallel, we can see from Fig. 9.a that the call blocking probability remains always stable. In this case, the number of paths (132 paths) is higher than in the case of the peer-to-peer topology. In this second case, the per-path request rate is smaller. The adaptation time interval should then be chosen carefully in accordance to the per-path expected session arrival rate.

Fig. 8.b and Fig. 9.b show that the call blocking probability obtained with PTT-BB stabilizes for quota sizes between 2Mbps and 5Mbps. Furthermore, for this interval, the call blocking probability is slightly higher than the one obtained with a single BB. However, for both cases: quota sizes smaller than 2Mbps or quota sizes higher than 5Mbps, the call blocking probability increases:

1. In the first case, this is due to the fact that PBBA tries to maintain the amount of available bandwidth within the [5*Quota, 10*Quota] interval. This interval is very small when the quota size is small. Consequently, the available re-

sources for each path are rapidly consumed. The number of rejected requests will then be elevated.

2.   In the second case, elevated quota sizes implies that an important part of the bandwidth is maintained unused by certain paths. Indeed, in this case also PBBA tries to maintain the amount of available bandwidth within the [5*Quota, 10*Quota] interval. Therefore, all the link-bandwidth can be allocated by the cBB to its paths. However, some paths will have a higher available bandwidth while others are running under the critical mode (i.e. rejecting resource request).

Hence, the quota size should also be appropriately dimensioned. It should be chosen according to the average bandwidth requirement of typical flows.

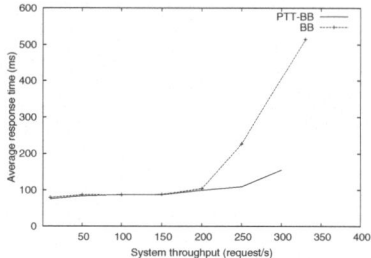

Fig. 10. Average response time to a request as a function of the system throughput

6.2 Scalability Gain

After demonstrating the performances of PTT-BB in terms of call blocking probability, let's now analyze its behaviour in term of scalability gain. Fig. 10 summarizes the results obtained in our scalability experimentations. It highlights the evolution of the time needed to handle a resource request obtained for different resource request rates (system throughput). This time is referred to as overall-system delay in the following. Note that for these experimentations, PTT-BB uses two eBBs, the quota size is set to 5Mbps while the adaptation time interval is set to 10s. We also used the same values for T_{REQ}, T_{REL} and N as in the previous experiments.

From Fig. 10, one can note that for rates over 200 requests per second, the slope of the response time obtained with a single BB increases drastically. Indeed, the BB element has to process one resource allocation request (REQ) or resource release request (REL) at a time (sequential treatments). Moreover, one should note the load of the BB is doubled compared to the system throughput, i.e. the BB has to process sequentially 400 requests per second (REQ or REL) when the system throughput is 200 requests per second. On the other hand, the slope of the response time obtained when using PTT-BB remains almost stable over time. This is due to three main reasons. The first one is that a per-path resource management at the eBB level involves smaller processing overhead than a per-link resource management as realised by the single BB. Furthermore, two resource requests involving two different paths are treated in parallel as they do not use the same "resource". This can not be the case with a single BB as we have also to check if the two set of links involved by the two paths are mutually exclusive or not. Last but not least, the bottleneck in the system, which is the cBB, is heavily loaded as each eBB sends path-quota requests each 10s. The fact that PTT-BB is more scalable than a single BB is therefore not a surprising conclusion.

7 Conclusion and Future Work

In this paper, we presented a novel approach to achieve a scalable resource management within the scope of the on-demand policy based resource allocation process. The scalability property of the proposed solution (PTT-BB) has been achieved through the distribution of the bandwidth brokerage operation among several mutually exclusive components. PTT-BB is based on a hierarchical management of network-resources. This management involves several edge-BB that realize a per-path resource management and a centralized-BB which proactively allocates/de-allocates link-resources to paths. Hence, a set of algorithms have been designed in order to: (i) realized a per-path admission control within the eBB, (ii) proactively adapt the amount of resources allocated to each path, and finally (iii) realize a per-link resource allocation/de-allocation to paths within the cBB.

In order to demonstrate the performance features of PTT-BB, an intensive set of experimentations have been carried out and the performance results have been compared to those obtained when a single BB is used. These experimentations have demonstrated that a system using PTT-BB is more scalable than a system using a single BB. Indeed, the average response time to a request remains almost stable with PTT-BB and this remains true in spite of the system throughput increase. This is not the case when using a single BB. Furthermore, we depicted throughout our experimentations that the call blocking probability of PTT-BB can be similar to the one obtained with a single BB. However, in the case of PTT-BB, two parameters have to be carefully chosen in order to control the call blocking probability: the adaptation time interval and the bandwidth unit (or Quota) size.

As a perspective to the work presented in this paper, we target to investigate the dynamic optimization of the parameters used in the proactive path bandwidth adaptation algorithm. The objective of this future work is to minimize the call blocking probability while optimizing network resource usage.

References

1. Haddadou, K., Ghamri-Doudane, S., Ghamri-Doudane, Y., and Agoulmine, N.: Designing Scalable on-demand Policy-based Resource Allocation in IP Networks. Technical Report under submission (2005).
2. Verma, D.C.: Policy-Based Networking–Architecture and Algorithms. New Riders Publishing, Indianapolis (2000).
3. Boyle, J., et al: The COPS (Common Open Policy Service) Protocol. RFC 2748 (2000).
4. Zhang, Z.-L., Duan, Z., and Hou, Y. T.: On Scalable Design of Bandwidth Brokers. IEICE Transactions on Communications, Vol. E84-B, No. 8 (2001).
5. ITU-T Recommendation No. E.721: Network grade of service parameters and target values for circuit-switched services in the evolving ISDN. (1999).
6. ITU-T Recommendation No. E.500: Traffic intensity measurement principles. (1998).

Short-Delay Video Streaming with Restricted Supplying Peer Bandwidth

Hung-Chang Yang[1], Hsiang-Fu Yu[1], Li-Ming Tseng[1], and Yi-Ming Chen[2]

[1] Dep. of Computer Science & Information Engineering, National Central University,
Jung-Li, Taiwan
{cyht, yu}@dslab.csie.ncu.edu.tw, tsenglm@csie.ncu.edu.tw
[2] Dep. of Information Management, National Central University, Jung-Li, Taiwan
cym@im.mgt.ncu.edu.tw

Abstract. With the growth of bandwidth, real-time video streaming service becomes popular. Such application is also considered a future killer application on Internet. Recent research efforts have demonstrated the promising potential of building cost-effective video streaming systems on top of peer-to-peer (P2P) networks. Since the peers have limited capacity, such as upstream bandwidth, each streaming session may involve multiple supplying peers. In this paper, we propose a novel strategy to retrieve a long-duration video from multiple peers which have arbitrary and restricted upstream bandwidth, such that the waiting time is minimized. In comparison with the previous work [13], our strategy can greatly improve the waiting time. In the arbitrary given examples, our strategy can improve the waiting time by 67%. To take into account the popular compressed video with variable bit rate, we also show how to apply our strategy readily to the VBR videos.

1 Introduction

With the advancement of broadband networking technology, and the growth of processor speed and disk capacity, real-time video streaming service is getting increasingly popular among users and contributes a significant amount of today's Internet traffic. However, there are still many challenges towards building cost-effective, robust and scalable video streaming systems due to the huge size, high bandwidth and delay requirements for video streaming.

A majority of video streaming architectures follows a client-server design. The server may have as many streams of each program as the current number of potential viewers (i.e. users currently connected to the service). Since the growth in bandwidth can never keep up with the growth in the number of viewers. It may easily run out of bandwidth and result in tremendous demand for communication bandwidth on the system and underlying network To alleviate the stress on the bandwidth, there are many researches have been stimulated in the recent years. One way is to broadcast popular videos [8-11, 14, 15]. According to [6], 80% of demands are on a few (10 or 20) very popular videos. Because the server's broadcasting activity is independent of the arrivals of requests, the approach is appropriate to popular or hot videos that may interest many viewers at a certain period of time. These approaches are using IP multicast technique to achieve serving multiple viewers using the same stream. However, the IP multicast has not been widely employed until now due to the increased control

J. Dalmau and G. Hasegawa (Eds.): MMNS 2005, LNCS 3754, pp. 362–370, 2005.

overhead and computational complexity at the routers. It is unlikely that IP multicast will be widely employed in the near future.

Broadband access to the Internet through services such as ADSL (asymmetric digital subscriber line) and FTTH (fiber to the home) has recently become very popular. Such services allow a large number of users to have their computers constantly connected to the Internet. Most computers are capable of storing many large files of digital content for the user, and many users are making such content available to others. Such technique is called peer-to-peer (P2P) networks. Each peer (i.e. user constantly connected to the Internet) can be a server to share its resources (supplying peer), while it is a client to obtain data from others (requesting peer). Due to this characteristic, application layer multicast (ALM) has recently proposed to implement the multicast functionality in application layer instead of IP layer, i.e. some of peers participating in the multicast play the role of the multicast router. Thus, ALM can be directly applicable to the current Internet since it does not need any new additional modification at IP routers. Application-level multicast techniques, such as NICE [1], SplitStream [2], SCRIBE [3], Narada [4], oStream [5] and Zigzag [12], construct the distribution trees over the peers to deliver video streams. However, it introduces another problem: it may overload some peers beyond their capacities. A peer in the tree may become a parent of several other peers. In the peer-to-peer networks, peers typically have limited capacity, especially of the upstream bandwidth. In many cases, peer cannot even provide the full stream rate to another peer.

In general, a P2P video streaming system has the following characteristics [7,13]: (1) peers have limited capacity, such as the restricted upstream bandwidth; (2) peers are heterogeneous in their bandwidth contribution. Therefore, each streaming session may involve multiple supplying peers. Xu [13] first proposed how to assign video data to multiple supplying peers in one streaming session. The goal is to ensure requesting peers can quickly initiate and then continuously playback a video, while it is being downloaded. However, Xu's work assumes the upstream bandwidth offered by a supplying peer must be one of the following values: $b/2$, $b/4$, $b/8$... $b/2^m$, b is the video consumption rate. This assumption is not flexible. To solve this problem, in this paper we propose a novel strategy to retrieve a long-duration video from multiple peers which have arbitrary and restricted upstream bandwidth, such that the waiting time for the requesting peer is minimized. In comparison with the Xu's work, our strategy can greatly improves the waiting time. For example the upstream bandwidth of supplying peers are $b/2$, $b/4$, $b/8$, and $b/8$, our strategy can improve the waiting time by 67%. To take into account the popular compressed video with variable bit rate, we also show how to apply readily to the VBR videos.

The rest of this paper is organized as follows. In Section 2, we review the Xu's work in detail. In Section 3, we present and analyze our strategy. How to apply our strategy readily to the VBR videos is also discussed in this section. In Section 4, its performance comparison is presented. Finally we make brief conclusions in Section 5.

2 Related Works

To the best of our knowledge, only the Xu's work [13] deals with problem which assign video data to multiple supplying peers in one streaming session such that the waiting time is minimized. Here, we first review some ideas used in it.

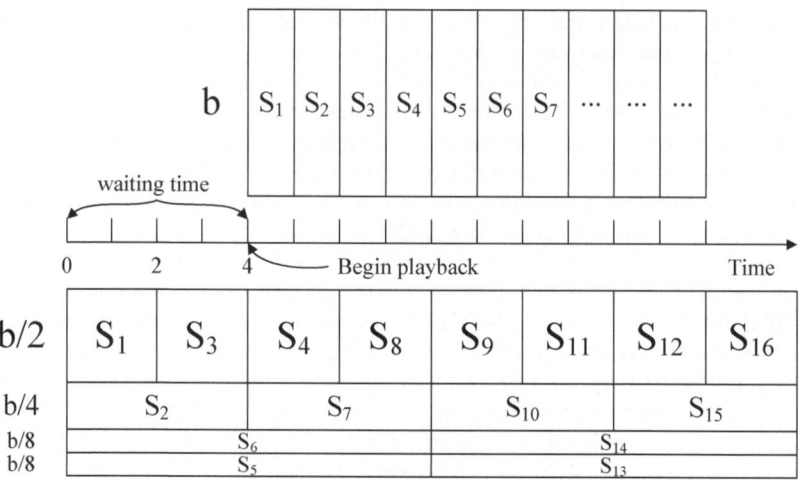

Fig. 1. Video data assignment of Xu's research

Suppose the upstream bandwidth offered by a supplying peer must be one of the following values: $b/2$, $b/4$, $b/8$... $b/2^m$, b is the video consumption rate and m is a positive integer. If there are n supplying peers which have been sorted in descending order according to their upstream bandwidth, and the lowest is $b/2^m$. Then it computes the assignment of the first 2^m segments, and the assignment repeats itself every 2^m segments for the rest of the video file. The segment assignment is in reverse order, such as 2^m, 2^m-1,..., 1. Its assignment strategy is from top to bottom and from right to left. The minimum waiting time will be n * the length of a segment. An assignment example is shown in Figure 1. There are four supplying peers. The upstream bandwidth of supplying peers is $b/2$, $b/4$, $b/8$ and $b/8$; and the video playback time scale is described in top side.

3   Real-Time Video Streaming Data Assignment

In this section, we first present the problem more detail. Let the total length of the requested video be L, measured in seconds. Let the video consumption rate be b, measured in bits per second. Assume there are n supplying peers which the sum of upstream bandwidth is equal to the video consumption rate. The upstream bandwidth of supplying peers are denoted as b_i, $i = 1, 2, 3, ..., n$, measured in bits per second. The problem is: if we want to partition the whole video data into m segments (equal length is unnecessary), how to partition the video data and how to assign the segments to each supplying peer, such that the waiting time w is minimized. In other words, if we want to ensure the waiting time will be w, how to partition the video data and how to assign the segments to each supplying peer, such that the number of segments m is minimized. That is, the length of each segment must be as long as possible.

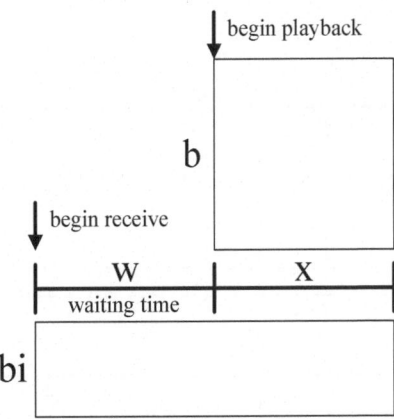

Fig. 2. The basic principle of our strategy

3.1 Description of the Basic Principle

Now, we describe the basic principle of our strategy: Consider we want to retrieve video data from some supplying peer which upstream bandwidth is b_i, and the waiting time is w Figure 2 shows this concept. From the figure, we observe that in order to guarantee continuous playback, the time x to retrieve the remaining portion must be not greater than the entire playback duration of the segment. In other words,

$$x \le \frac{b_i(w+x)}{b} \tag{1}$$

Thus, by satisfying this condition (1), we ensure that the retrieval of the remaining portion will not affect the continuity of the playback at any time instant. Therefore the longest length of the segment will be $x = \dfrac{b_i}{b - b_i} w$, while

$$x = \frac{b_i(w+x)}{b} \quad => \quad bx = b_i(w+x) \tag{2}$$

3.2 The Design and Analysis of Video Retrieval Strategy

In this section, we present our retrieval strategy in detail and determine the minimized waiting time w of requesting peer which retrieve m segments from all the n supplying peers, which have been sorted in descending order according to their upstream bandwidth.

According to the equation (2), if the upstream bandwidth of the supplying peer p_1 is b_1 and the waiting time is w, then the longest length x_1 of segment S_1 must satisfy the equation, $bx_1 = b_1(w + x_1)$. Now the waiting time for playback segment S_2 will equal to $w + x_1$. Hence the longest length x_2 of segment S_2 must satisfy the equation,

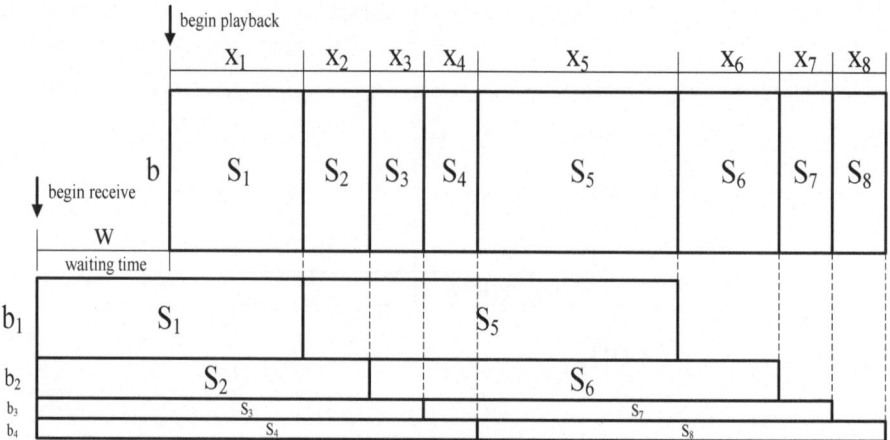

Fig. 3. An example of the video retrieval strategy

$bx_2 = b_2(w + x_1 + x_2)$, while the upstream bandwidth of the supplying peer p_2 is b_2
Figure 3 shows an example of the video retrieval strategy, while $m=8$ and $n=4$. Then
we have the following recursive equations for the segments 1 to n.

$$
\begin{cases}
bx_1 = b_1(w + x_1) \\
bx_2 = b_2(w + x_1 + x_2) \\
bx_3 = b_3(w + x_1 + x_2 + x_3) \\
\quad \bullet \\
\quad \bullet \\
bx_n = b_n(w + x_1 + x_2 + \ldots + x_n)
\end{cases}
$$

$$
\Rightarrow
\begin{cases}
x_1 = \dfrac{b_1}{b - b_1} w \\[2mm]
x_2 = \dfrac{b_2}{(b - b_1)(b - b_2)} wb \\[2mm]
x_3 = \dfrac{b_3}{(b - b_1)(b - b_2)(b - b_3)} wb^2 \\[2mm]
\quad \bullet \\
\quad \bullet \\
x_n = \dfrac{b_n}{\prod\limits_{i=1}^{n}(b - b_i)} wb^{n-1}
\end{cases}
$$

If the number of the segment m is larger than the number of supplying peers n, then
we can further have the following n recursive equations for the segments $n+1$ to $n+n$.

$$\begin{cases} bx_{n+1} = b_1(x_2 + x_3 + ... + x_{n+1}) \\ bx_{n+2} = b_2(x_3 + x_4 + ... + x_{n+2}) \\ \bullet \\ \bullet \\ bx_{n+n} = b_n(x_{n+1} + x_{n+2} + ... + x_{n+n-1}) \end{cases}$$

$$\Rightarrow \quad x_{n+i} = \frac{b_i}{b - b_i}(x_{i+1} + x_{i+2} + ... + x_{i+n-1}) , \quad i=1\sim n$$

For the segments $2n+1$ to $2n+n$, we can have the following n recursive equations.

$$\begin{cases} bx_{2n+1} = b_1(x_{n+2} + x_{n+3} + ... + x_{n+n+1}) \\ bx_{2n+2} = b_2(x_{n+3} + x_{n+4} + ... + x_{n+n+2}) \\ \bullet \\ \bullet \\ bx_{2n+n} = b_n(x_{n+n+1} + x_{n+n+2} + ... + x_{n+n+n-1}) \end{cases}$$

$$\Rightarrow \quad x_{2n+i} = \frac{b_i}{b - b_i}(x_{i+n+1} + x_{i+n+2} + ... + x_{i+2n-1}) , \quad i=1\sim n$$

And so on. Finally, we can induce the following recursive formulas (3) to determine the minimized waiting time w.

$$\begin{cases} x_p = \dfrac{b_p}{\prod\limits_{i=1}^{p}(b - b_i)} wb^{p-1}, \quad p \le n \\ x_p = \dfrac{b_{[(p-1)\bmod n]+1}}{b - b_{[(p-1)\bmod n]+1}}(x_{p-n+1} + x_{p-n+2} + ... + x_{p-1}), \quad n < p \le m \\ \sum\limits_{i-1}^{m} x_i = L \end{cases} \tag{3}$$

3.3 Apply Our Strategy to VBR Videos

Since the consumption rate of VBR videos usually varies with time. In order to guarantee continuous playback, we must initiate playback after finishing the retrieval of whole segment. Therefore, the size of segment S must be not greater than the size of retrieval data during the waiting time w. The equation (1) must be modified by following.

$$b_i w \ge \sum_{j \in S} f_j , \text{ where } f_i \text{ is the frame sequence, measured in bits} \tag{4}$$

Thus, by satisfying this condition (4), the longest length of the segment will be computed while

$$b_i w = \sum_{j \in S} f_j \tag{5}$$

Figure 4 shows an example of the video retrieval strategy, while $m=8$ and $n=4$. We can induce the following recursive formulas (6) to partition the video and assign to the supplying peers for a given waiting time w.

$$
\begin{cases}
b_p \left(w + \dfrac{\sum\limits_{k=1}^{p-1} |S_k|}{F} \right) = \sum\limits_{j \in S_p} f_j, \, p \le n \\[4ex]
b_{[(p-1) \bmod n]+1} \dfrac{\sum\limits_{k=p-n}^{p-1} |S_k|}{F} = \sum\limits_{j \in S_p} f_j, \, n < p \le m
\end{cases}
\tag{6}
$$

where $|S_k|$ is the length of segment S_k, measured in frames; F is the video consumption rate, measured in frames per second.

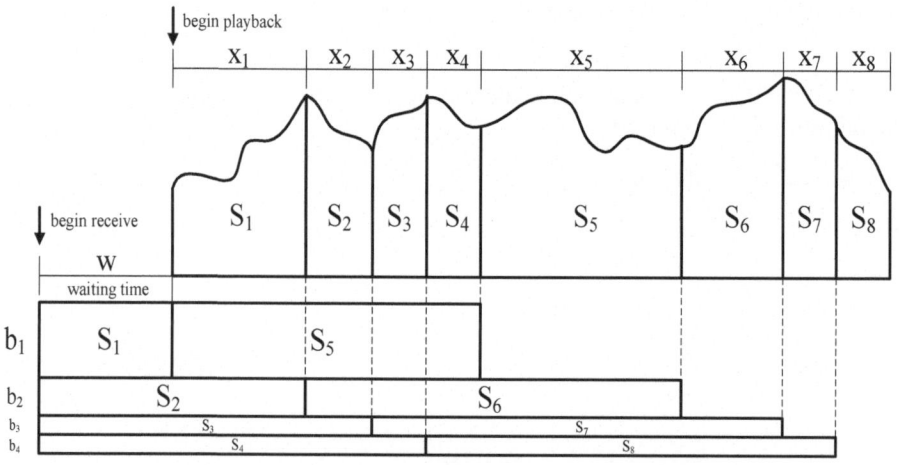

Fig. 4. An example of the VBR video retrieval strategy

4 Performance Comparison

Review the goal is: if we want to partition the whole video data into m segments, how to partition the video data and how to assign the segments to each supplying peer, such that the access time w is minimized. Herein, we'll compare the viewers' waiting time with the Xu's work [13]. Assume the number of segments m is from 100 to

1000. Two arbitrary examples of upstream bandwidth of supplying peers are given as $b/2$, $b/4$, $b/8$, $b/8$ and $b/4$, $b/4$, $b/8$, $b/8$, $b/8$, $b/16$, $b/16$. Figure 5 show the first example, we can observe our strategy can greatly improve the viewers' waiting time by 67%. The second example is shown in Figure 6. Our strategy can still improve the viewers' waiting time by 59%.

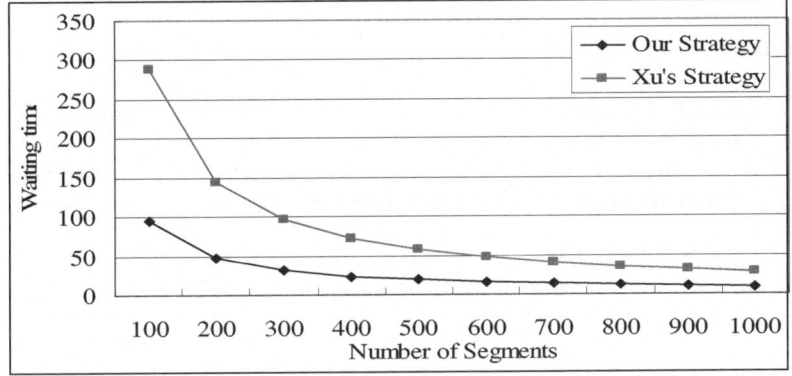

Fig. 5. Compare with viewers' waiting time with the Xu's work

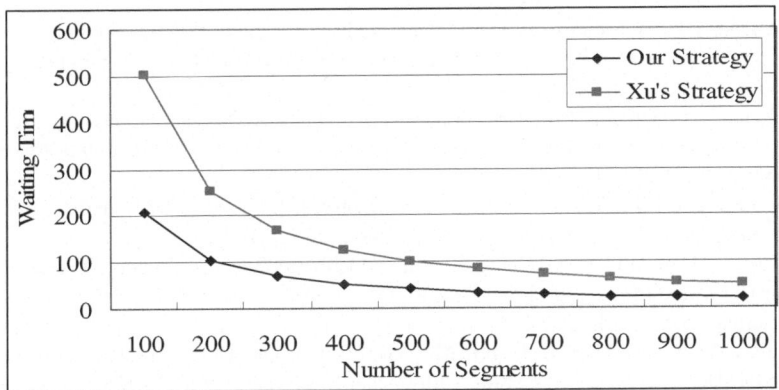

Fig. 6. Compare with viewers' waiting time with the Xu's work

5 Conclusions

With the advancement of broadband networking technology, and the growth of processor speed and disk capacity, real-time video streaming service is getting increasingly popular among users and contributes a significant amount of today's Internet traffic. Recent research efforts have demonstrated the promising potential of building cost-effective video streaming systems on top of peer-to-peer (P2P) networks. Since the peers have limited capacity, such as upstream bandwidth, each streaming session may involve multiple supplying peers. In this paper, we propose a novel strategy to retrieve a long-duration video from multiple peers which have arbitrary and restricted upstream bandwidth, such that the waiting time is minimized. In comparison with the previous work [13], our strategy can greatly improve the waiting time. In the above-mentioned two arbitrary examples, our strategy can improve the waiting time by 67% and 59%. To take into account the popular compressed video with variable bit rate, we also show how to apply our strategy readily to the VBR videos.

References

1. S. Banerjee, B. Bhattacharjee, C. Kommareddy and G. Varghese, "Scalable Application Layer Multicast," *ACM SIGCOMM*, Aug. 2002.
2. M. Castro, P. Druschel, A. Kermarrec, A. Nandi, A. Rowstron and A. Singh, "SplitStream: High-Bandwidth Content Distribution in a Cooperative Environment," *In Proc. of IPTPS*, Feb. 2003.
3. M. Castro, P. D ruschel, A. Kermarrec and A. Rowstron, "SCRIBE: A Large-Scale and Decentralized Application-Level Multicast Infrastructure," *IEEE Journal on Selected Areas in Communications*, Oct. 2002.
4. Y. Chu, S. Rao, S. Seshan and H. Zhang, "A Case for End System Multicast," *IEEE Journal on Selected Areas in Communications*, Oct. 2002.
5. Yi Cui, Baochun Li and Klara Nahrstedt, "oStream: Asynchronous Streaming Multicast in Application-Layer Overlay Networks," *IEEE Journal on Selected Areas in Communications*, vol. 22, no. 1, Jan. 2004.
6. Asit Dan, Dinkar Sitaram, Perwez Shahabuddin, "Dynamic batching policies for an on-demand video server," *Journal of Multimedia Systems*, vol. 4, no. 3, pp. 112–121, June 1996.
7. Mohamed M. Hefeeda, Bharat K. Bhargava and David K. Y. Yau, "A Hybrid Architecture for Cost-Effective On-Demand Media Streaming," *Journal of Computer Networks*, vol. 44, pp. 353-382, 2004.
8. L.S. Juhn and L.M. Tseng, "Harmonic broadcasting for video-on-demand service," *IEEE Trans on Broadcasting*, vol. 43, no. 3, pp. 268-271, Sep 1997.
9. Julian Liu, Su-Chiu Yang, Hsiang-Fu Yu, and Li-Ming Tseng, "Content Delivery Network with Hot-video broadcasting and Peer-to-peer Approach," *Journal of Information Science and Engineering*, Vol. 20, No. 6, 2004.
10. Anirban Mahanti, Derek L. Eager, Mary K. Vernon and David Sundaram-Stukel, "Scalable On-Demand Media Streaming with Packet Loss Recovery," *IEEE Trans. on Networking*, vol. 11, no. 2, pp. 195-209, April 2003.
11. Yu-Chee Tseng, Ming-Hour Yang and Chi-He Chang, "A Recursive Frequency-Splitting Scheme for Broadcasting Hot Videos in VOD Service", *IEEE Transactions on Communications*, vol. 50, issue:8, pp. 1348-1355, Aug 2002.
12. Duc A. Tran, Kien A. Hua and Tai T. Do, "A Peer-to-Peer Architecture for Media Streaming," *IEEE Journal on Selected Areas in Communications*, Jan. 2004.
13. Dongyan Xu, Mohamed Hefeeda, Susanne Hambrusch and Bharat Bhargava, "On Peer-to-Peer Media Streaming," *IEEE ICDCS*, July 2002.
14. Hung-Chang Yang, Hsiang-Fu Yu and Li-Ming Tseng, "Adaptive Live Broadcasting for Highly-Demand Videos," *Journal of Information Science and Engineering*, vol. 19, no. 3, pp. 531-549, May 2003.
15. Hsiang-Fu Yu, Hung-Chang Yang, Li-Ming Tseng and Yi-Ming Chen, "Simple VBR Staircase Broadcasting (SVSB)," *Journal of Computer Communications*, 2005.

Initial Approach Toward Self-configuration and Self-optimization in IP Networks

Elyes Lehtihet[1,2], Hajer Derbel[1], Nazim Agoulmine[1],
Yacine Ghamri-Doudane[1], and Sven van der Meer[2]

[1] Laboratoire de Réseaux et Systèmes Multimédia,
Institut d'Informatique d'Entreprise and Université d'Evry-Val d'Essonne,
Evry, France
{derbel, ghamri}@iie.cnam.fr
Nazim.Agoulmine@iup.univ-evry.fr
[2] Telecommunications Software & Systems Group,
Waterford Institute of Technology, Cork Road, Waterford, Ireland
{elehtihet, vdmeer}@tssg.org

Abstract. The growing heterogeneity and scalability of Internet services has complicated, beyond human capabilities, the management of network devices. Therefore, a new paradigm called autonomic networking is being introduced to control, in an efficient and automatic manner, this complex environment. This approach aims to enhance network elements with capabilities that allow them to choose their own behavior for achieving high-level directives. This so called autonomic network element should be able to optimize its configuration, ensure its protection, detect/repair unpredicted conflicts between services requirements and coordinate its behavior with other network elements.

In this paper, we present a research activity that investigates this new concept, and applies it to facilitate the configuration and the optimization of a multi-services IP network. This approach is a first step toward building a self-configured and self-optimized IP network that automatically supports the QoS requirements of heterogeneous applications without any external intervention. Different paradigms have been explored in order to model this behavior and to render network equipment autonomic. A laboratory prototype has been developed to highlight the autonomic behavior of the network to achieve heterogeneous QoS requirements of multimedia and data applications.

1 Introduction

The explosion of Internet technologies, services and applications and their corresponding heterogeneity has exacerbated, beyond human capacity, the complexity of managing the Internet. Traditional management and control techniques are no longer capable of ensuring the efficiency and cost effectiveness of existing and more probably future networks. This problem is already considered as crucial by the research community in almost all computer systems and recently a

J. Dalmau and G. Hasegawa (Eds.): MMNS 2005, LNCS 3754, pp. 371–382, 2005.

new paradigm has emerged as a potential solution. This paradigm, called self-ware, is a novel approach to perform network control, as well as management of middle box communication, service creation and composition of network functionalities. It is based on universal and fine-grained multiplexing of numerous policies, rules and events that is done autonomously to facilitates desired behavior of groups of network elements [1]. This approach focuses on the application of analogies from biology and economics to massively distributed computing systems, particularly in the domains of autonomic computing. IBM is considered as the first to introduce this term into the field of computing in 2001. This initiative aims to unify research related to selfware computer systems that are a capable of being self-managed [2]. Self-management encompasses a number of selfware management capabilities such as: Self-configuration, Self-optimizing, Self-healing, Self-protection, Self-awareness, etc.[3].

The concept of selfware is not only applicable to computers but to any system with processing, memory and communication capabilities. It not only affects the design of the system but also the applications, middleware, network equipment, etc. In the networking realm, the objective is to design autonomic networks that are able to manage themselves in an autonomic way and exhibit a global "intelligence" through their interactions. Our objective in this research is to investigate this concept and apply it in order to simplify the control and management of operators' IP networks. The aim is to aid the operator in the complex task of managing their networks by allowing them to control the networks behavior through only high-level goals. The network will automatically adjust its configuration to fulfill these goals without any intervention from the operator. This approach can facilitate cooperation between different administrative domains that share network devices.

This paper is organized as follows: Section 2 presents the limitations of current management approaches that have motivated the investigation of a novel approach. The following section presents the proposed management architecture. Section 4 describes the language we have designed to capture the high-level management goal. The following section details the architecture of the Autonomic Element (AE) as well as the internal functionalities. A prototype of the system as well as a set of conducted tests are presented in section 6. The following section 7 presents general discussions as well as concluding remarks about this work and future directions.

2   A Complexity Beyond the Capacity of Existing Management Systems

Policy Based Management (PBM) is defined as the usage of policy rules to manage the configuration and behavior of one or more entities [4]. In the PBM approach, decisions related to the allocation of network resources and/or security are taken by a central control entity called PDP (Policy Decision Point), which concentrates the entire decision-making activity of the system. However, as the network becomes larger and more heterogeneous and the provided service varies with different QoS requirement, these approaches become very difficult to specify, design and deploy. In the PBM approach, the number of policy rules, the consistency between the rules and the knowledge expected from the operator to control the entire network render it very complex to achieve. The only known solution to deal with this growing complexity in the realm is the complete decentralization of the decision-making process among the distributed entities.

We consider that the operational parameters (Routing services, QoS services, Connectivity Services, . . .) offered by individual network devices must be modeled in accordance with an **agreed-upon data model**. The definition of a common data model enables the network administrator to map business rules to the network by refining abstract entities into concrete objects/devices [5]; and the network designer to engineer the network such that it can provide different functions for different requirements which is equivalent to the refinement of high-level goals into operations, supported by the concrete objects/devices, that when performed will achieve the high-level goal [5].

In our approach we aim to achieve two main objectives; (1) to avoid the centralization of the decision making process and (2) facilitate the specification and the enforcement of operators objectives. We argue that every element in the network should be autonomic i.e. having the capability to take its own decision and to supervise several management objectives. The enforcement of this autonomy is achieved by (1) the specification of high-level goals (we have used an approach based on Finite State Machine theory, where each state represents a target behavior of the autonomic elements in a particular context), and (2) the specification of an interaction schema between AEs to coordinate their behavior and achieve their goals.

3   Autonomic Management Based on Goals

The management of today's communication systems needs more autonomy and decentralization. With this in mind, we propose a new management approach called "Goal-based management". The aim of this approach is to design a network capable of to organizing itself in such way that the aggregate behavior of each autonomic element satisfies the high-level operational goals defined by the administrator.

We define a goal as a semantic association between system resources. By subscribing a Goal, an autonomic element becomes a part of an entire autonomous domain (i.e. regrouping of elements with a single objective). All the elements associated with a single Goal are viewed as a single autonomic entity though an element can be associated to multiple Goals. Consequently, the behavior of an autonomic element can be driven by one or multiple Goals. The ability of the autonomic element to deal with multiple Goal definitions (multiple business requirements) is handled by the goal language. The setting of the managed element allows him to detect unpredicted conflicts between different objectives.

Systems resources (autonomic elements) inherit their properties and relationships from a general information model, which we have defined to model both

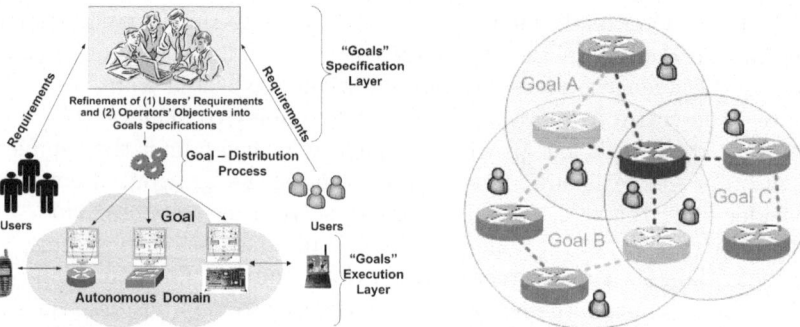

a. Goal-based network architecture   b. Multiple overlapped autonomous
domains sharing common resources

Fig. 1. Goal-based Management

AE behavior and communication mechanisms. The knowledge associated with
these relationships is essential for almost all autonomic management functions.
However, it is not sufficient to only establish the relationships between resources
but it is also important to capture the semantics of these relations. In fact,
without this explicit meaning the resolution of a problem is not possible [6]. As
depicted in fig.1, our framework is organized into two layers:

- *"Goals"* specification layer: its aim is to define the high-level objectives
  (Goals). This layer introduces a number of "goal specifications" in the network that allows the specification of Goals in terms of explicit behaviors
  expected from the target autonomic elements in various contexts. . In this
  first approach, the goals are specified as a state machine representing different possible network element behaviors as well as transition conditions
  between these states. These Goals drive the network equipment's behavior
  to exhibit self-management capabilities. This entity is called "Goal Server".
- *"Goals"* execution layer: the lower layer contains a set of autonomic network
  elements (AE) that behave in an autonomic manner while trying to achieve
  the high-level goals. The autonomic equipment is self-managed and capable
  of adapting it's behavior according to the context. The context of an AE
  corresponds to all the information about its environment i.e. its local state,
  remote AE states, active services, etc. AEs are able to interact in order
  to exchange knowledge and update their context. In real networks, these
  elements can be routers, switches, gateways, software,. . .

4   A Language to Capture Goals Description

In order to facilitate interoperability between management entities in the context
of autonomous management, it is necessary to define a shared understanding of
both domain information and the problem statement. Unless each autonomic
entity in a system can share information with every other autonomic entity and

so contribute to an overall system awareness, the vision of autonomic communications will not really be reached. Thus, we need a common data model to represent all resources in a uniform manner [6].

To achieve this objective, we need a language to express the specification of the Goal. Instead of developing a specific language, we have chosen to extend an existing one. This extension of the language is done at the metamodel level i.e. where the language itself is defined. We have added the necessary primitives to the language to model a Goal. Our reference information model is the Common Information Model (CIM) from the DMTF [7]. In the following, we will describe how we have extended this model to fulfill our requirements. As shown in the fig.2, the Goal concept is a specialization of a CIM Class. Like the CIM Notification concept depicted in the CIM Meta Schema, the managed elements have to subscribe, via an association, to a particular Goal. This subscription is called the Goal-distribution process and is detailed in section 5. The instances of the Goal conform to the CIM-XML mapping for the CIM Classes as provided by the DMTF [8], see fig.3. The Goal structure aggregates new extensions to the CIM Schema. Every extension is a specialization of a CIM Named Element and conforms to the CIM-XML representation of the properties, methods and parameters. We have added specific Qualifiers to every new structure of the CIM Meta Schema in order to capture the additional semantics to represent a Goal. The Goal concept is in fact a grouping of elements that permit to achieve a set of management objectives in specific contexts. We have structured the Goal as an aggregation of "Goal-Behaviors" and a "Goal-Setting". The Goal-Setting determines the behavior of the Goal according to a particular context and describes the AE's Role, Location and Identifier. It is also a composition of management data locating the other peer AEs sharing the same Goal (Element-Setting) and describing the management context of the user's application services

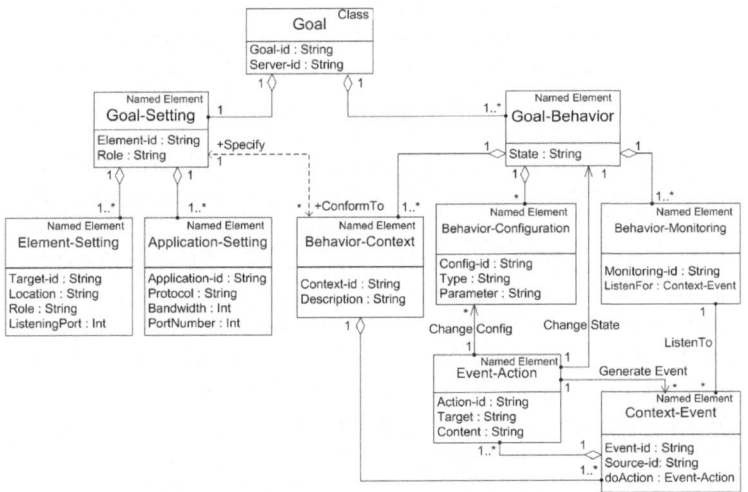

Fig. 2. Specification of the Goal Language

(Application-Setting). The Application-Setting aims to represent the user-level and the business-level requirements. This Application-Setting is specific to our case study; a more generic representation of the management context should be proposed in future work.

Every Goal-Behavior aggregates a set of Configuration, Monitoring, and Context specifications. The State is the unique identifier for the behavior of a Goal. The Behavior-Configuration of an AE corresponds to the execution of platform specific code correlated with the expected behavior. The Behavior-Monitoring implements the listeners for the exact type of Context-Events that need to be considered by the element in a particular state. Context-Event defines the occurrence of (1) low-level events collected by the sensors and provided by the platform-specific listeners, and (2) high-level events (messages) coming from goal servers and/or other AEs. The Behavior-Context part conforms to the Goal-Setting and identifies the collected events (Context-Event), and the equivalent actions (Event-Action), to achieve the Settings of the Goal in a particular context (behavior's state). A Context-Event is triggered from the monitoring module when sets of conditions are realized. These conditions are implemented in the system level of an AE by a set of activated sensors. When a Context-Event is verified, it triggers the execution of a set of Event-Actions according to the new context. An Event-Action specifies the execution of some platform-specific code and/or the emission of messages to the Goal Servers and other AEs. Here again, the internal implementation of the AE, which is specific to an execution environment, must match the description of the Event-Action. These actions can be reflexive i.e. change behavior state, or reactive i.e. change the Behavior-Configuration of the element and/or trigger changes in the behavior of other AEs. Changes in the AE's state trigger a specific re-configuration of the element, to apply the Context related to this new state.

The Behavior-Context module specification conforms to the Goal-Setting and it identifies the collected events, and the equivalent actions for realizing the settings of the Goal in a particular context (behavior's state).

The Goal representation as a Finite State Machine seems to be implicit in our case. The Goal aggregates multiple behaviors. Each behavior represents a State and is modeled by a set of configurations and policies to enforce as well as a set of sensors to activate. The transition between the states is defined by the Context according to the Setting. In simple terms, autonomic elements tailor their behavior to user- and business-requirements. The complete XML representation of the goal is presented in the fig.3. The AE is aware of the network context via the Goal-Setting. Conflicts are detected when the Context-Events, from different Goal instances, reported by the Behavior-Monitoring module do not conform to the Application-Setting of all the Goals. In this case the AE collects the Behavior-Context identifiers and sends them to the Goal Servers. The problem can be temporarily solved by assigning priorities to the goals depending on predefined policies between autonomic domains.

The Goal-language supports the communication mechanism between AEs and the Goal Servers. Every element exchanges information (knowledge) in a

```
<?xml version="1.0"?>
<CIM CIMVERSION="2.2" DTDVERSION="2.1">
<DECLARATION>
<DECLGROUP>
<VALUE.OBJECT>
<GOAL NAME="QoS_Goal">
 <QUALIFIER TOSUBCLASS="false" TRANSLATABLE="true" NAME="Version"
 TYPE="STRING"><VALUE>1.0</VALUE></QUALIFIER>
 <QUALIFIER TRANSLATABLE="true" NAME="Description" TYPE="STRING">
 <VALUE>Definition of our Goal that consider the interactions of
 Three Router to ensure QoS requirements</VALUE></QUALIFIER>
 <QUALIFIER NAME="Goal-id" TYPE="STRING">
 <VALUE>http://www.tssg.org/#scenario-QoS-requirements</VALUE>
 </QUALIFIER>
 <QUALIFIER NAME="Server-id" TYPE="STRING">
 <VALUE>To be defined after the Goal-distribution process.</VALUE>
 </QUALIFIER>
------------------------------------------------------------
<GOAL-BEHAVIOR CLASSORIGIN="QoS_Goal" State="Best Effort">
<QUALIFIER NAME="Description" TYPE="STRING">
<VALUE>The description of the behavior</VALUE></QUALIFIER>
------------------------------------------------------------
<GOAL-BEHAVIOR CLASSORIGIN="QoS_Goal" State="Priority Queuing">
```

```
<BEHAVIOR-CONTEXT
 Context-id="http://www.tssg.org/#scenario-QoS-requirements_Context_0001">
 <QUALIFIER TRANSLATABLE="true" NAME="Description" TYPE="STRING">
 <VALUE>Describe how this context is conform to the Goal-Setting
 and explain how the User- and business-level objectives are realized</VALUE>
 </QUALIFIER>
 <CONTEXT-EVENT
 Event-id="http://www.tssg.org/#scenario-QoS-requirements_Event_0001">
 <QUALIFIER NAME="Source-id" TYPE="STRING">
 <VALUE>Indicate the Source of the Event and it's defined by the
 Goal-Distribution process in the case of the Event is coming
 from another Autonomic Element or from the Goal Server</VALUE></QUALIFIER>
 <EVENT-ACTION
 Action-id="http://www.tssg.org/#scenario-QoS-requirements_Action_0001">
 <QUALIFIER TRANSLATABLE="true" NAME="Target-id" TYPE="STRING">
 <VALUE>Indicate the Target of the Action and it's defined by the
 Goal-Distribution process in the case of the Target is another
 Autonomic Element or the Goal Server</VALUE></QUALIFIER>
 <QUALIFIER TRANSLATABLE="true" NAME="Content" TYPE="STRING">
 <VALUE>Indicate the Content of the Action and it's defined by the
 administrator of the Goal.</VALUE></QUALIFIER>
 </EVENT-ACTION></CONTEXT-EVENT></BEHAVIOR-CONTEXT></GOAL-BEHAVIOR>
```

```
<GOAL-SETTING CLASSORIGIN="QoS_Goal">
 <QUALIFIER NAME="Element-id" TYPE="STRING"><VALUE>Indicate
 the unique Identifier of the Autonomic Element in the Goal
 and it's defined by the Goal-Distribution process</VALUE>
 </QUALIFIER>
 <QUALIFIER NAME="Role" TYPE="STRING"><VALUE>Indicate the
 Role of the Autonomic Element in the Goal and it's also
 defined by the Goal-Distribution process</VALUE></QUALIFIER>
------------------------------------------------------------
<SETTING-APPLICATION Application-id="VoIP">
<QUALIFIER NAME="Application-id" TYPE="STRING"><VALUE>The
description of the Application</VALUE>
</QUALIFIER>
<QUALIFIER NAME="Protocol" TYPE="STRING"><VALUE>Type of
the Protocol</VALUE></QUALIFIER>
<QUALIFIER NAME="Bandwidth" TYPE="STRING"><VALUE>Percentage
of bandwidth</VALUE></QUALIFIER>
</SETTING-APPLICATION>
------------------------------------------------------------
<SETTING-APPLICATION Application-id="VoD">
```

```
<SETTING-ELEMENT Element-id="http://www.tssg.org/
#scenario-QoS-requirements_Element_Edge01">
<QUALIFIER NAME="Location" TYPE="STRING"><VALUE>Defined
by the Goal-Distribution process</VALUE></QUALIFIER>
<QUALIFIER NAME="Role" TYPE="STRING"><VALUE>Defined by
the Goal-Distribution process</VALUE></QUALIFIER>
<QUALIFIER NAME="ListeningPort" TYPE="STRING">
<VALUE>Defined by the Goal-Distribution process</VALUE>
</QUALIFIER>
</SETTING-ELEMENT>
------------------------------------------------------------
<SETTING-ELEMENT Element-id="http://www.tssg.org/
#scenario-QoS-requirements_Element_Edge02">
------------------------------------------------------------
<SETTING-ELEMENT Element-id="http://www.tssg.org/
#scenario-QoS-requirements_Element_Core">
```

Fig. 3. Goal Representation in CIM-XML format

common specification. The Element reasons with this knowledge by applying the Goal configurations, monitoring the system events, detecting/reporting configuration conflicts and adapting its behavior (changing state).

5   Autonomic Element Architecture

The role of an AE is to satisfy the goals specified by the administrator through the Goal Server during its initialization, to interact with its peers in order to propagate knowledge, and provide a global "intelligence" for achieving the desired goal in a cooperative manner. The AEs can assign priorities to the enforced goals and reason with them i.e. loading behavior modules, configuring state and apply settings conforming to the contexts of the behavior. Therefore, the business-level and the user-level objectives are managed in a completely decentralized manner and conflicts can be solved more easily. When an AE faces a conflict, it takes it own decision depending on its knowledge and sends an event containing a Goal and Behavior-Context Identifiers, responsible of the conflict, to the Goal Servers. This event will help the administrator to understand the behavior of its network in order to enhance the specification of his goals and solve the unpredicted configurations conflicts.

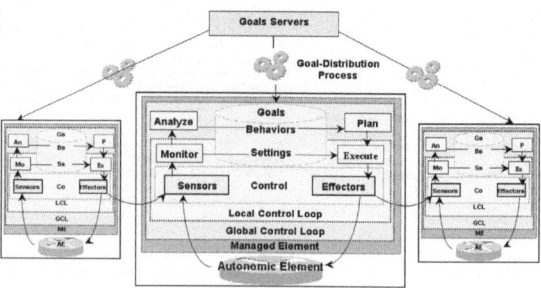

Fig. 4. Autonomic Element Architecture

As shown in fig.4, the reasoning capabilities of an AE are distributed between four functional modules that compose its internal architecture: monitoring; analyzing; planning and execution. Hence, the AE exhibits communication capabilities that allow it to interact with its environment. At initialization, the AE subscribes to autonomous domains via the Goal-distribution process. This process defines how an AE is associated to an autonomous domain and corresponding goal. A Goal can be enforced in many AEs (1-N) and an AE can be associated to several Goals (M-1). The administrator defines the set of elements that are required to achieve a Goal. This is accomplished using our defined Goal-language. Once a goal is specified, the Goal-distribution process is performed in two phases. In the first phase, every AE subscribes to a Goal via the Goal Server (GS). The role of the GS is to complete the Setting of the Goal by referencing every entity participating in its realization (autonomic domain elements). The identification process assigns a unique ID and a role to every AE (this can also be configured directly in the AE during its local configuration). The interactions between AEs are determined by their role, thus every AE is aware of its role in the autonomic domain. Once the Goal-Setting is completed, the AEs download the goal specification and use it to drive their behavior.

The internal architecture of our Autonomic Element is presented in fig.4. This architecture is aligned with the one presented in [2] and is composed of a number of functional modules that enable the expected autonomic behavior. The **Control Module** allows an AE to interact with other AEs as well as with its internal and external environment. It introduces two entities called sensors and effectors. Sensors provide mechanisms to collect events from the environment while the effectors allow the configuration of its managed resources. In our work, the Control module affects mainly the configuration of the underlying traffic engineering mechanisms of the IP router; in our test-bed, we have used the Linux Traffic Control TC tool [9]. The **Monitoring Module** provides different mechanisms to collect, aggregate, filter and manage information collected by sensors. Whereas, the **Analyze Module** performs the diagnosis of the monitoring results and detects any disruptions in the network or system resources. This information is then transformed into events. The **Planning Module** defines the set of elementary actions to perform accordingly to these events. These actions can be atomic Behavior-Configuration (e.g. QoS class modification, QoS class creation/removing,...) or Event-Action installation (e.g. configuration actions, messages, change behavior). The **Execution Module** provides the mechanisms that control the execution of the specified set of actions, as defined in the planning module. It mainly translates the Behavior-Context into calls in the Control module.

Once the goals are specified, the workflow interaction between the different modules of the AE allows the router to behave in an autonomic manner without any human intervention. The behavior defines two levels of control over the instrumented managed resources and the AE as a whole. The local control loop of the AE (change Behavior-Configuration) allows **reactive behavior**, to situation changes in the AE, to be enforced. Another general loop, called global control loop permits to achieve a **reflexive behavior** in the AE (behavior changes) according to more important changes in the context.

6   Experimentation

We have implemented a proof-of-concept prototype of an autonomous network that exhibits self-configuring and self-optimizing behaviors in fulfilling high-level goals. The aim of our prototype is mainly to demonstrate the ability of the network to control its own behavior, without human intervention, while all the time meeting the QoS requirements of heterogeneous user applications. The supported applications are FTP, Voice over IP and MPEG Video streaming. Our deployed test-bed, as shown in the fig.5, is composed of three routers (Edge Router ER1, Core Router and Edge Router ER2), a Goal Server, an Application Server and two client terminals supporting different types of applications (FTP, VoIP, Video Streaming). In this example, we have used a simple application identification technique based on a combination of layer 3 and 4 information (Port numbers and IP Address).

The high-level goals are defined by an authorized authority using the Goal Server (GS). The goals are specified to ask autonomic routers to adapt automatically their behavior and exhibit a self-configuration and self-optimizing properties according to the applications that are running in the network and the network capacity. In our scenario, the goal specification defines three behaviors for the AEs: BE (Best Effort), PQ (Priority Queuing) and DiffServ (Differentiated Service). The goal is enforced in the autonomic router using the GS.

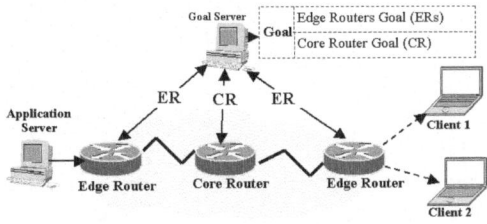

Fig. 5. Test-bed Architecture

This goal is interpreted by the autonomic router, which in turn enforces it locally i.e. execute corresponding low-level configurations, monitoring actions and enforce the corresponding context rules. These rules define the local configuration parameters of the router. More particularly, it defines the configuration of each router interface in term of scheduler, queue management, and buffering according to the context i.e. running applications streams, traffic load, etc.

At the starting of the experimentation, every router interacts with the GS to download their associated goal. The goal specification contains (1) the behavior specification of the autonomic router according to its role, (2) the applications identification and QoS requirement specification. In our experimentation, we have only two roles: Edge Router role and Core Router role. During time, an autonomic router interacts with a peer autonomic router to exchange context information, which allows him to have a global view of the network behavior and reacts immediately when any change occurs (new application launch, per class QoS degradation, etc.). The objective of this experimentation is to highlight the capability of an autonomic router to evaluate a situation and react accordingly to try to fulfill its assigned Goal. Figure 6 shows the evolution of the configuration of Classes of Service (CS) as well as the distribution of bandwidth between these classes. This evolution of the CS configuration corresponds also to a self-adaptation of the autonomic router behavior. Once the initialization phase is complete, all the routers initialize their behaviors to BE. This default behavior is motivated by the existence of only one type of application stream in the network (same priority); therefore only one class of service CS is needed (BE) to support this application. All the available bandwidth is allocated to the BE class. During time, ER1 detects the launch of a new application (VoIP application) through its sensors and using its knowledge base identifies its Settings i.e. the targeted QoS. Based on these properties, it determines the most accurate actions to adopt in order to maintain the QoS objectives (reflexive behavior). This situation is depicted in fig.6 at t=60 sec. At this instant, ER1 informs the peer Core router about this new situation (cooperative behavior) so that they cooperatively find a solution and take the most accurate actions. In this case, the cooperative decision is to adopt the "PQ" behavior, which allows to support the QoS for two classes

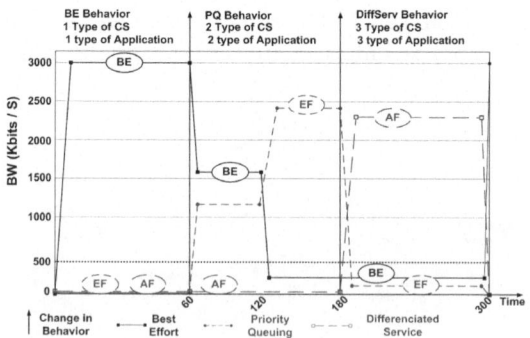

Fig. 6. Experimental Results

of application, one with low delay requirement and the other with best effort requirement. The bandwidth distribution between the two classes is controlled by a shaper, which ensures that the low priority class is not starved by the high priority class. Thus, the routers synchronously change their behaviors from BE to PQ.

ER1 continues to monitor any new application traffic using its sensors while the Core router controls the aggregated QoS for each class of service. In the case where it detects a high loss rate for the higher priority service class, it sends a notification (PQ) to the ER1 and a reconfiguration automatically occurs to redistribute the bandwidth between the two classes more efficiently. In the same figure, we can see that at t=126 sec ER1 has detected the launch of a second VoD application and immediately triggers a notification to inform the core router. The later then reconfigures itself automatically by changing the bandwidth distribution between the higher and the lower classes. At t=180 sec, a new application with the highest priority is detected. Three types of application are now running at the same time in the network. In order to maintain the QoS objective of each application, three different classes of service are necessary. The autonomic router's behavior then changes automatically from "PQ" to "Diff-Serv" and three classes of services are defined: Expedited Forwarding for VoIP; Assured Forwarding for VoD and Default Class for Best Effort traffic.

For our prototype to have a global view of the network, a number of monitoring sensors have been installed in the autonomic routers that collect information about their behavior and their context. This information is collected by a monitoring application and presents it in a useful manner to the administrator. The monitoring application presents also a topology map of the autonomic network as well as tables, statistics and graphs related to the autonomic routers' behavior, existing service classes, bandwidth occupation per class, and loss rate per service class.

The objective of this experimentation was to highlight the adaptive behavior of the routers based on the context. The tests have shown that the network effectively has achieved the enforced goal through the local behavior adaptation of AEs and their exchange of context information. Nevertheless, it is important to note here that the objective was not to highlight the benefit of having three types of scheduler in the network but rather the benefit of autonomous and coordinated behavior-adaptation, causing automatic router re-configuration based on the network context.

7   Conclusions and Perspectives

In this paper we have introduced an initial approach for introducing autonomous capabilities into IP routers. The idea behind this work is to show that it is possible to model a goal in terms of a state machine that specifies the expected behaviors from target autonomic elements in various situations. Conforming to the goal, network elements take stand-alone decisions based on their local information collected from cooperative autonomic peers. We have extended the

CIM in order to introduce the new concepts necessary to model a goal and we have specified a global architecture based on a Goal Server (GS) and Autonomic Elements (AE). We have implemented this concept in a small-scale test bed that allowed us to validate some aspects of the model and highlight the AEs autonomous behavior. The obtained results are very promising and have shown that some aspects of autonomic networks are realizable and simplify the tedious work of IP network configuration and optimization. However, this work should be seen as a first step towards the achievement of a truly autonomic network.

In the future we aim to use our model for a large scale IP network where the interactions and the behavior coordination between autonomic routers will be more complex. We will consider the case of a unique domain or multiple overlapped autonomic domains fulfilling different goals. The modeling of autonomic behavior and the introduction of cognitive and cooperative capabilities based on a generic representation of the management context are certainly the most important issues that we will address in future work.

References

1. Smirnov M., Popescu-Zeletin R.: Autonomic Communication, Communication Paradigms for 2020, Future and Emerging Technologies (FET), 22/07/2003, Brussels.
2. Kephart J. O., Chess D. : Vision of Autonomic Computing, Computer Magazine, IEEE, 2003.
3. Kephart J. O., Walsh W. E. : An Artificial Intelligence Perspective on Autonomic Computing Policies, in Proceedings of the 4th international Workshop on Policies for Distributed Systems and Networks, June 07 - 09, 2004, New York.
4. Strassner J. : Realizing on demand networking, in Proceedings of the 6th IFIP/IEEE International Conference on Management of Multimedia Networks and Services, 7th-10th September 2003, Queen's University of Belfast, Northern Ireland.
5. Bandara A. K., Lupu E. C., Moffett J. D., Russo A. : A Goal-based Approach to Policy Refinement, IEEE 5th International Workshop on Policies for Distributed Systems and Networks, POLICY 2004, June 7-9, 2004,
6. Stojanovic L., Schneider J., Maedche A., Libischer S., Studer R., Lumpp Th., Abecker A., Breiter G., Dinger J. : The role of ontologies in autonomic computing, Published in IBM Systems Journal, Volume 43, Issue 3, 2004.
7. DMTF : Common Information Model (CIM) Specification, V2.2, DSP0004, June 14, 1999.
8. DMTF : Representation of CIM in XML, v2.2, DSP0201, December 09, 2004.
9. Brown M. A. : Guide to IP Layer Network Administration with Linux, Traffic-Control-HOWTO, http://linux-ip.net/articles/Traffic-Control-HOWTO/.

Author Index

Lecture Notes in Computer Science

For information about Vols. 1–3665

please contact your bookseller or Springer

Vol. 3711: F. Kishino, Y. Kitamura, H. Kato, N. Nagata (Eds.), Entertainment Computing - ICEC 2005. XXIV, 540 pages. 2005.

Vol. 3710: M. Barni, I. Cox, T. Kalker, H.J. Kim (Eds.), Digital Watermarking. XII, 485 pages. 2005.

Vol. 3709: P. van Beek (Ed.), Principles and Practice of Constraint Programming - CP 2005. XX, 887 pages. 2005.

Vol. 3708: J. Blanc-Talon, W. Philips, D. Popescu, P. Scheunders (Eds.), Advanced Concepts for Intelligent Vision Systems. XXII, 725 pages. 2005.

Vol. 3707: D.A. Peled, Y.-K. Tsay (Eds.), Automated Technology for Verification and Analysis. XII, 506 pages. 2005.

Vol. 3706: H. Fuks, S. Lukosch, A.C. Salgado (Eds.), Groupware: Design, Implementation, and Use. XII, 378 pages. 2005.

Vol. 3704: M. De Gregorio, V. Di Maio, M. Frucci, C. Musio (Eds.), Brain, Vision, and Artificial Intelligence. XV, 556 pages. 2005.

Vol. 3703: F. Fages, S. Soliman (Eds.), Principles and Practice of Semantic Web Reasoning. VIII, 163 pages. 2005.

Vol. 3702: B. Beckert (Ed.), Automated Reasoning with Analytic Tableaux and Related Methods. XIII, 343 pages. 2005. (Subseries LNAI).

Vol. 3701: M. Coppo, E. Lodi, G. M. Pinna (Eds.), Theoretical Computer Science. XI, 411 pages. 2005.

Vol. 3699: C.S. Calude, M.J. Dinneen, G. Păun, M. J. Pérez-Jiménez, G. Rozenberg (Eds.), Unconventional Computation. XI, 267 pages. 2005.

Vol. 3698: U. Furbach (Ed.), KI 2005: Advances in Artificial Intelligence. XIII, 409 pages. 2005. (Subseries LNAI).

Vol. 3697: W. Duch, J. Kacprzyk, E. Oja, S. Zadrożny (Eds.), Artificial Neural Networks: Formal Models and Their Applications - ICANN 2005, Part II. XXXII, 1045 pages. 2005.

Vol. 3696: W. Duch, J. Kacprzyk, E. Oja, S. Zadrożny (Eds.), Artificial Neural Networks: Biological Inspirations - ICANN 2005, Part I. XXXI, 703 pages. 2005.

Vol. 3695: M.R. Berthold, R. Glen, K. Diederichs, O. Kohlbacher, I. Fischer (Eds.), Computational Life Sciences. XI, 277 pages. 2005. (Subseries LNBI).

Vol. 3694: M. Malek, E. Nett, N. Suri (Eds.), Service Availability. VIII, 213 pages. 2005.

Vol. 3693: A.G. Cohn, D.M. Mark (Eds.), Spatial Information Theory. XII, 493 pages. 2005.

Vol. 3692: R. Casadio, G. Myers (Eds.), Algorithms in Bioinformatics. X, 436 pages. 2005. (Subseries LNBI).

Vol. 3691: A. Gagalowicz, W. Philips (Eds.), Computer Analysis of Images and Patterns. XIX, 865 pages. 2005.

Vol. 3690: M. Pěchouček, P. Petta, L.Z. Varga (Eds.), Multi-Agent Systems and Applications IV. XVII, 667 pages. 2005. (Subseries LNAI).

Vol. 3689: G.G. Lee, A. Yamada, H. Meng, S.H. Myaeng (Eds.), Information Retrieval Technology. XVII, 735 pages. 2005.

Vol. 3688: R. Winther, B.A. Gran, G. Dahll (Eds.), Computer Safety, Reliability, and Security. XI, 405 pages. 2005.

Vol. 3687: S. Singh, M. Singh, C. Apte, P. Perner (Eds.), Pattern Recognition and Image Analysis, Part II. XXV, 809 pages. 2005.

Vol. 3686: S. Singh, M. Singh, C. Apte, P. Perner (Eds.), Pattern Recognition and Data Mining, Part I. XXVI, 689 pages. 2005.

Vol. 3685: V. Gorodetsky, I. Kotenko, V. Skormin (Eds.), Computer Network Security. XIV, 480 pages. 2005.

Vol. 3684: R. Khosla, R.J. Howlett, L.C. Jain (Eds.), Knowledge-Based Intelligent Information and Engineering Systems, Part IV. LXXIX, 933 pages. 2005. (Subseries LNAI).

Vol. 3683: R. Khosla, R.J. Howlett, L.C. Jain (Eds.), Knowledge-Based Intelligent Information and Engineering Systems, Part III. LXXX, 1397 pages. 2005. (Subseries LNAI).

Vol. 3682: R. Khosla, R.J. Howlett, L.C. Jain (Eds.), Knowledge-Based Intelligent Information and Engineering Systems, Part II. LXXIX, 1371 pages. 2005. (Subseries LNAI).

Vol. 3681: R. Khosla, R.J. Howlett, L.C. Jain (Eds.), Knowledge-Based Intelligent Information and Engineering Systems, Part I. LXXX, 1319 pages. 2005. (Subseries LNAI).

Vol. 3680: C. Priami, A. Zelikovsky (Eds.), Transactions on Computational Systems Biology II. IX, 153 pages. 2005. (Subseries LNBI).

Vol. 3679: S.d.C. di Vimercati, P. Syverson, D. Gollmann (Eds.), Computer Security – ESORICS 2005. XI, 509 pages. 2005.

Vol. 3678: A. McLysaght, D.H. Huson (Eds.), Comparative Genomics. VIII, 167 pages. 2005. (Subseries LNBI).

Vol. 3677: J. Dittmann, S. Katzenbeisser, A. Uhl (Eds.), Communications and Multimedia Security. XIII, 360 pages. 2005.

Vol. 3676: R. Glück, M. Lowry (Eds.), Generative Programming and Component Engineering. XI, 448 pages. 2005.

Vol. 3675: Y. Luo (Ed.), Cooperative Design, Visualization, and Engineering. XI, 264 pages. 2005.

Vol. 3674: W. Jonker, M. Petković (Eds.), Secure Data Management. X, 241 pages. 2005.

Vol. 3673: S. Bandini, S. Manzoni (Eds.), AI*IA 2005: Advances in Artificial Intelligence. XIV, 614 pages. 2005. (Subseries LNAI).

Vol. 3672: C. Hankin, I. Siveroni (Eds.), Static Analysis. X, 369 pages. 2005.

Vol. 3671: S. Bressan, S. Ceri, E. Hunt, Z.G. Ives, Z. Bellahsène, M. Rys, R. Unland (Eds.), Database and XML Technologies. X, 239 pages. 2005.

Vol. 3670: M. Bravetti, L. Kloul, G. Zavattaro (Eds.), Formal Techniques for Computer Systems and Business Processes. XIII, 349 pages. 2005.

Vol. 3669: G.S. Brodal, S. Leonardi (Eds.), Algorithms – ESA 2005. XVIII, 901 pages. 2005.

Vol. 3668: M. Gabbrielli, G. Gupta (Eds.), Logic Programming. XIV, 454 pages. 2005.

Vol. 3666: B.D. Martino, D. Kranzlmüller, J. Dongarra (Eds.), Recent Advances in Parallel Virtual Machine and Message Passing Interface. XVII, 546 pages. 2005.